England and the Discovery of America, 1481–1620

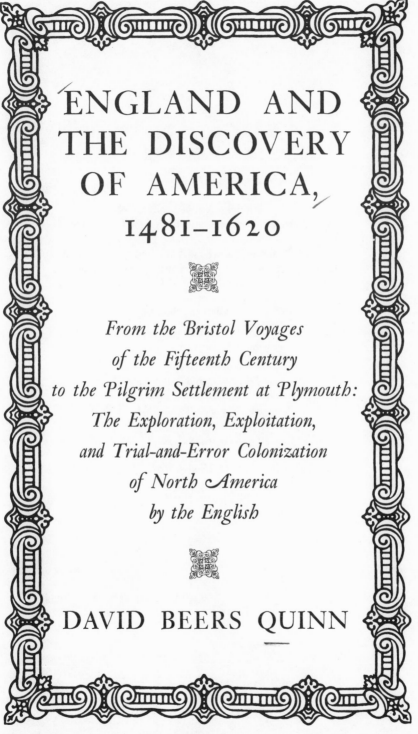

ENGLAND AND THE DISCOVERY OF AMERICA, 1481–1620

From the Bristol Voyages
of the Fifteenth Century
to the Pilgrim Settlement at Plymouth:
The Exploration, Exploitation,
and Trial-and-Error Colonization
of North America
by the English

DAVID BEERS QUINN

Alfred A. Knopf *New York* 1974

THIS IS A BORZOI BOOK
PUBLISHED BY ALFRED A. KNOPF, INC.

Published in the United States
by Alfred A. Knopf, Inc., New York, and simultaneously
in Canada by Random House of Canada Limited, Toronto.
Distributed by Random House, Inc., New York.

Library of Congress Cataloging in Publication Data:

Quinn, David Beers, date.
England and the discovery of America, 1481–1620.

Bibliography: p.
1. America—Discovery and exploration—English.
2. Great Britain—Colonies—America.
3. America—History—To 1810. I. Title.
E127.Q49 973.1'7 70–71123
ISBN 0–394–46673–X

Manufactured in the United States of America

FIRST EDITION

To Alison

Contents

A Bibliography of Books and Articles on American Exploration and Colonization by David Beers Quinn

Illustrations

MAPS

PLATES

Acknowledgments

IN A BOOK of this sort, representing studies carried on over many years, an enormous number of debts have been accumulated for which no adequate acknowledgment can be given. Alison Quinn has lived with my work longer than any and has had a great deal to do with its form and content. Bernard Bailyn was a primary influence in bringing it together, not least in introducing it to Jane Garrett, who made it in a real sense her own and, with Annabelle Learned as copy editor, did much to bring its pieces together. Alan Hodgkiss lent his great cartographical skill to making the sketch maps, while Beryl Hart and Brigid Quinn helped out at crucial times. Further back in the past, a great deal is owed to R. A. Skelton, J. A. Williamson, and Lawrence C. Wroth, all now dead, alas, and to Louis B. Wright, L. A. Vigneras, Philip Barbour, and Thomas R. Adams, Jr., among the living. Mr. Philip Robinson and the Robinson Trust showed me especial kindness in opening their treasures to me. My debt to many libraries and librarians, archives and archivists should be obvious.

Permission to reprint materials has been received from the Society for Northern Research and Professor P. G. Foote; the Royal Geographical Society and Sir Laurence Kirwan; the Bristol Branch of the Historical Association and Mr. Patrick McGrath; Cambridge University Press and Professor Kenneth Muir (editor of the *Shakespeare Survey*); The Historic Society of Lancashire and Cheshire and Dr. Michael Power; The Royal Historical Society and Mr. A. G. Watson; Professors H. A. Cronne and T. W. Moody jointly; The James Ford Bell Library and

Mr. John Parker; *The William and Mary Quarterly* and Professor Thad Tate; *Terrae Incognitae* and Mr. N. Israel and Professor Bruce Solnick; The Folger Shakespeare Library and Dr. O. B. Hardison, Jr.; *The New England Quarterly* and Professor Herbert Brown. For precise bibliographical information on the reprinted material and where it appears in this book, see the list of books and articles in the Bibliography, pp. 493–7.

Foreword

THIS BOOK IS mainly about the English and their part, or presumed part, in the discovery of North America and its eventual exploitation and settlement. It is a risky theme for an Irishman to undertake: he is liable in Ireland to be thought biased toward that sister isle which has not always seemed part of the same family; or in England he may well be thought to have a natural desire to keep in his place any Englishman who comes within his view. It is certainly not my intention to give the English more than their due. At the same time it is clear that, however much we debate about the details, they took a significant and exciting part in the discovery of North America, which in the end attracted so many Englishmen and Irishmen alike. Then, after a longish interval, Englishmen also took a substantial share in the exploration, description, and mapping of the eastern part of that continent, filling in with telling detail shores that, for the most part, Frenchmen or Spaniards already had seen but had not sufficiently remarked. In the end it was the English who were to lead the way where the Spaniards had already pointed, toward permanent settlement, to be followed very closely by the French.

It seems, too, that they had the further distinction of first planting viable communities of men, women, and children in North America who could put down roots there and create a new society, untrammelled—or at least not hampered unduly—by the homeland that had given them birth. The first colonies, for some little time weaker than the footholds of Spain and France, were in the end to prove the dominating element in the unified exploitation of the whole of America north of Mexico by the United States and Canada.

The treatment that follows is not in the form of a detailed connected narrative and analysis, but rather an exposure of successive points of interest, information, or synthesis which exemplify some of the problems of documenting and understanding a process which we know even today very imperfectly. The reader may regard it as a series of attempts to probe particular problems of a type illustrative of many more which could be studied in comparable ways—combined with attempts to formulate some general statements, which do not however pretend to cover exhaustively anything like the whole field.

It represents indeed a gathering together of certain papers and lectures prepared over a number of years, some previously published, others unpublished, which focus on the problems of discovery and the achievement of some degree of permanent settlement. The individual papers have not been treated with any great reverence. Where they seemed to represent what I wished to say, they have been left untouched except for necessary corrections of fact or reference, but there has been no reluctance to cut, enlarge, or alter where advantage in exposition was to be gained. Some degree of overlapping has been eliminated where it would seem silly to say virtually the same thing twice on the same scale, but where repetition has seemed necessary to a particular argument it has been allowed to stand. What unity the book has must be derived from its overall theme rather than from its detailed treatment of particular issues and developments.

It cannot be too strongly stressed that the last word has not been said on any aspect of early North American discovery. It is a field which attracted much effective interest from historians, bibliographers, and cartographers in the latter part of the nineteenth century. In the present century it has produced important and excellent documentary publications from historians such as H. P. Biggar, Jeanette Connor, J. A. Robertson, and H. I. Priestley. But it has scarcely drawn the serious attention it deserved from either narrative or analytical historians in the past generation. Without being neglected, it has been looked at more as a preface to the history of the North American nations than as history itself—a necessary prelude to be skipped over lightly and rapidly before the writer gets down to his main task of developing a historical theme in detail for a later period. It has not been taken seriously enough as a significant part of the historical discipline in its own right. Something of this has been due to the feeling that all that could be known was known, and there was little to do but repeat what has already been said. Nothing could be further from the truth.

Another cause for the neglect of the early history of eastern North America (for the West has been much more exhaustively and effectively covered) is the long-continued neglect of geographical studies in the eastern United States, in particular. It is true that this is geographical history rather than historical geography as it has developed in European universities, but its background is an informed knowledge of the natural environment, which has often been lacking among history students of New England and Southern universities. One consequence is that much of the attention paid to the early period has been at the local level, sometimes valuable but often pedestrian and repetitive, or focused on a few major issues like the voyages of the Cabots, which have drawn the attention of such outstanding names as Biggar, G. P. Winship, J. A. Williamson, and L. A. Vigneras, all associated with the uncovering of vital evidence or the setting out of new interpretations. But there are many signs of a renewed revitalized interest among historians in the larger area: both in detailed problems of documentation and interpretation and in the broader historical issues of the early phases of North American discovery and the pioneering of the first European settlements.

The process of early exploitation in the case of the territories that spawned new European societies is of particular interest in the world-framework of early modern history when set against the patterns of exploitation in countries which have more recently broken away, under indigenous rulers, from the domination of Europe-centered empires. Though the focus here is on England and English enterprise, this does not mean that the significance of either Spain or France in the early emergence of the North American continent is played down—or the smaller contribution of Portugal forgotten. While the work of Maurice Trudel has done much to pull together our knowledge of French interests in North America in the sixteenth and early seventeenth centuries, we have had so far no Woodbury Lowery of the present generation to do the same for the Spaniards. If the Amerindians and Eskimos of North America in the fifteenth and sixteenth centuries, and the bitter realities of their intercourse with the Europeans, which in the end robbed them not only of their lands but of their whole way of life, built up by centuries of communal effort, find little place in this book, this is accidental rather than deliberate. It is an important theme, essential for the full knowledge of what happened and what it meant. Ethnohistorians are illuminating it as historians in general become more conscious of anthropology and anthropologists of history; it will soon be possible to write in this field on a broad scale and in detail. Until this is done the appearance of the Europeans and their activities on the American coasts and rivers has a certain two-dimensional character; the missing dimension will make possible much better history when it is supplied.

This book is offered, then, as a small step forward in knowledge and understanding in an extensive area of study, providing an introduction to certain problems of content and method in a particular sector. It is in this respect complementary to the documentary work done elsewhere by my valued collaborators and myself on the English voyages and colonizing enterprises from 1578 onward, on John White and Richard Hakluyt in particular. What is set out in narrative and exposition has in almost all cases a deservedly limited life: it is right that it should pass into virtual oblivion within the space of, at most, a quarter of a century so far as the student is concerned. Documentary editions have, perhaps, a somewhat longer life if the presentation of the materials has been reliable and comprehensive and the annotation extensive and scrupulous. But neither should they, any more than secondary works, be allowed to become permanent fixtures.

Editing of texts, no less than expository writing, needs to be reshaped to the changing—often rapidly changing—needs of each generation of students and teachers. The value of reprint editions in stocking new libraries and filling out the collections of older ones need not be underestimated, but it has to be said against them that they also tend to bind the student and scholar to the use of decaying and often completely out-of-date material. This danger, with the continued rise in the costs of narrowly scholarly works, is a genuine one, preventing the young scholar from bringing the resources of the constantly accumulating and spreading scholarship in his field to bear on the detailed elucidation of the documentary sources. In few fields is the need for reediting texts reasonably frequently more important than in this one. The detailed growth of knowledge has a considerable future before it here; new materials can still emerge, however minute in quantity in crucial areas; the bringing of scholarly energies to bear on their assimilation to the old, the bringing out of new techniques of textual criticism and the elucidation of novel themes and approaches—these are all essential if the history of this fascinating and significant period is to avoid being stereotyped. If this book is a collection of secondary materials, it is at least possible to point here to the continued need for new, thoroughly annotated editions of documents as the main impetus to effective historical writing on the early discoveries and settlements.

In the study of the early moves westward in the fifteenth century and in many episodes of the sixteenth century, the conscientious historian who relies only on explicit evidence must continually say "I don't know" when confronted with a problem where evidence is incomplete, untrustworthy, or entirely lacking. At the same time, I believe, the historian should attempt to do all he can with the materials he has. The role of hypothesis in this type of study must inevitably be large. Imperfect data, strung together in a conceptual framework, have a great attraction for the unorthodox investigator. And in no historical field has there been more speculation—much of it of an almost wholly meaningless character—than the discovery of America. The most common temptation is to seize on some supposed "fact" and build a theory on it, assume that the theory provides a firm platform for further speculation, and continue with this process until a complete story of "what happened" emerges. The difficulty here is that the historical credentials of the initial "fact"—the disappearance of Atlantis, to take a commonly exploited example—are so poor that the structure raised upon it is entirely of fantasy, not history.

Fantasy-building is a perfectly acceptable human activity, but its involvement in the construction of alleged historical sequences introduces an element of pure fiction which must be unacceptable to the historian. At the same time, historians are often reluctant to reject such chains of fantasy altogether if they are strung together in language compatible with historical discourse. The result is that many books on the discovery of America before Columbus occupy shelf-space in the historical rather than fiction sections of research libraries, because they "just might have something in them." On the other hand, many historians will go to the opposite extreme and take the pragmatic view that we know nothing of Atlantic crossings prior to Columbus—nowadays perhaps making an exception for Eric the Red—and that all discussion of such voyaging is a dubious attempt to intervene in historical activity without having the essential bricks of factual information with which to do so.

It is arguable however—and this view will be followed in the discussion—that the critical approach to imperfect data, if pursued with a reasonably open mind, can take us some way toward conclusions which may have a certain historical validity. What is essential is to retain a many-sided approach to each fragment of material available, so that there is no undue preoccupation with one facet to the obscuring of others, and also that each chain of association and inference should be built up so far as possible without piling hypothesis on hypothesis so that prior hypotheses take on the character of established fact rather than that of conjectural bricks in an unsubstantial construction.

Or, if this is done at any time, it should be made explicit. It is perfectly reasonable to sketch out the less likely implications of a particular chain of thought as well as the more likely, but clear indication should be given of the significance it is thought right to place on each such construction. What we may do then is to defend speculative history in this area of discussion provided it does not pretend to any exclusive revelation and remains attached to documentary evidence.

All this may sound rather heavy-handed or an overstressing of the obvious. It is intended merely to suggest that speculative investigation of a field in which the evidential value of much of the data is imperfect is legitimate, so long as critical standards on evidence and in the construction of an argument are maintained as rigidly as possible. While the writer must be free to express preferences, he should avoid dogmatism. A very slight shift of emphasis or a minute change in the interpretation of a particular document may make it possible to restore to acceptability an argument or interpretation which has hitherto been put aside as imperfect or unacceptable. To keep all reasonable options open without making further critical study of the field worthless or self-defeating is not easy. It can, however, lead slowly and cumulatively to the expansion and consolidation of our pattern of knowledge, so that we will be able in the end to absorb new information, when and however it appears, into a meaningful sequence of events.

DAVID BEERS QUINN
December 1972

A List of Footnote Abbreviations

A.G.I.	Archivo General de Indias, Seville
A.G.S.	Archivo General de Simancas
A.N.L.	Accademia Nazionale dei Lincei, Rome
A.P.C.	*Acts of the Privy Council*
B.M.	British Museum, London
B.N.	Bibliothèque Nationale, Paris
Brit.R.S.	British Record Society
B.R.S.	Bristol Record Society
Cal.CarewMSS	*Calendar of Carew Manuscripts*
Cal.S.P.,Dom.	*Calendar of State Papers, Domestic*
Cal.S.P.,For.	*Calendar of State Papers, Foreign*
Cal.S.P.,Ire.	*Calendar of State Papers, Ireland*
Cal.S.P.,Span.	*Calendar of State Papers, Spanish*
Cal.S.P.,Ven.	*Calendar of State Papers, Venetian*
C.I.H.D.	Congresso Internacional de História dos Descobrimentos, Lisbon
D.C.B.	*Dictionary of Canadian Biography*
D.N.B.	*Directory of National Biography* (British)
H.C.A.	High Court of Admiralty

Hist.MSSComm.	Historical Manuscripts Commission, London
Lancs.R.O.	Lancashire County Record Office, Preston
L.R.O.	Liverpool City Record Office
N.R.S.	Navy Records Society
P.M.L.A.	*Proceedings of the Modern Language Association*
P.R.O.	Public Record Office, London
S.T.C.	A. W. Pollard and G. R. Redgrave, *A Short-title Catalogue of Books Printed in England, Scotland and Ireland 1475–1640*

PART I

Searches in the Atlantic

Prologue

The British Isles lie well forward on the eastern Atlantic rim. They are water-encircled but not waterbound. The growth of the English economy in the later Middle Ages was achieved through increased mastery of the seas that surrounded the islands and made inevitable the outward spread of English interests in the Atlantic. If we center our compass at the heart of England we can find, point by point, from the north almost to south the directions along which English interest, English ships, and English commerce were to travel between 1400 and 1600: Iceland to the northwest—reached in the fourteenth century and exploited by the Bristol men in the fifteenth; Labrador due west, a cold barrier to the Northwest Passage enthusiasts of the sixteenth century; Newfoundland west-southwest, to which Englishmen reached out in the fifteenth century, perhaps before John Cabot's voyage of 1497; New England and Virginia to the southwest, focus of the earliest English colonizing ventures; the Caribbean, south-southwest, to which Elizabethan privateers and later island-settlers were drawn.

The process which led along these compass points into the west was long and often discontinuous; at times the English were in the vanguard of western European peoples, at other times they trailed behind where Spain, or Portugal, or France led. In the end the greater part of North America was to fall to them, while the stronger empire of Spain in the New World resisted them successfully. But this took a long time, even after 1600, to work out.

The early chapters of this book are attempts to make arguments out of incidents and patterns out of what may often be only isolated events. The general effect of the discussion, whatever weight may be put on particular points, is to suggest that England had a more active and positive role in the exploration, discovery, and exploitation of the Atlantic in the fifteenth century than is usually recognized, even though we have still too little evidence to be dogmatic about many aspects of the story.

CHAPTER ONE

The Argument for the English Discovery of America Between 1480 and 1494[1]

I

In 1956, Dr. Louis André Vigneras published a letter he had found in the archives at Simancas which has greatly affected and will continue to affect consideration of the circumstances of the discovery of America.[2] In Spanish, and undated, the letter was addressed by John Day, an Englishman, to a Spanish official, the "Almirante Mayor," who is to be identified either as Fadrique Enriquez, Grand Admiral of Castile, or as Christopher Columbus, Admiral of the Ocean Sea, often referred to also as the "Almirante Mayor." Vigneras prefers the Columbus

[1] The text is unaltered (apart from a few typographical and minor stylistic details) from that in *The Geographical Journal,* CXXVII (1961), 277–85, but the notes have been updated.

[2] Vigneras first published the Spanish text in "New Light on the 1497 Cabot Voyage to America," *Hispanic-American Historical Review,* XXXVI (1956), 507–9, and an English translation in "The Cape Breton Landfall: 1494 or 1497? Note on a Letter by John Day," *Canadian Historical Review,* XXXVIII (1957), 226–8. He reprinted the Spanish text in "État présent des études sur Jean Cabot," Congresso Internacional de História dos Descobrimentos (C.I.H.D.), *Actas,* III (Lisbon, 1961), 664–6. Robert Almagiá, "Sulle navigazioni di Giovanni Caboto," *Rivista Geografica Italiana,* LXVII (1960), 2–3, also printed the Spanish text, and J. A. Williamson, in *The Cabot Voyages and Bristol Discovery Under Henry VII,* Hakluyt Society, 2d ser., no. 120 (Cambridge, Eng., 1962), pp. 212–14, the English translation. A further version is given in S. E. Morison, *The European Discovery of America. The Northern Voyages A.D. 500–1600* (New York and London, 1971), pp. 206–9.

identification and it seems the much more probable one. The letter is the work of a man of some learning, familiar with the geographical knowledge of the time, who has been carrying on a correspondence with the Grand Admiral, exchanging books with him, and sending him information on English voyages on at least one earlier occasion. Where its information can be checked against other evidence it is correct, which suggests that its unsupported statements are serious and probably authoritative ones.

The letter is mainly concerned with reporting a successful voyage from Bristol by an unnamed explorer who has found across the ocean a land that Day identifies with "the Island of the Seven Cities." Both by its general character and by specific details—the grant, for example (on 13 December 1497) of a pension of twenty pounds by the king to the explorer on his return[3]—this voyage can be clearly and unambiguously identified as that made by John Cabot in 1497, during which he coasted a substantial part of the Newfoundland and mainland shores across the Atlantic. The letter, moreover, states that the explorer had earlier made an unsuccessful voyage from Bristol, thus adding a piece of hitherto unknown information on John Cabot, while it also gives some details of the preparation for a further voyage which Cabot was making to follow up his discovery. From this last information it is possible to tie down the composition of the letter to the latter part of December 1497 or the opening month or so of 1498. The general considerations are discussed by Vigneras.[4] For the Cabot voyages the letter is an important source, the most important, indeed, to be published in the present century, while the details it gives of the 1497 discoveries will continue to provide material for interpretation and controversy. One passage in it goes beyond the Cabot voyages themselves and raises the question of the priority of the discovery of America in a novel form. Its interest is such that it is worth segregating it from the Cabot material and considering what its implications may be if it is taken literally as a statement of fact.

The text reads, in translation: "It is considered certain that the cape of the said land [that found by Cabot in the 1497 voyage] was found and discovered in other times by the men of Bristol who found 'Brasil' as your Lordship knows. It was called the Ysle of Brasil and it is assumed and believed to be the mainland that the Bristol men found." (The Spanish being: "Se presume cierto averse fallado e descubierto en otros tiempos el cabo de la dicha tierra por los de Bristol que fallaron el Brasil como dello tiene noticia Vra S^a la qual se dezia la Ysle de Brasil e presumese e

[3] Williamson, *Cabot Voyages* (1962), p. 217.

[4] "New Light," pp. 503–6; "État présent," pp. 655–6.

creese ser tierra firme la que fallaron los de Bristol.") [5] The Spanish of the letter shows few signs of being written by a foreigner, but Vigneras has found that John Day, its author, as an English merchant, appears also in a Spanish document of 1500.[6] The literal meaning is clear enough. The land, or part of the land, which Cabot found in 1497 is equated with "Brasil" or the "Isle of Brasil," which the Bristol men had found already some time before. Cabot's discovery, although the possibility of a rediscovery of land found and lost again is not ruled out, had not, Day is asserting, any claim to absolute priority. When, then, could this first discovery have taken place? Or between what limits can we place it? The major ambiguity lies in the words "en otros tiempos," with which Vigneras has already wrestled.[7] The expression is a vague one, "in times past," rather than "in past times," having only the implication that the "times" were not very recently past, but even that not very clearly. Certain dates, 1480, 1481, 1490, give us a framework of known facts in which to insert a series of questions and an argument on the implications of the statement.

1. Could the discovery have taken place before 1480? Clearly it could have done so, but no evidence whatever of specific English voyages of discovery into the Atlantic before that date has yet come to light. That being so, nothing useful can be said except that the first positive evidence we have, that for 1480, which follows, is slightly weighted against a discovery before that date, and that for 1481 more heavily.
2. On 15 July 1480 a ship, partly owned by John Jay the younger and with "Thloyde" (identified as John Lloyd with some probability, though it could be Thomas Lloyd) as master, left Bristol for the Island of Brasil, west of Ireland, and returned by September 18 following, having through bad weather failed to find the island. The Latin of William Worcestre on its objective reads: "usque ad insulam de

[5] Archivo General de Simancas (A.G.S.), Estado de Castilla, legajo 2, fol. 6.

[6] Cédula of 20 December 1500 (A.G.S., Cédulas de la Cámera, libro 4, fol. 252) printed by him in "État présent," pp. 666–7. Dr. Alwyn A. Ruddock, "John Day of Bristol and the English Voyages Across the Atlantic Before 1497," *Geographical Journal*, CXXXII (1966), 225–33, identified "John Day" as a name used in Bristol and in Spain during the 1490's by Hugh Say, a mercer and a member of a prominent London merchant family. She cites documents of 1502 and 1503 in the Public Record Office, London (P.R.O.), Early Chancery Proceedings, C 1/265/2, 268/1, 271/29, in which "John Day now calling himself Hugh Say" is referred to; Hugh Say himself mentions having been in Spain some three years before. The identification would appear to be almost conclusive, though a small caveat is inscribed on p. 56 below.

[7] "Cape Breton Landfall," pp. 224–5.

Brasylle in occidentali parte Hibernie."[8] Since the Island of Brasil appeared on many maps, in many different locations, from 1325 onwards, without apparently having been discovered in practice, this would appear on our present information to have been an unsuccessful voyage of discovery to an island known only in theory. Nevertheless, the alternative, that it was an unsuccessful voyage to an island or land already known and discovered before 1480, cannot be entirely ruled out. At least, however, the discovery did not take place in 1480 as the result of this expedition.

3. On or shortly after 6 July 1481 two ships, the *George* and the *Trinity* of Bristol, partly owned and victualled by Thomas Croft, one of the collectors of custom for Bristol, left the port "to serch & fynde a certain Isle called the Isle of Brasile."[9] The terms of their objective would, more strongly than the document of 1482, indicate that the Isle of Brasil had not been located and that this was another voyage of discovery. Moreover, on 18 June 1480, probably too late to be connected with the 1480 voyage, a license was given to Croft and three Bristol merchants, William Spencer, Robert Strange and William de la Founte, to trade for three years to any parts, with any goods except staple goods, despite any statute to the contrary, with two or three ships, each of sixty tons or less.[1] Since Croft was precluded by his

[8] William Worcestre, "Itineraria," Corpus Christi College, Cambridge, MS 210, p. 195, trans. in Worcestre, *Itineraries* (Oxford, 1969), ed. John H. Harvey, pp. 308–9. He noted also that "he who wishes to sail to the island of Brasyle must [at Blasket Island, Kerry, Ireland] set his course" (*ibid.*). This statement clearly needs further examination.

[9] Three versions of proceedings relative to Croft's participation in the venture survive in the P.R.O.: (1) Exchequer K.R. Customs Accounts, E 122 19/16, (2) Exchequer K.R. Memoranda Roll, E 159/259, 22 Edward IV, Hilary m. 30; (3) Exchequer, L.T.R., Memoranda Roll; E 368/215, 22 Edward IV, Hilary m. 10. The first was first printed by W. E. C. Harrison in "An Early Voyage of Discovery," *Mariner's Mirror*, XVI (1930), 198–9 (though mistakenly assigned to 1480); it was reprinted with the first printing of no. 3 in D. B. Quinn, "Edward IV and Exploration," *Mariner's Mirror*, XXI (1935), 283–4; no. 2 was first printed in Eleanora M. Carus-Wilson, *The Overseas Trade of Bristol in the Later Middle Ages*, Bristol Record Society (B.R.S.) (1937), pp. 157–65.

[1] Calendared from P.R.O., Treaty Roll, C 76/164, m. 10, in Carus-Wilson, *Overseas Trade of Bristol*, p. 157. See pp. 52–7 below. Brief biographies of Thomas Croft (d. 1488), William Spencer (d. 1495), and Robert Strange will be found in J. C. Wedgwood and A. E. Holt, *History of Parliament: Biographies of the Members of the Commons' House, 1439–1509*, 3 vols. (London, 1936), I, 239–40, 787, 819–20, each having been a member of Parliament at one time. William de la Founte's will was dated 11 September 1496, and he may be presumed to have died in that year. Cf. E. A. Fry, ed., *Bristol Wills*, British Record Society (Brit.R.S.), XVII (London, 1897), 123.

office from engaging in trade and was questioned on 24 September 1481 about shipping forty bushels of salt in the *George* and *Trinity* on 6 July 1481, it would appear that this license was for exploration, not commerce, while Croft's excuse that the two ships which he had helped to victual were intended not for commerce but for the search for the Isle of Brasil, was accepted. The 1481 voyage, of the failure of which there is no record, and of the return of which the proceedings against Croft are probably circumstantial evidence, is one which could have resulted in the English discovery of America. A discovery by this expedition would fit, without straining, the requirements of John Day's letter. Moreover, it is the earliest known voyage which could have so succeeded. 1481 is therefore the earlier limit on our present information for a successful discovery and could be the year of the discovery itself.

4. If the discovery did not take place in 1481, Croft and his partners, provided the license of 1480 was for the purpose which has been presumed, had still authority to set out ships in 1482 and in 1483 up to 17 June. Evidence is still entirely lacking that any such further voyages were made or, if made, that they had any results, but it is within the years of the currency of the license that the English discovery of America is least unlikely to lie.
5. The years between 1483 and 1490 are as blank of even the suggestion of evidence for a voyage as those before 1480, but they are still within the period of discovery appropriate to the Day letter.
6. One of the Spanish representatives in England provides a well-known piece of evidence about English western voyages which reaches back, perhaps, to 1490. Pedro de Ayala wrote from London to Ferdinand and Isabella on 25 July 1498 to report on Cabot's discoveries in 1497 and on the progress, so far, of his 1498 expedition. He added: "Los de Bristol ha siete años que cada año an armado dos, tres, quatro caravelas para ir a buscar la isla del Brasil, i la Siete Ciudades con la fantasia deste Ginoves," which has, since 1862, been invariably translated: "For the last seven years the people of Bristol have equipped two, three, four caravels to go in search of the island of Brazil and the Seven Cities according to the fancy of this Genoese." [2] It is not certain which years are meant. Is Ayala writing of seven years before Cabot's voyage of 1497 or of seven years before his letter? The range is either 1490 to 1496 or 1491 to 1497, and choice between the alternatives is not easy to make; both must be regarded as possible. How far Ayala was

[2] A.G.S., Estado, Tratados con Inglaterra, legajo 52, fol. 196. First published in *Calendar of State Papers, Spanish, 1485–1509* (London, 1862), p. 177; H. P. Biggar, *The Precursors of Jacques Cartier, 1497–1534* (Ottawa, 1911), pp. 27–9 (Spanish and English); Williamson, *Cabot Voyages* (1962), pp. 228–9 (English).

speaking precisely and authoritatively it is also impossible to say, but it is reasonable to take his statement at its face value that a series of Bristol voyages began in 1490 or 1491 and was continued in, perhaps, each of the six years following.

To determine how much or how little John Cabot had to do with these voyages is a delicate matter. "According to the fancy of this Genoese" has been taken, almost invariably, to mean that John Cabot, Genoese by origin though Venetian by adoption, inspired this series of Bristol voyages and proposed their objectives to those who took part in them. This does not necessarily follow. The phrase as it stands can mean simply that in Cabot's "fancy" the objectives of the Bristol voyages were the Isle of Brasil and the Seven Cities. He would stand outside the voyages entirely and his comment would be that of an observer only, made to Ayala's informant near to the time of writing in 1498. An alternative translation of the passage could read: "The Bristol men for seven years have fitted out yearly two, three, or four small ships to go in search, as this Genoese fancies, of the Isle of Brasil or the Seven Cities." Which interpretation is correct must remain a matter for argument. Each appears to be legitimate.[3]

The alternative interpretation fits usefully into a pattern formed by the newer documents. It is in line with the evidence already used on the 1480 and 1481 voyages. The English are continuing in the 'nineties their westward voyages from Bristol, only now they are using as many as three or four little ships instead of one or two; they are said to be looking for the Seven Cities in addition to their old objective, the Isle of Brasil. Moreover, the evidence found by Professor M. Ballesteros-Gabrois in the Aragonese archives, if it is to be accepted, puts John Cabot in Valencia between the middle of 1490 and the end of February 1493 at least, and so rules him out from influencing some of the earlier voyages of the series. This involves identifying the Juan Caboto Montecalunya, a Venetian engaged on harbor works at Valencia, with the "English" John Cabot. While this is not certain it is highly prob-

[3] I am indebted to Dr. A. E. Sloman, former head of the School of Hispanic Studies, University of Liverpool, for his support for this interpretation. "Fantasia," with the meaning of fantasy, fancy, imagination, also carried a nautical meaning of reckoning or estimation of direction or distances (A. Jal, *Glossaire nautique* [Paris, 1848], s.v. *Fantasia, Estime*). Dr. Vigneras has written to me of finding the word with this meaning in Pedro de Medina, *Arte de Navegar* (Madrid, 1545), fols. xxxii*v*–xxxiii*r*. This would give a meaning to the ambiguous phrase of "according to the reckoning of this Genoese" which would favor the second explanation, accordingly, as the most likely one.

able.[4] The discoveries of R. Gallo [5] on the "English" John Cabot's activities in Venice between 1476 and 1485 make it unlikely that there was a second John Cabot with Venetian nationality, though the cognomen "Montecalunya" remains mysterious. The consequence of accepting this identification would be that the voyages of 1490 (if there was one), 1491, 1492, and 1493 (probably) of the series were purely English expeditions, and so they could be considered as coming within the range of the independent English discovery described by John Day. Dates as late as 1490 and 1491 could be covered by his "en otros tiempos"; later dates, 1492, six years, and 1493, five years, before the Day letter, seem too near, or at least to be at the outer limit of credibility; 1494, if worth considering, would be rather absurd. We are entitled to say, remembering that we have selected one meaning of two from the Ayala letter and have accepted the Valencia material, that 1490 and 1491 come within the probable range of the independent English discovery of America, and 1492 and 1493 within the possible limits.

7. Robert Thorne the younger, in 1527, claimed that his father, Robert Thorne the elder, and Hugh Elyot, merchants of Bristol, were "discoverers of the New Found Landes.[6] The claim appears to have been made in good faith and, accepting Day's statement of a pre-Cabotian English discovery, it seems not unlikely to be true, or at least to indicate that these men had something to do with a voyage to the Isle of Brasil before Cabot came on the scene. No date is associated with the claim, but John Dee in 1580 [7] adopted it and associated it with the date 1494, doing so only tentatively, placing it "Circa An. 1494," and leaving no evidence to show whether or not he had specific reasons for the choice of date. "1494" therefore has no special authority: a Thorne–Elyot voyage before 1494 which had a successful outcome is as possible as one in that year if not more so. 1494 can, however, be dragged in as the furthest forward limit of the discovery recorded by John Day and, as already indicated, it is already so late that it can legitimately be thought of as beyond the limit.
8. John Cabot, if he still had unfinished business at Valencia at the end of

[4] Manuel Ballesteros-Gabrois, "Juan Caboto en España," *Revista de Indias,* IV (1943), 607–27; Ballesteros-Gabrois, "La clave de los descobrimientos de Juan Caboto," *Studi Columbiana,* II (1952), 553–60.

[5] Rodolfo Gallo, "Intorno a Giovanni Caboto," Accademia Nazionale dei Lincei (A.N.L.), Rome, *Rendiconti della classe di scienze morali, storiche e filologiche,* ser. 8, III (1948), 209–20; and see Williamson, *Cabot Voyages* (1962), pp. 192–5.

[6] *Ibid.,* p. 201. [7] *Ibid.,* p. 202.

February, 1493, is unlikely to have come to England in time to take part in westward voyages from Bristol before the end of the sailing season (September) in that year. 1494 is therefore the first year in which he, if the Valencia evidence be accepted, is likely to have been available to make a voyage from Bristol. John Day records that he did make one unsuccessful voyage before 1497. On the arguments advanced so far this would leave 1494, 1495, and 1496 open to him for it. It is difficult to say with any confidence that one year is much more probable than another. The first is still a possible Thorne–Elyot year and is therefore a shade less likely for a Cabot voyage. Vigneras argues that Cabot would not have made a voyage until he had got a royal license to do so and so could not have made his first, unsuccessful voyage until 1496.[8] This is reasonable but it does not exclude alternative suppositions. If Cabot intruded himself at Bristol he may have found himself handicapped by secrecy and obstruction so that his first venture had little chance of success and he may therefore have sought a royal license so that he could overcome it. This is pure speculation, but it is made to show that Cabot could have made his first voyage in, for example, 1495. If 1496 is regarded as more likely, however, following on Cabot's petition to Henry VII and the issue of a patent on 5 March granting him powers to occupy and govern lands found, and to trade with them through the port of Bristol,[9] a further point remains. In that case Bristol voyages made in 1495 as well as in 1494, in Ayala's series, would have been purely English voyages. The limiting date of an English discovery could therefore be pushed up to the very eve of the Cabot grant but, if it is, John Day's "in other times" must be called in question because if 1494 is an absurd date to associate with it, 1495 is impossible. A run of annual Bristol voyages, beginning about 1490 and continuing to include 1495, though not including a discovery in the later years, seems credible. The series would then be continued or paralleled by an unsuccessful Cabot voyage in 1496.

9. In summary then, since, according to John Day, the English discovered America before 1497 they must have done so either before 1480 or between 1481 and, at the furthest limit forward, 1494. 1481 or a date near it would best fit the phraseology of the Day letter on the information now available. A date of 1490 or 1491 is still possible though less likely, but it seems desirable to bring in at least one of the years covered by Ayala's evidence. A date between 1492 and 1494 appears

[8] "Cape Breton Landfall," p. 222.

[9] Williamson, *Cabot Voyages* (1962), pp. 204–5.

progressively less acceptable and 1495 unacceptable (though of course the drawing of a line in this case must be at least partly subjective). Allowing ourselves room for speculation on years both before and after, we can say that an argument on the present basis indicates that the English discovery could reasonably have taken place between 1481 and 1491, with the initial date, 1481, and the concluding one, 1491 (if it is the first of Ayala's series), as slightly less unlikely than the others, though with the chances otherwise in favor of a year in the early part of the series rather than the later. Further than this it would seem undesirable to go until something fresh can be adduced. The sequence of information is so fragile and incomplete that any single scrap of new evidence can upset it. It does not provide a basis for any dogmatic statement other than that made by John Day himself. Nevertheless, with all its limitations, it does provide a rational case for placing the English discovery of America in the decade before Columbus sailed in 1492, and possibly as early as 1481.

II

In what has been said above, the possible implications of one statement only in the Day letter were followed. But with that done it may be worth considering what kind of speculation may seem appropriate to the information which can be squeezed out of this statement. The main and obvious point is that we should ask what kind of a discovery was it that remained so little remarked before Cabot's patent brought the search for land in the west into the open. The descriptions in the documents of 1480 and 1481, in the Day letter and in Ayala's, mention the insular character of Brasil and the last two of them of the Seven Cities as well, though John Day also indicates each island, after the Cabot voyage of 1497, as a mainland (*tierra firme*) as well. The insular nomenclature is in accordance with the appearance of these names as denoting islands in the cartographic record, into which it is not proposed to enter, except to emphasize that charts of the fourteenth and fifteenth centuries do not give stable locations for Brasil and seldom specify the Seven Cities as such,[1] and so cannot be convincingly tied to discoveries. But whatever the English discovery was, in fact, the old insular name (or names) was applied to it.

A discovery of the Isle of Brasil by the English between 1481 and 1491 would lead us to expect some publicity, or else some attempt to exploit the discovery by further voyages of exploration, but until 1956 no

[1] Armando Cortesão, *The Nautical Chart of 1424* (Coimbra, 1954), pp. 68–74.

unambiguous statement of even an initial discovery had come to light. The implications of this appear to be twofold; either there was a discovery, which was quickly lost sight of and which subsequent searchers failed to disclose until 1497, or the discovery, when made, was valued only as incidental to some other purpose or objective. The first is possible; navigation in northern waters at this time was anything but accurate. Yet Day's statement does not easily admit of such an interpretation. The alternative seems rather more attractive in view of the later history of the waters between lat. 45° and 50° N off the North American continent. Fishing was contemplated in 1481, as can be clearly seen from the amount of salt shipped [2]; the discovery of land, believed to be an island, at Newfoundland or even Cape Breton, would attract attention and interest primarily as a landmark for fishermen intending to operate on the Banks nearby.

The history of the Newfoundland fishery, from the time it emerges in the early sixteenth century, demonstrates how incidental and casual was the attention of the fishermen of four nations to the land which bordered the fishing grounds. Speculation about the English-found Isle of Brasil which regards it as likely to be a territorial key to a fishery on the Banks and valued primarily as such, may well be fruitful. This could explain the lack of publicity about the land, if it was not thought to be of great importance in itself. Moreover, the silence about the fishery, the lack of publicity about the discovery of new and extremely rich grounds, would be entirely intelligible and could be supported by analogies from the sixteenth century. Bristol merchants and fishermen would not wish to have even their countrymen, let alone foreigners, as their competitors. But, given this possibility, the yearly expeditions of "discovery" mentioned by Ayala from 1490 (or 1491) would look, instead, like annual fishing fleets on their way to and from Newfoundland waters. If the English discovery can be pushed back into the period 1481–91, as it can if the argument above is reasonable, then so, it is likely, can the history of the English Newfoundland fishery, always supposing that the Isle of Brasil was not found and lost again, but was used mainly, perhaps solely, as a landmark for the fishing grounds.

The intrusion of John Cabot into the sequence of westward English voyages becomes more difficult to explain now that the Day letter gives a clear statement that there was an earlier English discovery. Before it appeared, John Cabot could be seen as the expert Italian navigator who came to Bristol to teach the local seamen how to cross the Atlantic and

[2] Carus-Wilson, *Overseas Trade of Bristol*, p. 114.

succeeded in doing so after they themselves had failed. But if they had already succeeded, why should they permit him to intervene, or, when the patent had been issued giving him rights to rule lands found, associate themselves with him? The answer, if the land first found had been rapidly lost again, might well remain the traditional one, but if the Isle of Brasil continued to be known and to be used to mark a fishery the difficulty is a real one. Cabot is unlikely to have got his patent or to have been able to operate from Bristol from 1496 onward without having something new to offer.

In trying to answer what John Cabot may have had to offer, speculation can, at least, state probabilities rather than possibilities. Cabot, like Columbus, Ayala said in 1498, had been in Lisbon and in Seville seeking support for his plans for exploration. This would have been either before 1490, probably after his journey to Mecca of which Soncino wrote in 1497,[3] or in intervals during the period when he was mainly engaged in Valencia in planning harbor works, if he is indeed Juan Caboto Montecalunya—from 1490 to 1493. It is less likely that he should have begun to press for support in either Spain or Portugal for his own plans after Columbus had returned, as he would know in 1493, triumphant in his belief that his island discoveries lay just off the shores of Asia. For the nature of these plans we have no documentary evidence prior to the 1497 voyage, but it is highly probable that they were similar to those of Columbus: a westward passage to Cathay and the rest of Asia on a sea route thought to be shorter than it actually was. The reports of Cabot's discoveries in 1497 [4] leave little doubt that he believed he had found a way to Asia. His departure from the Iberian peninsula in 1493 or 1494 for England in pursuit of his plans would therefore fit in with a belief that he could still compete with Columbus in the exploitation of his route to Asia by an approach from a somewhat different direction.

To pursue this film of speculation it is now necessary to presume the leakage of news of a Bristol discovery of the Isle of Brasil to either Portugal or Spain. Trading contacts make it possible. The need for Cabot to have some specific incentive to come to England makes it, perhaps, probable. We have John Day's statement to the Grand Admiral, who is likely to be Columbus himself, that the English had discovered the land found by Cabot in times past, "as your Lordship knows." This could mean recent knowledge on Columbus's part, imparted to him perhaps by Day not long before the surviving letter, but it could also mean knowledge which had been in his possession for some years, conceivably at the same

[3] Williamson, *Cabot Voyages* (1962), p. 216. [4] *Ibid.*, pp. 207–11.

time as John Cabot could have obtained it. If it was circulating as a story in Lisbon or Seville it is as likely that one would have heard it as another. All that is necessary here is to permit the inclusion of a leakage about the English discovery into the possible sequence which brought Cabot to England.

With this kind of background, John Cabot's appearance at Bristol would seem logical. He would be able to point to the success of the Columbus voyage of 1492, although he could well have expressed some skepticism as to whether the islands found were so near the Asiatic mainland as Columbus claimed; he could propose to use the Isle of Brasil as a halfway house to a more northerly part of the Asiatic coast, with a still shorter sea passage than that followed by Columbus, so as to tap the commerce of Cathay and the Spice Islands. It could have taken him several years to establish himself in Bristol and the suggestions already made that he might have had to overcome secrecy and even obstruction in his plans and in his initial voyage would remain relevant, but his success in getting the backing of Bristol merchants and of Henry VII would rest on convincing them that he could exploit the earlier discovery as a major trading route across the ocean, thus overlaying fishing by commerce. He came back from the 1497 voyage convinced that he had found the land of the Great Khan and that a further penetration down the coast of Asia would bring him to Marco Polo's Cipango.[5] He also revealed the existence of vast quantities of fish in the American waters through which he sailed, thus publicizing perhaps, rather than discovering, the Banks. It should be remarked that his patent of 1496 gave him rights over lands hitherto unknown to Christian peoples.[6] This would not strictly give him any rights over the Isle of Brasil as previously found; that would still, if the speculations above prove to have any foundation, remain in the charge of its discoverers if they cared to assert rights to it or continued to use it to mark the approach to a fishery or as a shore base of any sort. The patent of 1496 (and indeed those of 1501 and 1502 to other grantees which followed[7] made no mention whatever of a fishery. If it had been established before 1497, on the basis of the discovery of the Isle of Brasil, it presumably would continue as before, separate from and independent of the expeditions to search for a route to Asia or for other lands along that route, such as the island and mainland of the Seven Cities which Day thought Cabot had found. A prior English discovery of land to the west, which was not publicized before or after 1497, though information about it could have leaked out at some stage before 1497, would provide the

[5] Williamson, *Cabot Voyages* (1962), p. 210. [6] *Ibid.*, p. 210.
[7] *Ibid.*, pp. 236–47, 250–61.

basis for an English claim to a footing across the Atlantic anterior to and separate from Cabot's discoveries. Finally, if the leakage by which it is suggested John Cabot learned of the English discovery of the Isle of Brasil reached Christopher Columbus before he sailed to America in 1492, and he was well aware of it, in John Day's terms, so long before the Day letter was written, then the English discovery could have been one of the more significant pieces of information which led Columbus across the Atlantic with the conviction that there was land to be found within the range of distances which he anticipated. The Isle of Brasil as found by the English can therefore join the tales by the Unknown Pilot and the traditions of the Vinland voyages among the data which Columbus could have had at his departure.[8] Though the Day reference is suggestive, rather than conclusive, it is more specific than other indications of knowledge of pre-Columbian voyages at the disposal of the discoverer in 1492 and may therefore find a place in the Columbus story.

III

It should, in conclusion, be emphasized that the two parts of this argument ought to be sharply differentiated. The first part is merely a common-sense attempt to see where an argument from known evidence can lead. The second is a purely speculative reconstruction, novel only in its attempt to include the Day evidence of an earlier English discovery of America inside a larger perspective, but claims no objective validity. It may be useful, however, as indicating one new perspective which the Day letter had made possible. There will, no doubt, be many others.

IV

In the years since the first publication of the John Day letter in 1956 and following my "Argument" in 1961, the document and its interpretations have produced, as has been shown, a considerable literature. To

[8] Mr. G. P. B. Naish has pointed out to me that I have almost returned to the position reached by Bacon when he published *The history of the reign of King Henrie the Seventh* in 1622: "And there had beene before that time [1492] a discouerie of some *Lands*, which they tooke to bee *Islands*, and were indeed the *Continent* of *America*, towards the *Northwest*. And it may be that some Relation of this nature comming afterwards to the knowledge of COLUMBUS, and by him suppressed, (desirous rather to make his Enterprise the *Child* of his *Science* and *Fortune*, then the *Follower* of a former *Discouerie*) did giue him better assurance, that all was not *Sea*, from the *west* of *Europe* and *Africke* vnto *Asia*." First edition (London, 1622), p. 188.

some extent this has been focused on the very important evidence that the letter furnished on the Cabot voyages, yet the indications it gives for a pre-Columbian discovery of transatlantic land by English seamen are arguably of as great or greater interest.

One of the exceptional features of the John Day letter is that it offers us certain clear and precise statements on events which had occurred either very recently (in the case of Cabot's 1497 voyage) or at an indefinite period in the past (in the case of the first English discovery). There is very little material on fifteenth-century voyaging beyond the Azores before 1492 which enables us to make any precise statements whatsoever. We are left with hints, inferences, associations of men, trade goods, and events which we must try, with some historical conscience, to dispose in patterns which may have meaning.

The academic responses that followed the publication of the John Day letter provide a useful conspectus of critical opinion in the field of Atlantic studies in the fifteenth century. Broadly, of course, its major importance has been to provide a fuller and more satisfactory source for the Cabot voyage of 1497; although reaction to this aspect was somewhat tentative at first, the document has established itself as a classic, the most important discovered in the present century on this significant episode. But our more immediate concern is with the information it provides on a prior English discovery of the Isle of Brasil. It is here that response has been most varied.

The interpreter of Cabot voyages who had a major influence on some fifty years of Cabot studies, the late James Alexander Williamson, in his last completed work, *The Cabot Voyages and Bristol Discovery under Henry VII* which the Hakluyt Society published in 1962, was able to make the fullest and most distinguished commentary on the Day letter and its setting that has so far appeared. During the compilation of that volume the present writer, with the late R. A. Skelton, was able to take some appreciable part in revising the material reprinted from Williamson's earlier *The Voyages of the Cabots* of 1929, and in collecting new materials to be added to it. (It should not be inferred that Williamson accepted uncritically texts which were put before him by others. He sedulously and correctly checked them himself from their sources.) But it appeared desirable to both Williamson and this writer that they should formulate their own reactions to the Day letter independently in so far as it concerned the prior discovery of land in the western Atlantic. Consequently Williamson's long introductory discussion and the "Argument" set forth here were composed separately though simultaneously, and Williamson was able to include a reference to the latter in the final proof of his discussion.[9] In spite of differences of emphasis and direction, the two accounts are very close, though Williamson concluded that one alternative left open in the "Argument" had more weight than the others.

He took the view that John Day wrote the letter in English and that it was translated for him into Spanish (this is not universally accepted, since a case can be made for his having written it as we have it). Consequently Williamson did not think too much ought to be made of the crucial statement that the discovery of the "Isle of Brasil" had been made *en otros tiempos;* he regarded it as an attempt to put into Spanish a somewhat vague and general English phrase such as "formerly" or "for several years past." This enabled him to consider the Day letter reference as most probably associated with the voyages mentioned by Ayala in 1498 as having been made during the previous seven years (or in the seven years before Cabot's successful voyage of 1497). While Ayala may not have been accurately informed on what had been going on in England from 1490 or so onward, Williamson held that "if he is right in saying that from two to four ships had been sent out yearly for several years, we have an indication that something promising had been discovered, for it was hardly credible that the merchants concerned would have spent their money at that rate on a series of failures." His conclusion was therefore that "the whole statement, coupled with what we otherwise know, suggests that the discovery was in the early 1490's. But, for all we know to the contrary, there could have been a discovery in the early 1480's, perhaps by the expedition of 1481; but that is speculation without evidence."

He thought there were two possible explanations of the reference to the discovery of the Isle of Brasil in the Day letter and to the implications of the Ayala letter that in the 1490's the Bristol men were still searching for it. One was that "Brasil had been discovered long ago and subsequently lost, and . . . the voyages noted by Ayala were attempts to rediscover it, fruitless until John Cabot succeeded in 1497." The other was that "the 'Island of Brasil' came into permanent relations with Bristol and . . . voyages were successfully made to it." While both were possible, there were considerations of some weight to be urged against the first view: "Mariners who had found a western coast, not by chance but by deliberate purpose, as the record of 1480 and 1481 makes clear, would have known the compass course that led them to it and home again, and would have made an approximate estimate of their latitude on arrival. It does not seem likely that such a discovery, of a large country

[9] Williamson, *Cabot Voyages* (1962), p. 32.

and not a tiny island speck, could have been 'lost' in spite of annual attempts to recover it." Consequently, he concluded, "we must regard the Island of Brasil as a certainty and not a fading possibility in Bristol at the time that John Cabot came there."[1] The distinguished discussion and astute conclusions will make Williamson's response to the Day letter a classic one, irrespective of what precise turns orthodox opinion, that of the majority of workers in the field, may take. It is hard to controvert his opinion that the discovery of the Isle of Brasil was known in Bristol when John Cabot arrived there. On the other hand, the questions of what precise interval of time *en otros tiempos* implied (if any precision is possible), and what constituted a reasonable indication that the voyage of 1481 had or had not produced a discovery, were left open for further debate.

It remained possible for other students in the field to take a very different point of view and to argue that discovery of the Isle of Brasil, while taking place as Day indicated, was so far back in time that everything except a memory of it, rather vague and imprecise, had been lost. Alwyn A. Ruddock began her discussion of the document by the statement that "the date of the discovery of the land alluded to by John Day was quite unknown."[2] She held that the "amazing persistence" of the Bristol men, extending through 1480 and 1481 and continuing annually in the 1490's, was due to the fact that the vague memory of a still earlier discovery spurred them on to these repeated though unsuccessful attempts because during this period—that is, between 1480 and 1495—Bristol was badly in need of new fishing banks to maintain its traditional place in the fishing industry. Her view was that the original discovery "was most probably entirely accidental" and not, therefore, the result of any conscious program of exploration in Atlantic waters, but the consequence perhaps of a spell of exceptional weather—thus "an unusual meteorological situation at some date prior to 1480 could have driven an isolated Bristol ship all the way across the Atlantic to the North American coast." Such a situation would be the occurrence of strong, persistent easterly winds for an extended period all the way across the ocean. Such a phenomenon has indeed been known very occasionally in modern times (but instances from the fourteenth and fifteenth centuries have not yet been identified).

By placing the discovery well before 1480, or even a long time before, she could argue that the methods of navigation at the disposal of Bristol

[1] Williamson, *Cabot Voyages* (1962), pp. 24, 30–1.
[2] "John Day of Bristol," pp. 229, 231–2.

seamen were still too primitive to allow them to repeat their lucky western voyage with any appreciable hope of success. At the same time it seems fair to point out that repeated English voyages from Bristol to Iceland, which also involved open sea navigation for extended stretches, had not in the half-century before 1480 been connected with exceptional losses at sea or any notable uncertainty in finding their way. If the argument of primitive sailing methods is to have much force it must push the voyage back to a period when compass navigation was in its most elementary stages; but in that case the survival of the memory of a discovery and its renewal in such intensity as to justify a long run of unsuccessful voyages from 1480 onward does not carry any great conviction. This does not mean, however, that discussions which would take the discovery of the Isle of Brasil back before 1480 have no validity. What they require is either a convincing demonstration that *en otros tiempos* must mean as much as, say, a generation earlier—which might well be possible to make on creditable linguistic grounds—or that some evidence should be uncovered of an appropriate freak weather situation within a relatively limited period before 1480.

The repeated appearance of the same ships in the customs accounts of the fourteenth and fifteenth centuries does not suggest any undue incidence of loss or the making of voyages which it was not possible to repeat. While it may be said that these reflect mainly coastwise activity, this would not hold for trips to Lisbon or Iberian ports farther south which can best be undertaken by sailing some distance from land a good part of the way; and it cannot be said at all for the Iceland voyages, begun from east coast ports in the fourteenth century and taken up with conspicuous success by Bristol ships in the second quarter of the fifteenth. It may of course be suggested that even these statements require statistical proof related to the number of ships involved in the respective trades, and it would indeed be desirable if such proof could be given, but the persistence of a particular branch of commerce is in itself an indication that it has continued without an exceptionally high rate of loss.

A somewhat more complex approach to the problem is developed by Dr. Björn Thorsteinsson in his book *Enska Öldin:* to wit, that English ships had made voyages to the Norse colony in Greenland, that they continued to make them in the early and mid-fifteenth century when contact with Norway had come to an end, and that the voyages of 1480 and later which had the Isle of Brasil in view were in fact destined for Greenland—the alleged destination, the Isle of Brasil, being only a blind.[3] In this view

[3] *Enska Öldin í Sögu Islendinge* (Reykjavik, 1970).

the discovery of the Isle of Brasil *en otros tiempos* referred to the much earlier discovery of the route from England to western Greenland, and the voyages of 1481 and later to its resuscitation in the late fifteenth century. At the moment this seems a rather far-out approach, not sustained by firm evidence of any direct contact between England and Greenland, but solid proof that the Greenland settlement was viable in the middle and late fifteenth century might lend the view more authority as a hypothesis. Without explicit evidence of a single English artifact from either the Eastern or the Western Settlement, it is hard to believe that we can meaningfully discuss English voyages to Greenland—which, however, might have taken place, more plausibly perhaps than direct transatlantic passages at a relatively early date, but on which we are so far totally uninformed.

The attitude of complete rejection of a pre-Columbian discovery in the fifteenth century is nowhere better illustrated than in *The European Discovery of America: The Northern Voyages*, where Samuel Eliot Morison sweeps all evidence and argument under the carpet in a bluff, amusing comment on John Day's *en otros tiempos:*

There is no English or other evidence of this alleged pre-Cabotian discovery of America. The probability is that Day picked up the usual post-discovery yarns about "Of course, we know all about that, old So-and-So went there years ago," etc., and that he thought it would please Columbus to report that Cabot's discovery was no part of the Indies but had been discovered before. David B. Quinn, assuming that *en otros tiempos* means "a long time ago" [compare pp. 7 and 12 above] (whilst it may mean simply a couple of years earlier), has built up a theory, based entirely on this statement, that there was a "secret voyage" from Bristol to North America which discovered Newfoundland before 1492. This puts Quinn as a dialectician in a class with the Cortesão Brothers, and Henry VII in the "keep it secret" category with João II! . . . My comments are (1) that if America had been discovered by men of Bristol before 1497, there would certainly have been some record of it, somewhere; nor would that prudent prince Henry VII have granted letters patent to the Cabots in 1496 and rewarded John for discovering a *new* isle in 1497. And (2) if the men of Bristol discovered Newfoundland and waters teeming with codfish in 1490, why did they have to send vessels out yearly to search for "Brasil"? [4] [See pp. 9–11 above.]

This rejection of any pre-Columbian movement across the Atlantic apart from the Norse voyages leaves the ocean peculiarly empty for many

[4] Samuel Eliot Morison, *The European Discovery of America: The Northern Voyages, A.D. 500–1600* (New York and London, 1971), p. 208 *n.*

centuries, but it is a justifiable reaction in an outstanding historian whose great merit is that he sees sharply in black-and-white terms, and is therefore uniquely qualified to expound what is already known. He is perhaps too impatient to study the nuances of pre-Cabotian enterprise. The discussion of the evidence which does exist on possible voyages across the Atlantic before 1492 has been pursued at a somewhat more sophisticated level than he suggests. But it cannot be denied that no specific details of a voyage of discovery across the Atlantic before 1492 have yet been found. What has emerged is a certain amount of evidence which is worth taking seriously, though without the dangerous medicines of national or other dogmatisms. John Day's letter is, so far as it can be checked, a responsible and meticulous document; to suggest that on one specific point only he was lying appears very much in the nature of special pleading. We are left rather with two alternatives: either John Day is saying what he believed to be true, and it was true, or he was mistaken and the discovery of which he wrote was a false landfall. This is by no means impossible, but the framework into which the former alternative can be fitted gives supporting evidence for Day's statement even if, in the absence of further documentary discoveries, it is not—cannot yet be—wholly conclusive.

It is apparent that the question of when the early English discovery mentioned in the Day letter took place cannot be answered with any degree of finality unless and until further evidence can be found to clarify the matter beyond doubt. What can be done is to put the discovery, as far as possible at present, into a broader setting, considering some of the problems of Atlantic exploration in the fifteenth century, and see how far inferential evidence can take us in understanding the situation at the time. For this purpose a broad-ranging sketch follows of the relations of European powers to oceanic voyaging in the fifteenth century, and in particular of the associations of the Bristol men, narrowing down to the situation in the period between about 1480 and the Cabot voyage of 1497. This continues on the assumption that the least unlikely date for the discovery outlined in the Day letter was 1481 or thereabouts. It does not exclude the possibility that it took place either before or after that date. Circumstantial indications are used here to point to the 1481 date as one which makes sense within what we know of the context of Bristol activities at this period. The discussion does not claim that we know it to be the precise date, but continues and perhaps develops the argument that it may be so.

CHAPTER TWO

The Atlantic Perspective

I

In the process of discovery in the Atlantic three elements are to be distinguished: legend—experience—science. A rationalist scheme might assume that legends about the Atlantic and what it contained came first in order, experience second, and scientific proof last. This would not be correct. If there was a basic stock of inviting legends about the ocean circulating through the greater part of the Middle Ages—those, for example, of the voyages of St. Brendan—these tales of marvels to the west were counterbalanced by horror stories of what would happen to unwary voyagers into the unknown. There is no evidence of which I am aware that points to legend being the direct cause of Atlantic voyages.

The direct cause was, before Columbus, experience. Confidence in their ships and capacity to navigate, the following of economic incentives such as deep-sea fishing, and the search for fertile islands on which to grow sugar and vines were what brought men away from the shores of Europe into the oceans. But the finding of islands, from the Canaries onward, produced fresh legends or revived old ones, and enlarged by imagination the actual discoveries. Science came in as academic discussion, not of the sphericity of the earth but of its circumference, the precise layout of land and water on its surface and their relative dimensions, and also the question of reaching the easternmost point of the inhabited world —the Eurasian landmass—by voyages into the west. But science, too, encouraged legend: if wishful thinking brought Asia nearer to Europe, legendary islands as well as real discovered ones could be found to bolster up such wishes and harden them into beliefs. To follow this process in detail would take us far afield, but it is, in broad outline, what took place.

It is difficult to disentangle the history of the discovery of the Atlantic islands from the evolution of the sea chart of the Atlantic Ocean. Both played a part in the eventual discovery of America, and for the time being they may be treated together. Almost as soon as charts used in the navigation of the western coasts of Europe began to be assembled into a single picture of the eastern limits of the North Atlantic Ocean, and were left with a fairly wide expanse of sea on their western margin, there was an incentive to fill the vacuum. From the early fourteenth century on, legendary islands are boldly inserted on the chart. To them are added records of early discoveries or relocations of older finds, such as the Canaries and the so-called "false Azores." The firm discovery of the Madeiras before 1420 is what led, I believe, to the appearance of large new islands, well out to sea and associated with legendary happenings not hitherto shown on the charts.

Among these were the islands of Antilia and Satanazes on the Zuane Pizzigano map of 1424, about which Professor Armando Cortesão has written in such careful detail.[1] The desire to find them in actual fact may have led to the discovery of the eastern islands of the Azores group, probably in 1427. These in turn led on to completion of the discovery of the western Azores shortly after 1450. But none of the new islands was thought large enough to be Antilia or Satanazes. On some maps thereafter we find these names taking a position still farther west (also farther south), which they held until the Columbian discovery in 1492 of that western archipelago which was to bear the name of Antilia by transference from the myth to the real. At the same time, as we shall see, Antilia appeared on certain maps in a more northerly location as well. It may, however, be significant that no new islands were added, at least before 1490, to the map of the central North Atlantic after the Azores were finally entered on the charts in the 1460's. A number of voyages made after their discovery failed to locate further islands to the west. Speculation about the ocean was shifting in this period from insular searches to consideration of what lay on the other side.

Meanwhile a number of factors operated in the first half of the fifteenth century to bring nearer to Europe on the maps the mainland of Asia and its attendant islands. The translation into Latin of Ptolemy's geography brought into prominence the techniques of exhibiting a curved surface

[1] *The Nautical Chart of 1424* (Coimbra, 1954). See especially p. 20.

on a single plane. Exercises in map projection excited renewed interest in the globe. Moreover, the emphasis Ptolemy placed on the representation of latitude and longitude by a graticulated network created additional interest in the unexplored segments of the oceanic areas of the earth.

These are elementary points which applied mainly to academic students of geography, of whom there was an increasing number. More influential were Ptolemy's maps, which were copied and recopied. To them were soon added modern maps of regions he had not dealt with, and finally his representations (or those of his Byzantine redactors) were taken over and joined with marine charts to make a more comprehensive as well as more accurate world map—or at least a map of the inhabited world, the Eurasian landmass. Ptolemy's maps extended India farther to the east than had been customary. This opened up discussion of the extent of the landmass. His geography also brought renewed discussion of the circumference of the globe. He had lent his authority to the estimate of Posidonius, which was 16⅓ percent too low, rather than that of Eratosthenes, which was 20 percent too high. The general effect of these studies was to narrow the gap on the globe between western Europe and eastern Asia.

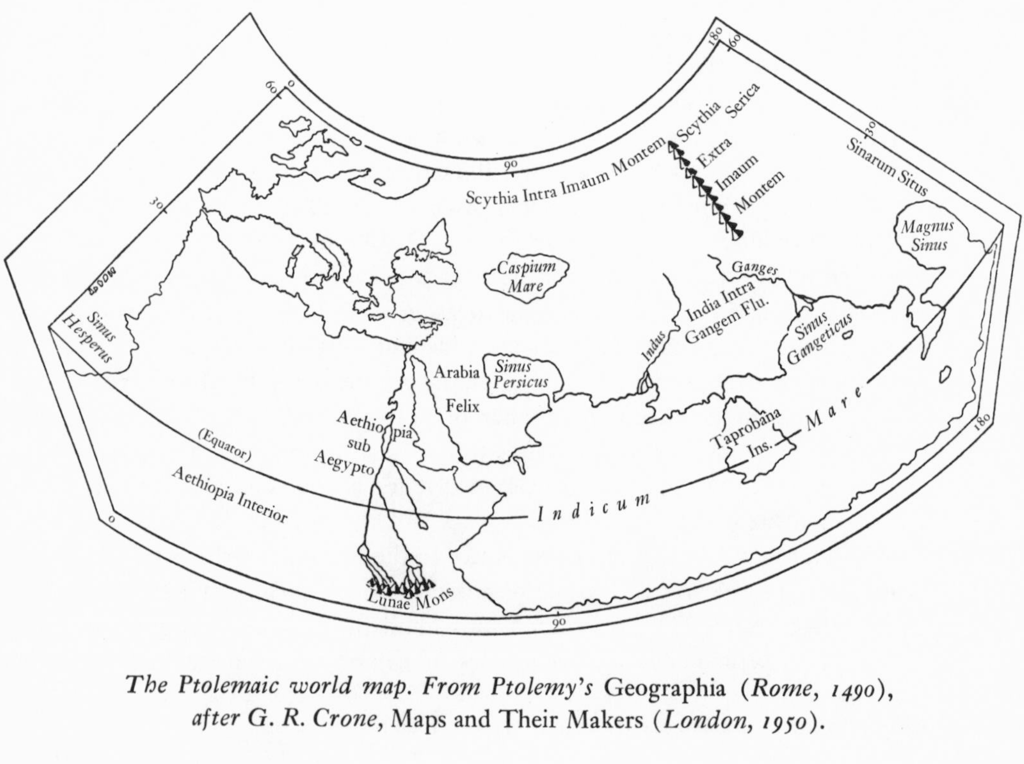

The Ptolemaic world map. From Ptolemy's Geographia *(Rome, 1490), after G. R. Crone,* Maps and Their Makers *(London, 1950).*

Once the practice of adding modern maps to Ptolemy commenced (before 1430) with the appearance on manuscripts of the "Geographia" of the Claudius Clavus map of northern Europe—and the Ptolemaic world picture was conflated (in the 1430's) with the coastlines shown on nautical charts, as in the Bianco map of 1436—the way was open for the assimilation of additional material from voyage narratives. The greatest impetus to extend Asia still further eastward came from the study of manuscripts of Marco Polo's travels. These may well have exercised a subjective influence on European cartography of Asia before 1450, but no specific evidence of their use in the first half of the century has so far been found. On the other hand the discovery of an additional manuscript, the "Tartar Relation," recounting the thirteenth-century expedition to Asia of Giovanni de Plano Carpini,[2] led to the modification of at least one version of the Bianco map. This is the recently published and much discussed Yale or Vinland Map, apparently of about 1440. Here Ptolemaic Asia is modified and extended further eastward by an additional group of islands. When we remember that the islands already discussed were being pushed out westward from Europe, it will be clear that the gap between Europe and Asia—at least to academic eyes—was already by 1440 being substantially narrowed. The incentive to attempt passages across it was increasing.

We should be on our guard against thinking that Atlantic voyaging was chiefly the result of academic theorizing, with no specific economic objectives. All the islands found in the Atlantic in the fourteenth and early fifteenth centuries proved extremely fertile. Madeira enriched its settlers rapidly from sugar and wines. The same was true of the Azores. These islands (and the Canaries and Cape Verde Islands farther south) also proved to have good offshore fisheries. Iberian nationals, therefore, had quite specific economic motives in seeking out other Atlantic islands after the ultimate Azores had been reached—though so far as we can tell there was a frustrating, generation-long gap before new discoveries were made.

Farther north, from the Basque shores of northern Spain to England at least, economic objectives were narrower still, confined largely to fishing. But the Basques pioneered whaling into the Atlantic and may have made voyages farther west than we have any record of. French and English fishermen in the later Middle Ages were ranging well out to the limits of the continental shelf west of Ireland and obtaining experience of oceanic conditions. During the first quarter of the fifteenth century English fishing voyages to Iceland were established on a regular basis both

[2] See pp. 33–4 below.

from east coast ports and from Bristol on the west. The fishermen traded English woollens for fish caught by the Icelanders, as well as exploiting the fisheries themselves. But competition tended to drive them to look for new fishing grounds. Since these were to be found only around islands or a mainland, the discovery of new fisheries away from the seas fringing western Europe implied finding land as well. But fishermen were often fanatically secretive and did not easily share their discoveries of new grounds. Moreover, whatever land they discovered in northern waters was of little value to them economically, except perhaps as shores on which to dry their fish (so saving expensive salt) during the summer months.

II

THE CLAUDIUS CLAVUS MAP of the northern regions which was first constructed in 1427 and revised and made available to southern Europe in 1430 showed a somewhat more realistic Scandinavia than had previously been seen, and also publicized the existence and location of Greenland. This was shown as the terminal arm of a peninsula extending northwestward and west from Scandinavia; within the great gulf so formed, Iceland was located. Clavus's ideas dominated the fifteenth-century maps which concerned themselves seriously with the north, notably those of Henricus Martellus in the 1480's. The broader importance of such maps for our subject is that they extended Europe significantly toward Asia, tended to stimulate wider interest in northern and especially northwestern waters, and may well have played a part in the discussions—extensive in the 1470's and 1480's but possibly emerging a generation earlier—of the possibility of access to Asia by a voyage to the west. *The Vinland Map and the Tartar Relation*, a study brought out in 1965 by R. A. Skelton, T. E. Marston, and G. D. Painter,[3] with its first publication of the Vinland (or Yale) Map, must be taken into serious consideration in any mention of these issues.

For a world map of the mid-fifteenth century (a date of between 1440 and 1448 has been claimed for it), the Vinland Map has some unusual features. It is derived, so far as the Eurasian landmass is concerned, from the circular Bianco map of 1436, roughly reshaped to fit a rectangular frame, but it has a much wider range of ocean to east and west than other world maps of this time. In the east the fringes of the Asiatic landmass have been torn off to make new islands in the extended ocean, while

[3] New Haven, Yale University Press.

in the west a group of great islands occupies a good part of the northern Atlantic. The first of these, Iceland, was not unknown to southern European mapmakers, but here appears much larger, recognizably shaped (more like a late sixteenth-century form, as some commentators have remarked), and lying off a peninsular, westward-pointing Scandinavia. Well spaced out farther west is a substantial Greenland, insular (where Clavus had brought Scandinavia around the north of Iceland to make it a peninsula); complete, as if circumnavigable; and again startlingly modern in form.

Greenland is probably the greatest single item of interest on the map for students of the North. Commentators have found its northern shore incredible (though arbitrary completion of partly-known landmasses was invariable on maps before 1500) and its fidelity on east and west coasts alike, baffling. Spaced out still farther west is an additional enormous island (where Greenland is some three times the size of Iceland, this is three times the size of Greenland) extending southward from a point two-thirds of the way up Greenland to the latitude of Brittany (over twenty degrees, some fifteen hundred miles). The inscriptions on the islands are, respectively, "isolanda Ibernica," a corruption which puzzles the commentators, "Gronelanda," and "Vinilanda Insula." There are further inscriptions: one, glossing the name Vinland, says it was found by Bjarni and Leif in association; another, longer and above Greenland, again recording the discovery of a land by Bjarni and Leif, declares it to have been fertile and to have had vines growing there; while later, in the last year of Pope Paschal (1117–18), Henry (Eiríkr), bishop and papal legate, is said to have visited extensively this great land to the south and west, returning afterward to Greenland and presumably to Europe.[4]

R. A. Skelton, in discussing the map, goes into considerable detail on the historical geography and cartography of the northern lands in the Middle Ages, and has made an enduring contribution in this field altogether apart from the Vinland Map. He demonstrates that much of the Greenland coastline implies that coastal sketches were done, and that the nature of the landmass shown required the making of at least a limited number of astronomical fixes. All this was quite within the capacity of Mediterranean cartographers in the fourteenth and early fifteenth cen-

[4] Some revisions of the captions on Greenland and Vinland are proposed by Quinn and Foote, "The Vinland Map," *Saga-Book*, XVII, 73–89, and by V. Slessarev and P. Sublett, "The Vinland Caption Re-examined," *Terrae Incognitae*, I (1960), 58–67. See also Einar Haugen, "Bishop Eric and the Vinland Map," *Proceedings of the Vinland Map Conference* (Chicago, 1971), ed. Wilcomb E. Washburn, pp. 137–42.

turies, but if done in the north would imply either a Norwegian school of cartography in that period (Norwegian ships were certainly at Greenland as late as 1410), or conceivably Italian participation in northern navigation (which is so far totally undocumented). Skelton argues fairly and undogmatically that there are a few known indications of Norwegian skill in geography which may make the map credible in its representation of Greenland. He has received independent support from Roald Morcken, who considers Bergen to have been an active center of geographical knowledge between the thirteenth and fifteenth centuries,[5] and who argues that Norsemen had apparently accurate distance tables at this period for northern voyaging, which would in turn make possible the coastal sketching from which the Greenland of the Vinland Map could have been compiled. There is still a considerable question mark over these issues, but there is no doubt that the Vinland Map has led to both critical and constructive discussion of northern geography in the later Middle Ages and has opened the way to a further extension of knowledge in this field.

So far the realistic outlines of Greenland on the Vinland Map remain unique: they have not been found strictly paralleled on any other fifteenth-century map. This is not true of the equally realistic outline of Iceland, which does reappear—or appears in a very similar form—in other maps of the 1400's; though, so far as has been remarked, only on maps of the last twenty years or so of the century. But the realistic outline of Iceland on the Vinland Map is the earliest of its type to be traced so far, if the map itself is indeed to be dated between 1440 and 1450. Skelton says of the model that "it may be held to have originated before about 1440."[6] It may now seem worth suggesting that this was an early fruit of the Bristol voyages to Iceland—begun before 1425—communicated through Italians in England or Portugal. Though east coast English fishermen and traders had been going to Iceland in the fourteenth century, Bristol trading operations were more extensive and, being linked with the fishery (as will be discussed further), brought them into close contact with the Portuguese. Whether it is necessary to attribute to English seamen a sufficient degree of cartographical skill at this early stage is uncertain. They might have picked up such skills in Lisbon, or—alternatively and more likely—could have carried with them to Iceland Portuguese or Italians living in Portugal who had learned enough of the Mediterranean

[5] *Den nautiske mil gjennom tusen år: Sagatidens distansetabeller fra vestkysten av Grønland til Hvitehavet* (saertryk av Bergens Sjøfartsmuseums Arshefte, 1964); see also his "Norse Nautical Units and Distance Measurements," *Mariner's Mirror*, LIV (1968), 393–401.

[6] Skelton, Marston, and Painter, *Vinland Map*, p. 167.

techniques of compiling marine charts to bring back an accurate outline of Iceland.

The working out of the pattern of Bristol-Iceland-Lisbon trade appears to have been complete about 1430; the following decade might therefore have seen the transmission of such an outline by way of Portugal to Italy. This is a speculative matter, but it seems a likely explanation. The Milan Catalan map, which Skelton says is "usually dated fairly late in the century,"[7] has a very similarly shaped Iceland, as have the Paris Map of about 1490 and the Behaim globe of 1492, both of which have legends referring to Bristol activity in and around that island. If this element in the Vinland Map can then be associated (though not certainly) with the Milan Catalan map we can link it indirectly with the complex of trade and exploration which brought the English northward and the Portuguese westward into the Atlantic in the second quarter of the fifteenth century, and gave the English—more particularly Bristol men—a specialized knowledge of Icelandic waters and shores.

If the Icelandic and Greenlandic outlines are realistic, the shape and dimensions of Vinland are entirely notional and do not correspond to North America as we know it, but to the saga accounts which distinguish three lands in the west. These seem here to be indicated, by the divisions caused by two large inlets on the east coast (though without inscriptions to say so), as Helluland, Markland, and Vinland. The last is brought far enough south on the map to correspond roughly with the more northerly vine-growing areas of Europe, so that there is here no ambiguity in the

[7] *Ibid.*, p. 167 *n.* It may be worth observing that English knowledge of the nomenclature of the northern waters was not confined to Iceland. They knew the name Greenland and, it might now appear, that of "Wyneland" even if not the correct location of the latter. In William Worcestre's *Itineraries* (ed. John H. Harvey [Oxford, 1969], p. 390) there appears a list of King Arthur's supposed conquests, later printed by Hakluyt in his *Principall navigations* (1589, pp. 244–45) the date of composition of which is unknown except that it was before 1481, which includes "Wyneland" for the usual "Wendland" among the islands "vltra Scanteam & Islandiam, Grenelandiam que sunt de appendicijs Norweie, et Sutheidam et Hiberniam et Guthlandiam et Daciam et Semilandiam et Wynelandiam et Emelandiam et Ree et Femelandiam et Wirlandiam et Estlandiam et Therrelam et Lappam et omnes alias Insulas et terras orientales ecciam vsque ad Russiam." If the inclusion of "Wynelandiam" by William Worcestre was a mistake (the editor says the hand is not his), the indications are nonetheless good, if the transcription is correct, that he knew the name. This is the first suggestion in the fifteenth century that any Englishman knew of Vinland as the name of a place, and it could be of considerable significance, since Worcestre was the source for the details of the 1480 voyage and had some ideas on where Brasil lay (p. 8 above). It would be unwise to comment further on it, however, until the provenance of the document on the Arthurian "conquests" has been fully investigated.

name of Vinland, or "Vineland." For the sagas to have been known outside Iceland at this time is somewhat surprising, while their use to lay out the lands of the saga voyages on the map argues a fair degree of sophistication, though not necessarily anachronistic, on the part of the compiler. If it is authentic, it certainly puts parts of North America, however notionally, on the map for the first time, although it has nothing to do with the priority of Columbus in opening up the New World. For northern studies, its relevance is that it adds a new, cartographic dimension to the saga and chronicle material on the westward expansion of the Greenlanders. No continuity between the end of the Greenland settlement about 1400 and the reopening of Greenland and North America to European contact in the sixteenth century has yet been firmly established. But if the Vinland Map was circulating in southern Europe in the fifteenth century—for which there is no firm evidence—then an element of continuity, if only in notional cartographic terms, may be traceable.

The story of the discovery of the Vinland Map, as told in the volume under review, left many questions in the reader's mind. In 1957 Laurence Witten, a New Haven bookseller, bought in Europe a volume in a modern calf binding containing the Vinland Map and the "Tartar Relation." In April 1958 Thomas Marston, curator of manuscripts in Yale University Library, to whom Mr. Witten had already shown his purchase, bought for his own collection from a London bookseller's catalogue an incomplete manuscript of the thirteenth-century world history by Vincent of Beauvais, the "Speculum historiale." He showed it to Mr. Witten, who soon established to his satisfaction that it and the "Tartar Relation" (and hence the Vinland Map) had originally formed parts of the same manuscript, a multivolume version of Vincent, with addenda: a notation on the outer leaf of the Vinland Map referring to the "Speculum" and showing it to be an integral part of the original. On this basis the reunited documents, after a series of extraordinary coincidences, were eventually acquired for Yale University.

For over a year after the publication of *The Vinland Map and the Tartar Relation,* Mr. Witten and Mr. Marston remained unwilling to say anything about the source of either group of documents, but in November 1966, at a conference in the Smithsonian Institution in Washington, Mr. Witten gave an account of what he could reconstruct of their history and so answered many questions which have been asked since the book's appearance.[8] The manuscripts came, it seems, from a single source, a pri-

[8] Laurence Witten, "Vinland's Saga Recalled," in *Proceedings of the Vinland Map Conference* (Chicago, 1971), ed. Wilcomb E. Washburn, pp. 3–14, and see also pp. 26–7.

vate library, where he was told they had remained for "a couple of generations" more, though nothing was known there of their earlier provenance. In the early part of 1957 Enzo Ferrajoli de Ry offered for sale on behalf of their owner certain materials which included both parts of the reassembled documents, to Messrs. Davis and Orioli, the London booksellers, who bought part of the collection (including the incomplete text of Vincent). But the Vinland Map, bound with the "Tartar Relation," after being shown to officials at the British Museum, was rejected as insufficiently authenticated.

In September of the same year, Mr. Witten met Mr. Ferrajoli at Geneva, learned from him of the map and "Relation," and was taken to see them in the library to which they had been returned. Mr. Witten bought them from the owner as apparently genuine, though unauthenticated, for $3,500. He did not see the Davis and Orioli catalogue of April 1958 until Mr. Marston had ordered the manuscript of Vincent of Beauvais from it. A further visit by Mr. Witten to the European library from which the reunited manuscripts came produced no trace of the missing portions of the "Speculum." The location of this library and the name of its owner have not yet been disclosed, and it is clear that scholars investigating the provenance of the documents will not be satisfied until they can test for themselves what may be learned from the former owner, since to press the inquiry further back in time may materially assist their interpretations. At the same time, Mr. Witten's statement is to be greatly welcomed as clearing away some of the mystery that surrounded the appearance of the map and the "Relation."

In August 1959 the documents passed out of Mr. Witten's possession, purchased by a private collector who deposited them with Yale University and, in collaboration with the Yale authorities, put in hand a full investigation of the map and its appendages. This was completed when the owner presented the manuscripts to Yale in 1964, the book by Skelton, Marston, and Painter being finally published in 1965.

R. A. Skelton, then superintendent of the map room of the British Museum, was given responsibility for the cartography, Mr. Painter for the "Tartar Relation," while Mr. Marston, curator of manuscripts at Yale, was left to deal with the texts, inks, paper, parchment, and handwritings. Mr. Marston put down a number of conclusions which will need further scrutiny before they can be fully accepted, but which form an interim report on these topics. He states that the ink is not modern, and it is certainly not made from a modern formula. He regards the paper found in the "Speculum" and mingled with parchment in the "Tartar Relation" as having been manufactured in the Upper Rhineland, possibly at Basel, about 1440. For this there appears to be good technical evidence. He considers that the hand is uniform between the three documents. There is no doubt that the hand of the "Tartar Relation" and the "Speculum" is identical, but it is far from certain that the hand on the map, though broadly similar in type, is identical with the other. That the bookhand is from the mid-fifteenth century is clear enough, but it may not have been confined, as is claimed, to the Upper Rhineland.

Both paper and handwriting, however, offer only earlier limits on the dating: either or both could have been employed some time later. Mr. Marston insists that the pair of leaves making up the map are conjugate with a pair of parchment leaves in the "Tartar Relation," which has seemed to other students of the map somewhat or even highly improbable. The suggestion is put forward that the documents may have been put together, and the map compiled, during the course of the Council of Basel in 1431–49, which certainly offers a field of inquiry that may in the end prove fruitful. No scientific tests were devised at the time which could assist in demonstrating whether in fact the map was five hundred years old or fifty, and though the "Tartar Relation" and the "Speculum" are, almost without possible doubt, original, a certain question must still hang over the authenticity of the Vinland Map.

The map as reproduced shows sharp contrasts of light and dark; it is not specified in the book that these are misleading. On personal inspection, the map seemed pale and faded. A good deal of the natural surface of the parchment appears to have been removed; the material is unusually translucent, the surface a light grayish-brown color on which the map outlines are frequently light, while the legends, in brownish ink like the outlines, are slightly faded and rubbed. The inner fold, now held by an external guard, differs in appearance from the rest of the surface. The texture seems coarser, the inking sharper, and the surface very dirty (though some of the darkness appears to come from mucilage on the guard). This suggests that the map, at some stage since it was bound up with the "Tartar Relation" in its present form, has been subjected to heavy cleaning, which spread a little of the ink color over the surface, though sparing the inner fold which was not so accessible to the cleaning instrument. A possible explanation is that the map was originally reversed, map side out, being used in this way as an outer cover for the "Tartar Relation," and became so soiled that its significance was not at first perceived. This might explain why it has been only recently identified as of interest for its own sake. If this is indeed the fact, it might help to strengthen the map's claim to authenticity—though it may also be argued that if the map is not genuine, cleaning could have been used to eliminate modern features.

If the map is authentic, we may then ask what its function was. The simplest answer is that it was intended to revise the world picture given in Vincent's text by demonstrating that mid-fifteenth-century knowledge of the spread of Christianity was greater than Vincent of Beauvais had at his disposal two centuries earlier, including as it did more specific information on eastern Asia from the "Tartar Relation" than his account of Carpini's mission had given. By setting out the "Relation's" contributions to missionary history on a map of the Eurasian landmass, and by using also the evidence of Bishop Eiríkr's residence in Greenland and his visit to Vinland, it could be shown how far Christians had gone in the west: namely, to the forgotten lands of the Norse dispersion. Because it is so simple and obvious, this could well be an adequate explanation of the compilation of the map.

A more sophisticated answer is also possible. R. A. Skelton has shown beyond reasonable doubt that the Vinland Map contains many of the basic features of the world map in the Bianco atlas of 1436, compiled in Venice and still preserved there. This circular map has been rather rudely adapted to fit the rectangular shape of a folio opening—some say it was redrawn as an ellipse, though Mr. Skelton has denied that the form is consistent enough for this. West is to the left, east to the right, and orientation to the north. The date 1440 assigned to it seems rather early for a map of this sort.

Characteristic of the period are the islands which are shown some considerable way out in the Atlantic Ocean, off the Iberian lands, but the breaking up of the eastern borders of Asia is unusual, while the three great islands in the North Atlantic—Iceland, Greenland, and Vinland—are unparalleled in their extension of the island pattern far to the west of anything shown on other pre-Columbian maps. Though the outlines of both Iceland and Greenland are realistic, the distances between the three islands are much exaggerated. Iceland is about the same distance from Greenland as Greenland from Vinland and Vinland (if the edges of the sheet have not been substantially trimmed) from Postrema Insula—the most prominent of the islands carved out of eastern Asia. This in turn is a similar distance from farther Tartary, the Asiatic mainland across the Great Sea of the Tartars. The spacing may be coincidence only, but if it is not, and if the scale is uniform (both only assumptions on present knowledge), then this map may be taken as showing a line of access from northern Europe to Asia by way of a series of thousand-mile steps from Scotland to the Far East.

The proportions of land and water shown on the map may also be worth our attention. The extent of the oceans both to the east of Asia and to the west of Europe is unparalleled in world maps of such an early

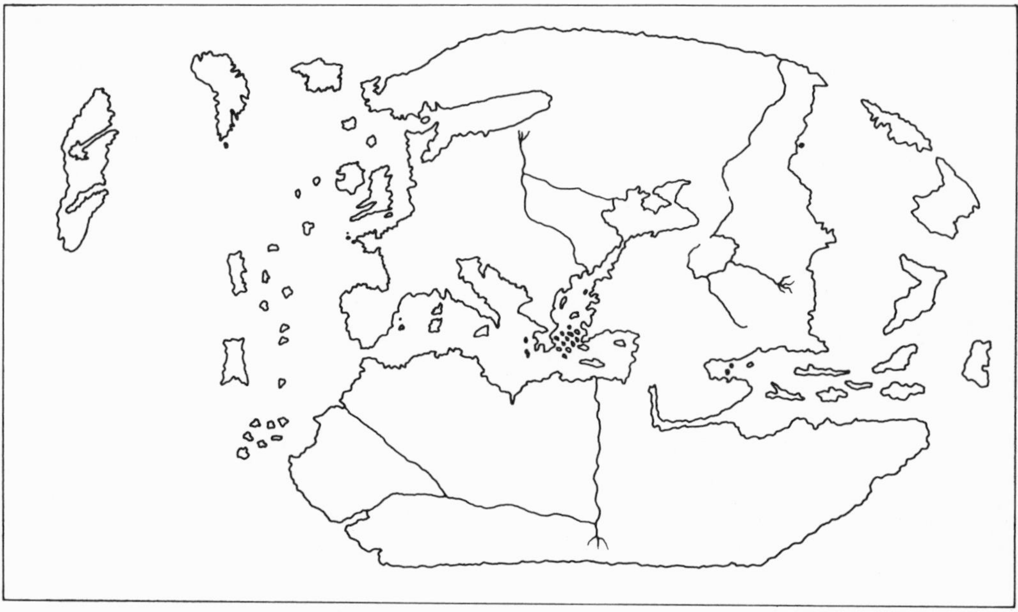

Outline of the Vinland Map, ca. *1444–1450*.
The original is in Yale University Library.

date. If a reproduction of the map is divided and rejoined so that the oceanic portion is in the middle, the layout takes on rather a different appearance. Not only does a series of northern steppingstones stand out as a possible inference from the disposition of islands on the map, but measurement of the proportions of land and water in tropical latitudes becomes possible. On this basis the known world, including the islands off the coast of Asia, occupies approximately two-thirds of the distance, the ocean one-third. It would be unwise to attempt to be more precise, both because of the rather irregular projection of the land surfaces on the plane surface and also because the edges of the leaves may well have been trimmed. From what can be seen it may appear that the known world was credited with an extent of some 240° and the oceans with some 120°. Of the classical estimates, that of Ptolemy had been 180° and 180°, but Marinus of Tyre had chosen 228° and 132°, respectively.[1] This last was the estimate from which Columbus started in the calculations that brought him to a still more optimistic view of the distance between Europe and Asia. But already—if it is authentic—the Vinland Map was making a similar assumption before 1450 and taking a proportion at least very close to

[1] See J. O. Thomson, *History of Ancient Geography* (Cambridge, Eng., 1948), p. 334.

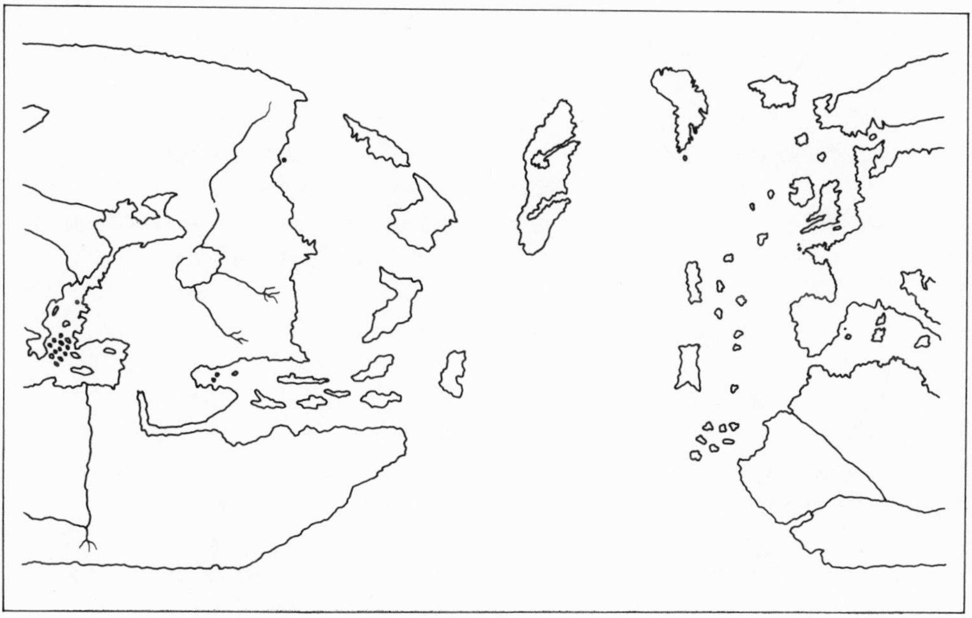

Outline of the Vinland Map, reversed
(compare p. 36 above).

that of Marinus. If we consider this fact together with the disposition of the islands in the north, dominated by the vast Vinilanda Insula, the Vinland Map must be considered as possibly the earliest map to lay down a practicable sea route from Europe to Asia.

There are, moreover, hints at conclusions about the lands beyond the farther eastern limits of Asia. Ptolemy's "Geography" in book VII, chapter iii, contained the rather cryptic statement that "Sinae is terminated in the north by the accessible part of Serica; on the east by the meridian marking the unknown land (*terra incognita*); on the west by India beyond the Ganges." [2] In other words, Ptolemy or his redactors allowed for an "unknown land" beyond China (which did not appear on his world map), with no terminal limit except the edge of the map on the northeast. This may in turn have been the origin of the Horn of Asia, which appears appended to the Ptolemaic outline and completes the Asiatic coastline on those fifteenth-century maps which do show a completed Asia. The "Horn" on the Vinland Map is very small, almost vestigial, though the islands into which eastern Asia has been fragmented extend some way

[2] *The Geography of Claudius Ptolemy* (New York, 1911), trans. and ed. E. L. Stevenson, pp. 157–8.

beyond it to the east, but one of the legends on the map has drawn the attention of the learned reviewer in *The Times Literary Supplement,* who regards it as "the most puzzling thing" in the book.[3] This legend states that "the Tartars affirm beyond doubt that a new land is situated in the outermost parts of the world and beyond it no land is found but only the open sea." This, curiously enough, is derived from a passage in the "Tartar Relation" which does not refer at all to "new land" (*nova terra*), but to "the said land" (*dicta terra*), and so alters entirely the original implications of the passage. Though Skelton did not note any influence of Ptolemaic thinking on other aspects of the Vinland Map, it might seem here as if the compiler of the legends had Ptolemy's statement about the "unknown land" in mind and adapted it to the concept of a terminal land, either on the mainland as Ptolemy intended, or beyond it and isolated from it, in the character of the great insular Vinland which lay to the extreme east—as also the extreme west—of the world map.

The concept of an ocean route from Europe to Asia is possibly involved to some degree in the Florentine map of 1459, even if we do not accept all of S. Crino's interpretations in *Comé fu scoperta l'America* (1943), and is clearly present in the Toscanelli letter of 1474 and doubtless in his lost map of a similar date. It is implicit in the Yale Martellus map of 1489–90, and set out in the round on the Behaim globe of 1492. If the Vinland Map is seen as a forerunner of these great cartographical landmarks of the latter part of the century, the inclusion of the northern islands, the fractionalizing of eastern Asia, and the disposition of the islands between the two extremes of the main landmass make up an intelligible pattern. Skelton repeatedly drew attention to the amateur quality of the cartography of the Vinland Map, but this is not in itself an obstacle to its embodying the speculations of a mid-fifteenth-century cosmographical theorist. That it may do so, and that these views may well be in the line of debate and experiment that led (accidentally) to the discovery of America, is clearly worth further examination and discussion.

Provided that both the Vinland Map and the "Tartar Relation" belong with Vincent of Beauvais's text, then the Council of Basel was a likely point of origin. Missionary enterprise was under active discussion there; those parts of Europe from which the "Tartar Relation" is believed to have derived (Silesia or thereabouts) were represented; there were numerous Italian humanists present whose interest in cartography can be plausibly demonstrated. There was even a northern delegation which could have brought news of the sagas and sketches of the northern islands.

[3] November 25, 1965, p. 1076.

Erik VII united in his person the lands of Denmark, Sweden, Norway, Pomerania, Iceland, and Greenland (the latter only in title); his four ambassadors arrived at Basel on 15 March 1434 with a guard of 150 men bearing the motto *Rex Datiae cuius regni non est finis*,[4] conceivably implying not only that the Union of Kalmar would last forever but that its limits were unbounded (as in theory they could claim to be in the west).

Without expressing any opinion on its precise value, it may be worth pointing out that G. Uzielli in 1894 set out an elaborate argument that Nicholas of Cusa, prominent in the Council of Basel until 1438, had thereafter, possibly as early as 1440 during the meetings of the Council of Florence, communicated information on Vinland to Toscanelli.[5] Other churchmen who left the Council of Basel also retreated to the rival Council held successively at Ferrara, Florence, and Rome between 1438 and 1443, and they had, besides their theological debates, time on their hands to embark on such scholarly pursuits as bringing Vincent of Beauvais's "Speculum" up to date and setting out graphically cartographical knowledge and cosmographical speculation such as the Vinland Map may incorporate. The Vinland Map could have arisen just as well in Florence where, as in Basel, there was much discussion of the range of Christian activity and of Christian unity, being recopied a little later in or near Basel,[6] especially as both R. A. Skelton and Mr. Painter thought that both map and "Relation" were second or later versions of the original compilations. Intensive research over some considerable period will be needed to follow through the association of the documents with Basel or Florence or both.

All three writers are convinced that the Vinland material has not been inserted recently on an older map; they are satisfied that the pair of parchment leaves on which the map appears are an authentic part of the group of documents. In these circumstances, it may appear ultraskeptical to suggest that the map could still be a forgery. That a map accompanied the "Speculum" and "Tartar Relation" is likely in itself. If it was of the known world, without Greenland or Vinland though with legends drawn from the "Tartar Relation," it could have been copied on another pair of blank parchment leaves, if any were available in the "Speculum." Ice-

[4] *Consilium Basilense: Studien und Documente*, 8 vols. in 9, 1896–1936, V, 397. The presence of Scandinavian clergy, 1434–6, is fully attested.

[5] Gustavo Uzielli, *La vita ed i tempi di Paolo Pozzo Toscanelli* (Rome, 1894), pp. 97–119. Cf. Giuseppe Saitta, *Nicolo Cusano e l'umanismo italiano* (Bologna, 1957), pp. 18, 35.

[6] See T. E. Goldstein, "Conceptual Patterns Underlying the Vinland Map," *Renaissance News*, XIX (1966), 321–30; Goldstein, "Some Reflections on the Origin of the Vinland Map," in *Proceedings of the Vinland Map Conference* (Chicago, 1971), ed. Wilcomb E. Washburn, pp. 47–52.

land, Greenland, and Vinland, with perhaps other novelties, could then have been composed and added to this copy, which would thus have a completely homogeneous appearance. It would thus be possible to dispose of the original map and pass off the copy with its striking additions as the original. This could not have been accomplished without both scholarship and skill in execution, but forgery has frequently been the result of an excess of scholarly vanity as well as greed. There is, until now, no positive evidence whatever, so far as is known, that such a forgery was made. On the other hand, there is as yet no satisfactory physical evidence that the map is genuine.

If in the end the Vinland Map is more fully authenticated, and is firmly rather than provisionally admitted into the body of sources alike of Norse history and of Atlantic cartography and world cosmography, it will open up a more searching inquiry into what precisely was known in western and southern Europe of the lands of the Norse dispersion toward the end of the Middle Ages—and also offer a possible stage in the direction of the fruitfully mistaken cosmography of the Columbus voyages. R. A. Skelton regarded the map as representing older rather than novel concepts, both of cosmography and of cartography, into which the new data on the northern islands have been fitted somewhat ineffectively as an extension of an established pattern. Mr. Goldstein sees it, on the other hand, as the first cartographic expression of a new concept of the globe, hammered out by critical discussion in the milieu of the Council of Florence. I should like to suggest here that it was, rather, an empirical attempt by a somewhat amateur hand to see whether and how the new data on northern and western islands could be used to extend existing cosmographical and cartographic concepts, but that the experiment need have been no more than an exercise. That the result had novelties in its appearance and implications could, but may not necessarily, have been accidental.

It cannot be claimed that the Vinland Map had any direct influence on English overseas activities before Columbus reached the outlying islands of a New World in 1492, but it is clear that, if it is genuine, it belongs to a chapter in the growth of Atlantic concepts which is relevant to English experience. It may also—indirectly, it is true—enshrine something of English enterprise in its outline of Iceland.

III

THE DISCOVERY OF the Americas in the fifteenth century was the work of Renaissance Europe rather than of any one nation. At the same time, it has proved difficult in subsequent scholarship to keep nationalistic claims out of discussions of what exactly was found, and when. The Portuguese made their major contribution to discovery in their voyages down the African coast and eventually to Asia; nonetheless their activity in the Atlantic, and success in finding and colonizing islands there, were an essential prelude to the discovery and settlement of the North American mainland. Whether, in fact, the Portuguese made an American landfall before the English or before Columbus is an important historical problem, but it has tended to get bogged down in nationalistic claims which have only marginal connections with academic scholarship.

Here the evidence is probably not conclusive enough for us to say with any real confidence that Portugal did make a mainland discovery before 1492. At the same time, the indications that she may have done so are not negligible. As will be seen when English activities in the Atlantic are considered, except in the northwest, England stepped gingerly into that ocean in the wake of the Portuguese. The greater part of what the English knew of Atlantic islands, except for Iceland, depended on information from Portugal. The maps we believe the English knew may have been made mainly by Italian cartographers, but the information they contained about the Atlantic came almost solely from Portuguese sources. At the same time, the English expeditions in search of the Isle of Brasil in 1480 and 1481 and after 1490 appear to have been made without the direct assistance of Portuguese personnel until the appearance of some Azorean Portuguese at Bristol in 1500.

The presence of the great island of Antilia on the Zuane Pizzigano marine chart of 1424 cannot in itself prove a Portuguese discovery, as it is totally unsupported by legends on this map or those that copied it, or by collateral evidence. Portugal played a part in the rediscovery of the Canary Islands in the fourteenth century; by 1420 she had discovered and begun to develop the Madeira group. Her first major move westward came with the discovery of the Azores, perhaps as early as 1427, and her gradual moves through those islands until 1453, when the discoveries were complete, brought her halfway across the ocean. As S. E. Morison pointed out in 1940, Corvo is only 1054 nautical miles from Cape Race by a great circle course.[7] And before the discovery was complete, Diogo de Tieve was already searching westward for further islands. Sailing westward or northwestward from the Azores to Newfoundland has its own special difficulties and problems. Tieve lost all sense of direction; the island he saw may have been an illusion, and is unlikely to have been America since the land he eventually reached was Ireland. After 1460, grants for western

[7] *Portuguese Voyages to America in the Fifteenth Century* (Cambridge, Mass., 1940), p. 15.

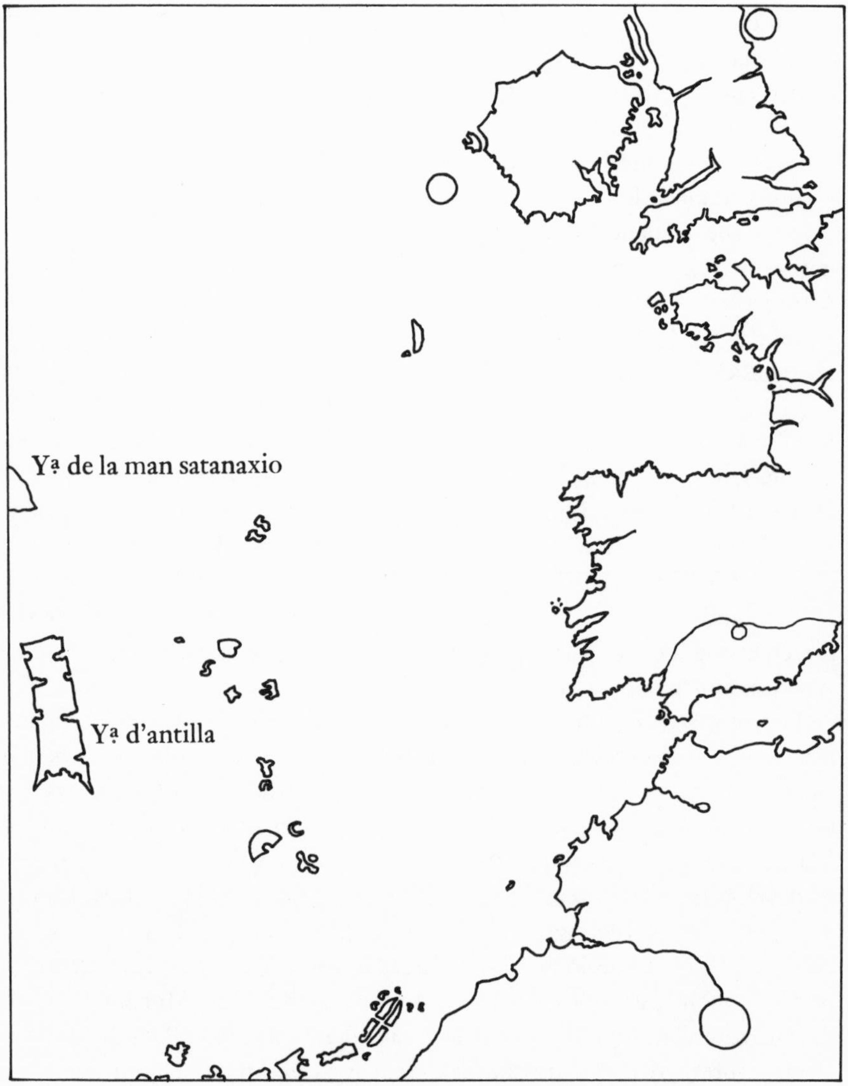

Antilia and Satanazes in a normal fifteenth-century position.
As they appear on the map by Andrea Bianco, 1436,
after J. A. Williamson, The Voyages of the Cabots *(London, 1929).*

searches become more frequent. João Vogado was granted in 1462 "two islands called after the sea chart, Lovo and Capraria," though there is no indication that he found them. In the same year Fernandes de Tavira reported sighting land "northwest of the Canary Islands and Madeira," though he was unable to rediscover it. In 1473 Ruiz Gonsalves de Camara was given rights to "an island which he or his ships may be able to discover."

It was in the following year that Paolo Pozzo Toscanelli, having established to his satisfaction that the ocean gap between Europe and Asia was less than anyone else had anticipated, and having drawn a map to demonstrate this, wrote his celebrated letter to the Portuguese priest Fernão Martins, for the use of King John, telling him that "from the island of Antilia, known to you" and itself some 2500 miles to the west, Japan was only 2500 miles away, and that from it the mainland coast of Asia was accessible. With Antilia the Portuguese were more familiar under the name of the Island of the Seven Cities, on the strength of a legend of cities founded by an early bishop who escaped from Portugal at the time of the Moorish invasion. If the name was known to the Portuguese, it is more likely to have been from hearing the story or from seeing the island marked on a map than from physical discovery.

The search for Antilia appears to have been undertaken by the Portuguese almost at once after receipt of the Toscanelli letter. Fernão Telles was granted a charter in January 1474 to proceed from the Azores in search of unspecified islands. In November 1475 he was granted a supplementary charter explaining that in the earlier one it had not been made clear that his rights extended to inhabited as well as uninhabited islands, provided they were not in the seas of Guinea—because "it might happen that, in sending out to seek them, his ships or people might find the Seven Cities or some other inhabited islands which at the present time have not been navigated to or discovered or traded with by my subjects." From this it does not appear that the Portuguese king believed that Antilia had been rediscovered, but it is clear that (perhaps because of the Toscanelli letter) he considered it worth rediscovering. However, Telles is in fact not thought to have made any insular discoveries.

The records of the period 1472–6 constitute possibilities of a discovery: a claim that a discovery probably took place in 1472 or 1473 as the result of a joint Portuguese-Danish expedition is substantial enough to have appeared in many surveys during the past forty years as reasonably well established. The argument, first fully advanced by Sofus Larsen,[8] begins

[8] *The Discovery of North America Twenty Years Before Columbus* (Copenhagen and London, 1925), and see Richard Hennig, *Terrae Incognitae*, 2d ed. (Amsterdam, 1956), IV.

with several indications of Danish-Portuguese contacts over West Africa between about 1440 and 1461. It then jumps a century to a letter of 1551 from the burgomaster of Kiel, Carsten Grypp, to the king of Denmark. Grypp claimed there was evidence on a map recently published in Paris of a voyage by two men in the Danish service, Pining and Pothorst, "who were supplied with a few ships and sent by your Majesty's grandfather, Christian I, at the request of the king of Portugal, to sail and find new islands in the lands of the north." No map with such an inscription has been identified, so that nothing is known about Grypp's authority for his statement, which is nonetheless interesting. Diddrik Pining and Hans Pothorst were Germans in the Danish service; they were employed in northern waters, Pining for some years acting as governor of Iceland. There is adequate evidence that they were engaged in the exploitation of the Greenland coasts adjacent to Iceland, probably for fish and seals, both before and after 1480, and are not unlikely to have visited West as well as East Greenland, though there is no evidence that they attempted to sail farther west. The Frisius-Mercator globe of about 1537 adds indications of lands to the west of Greenland and the legend: "These people to whom Joannes Scolvus, the Dane, came about the year 1476." ("Quij populi ad quos Iohannes Scolvus danus pervenit circa annum 1476.") No one knows who John Scolvus was, or whether he made a voyage or had any links with Pining or Pothorst.

Larsen put the whole boiling together, alleging that Scolvus was pilot of the Pining-Pothorst voyages and that he conducted an expedition to America in these years. An independent story, recorded by Gaspar Frutuoso in the Azores as late as about 1590, alleges that João Vas Corte Real, father of the celebrated brothers Gaspar and Miguel, "went to discover the New Land of the Baccalao by the king's order," but Larsen links him with the Grypp letter and sends him with Pining, Pothorst, and Scolvus to make an American discovery in 1472 or 1473. This statement of the data patched together by Larsen shows that the story he constructs has no unity or continuity. If a discovery was made as the result of independent action by these various parties, more evidence will be needed to raise any of these possibilities to a substantial degree of probability.

If João Vas Corte Real made any landfalls in the west, it is most unlikely that it was in company with the Danes or Germans. On the other hand, the Paris Map of about 1490, discussed below, puts the island of Antilia well to the northwest of the Azores and states that it had already by this time been settled by the Portuguese—and this is a pre-Columbian document. If any discovery of "Antilia" was made by the Portuguese, it is more likely to have been Nova Scotia or Newfoundland than a Caribbean island. But on present evidence this can only be taken as a possibility, sufficient to raise a query about S. E. Morison's conclusion in 1940 that this story of Portuguese voyages in search of new land or islands to the westward before 1500 is a chronicle of failure.[9]

The grant on 12 July 1486 to Fernão Dulmo, now usually identified as the Flemish Ferdinand Van Olmos, reflects the growing confidence on the part of adventurers, and perhaps of the Portuguese crown, that there was land to be found in the ocean west of the Azores. We are told that he received it because "he wishes to go to discover a great island, or islands, or mainland nearby the coast which is supposed to be the island of the Seven Cities, at his own costs." Moreover, in 1487 he made elaborate arrangements with his Madeiran partner, João Afonso de Estreito, to follow him with a second expedition. Dulmo's confidence may have arisen from knowledge of the plans Columbus had recently presented to the Portuguese court. Toscanelli and Columbus alike had been sure that Antilia lay well on the fairway to Asia.

Dulmo is not known to have sailed successfully. One theory is that he was driven back by unfavorable winds; another that he did not go at all, since he would have to relinquish his captaincy in Terceira. The second seems at least probable. The grant shows, however, that the Portuguese were continuing their westward probing until almost the eve of Columbus's voyage. The return of Dias in 1488, with news of the long-sought eastern turning of Africa, concentrated almost all the attention of the Portuguese thereafter on the opening of the main road to Asia, the way to the west being left for the Castilians.

The ideas of Columbus were formed in a Portuguese environment between about 1476 and 1485. The lore of the oceanic islands which he accumulated—where not based on traditionalist writers—was Portuguese; the Toscanelli letter was a Portuguese artifact in that it derived from Portuguese inquiries in Italy concerned with the extension of Portuguese activities in the Atlantic, and was probably being exploited by them before Columbus attempted to do so. Whether he had access to the Fra Mauro map in Lisbon is not certain, but he may have had. How much he added to his knowledge by his voyage to Iceland in an English ship, or expanded the range of his Atlantic interests by conversations with Bristol men, remain wholly matters of conjecture—so are speculations about whether in Iceland he picked up anything on Greenland or Vinland. The totality of his knowledge and speculations was his own, as was his

[9] *Portuguese Voyages*, p. 50. The hilarious treatment accorded this alleged episode in his *The European Discovery of America. The Northern Voyages* (New York, 1971), pp. 89–94, 108–9, may be noted: it seems at least partly justifiable.

burning enthusiasm to put his theories into effect. Here it is necessary to stress only that the information he had was also at the disposal in these years both of the Portuguese and, to some extent at least, the Bristol men.

The Spanish background of the Columbus voyage is relatively simple so far as our knowledge extends. We are left with the story of the Unknown Pilot (Alonzo Sanchez or another), who as master or pilot of a vessel was carried westward on the trades and survived the homeward passage from a Caribbean island, but only long enough to tell his secret of the western winds, currents, and islands to Columbus before his voyage. This story seems to have been current before Columbus's death in 1506 and was repeated by historians of the second quarter of the sixteenth century, notably Oviedo and Las Casas. It might well have been invented by his enemies to discount his fame, but there is a grain of possibility which makes it impossible to discard it completely, however unlikely it may be. And what Spanish sailors could report before 1490 about the sands of the Island of the Seven Cities, which the Paris Map says they could do,[1] is still an impenetrable mystery.

A recently discovered set of accounts for a Bristol voyage by the ship *Trenete* (not that involved in the 1481 Brasil voyage) to Spain and Oran in 1480–1, in which a John Dee, mariner, took part—though apparently not the John Day of the Cabot voyage letter—shows that the ship put in at Huelva, and a payment was made to the friars of the Franciscan house of Santa Maria de la Rábida for their prayers. Since this was a place where Columbus found advice and help, it has been suggested that perhaps the Bristol men gained there some news of Spanish knowledge of lands in the Atlantic, or—alternatively—supplied information on islands already found by the English.[2] The ship was owned by a consortium which included one of the several John Jays of Bristol, one of whom was associated with the 1480 Brasil voyage, though not, so far as is known, with that of 1481. Whether the Spaniards at Rábida had anything to give or to receive from the Englishmen is so far entirely unknown.

[1] See p. 60 below.

[2] T. F. Reddaway and Alwyn A. Ruddock, eds., "The Accounts of John Balsall, 1480–1," *Camden Miscellany*, XXIII (1969), 1–28.

CHAPTER THREE

England and the Atlantic

I

THROUGHOUT THE GREATER PART of the fifteenth century the English had a substantial trade with Iceland and were also active in the cod fishery off her shores. The larger share of the fishing and probably of the trade as well was done from east coast ports, but Bristol had a lively concern in both from about 1424 onward and retained a considerable interest in the Iceland trade until after 1480. Of the royal licenses issued in England from 1439 to 1484 to trade with Iceland, about 40 percent were to Bristol men for Bristol ships—though this represented only a fraction of the numbers who went there unlicensed. During most of the reign of Edward IV this trade continued. It is documented for the years 1461, 1466–7, 1469–72, and 1478–81, but there is nothing in the customs accounts for 1483; one ship (from London but calling at Bristol) in 1486, nothing in 1487, one ship in 1493, and then nothing at all is known for a generation. Even if only by negative evidence, it would appear that 1481 represented the virtual end of the Bristol trade.[1]

[1] See Eleanora M. Carus-Wilson, *Medieval Merchant Venturers* (London, 1954), pp. 98–143, and *The Overseas Trade of Bristol in the Later Middle Ages*, B.R.S. (1937), *passim;* Björn Thorsteinsson, *Enska öldin* (Reykjavik, 1970), on the English century in Icelandic trade, following his "Islandverzlun Englandinga afyrra hluta 16. aldar," *Skirnir,* CXXIV (1950); Thorsteinsson, "Islands—og Graenlandssiglingar Engelendinga á 15. öld og fundur Nordhur-Ameríku," in *Saga,* IV–V (Reykjavik, 1964–7), 3–72 (an English version of which I saw through

During the period when it flourished, Bristol merchants had close contacts with Icelandic ports, particularly with Snaefellsnes. They reached Iceland normally by way of the Irish sea and western Scotland, though there is some evidence of voyages round Ireland, where vessels could more easily be swept out into the ocean. Fishing vessels (doggers as they were often called) might be as small as fifty tons, trading ships as large as three hundred tons.

As we have seen (pp. 21–2), attempts have been made to show that English vessels may have had direct contact with the Norse Greenland colony before links with Iceland and Norway were finally broken, but though there are hints that this may have happened, there is no reliable evidence. We do not know whether, in the late fifteenth century, the colony still existed or not. The involvement of Englishmen in Iceland might, however, have put them in possession of some knowledge of it and conceivably of the sagas relating stories of the ancient Vinland voyages. The presence of English ecclesiastics in Icelandic benefices in the first half of the fifteenth century carried with it entry into the households of the older leading families of the island, where stories and documentary records of Greenland were maintained, so that a plausible intellectual channel for the transmission of information to England is indicated.[2] In 1475 John Goodman, a Bristol merchant whose trading interests ranged from fish to French and Portuguese wine and Spanish fruit, when involved in violent conflict with the Hansards could draw on evidence from leading Icelanders who knew him.[3] Such a man might also have brought information on Greenland and on western voyaging to Bristol, but proof is still lacking that such connections were in fact made.

Relations between the English and Icelanders were not always easy. There was fighting in 1467, and a state of war between England and Denmark which tended to affect the Iceland trade between 1468 and 1473. The admission by Denmark of Hanseatic vessels to the Iceland trade complicated the activities of both English traders (their virtual monopoly threatened) and fishermen. There was fighting again in 1475 after the truce between England and Denmark. The German governor

the courtesy of Professor Peter Foote); Thorsteinsson, "Henry VIII and Iceland," *Saga-Book*, XV (London, 1957–9), 67–101. I am much indebted also for personal letters from this scholar dated 15 May 1967 and 2 August 1969, and to Professor Gwyn Jones for his introduction.

[2] Thorsteinsson, "Íslands—og Graenlandssiglingar," pp. 34–5; Carus-Wilson, *Medieval Merchant Venturers*, pp. 121–4.

[3] Thorsteinsson, "Íslands—og Graenlandssiglingar," p. 52; Carus-Wilson, *Overseas Trade of Bristol*, pp. 134, 155–6, 209, 221–2, 226, 232, 240, 267, 273, 277.

installed in Iceland by the Danes, Diddrik Pining, who served from 1478 to 1490, waged war on the English, driving them from many harbors. In 1486 the London ship *Trinity* (which put in at Bristol on its return) was accused of seizing a Hanseatic ship in Hafnarfjördhur and selling it and eleven members of the crew at the Irish port of Galway. Some years before, after 1480, contact with Iceland was already declining, and when in 1490 a firm peace was made it was too late to revive the Bristol trade.[4] When Henry VII was in Bristol in 1486 he was told that the town's trade was depressed largely owing to the decline in the Iceland connection.[5]

The difficulties of the Icelandic trade helped to impel Bristol men to find both new markets and new fishing grounds. By 1480 they were turning for markets to the Atlantic islands—Madeira at least, colonized by the Portuguese; and for a fishery they were searching the Atlantic for the Isle of Brasil. If they found the Newfoundland Banks in 1481, as seems quite possible, they had every incentive to keep their discovery to themselves in the hope of keeping out competitors as long as possible.

The English ships which traded with Iceland tended to bring Icelanders to England—some, it was alleged, kidnapped and treated virtually as slaves, apparently for apprenticeship. Behaim, on his globe in 1492, says the Icelanders sold their own children into slavery to the English. The evidence of this being done in the east coast ports in the first part of the fifteenth century is considerable, but nothing has shown hitherto that it was done in Bristol.[6] This makes it the more surprising that in fact forty-eight or forty-nine Icelandic males, boys and men, were to be found in the service of Bristol households in 1484. The alien subsidy roll for the city in that year records the names of their masters with the payment of two shillings in subsidy for each person.[7] The collectors took the trouble to record only two of the names by which these servingmen were known in Bristol: William Yslond and John Yslond—for the rest, they are described as boys who were servants (*puerum sibi servientem de Islond*) of whom there are ten, or else as servants without qualification (*pro uno serviente eiusdem patrie*), of whom there are thirty-six, which, with one unspecified (the sum of two shillings is charged to the master and so is

[4] Carus-Wilson, *Medieval Merchant Venturers*, pp. 138–41; Thorsteinsson, "Íslands—og Graenlandssiglingar," pp. 46–9; "Henry VIII and Iceland," pp. 71–2.

[5] R. L. Storey, *Henry VII* (London, 1967), p. 170 (citing John Leland, *De Rebus Britannicis Collectanea*, 6 vols. [London, 1774], ed. Thomas Hearne, IV, 200).

[6] See Carus-Wilson, *Medieval Merchant Venturers*, pp. 116–17.

[7] P.R.O., E., 179 270, 54. I am indebted to Miss Mary E. Williams for a careful transcription. The roll is to be edited by her for the B.R.S.

probably for the same class of person), and the two named, make up thirty-nine presumably adult servants.

The masters comprise forty-nine separate persons, indicating no more than one Icelander to the household. Two of the persons named as having Icelandic servants are women. While by no means all the men can be readily identified, those who can form a broad spectrum of the mercantile community of Bristol—men who can be traced trading to France, Spain, and Portugal, and in one instance to Madeira. Curiously, none has any obvious association with the Iceland trade. They do not include many of the names which may in some way be associable with the Brasil voyages, such as John Jay, a Lloyd, Thomas Croft, Robert Strange, William de la Founte, Robert Thorne, or Hugh Elyot. William Spencer, who was among those to whom the special trading privilege of 1480 was given, is there; there is a John Eliot; and Richard Ameryk, later one of the customers of Bristol and a local favorite son for the naming of America;[8] also a John Pynke who was trading to Madeira in 1480.[9] There is therefore only a little correlation, insufficient for any conclusions, between the masters of Icelandic men and boys in Bristol in 1484 and the planning and execution of the Brasil voyages.

Nor do we know whether this group of males had been brought to Bristol in one group or how long they had been there—for the account is very much an isolated document—or whether they had come willingly or had been brought by force. Dr. Thorsteinsson pointed out to me that there were frequent allegations in Iceland in the early fifteenth century of the kidnapping of boys, men, and girls by English ships. None of these applied specifically to Bristol, though the London ship noted above which came into Bristol in 1486 was accused of disposing by sale of Hanseatic seamen in Ireland on its way. As late as 1536–7, at Yarmouth, an Icelandic boy aged eleven years was formally apprenticed as a seaman for the exceptional term of thirteen years—which might almost be seen as a type of legalized serfdom. Bristol, however, attracted an appreciable number of apprentices from Ireland in the first half of the sixteenth century, and it may well be that a number of the young Icelanders of 1484 had come to learn trades or crafts in the relatively more sophisticated English seaport. If so, we would expect the boys to return to Iceland when their apprenticeship was completed.

The adult servants may, however, represent a deliberate movement of Icelandic labor to Bristol. It is possible that a considerable volcanic

[8] See A. E. Hudd, "Richard Ameryk and the Name America," in *Gloucestershire Studies* (Leicester, 1957), ed. H. P. R. Finberg, pp. 123–9.

[9] See p. 57 below; also Carus-Wilson, *Overseas Trade of Bristol*, p. 285.

eruption—that of Mt. Katla, dated (approximately) 1490 or earlier—had already taken place and that some men had lost their homes and gone to work in England. The population, too, depleted by plague at the beginning of the century, may already have been sufficient to create demographic pressure for emigration.[1] At the same time the possibility exists that some of them had been seized and were held in Bristol against their will. If so, it might provide a reason why Bristol ships were, after 1484, except in a few cases apparently reluctant to return to Iceland. Aroused local hostility might have kept them from their accustomed ports. It may be that future research will provide some answers to these questions.

Whether free or enslaved, it is certain that there were in Bristol in this year (and probably for some years previously as well) a substantial number of adult Icelanders. If they had grown to maturity in their own homes, they would inevitably have brought with them much knowledge of the northern seas and conceivably of northerly and western lands. They provide one of the stronger indications that Bristol men, before the discovery of America, might have learned the traditional Icelandic stories of the Greenland colony and the routes to it, and even—just possibly—of the ancient voyages to Vinland.

Not all Icelanders were necessarily in a condition of dependence. One at least of those on the 1484 roll can be shown to have become completely assimilated into the Bristol merchant community. William Yslond, listed as servant to the merchant Thomas Devynshire, was by 1492 a naturalized Englishman and himself a Bristol merchant. On 6 October 1492, "Willelmus Islonde indigenus" shipped six cloths to Lisbon on the ship *Nicholas* of Toure, Nicholas Walsh, master.[2] Among other shippers were Robert Thorne, William Spencer, and John Pynke, who all at various times come into our roster of enterprising, westward-voyaging merchants. The appearance of this anglicized Icelander provides an excellent example of the close ties that bound merchants and merchandise between Bristol, Portugal, and Iceland.

II

THE CLOSE CONTACTS between England and Portugal in the fifteenth century—the "old friendship" was stressed in 1488 when an English treaty

[1] Much of this information is summarized from Dr. Thorsteinsson's letters of 15 May 1967 and 2 August 1969, acknowledged earlier. The Yarmouth apprenticeship appears in Dorothy Burwash, *English Merchant Shipping, 1450–1540* (Toronto, 1947), p. 69, and apprenticeships of Irish boys at Bristol in D. Hollis, ed., *Calendar of the Bristol Apprentice Book, 1532–1542* (Bristol, 1949).

[2] P.R.O., Customs Account, Bristol, 29 September 1492–25 March 1494, E. 122/20/9.

with Spain was being discussed[3]—made trade relations between the two countries easy. Yet the Portuguese did not make any concessions to the English in their exclusion of most foreigners from their West African ventures, and when in the 1480's there were some tentative approaches by English merchants in this area they were rapidly discouraged.[4] How much information on what the Portuguese were doing in West Africa trickled through to England there is so far no means of knowing with any certainty; though, trade relations being close, a certain amount of contact with Portuguese expansion was probably achieved.

There were also intermittent diplomatic contacts which could have been fruitful. It may be noted that when in 1443 Prince Henry the Navigator (Dom Enrique) was appointed a member of the Order of the Garter, William Bruges, Garter King of Arms, set out from England in October, in company with a Portuguese pursuivant who was in England on a mission, to confer the insignia of the Order on both Alfonso V of Aragon and Prince Henry. He did not return until July 1444, having spent some part of the interval in Portugal.[5] The years 1443 and 1444 were ones of intensive Portuguese activity both on the West African coast and in the Azores and it is highly likely that Bruges was able to bring back to England circumstantial accounts of what Portuguese explorers and traders were doing. If any more continuous trickle of news on African and Atlantic activity was reaching England it was more probably by way of Bristol than by any other route. Bristol ships were regularly going to Lisbon, Oporto, and the Algarve—the southernmost province, where the port in use was most probably Faro. Portuguese vessels were also coming to Bristol, as they were to Galway and probably Limerick on the western shores of Ireland. Portuguese vessels do not seem to have sailed direct to Iceland. But close links and overlaps existed in the trade between Portugal, Bristol, and Iceland, with Bristol as the distributing center between them.

Bristol's line of trading connections along the eastern Atlantic seaboard is well illustrated in 1479–80. On 11 December 1479, the *Christopher* of Bristol, Thomas Sutton master, put into Bristol from the Algarve with

[3] *Calendar of State Papers, Spanish, 1485–1509* (*Cal.S.P.,Span.*) (1862), p. 8.

[4] D. B. Quinn, "Edward IV and Exploration," *Mariner's Mirror*, XXI (1935), 275–84; J. W. Blake, *Europeans in West Africa, 1450–1560*, 2 vols. (London, 1942), II, 263–9, 295–8. See also T. F. Reddaway and Alwyn A. Ruddock, eds., "The Accounts of John Balsall," *Camden Miscellany*, XXIII (1969), 9–11, for English trade with Oran (not in Portuguese zone) in 1480–1.

[5] H. S. London, ed., *The Life of William Bruges*, Harleian Society Publications, nos. 111–12 (London, 1970), pp. 22–73.

a cargo of fruit, probably mainly figs from Faro.[6] Among the shippers were William Spencer of the 1480 trading license [7] and John Pynke, who was in 1480 to trade direct with Madeira—both of whom in 1484 had an Icelander as a servant. There was also a Spaniard, Martin Bermedo. When she had unloaded and reloaded, on 14 February 1480,[8] with Sutton still master, the *Christopher* set out for Iceland. There was a general cargo and no indication of Portuguese goods on board, and the whole was shipped by one man, John Shipward. Thus within a few months the same ship was trading from, say, Faro at 37° N to Snaefellsnes at 65° N: largely coastal sailing, but with an appreciable part of it on the open sea route to Iceland. Sutton was at the same time in a position to learn of Portuguese activities on the African coast, since the ports of the Algarve were important centers for West African commerce, and to inform the Portuguese—in so far as they might be interested—about Iceland and the conditions of the Iceland trade, some of whose dried cod came south to Portugal in English ships, while much of the salt brought to Bristol, some of which was reexported to Iceland, came from Portugal.[9] A considerable knowledge of this long stretch of the Atlantic littoral was thus shared by masters and pilots of the two countries.

In December 1485, as the *Christopher* was making her way along the Irish coast, quite probably on another Iceland voyage, she was attacked and captured in harbor at Inishbofin by a Galway vessel. Some of her men got away to Bristol, and when their complaints had been heard the town quickly placed an embargo on the goods of Galway traders in Bristol. After an appeal to the king's council by the *Christopher*'s owners, Henry Toller and William de la Founte (one of the 1480 licensees), an order was issued that the ship be restored to them.[1]

As late as 1492–3, the same William de la Founte was exporting cloth to Andalusia and Lisbon and importing to Bristol fruit from the Algarve, wine from Seville, and oil and salt from Lisbon; meanwhile exporting to Iceland on the *Michael* (Roger Tege, master) on 8 May 1493 flour, malt, and cloth [2]—showing, even when the trade with Iceland was far in de-

[6] Carus-Wilson, *Overseas Trade of Bristol*, pp. 232–3. [7] See pp. 7–8 above.

[8] Carus-Wilson, *Overseas Trade of Bristol*, p. 253.

[9] A. R. Bridbury, *The English Salt Trade in the Later Middle Ages* (London, 1955), pp. 114–5, has shown that while most of the salt used in England came from Bourgneuf Bay, Brittany (hence "Bay" salt), and from La Rochelle, considerable quantities were picked up by Bristol ships at Lisbon and Oporto, as well as a certain amount in Andalusia.

[1] *Select Cases in the Council of Henry VII*, Selden Society, no. 75 (London, 1958), ed. C. G. Bayne and W. H. Dunham, Jr., p. 5.

[2] P.R.O., E. 122/20/9.

cline, its continuity in hands engaged at the same time in trade with the Iberian lands, and especially with Portugal.

The men, and perhaps the ships, involved in the Bristol voyages of 1480 and 1481 had links with the Portuguese trade. It is not possible to be sure that either the *George* or the *Trinity* which went on the 1481 Brasil voyage can be identified specifically as trading to Spain or Portugal, since there were at least two vessels with each of these names trading from Bristol. One *George* of Bristol, for example, left for Spain on 4 February 1480 and returned on 17 May following; the other *George* sailed for Bordeaux on 12 January 1480 and returned on 24 April, William Spencer of the 1480 license and Robert Thorne having wines aboard her. One *George* of Bristol ownership was rated at two hundred tons, and it is not clear which was the larger and which the smaller ship, neither being linked firmly by surviving evidence with the Portuguese trade.

One *Trinity* of Bristol came in from Lisbon on 4 March 1480 with a large cargo. This included 350 pounds of wax and 2 tons of salt (customs valuation £8 6s. 6d.) for John Jay. This would suggest that she was the 300-to-350-ton ship in which a John Jay owned a share. If this was the same John Jay who had a part in the 1480 Brasil voyage, or heir of the man of that name who died in 1480, then part of the lading of salt from the *Trinity* may have gone on board the unsuccessful searcher for the Isle of Brasil in that year. Other names now well known in the Atlantic trade had goods in her also: Robert Strange, wine; John Pynke, oil, wine, and vinegar; Richard Ameryk, oil and sugar. She sailed for Lisbon again on 4 May, this time shipping eight cloths for John Jay. She made a rapid voyage and was evidently back in Bristol by mid-October at latest. Another *Trinity* sailed from Bristol to Ireland, the port not being named, on 20 March 1480. She had a fairly modest cargo, and since she was engaged in a comparatively local trade would, with reasonable probability, have been the *Trinity* of the 1481 voyage. Richard Ameryk laded in her two tons of salt and six tons of corrupt wine. The most interesting thing about her is that her master was a foreigner, Gunsalvus de Sayt, whose name (Gonsalves de Sayta?) strongly suggests that he was Portuguese.[3] We might think he could have been master of the *Trinity* in the 1481 Brasil voyage.

An interesting attempt has been made to identify the first of these two ships with the *Trinity* which sailed with the *George* in search of Brasil in 1481.[4] That *Trinity*, a large ship rated at 300 to 360 tons, had as part-

[3] Carus-Wilson, *Overseas Trade of Bristol*, pp. 156, 236–7, 246–7, 260–4, 268, 276–9, 281, 285.

[4] Reddaway and Ruddock, eds., "Accounts of John Balsall," pp. 1–28.

owner a John Jay II, who died in 1480, and it appears that his share passed to John Jay, junior (John Jay III?). After apparently returning once again to Bristol from Lisbon—the customs accounts for this period are lacking—she set sail again for Andalusia (Huelva, Palos, and Gibraltar) and the Moorish port of Oran. She left Bristol sometime after 18 October 1480 and returned on some date in 1481, not specified. The accounts of John Balsall, her purser, show she carried cloths for William Spencer and Robert Strange of the 1480 license, and also for Richard Ameryk and for whichever John Jay still had a share in her.

Mr. T. F. Reddaway and Miss A. A. Ruddock, who edit this account, make the suggestion that she was the ship that accompanied the *George* on the Brasil voyage of July–September 1481. But the arguments are not convincing. If Croft, de la Founte, Spencer, and Strange had a license to send out small ships in 1480 and the following years, it is most unlikely that they would have chosen the largest ship Bristol had in contravention of their license. The salt which Croft shipped in the *Trinity* and *George* suggests that they were small fishing vessels; we know that Croft was involved, but the editors say that John Jay was also. If he was, there seems to be no evidence of it since the item they quote in fact refers to 1480, when he was concerned in the earlier Brasil voyage. We would at least need to know when the *Trinity* returned from her long and arduous voyage to North Africa and back before we could usefully consider her as one of the ships which set out for the isle of Brasil in 1481, even if her size could be reconciled with what we know of the 1480 license.

Little record has so far been found of Iberian merchants or seamen residing in Bristol, though we would expect a certain number to be established there. A "Fornand of Spain" trading in 1480 was a naturalized Englishman; while a "Peter Gunsalvus" (Pedro Gonsalves) was exporting cloth to Oporto on 4 January 1480. Later, "Johannes Fornandus" (João Fernandes) was exporting from Bristol to Lisbon on 26 January 1493.[5] Further collation of materials may well throw up clearer patterns of association between Bristol and Portuguese merchants and shippers. It is sufficient here to indicate that through the normal trading channels information on Atlantic voyaging and possibly the interchange of a certain number of individuals on exploring expeditions could well have taken place, and the small group of men concerned in the Brasil voyages whom we are able to trace in some detail were involved in the Iberian and especially in the Portuguese trade.

[5] Carus-Wilson, *Overseas Trade of Bristol*, pp. 236, 286; J. A. Williamson, *The Voyages of the Cabots* (London, 1929), p. 204; Williamson, *Cabot Voyages* (1962), p. 118; P.R.O., E. 122/20/9.

How small that circle was may be seen from any of the surviving Bristol customs accounts. Between September 1492 and September 1493, for example, William Spencer, Robert Thorne, John Jay, and William de la Founte are all found engaged in the trade with Portugal. The same merchants, along with Hugh Elyot and Thomas Asshehurst, both of whom overlap into a later period of exploration activity, are found trading to Andalusia, mainly to San Lucár and Seville. One of the more interesting voyages is that of the *Nicholas*, which arrived at Bristol from Lisbon on 30 April 1493 carrying cargoes for John Jay (wine and oil), John Dey (Dee or Day?—oil and wine), Robert Thorne (oil), and William Spencer (wax and wine). John Dee (Day?—wine and alum) appears as importing in the *Mary Bird*—Richard Parker, master—from Bordeaux on 12 June 1493 and exporting (cloth) on the same ship to the Algarve on 26 September.

If John Dee and John Dey and John Day are all the same man who was also Hugh Say and the author of the Day letter of 1497, we can see how closely he was tied in with the small circle of Bristol merchants involved in the Iberian trade. The separate existence of a John Dee who was trading from Bristol as early as 1480 in the *Trinity* might lead us to be a little cautious in concluding that these references are all to one man (even just possibly in concluding that John Day who wrote the letter was really Hugh Say or just a Bristol John Dee who was nothing else). But even so, it is clear that this group was in constant contact with Spain and Portugal and so was in a position to learn of expeditions in preparation by those countries, in that vitally important decade which reached from Dias to Vasco da Gama and included Columbus as well. And they were in a position to let slip information about discoveries by Englishmen of islands in the western ocean in the near or more remote past.

It is worth going back at this point to the Exchequer inquisition of September 1481 [6] on which our knowledge of the 1481 Brasil expedition is based, as it shows how many of the jurors involved in the Iberian and Icelandic trades were chosen to present their report on Thomas Croft's involvement in it. For the purposes of the inquiry, to which I shall revert again in another connection, a list of eligible jurors, including seventy-five names in all, was drawn up. They included one of the John Jays, presumably he who had invested in the 1480 voyage; Richard Ameryk, who was deeply involved in the Iberian trade and also had an Icelandic servant in 1484, and who was still engaged in the trade to

[6] P.R.O., E. 122/19, 16.

Lisbon after 1490; John Goodman, who traded with France, Spain, Portugal, and Iceland; and Philip Greene, later John Cabot's landlord in Bristol, who forms a link between the earlier and later voyagers and has not, perhaps, been sufficiently investigated. All those mentioned except Richard Ameryk were eventually selected to serve. It may appear that the omission of Strange, de la Founte, and Spencer, the licensees of 1480, was because they might, like the fourth licensee, Thomas Croft, be interested parties. The investigation into the ships *George* and *Trinity* and the participation of Thomas Croft in their expedition was carried through by members of a small circle of men who were accustomed to trade to the same destinations and to use the same ships. They would therefore be familiar with the fact that, not only had the ships gone to "search" for the Isle of Brasil in July 1481, but the second objective—to "find" the island—had also (if it had) been achieved. And they would be fully familiar with the background of the Brasil voyages in the Icelandic and Iberian trades of the port of Bristol.

How much contact the Bristol men had before 1480 or even before 1500 with the Atlantic islands discovered and settled by the Portuguese in the fifteenth century—Madeiras, Azores, and Cape Verdes—is difficult to establish from documentary records. It would be surprising if the voyage from Bristol to Madeira of the *Mawdeleyn* of Quimperlé in Brittany—John of Chayson, master—on 18 May 1480[7] were the first, though it is the earliest of which record has been noticed in print. William Weston and the John Pynke already mentioned were the shippers, and the cargo cloth. A ship inward from Madeira in 1486, the *Mare Petat*, had sugar and bowstaves on board, and among the shippers were men named Gunsalves (Gonzales?) and Fornandus (Fernandes?),[8] two of the commoner Portuguese names. (A John Furnandus—João Fernandes—shipped sugar in the *Petrus* of Lisbon, Gonsalus Dido, master, to Bristol on 12 November 1492, and shipped cloth from Bristol to Lisbon in the *Marie* of Lisbon, Gonsalus Dido, master, on 26 January 1493.[9]) No voyages from Bristol to the Azores or from the Azores to Bristol have been traced, though some almost certainly took place, before a group of Azorean Portuguese appeared in the city in 1500.

If physical contact with the Portuguese Atlantic islands is attested only in a very sketchy manner, interest in the islands as they appeared on the maps can be demonstrated from 1479–80 or thereabouts. R. A. Skelton and John Harvey have analyzed two sets of jottings in William Worces-

[7] Carus-Wilson, *Overseas Trade of Bristol*, p. 285; Williamson, *Cabot Voyages* (1962), p. 187.

[8] Williamson, *Cabot Voyages* (1962), p. 187.

[9] P.R.O., E. 122/20/9.

tre's notebooks which throw some light on what one Bristolian thought worth recording who was himself sufficiently interested in the Brasil voyage of 1480 to leave us our only record of it.[1]

One set of notes is a series of mentions of Atlantic islands on a chart which R. A. Skelton considered was drawn by an Italian cartographer about 1470 or not long after, and the notes put down by Worcestre about 1479. This list covers all the islands found on the chart north of the kingdom of Guinea, including the Cape Verdes. There are the seven eastern islands of the Azores group, demonstrating for the first time a Bristol concern with islands well out into the Atlantic. There are three islands described as uninhabited, and a "large island of St. Brandan" to the east of Terceira. There is no Isle of Brasil. The list shows that sea charts were being visually searched for islands before the first Brasil voyage.

The second set of notes is shorter and appears to belong to 1480. It ranges from the Canaries to the Azores, several of which are located very much too near Madeira, others described as to the north of it. One entry (translated) is: "The island of Pyke (Pico) and other islands called the Isles of Hawkes where people of Portugal inhabit, otherwise called the Stowres (Azores) Islands." Skelton concludes that in this case Worcestre's source is hearsay, "doubtless from seamen who had sailed to the islands or had spoken with those who had. His note is therefore primarily a report of a conversation; and we may observe that all the islands cited, with one exception, were most probably frequented for trade by Bristol ships by the end of the 15th century." This valuable conclusion would suggest that before Worcestre's death, about 1481, it was possible to discuss at Bristol a considerable spread of Atlantic islands to which Bristol seamen had been or of which they had heard from Portuguese sailors who had sailed there. These notes obviously reflect the kind of interest in the Atlantic which was growing up in Bristol at the precise period when her more adventurous seamen were about to go in search of further islands for themselves.

The many sea charts which from 1424 onward record the location of the island of Antilia in the Atlantic (and also Satanazes and some other satellites) have been studied in detail by Armando Cortesão.[2] Up to about 1480 and sometimes later than that date, they place Antilia below or even well below 40° N, making a voyage westward from the Iberian

[1] R. A. Skelton, "English Knowledge of the Portuguese Discoveries in the Fifteenth Century, A New Document," C.I.H.D., *Actas,* II (1961), 365–74; William Worcestre, *Itineraries* (Oxford, 1969), ed. John H. Harvey, pp. 371–7.

[2] *Nautical Chart of 1424* (Coimbra, 1954).

peninsula the obvious means of access. But it becomes clear that after the western Azores were reached, about 1450, further islands were being sought in higher latitudes to the north or northwest of the Azores themselves, a process which probably began during the last stages of the discovery of the Azores chain itself. Thus Diogo de Tieve in 1452 was clearly at 50° N or beyond when he lost direction and ended up on the Irish coast. As S. E. Morison points out,[3] all the arguments used to indicate a Portuguese approach to Newfoundland before 1488 maintain that the searchers were operating in the general area to the northwest and west of the Azores, though the evidence for this is somewhat exiguous. It seems not unlikely that some of the sea charts were showing substantial islands in this direction well before 1470, though the first surviving one to do so is the Catalan chart at Milan, already mentioned, which R. A. Skelton considers may be as late as about 1480.[4]

The Isle of Brasil had appeared on many earlier sea charts in much the same region, namely, at no great distance westward from Ireland, usually in the form of a small disk or circle. But a small island of this sort, the result of many mirage sightings in this general area, would in itself provide little incentive for voyages from Portugal, Ireland, or Bristol. The Milan Catalan chart shows something different. Here Iceland is placed well to the south of its usual position and within the latitude of Ireland (of this something more will be said), while far out to the west, beyond the tiny Brasil off the west of Ireland, is another Isle of Brasil—larger, circular, and associated in a crescent-shaped bay with another, still larger island. The latter is very similar in appearance to the traditional rectangular shape of Antilia, but is placed more than ten degrees farther north, and also north instead of southwest of the western Azores. The name is given as Illa Verde.

This would seem to represent a distinct cartographical tradition. Skelton saw Illa Verde as perhaps a residual Greenland. But one might also regard it as a residual Vinland or, as indicated, a displaced Antilia. Such an island, in latitudes westward from Ireland, provided for the Bristol men, if they had access to a chart of this type, a much more adequate

[3] *Portuguese Voyages to America in the Fifteenth Century* (Cambridge, Mass., 1940), *passim.*

[4] It is reproduced in R. A. Skelton, T. E. Marston, and G. D. Painter, *The Vinland Map and the Tartar Relation* (New Haven, 1965), pl. 12 (from Biblioteca Ambrosiana, Milan, S.P. II 5), and discussed pp. 139, 166–7, 182, and in R. A. Skelton, *The European Image and Mapping of America, A.D. 1000–1600* (Minneapolis, 1964), p. 12. See also Fridtjof Nansen, *In Northern Mists,* 2 vols. (London, 1911), II, 279–81.

incentive than the traditional Isle of Brasil: namely, a pair of islands one of which, Illa Verde, was of a size approaching that of Iceland and a likely center for a major fishing bank.

So far it is not possible to point to a chart of specifically Portuguese origin which is early enough to have been used by the Bristol men as a pointer to their Isle of Brasil, but that such a tradition existed in Portugal is shown by the Paris Map.[5] This combines a sea chart of the Atlantic with a smallish *mappemonde* (or medieval world map) placed inside a series of Ptolemaic planetary spheres. The sea chart shows the traditional Isle of Brasil to the west, but in this case a little to the southwest of its usual location—while far to the west, and related to an Iceland which is reasonably well placed for latitude, is another large island, the Island of the Seven Cities. There are thus three islands, almost interlocking into a square configuration.

The date of the map can be defined with some approach to precision. The explorations of Diogo Cão are unlikely to have been recorded in this form before 1486 at earliest, and this provides the earliest date for the sea chart. The mappemonde shows a completed Africa, though a Ptolemaic India, so that it is subsequent to the return of Bartolomeu Dias from the Cape of Good Hope in December 1488, but earlier than Vasco da Gama's return from India in 1499. Moreover, the absence of any signs of land in the region to which Columbus sailed in 1492 means that it was completed before he arrived in Lisbon with an account of his new discoveries in March 1493. An approximate date of 1490 seems justified. The map is now classed authoritatively as one of a Genoese type which was strongly influenced by Portuguese sources and was probably composed in Portugal.[6]

The legend on the Island of the Seven Cities translates as follows: "Here is the Island of the Seven Cities, now settled by the Portuguese, where, the Spanish seamen say, silver is found in the sands." The story is found in Fernando Colón and in Portuguese histories of the sixteenth century, but this is its earliest known appearance. The Island of the Seven Cities is used by the Portuguese as a synonym for Antilia, whose occupation by the Portuguese occurred supposedly during the early Middle Ages, when a bishop led refugees from the Moorish invasion to it across the seas. The inscription points, however, to a more recent occupation and provides evidence of a sort for a Portuguese discovery of land north-

[5] Bibliothèque Nationale (B.N.), Paris, Département des Cartes et Plans, Rés. Ge AA. 562. I am indebted to Mlle Monique de la Roncière, Curator of the Department, for an excellent reproduction.

[6] Marcel Destombes, ed., *Mappemondes A.D. 1200–1500* (Amsterdam, 1964), p. 51.

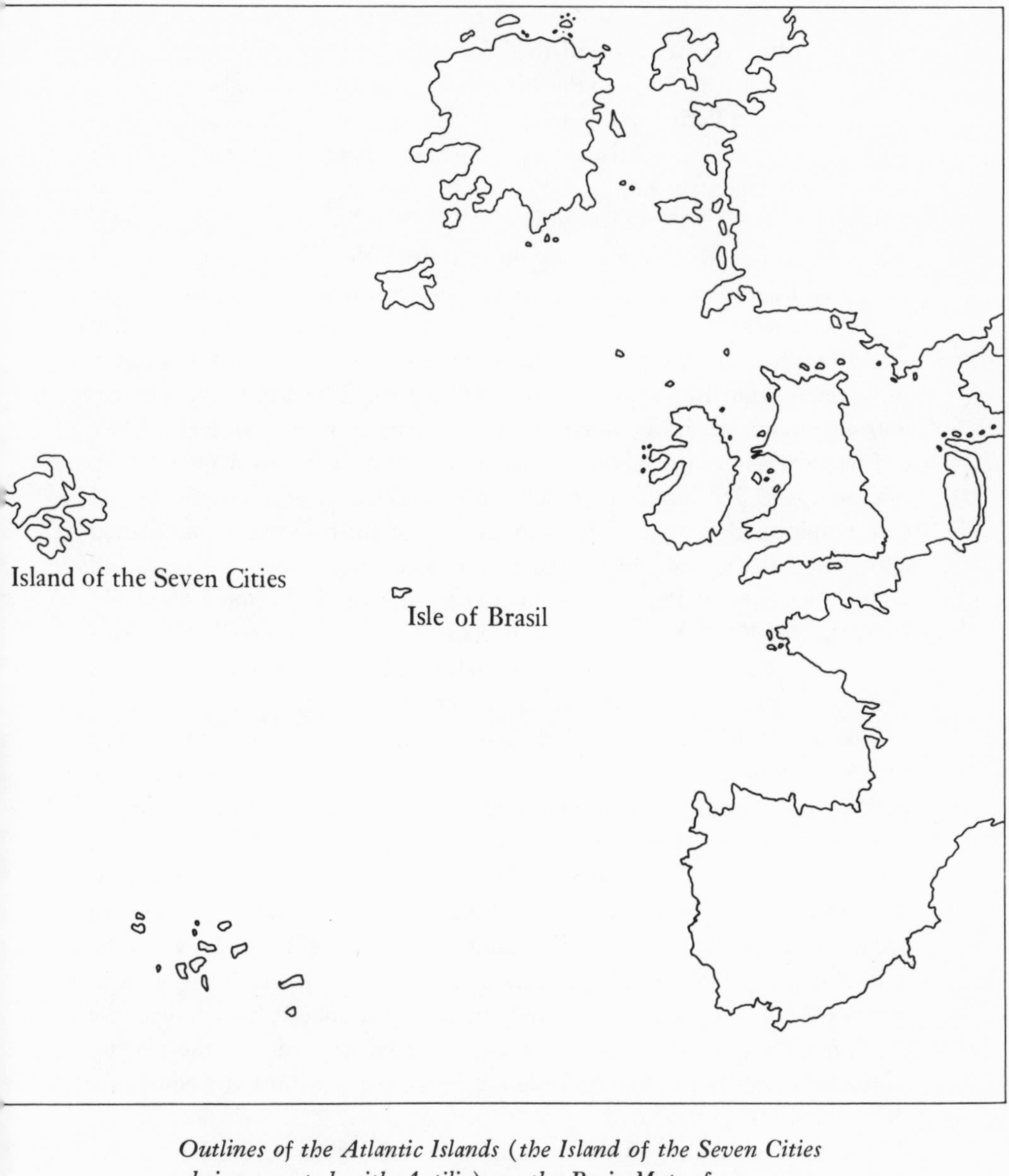

Outlines of the Atlantic Islands (the Island of the Seven Cities being equated with Antilia) on the Paris Map of ca. *1490. The original is in the Bibliothèque Nationale, Paris.*

westward from the Azores before 1490. Where the Spanish seamen come in it is impossible to say—had they been there themselves, or was this a tale picked up on a Spanish ship or in a Spanish port? Whatever its relevance to Portuguese discoveries, this was essentially the type of chart which would have led Bristol men into the Atlantic, and it may be remembered that Ayala reported that the ships going out after 1490 were looking for (or making for) the Isle of Brasil or that of the Seven Cities. We may use the Paris Map, with the earlier Catalan chart, as cartographical indications of the Atlantic as John Jay, Thomas Croft, and their successors of the early 1490's saw it.

The Paris Map also shows signs of English influence in its representation of Iceland and carries a legend attesting the virtual monopoly of fishing and commerce the English had enjoyed for more than half a century. "The inhabitants," we are told, "exchange their dried fish, as if they were money, for wheat, flour and other necessaries which the English bring them annually." In view of the range of English seamen like Thomas Sutton, whom we have noted, from southern Portugal to Iceland, we can see how such information on the north could get into maps made in Portugal, and indeed it is evident that something of an exchange of cartographical data was under way, with the Bristol men accumulating knowledge of the real and imaginary islands on the Portuguese maps and within the range of Portuguese experience, and the Portuguese obtaining from the English details of the important northern sources of the dried cod which was so important, even before the Newfoundland fisheries were developed, for winter protein in western Europe.

The world picture developed in the mappemonde may have some relevance to both Portuguese and English views, during the period from perhaps 1460 to about 1510, of the far western and far eastern limits of the landmass that lay beyond the Atlantic islands. The schematic, Jerusalem-centered world maps of the thirteenth and fourteenth centuries, with their T-shaped water-outline in a circular frame (T-O), had accustomed men to seeing the landmass spread out inside a circle. Those who understood what such a world map meant knew that it represented approximately half the surface of a sphere, which was the earth, but though there was a modicum of book learning on the placing of the "climates"—the successive zones north and south of the equator—there was no ready way of relating them to the land shown on maps of this type. The marine charts gradually introduced a degree of realism into representation of the Mediterranean and western European coasts from the late thirteenth century on, but they gave no clear guidance on the distribution of land to north or south. When the marine chart representations were transferred to the world map and it was centered around the Mediterranean rather than Jerusalem, the relative positions of the landmass east and west became more clearly evident, though its extent to north and south remained rather imprecise.

The Ptolemaic grid of latitude and longitude, which very gradually became current in the west during the early part of the fifteenth century, forced such Europeans as were aware of the problem into a more serious consideration of northing and southing, though the traditional "climates" did not extend farther than 54° north or south of the equator. The graticulation of the Ptolemaic map carried the landmass of Europe only as far as something like 60°, leaving open sea in the polar regions, except that toward the northeast and east the land was allowed to run off the map at a latitude approximating to the Arctic Circle. Yet world maps which included observed "modern" features were not fitted into the Ptolemaic framework until near the end of the century.

Until the making of the Yale Martellus map of 1489 or thereabouts, and the Behaim globe of 1492, therefore, clear indications of how far north the landmass might extend were seldom if ever given on fifteenth-century maps. It remained unclear in many of them whether it extended over the Pole or terminated some way to the south of it in fairly high latitudes. The Yale Martellus map is the first surviving example of a world map to give us a clear impression of what land was thought to lie within the Arctic Circle, which is shown cutting deep into the Norway-Greenland peninsula, also through a peninsula extending northward from Russia and through the tip of one promontory in Siberia. On it a substantial part of the route eastward from Europe to Asia is clear below 66°, westward a smaller but still considerable portion. The projection used makes it difficult to estimate precisely how far north the Norway-Greenland peninsula was considered to extend, but it would be in the neighborhood of 75°. To the north of it, and elsewhere round the top of the landmass, the sea is open beyond about 70°. We cannot however assume that these limits were in fact accepted in Portugal at the time when her cartographic influence had extended to Bristol—that is to say, some little time before 1480.

The rationale of Portuguese maritime progress down the African coast in the later years of Prince Henry's influence was the pursuit of the southern and southeastern rim of the landmass. This in turn was bound to raise speculation as to its southern limit, which was not resolved until done so empirically by Bartolomeu Dias in 1488. One way of regarding the Vinland Map, always with the proviso that it is what it purports to be, is to think of it as setting out land and water relationships in the northern hemisphere, and so giving details well to the north of those shown on the more usual world maps of the first half of the fifteenth century. This suggests that speculation on the specific northern limits of land had also begun. The Vinland Map showed an open Pole, but with some land—

the insular Greenland—extending north into what we might take, in the absence of latitude parallels, to be the low seventies. Yet even on the Vinland Map a voyage round the northern rim of the landmass in either direction could be contemplated, if the concept of a maritime approach to the Far East—more specifically to Marco Polo's Cathay—was already being seriously envisaged at this time.

To Pierre d'Ailly, writing his *Ymago Mundi* about 1415,[7] Iceland ("Tyle") was the most northerly inhabitable land. Inside his "post-climate," the zone which lay between 54° N and the Arctic Circle, there was to the northeast "a region uninhabitable on account of the cold," but there were no indications of this sort, and several to the contrary, on the northwest sector of his world-diagram of the "climates," which might therefore appear as a possible area open to exploration. This opening toward the northwest was even more explicit on the few maps that included Iceland as an island and Greenland as a peninsula attached to Norway (in the series leading from Claudius Clavus about 1427 to the group of Henricus Martellus maps which have survived for the period 1485–90), since no obstacle to a voyage to the northwest of the Greenland peninsula is anywhere shown. In the Fra Mauro map of 1458 or 1459, which attempted to lay out the known landmass according to a complex of conventions new and old, though not including latitude or longitude, there was a long series of named places and inscriptions along the upper edge of the landmass between Europe and farther Asia. These suggested not only that the Pole was off the map in the other oceanic hemisphere, but that there was a route, already largely known and explored (even if such an interpretation should prove erroneous if examined very closely) most of the way westward from Iceland toward the farthest known parts of Asia.

If we follow the northern rim of the Fra Mauro map westward in a little more detail, we have Iceland ("Ixlanda") lying rather far south and west of its correct position, while somewhat west and north of it a peninsula extends from the landmass with the name "Islant" (by a simple mistake), intended for Greenland. On it an inscription states that it is inhabited by evil men who are not Christians (an echo perhaps of the Eskimo, who wore down and destroyed the Greenland colony). Well beyond "Islant" is the Cape of "Rossia," beyond which again is an inscription that a Catalan ship had brought a cargo of skins from there. Finally, not far from the legend ("Septen Trio") which marks the northern, apparently polar limit, there is a further inscription which

[7] Pierre d'Ailly, *Ymago Mundi*, 3 vols. (Paris, 1930), ed. Edmond Buron, II, 383–5.

states that a merchant has come from there with skins of ermine and sable (though it is not stated whether by sea or by land). If, therefore, the viewer follows the coast beyond this northern limit he will soon pick up indications of the Earthly Paradise and, in the interior, of Cathay ("Chatai"), which would suggest that they were within reach from the north.

The significance of such a map therefore was that it gave chapter and verse for an apparently viable route along the northern edge of the landmass, with indications that merchants had already used a good part of it in their attempt to extend the fur trade, and that it should be possible to reach farthest Asia by the same means. Set out in great detail, such a map could pose the problem of a northern route, eastward or westward, to Asia just as explicitly as it indicated—with remarkable prescience and accuracy—a southern limit to the landmass. Along the southern route lay, as the Portuguese found from the 1440's on, riches in slaves and gold and ivory to sweeten their long and expensive voyages, before at last the spices and jewels of the Orient could be attained. By the northern route, if so it could be called, there were cod, whale, and other sea mammals, as well as hawks and rich furs such as ermine and sable, before the legendary wealth of the Earthly Paradise could be attained or the more tangible jewels and silks of Serica and Cathay come within their reach.

By 1460 Portugal had learned that application and the steady sending of expeditions farther and farther along the African coast could in the end produce returns; in the north the English, and through them the Portuguese, had learned to exploit the cod and other marine products of Iceland. They were able to envisage also the acquisition of valuable furs not too much farther away. The concept of a northern approach to Asia at this time is somewhat novel, one which must be put forward very tentatively, but it was clearly a notion that could fairly easily be obtained by examining world maps of the scale and detail of Fra Mauro's—moreover, this particular map was available to the Portuguese.

It had originated in a commission to its maker in Venice to construct a map which would lead the Portuguese down the coast of Africa toward Asia. In fact it set out to do much more: namely, to show as much detail about the world as a whole as Venetians were capable of assembling and putting down on a single surface at the time. It was sent to Portugal, complete, in either 1458 or 1459. A second version of it was in course of preparation and well advanced, though still incomplete, when Fra Mauro died in 1459. Finished by his assistants, it has remained at Venice ever since, influencing a limited number of Italian-made maps over the following generation. The Portuguese original long ago disappeared into the oblivion which has devoured so many other landmarks of Portuguese and Italian cartography devoted to charting routes for the great oceanic explorers and the discoveries they made. It left an heir, however: it comes to light and life again in the mappemonde on the Paris Map of about 1490. Made in Portugal by a Genoese chartmaker, the dual map—marine chart with a mappemonde inserted—combines empiricism in the one with tradition in the other. The sea chart records the African voyages of Diogo Cão and the recent explorations of the Atlantic islands; the mappemonde assimilates a substantial part of the Fra Mauro tradition and represents without doubt the influence of the lost original, which may well have survived in Portugal down to about 1490 at least. It has Fra Mauro's view of a completed Africa, now made manifest through the voyages of Cão and Dias; in this his representation of the east African coast (backed by shrewd assessment of Arab evidence) had been verified—the southern rim of the landmass was open eastward to Asia. But in the north new prospects seem to have been opening also.

The northern rim of the landmass on the mappemonde in the Paris Map sticks closely to that of the surviving Fra Mauro map. The peninsula which the Venice map names "Islant" is firmly labeled Greenland ("Gronland") and carries a very similar inscription about the bad non-Christian men who live there. There are convenient offshore islands, a number being added to Fra Mauro's stock, all the way westward. On the far eastern side of the map Cathay (again "Chatai") appears inland, while off the shore of the landmass, well past the Arctic lands and islands, we see the archipelago of the Earthly Paradise, beyond which (coming back westward) is the Golden Chersonese. This is a Malay Peninsula which leads on toward a Ptolemaic India, and so picks up the line of the land back to Africa and home to Portugal which Fra Mauro was the first to draw clearly.

One of the novelties of the Paris Map—it appears both on the sea-chart and on the mappemonde—is the placing of the Island of the Seven Cities. In the marine chart, as we have seen, this lay well out in the ocean to the west in the latitude of the British Isles. On the mappemonde it would seem to be in rather lower latitudes, perhaps westward from northern Spain or the Bay of Biscay rather than Ireland, but offering—if not dramatically—a useful steppingstone for a voyager attempting to find his way westward to Asia. It could cut down the distance, though not by a great deal, on the long haul, which men were now estimating at some eleven thousand miles in the latitude of Spain. If in fact anyone in Portugal was thinking of such a voyage (Columbus was publicizing the idea there by 1484 if not before, and may not have been the only one),

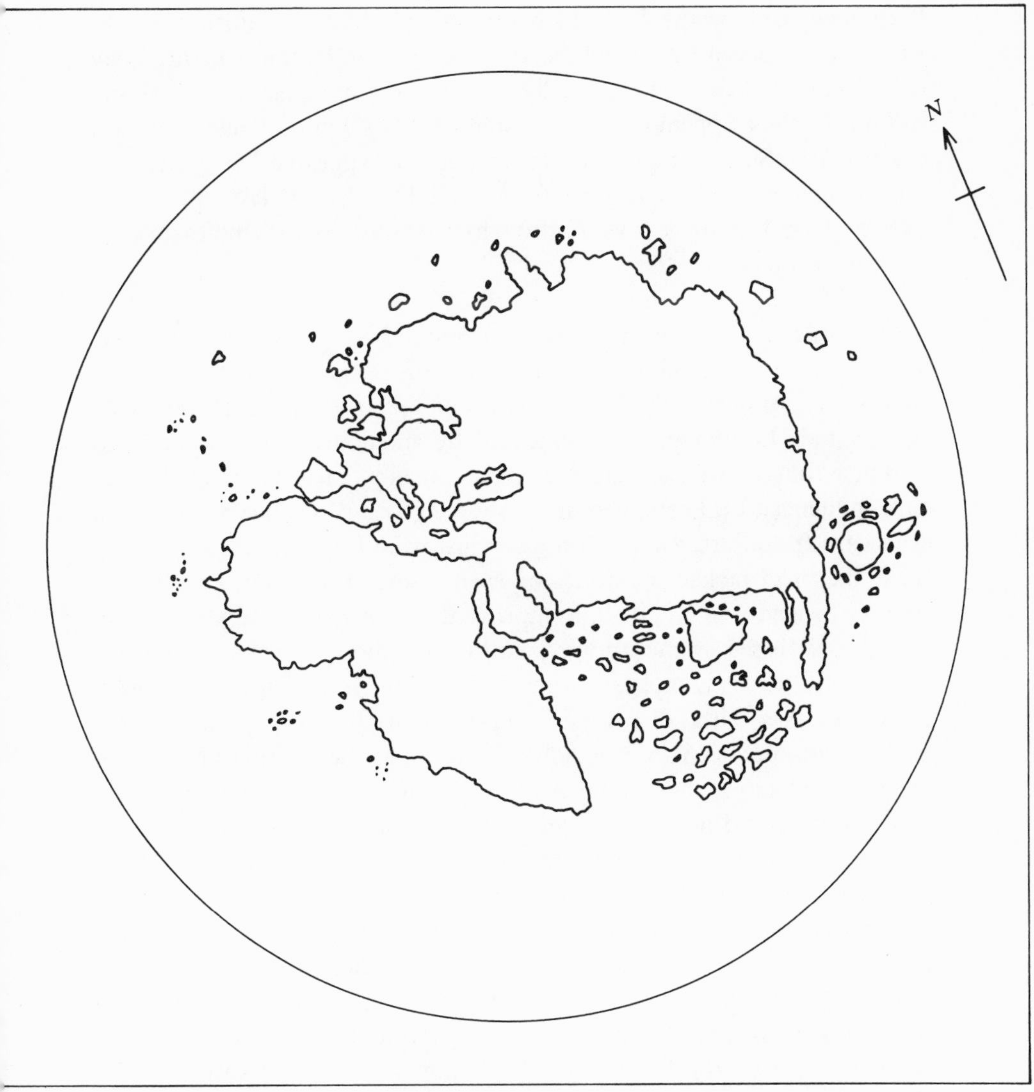

Outline of the mappemonde *inset in the Paris Map of* ca. *1490.*

the prospect offered by the discovery of the Island of the Seven Cities, whether by English or Portuguese, was not that of an easy steppingstone direct to Asia, like the Japan of Toscanelli and Columbus, but only a small advance along a longer route following the rim of the landmass, using islands where there were any standing off the coast, and eventually reaching Cathay by a long haul comparable with that which the Portuguese were making, step by painful step, along the African coast. If the

Portuguese had, as the Paris Map asserted, discovered before 1490 the Island of the Seven Cities (wherever this might be in reality), then they would regard themselves in the light of the cartographic world picture laid out in the mappemonde as one step—but a significant one—forward toward Asia. Such a step, however, would have appeared less enticing in this context once the voyages of Cão and Dias had at last opened the equally long but more specifically charted way to the Indies by the southern route.

The English, we have seen, were already in touch by 1480 and possibly a little earlier with the voyages and maps of the Portuguese in the Atlantic. Whether they were thinking on any such broad oceanic lines when the Bristol men set out on the Brasil voyages of 1480 and 1481 may very well be doubted. That they were influenced by the desire, even the need, to find new fisheries we can state fairly categorically. That they were by this time influenced by Portuguese maps showing islands far out in the ocean westward from Portugal and also westward from Ireland is almost certain. That they had picked up stories or even information about land to the west of Iceland is likely, though unproven. But that they had already any world view, based on the study of world maps and influenced by projects for Asiatic voyages, appears improbable, though perhaps not wholly impossible. Yet if the discovery of 1481—if that is accepted at least for purposes of discussion—was mainly of interest as the location of a fishing bank, as suggested, there is no need to assume that English perspectives and objectives did not expand during the decade following.

Ayala wrote that in the voyages of 1490 (or 1491) onward the Island of the Seven Cities had been joined to the Isle of Brasil and had come within the range of the Bristol men's efforts. However highly speculative it may be, it is, therefore, not out of the question to link the Bristol voyages of the pre-Cabot years—between, say, 1490 and 1496—with both the exploitation of a fishing bank and the utilization of the land that lay beyond it, in the location of the Island of the Seven Cities on the Paris Map, as the basis for a broader English world view. The latter would be similar to the notion I have ascribed to the Portuguese about 1480, of using this land—thought to be an island as it appears on the Paris Map—as a basis for oceanic exploration and even an approach to Asia. Too much, of course, hangs on a single piece of cartographic evidence for this to be pursued, but it is not wholly to be ruled out when we come to consider the activities of Bartholomew Columbus in England.

Such a view of a western approach to Asia might well help to make sense of the later voyages of the Corte Reals—why else, if they were not making for Asia, did they take their ships into such high latitudes? It would help us to understand the Anglo-Portuguese voyages, at the very least those of 1501 and 1502. And it would explain how Sebastian Cabot came to pin his hopes on a Northwest Passage, and to attempt it between 1507 and 1510. But it may very well have sprung in the end from Fra Mauro, being handed down through the Paris Map and others like it, communicated to the English and acting as a driving force behind both Portuguese and English voyages between 1490 (perhaps 1480) and 1510 at least. This makes an interesting prospect for investigation, but it would be undesirable to pursue it further here.

So far attention has been paid to what are thought of as neglected aspects of the Paris Map and its reflection of a particular Italo-Portuguese tradition of cosmography and cartography: the main nettle has not been grasped. When Charles de la Roncière published his argument in 1924 that the Paris Map was composed by Columbus, or with his supervision by his brother Bartholomew, "under the walls of Granada in 1491,"[8] almost as large a spate of scholarly words emerged to attack or criticize this opinion as welcomed or derided the Vinland Map on its appearance in 1965.[9] La Roncière was able to show parallels between what is recorded of Columbus and Iceland, and Columbus and the Island of the Seven Cities, and above all between Columbus and the extracts from Pierre d'Ailly's *Ymago Mundi* which flanked the mappemonde on the Paris Map (even down to the misunderstanding of a phrase relating to the length of the passage down the Red Sea).[1] There was, too, in the mappemonde a combination of extreme traditionalism and considerable innovation—typified in the use of nomenclature from St. Brendan (the "Navigatio Sancti Brandani") and Marco Polo alike in the northern and eastern sections of the map—which was not untypical of Columbus. But the location of the Island of the Seven Cities (Antilia) at about 53° N, instead of about 28° N where Columbus expected in 1492 to find it; the complete absence of Japan, a key element in his argument on the accessibility of the Asian mainland by an island-hopping program, and above all the indications on the mappemonde that there was no short route to Asia but only a slow combination of island-hopping and very long coastal voyages—these seemed to most reviewers adequate reasons for skepticism or rejection. We can say, indeed, that this is not the world picture Columbus sold to Ferdinand and Isabella in 1492, nor that revealed in his surviving notes or in the admittedly confusing picture drawn by his son Fernando Colón.

It may also be said that with Columbus we cannot state precisely what

[8] Charles de la Roncière, *La Carte de Christophe Colomb* (Paris, 1924).

[9] A bibliographical study of this controversy is overdue.

[1] La Roncière, *La Carte de Christophe Colomb*, pp. 9–14, a point in favor of his view with which critics do not appear to have dealt adequately.

influences operated to produce his views. He could have drawn many of his notions about the Atlantic and the world at large from the Portuguese and from other Italians like himself whom he met in Lisbon. The so-called Columbian features of the Paris Map may, therefore, be indirect reflections of the influence Portugal had on Columbus. At the same time, we need not rule out all possible association of the map with the Columbus brothers. For if Bartholomew Columbus, in seeking support from Henry VII, had put to him the view that Christopher successfully asserted in Spain in 1492—namely, that a relatively short voyage in the latitude of the Canaries would bring him to Japan and Asia—he would have been laughed out of court (and perhaps was), for England had no access to bases in these latitudes, which in any event were already walled off (by a papal bull of 1481) for Spain and Portugal. If Bartholomew was making a serious case for a western voyage to Asia from English latitudes, he would have to present a different picture.

We have in our minds only a single world picture drawn by Columbus: that which he presented to the Spanish sovereigns. He may have had alternatives in his mind. One which showed the Island of the Seven Cities (Antilia) due west of Ireland, as shown on the Paris Map, is a likely one. But if so, the mappemonde does not give much support to the view that even from the Island of the Seven Cities access to Cathay and the Earthly Paradise would be short and easy. If something like the Paris Map was being used in 1489 or 1490 by Bartholomew Columbus to tempt Henry VII, he would have to justify English participation, not by the incentives of a quick voyage, but by the news that the Island of the Seven Cities—the Isle of Brasil, perhaps already found by the English—was only one stage in a long process of voyaging comparable to that of Portugal down the African coast, at the end of which Asian riches could be reached.

Rejection of such a scheme in 1490 would be as understandable as having second thoughts about it would be in 1492—more especially if the western voyages from Bristol in 1490 or 1491 had brought back some encouraging news about the Isle of Brasil. I do not assert that these considerations were raised by Bartholomew Columbus with Henry at any time, from 1489 on; the evidence of the Paris Map merely indicates that such views were in the air in Portugal and may have been put down in cartographical form by the Columbus brothers as by others. The inference that Bristol voyages made before John Cabot came to England were influenced by some such cartographical and cosmographical considerations is much stronger than that either of the Columbus brothers was identified with these views or ever asserted them.

While it might seem unwise to draw what may well prove to be a red herring across the already tangled trail of contact between the Columbus brothers and England, there is another reference which requires at least mention. It would appear that before Columbus's son, Fernando Colón, set down what he could find of his father's and his uncle's contacts with England, Alexander Geraldinus (Alessandro Geraldini), first Bishop of Santo Domingo, who died in 1525, had already written something on this question in his *Itinerarium*, although this was not published until it appeared at Rome in 1631. He surveys briefly the early career of Christopher Columbus before he set out on his transatlantic voyage in 1492. He says that it was Christopher who visited France and England, and that in these countries he first expounded his theory of a New World beyond the ocean. On being rejected by the king of France he went to England, and only after a further rejection there applied for aid to John II of Portugal.

This tour of France and England is set forth as if quite distinct from Bartholomew's and taking place much earlier. It rather seems to coincide with Christopher's to Iceland and Galway (the first according to his son's account, the latter by his own note). This, one may suggest, would have brought him on board a Bristol ship to Galway going to Iceland, and possibly returning from it also, perhaps about the year 1477. Even if this journey described by Geraldini is held to have taken place a little later, it still brings Columbus much nearer in time to the years 1480–1, when the Brasil voyages were taking place. It would make the English king who rejected him Edward IV (or conceivably Richard III) and in France Louis XI, not Charles VIII. If there had been such unfavorable reactions during the years, say, between 1477 and 1483, then they might have been revived and referred to either by Henry VII or by Charles VIII (or rather Madame de Bourbon) when Bartholomew appeared later. Christopher's first return to Portugal could then have taken place in 1484 or 1485 and have preceded his campaign to get John II as a backer.

The coincidence of two parallel visits of Christopher and Bartholomew to England and France, separated by some seven to ten years, may appear unlikely. The earlier visit by Christopher would certainly involve a considerable rearrangement of the accepted biography of the discoverer; it could also upset a good deal of what I have already said about the Bristol ventures, which would then appear to have had possibly much closer links with the Columbus plans and to have been parallel to them from an early stage. All that seems worth saying here is that perhaps the credentials of the Geraldini story have not been scrutinized as closely as most other aspects of the Columbus story and legend. On the face of it, Alessandro Geraldini appears to have some qualifications to set down an authentic narrative. He had accompanied his brother Antonio Geraldini from Italy and his native Amelia in 1487, when the latter went to Spain as papal nuncio, and had settled down in Spain. Much later, before going to Santo Domingo as bishop in 1520, he was in the service of the Emperor Maximilian and went on a diplomatic mission to England to carry on a negotiation with Henry VIII. When, in Santo Domingo, he wrote the account of Columbus, he had been in a position to know something both of Columbus and of England. Whether he was guessing, recollecting, or confusing the later visit of Bartholomew, or was in fact correct, is at present very difficult to say.[2] The Geraldini evidence therefore adds only another strand of confusion to the misty English background of American exploration.

III

THOUGH THE VOYAGES in search of Brasil of 1480 (unsuccessful) and 1481 (possibly successful), and the westward voyages from 1490 to 1495, together with Cabot's known voyages of 1497 and 1498, were all from Bristol, they were not purely local ventures. The permission of the crown or at least of fairly prominent persons and some encouragement from official circles were essential if adventures into the Atlantic were to be made with purpose and under legal protection. At the same time the material for telling the story is very limited and therefore susceptible of a considerable number of differing interpretations—the fact being that the less material there is, the larger the number of deductions that can be made from it: a kind of Parkinson's Law of historical study. Such analysis as is contained in this section consequently has a much higher proportion of theorizing to information than would normally be permissible. The justification is that official knowledge of western voyaging is an aspect which must be taken into account and has not hitherto been examined; if discussion is to go forward, there must be something to discuss.

If there was a key figure in the 1480–1 voyage pattern it would appear

[2] ". . . primo Galliam, & postea Britanniam Insulam adivit, & proposita spe novi mundi inveniendi cum hac expeditione ab utroque Rege velut incerta reiiceretur, ad Joannem Lusitaniae Regem." Alessandro Geraldini, *Itinerarium* (Rome, 1631), p. 203. Cf. Samuel Eliot Morison, *Admiral of the Ocean Sea*, 2 vols. (Boston, 1942), I, 102, where the reference is mentioned but not discussed; and Conte Belisario Geraldini, *Cristoforo Colombo ed il primo vescovo de S. Domingo, Mons. Alessandro Geraldini d'Amelia* (Amelia, 1892).

to be Thomas Croft.[3] This Herefordshire landowner, who was also a lawyer, had had himself elected as member of Parliament for Leominster, center of the area in which his family's interests lay. Whereas before 1478 he had gained from being "the king's servitor" only some small perquisites in the way of office, he evidently tapped during the Parliament of 1478 some appreciable sources of official influence. He emerged with a number of offices which were lucrative rather than prominent; amongst them, bestowed in 1478, that of joint collector of royal customs and also water bailiff for Bristol. Later, in 1483, he became joint deputy butler for Bristol and a number of other ports. In the grant made by the royal Chancery on 18 June 1480, to himself and three Bristol merchants to trade without normal restrictions in not more than three small vessels (which sound like fishing doggers),[4] his name comes first, and it would be reasonable to conclude that the idea of the grant and its acquisition were his.

If the grant is connected with voyages to look for and locate western islands, as seems the only probable deduction on our present information, then Croft would have had to expound some reasons for it to officials at court or in the Chancery. This seems to make it clear that between 1480 and 1483, the duration of the grant, there were some officials—they may not have been very important, and need not have included the king, Edward IV—who knew and approved of the Bristol projects. While our knowledge of the unsuccessful 1480 voyage rests on the private diary of William Worcestre, uncirculated at the time (though its author was not without contacts among prominent men outside Bristol), all we know of the 1481 voyage comes from official documents, a fact which in turn implies a certain amount of official knowledge of what went on in the voyage, or at the least what it was about.

A substantial number of high-ranking legal officials were made aware of the Brasil voyage of 1481 by a royal commission under the Great Seal which was issued on 25 February 1481 to William, Lord Berkeley (who did not act); Sir William Notyngham, chief baron of the Exchequer; Sir Richard Cheke, a justice of the court of King's Bench; Thomas Whytingdon, a secondary baron of the Exchequer; John Mynche, and Kenelme Dyges (the last of whom did not act); empowering them to inquire into the king's rights in the port of the city of Bristol, including ships and

[3] See J. C. Wedgwood and A. E. Holt, *History of Parliament: Biographies of the Members of the Commons' House, 1439–1509*, 3 vols. (London, 1936), I, 239–40; brief article by D. B. Quinn, *Dictionary of Canadian Biography*, I (Toronto and Quebec, 1965), 239–40; O. G. S. Croft, *The House of Croft of Croft Castle* (Hereford, 1949), pp. 36–8.

[4] See pp. 8–9 above.

shipping, merchandise, and the dues associated with the trade and shipping of the port.[5] No great haste was shown in bringing the commission into effect, but on 25 August letters under the privy seal were issued to the sheriffs of Bristol warning them that the commissioners would arrive on 4 September and instructing them to facilitate their work.

After the commissioners arrived in Bristol (the exact date is not known), some time was probably spent in private investigation and in the compilation of the list of seventy-five potential jurors who might be called to assist in the presentation of evidence about affairs in the port. Eventually, by 24 September, a jury of presentment of forty-four persons was empaneled, including the men noted above. The surviving inquisition deals with only a limited part of the commission's ostensible business, namely, with the evasion or nonpayment of customs and other dues on goods imported to or exported from the port, with the alleged participation (contrary to the prohibitions placed upon them) of royal officials engaged in customs control of trade through the port. It may be said that the four cases of alleged evasion of duty payment were all minor ones; the case against John Shepard, one of the customers, for placing two dozens of cloth in his barge, the *Christopher*, was explained away by the fact that the cloth was to be used for fitting out the vessel (apparently with sails) for his personal use.

The most interesting case, clearly (mentioned earlier, p. 8), is that of Thomas Croft, charged under two headings: first, of owning shares (one-eighth in each instance, thus indicating that he had a number of associates) in the ships *Trinity* and *George*, which were assumed to be engaged in trade; and second, for lading in them forty bushels of salt worth twenty shillings, presumably for trade and to his own profit. Had these charges been supported by the jury, Croft would have been liable to trial in the court of Exchequer and, if found guilty, subject to loss of office and other penalties. The jury exonerated Croft on both counts, declaring that the part-ownership of the ships and the investment of the salt in their voyage were not for purposes of trade or profit but *causa scrutandi et inveniendi quandam insulam vocatam le Ile of Brasile*, which may be translated "on account of searching for and finding an island called the Ile of Brasil," though it may also appear in the form in which we find it in 1483 in English, that is, "to serche and fynd a certaine Ile callid the Isle of Brasile." The latter derives from an occasion when Croft appeared in the court of Exchequer at Westminster to answer for his accounts, or nondealings as it turned out, as sheriff of Merionethshire and under a

[5] All the documents cited are in P.R.O., E. 122/19, 16.

commission for the seizure of the goods of the Earl of Warwick, while at the same time he asked for a formal pardon, which he received in the terms just given, for taking part in the 1481 Brasil venture.[6]

In the course of these proceedings in Bristol a considerable number of local merchants and others had reason to discuss and comment on the voyage of 1481, and it seems difficult to deny the probability that this was about a voyage achieved as well as attempted. At the same time, both then and in 1483, a substantial number of important legal officials employed in the courts and at the court of Edward IV were also well informed about the voyage and its part-sponsor, Thomas Croft. This knowledge would remain with them for some years and be available, in so far as they survived the political turmoils of the reigns of Edward V, Richard III, and the invasion and establishment of Henry VII. They would, in particular, be aware of whether or not the voyage was completed within the seventy-nine days between July 6, when the ships are said to have set out (or within a day or two of this), and September 24, when the inquisition was held. This knowledge might have been passed on to King Edward, though we do not know that it was.

If another voyage was attempted from Bristol by the licensees of 1480 in either 1482 or 1483, nothing so far has come to light. But Thomas Croft was one of those who switched his allegiance in 1484, during the reign of Richard III, to the Lancastrian challenger Henry Tudor. He duly received rewards for his services to King Henry on his "most victorious field" at the Battle of Bosworth[7] and continued to enjoy the royal favor, though not in any very exalted position, until his death in 1488. The political unsettlement of the years after 1483, the lack of drive which Thomas Croft had shown toward following up the voyage of 1481, and the caution of the new king in committing himself to doubtfully profitable western ventures may all be suggested as reasons for official inaction during years when the Portuguese were intensively and successfully active in their progress into the South Atlantic. What went on in Bristol itself in these years in regard to western voyaging we have, so far, no means of knowing.

In 1488 or at the opening of 1489, London received a visitor who brought to its merchants and officials and to the king news of the plans which Christopher Columbus was trying to sell, first to Portugal (if we put aside the Geraldini account), then to the Spanish sovereigns, and

[6] Carus-Wilson, *Overseas Trade of Bristol*, pp. 261–5.

[7] See, for example, William Campbell, *Materials for a History of the Reign of Henry VII*, I (London, 1873), 191; II (London, 1877), 61.

finally to the king of England. Bartholomew Columbus, his younger brother, was a chartmaker in Lisbon from about 1477 onward and was closely associated with his brother in the development of his views of the ocean.[8] He is likely to have been involved in the presentation of the first plans for a western voyage in 1484 or 1485 to be put before John II of Portugal, which were rejected. He was with Christopher during at least the early part of his long and unsuccessful ordeal in Spain between 1485 and 1488,[9] and the brothers were both in Lisbon again before the end of the latter year and saw together the arrival of the caravels of Bartolomeu Dias, with the report that the way to the East around Africa lay open. This detached Portugal from her intermittent western quest. Christopher determined to turn to England. It is highly probable that he had some contacts in Bristol, if not in London, but he determined to stay to watch events and sent his brother with such data as he thought necessary to convince King Henry.[1] On his way to England by sea Bartholomew's ship was attacked by Hanseatic pirates. (If this was a Bristol ship she may have been the victim of reprisals rather than simple robbery, since the *Trinity* in 1486 had, as we have seen, taken a Hanseatic ship in Iceland and disposed of it and its crew in Ireland.) Bartholomew had been robbed and was in poor physical shape before he reached London about the beginning of 1489.[2] To his material he added Latin verses to tell the king that the map would reveal to him what Strabo, Ptolemy, and Isidore had taught (presumably that the earth was spherical and that by going west one could arrive at the east), and also that Hispanic ships had newly penetrated the hitherto unknown torrid zone.

Apparently Bartholomew was unable to present this map to the king

[8] For Bartholomew Columbus see Morison, *Christopher Columbus, Admiral of the Ocean Sea* (1942), pp. 12–14, 35–6, 90–1, 481–2; Salvador de Madariaga, *Christopher Columbus*, 2d ed. (London, 1949), pp. 30, 72–3, 259–64 (with some mistakes in chronology).

[9] Deposition of Bartholomew Columbus, 1512, in Césareo Fernández Duro, ed., *Pleitos de Colón* (1894), I, 185; Madariaga, *Columbus*, pp. 261, 462.

[1] The documentation on Bartholomew Columbus's visits to England and France is from Hernando Colón, *The Life of the Admiral Christopher Columbus* (New Brunswick, N.J., 1959), ed. and trans. B. Keen, pp. 36–7 (also Williamson, *Cabot Voyages* [1962], pp. 199–200), 40–1, 146; Bartolome de Las Casas, *Obras Escogidas* (Madrid, 1957), ed. J. Perez de Tudela, I, 108–10, 280–1; G. Fernández de Oviedo, *Historia General y Natural de las Indias* (Madrid, 1959), ed. J. Perez de Tudela, I, 21.

[2] The date, according to Hernando Colón, was London, 10 February 1488, by the English reckoning (with the year running 25 March–24 March), the calendar year being 1489.

for some considerable time. He was impoverished and had to establish himself as a chartmaker in London. He had also to accumulate a small competence before he could, no doubt by suitable presents, win access to the king. According to Las Casas, when he did, the king received the map and the verses "and showed towards Bartholomew Columbus always a cheerful countenance and took pleasure in talking of that matter with him." But at the same time, Las Casas admits that Bartholomew got no answer within a short time and suffered he knew not what repulses and setbacks at the king's hands. Oviedo gives a further indication of what may well have happened, saying that "the King having been reported to by the councillors and other persons to whom he had committed the examination of this matter, laughed at all that Columbus had said and held his words as vain." It is by no means certain that Las Casas, Fernando Colón, and Oviedo are not simply filling historical gaps in a plausible manner, but it is quite possible that the report is based on fact. An initial show of interest by Henry, followed by reference to a committee, and then the laughing of the project out of court may very well represent what took place.

If there was a committee of the sort Oviedo describes, one may suggest that it would contain at least one member who could cope with the mathematical demonstrations of the length of a degree and the circumference of the globe, on which the Toscanellian sequence adopted by Christopher Columbus—bringing the Canaries, Antilia, Japan, and Cathay neatly into line along a practicable sailing route westward—would be critically considered. Second, someone with a reasonably recent experience of Spain and Portugal would be needed, to keep the diplomatic aspects of a commitment to the Columbus brothers in mind and also possibly to report on what was being done in the Iberian lands about overseas voyaging. Third, there would need to be a merchant with some knowledge of what products might be expected from direct contact with the East—probably someone concerned in the Italian-borne overland Oriental trade. Fourth, a man who knew what had gone before, in the way both of royal grants and of Bristol voyages and discoveries. Finally, if Henry was adopting a characteristic realistic attitude, someone to look after possible costs would be regarded as essential.

To suggest members for a hypothetical committee whose membership is in any case entirely unknown may seem rash, but there may be some value in establishing that such talent could be found in or near the court.[3]

[3] All English persons mentioned in this paragraph, except Sir Richard Croft, are noticed in the *Dictionary of National Biography* (*D.N.B.*).

Archbishop Morton, the Lord Chancellor, or (if he was too lofty for such a body) Richard Foxe, Bishop of Exeter, were both learned clerics whose mathematics might be adequate to sift the theoretical claims of the Columbus brothers. Dr. Thomas Savage, the king's chaplain, and Sir Richard Nanfan, a member of his council, are also possibilities for membership under the second category. They had been the English representatives at the signing of the Treaty of Medina del Campo with the Spanish sovereigns on 27 March 1489,[4] and had then gone on to complete a further treaty with John II of Portugal (to whom they brought the insignia of a Knight of the Garter) on 18 August. They not only knew the diplomatic situation very well, but were almost certain to have heard reports of the recent Portuguese voyages to the south, and may even have picked up some traces of the Columbus brothers during their three months or more at the Iberian courts. Lord Daubeney was also a possible member. Warden of the Mint, he was also Constable of Bristol Castle and might well have knowledge of overseas activities from that city.[5] He had had recent diplomatic contacts with Spain in the negotiations leading to the 1489 treaty.

On the financial side a very strong candidate would appear to be Sir Richard Croft, treasurer of Henry's household.[6] He was the elder brother of the Thomas Croft who had died in 1488, and would know of his Brasil entanglements between 1480 and 1483. That in one way or another he was in touch with Bartholomew Columbus at this time seems very likely. For an outside contact, we might expect some prominent member of the Mercers' Company or the Merchant Adventurers of London, though no names can easily be suggested. Bartholomew Rede, the goldsmith, was associated with Daubeney in running the Mint and would share what he may have known of the Bristol situation; he would also, as a goldsmith, be aware of what credit could be raised for a speculative venture from private sources. I mention him because some thirteen years later he is found helping to finance an American expedition.[7] Whether John Day,

[4] A. F. Pollard, *The Reign of Henry VII*, 3 vols. (London, 1914), III, 2–6.

[5] Daubeney was associated with William Spencer in regard to property in Bridgwater in 1487, and was in a position to have learned of the 1480 license (Robert Strange had earlier, in 1481, been concerned with the same property); *Calendar of Inquisitions Post Mortem, Henry VII*, II (London, 1915), 257.

[6] For Sir Richard Croft (d. 1509) see biography in Wedgwood and Holt, *History of Parliament: Biographies*, I, 237–8. He was treasurer of the household from 1485 to about August 1492 (W. C. Richardson, *Tudor Chamber Administrative* [Baton Rouge, 1952], p. 484). See also Croft, *House of Croft*, pp. 40–6.

[7] See pp. 122–3 below.

in his respectable London guise of Hugh Say,[8] was available or already interested in voyaging, we have as yet no evidence to indicate. But these do not exhaust the list of possibilities. They are worth noting only to show that Henry could readily have found useful advisers from among his counselors and in the mercantile community of London.

Why should the proposition of Bartholomew Columbus to the English king have been rejected sometime in 1490, or possibly as late as 1491? The most obvious reason is that for anyone in England who had a reasonable knowledge of current and classical ideas of cosmography, a proposal to sail from England to Asia by a transoceanic voyage was absurd on the face of it. It was well known that a journey of some ten thousand miles at least lay between Europe and "Further India" (eastern Asia). Taking an equatorial circumference of some twenty-five thousand miles and a Ptolemaic ratio of 180° land to 180° water, it would be twelve thousand miles or more, though other estimates could have reduced it a little. An ocean voyage of this length would certainly be a laughing matter.

But if Bartholomew Columbus's proposal was for a voyage westward in latitudes where Antilia and Cipango were believed to lie—the two steppingstones to Asia in the Toscanelli theory of 1474—namely, about 28° north latitude, then diplomacy as well as distance would be involved. Portugal and Castile between 1478 and 1481 had sealed off the seas southward from the Canary Islands by both treaty and papal bull. Any intervention in the Atlantic which involved penetration of the Iberian sphere would be the prelude to a diplomatic and possibly a naval struggle which Henry VII was neither equipped for nor ready to envisage. There was the additional point that English access to Asia in latitudes as low as this meant a long southward addition to the westward voyage, which helped to put it still further out of account. A cause for laughter, too, might have been the solemn, prophetic, messianic manner which Christopher Columbus himself was inclined to adopt and may have passed on to his brother in presenting what appeared to be his more outrageous propositions. The first two of these considerations in themselves were concrete and specific reasons for ridiculing the whole project.

A different frame of reference for the rejection may also be imagined. A proposition set out in the context of the Paris Map, when an island far to the west of the British Isles gave some hope of shortening the distance to Asia—also shortened by the convergence of the meridians in northerly latitudes—would have a more realistic setting. If it was combined with

[8] See p. 7 above and p. 94 below.

assurances, as Christopher Columbus's to the Iberian monarchs were, that the total distance by sea westward to Asia was much less than classical geographers said, then coastwise sailing along the rim of the landmass to Asia, using such islands as lay out to sea on the way, might have sounded at least plausible. But if Henry VII and his advisers were in possession of knowledge that far out in the Atlantic there was indeed the Isle of Brasil, which marked a fishing bank but was much farther off than Columbus suggested; and if, too, there was some vague awareness that beyond it again lay only Greenland, noted in the past for hawks and furs but too cold for sustained mercantile contact—then the Columbus overtures might have been rejected because the Englishmen who reviewed them felt they knew more about the Atlantic than Bartholomew, and that the problems and distances involved were far greater than he supposed. A refusal for such reasons need not have involved ridicule, but only rejecting the proposal after serious consideration, on the grounds that the English knew more about the Atlantic in northern latitudes than the Genoese brothers, who were mainly theorists.

We can, however, say two things. The first is that after the visit of Bartholomew Columbus to England, Henry VII and some members at least of his circle were reasonably well briefed on the issues presented by the Genoese. In addition—but here we come to matters of conjecture rather than fact—if Henry and his entourage were aware of an Isle of Brasil out in the Atlantic, discovered by Englishmen, and to which English fishing vessels were already going, then the Columbus overtures might well have quickened their interest in this discovery. This might even have led them to back further voyages in 1490 and 1491 (the initial ones of Ayala's series) to determine whether the Isle of Brasil was merely an island, after all, or might be associated with a larger insular landmass: namely, the Island of the Seven Cities, located more or less as on the Paris Map.

Bartholomew Columbus, discouraged, went to France. At the Fontainebleau court of the regent, Anne de Beaujeu, Madame de Bourbon, he was accepted as a chartmaker, though we do not know to what extent he attempted to influence her or the young Charles VIII to consider his brother's now fading propositions. Between the evidence provided by Las Casas and Bartholomew's own nephew, Fernando Colón, S. E. Morison has pieced together a possible story of his activities, to the effect that he lost touch with his brother and did not know of his final success in getting support from the Spanish sovereigns; that he learned of his return from his initial voyage in 1493, first from Charles VIII and then through an invitation from Christopher himself, but reached Spain only in time to hear that his brother had left on a second voyage. Bartholomew found a ship in which he could follow him and in September 1494 reached the outposts of the new lands which were to involve him for the rest of his life.

Christopher Columbus insisted that he had received offers from both France and England before he finally closed with the Spanish sovereigns.[9] We have one picture of him, presumably in 1491, in sufficient despair to be ready to run off himself with an offer to Charles VIII and thence to England to look for his long-lost brother.[1] Another story is that Henry VII's acceptance finally reached Bartholomew when he was at the French court in 1493, and as he was about to hurry off to Spain with it, the French king gave him news of his brother's triumphant return from the Indies.[2] These tales are sufficiently contradictory to make it difficult to classify them as anything but different versions of a family myth, embodying the belief that if Spain had not backed Columbus, then other rulers would have been only too glad to do so. At the same time, the possibility that Henry VII had changed his mind between (perhaps) 1490 and 1493 cannot be altogether ruled out. If his advisers put it to him that the convergence of the meridians might make the distance between England and Cathay significantly shorter for a voyage to be worth considering; or if a Bristol reconnaissance in 1490, 1491, or even 1492 had revealed that the Isle of Brasil was sufficiently substantial to be important in its own right and was adjacent to an island thought to be the Island of the Seven Cities; then a renewed interest in a proposition by Bartholomew Columbus by letter or by a second visit might appear possible.

The fact remains that Columbus discovered what he believed to be the outliers of Japan or some other part of Asia and returned to tell the tale, first at Lisbon in March and then at Barcelona in April 1493. We have no evidence of when the vindication, as it was thought, of his cosmographical propositions got to England. Las Casas said it reached Charles VIII quickly "because kings hear news before other people";[3] it is unlikely that the English court was far behind the French. This information put a different complexion on the situation: the new islands, even if they had not yet led to the spices of mainland Asia, were reported rich in gold and spices in their own right. Now any proposition which could keep England in the running would be listened to with an entirely new respect, while the diplomatic aspects of the discovery would be kept especially

[9] Colón, *Life of Columbus*, p. 41. [1] *Ibid.*, p. 40. [2] *Ibid.*, p. 146.

[3] *Obras Escogidas*, I, 281. For Bartholomew Columbus's own reference see Manuel Fernández de Navarrete and others, eds., *Colección de Documentos Inéditos para la Historia de España*, XVI (1850), 559; Madariaga, *Columbus*, pp. 263–4.

in mind. How rapidly the news arrived of the papal bulls of 1493, recognizing a division of spheres of interest between Spain and Portugal in the west and east respectively, is not known, but it is reasonably certain that the Treaty of Tordesillas concluded between Spain and Portugal on 7 June 1494, about which Henry VII was to discourse in detail with the Spanish representative, Ayala, in 1498,[4] was very soon known in England. Few if any may have understood where the meridian lay which was to mark the boundary between the spheres of interest, 370 leagues west of the Cape Verde Islands. But it clearly affected both English opportunities to sail west to look for Cathay and also analogous rights, however little regarded so far, in the Isle of Brasil and whatever other lands had been sighted in the annual voyages from Bristol to the western ocean. The way, indeed, was now open for John Cabot, that other Venetian who had been trailing a very similar plan before mercantile interests in Seville and Lisbon,[5] probably putting it to John II also at some stage before Christopher Columbus sailed and returned with his discoveries. This time propositions for a voyage westward to Cathay, in the latitude of Ireland, would receive from even the cautious Henry VII a more serious hearing.

Before John Cabot reached England, however, there was at least one visitor—an unwilling one—who was in a position to explain the Atlantic situation fully to English officials or the English king. Martin Behaim of Nürnberg had lived in Portugal as a trader and had been in the service of John II.[6] He developed ideas similar to those of Columbus on the accessibility of Asia, and on his return to Germany provided the material for his famous globe in 1492. This showed not only Antilia, though far to the south near the equator, but Cipanga to the west of it and Asia beyond—a series of steppingstones by easy stages from Portugal to the Canaries, the Cape Verdes, Antilia, Cipanga, and across the *Oceanus Indie superiore* to Asia, not unlike those discernible much farther north and nearly half a century earlier on the Vinland Map. Behaim was familiar

[4] See pp. 9–11 above, and Williamson, *Cabot Voyages* (1962), pp. 228–9. Ayala had been on a mission to Portugal in September 1493 to discuss the papal bulls dividing the Spanish and Portuguese spheres of influence. He was apparently not present for the treaty negotiations at Tordesillas in June 1494. Cf. Florentino Perez Embid, *Los Descobrimientos en el Atlántico hasta el Tratado de Tordesillas* (Seville, 1948), pp. 242–3.

[5] Williamson, *Cabot Voyages* (1962), pp. 203, 228.

[6] E. G. Ravenstein, *Martin Behaim, His Life and His Globe* (London, 1907), and the critical account by G. R. Crone, "Martin Behaim, Navigator and Cosmographer; Figment of Imagination or Historical Personage," C.I.H.D., *Actas*, II (Lisbon, 1962), 117–32, and "Martin Behaim and the Globe of 1492," *Geographical Journal*, CXXIII (1963), 239–49.

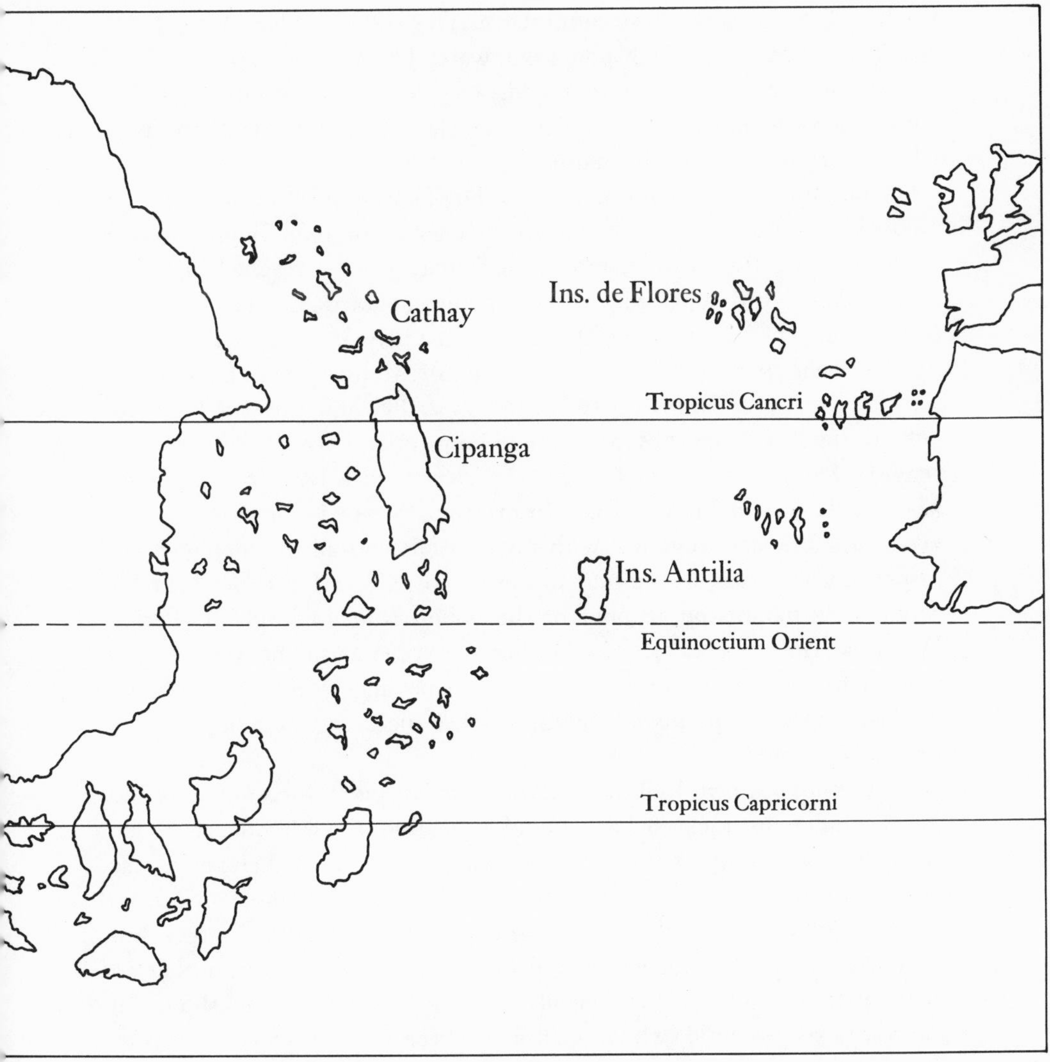

The ocean between Europe and Asia, as shown in the Behaim globe of 1492. The original is in Nürnberg, Germany. After J. A. Williamson, The Voyages of the Cabots *(London, 1929).*

with the medieval English source on the northern lands already discussed, the "Inventio Fortunata,"[7] and had had inscribed on his globe, at the North Pole, what has been translated as follows: "In the book 'De inventione fortunata' it may be read that there is a high mountain of magnetic

[7] See pp. 107–9 below; Nansen, *In Northern Mists*, II, 289.

stone, 33 German miles in circumference. This is surrounded by the flowing "mare sugenum" which pours out water like a vessel through openings below. Around it are four islands, of which two are inhabited. Extensive desolate mountains surround these islands for 24 days' journey, where there is no human habitation."

On 14 July 1493 a friend of Behaim, Dr. Hieronymus Müntzer, in ignorance of Columbus's successful voyage, wrote to John II proposing a western expedition by which "eastern Cathay can be reached in a few days' sailing," and suggesting that there be included on the voyage "a companion sent by our King Maximilian, namely D. Martin Behaim." [8] Behaim went to Portugal, but neither he nor Müntzer was employed in Atlantic voyaging. Instead, later in the year, Behaim was sent by King John to the Low Countries, probably in connection with Yorkist intrigues against Henry VII. He told of his experiences in a letter to his cousin Michael Behaim in March 1494. "In crossing the sea I was captured and taken into England, together with my servants and all the money I had to pay my expenses, amounting to quite 160 gulden. I was detained for about three months on account of the young King of England [Perkin Warbeck, the pretender]. . . . During that time I caught a fever, and twice I had a lighted taper in my hand, expecting to die, etc. When I was well again, a pirate one night carried me secretly in his ship to France." [9]

If this imprisonment took place during the last month or so of 1493 and the beginning of 1494, Behaim could have told English officials much about his own views of the western ocean, drawn them sketches of the Atlantic map as he saw it, and reported on Columbus's discoveries. No corroboration of his story has been found so far in English sources, but if his knowledge was not made available or exploited, it makes rather an ironic footnote to this highly speculative outline sketch of English official interest in the Atlantic, which is all it has been possible so far to reconstruct.

[8] Ravenstein, *Behaim*, p. 113. The Henricus Martellus world map of *ca.* 1490, now at Yale (p. 63 above), is a forceful addition to existing evidence for the belief in a short passage westward to Asia. Its indications of longitude show it to have been based on assumptions comparable to those of Toscanelli and Behaim. The islands shown in the Atlantic westward from Europe would appear to form steppingstones to Cipango, east of Asia (and apparently conflated with Antilia), which again is within reach of a protruding "Horn of Asia."

[9] *Ibid.*, pp. 113–14.

Summary

THE ARGUMENT FOR an English discovery of America is appreciably strengthened through the indirect evidence provided in the foregoing pages. The basis of this evidence is the close association of a small group of men, including those involved in the Brasil voyages of 1480 and 1481, in the overlapping Iceland and Portugal trade of Bristol. The decline of the Iceland fishery and commerce and the flourishing of the Portuguese trade affected to some degree the cloth exports of Bristol, though on balance the cloth trade in the last quarter of the century was expanding.[1] The decline in the amount of dried and wet salted cod available for sale to Portugal was a significant handicap to Bristol merchants in their trade with the Iberian peninsula. On the Portuguese side, the decline in cod deliveries from Iceland by English ships was even more serious.

The Bristol men had incentives of their own to look out into the ocean for new sources of cod and new markets for cloth. The Portuguese had equally great incentives to push their own fishing interests in the Atlantic, and it is probable that some Portuguese activity in sponsoring searches for islands to the west was influenced by such considerations. The Portuguese, however, also had reason to encourage English searches for alternative sources of fish in the western Atlantic, since the Icelandic fish trade had provided such an appreciable part of Portuguese imports. Thus we find English merchants making themselves familiar with Portuguese

[1] Eleanora M. Carus-Wilson and Olive Coleman, *England's Export Trade, 1275–1547* (Oxford, 1963), pp. 106–10, 143.

knowledge of islands in the Atlantic and sending out ships to look for further islands. Some degree of more active cooperation from the Portuguese side in this exploratory work might be expected. We know that some maps showing Atlantic islands were available in England by 1480, and we can legitimately assume that Bristol merchants could see on these maps major islands apparently still unexploited in the western ocean: Brasil, the Island of the Seven Cities, Antilia, Satanazes, Illa Verde, or whatever they were named. Their potential exploitation formed a joint Anglo-Portuguese interest.

A degree of shared knowledge is known for the period around the year 1480. Then after 1481 darkness falls over Bristol activities in the western ocean, lasting for the rest of the decade. One plausible explanation is that a discovery was made in that year and was being exploited under conditions of secrecy. It is not impossible that similar circumstances applied to Portugal also—that she too knew of or had made some such discovery, though she may not have been exploiting it herself. Such a find would not be, for the English, a potential market for cloth; it would be a fishery, and therefore something to keep secret in order to avoid intrusion by outsiders.

The close cooperation of a small group of merchants in the Iceland and Portugal trades and the Brasil voyages, and the joining of this group by Hugh Say, under the name of John Day, at the opening of the 1490's, strengthens his statement that an English discovery was made within what we may legitimately think of as the continuous existence of the group—also the likelihood that the 1481 voyage was the crucial one. A closer look at the circumstances of the commission of 1481 which brought to light the Brasil voyage of that year, and the jurors who took part in the investigation, makes it very difficult to believe that the voyage did not begin in July and end before 24 September 1481, and that its recorded purpose—to search for and find the Isle of Brasil—was not accomplished. However, final, specific proof is still lacking.

We have seen that J. A. Williamson was inclined to think the initial discovery (in spite of the phrase *en otros tiempos*) was made about 1490 or a little later. This has been considered in the initial argument of this volume and was shown to be progressively less likely after 1490, on any interpretation of the phrase. While Ayala's letter of 1498 says that voyages had taken place for the past seven years, he is more likely to mean the seven years before the successful voyage of Cabot in 1497—that is, from 1490 to 1496—than between 1491 and 1497. We can see that a renewed series of voyages might represent either a new initiative unconnected with the Brasil voyages of 1480 and 1481, or part of a series of voyages from 1481 onward, perhaps stepped up after 1489. An independent series beginning in 1490 or thereabouts could have relied on a discovery of the Isle of Brasil made in 1481 which had not been subsequently exploited; but this would not fit very well the conditions of Anglo-Portuguese trade which seem to have set off the earlier Brasil voyages. Continuity seems more likely, though there are no Portuguese trade records which enable us to test this theory.

As to Ayala's statement that the English "search" in these years was not only for the Isle of Brasil but also for the Island of the Seven Cities, we have seen that the Italo-Portuguese map of *circa* 1490—the Paris Map—brought an Island of the Seven Cities into the ocean far to the west of Ireland, already discovered, it was said, by the Portuguese. Such an island might well have been a new object of interest to English voyagers, fishing off Newfoundland, in the hope of finding a market for cloth in the west. Or it might have been thought of as a steppingstone on a long haul around the rim of the landmass to Asia. Bartholomew Columbus's views seem to have involved some such considerations, with a possible promise that the route to Asia by this means would be shorter than had hitherto been estimated. One may even suggest that the supposed change in attitude by Henry VII toward the Columbus plans, in 1491 or early 1492, might have sprung from some additional discovery of land to the west made by the Bristol men in 1490 or 1491. A firm discovery of what was thought to be the Island of the Seven Cities would put a different complexion on what had hitherto been regarded as a wholly impracticable route to Asia. These faint glimmerings of light—if they are even that—do no more in this area than open up a few novel possibilities. But they can help, even if they are not in any way established, to clarify the position that confronted John Cabot when he came to England, which made it possible for him to get both royal backing and Bristol support.

PART II

Discovery in the West

Prologue

Against the sparsely documented early background of English western enterprise—the expeditions of 1480 and 1481 and the revival or extension of western voyaging about 1490, plus an extensive framework of speculation on when the English may have discovered the Isle of Brasil—the events of the years from 1496 to 1505 have a more solid documentary foundation. They have the air at least of being firmly grounded on contemporary information. This is to some extent deceptive, since the number of questions which cannot be conclusively answered remains high. Where precisely did John Cabot's voyage of 1497 take him, and where was his landfall? What happened in 1498 besides the loss of Cabot himself? How exactly did the Azorean Portuguese become involved in Bristol voyages to the west from the year 1500 on? What happened in 1502 to widen the scope of English western enterprise—and why did so much of the English initiative come to an end after 1505?

These are only a few of the major questions to which, in spite of substantial evidence in each case, answers cannot be given categorically. Answers are indeed given below to some of them, but they are tentative. Yet there is less room for speculation after 1496: history dominates theory (if that is not too grand a name for it)—not theory history.

CHAPTER FOUR

The Conquest of the Atlantic

I

JOHN CABOT REACHED England after it had become clear to King Henry VII that to encourage a western venture was, or might well be, worth while. Something could be built on the knowledge of the Bristol men which would keep the English crown in the new fashion of finding—not merely talking about—steppingstones to Asia somewhere in the western ocean. The grant of 3 March 1496 to Cabot and his three sons is so reminiscent of Portuguese grants of a similar sort made over the previous seventy years that it might almost have been modeled on one of them. They were to find new lands anywhere to the west of England and Iceland, or to the north or the east (but not to the south, where Columbus was entrenched and Spanish and Portuguese authority effective), and to govern them in the king's name. As in the Portuguese grants, the discovery was to cost the king nothing. No official investment took place until it was clear that there was something to invest in, or at least something more than a fishery adjacent to some western island or islands known as the Isle of Brasil and the Island of the Seven Cities. When Cabot came back with the report of a discovered mainland, then investment could be contemplated by the king and the London merchants.

An unsuccessful voyage was made, and then, in 1497, a successful one. The only record of this in Bristol today is a note in the margin of a seventeenth-century town chronicle derived from an earlier one. In "A Summary or pettie Chronicle . . . written in Bristoll by William Addams in anno 1625" is the entry: "On the 24th of June 1496 [for

1497], was newfowndland fownd by Bristol men in a ship called the Mathew."[1] Local loyalties gave credit for the discovery to the men of Bristol and not to the foreigner, John Cabot. A generation ago this might have seemed ungenerous; since the discovery of the Day letter it seems just enough.

In piecing together the outline story of the 1497 voyage a special degree of authority must be given to the Day letter. This was written by someone who had a good deal of expertise in maritime matters to another, greater man who had an immense amount. The other records on which scholars had to make do before 1956 are communications of diplomatic agents in London who reported to Italy what they were told or picked up casually: they were not, so far as is known, maritime experts and knew little about the problems of the Atlantic. The exception is Pedro de Ayala, special ambassador of Spain, who was well informed of Columbus's discoveries, since he had been sent to Portugal in 1493 to discuss their implications. But his report on the 1497 voyage, if he made one, is missing, and what we have is mainly a roundup of information and comment on the background of the 1498 expedition.[2] Consequently, the reports of Lorenzo de Pasqualigo and Raimondo de Soncino, the old standbys for this voyage, will be treated as subsidiary only.

If we take the Bristol date for the landfall of the *Mathew*, 24 June, we can put her departure from Bristol at about 22 May. Cabot, after picking up the Irish coast at Dursey Head would, on our reading of the Day letter, sail southwestward until he was in the latitude his Bristol advisers said was most suitable for picking up the Isle of Brasil or the Island of the Seven Cities. Day gives her a good run westward, with an east-northeast wind for thirty-two or thirty-three days, that is, until 21 or 22 June, when he ran into a storm. He was then evidently on the continental shelf and may well have been sailing over the Newfoundland Banks.[3] He recorded a compass variation of 22°30′. On 24 June he made a landfall, the location of which is described as "west of Bordeaux River," the mouth of the Gironde being at 45°35′ north latitude, which would give a landing between, say, Cape Canso, Nova Scotia (45°19′) and Cape Breton on Cape Breton Island (45°57′). Cabot landed "near the place where land was first sighted"—whether north or south of it is not indicated. A cross,

[1] Bristol Record Department, Bristol Record Office (B.R.O.) 13748(4), first published in *The Times Literary Supplement*, 8 June 1967, p. 517.

[2] Williamson, *Cabot Voyages* (1962), pp. 207–14, 228–9.

[3] See John T. Juricek, "John Cabot's First Voyage," *Smithsonian Journal of History*, II (1967–8), 7–8. This paper has some very good critical material, but its positive suggestions are misconceived.

probably of wood rather than stone, was brought ashore and set up, and banners bearing the arms of the Pope, Alexander VI, and Henry VII of England were erected as tokens of Christian overlordship and English sovereignty, respectively. The explorers did not penetrate more than a bowshot inland, but they saw a stick about eighteen inches long of red wood (or painted red), pierced at both ends. This, together with a site where a fire had been, was good evidence of human occupation. There were trees suitable for masts, and good grass. (We are not told that Cabot took a sun sight on land, but a good many deductions as to locations depend on his having done so.)

The *Mathew* may then have coasted some little way to the south but soon turned northward again, since Day says "most of the land was discovered after turning back." Too much has subsequently been made of this phrase; the inference that Cabot went on sailing eastward for the rest of his coasting is quite unjustified in the context. Day is giving his correspondent a verbal commentary in general terms on an outline sketch (which has not survived) of the land Cabot found, and it does not follow from what he says that only an eastward course was kept after leaving his original landfall or some spot nearby. They followed their course, he says, "discovering the coast," remarking on the great quantities of cod, seeing at least one forest that appeared attractive, and trying to make out whether there were or were not fields on shore and whether the moving creatures they glimpsed were human or animal.

After about a month's sailing—that is, between about 22 June to 24 July—they reached what is described as "the cape nearest to Ireland . . . 1800 miles west of Dursey Head." Dursey Head is in County Kerry at 51°36′, and its opposite number on the North American coast would be Cape Bauld at 51°40′ or Belle Isle at 51°53′, at the northern tip of Newfoundland. They duly set out "from the above-mentioned cape of the mainland which is nearest to Ireland," with a wind behind them from the west, and made an especially fast passage; though the sailors confused Cabot by maintaining that he was sailing too far north, so that he fetched up on the Breton coast (at about 48°30′) after only fifteen days, i.e., between about 6–8 August. Their run to Bristol would take them about two days, according to the winds, so that from Day's letter we can make their return not later than 8–10 August,[4] a total absence of just over eleven weeks—a remarkably lucky and efficient voyage. In fact, they may well

[4] Samuel Eliot Morison, *The European Discovery of America: The Northern Voyages, A.D. 500–1600* (New York and London, 1971), p. 186, favors a departure date of not later than 20 July, a sighting of Ushant on 4 August, reaching Bristol on 6 August, which is possible, though not, as he states, certain.

have been in a day or two sooner, for Cabot got to London and had a reward credited to him from the king on either 10 or 11 August.[5]

The reports made from London, where Cabot talked freely to the Venetian Pasqualigo,[6] were that he claimed to have made his landfall seven hundred leagues away,[7] and to have coasted three hundred leagues before returning. He found on shore snares and a netting needle (perhaps the same as Day's stick pierced at both ends), and saw cuts on trees, so that he concluded there were inhabitants. He said the tides were slack off the shores he coasted. He saw two islands on the way back, at which he did not linger as his provisions were running low; he was said to have been away three months. The taking possession of the new land with a large cross is mentioned, as is the erection of two banners, though here one is said to have been Venetian (Cabot being a Venetian citizen and wishing to flatter his countrymen). There is little more in this letter, sent on 23 August, that is, within two weeks of Cabot's arrival in London.

The report sent by Soncino to the Duke of Milan on 18 December represents a later stage in the information process.[8] Cabot had by that time constructed both a mappemonde and a globe and was able to set out not only his route but his placing of his discoveries in Asia. The statement that "in going towards the east he passed far beyond the country of the Tanais" is nonsense, the river Tanais being in various contexts the Jacartes or the Don, and being confused on the Vinland Map with a region or kingdom in mid-Russia.[9] However, a few geographical points are made. On his outward voyage he "passed Ireland . . . and then bore towards the north, leaving the North Star on his right hand after some days."[1] (This has been used to challenge the route implied in the Day letter and to set Cabot on his voyage into the ocean at latitude 53° or 54°,

[5] Williamson, *Cabot Voyages* (1962), p. 214. [6] *Ibid.*, pp. 208–9.

[7] Calculations made on the basis of a Roman mile produce a conversion of 700 leagues into 2240 nautical miles from Bristol to Cape Breton Island, and, on the basis of the statute mile, of 1826 miles from Bristol to Cape Race. See J. T. Juricek, "John Cabot's First Voyage," pp. 9, 21; Melvin H. Jackson, "The Labrador Landfall of John Cabot," *Canadian Historical Review*, XLIV (1963), 131–4. Whether Pasqualigo's round figures have anything more than approximate relevance may be doubted.

[8] Williamson, *Cabot Voyages* (1962), pp. 209–10.

[9] See R. A. Skelton, T. E. Marston, and G. D. Painter, *The Vinland Map and the Tartar Relation* (New Haven, Conn., 1965), pp. 129–30, pl. 7.

[1] Mr. Jackson ("Labrador Landfall," p. 130) makes much of this: he corrects Williamson by translating "la tramontana" as "Polaris," not "north" (cf. Juricek, "John Cabot's First Voyage," pp. 9, 21). Morison, *Northern Voyages*, pp. 170–7, has him run down the latitude from Dursey Head to Cape Degrat (51°33′ and 51°37′).

which with a westerly course would bring him to a landfall on the coast of Labrador.) It was said Cabot thought that, with luck, after leaving Ireland the voyage should not take more than two weeks.

Day had in his mind an insular picture of the Cabot discoveries. The landfall opposite the Gironde River was at "the southernmost part of the Island of the Seven Cities." This would be farther north than the traditional location of Antilia and somewhat farther south than its equivalent, the Island of the Seven Cities, on the Paris Map.[2] But Day assumes that his correspondent will not be surprised at such a location. He speaks of the landing as taking place on a "mainland" and of their finally leaving the coast "from the above-mentioned cape of the mainland," that opposite to Dursey Head. It is not clear (and cannot be clear unless his sketch becomes available) whether his "mainland" is something distinct from the island; it may not be so. What is clear is that he equates the "cape of the said land" with the Island of Brasil, which is thought to be "the mainland that the men of Bristol found." If Cabot's discovery is a single tract of coast, then Day appears to be saying that it is at the same time the Island of the Seven Cities, the Isle of Brasil, and the mainland.

But he also refers to the sketch-chart as showing "the capes of the mainland and islands," leaving us, in the absence of his graphic representation of what he meant, in some confusion. He sent his correspondent "a copy of the land" which would tell him what he wished to know (we in our turn would very much like to know what this was): it "named the capes of the mainland and the islands, and thus you will see where land was first sighted." This would seem to be a rough copy of a running chart made by Cabot as he reviewed his journal and such detailed charting as he had time to make. It would compare closely with that of Hispaniola made by Columbus on his first voyage: a running survey with a coastline and names, but without scale, orientation, or graduation for latitude or longitude.[3] Day expected to clarify this sketch by placing it in its context on a more general map, but said "I do not send the map because I am not satisfied with it," as he had made it hurriedly before leaving England. Later, Ayala got hold of a copy of "the chart or mappemonde which this man [Cabot] has made," but it is not known whether he sent it on to Spain subsequent to his letter of 25 July 1498.[4] This was clearly either a general sea chart or else a mappemonde, and not a sketch.

[2] See pp. 66–8 above.

[3] Discussed by R. A. Skelton in "The Cartography of Columbus' First Voyage," in *The Journal of Christopher Columbus* (London, 1960), ed. Louis André Vigneras, p. 221, and see fig. 2.

[4] Williamson, *Cabot Voyages* (1962), pp. 228–9.

There is another nettle which must be grasped by all students of the English voyages: the celebrated map of Juan de la Cosa made in 1500.[5] Almost everything that can be said about it can be adduced to "prove" different landfalls and varying courses for Cabot.[6] The fact that it is now not wholly legible and that many earlier reproductions are suspect in detail does not make things easier. Two assumptions are made here. The first is that the basis for Cosa's inclusion of the English coasts on his map was the running survey sent by John Day of the coasts followed by Cabot, which Columbus might well have passed on to him, and which is now missing from the Archivo General de Simancas, where we would expect to find it still attached to John Day's letter. The second is that this sketch contained a coastline and names but no indication of scale and no latitudes or longitudes except those given by Day, namely, the landfall as opposite (that is, due west of) Dursey Head.

Cosa used an old world map on one scale and proceeded to construct an outline of the western lands so far discovered on a larger and more generous one;[7] nonetheless he integrated the two and treated them as if they were on the same scale. He showed a continuous coast on the west with one traditional feature, the Horn of Asia (which alternates with Greenland as a peninsula on mappemondes of the fifteenth century) west of Iceland (which is Frislanda in the Catalan map previously considered). The coast then picks up the "cauo de ynglaterra" and marks it with a flag. This cape is due west of Dursey Head. Three other features on the coast are flagged, and a fifth flag stands just beyond "Mar descubierto por inglese," which in turn stands west of the Gironde River. The "English Coast" is flattened and stretched out from east to west, but it can clearly be derived from just such an outline as it is suggested John Day sent.

[5] R. A. Skelton, "Cartography of the Voyages," in Williamson, *Cabot Voyages* (1962), pp. 297–307, discusses this map with authority; it is reproduced as a frontispiece to the volume.

[6] The classic discussions, written before the Day letter was published, are in W. F. Ganong, *Crucial Maps in the Early Cartography and Place-Nomenclature of the Atlantic Coast of Canada* (Toronto, 1966), pp. 3–45, and Williamson, *Voyages of the Cabots* (1929), pp. 185–97. Subsequent studies include Jackson, "Labrador Landfall"; Juricek, "John Cabot's First Voyage"; and Skelton, "Cartography."

[7] G. R. Crone, *Maps and Their Makers* (London, 1953), pp. 83–6. His emphasis on the distinctness of the two scales tended to divert attention from the concordance of the English coasts on the western portion of the map with the Day letter. A closer study will show that Cosa regarded the two portions as compatible. Father Lucien Campeau, S.J., in "Jean Cabot et la découverte de l'Amérique du Nord," *Revue de l'Histoire de l'Amérique Française,* XIX (1965), 398–408, was the first to argue the relevance of the Day letter to the Cosa map and to lay out the outward and homeward courses on that map.

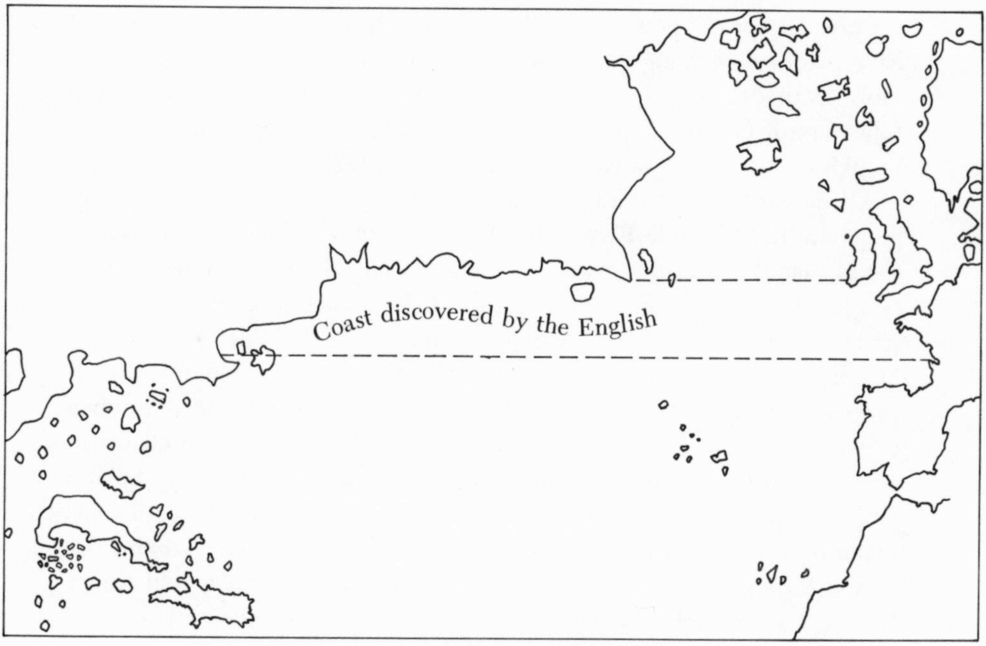

The coast discovered by the English, on the map of Juan de la Cosa, 1500, conforming to the limits indicated in John Day's letter. The original is in the Museo Naval, Madrid. After Lucien Campeau, "Jean Cabot et la découverte de l'Amérique du Nord," Revue de l'Histoire de l'Amérique Française, *XIX (1965), 398.*

It is, therefore, possible to say that the landfall is (approximately) Cape Breton and the point of departure (approximately) Cape Bauld. If this follows, the "Mar descubierto por inglese" is the water lying between Cape Breton and southern Newfoundland (including Cabot Strait). The spacing of the remaining three flags would therefore be somewhat arbitrary by our present knowledge. We can, very tentatively, associate them with major features of the coastline, "C° de S. Luzia," perhaps representing the Burin Peninsula; "C° de S. Jorge," Cape Race; "Illa de la trenidat," Bonavista or Fogo Island. Supposing an outward course along the parallel of 45°30′ to make a landfall at Cape Breton, subsequent courses would be northeast to the southern coast of Newfoundland, east along the Newfoundland coast to Cape Race, north-northeast to Bonavista, northwest to Cape Bauld, and finally east from Cape Bauld.

Such courses are not represented on the Cosa map: the trend of the coasts is from east to east-northeast with relatively minor bays and inlets. If Cosa had a sketch without scale and without any major distinguishing features except the points of arrival and departure, this is what he would have made of it. Such an attitude to what has often been regarded as Holy Writ can only be considered philistine by the more sophisticated followers of Cabot's ship and of Cosa's brush, but it represents a logical though deliberately limited interpretation of what the premises set out.

At the same time it must be indicated that it may well be untrue. Day pinpoints the Gironde River and Dursey Head as fixing the latitude of Cabot's landfall and departure. Cabot was using dead reckoning (everyone had to) and Polaris for navigation. It is questionable that he would, on the basis of these alone, be able to estimate his latitude with any approach to precision when he made his landfall. If he was only two degrees (140 miles) out, he was not doing too badly. An altitude sight when he went ashore could, if he was an expert in using astrolabe and quadrant, give him an observation within 30′ or 40′ of the actual position. Such a range (25 to 50 miles perhaps) would not invalidate the topographical implication of following Day's leads, though it would complicate them in detail. An error of one or two degrees (70 to 140 miles) would throw them out completely. In the extreme event of a two-degree error either way, Cabot might have made his landfall either in Maine or in southeast Newfoundland, and his departure from Cape Race or from some point up the Labrador coast almost as far as Hamilton Inlet. We can say positively that the evidence points to Cape Breton, yet it may well be unreliable. The student may decide to say that acceptance of what one might call the Day limits gives us the only rational lead we have, though we must regard them as wholly conditional on a degree of accuracy in navigation and observation which would be unusual at the time. To assert their authority more positively would be to deprive future generations of scholars of the fascinating attempt to fit the map outlines into ever more detailed alternatives.

The expedition of 1498 which followed John Cabot's triumphant reconnaissance was the first—and indeed only—attempt by the English crown to emulate the overseas activities of the Portuguese and Spanish sovereigns. Ferdinand and Isabella saw to it that Columbus sailed with seventeen vessels on his second voyage in 1493: the second fleet which Manuel V equipped for the Indies voyage after Vasco da Gama's return in 1499 was to comprise thirteen vessels. Both enterprises were major commitments of the state. By comparison, the scale of Henry VII's response to Cabot's request for assistance to reach the shores of Cathay and trade with the dominions of the Great Khan was puny.

The Bristol men who had pioneered the sea route to the west and linked their fortunes to Cabot in 1497 were willing to make a considerable

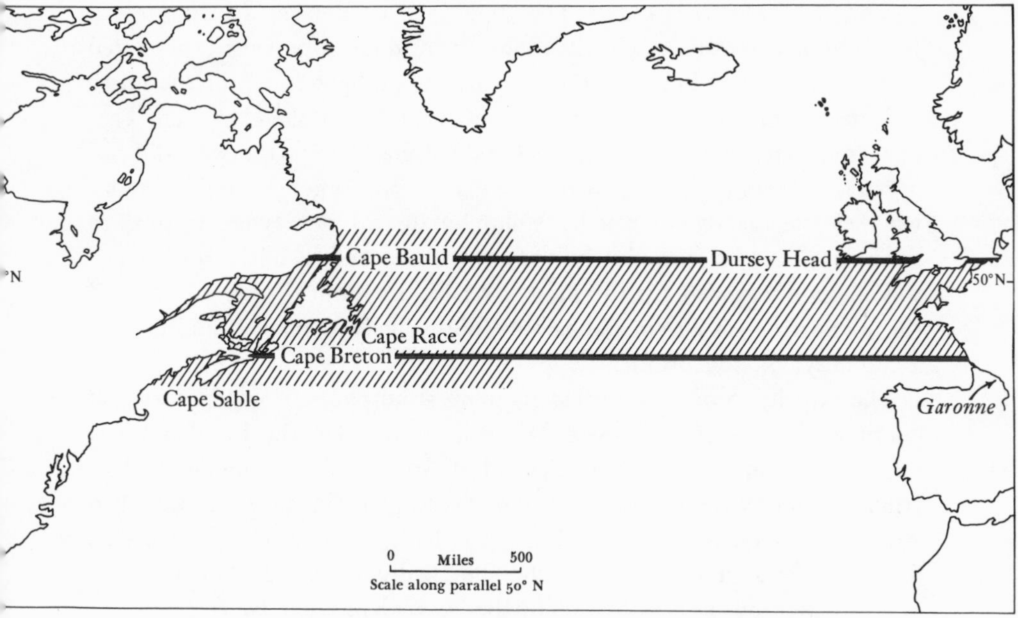

The north-south limits of John Cabot's voyage of 1497, according to the John Day letter (allowing for an error of up to two degrees in latitude determination).

effort to exploit the commercial riches which he was sure were to be found. They were prepared to find and equip four vessels—as many as they had hitherto risked in any one year, so far as we can tell—on an Atlantic voyage. King Henry would not go beyond one vessel. Between 17 March and 6 April 1498 he advanced the sum of £113 8s. to Lancelot Thirkill to fit out his ship (its name is not known), along with Thomas Bradley, "going towardes the new Ilande." [8] The ship itself and its lading were the adventure of such London merchants as had been sufficiently impressed by Cabot's story to be willing to invest a little money in a further expedition.[9]

Cabot himself received an award of £10 in cash and a pension, to be paid from the receipts of Bristol customs, of £20 a year [1]—not ungenerous by Henry's standard but unaccompanied by any substantial royal investment. The whole affair must have been a deep disappointment to him. John Day reported that when he wrote (about December 1497), Cabot expected to have a fleet of ten to twelve vessels; another report

[8] Williamson, *Cabot Voyages* (1962), pp. 214–25. [9] *Ibid.*, p. 220.
[1] *Ibid.*, pp. 214, 217–8.

suggested fifteen to twenty.[2] The superficial excitement which greeted John Cabot's return was clearly followed by doubts, perhaps engendered by those interested in cosmography, that the authentic map of the north and west might be very different from what Cabot sketched out. That he was credited with exploring a substantial coastline to the west did not necessarily mean that he had reached Asia. Some skepticism about whether the islands reached by Columbus in the west were as near to the Spiceries as he alleged may also have been present. The 1498 voyage was clearly regarded by the king—and by Londoners who adventured for investment—as an outside gamble, not a likely winner: a chance, not a certainty, of rich profits.

The expedition of 1498 thus starts in an atmosphere of uncertainty and continues in one of anticlimax. We can assume that the London vessel made its way to Bristol toward the end of April or the beginning of May, from which city the little fleet of five vessels, provisioned for a year, then set out. Ayala reported on 25 July, "News has come that one of these . . . has made land in Ireland with the ship badly damaged. The Genoese [Cabot] kept on his way." [3] No further news had come by late September.[4] Polydore Vergil much later, about 1512, summed up what was thought to have happened to John Cabot: "In the event he is believed to have found the new lands nowhere but on the very bottom of the ocean, to which he is believed to have descended together with his boat, the victim himself of that self-same ocean; since after that voyage he was never seen again anywhere." [5] With this simple narrative John Cabot—his pension and his rent in Bristol conscientiously paid up to Michaelmas 1499 in case, after all, he returned—disappeared, and his expectation of getting speedily to Asia by a western voyage with him.[6]

John Day had thought of Cabot's discoveries in 1497 in terms of a large insular mass or masses found far out in the Atlantic. He expressed no opinion on their relevance or otherwise to the problem of access to Asia, though he would have put down his views of this question on the general map which, when he wrote, he had not finished and with which

[2] *Ibid.*, pp. 213, 209. [3] *Ibid.*, p. 228. [4] *Ibid.*, p. 220. [5] *Ibid.*, p. 225.

[6] *Ibid.*, pp. 218–19. Thomas Bradley appears to have been the man who acted in 1503 as interpreter to an English mission in Spain (James Gairdner, *Memorials of Henry VII* [1858], pp. 223–4), while Thirkill was also alive on 6 June 1501 (judging by a bond made in 1505, British Museum [B.M.], AdditionalMS 21480, fol. 35v.). See articles by D. B. Quinn in *Dictionary of Canadian Biography* (*D.C.B.*), s.n. It would thus seem that both had survived the voyage, but evidently not in the vessel of which John Cabot was captain. It may of course have been the one that put back, damaged, to Ireland. Sebastian Cabot, also, could well have been on the voyage and have survived (see p. 138 below).

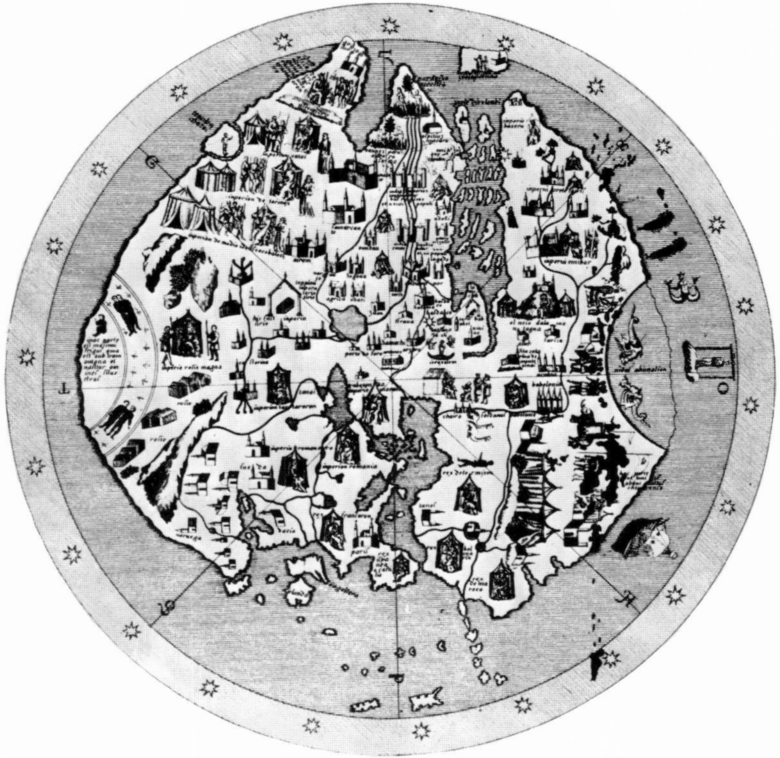

An engraving after the Bianco Map of 1436.
The original is in the Biblioteca Marciana, Venice.

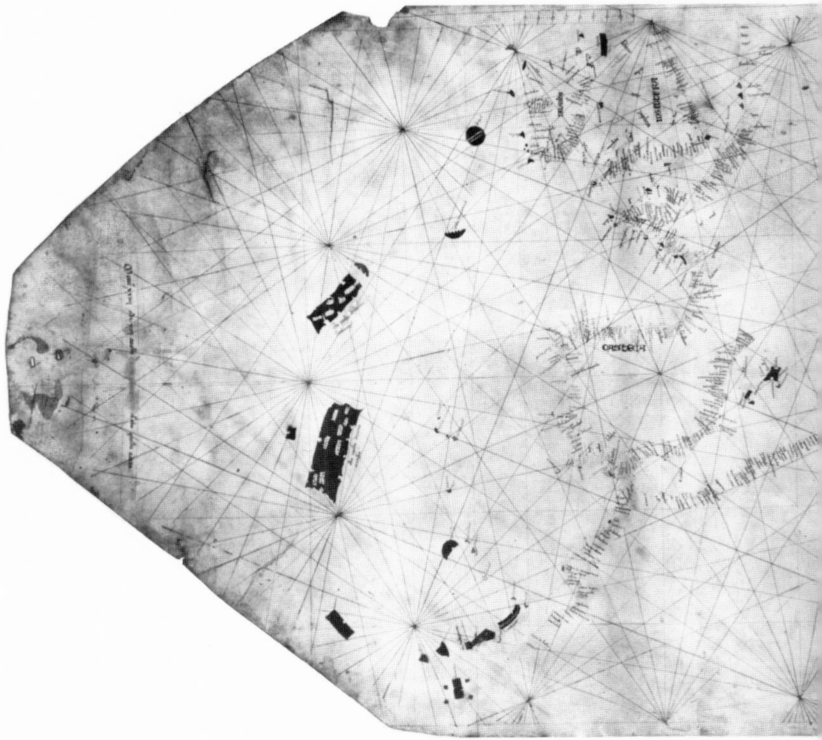

The Zuane Pizzigano Map, 1424, the first to show
Antilia and Satanazes. The James Ford Bell Library, Minneapolis.

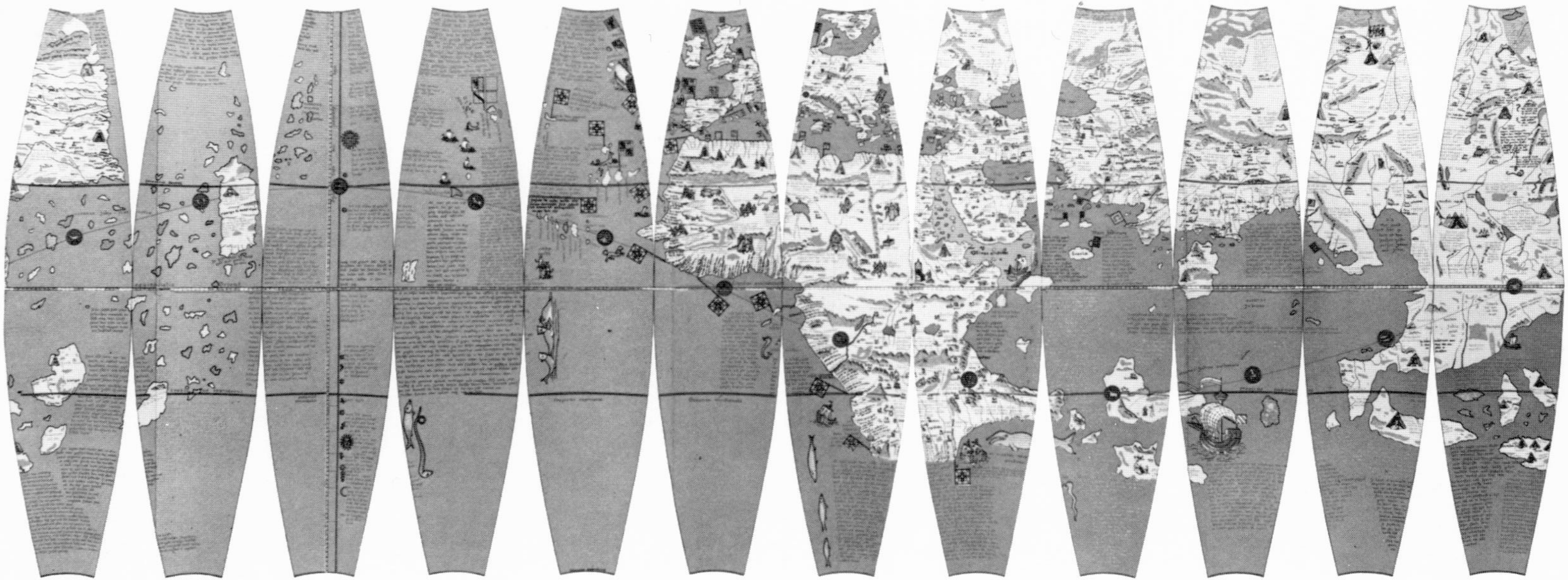

ABOVE: Gores of the Martin Behaim globe, Nürnberg, 1492.
After Edward G. Ravenstein, *Martin Behaim* (London, 1904).

BELOW: The Henricus Martellus world map of *ca.* 1490.
Yale University Library.

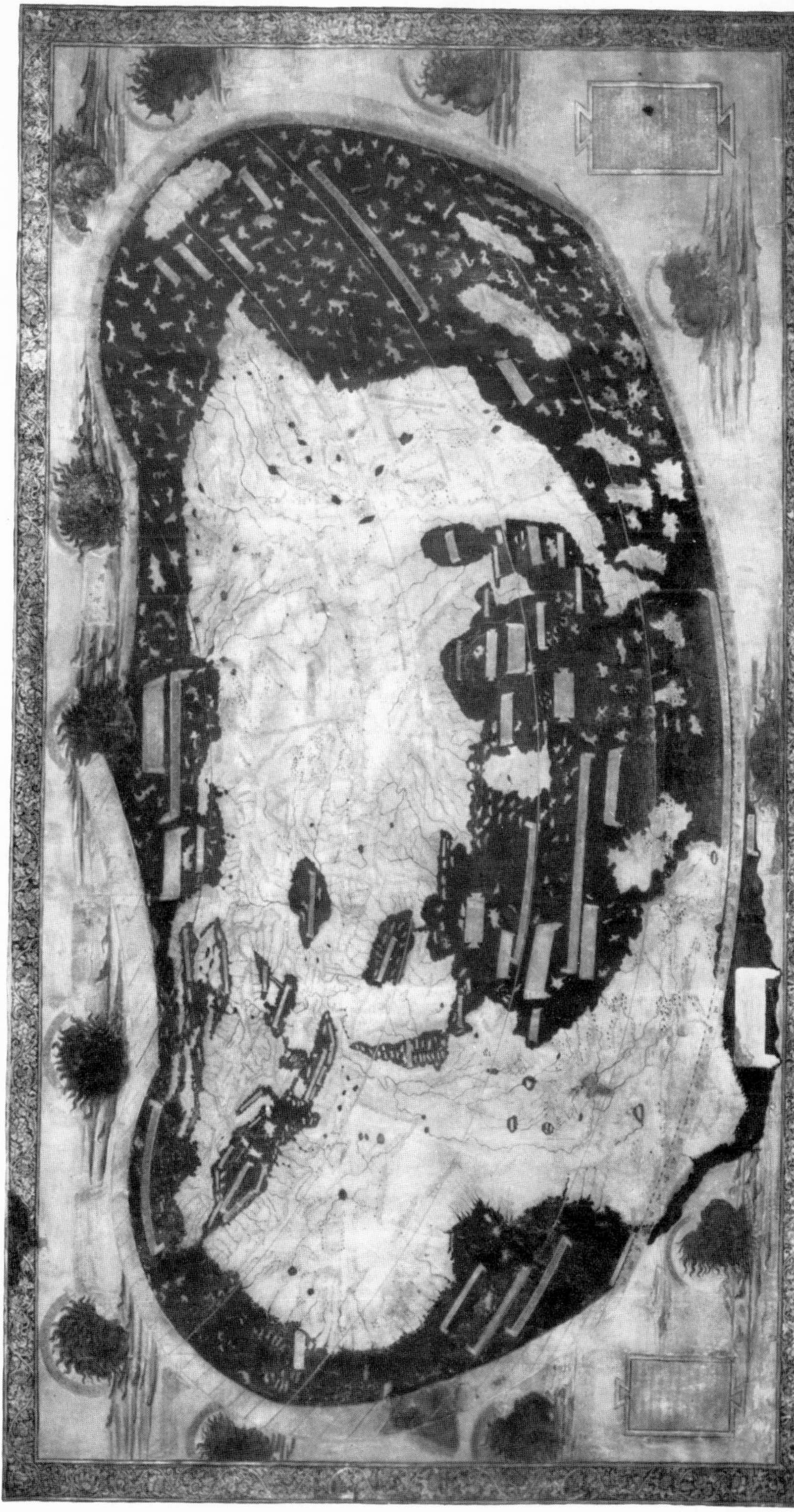

mar descubierta por ingleses
C. de s. Jorge
la española
cuba

ABOVE: The coast discovered by the English, on the Juan de la Cosa map of 1500. Museo Naval, Madrid.

BELOW: Tierra de Ayllón and eastern North America on the world map of Diogo Ribeiro. Original in the Vatican Library.

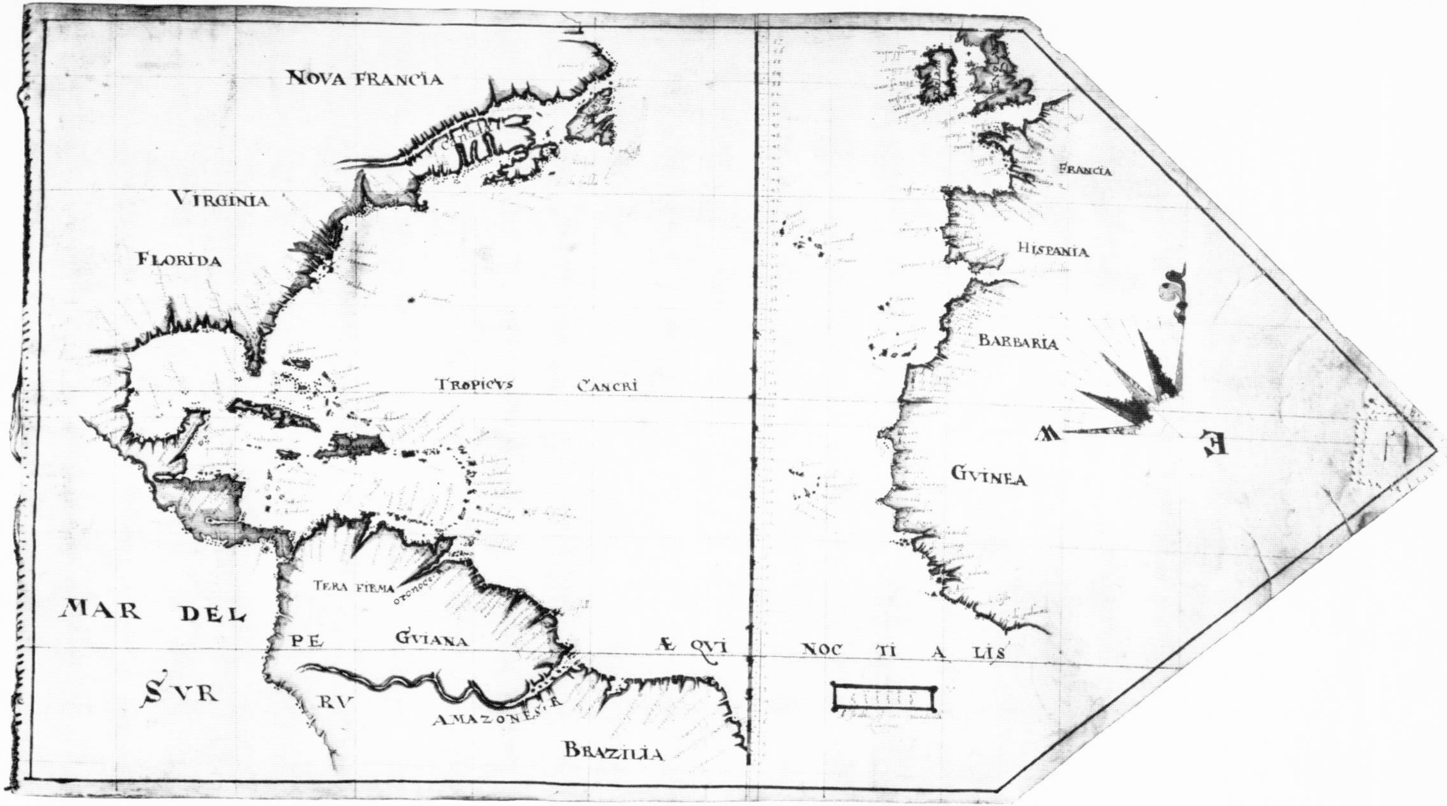

ABOVE: The Virginia Chart, *ca.* 1610. New York Public Library.

BELOW: New England on the Velasco Map, *ca.* 1610–1611.
Archivo General de Simancas.

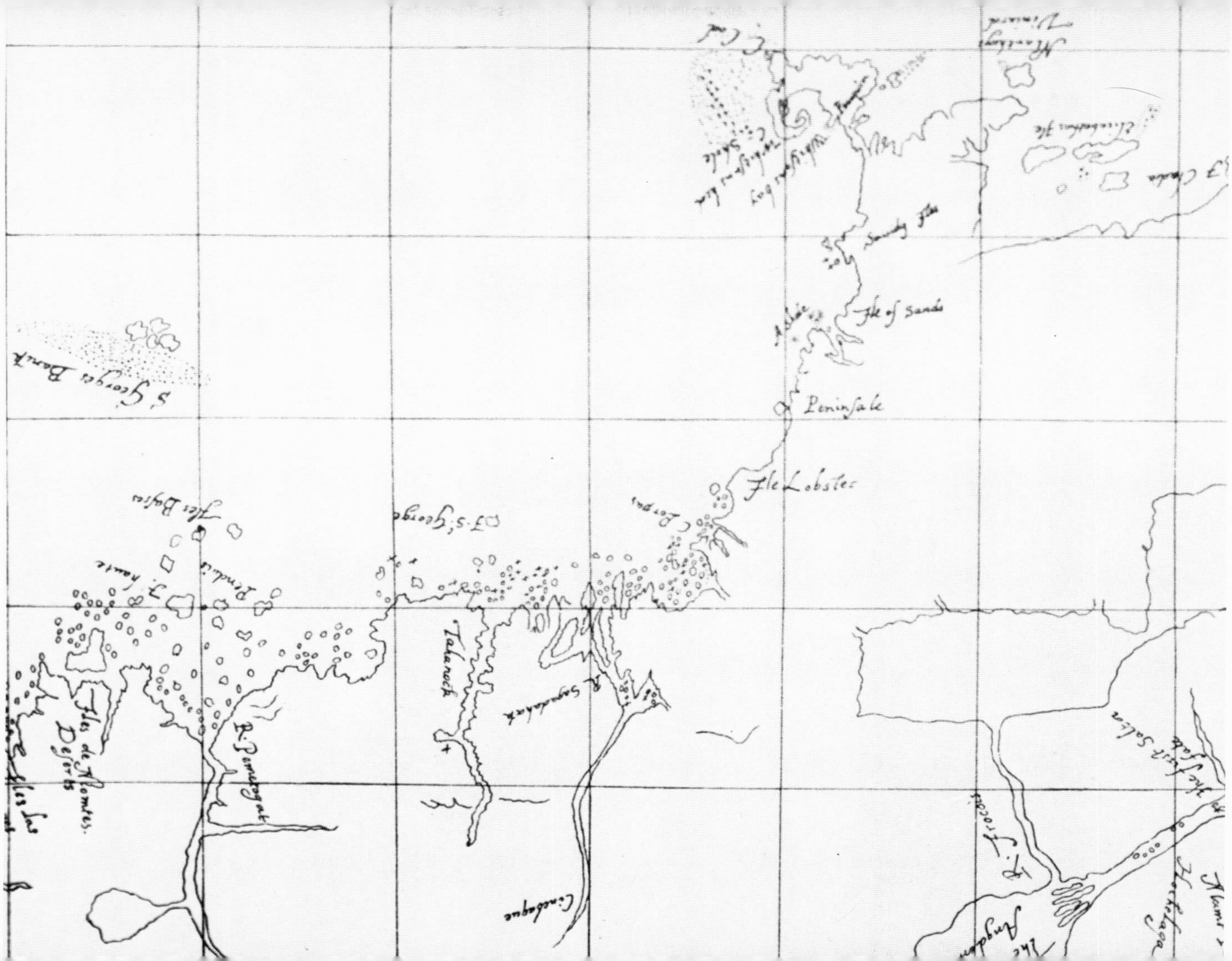

St Georges Bank
Iles Basses
Pendeis
I. haute
Iles de Nomades
Deserts
R. Pemetegoat
I. St George
Tahanock
R. Sagadahock
Cinebaque
C. Corpus
Ile Lobster
Peninsale
Ile of Sands
Sandy Ile
Elizabethes Ile
R. Irocois
The first Salton fale
Hochelaga

John Smith's map of Virginia, compiled 1608–1609.
From John Smith, *A Map of Virginia* (London, 1612).

he was not satisfied. He apparently found it hard to make up his mind as to the precise relevance of the Cabot discoveries to those already made by Columbus, and their place in the overall cosmographic picture he had in mind. This is more likely to have been conditioned by a circumpolar landmass such as appeared on the Paris Map, or by a peninsular projection of Europe to Greenland in the west and the corresponding eastward-pointing Horn of Asia of Henricus Martellus, than by the notion of island-hopping to the relatively nearby Asia (in latitudes of 25° to 30° N) of Behaim or Columbus. Cabot clearly believed he had reached Asia within two thousand miles of Bristol and had nothing more to do than follow the coast southward to arrive at Marco Polo's Cathay.

Whether any of the ships of the 1498 expedition returned to tell a different tale we do not know for certain. What we can say is that his idea appears to have died with him. All the indications we have—though admittedly slight—are that subsequent voyages made from England, in the years before 1508 at least, were for the purpose of exploiting for their own sake, so far as possible, the lands that lay to the west without considering them as leading to anything else. These voyages were governed by a pre-Columbian world picture, but one which could accommodate either a great island, a group of islands, or the projection of the northern landmass, eventually linked with Asia, in western seas.

II

THE LETTER OF John Day to the "Almirante Mayor" concerning John Cabot's American voyage of 1497 [7] is significant enough to invite continued comment and explanation. Since the name John Day has been identified as an *alias* for Hugh Say (d. 1517), a member of a widely connected and cultivated family of London merchants who had other footholds in Bristol and Spain, the close correspondence between this Englishman and an admiral of Spain no longer appears so anomalous as when the letter was first published in 1956. Louis André Vigneras, who found the Day letter in 1955, has already demonstrated that the "Almirante Mayor" to whom it is addressed was almost certainly Columbus,[8] whose title of "Almirante del Mar Oceano" was frequently generalized to "El Almirante Mayor," while he often signed himself "El Almirante." The other territorial official with a similar title was the hereditary

[7] See pp. 5–13 above.

[8] L. A. Vigneras, "The Cape Breton Landfall: 1494 or 1497? Note on a Letter by John Day," *Canadian Historical Review*, XXXVIII (1957), 226; "État présent des études sur Jean Cabot," C.I.H.D., *Actas*, III (Lisbon, 1961), 663, 669.

"Almirante de Castilla," Fadrique Enriquez, who was also addressed as "El Almirante Mayor," but had no associations with overseas voyages and was probably in Italy, as Vigneras has shown, when the Day letter was written. From the external evidence the letter makes better sense, indeed only makes sense, as part of the correspondence between an exceptionally well-informed Englishman and the now-famous discoverer, as he still regarded himself, of the offshore islands of Cathay.

On internal evidence also, the letter seems to fit into the Columbus picture. Why, we may ask, should Columbus have been so concerned with what the English were doing in 1497 as to be in contact by letter, and perhaps also in person, with John Day? The most probable reason is that he was engaged in a systematic revaluation of his ideas and discoveries for the first time since his departure on his first transatlantic voyage in 1492. Returning to Spain from his second voyage on 11 June 1496, he did not leave on his third until 30 May 1498. In the meantime he had opportunity to go over his books and notes and to search for fresh information. His new discoveries were puzzling. Though he had strenuously maintained on his second voyage that Cuba must be a peninsular extension of the mainland of Asia, he cannot have been altogether happy with the fact that in two expeditions, now, he had gone well beyond his calculated limits of the ocean and had still not found any north-south coastline which would allow him to place his discoveries on the globe as he knew it.

That he had rethought his position is to be seen from his southwest course in 1498, which he had intended to bring him south of the equator, since he expected the mainland of Asia to be within easier reach in these latitudes than from the Antilles. The evidence for his continued study of the older authorities is equally indirect but none the less convincing. In the letter he wrote to Ferdinand and Isabella from Hispaniola in October 1498,[9] he cites a long series of authorities in support of the claim that he had just discovered the Earthly Paradise on the shores of the Gulf of Paria. These include Aristotle, Strabo, Seneca, the younger Pliny, Ptolemy, St. Augustine, St. Ambrose, St. Isidore, Bede, Duns Scotus, and Pierre d'Ailly, all of whose works he is most unlikely to have had with him, but whom he is equally unlikely to have remembered in detail if he had not read them since before his first voyage. It is highly probable that the quota-

[9] Christopher Columbus, *Scritti* (Genoa, 1892), ed. C. de Lollis, II, 26, 40; Cecil Jane, ed., *Select Documents Illustrating the Four Voyages of Columbus,* II (London, 1933), 1–47; Christopher Columbus, *Oeuvres* (Paris, 1961), ed. Alexandre Cioranescu, pp. 219–39, 441–64; Samuel Eliot Morison, ed., *Journals and Other Documents on the Life and Voyages of Christopher Columbus* (New York, 1963), pp. 284–8.

tions represented a recent reading and rereading of his authorities, and the collection of a notebook of citations which represented what he could expect to find of the remote East by further exploration to the west. This would be comparable with the "Book of Prophecies" he put together after his third voyage, which has survived.[1] The list of authors shows little novelty, but on a subject such as the Earthly Paradise this is scarcely to be expected. It is not at all unlikely that he also briefed himself thoroughly on English activities before he set sail.

Well before he had any plans for a voyage to Asia, Columbus had shown an interest in the activities of the Bristol men who fished off the coast of Iceland and traded to it in the 1470's; he had probably visited England himself about 1477, though the evidence may not be entirely conclusive.[2] If he did, he almost certainly went to Bristol in a Bristol ship and thence to Iceland and back to Bristol, making a call at Galway on the way, and eventually back to Lisbon. We have seen that, when his oceanic plans had developed, he may just conceivably have come to England again. Later still he had sent his brother Bartholomew to England to explain to Henry VII his plans for an oceanic crossing to Asia (perhaps different plans from those he put before the rulers of Portugal and Spain). He later claimed he had thought of going personally to England about 1491, when things looked black, and had had written offers from Henry VII. It is difficult to assess the value of these references, except that they show his continued interest in England.[3] He several times compared the extent of the West Indian islands he had found with that of Great Britain, he mentioned the quality of English bows, and the market in England for dyewood—points of more interest cumulatively than in isolation.[4]

Columbus knew, according to John Day, that "in times past" (*en otros tiempos*) the Bristol men had discovered the Isle of Brasil out in the Atlantic Ocean. This knowledge may possibly have been in his possession before 1492,[5] and it links up with what we know of his continued concern with English commercial and maritime activity over some twenty years

[1] Columbus, *Scritti*, II, 75–160.

[2] *Ibid.*, I, 71, 11, 524; Fernando Columbo, *Le Historie . . . di Cristoforo Colombo* (Milan, 1930), ed. R. Caddeo, I, 29–32, II, 328–38; Fernando Colón, *The Life of the Admiral Christopher Columbus* (New Brunswick, 1959), ed. and trans. B. Keen, pp. 11–12; Marianne Mahn-Lot, "Colomb, Bristol et l'Atlantique Nord," *Annales*, XIX (1964), 528–30.

[3] See p. 81 above.

[4] Columbus, *Scritti*, I, 76, 99, 128; Jane, ed., *Select Documents*, I (1930), 12–13; *Journal*, ed. Vigneras, p. 117; Columbus, *Oeuvres*, pp. 127, 154, 164, 184, 240; Morison, ed., *Journals*, pp. 128, 132.

[5] See pp. 15–16 above.

before 1497. It was therefore very natural that, during a period of renewed reading and research, he should have been in touch with a merchant like John Day, who was trading between Bristol and Spain. Day's account of John Cabot's discovery in 1497 of a mainland and island, thought by Day to be the Island of the Seven Cities (or Antilia), was probably interesting, possibly gratifying, to Columbus in that it seemed to suggest that the north-south shore of Asia which he had so far failed to find in Caribbean latitudes was to be found between 46° and 51° N (the approximate limits of latitude indicated by Day) at about the distance from Europe he had long anticipated. He was less likely to accept Day's identification of this land with the Island of the Seven Cities, which he expected to find on his westward voyage from the Canaries in 1492, and is likely by 1497 to have consigned to limbo (unless he retained an alternative picture such as that shown on the Paris Map).

The existence of a substantial coastline opposite France and Ireland would have confirmed Columbus's belief that the Asian mainland lay not too far from his original discoveries, and may also have encouraged him to cast farther to the south, as he was to do in 1498, in the hope of finding the Asiatic mainland more quickly. The sketch which Day had enclosed gave him some indication of the extent of Cabot's discoveries, but we may doubt whether it helped him very much with regard to their location. The promised map, on which Day proposed to locate the new lands, was not ready, and we do not know that it was ever completed.

It may well be, as we have seen, that Columbus passed the sketch to Juan de la Cosa and that it was used for the English coasts on the famous map he began in 1500.[6] The news that Cabot intended to follow up his discoveries by a larger expedition in 1498 to the shores of Cathay (as he thought) would give Columbus an additional incentive to accelerate his own preparations and make a decisive bid to establish a foothold on the mainland of Asia ahead of the English. These various considerations may explain the nature of the association between Day and Columbus, though they do not provide final or explicit proof that it took place as suggested. The mention in the Day letter of two books, one by Marco Polo and the other the "Inventio Fortunata" already mentioned, may provide some additional support for the case that the two men were closely linked together.

Columbus owned a copy of the third printed edition of Marco Polo's travels, the short Latin version by Francesco Pipino published between

[6] Antonio Ballesteros (*La Marina Cantabra y Juan de la Cosa* [Santander, 1954]) was unable to find any information on the relations between Columbus and Cosa after their return together to Spain in June 1496.

1485 and 1490, it is thought by Gerard de Leeu at Antwerp.[7] This he annotated extensively, it is usually considered before 1492, though he may have added to his notes later. The proposition has been put forward that some of the notes are in the hand of Gorricio, a monk of the Carthusian house at Seville whom Columbus encountered only after his return in 1493.[8] These paleographical findings are not necessarily correct, but they offer some possibility at least that Columbus's copy of Polo was circulating among his friends. John Day informs his correspondent that he is sending him a book by Marco Polo (which cannot be anything but the travels). It might be argued that since Columbus already owned a copy, this weighs against his being Day's correspondent. But he might have lent this copy; if so it was returned, since it is still in the Columbian Library. The more likely possibility is that Day had obtained for him the new and more valuable Venetian edition (in the Venetian dialect) of 1496. There was also a manuscript version circulating in Spain.[9] The most interesting conclusion to be drawn from this item is that Day, like Columbus, was a student of Polo, the earliest Englishman known to be so; that they had discussed the travels together, and that these had remained a subject of common interest.

The reference in the letter to the other book is more puzzling. Day mentions it under the title "El libro ynvincio fortunati." This, according to Mercator, "an English Minorite from Oxford . . . gave the King of England [Edward III] . . . which he called in Latin *Inventio Fortunatae* [John Dee thought it might have been called "Inventio Fortunae"] which book began at the last climate, that is to say latitude 54°, continuing to the Pole." [1] (Columbus, following Aeneas Silvius and Pierre d'Ailly, put

[7] Biblioteca Columbina, *Cataloga de sus Libros Impresos,* 7 vols. (Seville, 1838–1948), ed. Simon de la Rosa y López, I, 53, V, 451.

[8] Columbus, *Scritti,* II, 446–70; F. Streicher, "Las notas marginales de Colón," *Investigación y Progreso,* III (Madrid, 1929), 51. Streicher's work on other aspects of Columbus's postils has been sharply criticized by Samuel Eliot Morison (*Admiral of the Ocean Sea,* 2 vols. [Boston, 1942], I, 127–8), so that his conclusions must be regarded with some caution.

[9] Morison considered (*ibid.*, p. 105) that Columbus was probably interested in Polo before the printed editions became available. He points to R. Steube, "*El Libro de Marco Polo*" *aus dem Vermachtnis des Dr. Herman Kunst* (Leipzig, 1930), which indicates that there were Spanish manuscript versions available in Spain, which Columbus might have seen. He could also have traced Polo influences on the Fra Mauro map of 1459 if he had access to the version sent to Portugal or to other maps derived from it (cf. pp. 64–70 above).

[1] E. G. R. Taylor, "A Letter Dated 1577 from Mercator to John Dee," *Imago Mundi,* XIII (1950), 59; Skelton, Marston, and Painter, *Vinland Map,* p. 179; Vigneras, "Cape Breton Landfall," p. 226.

the greater part of Germany and all Norway, England, and Ireland beyond the seventh climate.)[2] Somewhat confusingly associated with the name of Nicholas of Lynn, this document had something of a vogue in the sixteenth century, but it was never printed and has not survived except through Mercator's summary of what Jacob Cnoyen said of it and in a number of less specific allusions. John Day's is the earliest English reference to a work of this title, and as that book was of English origin and dealt with the northern regions it is reasonable to assume it is the one described above.

If this is so, Day had had a copy, which he had promised to let his correspondent see, but had mislaid it and was unable at the time of writing to send it to him. It was already known to Martin Behaim by 1492,[3] but whether from a copy seen at Lisbon or at Nürnberg we cannot say. The nautical interest that Day and his correspondent had in it might have arisen from the knowledge by one or the other of them that Behaim had used it. A copy of this book has been associated with Columbus, so that it might be thought that he would already have had it before the Day letter was written. But this association may very well be mistaken. Las Casas in his *Historia de las Indias*, in discussing late fifteenth-century tales of possible islands lying westward from the Cape Verde Islands and the Azores, says that St. Brendan had referred to such islands as also had a book called "Inventio Fortunata" ("de lo mismo se hace mención en el libro llamado Inventio fortunata").[4] There are two points to be made here: first, that there is no mention of Columbus having owned such a book, so that the reference may be to something Las Casas himself had seen, and second, that Las Casas is referring to islands between the latitudes of 15° and 40° N.

Fernando Colón makes an even more imprecise statement, saying that "Juventius Fortunatus tells of two other floating islands supposed to lie to the west and farther south than the Cape Verdes" ("E Juvenzio Fortunato narra, farsi menzione di due altre Isole volte al-l'Occidente a piú australi che le Isole di Capo Verde le quali vanno sopra l'acqua nuotando").[5] This has usually been taken as a corruption of the Las Casas passage, but it may be seen that though the location is similar the matter is different, and it remains doubtful whether the two writers are referring to the same thing. In any event, the reference in both cases is

[2] Columbus, *Scritti*, II, 293. [3] See pp. 82–4 above.

[4] Bartolome de Las Casas, *Obras Escogidas*, 5 vols. (Madrid, 1957–8), ed. J. Perez de Tudela, I, 48.

[5] Fernando Colombo, *Le Historie della vita e dei fatti di Cristoforo Colombo*, 2 vols. (Milan, 1930), ed. Rinaldo Caddeo, I, 69.

still to islands in the vicinity of latitude 15° N. There is in the second instance, as in the first, no mention of Christopher Columbus as the source. Since Mercator is most specific that the fourteenth-century English "Inventio Fortunata" dealt solely with parts of the globe north of 54°, and it was used by Behaim for the Arctic regions only, neither the Las Casas nor the Fernando Colón reference can very well be to this source but must surely be to another work. The identity of title, in the case of Las Casas, must be coincidence.

The "Inventio Fortunata" mentioned by John Day does not tie up with anything known to have been in Columbus's possession or even known to him. According to his own statement, Columbus had been in Iceland and had his own views about its extent and latitude.[6] His interest in "Thule" and in the northern regions is established by his frequent annotation of references to it in the texts he read. If John Day was able to tell him of the existence of a fourteenth-century narrative which dealt with Thule and other northern regions, he would no doubt be anxious to see it. Columbus was concerned, we can see from his statements in the course of the 1498 voyage, to establish the precise shape of the earth, which would suggest that he had become involved once more in cosmographical speculation. Just as evidence of Cabot's discovery of extensive shores westward from the British Isles and France would tend to confirm his views of where the coast of Asia lay, so a discussion of polar and subpolar topography would assist him to clarify his views on the distribution of land and water on the earth's surface.

Though such a treatise as the fourteenth-century "Inventio Fortunata" would certainly have aroused Columbus's curiosity, Day may not have been able to satisfy it. It may indeed be that he had the only copy in England (Cnoyen's was presumably in the Netherlands), and his mislaying of it in 1497 may have meant its final loss to English scholars such as Dee and Hakluyt, who searched for it in vain in the sixteenth century and found, in the end, that Mercator had lost contact with Cnoyen's manuscript, which also disappeared. The reference to this work provides no very clear evidence either way on the question of Day's links with Columbus, but his possession of such a manuscript once again shows the range of his interest in the documents of exploration, and makes more convincing the case that he had much in common with Columbus.

What is most evident from the letter, however, is the closeness with which the Admiral is in touch with events in England. He knows that the man about whom Day is writing (who we know is John Cabot) has

[6] Colombo, *Le Historie*, I, 29; Colón, *Life*, p. 11.

been in England for some time and has already made a voyage before 1497.[7] ("Since your Lordship wants information relating to the first voyage, here is what happened: he went with one ship, his crew confused him, he was short of supplies and ran into bad weather, and he decided to turn back.") Day does not bother to be specific about the Admiral's request for information on the voyage of 1497; his correspondent evidently knew of that too, and Day plunges in with reference to "a copy of the land which has been found." He has brought his information with him to Spain, so he must have left England at the end of August at earliest (probably a little later). He promises, "When I get news from England about the matters referred to above—for I am sure that everything has to come to my knowledge—I will inform your Lordship of all that would not be prejudicial to the king, my master"; in return he only asks his correspondent to write to him again "about such matters." It is clear therefore that very shortly after he reached Spain in June 1496, Columbus was fully informed about the activities of John Cabot in England, by a correspondent other than John Day. It would appear that he had either known Cabot himself or knew a good deal about him, and that he had made contact with John Day to keep in further close and intelligent contact with what was going on in England in regard to western voyaging. The Day letter, therefore, throws some light on Columbus as well as on the Cabot voyages.

The various considerations which can be brought forward strengthen the identification of the Grand Admiral with Columbus to such a point of high probability that they are almost evidentially conclusive. Some Columbus scholars may raise the objection that, since his views were becoming increasingly rigid in form and mystical in content, there is insufficient evidence that he was capable of being influenced in 1497 by new information such as John Day was able to give him. But the indications given above tend to show—though they do not prove—that the last moment when he was still capable of being curious about the realities of the world and receptive to new information about it had not yet been reached and that he was not yet a man with a completely closed mind, expecting the world to conform to his ideas and unable to accept other interpretations. That the rigid, mystical element was encroaching may be argued from a number of passages in his writings in 1498, as from his Book of Prophecies, compiled after his return in 1501–2. At the same time, his appreciation that his discovery in 1498 of a mainland was something new, "another world" in his own words, would indicate that he

[7] Williamson, *Cabot Voyages* (1962), pp. 212–14.

still retained some elasticity of mind and was, before he sailed, still capable of carrying on fruitful discussion with John Day. It may be that the correspondence with the Englishman, of which we have one surviving letter only, helped to keep awake a little of the lively curiosity he had shown in earlier life about the known world he was trying so hard to enlarge. If there is anything in this line of argument, the Day letter may well be considered as one of the sources for the Columbian concepts of the third voyage.[8]

III

BETWEEN CABOT'S VOYAGE in 1497 and the year 1506 there was a series of Portuguese voyages into the western Atlantic (an unknown number before 1500 and at least four between 1500 and 1506) and also a number of English voyages between 1501 and 1506 (at least five) in which Portuguese from the Azores as well as Englishmen were concerned, and which were not mere fishing voyages. The association of English and Portuguese in the expeditions made from England and their overlapping with those made independently from Portugal raise difficult problems of chronology which have not yet been satisfactorily sorted out. Together, the English and Portuguese voyages between 1501 and 1505 represent the first attempt, apart from the unknown success of Bristol ships in fishing on the Newfoundland Banks from the time of their first discovery of the Isle of Brasil, to exploit the lands lying westward in what we know as North America for their own sake, even if without conspicuous success.

After Dulmo had attempted in 1487 a westward voyage in search of the Island of the Seven Cities, there is a gap in known Portuguese efforts to explore the North Atlantic. The effect of the return of Bartolomeu Dias in December 1488, with his account of the turning of the Cape of Good Hope, was sufficient to divert Portugal for some time from the problems of searching for islands westward from the Azores. The Spanish sovereigns had induced Pope Alexander VI to take the meridian 100 leagues west of the Azores meridian and Cape Verdes as delimiting the overseas domain between Portugal and Spain. This could well have

[8] "Le texte [the Day letter] que nous avons présenté a le mérite, du point de vue colombien qui nous occupe, de témoigner des préoccupations et des connaissances du Génois. . . . Tout ce qui contribue à dissiper l'isolement dans lequel les biographes de Colomb, faute de documents nombreux sur la première partie de sa vie, ont trop souvent confiné le Découvreur (qui se serait, d'après eux, entouré d'un mystère volontaire) est précieux pour l'historien, qui est ainsi mieux en mesure de situer dans le réel l'aventure du Génois." Mahn-Lot, "L'Atlantique Nord," p. 530.

represented an honest attempt by Spain to estimate how far Portuguese mariners had, in fact, penetrated the western Atlantic, and is quite possibly a reasonable estimate of how far the voyages between 1452 and 1487 had actually reached beyond the Azores. The Portuguese reaction, however, was sharp and hostile. They insisted that Spain's zone did not extend south of the Canaries, but with negotiation of the Treaty of Tordesillas on 7 June 1494, accepted a line drawn along a meridian 370 leagues west of the Cape Verdes.[9] Whether this was an attempt by John II to keep as wide a sweep as possible to the west of his island dominions, so as to make possible further insular discoveries, or whether Portugal had any reason to believe that substantial territories lay within the extended sphere has been long and indecisively argued.

The Portuguese sent at least one expedition secretly to test the Dias route to India,[1] but it seems probable also that one expedition disappeared without trace; it was not until 1498 that Vasco da Gama was at length despatched with a sufficiently well-equipped fleet to enable him to reach India. In the meantime there may well have been a certain revival of Portuguese interest in testing the limits of the Atlantic zone reserved for her in 1494. The Cabot voyages as well—particularly that of 1497 about which no secrecy was maintained—are likely to have stimulated Portuguese curiosity about the Atlantic. What encouragement was given to explorers to probe the seas westward and northwestward of the Azores before 1499 is not known, but the grants given to Azoreans in 1499–1500 indicate that a certain amount of exploration had already taken place before the earlier of these two dates.

In the history of exploration formal grants are often deceptive documents. Grants were given to João Fernandes, farmer (*labrador*), of Terceira on 28 October 1599 and to Gaspar Corte Real, gentleman of the royal household, Captain of Angra (Terceira) and São Jorge and son of João Vas Corte Real, on 12 May 1500. Just how misleading they may be is not clear and has led to much discussion. Fernandes was authorized "to seek out and discover at his own expense some islands lying within our sphere of influence," and was promised the governorship of those he might find.[2] It has been argued that this meant he had been on no previous

[9] See F. Perez Embid, *Los Descobrimientos en el Atlántico hasta el Tratado de Tordesillas* (Seville, 1948), pp. 234–48.

[1] The basic data on the secret voyage, or voyages, is in T. A. Chumovsky, *Três Roteiros Desconhecidos de Aḥmad Ibn Mádjid o Piloto Árabe de Vasco da Gama* (Lisbon, 1960).

[2] H. P. Biggar, *The Precursors of Jacques Cartier, 1497–1534* (Ottawa, 1911), pp. 31–7.

voyages and had made no discoveries. While this is possible, it is by no means certain. On good precedent, Fernandes may well have made some western discovery before he made any application to the king. The grant to Corte Real is more specific. It states that he had already made attempts with ships and men to find "some islands and mainland" (*de buscar e descubrir e achar . . . algumas Ilhas e terra firme*): this is proof that he had already been active in exploration, but it suggests more positively than with Fernandes that no discovery had so far been made (again perhaps misleadingly). The grant goes on to say that if he succeeds in discovering such islands or mainlands it will redound to the honor of the crown, therefore he is to be encouraged by hereditary rights of governorship of any lands he may discover, and considerable detail is given of precisely what these rights covered. The grants are very different, that to Fernandes simple, nonspecific, conferring a life-interest in the lands discovered; the one to Corte Real elaborate and specific in conveying authority and endowing the discoverer with hereditary rights, also specifying "islands and mainland," not just islands in general.

Gaspar Corte Real sailed northward from the Azores in 1500 and discovered a mountainous cape which gave promise of an extensive landmass in its rear: this was depicted in the Cantino map, compiled in Portugal about the end of 1502, as a peninsula to which was attached the legend:

> This land is discovered by order of the excellent prince Dom Manuel King of Portugal, which is believed to be the point of Asia, and those who discovered it did not land, but saw it, and only saw mountain ranges very thick, and according to the opinion of the cosmographers it is believed to be the point of Asia.[3]

The usual deduction is that Corte Real sighted Cape Farewell, the southern tip of Greenland at 60° N, but was unable to make land and merely made such observation of its position as he could. The mapmaker is clearly relying on a Martellus-type (or just possibly a Paris Map type) map to indicate the supposed nature of the discovery. Corte Real returned to the Azores and set out in 1501 on a more protracted exploration from the new landmark, as we shall see presently.

João Fernandes came to England early in 1501 and, with his companions, offered his services to the Bristol men for the discovery of further lands to the west. His reasons have never been fully explained. It may be

[3] Armando Cortesão and Avelino Teixeira da Mota, *Monumenta Portugaliae Cartographica*, 6 vols. (Lisbon, 1960), I, 14. See also Samuel Eliot Morison, *Portuguese Voyages to America in the Fifteenth Century* (Cambridge, Mass., 1940), pp. 52, 70.

that before the grant of 1499 from Manuel I he had made a successful landfall, had hoped to exploit it under that grant, but was forestalled by the Corte Real discovery of 1500. Alternatively, he may have sailed in the same year as Corte Real, made a comparable discovery (though not necessarily so far north), and come back to find that his compatriot was asserting his own rights to the land he had sighted. Thus Fernandes would have left Terceira in the hope of obtaining support in some other seafaring land, since he was, after all, only a humble man and Corte Real a nobleman, all-powerful in Terceira itself and with access to the king. But through an alliance with the English, he might possibly be outmaneuvered by Fernandes and his associates.

Some such motive seems likely. What has not yet been explained is how close an association the Azoreans had with Bristol men before 1500. It appears highly probable that the latter were trading with these Atlantic islands as far back as the 1480's, but no documentary evidence of it has been published. An obvious basis for the appearance of Fernandes and his associates in Bristol would be that they knew personally a number of the merchants and seamen there who had traded with the Azores, or perhaps had themselves been on trading voyages to Bristol. Another possibility which has been canvassed is that Fernandes, after discovering land in the west, was driven by bad weather eastward to England and made Bristol instead of Lisbon, then informing Bristol merchants of his discoveries and agreeing to pool their respective knowledge of Atlantic voyaging. This is not impossible, yet it might seem that a more postive disincentive would be necessary before a group of Portuguese would agree to desert their own country and go into the service of her English rival. This would lie in Corte Real's assertion of personal influence to enforce his own claims to discoveries made by Fernandes and himself independently.

On the maps, the Terra Labradoris which gives credit to João Fernandes for his discovery, in some cases indicating that he led the Bristol men to it, is variously what appears to be Greenland or a land further west, apparently modern Labrador.[4] It is difficult to know what exactly is meant by Labrador in these cases. It should be stressed however that the knowledge of this land on the maps is drawn from Iberian rather than English sources and so may well be a poor guide to the precise discovery that was made. But whatever news Fernandes brought to Bristol in 1501, it must have appeared novel and have provided alternative incentives to

[4] The technical evidence is analyzed by Skelton, "Cartography of the Voyages," in Williamson, *Cabot Voyages* (1962), pp. 307–20.

the hopes raised by Cabot's first voyage and so soon dashed by his failure in 1498. It may have been a stretch of the western coast of Greenland, though trade with Eskimo there could not be made a very attractive prospect. It might, alternatively, have been some part of the Labrador coast, possibly including the northern part of Newfoundland, overlapping the Cabot coasting of 1497, where Eskimo and Indian contacts alike could have seemed, in summer at least, more promising. This is the least unsatisfactory of all the theories so far put forward. According to the map evidence, for what it is worth, the discovery was made generally to the north of the coastline explored by Cabot.

Corte Real had returned to Lisbon in 1500 with news of the discovery he had made of southern Greenland, and was able to get assistance from the crown in fitting out two vessels which set forth in the spring of 1501. They sailed north, resighted Greenland, and sheered off to the west and northwest to avoid icebergs, reaching land there and following it for some six hundred miles southward. There are cartographical arguments that they may have entered Hudson Strait,[5] but the letters which are the main documentary sources for the voyage suggest a passage fairly close to the western shore of Greenland, the crossing of Davis Strait to Labrador at a fairly high latitude, and a long coasting voyage southward by way of Labrador, Newfoundland, the Maritimes, and possibly Maine.[6] Landings were made, some information gained of the fauna, and native people were encountered. The size of the conifers suitable for masts impressed them particularly. This would suggest that a landing was made either at the Maritimes or in New England. Probably at the same place, an Indian community of some fifty people was seized and taken wholesale on board one of the vessels to be turned into cash as slaves on arrival in Portugal. The chances are that these were Micmac or members of some more southerly Algonkian tribe. But though one ship came back, the other with Corte Real on board, which had gone on coasting to attempt to find how far the long mainland landmass extended, failed to reappear, and he was given up for lost. Gaspar Corte Real's voyage of 1501 provides the first detailed record of a voyage from north to south along the North American coast since Norse times, Cabot's south to north voyage of 1497 overlapping it in part.

The picture built up by this voyage is that of a circumpolar landmass: ". . . the crew of this caravel [the ship which returned] believes that

[5] *Ibid.*, pp. 313–16.

[6] The letter of Alberto Cantino to the Duke of Ferrara, 17 October 1501, and of Pietro Pasqualigo to the Signory of Venice, 18 October 1501 (Biggar, *Precursors*, pp. 61–7), are the main authorities.

the above-mentioned land is mainland, and that it joins another land which was discovered last year in the north [Greenland] by other caravels belonging to this king." Moreover, Pasqualigo went on to indicate that they believed the land they had traversed to be connected both with "Antilie" [discovered by Columbus, the Caribbean Islands] and the recent discovery of land farther south [Brazil, found by Cabral in 1500].[7] The picture was thus built up of a landmass extending northwestward from Europe through Greenland to a long stretch of coast trending west and southwest, which would fill in much of the ten-thousand-mile gap between Europe and the Spiceries, though this view would have been complicated by the range of latitudes covered by all these discoveries, which would produce in the end an enormous peninsula barring Europe in almost continental fashion from the East Indies, to which the Portuguese had now obtained eastward access by way of the Cape of Good Hope.

The Oliveriana map of about 1503 most clearly expresses this view and the dilemma it created.[8] No fewer than three southern projections of land westward from Iceland are shown, extending south to perhaps 45° N with unfilled gaps between them, though all may be assumed to be probably projections from a circumpolar landmass. That to the west of Iceland is clearly Greenland; to the south is located the "Insula de Labrador" in the place and with the shape of the Island of the Seven Cities on the Paris Map. To the west a second peninsula has several islands off its shores and attempts to represent the Corte Real discoveries of 1501. Beyond that the third peninsular extension occupies the western portion of the map; it may represent Cathay, and is located north of the Spanish Caribbean discoveries, with the name "Costa Fermoza." The northern shore of South America is indicated as a detached mainland landmass to the south of the Antilles. The Oliveriana map is notable for leaving the coastlines incomplete.

The Cantino map of 1502 is the first to create a genuine confusion in the world picture. On the east, Asia extends northward to the Arctic Circle (above which the map goes only a little way). Greenland is a peninsula extending from Europe in the Clavus-Martellus tradition, containing the legend on the 1500 Corte Real voyage already cited. To the southwest of Greenland is shown the land discovered by Corte Real in 1501. This is an island on the Portuguese side of the dividing line, with similarities in its location to Vinland on the Vinland Map, though smaller.

[7] Biggar, *Precursors*, pp. 65–7.

[8] Williamson, *Cabot Voyages* (1962), p. 305, pl. 9.

In position it is also comparable with the Island of the Seven Cities on the Paris Map (though larger than that). On it are shown growing enormous mast trees. The inscription is:

> This land is discovered by order of the very high, most excellent prince King Dom Manuel, King of Portugal, which was discovered by Gaspar de Corte Real, a knight of the house of the said King, and when he discovered it he sent a ship with certain men and women whom he found in the said land, and he remained with another ship and never more returned, and it is believed that he is lost, and there are here many masts.[9]

Far to the west of this again, and extending southward to the tropic, is another land, unnamed, which is given no western limit and is quite impossible to fit into the Asian profile on the eastern part of the map. To the southwest, the Spanish-found islands lie between the tropic and the Equator, while to the south of them again is an insular landmass of continental dimensions. Through this the demarcation line passes, leaving a substantial portion on the Portuguese side. The way was being opened for distinguishing transatlantic landmasses from Eurasia.

In England a patent was issued on 19 March 1501 to three Englishmen, Richard Warde, Thomas Asshehurst, and John Thomas, and three Azorean Portuguese, João Fernandes, Francisco Fernandes, and João Gonsalves, to occupy lands which are at present "unknown to all Christians"—thus avoiding the charge of impinging either on Cabot's discoveries or on those made under Portuguese auspices.[1] Much was made of the ten-year monopoly of trade to newly-discovered lands which was granted them. All that is known is that a voyage was made in 1501 which made a landfall and returned, probably late in the year, since a reward of £5 to the Bristol men "that founde thisle" was made in January 1502.[2] Nothing can usefully be said about its destination, except that it was promising enough to lead to a further enterprise in 1502, which was probably on a larger scale.

Thus the year 1502 saw still another voyage. It seems possible that the mariners who were given small rewards in September for bringing hawks and an eagle to the king had been on the expedition, though it is not certain; more substantial was the £20 paid in the last week of September[3] "to the merchauntes of bristoll that have bene in the new founde launde."

[9] Cortesão and Teixeira da Mota, *Monumenta Portugaliae Cartographica*, I, 14.
[1] Williamson, *Cabot Voyages* (1962), pp. 235–47.
[2] *Ibid.*, p. 215. [3] *Ibid.*, p. 216.

This is the first time that the words that make up "Newfoundland" are found used together, but it is not, of course, diagnostic on where the merchants had been. However, it is interesting that these men are described as merchants, presumably engaged in or making a reconnaissance of some transatlantic commerce. There were also three captives, men "takyn In the Newe Found Ile," dressed in skins and eating raw (or perhaps half-raw) meat; their language could not be understood.[4] They remained at court, having been presented to Henry VII, and two of them were still there in 1504, when they were dressed like anyone else and appeared English even if they were not heard to speak the language. They were clearly North American Indians—not Eskimo—so that unless they were Montagnais caught while fishing off southern Labrador they were brought from Newfoundland or farther south. So far as we know, these were the first Amerindians to reach England from North America, just as those brought by Corte Real's men in 1501 were for Portugal. The voyage was felt to have been in some way a success, though in the absence of indications of trade goods brought back it is impossible to know in what degree. Furs may have come in some appreciable quantity. The grant of pensions of ten pounds each from the Bristol customs to Francisco Fernandes and João Gonsalves on 26 September was ostensibly for their service "as Capitaignes into the newe founde lande." [5] This indicates that each had been in command of a ship. Since nothing further is heard of João Fernandes, it is not unlikely that he was in command of a third ship which did not return; Richard Warde, who also fades out of sight, may have been with him. We lack altogether a clear indication of where they had been, but there is some probability that their coasting overlapped to an appreciable extent that done by Gaspar Corte Real in 1501, and comprised parts of Labrador, Newfoundland, and possibly coasts farther south.

Miguel Corte Real was authorized on 15 January 1502 to go to look for his younger brother Gaspar and to take over half his rights to his discoveries if he had died.[6] The same sequence followed his efforts; a voyage was made with two or more ships. One at least returned; that carrying Miguel Corte Real did not. It cannot be established that this voyage in any way enlarged the knowledge of western lands acquired in 1501. If this was not entirely the end of Portuguese exploration, it did mark the virtual termination of a brief and significant series of expeditions.

[4] *Ibid.*, p. 223. [5] *Ibid.*, pp. 248–9.

[6] Biggar, *Precursors*, pp. 67–70.

IV

THE YEAR 1502 signals a break in the sequence of known English voyages across the Atlantic, or was at least the occasion for a major reorganization of the business side of transatlantic ventures. It is also somewhat of a turning point as regards the sources from which most of our information on the next series of voyages—those from 1502 to 1505—comes. Our knowledge of the period between Cabot's first voyage and the beginning of his second derives to an appreciable extent from the rewards and other payments made by the king to him or to his associates in 1497–8. The same is true of the revived expeditions of 1501–2. These are derived from the king's Daybooks of Receipts and Payments, which are technically the Daybooks of the king's Treasurer of the Chamber, and which are for those years in official custody in the Public Record Office. It is well known that Henry VII preferred to carry on not merely the business of the royal household through the means of the Treasury of the Chamber but also to draw in and pay out a considerable part of the royal revenue for state purposes by the same channel.

His concern with money was so close that for many years he scrutinized the accounts. The meager eleven items which have obvious associations with the Cabot and post-Cabot voyages between 1497 and 1502 reflect Henry's personal concern with Atlantic exploration: his desire to reward discoverers and, in a limited way, assist them in their enterprises. Over these years we can say that Henry remained in reasonably close touch with what the Bristol men were doing. After 1502 we were in more difficulty. The surviving extracts from the Book of Payments for 1502 to 1505 did not come to us directly from the Book itself but from a derivative document; we could not tell, therefore, whether this source accurately recorded all items of American interest contained in the original Daybook, and were not even sure that the king continued during these years to make his page-by-page examination of the accounts, which would be some indication that he still maintained a personal interest in and knowledge of American voyages in the years 1502–5.

In 1833 Samuel Bentley, the London publisher, and his collaborators were engaged in collecting materials for a miscellany of historical sources, eventually published in that year as *Excerpta Historica*.[7] They wished to

[7] A. N. L. Munby, *Phillipps Studies*, 5 vols. (Cambridge, Eng., 1957–60), III, 51–3, 155; Sir Thomas Phillipps, *Catalogus* (reprint 1968), no. 4104; Sale Catalogue, Craven Ord, Manuscripts, 25 January 1830 (R. H. Evans, 93 Pall Mall, London), no. 1017; see B.M., *Catalogue of English Book Sales in the British Museum 1676–1900* (London, 1915), p. 179.

include extracts from the Daybooks already known to scholars, but found that, though books extending from 1491 to 1505 had been known to be extant, they were at the time inaccessible. They had therefore to fall back on a recently acquired item in the British Museum, Additional Manuscript 7099, from which they were able to give extracts extending over the years 1491–1505. This volume represented the rough but extensive copyings of one Craven Ord, a minor official in the office of the King's Remembrancer, whose collections had been sold at auction in London in 1830. The collections were disposed of at three sales by R. H. Evans on 25 June 1822, 25 January 1830, and 9 May 1832. A number of volumes might have been bought in for restoration to the archives but were not. The original manuscript, the "Privy Purse Expenses of Henry VII from 1503 to 1506," as the Daybook was henceforth to be known, appeared in the second sale, in 1830, and passed to the bookseller Thomas Thorp, from whom it was acquired shortly after by Sir Thomas Phillipps, in whose privately printed *Catalogus Librorum Manuscriptorum* it duly appeared as no. 4104. It seems to have attracted little attention while in Phillipps's possession and was still in the residue of the vast Phillipps collection when it was acquired by Messrs. W. H. Robinson, Ltd., in 1946. It is now owned by the Robinson Trust, and it is owing to the kindness of the trustees of the Robinson Trust, and more particularly of Mr. Philip and Mr. Lionel Robinson that it is possible to quote from it directly and to reproduce three of its attractive pages.

From the time of the appearance of the *Excerpta Historica* in 1833 down to 1962, Additional Manuscript 7099 remained the source from which the extracts relating to all the American voyages between 1497 and 1505 were repeatedly taken, until finally in 1962 James Alexander Williamson did extract them from all the books, those for 1495 to 1502 and from 1505 onward, in the Public Record Office. But like his predecessors, he had to resort to Craven Ord's version for the years 1502–5. It is thus very valuable that after such a long delay it should be possible to print the precise words and spellings of the appropriate items and to subject the volume to a detailed scrutiny which enables us to add something to the very little that is already known of the voyages of those years. By their nature, the entries of royal gifts and loans cannot tell us a great deal, but what they do tell has a greatly increased interest on account of the extreme scarcity of materials.

Craven Ord was reasonably thorough in his coverage of the Daybooks, though he did not include every entry—for example, that relating to Hugh Elyot given below. But he lumped each page of entries under a single date, whereas they frequently covered from several days to a week; he partly modernized the form of each entry; and he failed to interest himself in the record of loans by and obligations to the king which appeared toward the end of the book. It is possible, therefore, to be more precise about dates, to amend the form of each entry, and also to add one item, represented both in the daily series and in the section of loans and obligations, which enlarges significantly our knowledge of Henry VII's continued concern with American voyaging. The information that Henry VII made a loan to two of the persons involved in the ventures of 1502–5 (even though he required its repayment within a year) indicates that the continuation of westward voyaging commanded a degree of royal interest and support, on however limited a scale, that has not hitherto been suspected. This helps to add a new dimension to our understanding of these voyages, even if much about them remains wholly obscure.

The drastic reorganization of English western ventures took place in December 1502.[8] A voyage had taken place in that year, as we have noted. On 8 December a new charter was made out, to the two Portuguese captains who had recently been granted pensions; to Thomas Asshehurst, who had appeared in the 1501 patent; and to a newcomer, Hugh Elyot. It is a complex document. It implies that the three persons omitted from among those to whom the 1501 grant was made were still alive and entitled to anything they had hitherto discovered. This is reasonable if they had disappeared at sea but were not yet known to have died. The lands discovered by the subjects of the king of Portugal or by other friendly sovereigns were to be respected, but only if they were "in possession." The new grantees, in fact, were authorized to take over lands discovered by others but not yet occupied.

This could represent a challenge to the Portuguese, whose recent discoveries were almost certainly known in Bristol, to exploit their discoveries or else relinquish them, and also marked the explicit assertion of a doctrine of effective occupation. It also implied that lands discovered under the Cabot patent of 1497 were at their disposal. The syndicate was evidently being broadened to take in a wider range of Bristol adventurers, some of those who had aided Cabot having either abstained or been excluded from the 1501–2 ventures. It also, as we shall see, widened the range of the syndicate by including a London element as well as those from Bristol. So far as is known, the 1501–2 voyages were carried through only by a small group of Bristol men in cooperation with the Portuguese adventurers.

[8] Williamson, *Cabot Voyages* (1962), pp. 250–61.

The appearance of Hugh Elyot among the grantees of 1502 provides a link between this venture and the earliest North American voyages, since we have seen that Robert Thorne the younger declared in 1527 that his father, Robert Thorne the elder, and Hugh Elyot had been the first to see the New Lands across the ocean.[9] In January 1502 Elyot and the elder Robert Thorne and his brother William are found as partners in the purchase of a French ship of 120 tons which they had brought from Bordeaux to Bristol and renamed the *Gabriell* of Bristol.[1] A bounty of £20 to the Thorne brothers to be drawn from Bristol customs for the purchase of this ship was collected by William's son Thomas before Easter 1502.[2] Robert and William Thorne had interests in both London and Bristol, William being recorded in 1518 as a London master mason,[3] and both continued to be associated with the ventures for several years. William Clerk of London was also deeply involved:[4] he may have been the member of the Society of Merchant Adventurers of London of that name,[5] and perhaps the same William Clerk who had a house in Bristol not many years before.[6] A figure of considerably more importance was Sir Bartholomew Rede, a leading city figure and recently mayor.[7] Rede was associated in the working of the London Mint with Sir Giles Daubeney, later Lord Daubeney, Constable of Bristol Castle, as early as 1485. No earlier association of his with Bristol ventures before

[9] Williamson, *Voyages of the Cabots* (1929), p. 13; see p. 11 above.

[1] Williamson, *Cabot Voyages* (1962), pp. 247–8.

[2] *Ibid.*, p. 248; G. C. Moore-Smith, *The Family of Withypoll,* Walthamstow Antiquarian Society, no. 34 (1936), pp. 25, 28.

[3] Moore-Smith, *The Family of Withypoll,* pp. 24, 26, 28; Laetitia Lyell and Frank D. Watney, eds., *Acts of Court of the Mercers' Company, 1453–1527* (London, 1936), p. 464. This was in 1518. He died in 1519.

[4] Williamson, *Cabot Voyages* (1962) pp. 262–3.

[5] In 1509. Lyell and Watney, eds., *Acts of Court,* p. 333.

[6] Williamson, *Cabot Voyages* (1962), p. 219. It has not proved possible to trace the original document (a rental of 1498–9): it is not among the Chester-Master papers in Gloucester County Record Office, while inquiries among members of the family produced no indication that it now survives.

[7] There is a brief biography in J. Staples, "Members of the Goldsmiths' Company who have been Aldermen of Aldersgate," London and Middlesex Archaeological Society *Transactions,* VI (1881–90), Appendix, pp. 24–25. His association with Daubeney in 1485 is noted in William Campbell, *Materials for a History of the Reign of Henry VII,* I, (1873), 105, 107. He was mayor in 1502–3, was knighted, and died later in 1505. See John Stow, *Survey of London,* 2 vols. (1908), I, 305–6, II, 83, 179. The fragmentary account in P.R.O., E. 101/415, 16, pp. 3–4, indicates that he was still involved with coinage as late as April to June 1505. He died on 26 October 1505 (*Calendar of Inquisition Post Mortem, Henry VII,* III [1955], 97).

1502 is known, though it is possible there may have been one. It is clear, however, that as a goldsmith he was concerned in a small way with financing the ventures of 1502–5. Clerk, of the London group, was more deeply involved. The patentees and their associates, though not formally incorporated, were called either the Company of Adventurers into the Newfound Islands ("The Company adventurers in to the new fownde ilondes") or the Company of Adventurers prepared into the Newfoundlands ("the Company Adventurers preparyd into the new found londes").[8]

The only major discovery made about the ventures sponsored by this group is that at least the second of them, the voyage of 1504, was partly financed by a loan from the king.[9] On 26 April 1504 £50 was lent to Hugh Elyot, which was almost certainly toward fitting out the expedition of that year. The formal obligation, signed on 4 May, provided that the money be repaid within a year, and in this Elyot's name is joined with Bartholomew Rede's. The sum of £50 was duly repaid by Elyot and Rede in Easter term 1505. The king's participation, even if only on such a small and temporary scale, indicates clearly that, apart from occasional rewards, he also regarded the ventures as worthy of some financial assistance. That the aid was so small and given for so short a time may indicate also that Henry VII was not very optimistic of the London-Bristol associates developing a highly profitable trade. What part Sebastian Cabot played in the Company has not yet been clarified.

In mid-September 1503 Sir Walter Herbert's servant brought Henry "a brasell bowe & ij Rede arowez," for which he was rewarded.[1] (Herbert's precise involvement is not known, but he frequently sent the king gifts of hawks and other things.) These seem probable acquisitions from

[8] Williamson, *Cabot Voyages* (1962), p. 263.

[9] King's Daybook, October 1502–30 September 1505, PhillippsMS 4104, Trustees of the Robinson Trust:

fol. 53v. 26 April 1504. "Item to hugh Eliot opon lone by oblicacion

(Not in B.M., AdditionalMS 7099.)

fol. 237v. Hugh Eliot & bartilmew Rede are bounden in an obligacion
Solutus to pay at Ester Anno domini millesimo & v° for as moche money borrowed of the King l li iiij° die maij anno xx.

(Not in B.M., AdditionalMS 7099.)

[1] *Ibid.*, fol. 32v., 15–20 September 1503, "Item to sir Walter Herbert[s] seruaunt for bringin of a brasell bowe & ij Rede arowez vj s viij d."

(Williamson, *Cabot Voyages* (1962), p. 216, gave it from Craven Ord's transcript, B.M., AdditionalMS 7099.)

North America. Just possibly they could have been made of genuine brazilwood from newly discovered Brazil, already being exploited by the Portuguese, but they were more probably the product of a 1503 Bristol voyage, although they might also have come with the Indians who were at court in 1502. South of Cape Breton, at almost any place along the coast, Indians might have been found using bows and arrows made of red oak (*Quercus ruber*), which is both hard and of a color not dissimilar to the brazilwood that was already known in its Asiatic form. Either in 1502 or 1503, it seems, trading may have been carried on with the Indians along the coast of the Maritimes or of New England.

A further gift of hawks "from the newe founded Ilande" was rewarded in the latter part of November,[2] but these might have been acquired almost anywhere along the coast. The 1503 voyage (judging by the bow and arrows, if they have any diagnostic value), may have been directed to shores south of those which John Cabot coasted in 1497. The 1504 voyage, apart from the king's loan, produced even less information; a voyage was apparently made, since early in April a reward was given to a priest "going to the new Ilande,"[3] but this need scarcely indicate missionary activity—clergy went with Cabot in 1498, most probably as passengers and chaplains rather than as missionaries.

It was apparently for the voyage of 1505 that William Clerk laid out on Hugh Elyot's behalf £144 18s. 6d.[4] Much of this was for the fitting out of the *Michell* (or *Michael*) with ropes, sails, nails, flour, beer, and barrels (tuns, pipes, hogsheads). One at least of the ships was back early, since before the end of August certain Portuguese—most probably the Azorean members of the Company, Francisco Fernandes and João Gonsalves—brought to the king "popyngais and Cattes of the montaign with other stuff."[5]

[2] PhillippsMS 4104, fol. 38r, 24 November 1503, "Item to one that brought haukes from the newe founded Ilande in Rewards xx s."

(Williamson, *Cabot Voyages* [1962], p. 216, prints it from B.M., AdditionalMS 7099.)

[3] PhillippsMS 4104, fol. 53r, 7–10 April 1504, "Item to a preste that goith to the new Ilande xl s."

(Williamson, *Cabot Voyages* [1962], p. 216, prints it from B.M., AdditionalMS 7099.)

A present of 40s. to "a portingale" between 28 January and 31 January could have been made either to one of those who had been on the 1503 voyage or to one who was preparing to go on that of 1504.

[4] Williamson, *Cabot Voyages* (1962), pp. 262–3.

[5] PhillippsMS 4104, fol. 96v, 15–20 August 1505:

Popinjays are parrots. Known throughout the later Middle Ages and acquired largely it seems from East Africa by way of Egypt, they gave their name to tenements in London in the fourteenth and fifteenth centuries.[6] More recently the Portuguese in the mid-fifteenth century had brought back new and exciting varieties from Guinea which may have reached England before the end of the fifteenth century. Finally, in 1500, Cabral sent back from Brazil "very large and beautiful red parrots and two little green ones,"[7] so that in October 1501 Pasqualigo was able to write from Lisbon of "the Land of the Parrots" (*terra dei papaga*), recently discovered by Portugal.[8] An item in the royal Daybook for the period 14–19 January 1498 does not seem hitherto to have been noticed: it is a reward to Richard Dekons "for a popyngchay" of the substantial sum of £6 13s. 4d.[9] If Dekons could in any way be associated with John Cabot, it would be tempting to assign the bird to the 1497 voyage, which would then have to be brought down into latitudes where parrots existed. As it is, and without associating it with Cabot, it is important as showing that parrots were prized at court and were welcome presents, though it may be said that their rarity was presumably decreasing, since the Portuguese in 1505 merited a reward of only £5 for more than one popinjay and more than one "cat of the mountain" as well.[1]

The popinjays or parrots available in eastern North America were specimens of the Carolina parakeet (*Conuropsis carolinensis*),[2] which

---

Item to Clays goyng to Richemount with Wylde Cattes &
Popyngays of the newfound Island for his costes xiij s iij d
Item to Portyngales that brought popyngais and Cattes of the
mountaigne with other stuf to the kinges grace C s.

Clays was a messenger bringing the paroquets and bobcats from Westminster to the King at Richmond Palace. What the "other stuf" brought by the Portuguese was, we cannot say.

(Printed by Williamson, *Cabot Voyages* (1962), p. 216, from B.M., AdditionalMS 7099.)

[6] London had a brewery called "le Papageay" (1394), a tenement "le Popyngeay" (1424), and a brewery "la Popyngjay" (1486).

(R. R. Sharpe, *A Calendar of Wills Proved and Enrolled in the Court of Hastings*, 2 vols. [London, 1889–90], II, 311, 435, 590.)

[7] See W. B. Greenlee, *Voyages of Cabral* (London, 1939), pp. 26, 58–59, 120, while they appear on the Cantino map (1502).

[8] Biggar, *Precursors*, pp. 65, 67.

[9] King's Daybook, 1 October 1497 to 30 September 1499, P.R.O., E. 101/414, 16.

[1] See p. 124, *n.* 5, above.

[2] See E. H. Forbush and J. B. May, *Natural History of the Birds of Eastern and Central North America* (Boston, 1939), p. 256. A beak found in New England is in the collections of the Peabody Museum, Salem.

were southern birds (the last being killed in Florida about 1904) occasionally seen by early settlers of New York State, though their beaks have been found as far north as Casco Bay in Maine and in the St. Lawrence valley in the vicinity of Quebec. The "cats of the mountain" were the bobcats or lynx (*Lynx rufus*),[3] with a similar range to the Carolina parakeet, their northern limits being Maine and the southern part of Quebec province. For the English to capture parrots would be no more difficult than to take hawks: trapping lynx would be less easy—most probably trade was the answer. The 1505 expedition can then be plausibly considered to have traded with the Indians for birds and beasts to take home. The place would be New England or somewhat farther south, or conceivably well down the St. Lawrence River. Otherwise the only explanation would be that the Indians of, say, the Maritimes, had obtained specimens of these creatures by trade from farther south and had disposed of them to the English. This does not seem very probable. We can therefore locate this expedition reasonably firmly—perhaps the first English expedition for which this is possible—within the present boundaries of the United States.

We do not know what other trade was done. Furs are not mentioned, but are a possibility. The large barrels mentioned in Clerk's accounts, if not part of Elyot's wine-trading activities, could have been for the collection of fish or whale oil. Fishing, though again not specifically indicated, might have been attempted. What is clear, however, is that in 1505 the Company was coming adrift. Payments of the pensions of the two Portuguese are known for September 1502, and probably for the same time in 1503, but with no indication that they were paid thereafter. William Clerk took proceedings in the court of Chancery for the repayment of the money he had laid out for Hugh Elyot, and may not have obtained payment. Elyot proceeded in the Constable's court at Bristol for £100, alleged to be a debt owed him by Francisco Fernandes; the latter appealed to the Chancery against these proceedings, counterclaiming that Elyot owed him £160.[4] Again we do not know the result.

Until further evidence appears, the precise causes of the failure to carry on a profitable trade with the Algonkian Indians of eastern North America between 1501 and 1505 cannot be fully understood. It was probably a matter of expecting too much, of not knowing how to obtain furs, dyes, and suchlike from the Indians, being too concerned with exploration, perhaps, to concentrate on trying to make the voyages pay. By

[3] Cf. E. R. Hall and K. R. Kelson, *The Mammals of North America*, 2 vols. (New York, 1959), II, 968–72.

[4] Williamson, *Cabot Voyages* (1962), pp. 248–249, 262–264.

now they were not being subsidized and their final failure was complete. No other trading voyages can be traced for the remainder of the reign of Henry VII. Even the Newfoundland fishery remains entirely obscure for these years; probably it was being carried on each year by a few small fishing vessels from Bristol as it may have been from 1481 onward, but we do not hear of it directly again until a "fishing fleet" for Newfoundland is mentioned in 1522.[5]

A Portuguese expedition to look for the lost brothers Gaspar and Miguel Corte Real may have been sent out in 1503,[6] and it was followed in subsequent years by fishing vessels which were well established on the shores of Newfoundland by 1506. In that year Vasco Eannes Corte Real, the eldest brother of all, had his brothers' grants transferred to himself. He and his successors seem to have kept up some contact with North America voyaging, but their specific activities cannot be traced.

Similarly, the role of Pedro de Barcellos remains obscure. He is said in 1506 to have spent, at some time earlier, three years on a voyage of discovery along with João Fernandes.[7] This must have been before 1501, when Fernandes appears in Bristol; it could most easily have comprised the years 1498, 1499, and 1500, though it might have begun earlier. Barcellos went back to his lands in Terceira, though in 1509, after his death, his sons received a reward from the crown for the exploring done by their father in the north.[8] This again is another loose end, though we may if we wish contrast the loyal and pedestrian Barcellos with the ambitious and daring Fernandes, who risked the displeasure of his king and lost his own life in following up, in the company of a number of Bristol and London merchants and seamen, a transatlantic discovery.

The association of Englishmen and Portuguese from 1501 to 1505, draws together earlier indications of the community of interest which the latter and Bristol men had in the Atlantic. The papal bulls of 1493 and the Treaty of Tordesillas in 1494 broke that community of interest and began the alignment of Portugal with Spain in Atlantic matters. The cooperation of 1501–5 was a last expression of the old association with the Englishmen of Bristol.

There is clearly, as the result of successive voyages, separately or in conjunction, a gradual elaboration of the knowledge of the length and complexity of the North American coastline. From 1497, perhaps, English-

[5] We hear, August 1522, of "the commyng home of the new fownd Isle landes flete" (Biggar, *Precursors*, pp. 142–3; *Calendar of Letters and Papers of the Reign of Henry VIII* (1864), II, pt. 2, nos. 2458–9).

[6] Henry Harrisse, *The Discovery of North America* (London, 1892), p. 76.

[7] Biggar, *Precursors*, pp. 92–99. [8] *Ibid.*, pp. 100–2.

men could think of the land across the ocean as having continental dimensions. The Portuguese were clear that there was a division by sea between Greenland and the next land farther to the west. Whether Greenland was thought of as a peninsula projecting from Europe, or as a protrusion from a circumpolar land, or as the last easterly pointer of Asia, it was clear that a water passage went as far as had been explored toward the northwest. It was not surprising therefore, that this channel should become the focus of renewed interest a few years later, and that its search was to some extent independent of the clear representation on the maps of the continentality of North America.

The little group of Bristol merchants which was associated over part or the whole of the period from 1480 to 1505 with western voyages had a long trading life. Several of them—John Thomas, Thomas Asshehurst, and Hugh Elyot—appear in the surviving Bristol customs accounts (for 1512–13 and 1517–18) still trading with the Iberian peninsula during the first decade of Henry VIII's reign.[9] In 1524 representatives of the group are still found firmly rooted in Bristol: Hugh Elyot in Broad Street; John Thomas, merchant, in the Abbey and in Small Street; John Jay (a still younger one?) in Broad Street; William Thorne in Pyle End; and Joanna Thorne, widow (her husband Nicholas being not long dead), in St. Nicholas Street.[1] No evidence has yet come to light that, from 1505 to 1525 at least, any of them had any concern with America or with voyages in that direction. Their earlier experiences appear to have been decisive.

The king's Daybook for 1506–9 has none of the interest of its predecessor on the overseas voyages.[2] In the week beginning 10 July 1506, it is true, there is a payment "to the ladd that kepeth the Wylde Cattes" of 10s., which would suggest that the American bobcats were still alive, though of course these particular wild cats may have been home-grown. The Pierre Champion who received a reward of 6s. 8d. in the week beginning 28 August 1506 for bringing the king a "Basseleke" may or may not have brought a basilisk—which may or may not, in turn, have been an iguana from the Caribbean, though if so, it is most likely to have been picked up by a French merchant in Spain. Richard Dekons and Sir Walter Herbert continue from time to time to supply hawks to the

[9] Gordon Connell-Smith, *Forerunners of Drake* (London, 1954), pp. 60–61, 69.

[1] 10 January 1524 subsidy returns. P.R.O., E.179/113/192.

[2] P.R.O., E.36/214. This copy is probably one retained by the Treasurer of the Chamber as it contains no signatures by the King (though it is possible that Henry after 1505 ceased to take such an intimate interest in finance as he had done hitherto).

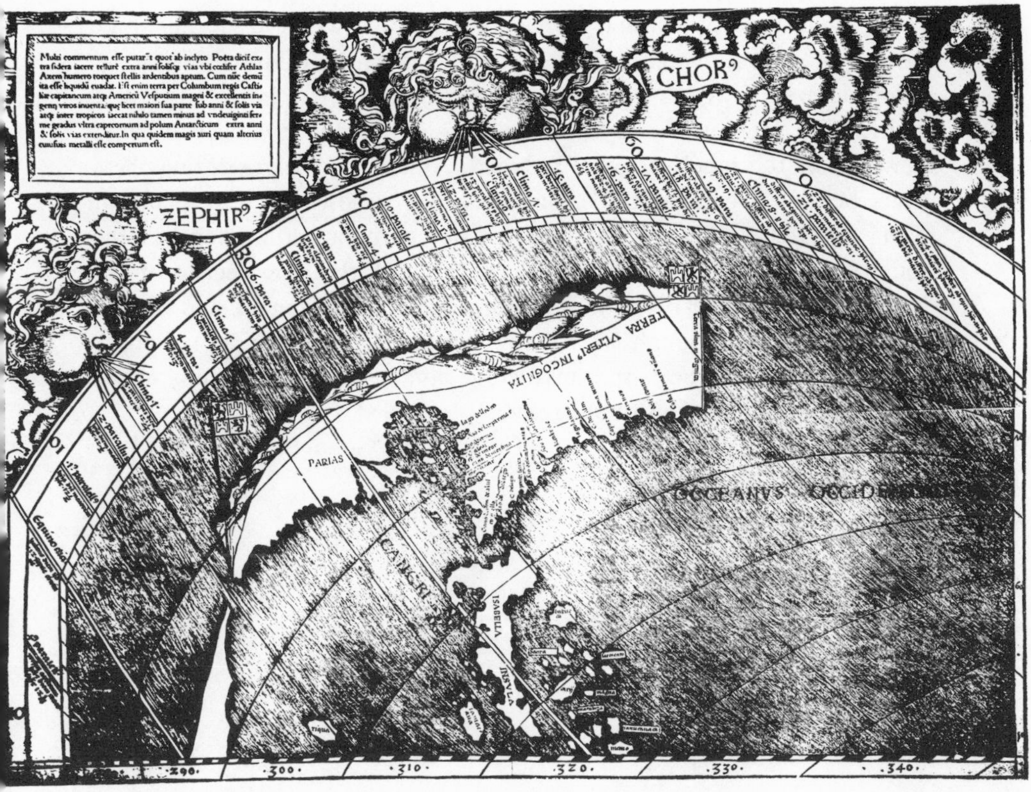

The first delineation of North America as a separate continent (the name America being given to the more southerly of the two new continents), 1507. From the world map of Martin Waldseemüller.

king, but this does not appear to mean that any hawks were coming from North America. The excitement of visits of voyagers from American expeditions which had run through the Daybooks from 1497 to 1505 is replaced by mere frivolities. There is no evidence in this volume that Henry VII spent a single penny during the years 1506–9 in the encouragement of those who were going or had gone across the ocean.

Taken together, the voyages considered above are of considerable significance. They established that it was possible for Portuguese and English to cross the intervening Atlantic and to find, not scattered islets but major islands and continuous landmasses extending for great distances. There is no hint in the evidence we have for the Portuguese voyages, or indeed in the exiguous evidence for English voyages as well, that this was the land of the Great Khan, or Cathay, or any part of Asia. The new lands were accepted as they were, countries inhabited by people in a precivilized stage of cultural development—lands where trade might be carried on, slaves acquired (in the case of Portugal), and fisheries developed. Even if we have no direct evidence to prove it, both Portuguese and English acted as if this was a new, hitherto undiscovered continent. It would be too much to say that North American voyages during these years became a commonplace, but they were shown to be capable of being repeated with some regularity, if not without peril. They laid the foundations therefore for the development over the next decade of the Newfoundland fishery, in which Portuguese and French, and almost certainly English (though we have no record of their fishing activities) gradually built up the first transatlantic commerce that was not under the control of the Spanish monarchy.

CHAPTER FIVE

Sebastian Cabot and English Exploration

I

THE PERSPECTIVE OF English attitudes and action regarding North America after 1505 is vaguer than for the previous decade. We have the activity of 1480–1 and 1490–6 in the preliminary phase, the rapid sequence of constructive and exciting discovery between 1496 and 1505, the occasional though rather rare concern with North American exploration evident from 1505 to 1510, and finally the still more intermittent concern shown between the older sequence of voyages and the eclectic and infrequent expeditions of the new era. During the period after 1505, England's prior claims to prominence in North American waters were resigned to France, Portugal, and Spain. Sebastian Cabot's own voyage in search of a Northwest Passage around America marks a new direction in exploration: the continental character of America has been established only to be rejected—it is to be circumnavigated by a voyage around its northern shores to Asia. The failure of that voyage meant the end of Cabot's efforts in England for many years. With his move to Spain we are left with the limited, though occasionally real, interest of Henry VIII, Cardinal Wolsey, and even Thomas Cromwell in sponsoring or permitting westward voyages of exploration. Those planned in 1517 and 1521 and those made in 1527–8 and 1536 are not of spectacular importance, yet the plans and achievements were not negligible either, only very widely spaced—worthy of attention but in significance, not to be set beside ventures like those of Verrazzano or Cartier or de Soto.

After 1536 there is a long gap even in planning, though there was some thinking of a Northwest Passage or polar voyages to Asia. Until Sebastian Cabot returned to England in 1548 there was little concern with the New World. But after that year a new vigor illuminated old planning. In the last decade of his life Cabot was concerned to stimulate not merely voyaging to North America but the widening of English commercial contacts overseas generally. The search for a passage to Cathay which he inspired led to Russia and to overland trade with Persia—not to a further bout with the American Arctic. Yet he set men thinking again about voyaging over the Pole, through Northwest Passages, up the Amazon; he was involved in the planning that led to the establishment of trading links with Morocco and Guinea. Under him the first suggestions of an overseas English commercial empire begin to take shape. A generation of younger men grew up under his inspiration who had wider views of exploration, commerce, exploitation, and eventually settlement overseas.

Sebastian Cabot spent a significant part of his life in Bristol, and made an appreciable contribution to her overseas activities in the reign of Henry VII and the opening of the reign of Henry VIII. It was from his Bristol period that his first overseas experience sprang, and the interest in exploration that dominated his life; the activities of pioneering Bristol voyagers provided inspiration for his lifework in the Spanish service and for his persistence as an old man in getting the first effective English overseas exploring and trading corporation under way.

During his lifetime Sebastian appears to have taken to his own credit some of the achievements of his father, John Cabot.[1] Consequently later generations, especially in the Elizabethan age, assigned to him alone major responsibility for the English voyages to America under Henry VII. Down to the present century he was credited with the leading part in the 1498 voyage of his father, and it is only comparatively recently that the majority opinion of scholars—itself a fickle thing—has narrowed down

[1] Sebastian's life story is well represented in published documents which, together with much commentary, appear in Henry Harrisse, *Jean et Sébastien Cabot* (Paris, 1882) and *John Cabot, the Discoverer of North America, and Sebastian Cabot His Son* (London, 1896); Williamson, *Voyages of the Cabots* (1929) and *Cabot Voyages* (1962); J. T. Medina, *El Veneciano Sebastián Caboto al servicio de España*, 2 vols. (Santiago, 1908). Roberto Almagià, *Commemorazione di Sebastiano Caboto nel IV centenario della morte* (Venice, 1958), is an excellent survey of his influence. R. A. Skelton's article on him in *D.C.B.*, I (1965), is the best short account in English. G. P. Winship, *Cabot Bibliography*, 2d ed. (London and New York, 1900), is still of great value. There remain many gaps in our knowledge of his life at certain periods.

his individual contribution to Bristol voyaging to a single venture, apparently made in the years 1508–9.

The greater part of his adult life, from 1512 to 1548, was spent in the service of Spain. The last years of his life, in England again, were passed mainly in London. Thus his Bristol connection covered only the early formative years of his manhood, extending from about 1494 to about 1510. It was revived fitfully in 1521, and for a time, after his return to England, in 1548–9. He is not known to have maintained continuous association with the city throughout his career in Spain, though he can be shown to have had contacts there with some Bristol men. But his connection with Bristol was sufficiently close for a long enough time to justify students of Bristol history in giving him an honored place among their great men.

Sebastian Cabot himself made three statements about his birth. The first, in 1522 to Gasparo Contarini, the Venetian representative in Spain, was that he was born in Venice and brought up in England. The second, at some time before 1550, to a gentleman of Mantua, was that he reached England from Venice only when he was old enough to have already mastered the classics and the sphere. The third, before 1555 to Richard Eden, was that he was born in Bristol, brought at the age of four years to Venice, and later came back to Bristol with his family.

His father, Giovanni (or Zuan) Caboto, was said in 1498 to have been originally a Genoese, but his family has never been positively identified in Genoa.[2] Let us try, nevertheless, to set in more or less continuous and narrative perspective the known, or generally accepted, facts of the elder Cabot's life (briefly touched on earlier—pp. 9–10). Perhaps as early as 1461 he settled in Venetian territories, and in 1476 was accepted as a Venetian citizen, at which time there was no mention of his having a wife or children. Between 1482 and 1484 he married, and early in 1484 gave his wife, Mattea, some property in security for her dowry; this suggests that his marriage was not very far behind him, though at the end of the same year Caboto is described as the father of sons. By December 1584, therefore, his wife had borne him either two or more sons in succession, or perhaps twins. This was at Chioggia, one of the Venetian islands. One of these children was almost certainly Sebastiano, the other

[2] On the early history of the Cabot family see Rodolfo Gallo, "Intorno a Giovanni Caboto," A.N.L., *Rendiconti della classe di scienze morali, storiche et filologiche*, ser. 8, III (1948), 209–20; Williamson, *Cabot Voyages* (1962), pp. 190–8; Manuel Ballesteros-Gabrois, "Juan Caboto en España," *Revista de Indias*, IV (1943), 607–27; Roberto Almagià, "Sulle navigazioni di Giovanni Caboto," *Revista Geografica Italiana*, LXVII (1960), 1–12.

his elder brother Ludovico. Whether their young brother Sancio was born in Venice we cannot tell.

Giovanni Caboto is described as a merchant and was employed in the Mediterranean trade, probably to Alexandria, where the Venetians collected spices, medicines, dyes, and silks brought by Arab traders from Asia. Like other venturesome Italians of the fifteenth century, he penetrated into the Muslim lands in the guise of a pilgrim to Mecca, and evidently returned safely without being unmasked and punished. This gave him an abiding interest in the source of the rich commodities that came from the East. It seems probable that sometime later, perhaps about 1490, he moved to Spain with his wife and family and finally settled in Valencia, where he was known as Juan Caboto Montecalunya, the Venetian. He was evidently building up some reputation as a cartographer and navigator, and it was probably shortly after he reached Spain that he approached officials and merchants, first in Seville and then in Lisbon, with plans for a westward voyage across the Atlantic to the Oriental land of Cathay, which he knew from Marco Polo's account. He equipped himself with both a world map and a globe, the latter made by himself, but evidently had no success.

We do not know where and how his quest crossed that of Columbus, who from before 1485 onward had been engaged on a similar enterprise and who eventually won the support of Queen Isabella and was thus enabled to make his decisive voyage to the West Indies in 1492. In that year Juan Caboto Montecalunya was advising the authorities at Valencia on the construction of a new harbor for the city. He designed and colored plans for this project, but in 1493 it was decided not to adopt them and the scheme dropped. It was apparently after Columbus's triumphant return with news that he had found the Indies by a westward voyage and had left a colony on an island, as he thought, off the shores of Japan, that Juan Caboto was forced, at the end of his consulting job, to leave Valencia.

He now decided that he could revive his project for an approach to Asia by a westward voyage if he could convince the merchants or rulers of one of the more northerly countries that a shorter and cheaper approach could be made to Asia in northerly latitudes, and that this would neutralize the initial advantage which Columbus had given Spain. Accordingly, he and his family left Spain for England and settled in Bristol. John and Mattea Cabot, with their children—now Lewis, Sebastian, and Sancius—take on an English guise.[3]

[3] The progress of modern research on this problem may be followed in R. A. Skelton, "English Knowledge of the Portuguese Discoveries in the Fifteenth Century, A

We have seen that the Brasil voyages of 1480 and 1481, and the fact that the English located the "Isle of Brasil" in the western Atlantic either before 1480 or (more probably) in 1481, put a different perspective on the Cabot voyages from Bristol. To sum up the remaining background, from 1490 or 1491, yearly for seven years, two to four ships sailed annually, we are told in 1498, into the Atlantic looking for the Isle of Brasil or the Seven Cities (another imaginary island on the charts, also called Antilia). This could mean that up to twenty-eight ships left Bristol in those years, not for commerce but for exploration alone. Such an investment was quite beyond the financial resources of Bristol as we know them at that time. The 1481 vessel had carried enough salt to indicate that its owners were making a search for new fisheries: the suggestion about later vessels is that they were going fishing across the Atlantic, perhaps to the Newfoundland Banks, and thought of the island they saw there—the Brasil of earlier discovery—as no more than an inhospitable landmark for the fishery, not worth recording in the annals (or "calendars") kept by so many of the town's merchant families. This situation changed sharply after the discoveries made by Columbus in 1492, which became known to Bristol traders who frequented Spain. If Columbus had found the Indies by a westward voyage, sooner or later it would occur to Bristol men that they could do the same, just as it must have been brought home to Henry VII and his advisers that the plans of Bartholomew Columbus which they had rejected were not wholly chimerical.

New Document," C.I.H.D., *Actas,* II (Lisbon, 1961), 365–74; Louis André Vigneras, "New Light on the 1497 Cabot Voyage to America," *Hispanic-American Historical Review,* XXXVI (1956), 503–9; Vigneras, "The Cape Breton Landfall: 1494 or 1497? Note on a Letter by John Day," *Canadian Historical Review,* XXXVIII (1957), 219–28; Vigneras "État présent des études sur Jean Cabot," C.I.H.D., *Actas,* III (Lisbon, 1961), 657–70; D. B. Quinn, "The Argument for the English Discovery of America Between 1480 and 1494," *Geographical Journal,* CXXVII (1961), 277–85; Quinn, "John Day and Columbus," *Geographical Journal,* CXXXIII (1967), 205–9; Quinn, "État présent des études sur la redécouverte de l'Amérique au XVe siècle," *Journal de la Société des Américanistes,* LV (1966), 343–82; Marianne Mahn-Lot, "Colomb, Bristol et l'Atlantique Nord," *Annales,* XIX (1964), 522–30; Melvin H. Jackson, "The Labrador Landfall of John Cabot," *Canadian Historical Review,* XLIV (1963), 122–41; Lucien Campeau, "Jean Cabot et la découverte de l'Amérique du Nord," *Revue de l'Histoire de l'Amérique française,* XIX (1965), 397–408; Alwyn A. Ruddock, "John Day of Bristol and the English Voyages Across the Atlantic Before 1497," *Geographical Journal,* CXXXII (1966), 222–33; J. T. Juricek, "John Cabot's First Voyage," *Smithsonian Journal of History,* II (1967–8), 1–22; Demetrio Ramos, "Los Contactos trasatlanticos decisivos, como precedentes del viaje de Colón," *Cuadernos Colombinos,* no. 2 (Valladolid, 1972), pp. 45–65.

How and when did the Cabots come on the scene? We should probably discount firmly Sebastian Cabot's statement as an old man that he was born in Bristol, lived there until he was four years old, and was then taken to Venice. This would put John Cabot's first residence in Bristol back to well before 1480, while there is no indication that he was in England much before 1496. It is true that on a map published in 1544 for which Sebastian Cabot supplied some information it was stated that the Cabot discovery of America took place in 1494, but there seems nothing to support this and a good deal to set against it. In connection with the Bristol voyages between 1490 and 1497, John Cabot was cited as giving his opinion that the English were looking for Brasil or the Seven Cities; it has therefore been thought that he inspired or directed these voyages himself and so was in Bristol by 1490. But this meaning does not necessarily attach to the text of the Ayala letter (pp. 9–10), while the evidence of Juan Caboto in Valencia in 1492–3 stands in its way. The earliest appearance of the Cabots in England is not yet firmly dated, but cannot apparently be earlier than late 1493 or early 1494.

Soon after his arrival in Bristol, John Cabot put to sea. A voyage was begun with one ship, but there was some confusion about the route; he was short of supplies and decided to put back. This is all we know of a voyage made between 1494 and 1496. The first datable evidence of the Cabots is when John, with his sons Lewis, Sebastian, and Sancius, on 5 March 1496, petitioned Henry VII for a royal patent, which was granted on the same day. The Spaniards had evidence in 1496 that he had arrived in England, and Columbus at least learned something of his first voyage. Henry VII knew enough to understand the apparent implications of Columbus's discovery. Cabot could put forward his own plan for reaching Asia more rapidly by a voyage from Bristol, using the islands that Bristol men had discovered as steppingstones on the way, with the certainty of being understood at court. The first patent empowered Cabot and his sons to find out lands not known to any Christian peoples, to the north, east, and west of Henry's dominions, and to annex them to the crown, taking authority themselves to govern the same lands and to receive certain customs privileges for goods brought thence to Bristol. The grant, which was valid for up to five ships, was sufficient to transform the position of John Cabot at Bristol. No longer a foreign interloper, he could be admitted to the secret of making an Atlantic crossing to the fishing banks (if the argument above is acceptable) and allowed to try his luck in going still farther west toward the Farthest East.

The second voyage, the first to be successful, was nevertheless made as described above, in a single ship. Was Sebastian Cabot on this ship?

It may appear that he was, though he was probably only thirteen or fourteen years old at the time, since a legend on the 1544 map gives the right date—June 24—though the wrong year (1494), and states that the discovery was made by both father and son. It should, however, also be clear that if this information came from Sebastian himself he was no longer wholly reliable about such distant events.

John Cabot brought overflowing news—or confirmation—of the great fishery off the Newfoundland coast, but he was set fair very soon for another voyage to Japan and Cathay, as the fishery was not directly his concern. A reward of £10 in August was followed by a pension of £20 a year—a large sum—in December. He is described as being, before his success, a poor man. Now he was rich by contemporary standards. It was probably at this time that he rented from Philip Greene, a prominent Bristol merchant and landowner, a house in St. Nicholas Street not far from the bridge, for which he agreed to pay the annual rent of forty shillings. Reunited with Mattea and his three sons, John Cabot, dressed in silk and courted by the crowd whether in Bristol or London, was suddenly a public figure. Like Columbus, he too was called the Grand Admiral, though it is unlikely that any such title was conferred on him by Henry VII. Cabot was busily disposing of islands in his new regime and jokingly granting his friends titles. The fleet sailed early in May.

The second expedition had been lucky, the third was unlucky. John Cabot was lost at sea. One ship at least got back. This is about all that can be said of the voyage, and the question of whether Sebastian accompanied his father in 1498 is quite unanswerable. If he did, he was not sailing on the same ship as his father, but on one of those that returned safely. Cathay, it was now evident, was not just across the Atlantic, where a convict squad might be set to construct a trading post from which ships could sail southward to tap the riches of the East. This 1498 expedition may even have provided the first inkling that the land to the west was not Asia but a new landmass of continental dimensions.

John Cabot's pension was paid up to the end of September 1499, and his rent up to the same date, as he might well have been expected to return at the end of a second season's sailing. But he was then, it seems clear, given up for dead. His family, fatherless, was left to begin a new, possibly somewhat poverty-stricken existence in Bristol. We know no more of Sebastian's mother or his brothers, and of himself nothing until 1505. In that interval further voyages from Bristol had taken place (though the Cabot patent of 1496 was still potentially operative): one series in 1501–1502, another in 1502–5. This is a tenuous link by which to bring in

Sebastian, yet it is not improbable that he was associated in some way with the new syndicate between 1502 and 1505. The inclusion of Hugh Elyot in the second syndicate, the Company of Adventurers to the New Lands, might suggest a new opening for the Cabots, since he with Robert Thorne may have been a link between the Brasil voyages of 1480–1 and the Cabot voyages of the 1490's.

Did Sebastian take part in any of these new voyages? He may have done, but so far we cannot prove positively that he did. As "Sebastian Caboot Venetian" he emerges as a person in his own right for the first time when he receives a pension of ten pounds a year from King Henry on 3 April 1505.[4] It was to be paid from the customs receipts of Bristol, indicating that Sebastian still had his home there, while the reason for the award was "in consideration of the diligent service and attendance that [he] hath done unto us in and about" the town and port of Bristol. It sounds as if these were local services rather than participation in overseas voyages, but even this is not yet clear. It is almost certain that by this time Cabot was a trained and practicing surveyor and cartographer. He may have assisted in drawing up plans for new fortifications or harbor works, as his father had apparently done earlier in Valencia. But it is possible also that he had made some enduring cartographic records of the voyages across the North Atlantic, down to and including that of 1504, whether or not he had been on any of them himself.

The evidence for this is most exiguous, but there were certainly extant one or more manuscript maps of his (as well as a version of his printed map of 1544 or 1549) in the Palace of Whitehall late in the sixteenth century, while a collection of his maps and discourses was in the hands of his associate in old age, William Worthington, as late as 1582 though they disappeared without being described in detail. His service to the king might at least partly have consisted in showing, by his cartographical work, that North America was not an island but a great independent landmass which extended far to the north and south, and which must be circumvented (if at all) by a long roundabout voyage to the northwest or southwest before Asia could be reached. In this case he would have anticipated Waldseemüller's epoch-making globe and map of 1507. But if Sebastian sketched out his idea of a Northwest Passage before 1508, no record of it appears to survive. On the other hand, his perspective might have been influenced by ideas, antedating the American discoveries, associated with old views of the landmass.

[4] A. P. Newton, "An Early Grant to Sebastian Cabot," *English Historical Review*, XXXVII (1922), 564–5; Williamson, *Voyages of the Cabots* (1929), p. 70; Williamson, *Cabot Voyages* (1962), p. 265.

There is adequate evidence, which we shall examine presently, that Sebastian Cabot set out on just such a voyage in or about 1508.[5] As this testimony refers to some "sixteen years before 1524," which does not give a very precise date, 1507 would not be an unlikely alternative. The indication that he returned in 1509 is rather late and may not be as substantial as it appears, so that a departure in 1507 with a return in 1508 would not be improbable. Nor does the figure of sixteen years before 1524 wholly exclude a departure in 1509 and a return in 1510. But on the whole, the burden of the evidence we have is that he set out in the last year of Henry VII's reign (1508) and returned in the first year of the reign of Henry VIII (1509); though the possibility that he was sent out by the young king shortly after his accession in April 1509 and returned in 1510 is a possible alternative. He did not need royal permission to go on such a voyage since the patent of 1496 was still sufficient authority, but he wrote much later to Ramusio—the great Venetian collector of voyage narratives—that the ships in which he sailed were supplied at the king's expense, while another account says that they were two in number and had three hundred men—a very high figure—on board. The complement might suggest that he intended to establish a trading post and port of call along his route to Asia, or conceivably a factory in Asia itself.

A number of the accounts agree that he sailed so far north that, as one of them said, "even in the month of July he found great icebergs floating in the sea and almost continuous daylight, yet with the land free by the melting of ice." How far north he went is difficult to establish. In one account he is said to have established his latitude by the quadrant (on shore?) as 55° N in July; in another, derived from a letter of his, he claims a latitude of 67°30′ on June 11. The master of his ship, it is said, was unwilling to go farther north, while the sailors turned mutinous, so that, though the sea was open and he thought he could pass through to Cathay, he had to turn back. At 55° he would be just north of Hamilton Inlet in Labrador, at 67°30′ well up the coast of Baffin Island. The indications of ice movement and of the freezing of the land while icebergs were still moving south would fit a landfall in the vicinity of Cape Chidley and conceivably a turn westward into Hudson Strait.

The second stage of Sebastian Cabot's expedition consisted of a long voyage down the east coast of North America. It may well be that he made probing ventures into various gulfs and bays as he went southward,

[5] The classic reference here is G. P. Winship, *Cabot Bibliography* (London and New York, 1900), pp. xvii–xviii. His interpretation was adopted independently by Williamson (*Voyages of the Cabots*) in 1929 and revised in detail by him (*Cabot Voyages*) in 1962.

but it is also possible that he coasted rapidly south in search of an alternative passage around southeastern North America, southwestward to Asia. André Thevet, recalling late in his long life a conversation he had with Cabot about 1550, reported that Cabot "gave me certain recollections of the mainland of Corte Real, as of the rivers within the Arctic circle [north, that is, of 66°33′] down to the Gulf of the Isle of Devils [the Gulf of St. Lawrence, south of 50°], where he took two ships and many English seamen and soldiers, and from there to the river of Ochelaga and Saguenay [the St. Lawrence River]."[6] This would imply that he made a reasonably close coastal survey down the Labrador coast and through the Strait of Belle Isle, which is not suggested elsewhere. Thevet also indicates that he was sent out by Henry VIII, that is, in 1509 or later. Thevet's memory was always bad, and he had what almost amounted to genius in confusing his information, but it may just be worth while to put his opinion on record.

If we knew even a little more about Cabot's ideas or his resources we should find it easier to make positive suggestions. If he knew, for example, of Waldseemüller's revolutionary map and globe, printed in 1507, he would see there a southern continental landmass quite detached from Asia and separated from it by a wide ocean (and named for the first time "America"). It had also an unnamed landmass in the place of North America, which had a similar relationship to Asia but with passages around it to both northwest and the southwest, through which access to Asia by an intervening ocean might be attained. Had this been in his possession, Cabot might well have found confirmation of his own concepts of a Northwest Passage and inspiration for a voyage in search of a Southwest Passage as well. At some place on his southward route it is probable that he wintered for several months, but how far south he was at this point cannot even be conjectured. We are told in the earliest surviving account of his voyage that "he extended his course furthermore to the southward owing to the curve of the coastline, so that his latitude was almost that of the Straits of Gibraltar [36° N—approximately the latitude of Cape Hatteras, but with a large plus or minus error to be allowed for] and he penetrated so far to the west that he had the island of Cuba on his left hand almost in the same longitude with himself"—which would have been true from Cape Hatteras southward, though few longitudes are even approximately accurate at this time. On his way Cabot remarked the great quantities of fish to be seen, and he made some contacts with North American Indians, finding "the men of those lands clothed in skins and

[6] "Le Grand Insulaire," B.N., Fonds Français 15452, fol. 176.

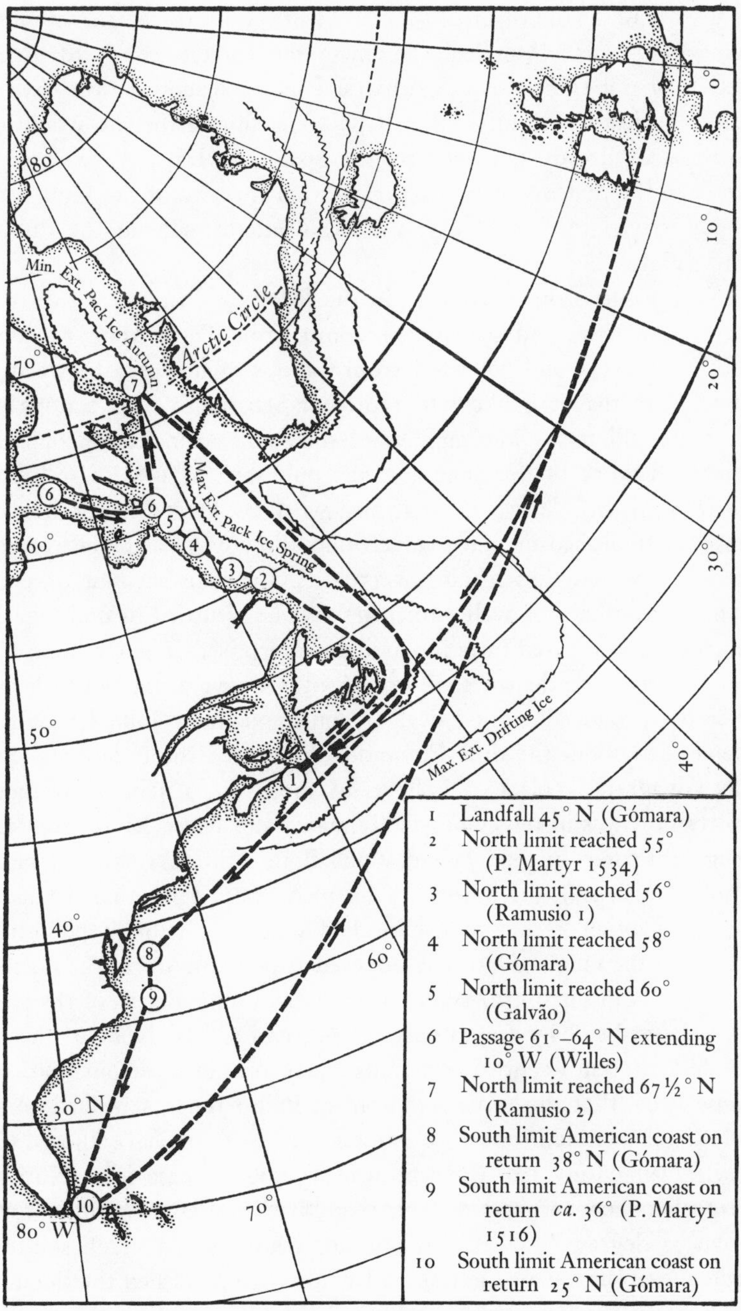

The northern and southern limits of Sebastian Cabot's voyage of ca. *1508–1509, according to the conflicting authorities. Courtesy of the Bristol Branch of the Historical Association.*

not anywhere devoid of intelligence." His decision to return without following the North American landmass far enough south to ascertain whether or not there was a Southwest Passage around it may have been because he feared—rightly—that if he went any further he would come into the area already occupied by the Spaniards. His voyage home may have been the first by an English expedition by way of the Gulf Stream, and he arrived to find Henry VII dead and his son on the throne as Henry VIII.

How reliable is this narrative? In the first place, the greater part of it (apart from dates and narratives) comes from Peter Martyr's account published in 1516 and collected from Cabot's own words between 1512 and 1515, so that it is likely to represent Sebastian's recollections when they were still fresh. The number of ships and an indication of latitude comes in a work of the same author's published in 1534; a still further indication of date derives from a third work by Peter Martyr written in 1524 (but published in 1530) which puts the voyage as taking place sixteen years earlier, thus making it 1508. A Venetian account of 1536 (a late one, but otherwise well informed) says he returned to find "the King dead, and his son cared little for such an enterprise." The rambling report by a Mantuan gentleman to Ramusio of a conversation with Sebastian Cabot has produced a good deal of confusion. In it John Cabot is said to have died about the time Columbus discovered the Indies, and Sebastian's voyage took place "I believe, in 1496"—it is quite clear that the conversation was ill-remembered. Ramusio later had a letter from Cabot giving him some specific information about latitude reached (the high 67°30′ in this case), the mutiny of his men, and a few other details. The Spanish historian Francisco Lopez de Gómera, in a book published in 1552, gives the range of latitudes covered as between 58° in the north and 38° or 25° N in the south. Willes in 1577 gives some details of the passage Cabot claimed to have found between 61° and 64° N. None of the other published sixteenth-century accounts seem, on close examination, to be of any value, though the veteran seaman Philip Jones, who had contacts inside Cabot's circle in the 1550's and is very likely to have known Cabot himself, claimed in 1586, when he was arguing the case for a Northwest Passage between 66° and 67° N, that "Bastian Caboto" did not reach "above 52 degrees."[7] J. A. Williamson, who devoted much skillful research and argument to the task and who twice published the documents on it (except the last cited), established the basic story of the first independent voyage by Sebastian Cabot, even if all surviving versions of it

[7] B.M., HarleianMS 167, fol. 107.

cannot be reconciled. At the same time, Sebastian's own story, as told at different times in his later life, was, like his account of his birth and childhood, inconsistent. His figures for attained latitude varied; his statements on whether he or King Henry (and which Henry) paid for the ships did not match; he may even have been inconsistent as to dates. His voyage, though we cannot follow its implications too fully in detail, was in many respects a milestone in English exploration. It marked the first long coasting voyage, so far as we know, along the greater part of the eastern shores of North America, and it also brought to an end one considerable chapter in the history of English westward venturing.

Sebastian's backing may have come wholly from London mercantile sources, though like the Company of Adventurers between 1502 and 1505, he may have had Bristol backing as well. It does not appear that the surviving records of Henry VII's reign—the king's Daybook for 1505–9 among them—contain any indications of royal loans, grants, or rewards relevant to his voyage. Nor do those of the early years of the reign of Henry VIII, so fully calendared in the *Calendar of Letters and Papers of the Reign of Henry VIII*, volume I. Though it is not impossible that royal vessels were hired out to him and his financial backers, this has so far found no evidential support. Bristol records do not appear now to contain any reference to his voyage, nor do any of the surviving town chronicles. The negative evidence might thus point to exclusive or almost exclusive London financing, and yet in 1521 important London merchants denied that he had ever been in American waters. Important as the voyage was, therefore, a screen of uncertainty hangs over almost all its aspects.

How much relevance Sebastian Cabot's voyage had for Bristol is not known. He may have taken his departure from Bristol, as all the other western ventures had done. His voyage is likely to have done much to delimit the northeastern shores of North America, provided he kept full records of his landfalls and drew his charts on his return. Bristol merchants and sailors, if he made them free of his knowledge, could have been more fully informed about the nature and extent of North America than almost all western Europeans of the time. What was known was not inviting, so that Bristol men stuck to a certain amount of fishing at Newfoundland and, so far as we know, gave up trading with the mainland and searching for new trades.

After Cabot's return which probably took place in 1509, the impulse toward further westward voyaging was not apparent. Clearly, young Henry VIII was not interested in carrying on a series of enterprises which had been, from the national point of view, conspicuously unprofitable. Married to a Spanish wife, he had no intention of competing in the Spanish Indies to the west, which Sebastian must have admitted, if questioned on his voyage, would be the inevitable result of trying to find a Southwest Passage around North America. There was no incentive whatever for Bristol merchants to spend further money on what must now have seemed quite vain hopes of trading directly with the Far East. If it is true that throughout these years a few Bristol ships were going out regularly each year to the Newfoundland fishery, this activity had settled into a few hands, had become routine, and had little to do with expensive speculation on voyaging to Cathay. If the suggestion is correct that Bristol men were quietly sailing to Newfoundland each year between 1491 and 1496, then the picture from 1496 to 1509 and later was probably more or less the same. We have no details, as fish does not appear on the few customs accounts that survive, but by about 1520 it is clear that Bristol had a hand in the fishing fleet that sailed annually from western ports to Newfoundland.

II

SEBASTIAN CABOT CUT MOST, though not all, of his ties with Bristol, so far as we can tell, not long after his return in 1509. He married a Londoner, whose Christian name was Joanna, and had at least one daughter (Elizabeth), but it seems almost as likely that their home was by the Thames as by the Bristol Avon. His daughter continued to live in London during the years following. Her godfather, William Mychell of London, chaplain, who may have been incumbent of St. Mary Abchurch, made his will on 7 May 1516 and left her three shillings and fourpence: "I bequeath to Elizabeth, daughter of Sebastian Cabot, my god child, 3*s* 4*d*." This will was proved on 31 January 1517.[8] Nothing more is known of her connections.

Shortly after the opening of Henry VIII's reign Cabot was in the service of the crown, being employed in 1512 with an English force in war against France. His cartographical abilities were recognized in a reward paid to him on 1 May for making a map of Gascony and Guienne, but this was to be his last direct service to the Tudors for some years. It would seem that he commended himself to Henry VIII's father-in-law, Ferdinand I, as a pilot and cartographer skilled in navigation in the Indies, and after some discussion at Burgos he was released by Lord Willoughby,

[8] Ida Darlington, ed., *London Consistory Court Wills, 1492–1547* (London, 1967), p. 22. Mychell's other bequests were to his sister Joan, wife of John Ireland of Great Weldon, Northamptonshire, and to another godchild, Margery, daughter of James Hawley, with residue to one of the witnesses, Richard Carleton, clerk. None of them seem, so far, to have had any connection with the Cabots.

his captain, for service in Spain—the letter Ferdinand wrote him mentioning specifically "the navigation of the Indies and the Island of the Bacallaos [Newfoundland]." For thirty-six years, after a short visit to England, including probably a little time in Bristol to wind up his affairs and collect his wife and family from London or Bristol, Sebastian Cabot settled down as a Spanish official, though he did not entirely lose his contacts with England, and specifically with Bristol.

In Spain he was employed as one of the pilots of the Casa de Contratación at Seville, from which the Indies trade was carried on. It would seem that his duties involved rather instruction of seamen in pilotage and in the construction of charts than exercise of his craft at sea. He was evidently highly successful, since he succeeded to the office of chief pilot in 1518. He was now not only head of the pilot school but also responsible for keeping up to date the official map of the Indies, the *padrón real*, on which instructions for voyages between Spain and the Indies were based.

The discovery of the Pacific Ocean across the Isthmus of Darien in 1513 set in motion a movement in Spain to find a direct sea passage to Asia, now that it was clear that an ocean voyage to the Spice Islands and Cathay was necessary once America was left behind. Sebastian Cabot was quite frank in telling Peter Martyr that he believed in the existence of a Northwest Passage. We may ask why he did not succeed in getting Spain to put his experience and theory to the test. The answer is that a Northwest Passage at, say, 60° north latitude would not suit the Spaniards. Northern waters were mainly the preserve of the English, the Portuguese, and the French, and there Spain would find seamen from these countries ready to challenge her monopoly of access to Asia by way of the west. Better no passage to Asia than one in such high latitudes. After various reconnaissances, Fernão de Magalhaes (whom we know better as Magellan), a Portuguese in the Spanish service, who had been round the Cape of Good Hope to southeast Asia with his countrymen, was sent off in 1519 to find a Southwest Passage around South America to Asia. We know that he succeeded, but the Spanish authorities did not learn that he had done so until the *Victoria* returned in 1522.

Sebastian Cabot had, in the meantime, revived his ideas of a Northwest Passage. There is no reliable evidence that he had anything to do with projecting English voyages between 1512 and 1520, but probably in the latter year he conceived the idea of reviving a northwest voyage.[9] Henry

[9] H. P. Biggar, *The Precursors of Jacques Cartier, 1497–1534* (Ottawa, 1911), pp. 134–42; A. H. Johnson, *The History of the Worshipful Company of the Drapers of London*, 5 vols. (Oxford, 1914–22), II, 264–7; Williamson, *Voyages of the Cabots*

VIII and his own master, Charles V, were for the moment on very good terms, and he was consequently able to get permission to go to England, probably on the pretext of family affairs, since possibly his mother and more probably other members of his family were still living there. If he could get Henry VIII's help for a northwest venture, then he could try to do for England what Magellan was trying to do for Spain and gain more glory and even profit than he had in Seville. If he could not find support in England he could return to Spain and hope his intended defection would not be suspected. A reward was paid to Cabot when he came to England early in 1521, and he rapidly got the backing of the king, Cardinal Wolsey, and the king's council. The English cloth trade was somewhat depressed at the time, and the Merchant Adventurers of London agreed on 7 March to supply one ship (of a hundred tons), victual her for a year, and pay the crew, while the crown would supply the rest of the equipment. There were to be five ships in all from London, and others were also promised by Bristol, with whose merchants Cabot must have been in touch directly.

On 11 March the plan ran into trouble from the Drapers' Company. The Wardens gathered from native-born English mariners that the voyage was hazardous and too far—it was described as being "towards the Newfound Island" or "into the newfound Island," while Sebastian himself was attacked: they thought it was too risky an adventure to send five ships, men, and goods "upon the singular trust of one man, called as we understand, Sebastyan, which Sebastyan, as we hear say, was never in that land himself." He was said rather to be reporting things he had heard his father and other men speak of in times past. The result was they would put up only two hundred marks (£133 6s. 8d.). Information from the other London companies is not available, but it seems that the overall response was too unfavorable for risks to be taken, and the plan was abandoned, perhaps only after it was clear that the vessels promised would not be ready in time to make a voyage that year—they would surely need to have set out in May.

This expedition was clearly intended to emulate Magellan's. Why then should there be such distrust of Sebastian? Possibly the London merchants knew nothing of the 1508–9 voyage but did recollect the abortive assistance given to John Cabot in 1498. Again we may ask why Sebastian Cabot was not produced to convince the merchants. The answer is probably that he was afraid to come into the open and confront them, because

---

(1929), pp. 97–101; Laetitia Lyell and Frank D. Watney, eds., *Acts of Court of the Mercers' Company 1453–1527* (London, 1936), pp. 524–9; *Calendar of the Letters and Papers, Henry VIII*, IV, pt. i, no. 366, p. 154.

this might lead to disclosure of his plans to Charles V. When the objections arose, he may in any case have been in Bristol. It is interesting to notice that his credit should have been as good there as it was bad in some circles in London. Before 7 March, we are told, "the towne of Brystowe hath sent up word and knowledge that they will prepare two ships," but there is nothing in the local records to show why this did not lead to an independent Bristol venture after the Londoners had become reluctant to continue. England was clearly not yet willing to invest in effective commercial challenges to Spain.

Sebastian went back to his duties in Spain. He claimed that the English fleet was almost ready, when his conscience smote him and he refused to go without Charles V's permission. This may just possibly be true, but he might equally well have seen that cordial relations between Henry VIII and Charles V were already breaking down and felt he would be safer on the Spanish side if it came to war. Lack of enthusiasm amongst the major companies in London meant that only a small London-Bristol venture was practicable, and this was not enough for him. His further explanation—that he suddenly remembered he was a Venetian by birth and should be working for his native city—was clearly invented when he put out feelers late in 1522 to see whether there was any Venetian money available for such an enterprise. But this was just after the *Victoria* had arrived back with news that the world could be sailed around and that there was, indeed, a Southwest Passage around South America to the South Sea.

III

IN 1523 SPAIN decided to determine whether, after all, there was a passage through temperate North America to the Far East, but it was the Portuguese Estevão Gomes, not Sebastian Cabot, who was chosen to lead the expedition. His voyage revealed much that was of interest about the North American coastline, but made it clear also that there was no passage westward to be found south of Newfoundland, the most northerly limit of Spanish interest. Cabot, therefore, put his Northwest Passage notions in cold storage and concentrated on preparing a great expedition to explore the coasts of South America and to attempt to find a passage to the Pacific in latitudes more temperate than those of the Strait of Magellan. Mobilizing both private and public resources for the voyage, he set sail only in 1526 "for the discovery of Tharsis, Ophir and Eastern Cathay." [1]

[1] Medina, *Sebastián Caboto,* is the prime authority for the Plate voyage, supplemented by Roger Barlow, *A Brief Summe of Geographie* (London, 1931), ed. Eva Germaine

In the course of his preparations Cabot had reinforced his connections with the English merchant community in Seville and San Lucár. He was closely in touch with Robert Thorne, whom he would have known in Bristol, and with Henry Patmer and Roger Barlow, both of whom continued to travel between Seville and Bristol in the 1520's. It is probable that discussions between Cabot and Thorne influenced the latter's project for an English voyage to Asia over the Pole, which was presented to Henry VIII in 1527 while Cabot was absent in South America. Thorne invested over three hundred pounds and Barlow over a hundred, both substantial amounts, in Cabot's expedition, while Barlow sailed with Cabot in the flagship. Henry Patmer, who evidently had some experience as a pilot, sailed in another vessel while a third Englishman, called Thomas Terman by the Spaniards, has not yet been identified. Cabot's command of the Southwest Passage expedition was thus a means by which Englishmen were enabled for the first time to penetrate south of the equator to the new western lands there discovered by Spain and Portugal.

The expedition was nearly four years away from Spain. Cabot showed considerable endurance and courage on the voyage, but he lacked the single-mindedness of Magellan and Sebastian Elcano, and demonstrated that his judgment was often imperfect and his temper arbitrary and tyrannical. In 1526 he made for Brazil by way of the Canaries and the Cape Verdes, losing his flagship (though saving her complement and part of her stores) and marooning some of his men on Santa Catarina Island. He entered the River Plate (then known as the Rio de Solis) in 1527, explored the estuary, penetrated far inland by the Uruguay, San Salvador, Cacaraná, and Paraguay rivers, building forts and gold-hunting, getting some information on the riches of the western mountains (the Andes), but taking no decisive action to conclude his search for a water passage to the Pacific.

In 1528 he sent the *Trinidad* home for reinforcements. Roger Barlow, described as Cabot's lieutenant, was an officer on board her. Calderón, her commander, and probably Barlow too, reported on their experiences to Charles V and set out the nature of Cabot's problems, but no reinforcements were in fact sent. Cabot sailed back in the *Santa Maria* in 1530, to face some seven years of judicial inquiry into his activities on the voyage, though he was allowed to take up his post as master pilot again in 1532. He was sentenced to four years' banishment to Morocco in 1531, but the

---

Remington Taylor, Hakluyt Society, 2d ser., no. 69, pp. xlviii–li. Professor Taylor's introduction is essential on Cabot's relations with the Bristol men, supplemented, on occasion, by Gordon Connell-Smith, *Forerunners of Drake* (London, 1954).

sentence was not put into effect. Barlow, having made contact with the English ambassador—probably Thomas Boleyn, Earl of Wiltshire, then on a special embassy to Spain—was recommended to Henry VIII and returned to England, apparently in 1530.

Thorne also was in England shortly after, and it is thought that Barlow joined him in a project to sail northward over the Pole, which came to an end with Thorne's death in 1532. Though Barlow was to retain close ties with Bristol, taking a wife from there (Julyan Dawes),[2] his main interests were to be in Pembrokeshire. Whether he kept contact with Cabot is not known, but in the winter of 1540–1 he wrote up "A brief summe of geographie" for Henry VIII, and he is likely himself to have been the "pilot from Seville well versed in the affairs of the sea" whom Henry VIII did not in the end agree to send on a northern voyage. Though Barlow gives an account of Brazil and the Plate based on his own experiences there in 1526–8, he does not mention Cabot by name but assumes that the king already knows the story. This suggests that he had already made some report to the king, now lost, of Cabot's South American voyage soon after his return to England.

In 1536 Sebastian Cabot placed himself firmly against the view that there was a passage through any part of North America.[3] The coast of Florida (which in Spanish reckoning could extend to 40° N) and the "Bacallaos" (Newfoundland and Labrador) were, he said, continuous. Whether or not this was the result of his experience in coasting southward—possibly even, as Thevet says, penetrating the St. Lawrence estuary—in the second stage of his 1508–9 voyage, we cannot say. He was not so certain that there was no passage westward from the Gulf of Mexico, even though by this date that coast had been thoroughly explored. He left out all reference to a Northwest Passage around North America. Since he is never found advocating that Spain should send him to penetrate such a passage, we may regard this report, prepared for the Spanish government, as negative evidence for his continued belief in a Northwest Passage, which he was anxious to keep to himself in the hope that he might some day be able to exploit it for his personal profit and renown.

[2] The Bristol Audit Book, 1532–3, p. 50 (in Bristol Record Department), has the following entry: "20th August 1533. Roger Barloo, merchaunt is admitted in to the liberties by cause he hath married with Julian the daughter of Mr Robert Dawys and hath paid his fee 3/4."

I am indebted for this reference to Miss Elizabeth Ralph.

[3] This report is cited, for the first time, from Archivo General de Indias (A.G.I.), Seville, Real Patronato 12. n. 7, in L. A. Vigneras, "A Spanish Discovery of North Carolina in 1566," *North Carolina Historical Review*, XLVI (1969), 399.

Clearly Cabot did not have an altogether easy time in Spain after his return from the Plate. To litigation by his former companions on the American voyage was added rivalry with Alonso Chaves, who had done most of his work as pilot major from 1526 to 1532, and who was an uneasy collaborator, especially after 1536 when he got the post of royal cosmographer. They did not, despite Charles V's orders, work effectively together on the revision of the *padrón real:* there were recriminations about Cabot's standards in chartmaking, and though he was upheld by an inquiry in 1545, his position was becoming less comfortable. As early as 1538 he canvassed the idea of coming to England to see the king and possibly return to his service. A northern expedition was discussed in England in 1540–1,[4] and had this been carried out he might have had his wish; he may even have been consulted. He was getting old—by 1545 he was over sixty—and was in recurrent financial difficulties the precise cause of which is unknown. As it was, Henry VIII was dead and Edward VI on the throne before positive inducements were made to him to come to England. When this happened, he responded quickly and favorably.[5]

The death of Cabot's second wife, Catalina de Medrano, in 1547 (his first wife had died long before) had lessened his ties with Spain still further, though he had sufficient property remaining in Seville to be somewhat apprehensive about its fate if he left Spain. In October 1547 the English Privy Council made money available to bring him to England, though perhaps only for a visit, and he got leave to travel to the Netherlands, i.e., within Charles V's dominions. While his salary was paid in Spain up to November 1548, it is probable that he was by then in England and intended, with occasional hesitations, to stay there. He had been conveyed to England by Henry Ostriche, a relative of William Ostriche, a prominent member of the Andalusia Company settled in San Lucár, who had had close trading relations with Bristol.[6] Henry is said (in 1586) to have been Sebastian Cabot's son-in-law and so may have married his daughter, Elizabeth.[7]

[4] See James Alexander Williamson, *The Voyages of the Cabots and the English Discovery of North America Under Henry VII and Henry VIII* (London, 1929), p. 280; Barlow, *A Brief Summe of Geographie,* pp. xlviii–li.

[5] Much of the material on Cabot in England, 1548–57, is in Harrisse, *Jean et Sébastien Cabot* and *John Cabot, the Discoverer of North America, and Sebastian Cabot His Son,* as well as Medina, *Sebastián Caboto,* II, and is supplemented by documents in *Cal.S.P.,Span.,1547–1558,* 5 vols. (London, 1913–54), and *Calendar of Patent Rolls, Philip and Mary,* 4 vols. (London, 1937–39).

[6] The Juan Estar (John Ostriche ?) with whom Cabot had business dealings in Spain, in company with Roger Bodenham, is likely to have been a member of the same family. Medina, *Sebastián Caboto,* I, 527–8.

[7] Barlow, *A Brief Summe of Geographie,* p. xxiii.

Cabot was to reside for the last decade of his life in England, and it seems clear that he spent the first months after his return at Bristol, which he may not have visited since before he had left for Spain in 1512 apart from a possible brief visit in 1521. He was residing there, for example, in May 1549. Whom he can have known there by this time is hard to say, and there are few surviving Bristol records for the period which can help us. John Barlow, Roger's brother, was a prebendary of Bristol Cathedral and is likely to have spent some time in the city, while Roger, although his interests were by then mainly in Pembrokeshire, had not broken off connections with Bristol. The Barlows are at least probable contacts, but we cannot say whether Sebastian had any property or relatives left in the city. He did not settle down permanently in Bristol, however, and after he was called to London in May 1549 we do not know that he returned to live there, though he may have paid brief visits and is likely to have remained in touch with his friends. It is perhaps significant that we can trace no Bristol investment in the major enterprises with which he was concerned, unless a possible contact with a Barbary voyage, and that Bristol in particular played no part in the northerly passage ventures with which Sebastian's English career reaches a late climax.

Somerset, Paget, Northumberland—such great men were his contacts in the government, 1549–53, and London magnates such as Sir George Barne, Sir John York, William Garrard, and Francis Lambert his associates among the merchant class. James Alday, a seaman, was in Cabot's service in 1550, when he was stopped by royal letters—at Cabot's instance he claimed—from going on a Mediterranean voyage as master on Captain Roger Bodenham's ship, the latter being himself an old contact of Cabot's in Spain. Richard Shelley, possibly a relative of the John Acheley or Ashley involved in the Guinea trade in the 1560's, accompanied Cabot once on a visit to the imperial ambassador and may have been his secretary, who is referred to on a similar occasion. We have no other information on his personal contacts, apart from a brief association with the French Huguenot pilot Jean Ribault, who was to die in Florida at the hands of the Spaniards in 1565.

It is in connection with Ribault that we get the first glimpse of Sebastian Cabot in 1550, engaged in discussions of a northerly venture. Edward VI was said by the imperial representative to wish to send two of his ships to the East. Cabot was retained for this purpose, and Jean Ribault had been released from prison in connection with it. "Some say, moreover, that the king intended to send a few ships towards Ireland [= Iceland] by the northern route to discover some island which is said to be rich in gold" [8]—this odd rumor is said to have been current for some six

[8] *Cal.S.P.,Span., 1550–2* (London, 1914), pp. 115, 217, 492–3.

months, that is, goes back to the latter months of 1549. It sounds like a plan such as that which Robert Thorne had advocated in 1527 for a voyage over the Pole, with a little color (gold-color) thrown in. Nearly six months later, at the beginning of 1551, we have a similar report. Jacques Ribault was said to be engaged in drawing up a marine chart, and Sebastian was working with him on it; they were to have a commission, or at least Ribault was, with some Englishmen experienced in navigation who had been with Cabot (Barlow perhaps being one of them) "to discover some islands, taking the way of the Arctic Pole"; two ships indeed were said to be ready, or almost ready. This was, more probably, a Thorne-style project, if the reports were not a mere blind for a more ambitious venture still, concocted between Northumberland and the French ambassador, Boisdauphin, for a joint Anglo-French expedition up the Amazon to take Peru in the rear—which Cabot revealed to the imperial ambassador in 1553 when it had long been a thing of only academic importance.

The South American project took Cabot on a visit to France. We cannot say whether the date was late 1550 or early 1551. The place was St. Malo. Our authority is André Thevet, whose "Grande Insulaire" was written between 1584 and 1590. Thevet, who was to accompany Villegaignon to Brazil a few years later, appears to have been already involved in discussions on the Amazon. He tells us that "when I was at St. Malo, in the Isle, lodged in the house of Jacques Cartier, there came the Captain Gabotte, son of the great Gabot [presumably John Cabot], worthy old man, with whom I talked for nine whole days, and, being a person of good understanding in marine affairs, lacking nothing of the merits of his father, familiarly discoursed with me about the whole coast from Canada to Florida." [9] Thevet did not carry away from these extended discussions, which should have revealed a great deal about American exploration and the careers of two of its most famous practitioners, more than vague indications of Sebastian Cabot's Northwest Passage voyage. These are probably the conversations to which he refers in his book, published after his return from Brazil, *Les singularitez de la France Antarctique,* in which he says that Cabot "proposed to go to Peru and America to people those countries with new inhabitants and establish there a New England." [1]

It rather appears that a joint Anglo-French enterprise to ascend the Amazon and take the Spaniards in Peru from the rear was in fact contemplated, and that Cabot was brought over to exchange views with the

[9] B.N., Fonds Français 15452, fol. 176. [1] Paris, 1558, fol. 148v.

doyen of French-American affairs, the aging Cartier, on the prospects of such a venture. Cabot may well have been a discouraging influence, since he knew something of the vast distances and dangers to be overcome before the Spanish empire could be penetrated in such a manner. Whether Jacques Ribault was also present at these discussions is not apparent; it is not unlikely. The project was soon abandoned, perhaps as a result of the St. Malo conference. Ribault found other employment, and Cabot returned to his preoccupations with voyages to the north.

He was a man strongly concerned with his own property rights. On 4 June 1550 he obtained an exemplification of the royal grant of 5 March 1496 to his father, himself, and his brothers, the original of which he said had been lost. We do not know what use he made of this, unless he employed it in getting a reward of £200 which he received from the crown soon after. Then in 1551 he began to worry about the property which his long-dead mother, Mattea, might have left in Venice, which had never been claimed. The seignory, after representations by the English ambassador, committed the matter to the secretary, Giovanni Battista Ramusio, who had already recorded Sebastian's earlier career in his *Navigationi et viaggi*,[2] but there were few documents extant and nothing could be traced. Cabot also kept a door ajar for his return to the emperor's service. From 1549 to 1554 frequent attempts were made to induce him to return to Spain or visit the emperor on the Continent. Cabot often visited successive imperial ambassadors, from time to time letting fall some information on his activities or bringing some tidbit of intelligence with him. He frequently expressed the desire to leave England, and offered to bring the emperor information on navigation and other topics he considered of great value. He was certainly concerned about his Seville property, which he feared might be confiscated, and it is said of him, correctly, by one ambassador in 1550 that he "tried to make his profit out of both sides."

As late as November 1553 Cabot sent the emperor a world map by the hands of a Spanish friend of his, Francisco de Orista, offering to come and demonstrate his theories (held, it may be said, for a long time before this) on the connection between magnetic variation and longitude, and a consequent method of determining the latter. But always when he was invited to Spain or the Continent he found a powerful English official who put obstacles in the way of his going; or he was ill; or he was too old and feeble. He may have gained a little by playing off his imperial ties against

[2] A rather confused account had appeared in the *Viaggi*, I (1550), fol. 398–403; it was corrected by a letter from Cabot (possibly as a result of fresh contacts engendered by Ramusio's task) in III (1556), 416–17.

his English employers, but there is no evidence that he seriously intended to go again to the Continent. Yet his conduct throws some light on his personality as an old man. He cast around himself an air of authority and mystery, as if he were the repository of many secrets, and if sometimes he seemed a little silly in his enigmatic manner, he did impress himself seriously on the London business community—which was by no means credulous, but had taken a beating in the commercial field since the collapse of the cloth trade after 1550, and was consequently open to suggestions for new lines of trade such as Cabot could make to them with unique knowledge.

The imperial representative in London in 1553 said that Cabot had been employed "on several occasions upon the equipping of certain vessels for the discovering of new land." He may indeed have had an investment in the bark *Aucher* for Roger Bodenham's Levant voyage of 1551,[3] in which Richard Chancellor served part of his sea apprenticeship, but like the voyages to Barbary and Guinea from 1551 onward, this was to an area not yet systematically frequented by English merchants rather than to "new lands." James Alday, Cabot's servant, claimed that he "invented" the voyage "for the trade of Barbary" which he set afoot—it might seem with Cabot's backing—in 1551. The ship's company was struck down while still in London by disease, and Alday and Henry Ostriche, Cabot's son-in-law, were among those affected—Ostriche fatally—so that it was Thomas Wyndham who sailed the *Lion* profitably to Barbary in 1551. The backing of major London merchants, Barne, York, Garrard, and Lambert, for the 1553 venture, when their association with Cabot on another venture was already established, makes it almost certain that he was one of the principal entrepreneurs in this series of voyages. The 1553 extension of trade from Barbary to Guinea in the third voyage of the series may have taken place under Cabot's influence, since his correspondence with Charles V shows him to have been particularly interested in this area.

Thomas Wyndham, who commanded the English ships on all three occasions, had a house at Marshwood Park, near Minehead, and so may well have had associates in common with Cabot at Bristol. We may suspect that there was a Bristol group interested in the 1552 voyage at least, though firm evidence for this is lacking. However, Wyndham brought the *Lion* round from London to the King Road, the Bristol anchorage, in 1552, acquiring there an additional vessel, a Portuguese ship brought in

[3] Richard Hakluyt, *Principal Navigations*, 12 vols. (Glasgow, 1903–5), V, 71–6, VI, 136–7.

as a prize to Newport and valuable as possible cover from Portuguese patrols on the African coast. She was fitted out at Bristol and the expedition sailed from there, the Bristol men noting that the *Lion* was "laden with merchandise, so and in like manner with munitions, as Morris pikes in great number, with hand guns, shirts of mail, with other artillery meet for the war." [4] Wyndham was prepared to fight the Portuguese if necessary, but a part at least of his warlike lading was for trade in Morocco itself. Cabot's link with the 1553 Guinea voyage is referred to specifically by Simon Renard, Charles V's ambassador, when he writes of its being directed to Guinea "on Cabot's advice"—perhaps with sardonic overtones, as he was stressing its ill-success, Wyndham and many of his men having perished on it.

Sebastian Cabot had a considerable reputation during his lifetime as a cartographer, but only a few traces of his work survive. The most important are in the printed world map of 1544, surviving only in a copy in the Bibliothèque Nationale.[5] He had signed in 1541 a contract with two Seville printers, Lazaro Noremberger and Gabriel Miçel, to produce a world map for them to publish. It appears that Cabot failed to get the emperor's approval for this scheme and so dared not use for it the *padrón real:* the secret master chart which was under his control as pilot major. Accordingly, a French world map was used as a basis for the 1544 map, and Cabot's contributions were confined to notes on his own and his father's voyages and to his views on navigation. After he came to England a new version of this map was produced by Clement Adams in 1549, and to this Cabot made some additions, particularly his claim to have reached on his northern voyage a channel between 61° and 64° N which extended westward for at least ten degrees of longitude. This was excellent publicity for his views, since the map was bought and displayed by many merchants and courtiers, though no copy has survived.

Cabot is not known to have received further public notice in print before 1553, when Richard Eden referred to his voyages in *A treatyse of the newe India* (1553) (and later made further references to him in *The decades of the newe worlde or west India* [1555]), but though Eden met Cabot, he gained his published information on him mainly from Ramusio and Peter Martyr. Clement Adams, who wrote on the 1553 voyage (*Noua*

[4] Bristol Archives Department, B.A.O. 00005 (3), text modernized.

[5] On the 1544 map, R. A. Skelton, "The Cartography of the Cabot Voyages," in Williamson, *Cabot Voyages* (1962), pp. 322–4, and *D.C.B.*, I (1965), 157–9, is authoritative. A copy of the Latin version of the legends, printed as a pamphlet, is in the Henry E. Huntington Library, San Marino, California.

Anglorum ad Moscouitas nauigatio [1554] [6]) tells how "certain grave citizens of London, and men of great wisdom, and careful of the good of their country . . . began first of all to deal and consult diligently with him" (Sebastian Cabot); he is described as "a man in those days very renowned." His growing reputation is attested also by the imperial ambassador, who wrote of him on 4 September 1553 that "the people of London set a great value on the captain's services, and believe him to be possessed of secrets concerning English navigation."

Cabot's greatest secret was his claim to know the routes through northern waters to Cathay, and the planning of expeditions to the north took place under cover of concealment between 1549 and 1553, emerging in the latter year with news that ships were at last ready to sail. As late as March 1553 a report to Charles V still confused the preparations for the Guinea and northern voyages, though they may well have overlapped. By 10 April clear information was available about three ships which had sailed down the Thames for the north: "they will follow a northerly course," it was reported, "and navigate by the Frozen Sea towards the great Chamchina,[7] or the neighbouring counties . . . and they believe the route to be a short one, and very convenient for the kingdom of England, for distributing kerseys in these far countries, bringing back spices and other rich merchandise in exchange." "Captain Cabot" had come to see the imperial ambassador, Jean Scheyfve, and finding him already well informed about the venture, submitted to being interviewed on its prospects. Was it as certain as it seemed? Yes it was, said Cabot. When it was suggested that "Chamchina" formed part of the Spanish overseas zone, "he said it was true; but that view only interested the Emperor and the King of Portugal, while the others would probably claim that the land would belong to him who first occupied it." This statement of the English view of effective occupation might suggest that the sponsors of the voyage envisaged imperial conquests as well as trade in the Far East. But Cabot was evidently unwilling to be too specific about routes, since Scheyfve on 11 May was still uncertain whether the vessels were going to the northwest, northeast, or over the Pole—"some said that they would steer to the north-east and pass the Frozen Sea, and others that their plan was to follow a westerly course and enter the Strait of the Three Brethern

[6] Hakluyt, *Principall navigations* (1589), p. 280; Hakluyt, *Principal Navigations*, II (1903), 239–40. No copy of the original edition is known to have survived.

[7] Marco Polo's version would have been translated as "Great Khan of Cathay." "Cham" came into English in 1553 and "China" in 1555 through Richard Eden (Edward Arber, ed., *The First Three English Books on America* [London, 1885], pp. 12, 260), but he did not join them into a single word.

[illustrated by Gemma Frisius, in the northwest], or pass Cape de Las Parras [possibly Barra Head, Hebrides, on the way to the Pole]." We do not know under what circumstances the most novel of the three routes, that to the northeast, was eventually chosen.

The combination of several hundred London merchants in "the mystery and company of the Merchant Adventurers of the city of London . . . for the discovery of Cathay, and divers other regions, dominions, islands and places unknown," to give it the nearest approximation to its earliest title, was a spectacular affair, at the head of which Sebastian Cabot emerged as governor.[8] On 9 February 1553 at Ratcliffe Cabot delivered to the expedition, which was about to sail downriver under its commander Sir Hugh Willoughby, a set of ordinances for the conduct of the voyage. They included many sensible provisions for discipline, consultation, and conduct during the voyage, with much detail on how its progress was to be recorded so that subsequent expeditions could retrace its course. Many of the precepts are likely to have sprung from Cabot's own experience, but collectively they were the work of the syndicate's executive, governor, consuls, and assistants. The ships made their way slowly out of the Thames and up the east coast, taking off from Orford Ness for Norway only on 23 June and thence making their way to the open sea north of Norway and ultimately to the White Sea and Muscovy, thus opening a new English trade, not with Cathay but, more prosaically, with Russia.

Sebastian Cabot's place in the company's development after Richard Chancellor's return in 1554 with news of his achievements in Russia may have been little more than nominal. No royal charter had been issued to the syndicate before Edward VI died, and when Queen Mary finally incorporated the company on 26 February 1555 its title was still couched in the most general terms as the "merchants adventurers of England for the discovery of lands . . . unknown, and not commonly frequented," which might cover ventures to almost any place outside western Europe. Cabot was honored by being made governor for life, as he had been "the chief setter forth of the journey or voyage." On 1 May 1555 he presided over a court meeting of the company, his last known appearance in this capacity, though the "good old Gentleman" gave a lively farewell to Stephen Borough's Muscovy expedition on 27 April 1556.

For Sebastian Cabot a life pension of two hundred marks (£133 13s. 4d.) a year for life granted on 27 November 1555 was his final reward.[9]

[8] The Hakluyt references are *Principall navigations* (1589), pp. 259–63, 311; and *Principal Navigations*, II (1904), 212, 195–205, 240, 281.

[9] Harrisse, *John Cabot*, pp. 458–460.

He may not have enjoyed it altogether peacefully, for a friend, Thomas Tyrell of Birdbrook, Essex, making his will in 1556 left a bequest to Sir William Petre, the Secretary of State,[1] "trusting that he will be good Master to Master Captain Caybote whensoever he shall have occasion to sue for his pension." On 29 May 1557 the pension was reassigned to be held jointly with William Worthington, and Cabot continued to draw his half-share of it until Michaelmas 1557, presumably dying between 29 September and 25 December in that year, since the next payment, of the full amount, was made to Worthington alone. Worthington, who enjoyed his pension for many years, acted apparently as Cabot's executor and retained in his possession in 1582, according to Richard Hakluyt, "all his own maps and discourses drawn and written by himself" which the great editor hoped to publish. A partial reversion of the pension to Mary Scudamore in 1584 indicated that it was not thought Worthington had long to live,[2] but he died without leaving any trace of Cabot's maps and papers, in the absence of which so many queries about his life and opinions remain unanswered.

The city of Bristol had, largely through John Cabot and his son Sebastian, a distinguished association with the overseas voyages of the great period of European expansion. This began about 1480 and was dominated by John Cabot between about 1494 and his death in 1498. Sebastian Cabot, who regarded himself very much as a Bristol man, continued his association until 1521. Thereafter it was peripheral and discontinuous, though the link survived until 1549 at least, and possibly until 1553. The city was thus one of the commercial centers outside Italy where the new type of Italian entrepreneur, who played such a vital part in the overseas movement, settled and from which he operated.[3] John Cabot, with some aid in a minor capacity from the boy Sebastian, we may legitimately assume, undertook three voyages into the Atlantic from Bristol. Only one of them, that of 1497, proved successful, but that sufficiently to put the Bristol discoveries in the European picture and give England a place on the maps and narratives of the slowly-revealed New World.

Sebastian remained aware that the 1497 voyage was a significant achievement and appears sometimes to have taken credit for it himself. His own northwest voyage was for so long wrapped in obscurity, partly of his own making, that it remained difficult to be sure when it took place. It con-

[1] Essex County Record Office, Chelmsford, T/A 256/8, for information on which I am indebted to F. G. Emmison.

[2] Bristol Archives Department, B.A.O. 5139 (406).

[3] C. Verlinden, *Les Origines de la civilisation atlantique* (Neuchâtel and Paris, 1966), p. 160.

tinued very persistently to be associated with John rather than Sebastian, and with 1498 rather than with 1508–9. But so far as it could be seen as an achievement distinct from that of 1497, it appeared in his own time, and must still appear to us, an important step in defining the eastern coastline of North America and in establishing its continental character, as well as being the starting point for a whole series of wild-goose chases in search of a Northwest Passage to Asia. These, though they led to a great waste of resources over more than two centuries, were a vital stage in the modern exploration of the Arctic. Unfortunately, Bristol did not have sufficient confidence in Sebastian Cabot, or he in her merchants, for them to build on the pioneer Cabotian achievements. His knowledge went instead to strengthen and develop the empire of Spain in America, and his solid achievement lay in the building up of pilotage into an essential instrument in running a maritime empire. After his return to England, Cabot revived his connection with Bristol, but had to turn to London with its greater mercantile resources and initiative to get effective backing for his plans. He turned away from his own earlier North American interests to an attempt to make contact with the Far East. But indeed, his concern with North America, and South America too, had always been subordinate to his long-term objective: access to Cathay. In so far as his projects helped English commerce to break out of its traditional mold and led to the diversification of English enterprise in the Mediterranean, Africa, and Russia, he is an important figure in economic and maritime history.

But he is an ironic figure too. His great vanity was that he had discovered a means of determining longitude; but this was a complete illusion. Apart from this, his great secret was his knowledge of passages from England to the Far East by the north, northwest, and northeast—but these were illusions also. His effective achievements were only by-products of his more visionary projects. It is not easy, given the surviving evidence, to estimate his character clearly. A man of many talents, competent and far-seeing in many respects, he was also vain, and in action arbitrary, while he lived a fantasy life of mysteries and dark secrets alongside his more prosaic everyday activities. Did he imitate Columbus in much of this, or was it derived from the mold in which the businessmen-mystics of the Italian dispersion were cast?

CHAPTER SIX

Henry VIII and Western Voyaging

I

THE MAJOR CONTRIBUTIONS to the exploration of North America were made under the auspices of the crowns of France and Spain. The reign of Henry VIII from 1509 to 1547 was not distinguished by any remarkable English addition to the process of discovery of the North Atlantic and its western borderlands. Englishmen did not become wholly indifferent to what was going on across the ocean, but the voyages of the Cabots and of the Company of Adventurers had revealed a land that was unprofitable—either because its inhabitants had nothing worth while with which to trade and showed no great enthusiasm for English goods, or because the seas were cold, their margins frozen, their promise after the rigors of exploration still unrevealed. Englishmen did, during this period, retain a share, though not a major one, in what was becoming a great international industry: the fishery on the shores of Newfoundland and on the Banks nearby. For the rest, English merchants concentrated more on Brazil, on penetrating legally the trade of the Spanish Indies through their resident merchants in Spain—even, late in Henry's reign, beginning the seizure of Spanish bullion ships coming from the western Indies. The European cloth trade remained the great magnet of English commerce, its expansion in the Mediterranean and in the Baltic a sufficient extension of the range of English commercial effort.

Henry VIII himself, it may be said, was preoccupied for much of his reign with his personal problems and enjoyment and with great affairs of state; yet commitments as great or greater did not prevent Francis I from patronizing Verrazzano's important survey of the North American coast, or from aiding the four important Cartier and Roberval expeditions into the St. Lawrence valley. French competition with the Hapsburgs, and the desire to rival even in a small way the achievements of Spain, perhaps spurred on their exploration of the North American coasts to see whether there might be something worth while to be found there, after all, if only a passage in temperate latitudes to the Pacific Ocean. It may be that the explorers who went out from France were more expert than those who left England for North American exploration—the latter country had indeed failed to hold its most learned and experienced venturer, Sebastian Cabot. But although Verrazzano and Cartier did not have their match in the England of Henry's day, there was not much difference in the scale of effort made by the two countries.

Henry VIII patronized mapmakers when they came to him; he commissioned a map from Girolamo da Verrazzano, gave lavish encouragement to complete his fine atlas to Jean de Rotz, was prepared to encourage a Northwest Passage voyage in 1521 if his London merchants would help, accepted a polar voyage scheme from Robert Thorne in 1527 (though he did not act on it); he accepted also a world geography with valuable notes on the New World from Roger Barlow in 1541. He sponsored such projects for the exploration of the North American coastline as came before him with sufficient support from his ministers, but so far as we can tell they were neither numerous nor very wide-ranging in intent. For those Englishmen who took part in western exploration, the chance that preserved the records of Verrazzano's and Cartier's voyages to be published in 1556 in Ramusio's great collection of *Navigationi et viaggi* (volume III) was unfortunate. Neither Rut's voyage nor Hore's was properly documented in its own time or later in the sixteenth century. Meanwhile we may anticipate our conclusions and suggest that both these voyages may have found inspiration in French achievements and have been to that extent derivative.

Three English ventures remain worthy of some detailed consideration: an attempted voyage of 1516 and its literary exploitation by John Rastell between 1517 and 1519; the voyage of John Rut, which was the first full north-to-south coasting of the greater part of the eastern North American shoreline; and the experiences of Richard Hore, whose effort in 1536 to show off the Gulf of St. Lawrence and the Newfoundland coast to a number of gentlemen from London was an interesting failure. With all of them Henry VIII had some connection.

In the early part of Henry's reign, Sir Thomas More was the most lively focus of intellectual interest in England. His range of scholarship in theology and philosophy was formidable, his interest in mathematics considerable, and he was appreciably concerned with natural history. More than most of his English contemporaries, he had a sense of the possible significance of the New World in the west, and he played on that sense in both the setting and the content of his moral fable *Utopia*, of which the first edition—in Latin—appeared in 1516. His feeling that there were other types of societies besides the European strikingly foreshadowed the impact of the Aztec and Inca civilizations on the Spaniards who first encountered them a few years later. His interest in colonies, not altogether derived from classical precedent, and his awareness that they would present both opportunities and problems to human society, were also in advance of almost all other Englishmen.

More was remarkable, too, as the focus of a circle of friends and scholars. A lawyer by profession, he drew some of his acquaintance from legal circles. Among them was John Rastell, whom A. W. Reed has described as "one of the more interesting members of the More circle."[1] Rastell was born about 1475, the son of Thomas Rastell of Coventry. He became coroner of Coventry, but moved away to London about 1512 to improve his fortunes. Here he met and married Elizabeth More, Sir Thomas's sister, and so was drawn by marriage as well as by inclination into More's orbit. He performed minor administrative jobs for the crown, within the circle of one of the royal ministers, Sir Edward Belknap. In a burst of restless versatility, he opened a printing business in London, to which he became greatly attached and from which he issued many law books. There seems little doubt that it was in the coterie around More that his interest was aroused in the possibilities of North America. He attempted to follow the literature of cartography, which was altering the traditional picture of the world's surface by the inclusion of a pair of western continents unknown to Europe before the sixteenth century, since the late-fifteenth-century discoveries were all thought to be Asiatic appendages. Moreover, he made contact with obscure fishermen and the merchants behind them who were pioneering Newfoundland fisheries in the Bristol tradition, and preserved knowledge communicated by them which throws some indirect light on English participation in the fisheries during the period for which no direct documentary sources have yet been found. Like More, he had some sense of the possibilities of colonizing the New World. Rastell is significant, therefore, as a seminal figure whose views were broader on geographical and North American issues than those of most of his countrymen in that period.

[1] "John Rastell's Voyage in the Year 1517," *Mariner's Mirror*, IX (1923), 137.

The end of 1516 or the beginning of 1517 marks the time when Rastell's general interests crystallized into a plan to lead an expedition himself to North America.[2] It is clear that he valued that dim, unknown region for its own sake and wished to exploit what he believed to be its riches, but it is also likely that he hoped to use a foothold on North America to make contact with Asia. We do not know exactly what world maps he had at his disposal and so cannot tell precisely what relation his view of America had to Asia. He probably thought it would be necessary to go fairly far north of the known extent of North America in order to reach Asia, and perhaps had some contact on this question with Sebastian Cabot before the latter left England in 1512—or by correspondence after he settled in Spain. But his primary aim was a colony in eastern North America.

On 5 March 1517 he received a passport for himself and two London merchants, Richard Spicer and William Howting, with whom he had associated himself. This gave a measure of official recognition to the project. He went on to borrow from the crown for himself and his associates the sum of five hundred marks (£333 6s. 8d.), and was able to hire one or more ships from the king. Whether Belknap was his sponsor or not is unknown, but it is reasonably certain that Sir Thomas Spert, whose responsibility for the king's ships was considerable, was one of his patrons and probably the most active in the chartering of the royal vessels for what was becoming at least a semiofficial venture.[3] The Earl of Surrey, the Lord High Admiral, was also involved, more especially in the ship *Barbara* in which he had a share, but his precise association with Rastell remains, as we shall see, obscure. One of the ships was the *Mary Barking* of London—Philip Tyse, master—in which William Howting was to sail. It would seem that Rastell had some share in the *Barbara* but was not the major owner, and that the ship was technically on charter for the expedition. Rastell and Richard Spicer were to sail in her, with John Ravyn as purser. The names and even the number of other vessels are unknown to us.

[2] The basic documents in the case, the proceedings in the Court of Requests in 1519–20, were printed by Reed in "John Rastell's Voyage," pp. 137–47. Above all, his treatment of Rastell's life and dramatic achievement in *Early Tudor Drama* (London, 1926), pp. 11–12, 187–201, forms the principal base for the study of Rastell. J. A. Williamson, in his *Voyages of the Cabots* (1929), pp. 85–93, 244–8, printed the passport, a selection from the Court of Requests documents, and the relevant parts of *An Interlude* (*ca.* 1519). There is a short article on the Rastells by D. B. Quinn in *D.C.B.*, I, 565–6.

[3] G. G. Harris, in *The Trinity House at Deptford, 1514–1660* (London, 1970), assembles some useful material on Spert.

Rastell sailed with a retinue of intended colonists and with the equipment to establish a small settlement across the Atlantic. We hear of his "company that he brought with him from London to the number of 30 or 40 soldiers, besides mariners." The taking of armed and disciplined men to initiate colonization in North America was to be the practice on much later occasions. We learn also of his "salt victual, tools for masons and carpenters and other engines [that is, equipment] that he had prepared for the New Lands," which makes quite explicit his intention of constructing a small colonial base. One gathers that he expected to be away some three years, but how much of this time was to be spent in his settlement and how much in reconnoitering for a route to Asia cannot be determined. Clearly, wherever he was bound, he expected fishing to provide economic returns. He may well have expected also to open up trade with American Indians in cloth in exchange for furs and other local commodities. He thought timber products could be profitably exploited.

We lack a convincing statement of the location of his intended settlement. He knew something of Newfoundland from fishermen who had been there. It is possible that he intended to touch Newfoundland and work southward until he found a suitable location. If he thought in terms of an American continent made up of a number of great and small islands through which he might pick a passage to Asia, we would expect him to begin by a fairly extensive coastal exploration. The most recent western exploration had been that of Sebastian Cabot, which had brought him into subarctic conditions on the Labrador coast but offered hope of a western passage if he persisted; it is possible that Rastell, too, aspired to follow the coast to the northwest. But his first intention was a settlement, an economic as well as a military base, in temperate latitudes in North America.

The expedition was not fated to reach its destination. We know what happened only from a court case against John Ravyn in which most of the evidence came from his accusers. According to them, Ravyn delayed the setting out of the expedition from Blackwall on the Thames and was not on board when they left Gravesend, so that the ships had to put into Sandwich to pick him up. On various pretexts—to buy stores, to repair leaks—Ravyn held back the *Barbara* and hence the rest of the squadron by stops at Dartmouth, Plymouth, and finally Falmouth, trying at the last port to induce Rastell to give up the voyage on the grounds that the season was too late, and make instead a trading voyage to Bordeaux. He proceeded to turn Rastell's factor, Richard Walker, out of the ship and is alleged to have converted to his own use a quantity of Rastell's goods worth more than £100. These are described as "fine white flour and bay salt, with certain packs of friezes and canvas and coffers of silks and 'tukes' and other mercery ware with divers other goods and household stuff as feather beds, napery, pans, pots and divers other wares as salt, hides, tallow and other things."

During the delay at Falmouth, it was alleged, Ravyn got one or two ships of the little fleet to turn back and apparently give up the voyage, while others were sent on to Ireland and were not seen again. This suggests that there were at least four or five vessels altogether. It also credits Ravyn and Richards, the master of the *Barbara,* with great power over the other masters. Ravyn claimed to have some authority from the Earl of Surrey, the Lord High Admiral, but even so it was clear that Rastell had little influence or control over an expedition of which he was nominally the head. The *Mary Barking* had meantime gone ahead and put in at Cork. There the master, Philip Tyse, and his sailors turned on Howting, locked him in his cabin, and took the ship back to England. Finally Rastell got the *Barbara* to sea in spite of the slights and losses he had endured. On the way from Falmouth to Ireland, Ravyn pressed Rastell to chase and capture one Henry Mongham, an Irish pirate who had captured a Portuguese ship, evidently with a view to seizing the prize for himself. He also urged him to give up his voyage and fall to robbing upon the sea ". . . and that it should be as profitable for him as fishing in the new lands." Rastell refused, but the *Barbara* put into Waterford on the pretext of obtaining stores. Rastell went on shore to lodge at the house of Thomas Dryvam (possibly for Bryver), and while there heard of Howting's fate and the defection of the *Mary Barking* at Cork. In fear of his life, he now refused to go on board the *Barbara* again. Ravyn then threatened Rastell that he would burn the ship if he (Rastell) would not do what he said. He also claimed that he had power of attorney from Surrey and a copy of the charter party and would see the ship occupied to his lord's best profit. This implies that Surrey was himself the owner or at least part-owner of the vessel and had gone into the venture either half-heartedly or with intent to ensure its failure—though this may be a gloss imposed by Ravyn or his accusers. Finally Ravyn and Richards, Rastell alleged, coerced him into giving Richards an acquittance for his bond to complete the voyage, and into writing to Surrey "to desire him to be good lord to him to perform his voyage the next year," while allowing Ravyn to take the vessel to France to trade.

We do not know what Rastell's own men were doing while this went on, but they clearly failed to give him any effective assistance. The ship sailed off in the end to Bordeaux and La Rochelle, the lading intended for the American venture was sold there, Ravyn keeping a record of it, while

Rastell stayed on in Ireland, probably still in Waterford.[4] In the meantime his factor, Richard Walker, had gone on his behalf to see the Earl of Surrey at Blechingly to complain of Ravyn's actions at Falmouth. Surrey is said to have admitted that he had authorized John Ravyn "to take the ship into his own hand," and instructed Walker not to meddle with Rastell's goods. The other vessels had presumably gone back to London by this time, as there is no indication that any of them attempted the Atlantic crossing.

The reasons for the miscarriage of this fairly elaborate venture are not clearly known. The indications that Surrey intended to sabotage it by means of his agent Ravyn are not conclusive, but they may represent some intrigue in official circles between elements favorable and unfavorable to the venture. The obvious cause of the failure was the unruliness of the seamen, but we cannot be clear whether this was due to their anxiety to launch out on a piratical career or to unwillingness to trust themselves to a long ocean voyage with possibly an attempt to reach Asia by sea as its final object. This same doubt as to the aim of the voyage may also have prevented the intended settlers, Rastell's "soldiers," from asserting themselves against the seamen. However, it would seem that one cause of the breakdown was the lack of effective direction and control by Rastell himself. He did not exhibit any exceptional qualities of leadership and allowed himself to be intimidated into giving up his goods and his enterprise.

Such a sequence of events would have had serious psychological effects on many an expedition leader, but Rastell took his misfortunes philosophically, even fatalistically. He appears to have found congenial companions in Waterford and recovered his nerve there as well as getting on with his writing. It may have been as much as two years after his original departure that Rastell returned to England. On 15 November 1519 he began the proceedings against Ravyn for damages in the Court of Requests from which almost the whole of our knowledge of the projected voyage and its unfortunate outcome derive. The case was adjourned until 2 February 1520 for the taking of witnesses' statements, but its outcome is not apparently on record, though it would appear that Rastell got some redress for his many injuries at Ravyn's hands. Challenged by Ravyn on why he did not take the case to the Lord High Admiral's court, where maritime causes were adjudicated, Rastell sidestepped this attempt to get

[4] See Peter J. Pivernous, Jr., "John Rastell's Proposed Voyage to America from Ireland, 1517–1519," *Terrae Incognitae,* III (1971), 59–65, who considers Rastell was planning a further voyage from Waterford.

him directly involved with the Admiral, the Earl of Surrey, by saying that since he had lost all his money he was unable to afford to do so, and had therefore to pursue his case in the poor men's court, the Court of Requests.

While he was in Ireland, Rastell had not been idle. He had completed the writing of an interlude, *A new interlude and a mery of the iiij elementes,*[5] which summed up his views on cosmography and provides some insight into his understanding of the New World, as well as throwing some light on his expedition. This may have been ready for his printers, who had presumably been turning out books to his profit during his absence, before the end of 1519 and was in circulation soon afterward. Its verse dialogues on world geography show that, up to the time of his departure on his voyage, Rastell had close contact with and an intimate knowledge of recent Continental works on world geography. This is presented in rather elementary terms for popular consumption, but it reflects a good understanding of the new world picture, so greatly altered since the crucial dates of 1488, 1492, 1498, and 1507 had brought into view the Cape of Good Hope, the islands of America, the sea route to India, and the epoch-making Waldseemüller map with its America and its so far unnamed sister continent in the ocean between Europe and Asia.

Baldly, in prose, Rastell's comments on the New World amount to this. The New World, now known as America (and he includes North and South in this term, though Waldseemüller had used the name for the southern continent only), was said to be five thousand miles long. Though much had been explored, very little was known of its commodities, especially in its northern parts. If his own expedition, dispatched with the assent of King Henry, had had a chance it would have been an honorable thing to take possession of these lands; but the adventurers were deceived by the sailors. It would have been meritorious to convert the peoples of the new lands. They were primitive, living in wood-cots and caves, having no houses, using no iron, though finding copper in the ground. In the south they went naked; in the north they dressed in the skins of beasts. How the people got there was a question for learned men. The great forests of fir and pine would produce pitch, tar, and soap-ashes, which up to now have had to be brought from the Baltic. Fish were so plentiful, they could be killed with sticks in the harbor. Now that the French and others had found the trade, they laded a hundred ships

[5] See George B. Parks, "The Geography of the 'Interlude of the Four Elements,'" *Philological Quarterly*, XVIII (1938), 251–62; J. Parr, "John Rastell's Geographical Knowledge of America," *Philological Quarterly*, XXVII (1948), 229–40.

or more each year with fish. Far to the east was the land of the Khan of Cathay. The new lands were called America because Americus found them[6]—they were not more than a thousand miles from Cathay. From the new lands men could sail to Cathay and come back to England again around the world.

A simplified world picture, not unrealistic by contemporary standards, is thus set forth, with primary emphasis on the need to have Englishmen occupy the lands directly west of the British Isles.

It may be useful to go over this again in so far as he tells us of his own venture:

But what commodytes be within
No man can tell nor well Imagin
But yet not longe ago
Some men of this contrey went
By the kynges noble consent
It for to serche to that entent
And coude not be brought therto
But they that were they venteres
Have cause to curse their maryners
Fals of promys and dissemblers
That falsly them betrayed
Which wolde take no paine to saile further
Than their owne lyst and pleasure
Wherefore that vyage and dyvers other
Such kaytyffes have distroyed
O what a thynge had be than
Yf they that be Englyshe men
Myght have ben the furst of all
That there shulde have take possessyon
And made furst buyldynge and habytacion
A memory perpetuall
And also what an honorable thynge
Both to the realme and to the kynge
To have had his domynyon extendynge
There into so farre a grounde
Which the noble kinge of late memory
The moste wyse prynce the vij. Herry
Causyd furst for to be founde.[7]

[6] Amerigo Vespucci was known as Americus.

[7] Williamson, *Voyages of the Cabots* (1929), pp. 89–90. The standard text, spelling modernized, is in John S. Farmer, *Six Anonymous Plays* (New York, 1915), pp. 24–7.

This first patriotic manifesto of the colonizing movement which brought Englishmen in the long run to North America was a feeble squeak only—no matter how interesting that it should have been made at all. It was small return to the king that his contribution to the first independent attempt to exploit North America should be repaid only in words, which do not indeed appear in this case to have traveled very far. The circumstances surrounding the failure of the 1517 expedition were not such as to encourage royal intervention in North America.

The only further contribution which the Rastell family made to American discovery was that John Rastell's son, John Rastell the younger, (born in 1511 in Coventry) was one of those who, under the auspices of Captain Richard Hore, saw Newfoundland and perhaps part of Labrador, in 1536. America on this occasion did not live up to the father's hopes of twenty years before.

A new interlude of the iiij elementes was not the earliest English literary work in which there is a reference to the New Found Lands, or at least the New Found Island. That priority, so far as is known at present, goes to an earlier Interlude, *Hyckescorner*, the first edition of which, printed in London by Wynken de Worde, has been tentatively dated either 1510 or 1512. Following this there were subsequent printings about 1520 and 1550, none of them dated, but showing that it enjoyed a measure of popularity. The hero-villain, Hycke Scorner, returns from an imaginary voyage and gives a list of all the places, real and imaginary, where he has been, what ships he has sailed in, and what has become of the personified vices, all eventually consigned to the waters off Ireland, with which the ships were laden. The whole passage, whatever its literary merits or lack of them, indicates a considerable degree of commercial and maritime knowledge, even if the reader is not expected to take what is said as literally true.

HYCKESCOR[NER]. *Syr I haue ben in many a countre*
As in fraunce Irlonde and in spayne
Portyngale seuyll also in almayne
Freslonde flaunders and in burgoyne
Calabre poyle and erragoyne
Brytayne byske and also in gascoyne
Naples grece and in myddes of scotlonde
At cape saynt vyncent & in the newe founde Ilonde
I haue ben in gene and in cowe
Also in the londe of rumbelowe
Thre myle out of hell
At rodes constantyne and in babylonde

In cornewale and in northumberlonde
Where men sethe rushes in gruell
Ye syr in caldey tartare and lude
And ye londe of woemen y^t^ fewe men dothe fynde
In all these countres haue I be

FREWYLL. *Syr what tydinges here he now on the sea.*

HYCKESCOR. *We mette of shyppes a grete nave*
Full of people that wolde in to Irlonde
And they came out of this countre
They wyll neuer more come to englonde.

IMAG[YNA]. *Whens were ye shyppes of them knowest y^u^ none*

HYCKESCOR. *Herken & I wyll shewe you thyr names eche one.*
Fyrst was the regent with the myghell of brykelse
The george with the gabryell and the anne of foye
The starre of salte ashe with the Ihesus of Plumoth
Also the hermytage with the barbara of darmouth
The nycolas and the mary bellouse of brystowe
With the elyn of London and Iames also.[8]

This curious catalogue reads like a combination of Mandeville's *Travels,* a series of extracts from a customs account, and a newsletter. It shows that before Henry VIII's reign was well under way the New Found Lands were known by hearsay to a London audience, and that it was not unheard of (perhaps only in an imaginary voyage) to put them alongside better-known places, real and imaginary. The author of the Interlude is unknown, but Hyck Scorner appears in a woodcut—the first representation of an Englishman, even if only a stage character, who claimed to have been in North America.

The plans for a Northwest Passage voyage in 1521, already mentioned (pp. 145–7), to further which Sebastian Cabot came unavailingly to England, show clearly that Cardinal Wolsey and King Henry were at that moment showing a specific and personal interest in western voyaging. It is interesting and significant of a temporary change of attitude that they were for a time willing to try to push unenthusiastic London merchant

[8] *Hyckescorner,* Tudor Facsimile Texts (London, 1908), ed. J. S. Farmer, sig. A6v.–A7. *Regent* and *Michael* of Brightelmstone (now Brighton); *George, Gabriel,* and *Anne* of Fowey; *Star* of Saltash; *Jesus* of Plymouth; *Hermitage* and *Barbara* of Dartmouth; *Nicholas* and *Mary Bellows* of Bristol; *Elyn* and *James* of London—all may have been names of serving ships. We hear, for example, of the purser of the *Anne* of Fowey in 1513 (Dorothy Burwash, *English Merchant Shipping, 1450–1550* [Toronto, 1947; Newton Abbot, Eng., 1969], p. 49).

companies into speculative investment in western expeditions. They did not keep up the pressure long enough to get any London vessels dispatched, and we do not learn that those preparing in Bristol ever got to sea. It would be unwise to conclude that this effort represented any direct interest in voyages to North America for its own sake. The evidence indicates that it was simply a plan to follow the northerly coasts of America to the Pacific in order to discover if possible a route parallel to Magellan's of 1519. Cabot, in his role as chief pilot in Spain, was concerned with the latter, but attempted through his English connections to follow his own theories, first tried in 1508–9 as we think, in pursuit of an opening to the northwest. The subsequent voyages of 1527 and 1536, though concerned to some extent with passages through or around North America, were involved to a greater degree in exploration of its coastline and estuaries and thus helped to bring England, if not into a renewed position of prominence in North American discovery, at least more or less up to date as regards French knowledge acquired in the interim.

II

THE VOYAGE BY John Rut IN 1527 to Labrador, Newfoundland, and down the east coast of North America to the Spanish islands in the West Indies is the most important English expedition to North America made during the reign of Henry VIII. The tracing of the North American coast from north to south was carried out with an apparent skill and competence lacking in both 1517 and the later voyage of 1536. At the same time the sources, though full enough on some aspects of the trip, are confusing.

The first we hear of a venture in preparation is when Lord Edmond Howard, son of the Duke of Norfolk, writes to Wolsey early in 1527: "I am enformyd ther shalbe a vyage made in to an newfounde land with dyvers shypps and cappetayns and sogears in them; and I am informyd the vyage shalbe honerable and profytable to the Kyngs Grace and all hys reame. Syr if your Grace thynk my poor karkes any thyng meet to serve the Kyngs Grace in the sayde vyage, for the bytter passeon of Kryst be youe my good lorde ther in, for now I doo leyff as wretchyd a lyffe as ever dyd jentylman being a true man."[9] Clearly the expedition was intended to be an elaborate one (complete with soldiers as well as seamen); it was under official auspices, or at least semiofficial ones—Cardinal Wolsey was believed to be involved in its preparation.

[9] Henry Ellis, *Original Letters*, 3d ser., I (London, 1846), 161–2; H. P. Biggar, "An English Expedition to America in 1527," in *Mélanges d'histoire offerts à M. Charles Bémont* (Paris, 1913), pp. 459–72.

There is a rather amusing personal association involved in this case. In 1517, as we saw, the Earl of Surrey was apparently closely concerned with the ship *Barbara* in John Rastell's abortive voyage, and it is possible that he may have been an investor in the voyage who changed his mind as to its viability and acted through John Ravyn to divert or sabotage it (though his role is by no means clear). In 1524 Surrey had become Duke of Norfolk, and it was his son, who had already had some naval and military experience, who was now anxious to involve himself on an American voyage—compare John Rastell's son's participation in the 1536 voyage. There is no indication at all that Howard's plea was successful or that he sailed with the expedition.

E. G. R. Taylor has argued that the expedition of 1527 was launched on the basis of a map which showed the Verrazzanian profile of eastern North America, compiled as a result of his voyage in 1524. This included the ambiguous Sea of Verrazzano, which seemed to offer a rapid passage over an isthmus to the Pacific at 34° N or thereabouts.[1] The evidence that such a map existed in England before 1527 is tenuous, though not negligible. In 1582 Richard Hakluyt in his *Divers voyages touching the discoverie of America* wrote "that master Iohn Verrarzanus, which had been thrise on that coast, in an olde and excellent mappe, which he gaue to king Henrie the eight, and is yet in the custodie of master Locke, doth so lay it [North America] out, as is to be seene in the mappe annexed to the ende of this booke, beeing made according to Verarzanus plat."[2] The Michael Lok map in that volume does indeed show Verrazzanian characteristics, though it is not at all likely that Giovanni da Verrazzano himself came to England. His brother, the cartographer Girolamo da Verrazzano, is more likely to have been the donor, if in fact the presentation was made before 1527. The Verrazzano brothers met a number of setbacks in France between 1524 and 1526, and it is possible that overtures to Henry VIII by Girolamo, with the gift of a map, may have been made during this period, though it should be pointed out that in May 1525 Giovanni rejected a Portuguese offer to transfer to their service.[3]

[1] *Tudor Geography, 1485–1583* (1930), pp. 11–12; see also Henry Harrisse, *The Discovery of North America* (1892), pp. 542–3.

[2] Sig. *2: see also E. G. R. Taylor, ed., *The Original Writings and Correspondence of the Two Richard Hakluyts*, Hakluyt Society, 2d ser., nos. 76–7, 2 vols. (London, 1935), II, 287, 283; Lawrence Counselman Wroth, *The Voyages of Giovanni da Verrazzano, 1524–1528* (New Haven and London, 1970), pp. 165–8.

[3] See Jacques Habert, "Jean de Verazzane: État de la question," in Manuel Ballesteros-Gabrois and others, *La Découverte de l'Amérique* (Paris, 1968), p. 55.

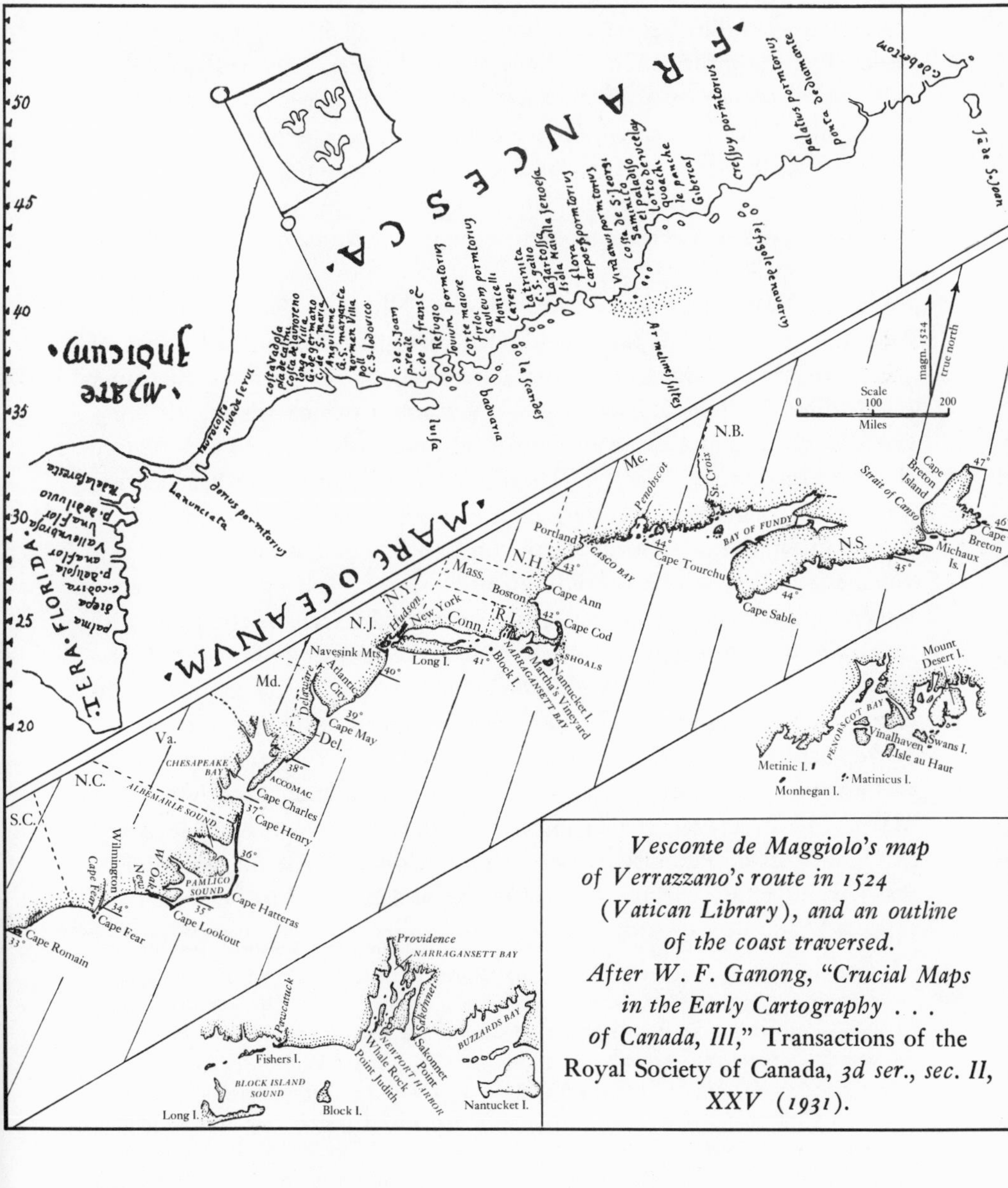

Vesconte de Maggiolo's map of Verrazzano's route in 1524 (Vatican Library), and an outline of the coast traversed. After W. F. Ganong, "Crucial Maps in the Early Cartography . . . of Canada, III," Transactions of the Royal Society of Canada, *3d ser., sec. II,* XXV *(1931).*

Some special incentive must have existed in the period immediately before 1527 to set in motion the expedition of that year. News of Verrazzano's voyage of 1524, less likely news of the comparable voyage by Estevão Gomes in the same year, or the appearance of a member of either of these expeditions with an offer to conduct an English venture along a track he had already followed, might all have operated to this effect. But the information we have about the map presented to Henry VIII makes sense as a major incentive, even if the chain of evidence is a little thin. If this is accepted, Henry VIII and his agent John Rut must be regarded as attempting to forestall French exploitation of the east coast of North America, and in particular to try to locate the mysterious and promising Sea of Verrazzano, which might offer an easy route to the East.

On 20 May, two ships with a pinnace left the Thames bound for North America: on 10 June they sailed finally from Plymouth.[4] One of the ships was the *Mary Guildford* (or the *Mary* of Gilford), the other the *Samson.* Nothing is known of the *Samson* or of her master; the *Mary Guildford* was under the command of Captain John Rut, an experienced shipmaster in the royal service. There is some difficulty about her identity. She was a royal ship of 160 tons, built in 1524.[5] Her main function was to go late in each year to Bordeaux to collect a cargo of wine from the new vintage for the king's household; normally she was laid up in the Thames under a maintenance party during the summer. In 1526, in company with the *Minion,* she was sent to Bordeaux under her master John Rut ("Johnn Rowte"), with a crew of twenty-eight including a master gunner (indicating that she carried some armament), returning before the end of November.[6] Rut had commanded a ship as far back as 1512, so that he was a very experienced seaman. In the grant of an annuity to him on 24 May 1527, after he left the Thames on the current voyage, he is described as "John Rutt of Ratcliffe, yeoman of the Crown." The first installment was payable at Michaelmas, so perhaps he was expected to be back from

[4] Williamson, *Voyages of the Cabots* (1929), p. 103. The main authority for the first is John Rut's letter from St. John's (Samuel Purchas, *Hakluytus Posthumus, or Purchas his Pilgrimes,* 4 vols. (1625), III, 809, and 20 vols. (1906), XIV, 304–5 (A. W. Pollard and G. R. Redgrave, *A Short-title Catalogue of Books Printed in England, Scotland and Ireland 1475–1640* [*S.T.C.*], 20509); Williamson, *Voyages of the Cabots* (1929), pp. 104–5, which will be used without further specific reference.

[5] Michael Oppenheim, *The Administration of the Royal Navy, 1509–1660* (London, 1896), pp. 50, 68, 91.

[6] Details of the *Mary Guildford* movements and payments in Biggar, "An English Expedition," pp. 462–4. They will subsequently be cited without further specific reference.

his voyage at the end of September or thereabouts. There is a complete absence of information of any voyage by the *Mary Guildford* for wine in the latter part of 1527; and she was described by Rut himself, in a letter from Newfoundland in August to Henry VIII, as "your Graces, The Mary of Gilford," which proves that she was the king's.

This would seem to provide ample indication that the king's wine ship was detached for the American voyage. But there are two difficulties. In the first place, the usual maintenance party was paid for her upkeep during the summer of 1527: John Griffith, keeper of the "Mary Gwylford," with three men, acting as shipkeepers, were paid for "keeping of the said shipp W^tin the Ryver of Themes," from 7 June (when Rut's ship was about to leave Plymouth) to 1 September (when he had certainly not returned). This J. A. Williamson regarded as proof that Rut's vessel was another ship, the *Mary* of Gilford, which he was nowhere able to identify.[7] The only plausible explanation is that the maintenance team was given the terms and wages they normally enjoyed during the summer for taking charge of the *Mary Guildford,* even though they did not have to do the work, the ship itself being on its American voyage.

Another difficulty raised by Bernard Hoffman is that the ship which eventually appeared in the West Indies and must have been Rut's ship was said by the Spaniards to be of 250 tons, not 160.[8] This however, in view of differing standards of measurement and the vagueness of estimates made by eye, should not be taken as a serious objection. The *Mary Guildford* was, almost certainly, the wine ship of that name.

The ships made a good passage from Falmouth and held a course to the northwest until 1 July. They then met ice at 53° (perhaps it should be 58°). This was apparently off the Labrador coast; the great icebergs and deep water alarmed them, and the men in the *Mary Guildford* were afraid to go farther north. The *Samson* had been with them until 1 July, but a storm had blown up and in foul weather she was lost sight of. By the time the icebergs were sighted on 3 July the *Mary Guildford* had definitely lost touch with her. When they turned southward, about 4 July, they finally left her to her own resources. Within four days, about 7 July, they sounded in 160 fathoms and fell in with the mainland, some ten leagues along the shore meeting a great iceberg close to land.

Soon after, they reached Cape de Bas. This place Rut describes as having nearby "a good Harbor, and many small Ilands, and a great fresh River going up far into the Mayne land." Such a description would fit

[7] Williamson, *Voyages of the Cabots* (1929), p. 256; Biggar, "An English Expedition," p. 471.

[8] B. G. Hoffman, *Cabot to Cartier* (Toronto, 1961), pp. 120–1.

many points of Labrador, but if his rough estimate of latitude is correct, St. Lewis Inlet (at 52°20′ N) would meet the requirements.[9] They spent ten days in the harbor, "ordering" the ship (though whether for food or for trade is not clear) and fishing. There follows in Rut's letter a passage too corrupt to be intelligible, but out of it emerges the fact that a rendezvous had been arranged at Cape Spear, well to the southeast on the Newfoundland coast, and that the first ship there was to wait six weeks for the other. We thus get a rough outline of the first stage of the voyage as laid out before the ships left England. This was that they should keep a northwesterly course into Arctic latitudes, presumably in the hope of sighting the passage which Sebastian Cabot, in his voyage to the northwest, believed he had found. It does not appear that they were to do more than reconnoiter its entrance. After that, they were to work their way south and be at Cape Spear well before the end of August. Once the *Samson* had separated from the *Mary Guildford*, Rut could only assume she would be able to make the northern reconnaissance alone and duly arrive at the rendezvous.

After ten days in the shelter of Cape de Bas and its adjoining inlet—that is, about 17 or 18 July—the *Mary Guildford* set sail southward. She reached and entered the harbor of St. John's on 3 August having some days on hand. She would have had her pinnace with her, though whether under sail or on tow we do not know. St. John's was a scene of activity: twelve French fishing vessels (eleven Norman, and one Breton) and two Portuguese were there. All were engaged on inshore fishing, and no doubt were also drying the fish they caught on flakes (or frames) on land. They provided a European contact which the Englishmen, no doubt, appreciated. But one reason for entering was to find a channel of communications, since to send letters by French vessels would not be difficult. Rut therefore sat down to write laboriously, "in bad English and Worse Writing," as Purchas said long after, to the king.[1] This letter, dated 3 August, is the first to be sent by an Englishman from a port in North America. It was accompanied by another from Albertus de Prato to Cardinal Wolsey, in a Latin "almost as harsh as the former English," of which Purchas thought it necessary to give only the beginning and end—had he given it all, Rut's letter, in its printed form at least, might not appear so opaque. The latter was dated 3 August; de Prato's "bearing the same date," according to Purchas, had the date printed as "die x

[9] On the Desliens Map of 1550, "C de basses" appears on the north side of what seems to be Hamilton Sound (54° 34′ N). See Henry Harrisse, *Histoire cartographique de Terre-Neuve* (London, 1900), pp. 199–200.

[1] Purchas, *Hakluytus Posthumus* (1906), XIV, 304.

Augusti," so it may be that they stayed at St. John's a little more than a week, though Rut described them as ready to sail on 3 August.

In either event, the *Mary Guildford* set sail for the rendezvous at Cape Spear. The letter actually says "we are readie to depart toward Cape de Bas, and that is twenty-five leagues." Read literally this is nonsense, as Rut's original Cape de Bas was now several hundred miles to the north; clearly there is a misreading or misprinting for "Cape de Ras"—that is, Cape Race—for which a distance of seventy-five nautical miles from St. John's is a reasonable estimate. Cape Spear was less than half the distance.

Why Cape Spear? It has often been remarked that it is strange that Rut found no English ships at St. John's, since when the curtain begins to lift on the English Newfoundland fishery in the 1570's, that is the real center of English activity. The answer lies probably in the fact that in the 1520's and 1530's the English fishery was centered round Cape Spear, the fishermen using the islands and the small harbors nearby for their stages. Thus it was that the *William* in 1536 made this area her base (though there were Bretons there, too).[2] The move to St. John's came sometime later. But by inference the *Mary Guildford* waited at Cape Spear in vain. The *Samson* did not appear and was never heard of again.

The next stage of the voyage was clearly intended to be an extended reconnaissance of the coast southwestward from Newfoundland. In his letter Rut had said that after making, as he hoped, his rendezvous with the *Samson* he would set out "toward parts to that Ilands that we are commanded by the grace of God as we were commanded at our departing." Whether the obscurity is due to Rut or to Purchas is not clear, but since he went southward, no doubt Rut's instructions told him to do so. From here on, however, our direct evidence breaks off and picks up indirectly in reports made by Spaniards who encountered him in the West Indies three months later. What the Englishmen then told of their voyage before and after August 1536 was carefully culled from individual Spaniards who had encountered members of the crew.[3] There were some difficulties of communication, but it is clear that some of the Englishmen could speak some Spanish, and there is a reasonable coherence about the answers reported, though with occasional obscurity about what actually was said.

[2] See p. 187 below.

[3] H. P. Biggar, *Precursors of Jacques Cartier, 1497–1534* (Ottawa, 1911), p. 167; Williamson, *Voyages of the Cabots* (1929), pp. 106–7; see also Irene A. Wright, ed., *Spanish Documents Concerning English Voyages to the Caribbean, 1527–1568* (London, 1929), pp. 29, 48, 55.

All the Spanish witnesses were agreed that the Englishmen said their ship was the king's and had been dispatched by him with a consort. Gines Navarro was asked if he could read Spanish or Latin, as if so he could read the instructions they had from the king (he said not).[4] If the instructions were available in Spanish, it may have been foreseen that the ships might end up in the Spanish zone—though there is room for misunderstanding here on Navarro's part. The ship is said to have been of 250 tons and with three masts ("de tres gavias"): she had a pinnace ("una pinaça") which held twenty-five to thirty men. The total complement was about seventy (where the normal crew of the *Mary Guildford* was under thirty). The ship, one witness said, "was well equipped for war with much heavy brass artillery, in two tiers."[5] She had, said another, "many small arms and cross bows and lombards and pikes and targets." She had also on board "carpenters, smiths and a forge, other artisans, tools to build more vessels in case of necessity and an oven for baking bread." She had wine, flour, and provisions for her men (though not all her captain desired), and she had woolen cloth, linen, and other goods for trade.

This adds up to quite a formidable picture: the ship was clearly prepared for many emergencies, including armed resistance, and had the equipment and men which would make a longish stay in a particular place possible. This might seem to raise the possibility that the *Mary Guildford*, with the *Samson*, may have intended to do more than reconnoiter a Northwest Passage if they found one, and were expected to follow it to the Pacific if it led there. The other evidence, which we have already considered, scarcely supports this view. What is clear is that, six months out from England and after a very long voyage, the ship and her men were still in very good shape.

The English spoke freely of their long-term plans.[6] They told Gines Navarro that "the king had fitted out that vessel and another to go and discover the land of the Great Khan ["*Gran Can*"], but that on their way, they met with a storm, during which they lost sight of their consort and had never seen her again." In another report they stated that they were "to make a certain exploration toward the north, between Labrador and Newfoundland ["entre la tierra del Labrador e los Baca-

[4] Biggar, *Precursors*, pp. 165–8 (see Williamson, *Voyages of the Cabots* [1929], pp. 106–7).

[5] Wright, *Spanish Documents*, pp. 55, 60; see also pp. 30, 36, 40, 48, 52, 55, for the other details on the ship.

[6] Biggar, *Precursors*, pp. 165, 167; for other references to objectives, see Wright, *Spanish Documents*, pp. 29, 48.

llaos"], in the belief that in that region there was a strait through which to pass to Tartary." Finally, they stated that they had been sent "to discover a certain strait that lay near Norway [*a descobrir cierto estrecho que estaba a la banda de la Noruega*]."[7] This made sense if Greenland was still regarded as a peninsular extension of Norway, and in fact all three statements cited hang together.

The most dramatic report on the next stage was that "they held on their course and reached the frozen sea where they met large islands of ice," which is confirmed by Rut's letter. However, they also said that "being unable to pass that way, they altered their course but ran into a sea as hot as water in a boiler. For fear lest that water should melt the pitch of their vessel, they turned about . . ."[8] This was either a misunderstanding or a tall story: it is unlikely to represent an underwater eruption and is not hinted at in Rut's letter. They then came south to explore Newfoundland, where they found some fifty Spanish, French, and Portuguese fishing vessels—fourteen, as we saw, at St. John's. Other reports add a few details: they were perhaps as far as 64° N (another said 50° and something more) when they turned back. Some of their men—four or five—died of cold.[9]

In their coasting south the English had attempted to make some contact with the Indians, but in one version, "on reaching the shore the Indians killed the pilot, who they said was a Piedmontese by birth." Since the English seemed to know their way about the West Indies in some detail, the Spaniards were inclined to doubt whether they had not skillful enough pilots on board, and expressed the opinion that they did not need a Spanish pilot, as they alleged, but could very well bring themselves back to England.[1] From the place where the pilot was lost, which is assumed to be the island of Newfoundland, but may have been much farther south, the English are said to have "made their way for some 400 leagues or more along the coast of the new land where Ayllón took his colony"[2]—Lucas Vásquez Ayllón's abortive Spanish colony in 1526 having been directed to what is now South Carolina, though a considerable part of the interior was called "Tierra de Ayllón." From the main-

[7] Miss Wright mistakenly translated "Noruega" as "Norumbega," Verrazzano's name for New England (thus giving support to the view that Rut had a Verrazzano map), but the Spanish and a correct translation appear in Biggar, *Precursors*, pp. 171, 176.

[8] *Ibid.*, p. 167 (Williamson, *Voyages of the Cabots* [1929], p. 107).

[9] Wright, *Spanish Documents*, pp. 29, 45, 48, 55.

[1] Compare Biggar, *Precursors*, p. 167, and Wright, *Spanish Documents*, pp. 38, 45, 54.

[2] Biggar, *Precursors*, p. 167. Williamson, *Voyages of the Cabots* (1929), p. 107.

land they crossed the Caribbean to San Juan de Puerto Rico, touched at Mona, and came on to Santo Domingo where the contact with the Spaniards which produced so much evidence took place. When asked why they had come to the West Indies in the first place they said they had wished to report to their king what the region was like; they had cloth to sell, and they wished to carry home a cargo of brazilwood. They could also do with water and some provisions and a new pilot.[3]

Friendly contact was made with Spaniards at Mona, where a Spanish ship was loading cassava and encountered the English in their pinnace, the men in which asked some questions and gave some explanations of their presence. The pinnace then made for Santo Domingo, followed by the ship, which remained outside the harbor. The pinnace entered, and the ship's master gave some account of himself and asked if he might enter harbor with his ship. Two Englishmen were left ashore and two Spaniards went out to pilot the ship in, but as she was about to enter the harbor, the fortress fired a stone shot at her. There was argument afterward as to whether this was a hostile act or merely a signal, but it alarmed the English. The Spanish pilots were put into their boat and the vessel sailed off, evidently leaving two of the crew behind. A few days later the ship appeared at Ocoa, farther along the coast; this time they seized without payment any food they could get hold of and sailed away. The ship appeared at Mona on 19 November and at Santo Domingo on 26 November: she left Ocoa about 30 November.[4] We have no account of the *Mary Guildford*'s arrival in England, but it would have been sometime late in February or in March, according to the weather she encountered.

The ship which had thus completed her voyage—perhaps the longest so far made by an English vessel—took up her accustomed task in the latter part of 1528, when with the *Minion,* and under her old master John Rut, she set out once more to Bordeaux for the king's wine just as if she never had been in foreign parts.[5] The chances that the vessel which made the voyage to America in 1527–8 was the king's wine ship seem so high that the identification appears fully acceptable.

Rut had proved capable of sailing the *Mary Guildford* up the coast of Labrador, but his reports on the approaches to the supposed Northwest Passage can only have been highly unfavorable, and were reinforced by the disappearance of the *Samson.* Thereafter Henry VIII, until the end of

[3] Cf. Biggar, *Precursors,* pp. 167–8, and Wright, *Spanish Documents,* pp. 29, 48, 55–6.

[4] Williamson, *Voyages of the Cabots* (1929), pp. 110–1; Wright, *Spanish Documents,* pp. 29–58 *passim.*

[5] Biggar, "An English Expedition," pp, 459–72, citing *Calendar of Letters and Papers of the Reign of Henry VIII,* IV, p. 2 (1872), no. 2215; B.M., RoyalMS 14 B XXIX.

his reign, resisted all suggestions that he should associate himself with further northerly voyages. So far as this aspect is concerned, royal participation in a search for the Northwest Passage began and ended in 1527. But Rut had also coasted a long stretch, several thousand miles indeed, of temperate coastline. He had probably little of promise to report about the native peoples he had met, since his pilot had been attacked and killed on shore. Why was not more made, by publication or by the sending out of further exploratory voyages, or even the circulation of maps, of the attractions of the warmer coasts of North America, traversed between the end of August and the beginning of November?

This remains something of a mystery. The *Mary Guildford* reached the West Indies in too good shape to have suffered from hurricane damage, so the weather does not seem to have been unfavorable. Her men made no complaints about the more southerly shores they had encountered. The only explanation which can be suggested is that the *Mary Guildford* was concentrating on finding Verrazzano's isthmus or else a passage through the continent in temperate latitudes, and so did not pay any great attention to the potentialities of the coast southward from Newfoundland to Florida for trade or settlement. Indeed, there may have been active discouragement by the inhabitants of any close reconnaissance since Rut tells us that his pilot was killed by the Indians on one visit to the land.

The identity of the pilot is not without interest. The Spanish report stated he was an Italian, a Piedmontese. Purchas gives us the name of one Italian, Albert de Prato, who was with Rut at Newfoundland, and Biggar believed he might be identified with a certain Alberto de Porto who had recently been in England, but neither can be associated with the art of pilotage.[6] Had this man been associated in any way with the Verrazzano

[6] We lack information on the personnel of the voyage. Richard Hakluyt (*Principall navigations* [1589], p. 517) said that a wealthy canon of St. Paul's, who was also "a great Mathematician," went on the voyage. This man has not been identified (compare John Le Neve, *Fasti Ecclesiae Anglicana, 1300–1541*, new ed. [1963], pt. 5) unless he was the rather elderly Polydore Vergil (who had written in 1512 of Cabot's death, p. 102 above). Denys Hay (*Polydore Vergil* [Oxford, 1952], p. 47) has suggested that as late as 1540 to 1543, when he wrote his dialogue *De Patentia* (published in *Dialogi* [Basel, 1545]), Vergil was still interested enough to remark: "I call those merchants to witness who make that adventure from which every man's courage shrinks and at which it trembles. For within the memory of men now living, some amongst them have had the bounty of beneficent princes, who have a care for the enlargement of the state, and have sailed out into the ocean to explore many islands which, hitherto, were unknown—even though before they did so they sustained immeasurable losses." (The translation owes much to Mr. Neil

voyage, he would have linked the English voyage more closely with the somewhat earlier French expedition, the map of whose discoveries had apparently, we have seen, come into English hands before Rut sailed.

The hostility with which the ship was received at Santo Domingo may have helped to deter further English interlopers: Henry's serious involvement with Charles V on the question of the dissolution of his marriage is likely to have underlined for him the unwisdom of penetrating the Spanish monopoly of sea and land power in the west unless it could be done with adequate force. Henry had not, indeed, been oblivious to the New World empire which the Spaniards had been building. In his treatise against Luther, the *Assertio septem sacramentorum*, printed in London in July 1521, there is a passage on the Indians of the Americas and their relations with the papacy: "For . . . the Indians themselves (separated from us by such a vast Distance, both of Land and Sea,) do submit to the See of Rome." Thomas More may indeed have drawn Henry's attention to the new extensions of papal influence and authority in the Americas in the course of the revisions of the king's drafts in which he took part.[7] In any event, Henry could not thereafter have remained in ignorance of what was happening in the Spanish empire: of the discovery of the Aztec Utopia and its destruction by Cortés, with the consequent spoil of gold, silver, and jewels, some at least of which had been intercepted and seized by French pirates. The appearance of Rut's ship in the West Indies in 1527–8 (Henry's own wine ship, as we have seen) was in all probability a planned reconnaissance of the new empire.

III

THE THIRD VOYAGE with which we are concerned, that of Richard Hore to Newfoundland in 1536, appears to have little political significance. It too may have been a follow-up of French discoveries in the west, though if so, no attempt was made to exploit the knowledge gained on the voyage. This in turn may well have been because so little novel information was acquired, and that little under such disadvantageous conditions that no use could be made of it.

Cheshire.) If Vergil is not harking back to Cabot, this may be a reference to the loss of the *Samson* on the 1527 voyage. But it does not establish that he took part in the expedition, which is in any event most unlikely.

[7] Translated in *Assertio Septem Sacramentorum* (New York, 1908), ed. Louis O'Donovan, p. 202. A good general account of the treatise and its significance is given in J. J. Scarisbrick, *Henry VIII* (London, 1968), pp. 110–15. See also F. L. Baumer, *The Early Tudor Theory of Kingship* (New Haven, 1940), p. 41.

The story, so far as we know it,[8] begins on 13 December 1535 when a Breton seaman, Alain Moine (or Moyne), undertook to enter the service of William Dolphyn "to be pylott of his seyd shippe for oon hole yere."[9] The ship was the *William* of London, and her owner a well-known London draper who lived in Leadenhall Street. In February 1536 Richard Hore (or Hoore), citizen and leather-seller of London and an experienced sea captain, opened negotiations to hire the *William* from Dolphyn for a voyage to Newfoundland. The charter party (or agreement for the use of the ship), according to a later statement by Dolphyn, was completed in March and provided that the *William* would go and return within six months.[1] Hore paid down £5 in earnest on signing it and entered into a bond for £500 to pay the charter—£160—on his return and to restore the *William* "immediately after the saife arryvyng of the said shipp in the said Ryver of Thamys as nye the Citie of London as she may sauffely arryve . . . with mastes saylles and all other necessaryes & furnamentes [furnishings] in the sayd inventory."

Richard Hore is described by Hakluyt as "a man of goodly stature and of great courage, and given to the studie of Cosmographie." He was associated with Dolphyn and Sir Thomas Spert—the naval official and shipowner mentioned earlier (p. 163) as interested in overseas exploration—in trade with Spain. Hore was in difficulties with his partners

[8] Sources for the voyage are the two imperfect narratives roughly combined by Richard Hakluyt in *Principall navigations* (1589), pp. 519–20 (reprinted in 1600; see *Principal Navigations*, 12 vols. [Glasgow, 1903–4], VIII, 3–7), one of them collected from Oliver Dawbeny by Hakluyt's older cousin sometime before its publication, and the other from Dr. Thomas Butts by Hakluyt himself not long before he printed it. These recollections of half a century back are not too reliable in detail. To them may now be added the libel, interrogatories, and schedule in a High Court of Admiralty (H.C.A.) case, Dolphyn *contra* Hoore, 1536 (P.R.O., H.C.A. 24/2, 13; H.C.A. 3/14, 15), and depositions, in a subsequent series of actions by William Dolphyn, from Alan Moyne, a Breton pilot, n.d. (H.C.A. 13/3, fols. 61–3); Richard Elyot, master mariner, of Fareham, Hampshire (formerly of London and Waterford), aged sixty, 20 July 1537 (*ibid.*, fols. 147–147v); William Butler, master's mate, of London, 29 March 1537 (*ibid.*, fols. 100–100v); Christopher Lord, seaman, of London, n.d. (*ibid.*, fols. 100v–101). (I am indebted to Miss E. J. Greeves for her careful editorial work on the depositions.) There are valuable biographical notes in H. P. Biggar, *The Voyages of Jacques Cartier* (Ottawa, 1924), pp. 273–7 (with which the article by D. B. Quinn on Richard Hore in *D.C.B.*, I, pp. 371–2, may be read). J. A. Williamson, *Voyages of the Cabots* (1929), pp. 268–71, is now largely superseded. E. G. R. Taylor, "Master Hore's Voyage of 1536," *Geographical Journal*, LXXVII (1933), 469–70, first called attention to some of the Admiralty material, though not all of her conclusions on it can be sustained.

[9] P.R.O., H.C.A. 13/2, fols. 61–3. [1] P.R.O., H.C.A. 24/2, no. 3.

throughout and may not have treated them, or at least Dolphyn, altogether honestly. The *William* was bent on fishing, but not only that, since Hore also hired the *Trinity* of 140 tons. According to the recollections of one of her passengers, Dr. Thomas Butts, as a very old man, the king gave his "favour and good countenance" to a plan put forward by Hore to bring with him "on a voyage of discoverie upon the Northwest partes of America" a number of gentlemen from the Inns of Court and Inns of Chancery and others who wished to see the New World.[2] Accordingly, some thirty gentlemen assembled. Of these, Hakluyt gives us as sailing on the *Trinity* with Hore as captain: a West Country gentleman named Wickes (or Weekes); a Master Tucke of Kent; men named Tuckfield, Hardie, Biron, Carter, Wright, and Ridley, but not otherwise specified; Thomas Butts, son of Sir William Butts of Norfolk; and "master Rastall Serieant Rastals brother," namely John Rastell the younger, son of the John Rastell who had made the vain attempt to get to America in 1517. On the other ship, which Hakluyt calls the *Minion* but which seems clearly to have been the *William*, of which Richard Eliot was master, sailed Oliver Dawbeny (who long afterward gave some account of the voyage);[3] a London merchant, Armigil Wade, "a very learned and vertuous gentleman" whose son William Wade (or Waad) became clerk of Queen Elizabeth's Privy Council; and a Master Joy, later a gentleman of Henry VIII's chapel. There were on the two ships also some ninety seamen, some of whom would be engaged for the line-fishing of cod at Newfoundland. They were mustered in warlike manner at Gravesend, formally received the sacrament, and set sail on Good Friday, 19 April.[4]

The voyage was slow, but the ships seem to have kept company for the two months it took them to sail from London to the vicinity of Cape Breton. They then changed their course and sailed back around the southeastern tip of Newfoundland and then north along the coast, coming to a well-known landmark for voyagers, Penguin Island—the modern Funk Island—off Cape Fogo. There they found quantities of sea-birds and birds' eggs. The Great Auk, being both large and unable to fly, was a regular source of meat for fishing vessels, and eggs and birds were sampled and some taken with them. Bears, black and white, were also killed and eaten.

At this point it may be asked what can be surmised about their destination. No evidence as to this has yet come to light. But Jacques Cartier had

[2] Hakluyt, *Principall navigations* (1589), pp. 518–19.

[3] Compare *ibid.* with H.C.A. 13/2, fols. 147–147v.

[4] Hakluyt, *Principall navigations* (1589), p. 518; H.C.A. 13/2, fols. 100–100v.

sailed this way in 1534, had also taken birds at Funk Island, and had entered the Strait of Belle Isle. From there he had gone on to explore the Gulf of St. Lawrence, and by contact with the Indians gained some knowledge of the great river that lay to the west of the Gulf. He returned to St. Malo on 5 September in the same year. In May 1535 he went out again, spent the following winter near modern Quebec, and returned in June 1536 by Cabot Strait, reaching France on 6 July.[5]

Alain Moine was a Breton, and if he came to England within the year before he signed on with William Dolphyn, he is almost certain to have known of Cartier's first voyage and of his departure on the second. One may suggest—no more is possible—that Richard Hore was preparing a fishing voyage when he learned from the pilot of the *William* of the discovery of the Strait of Belle Isle (already known to French fishermen before Cartier's first voyage) and of the interesting waters and shores beyond. Hore may then have decided to modify his plans, combining the more pedestrian fishing expedition with a sight-seeing excursion into the Gulf of St. Lawrence for a group of London gentlemen. This would make some sense of the subsequent rather obscure events, though it is not the only possible interpretation of the voyage. If Hore started out as captain of the *Trinity*, he remained in her throughout. Oliver Dawbeny, the informant for the next part of the story in Hakluyt, claimed to have been on the *Minion*,[6] which I have identified with the *William*, but his story makes sense only if his ship was the *Trinity*. Given the advanced ages of Butts and Dawbeny when their versions were published, it is clear that where these conflict with the record, they must give way; but not all the material is clear-cut as between one and the other.

Dawbeny says that when his ship was at anchor in a bay some time after their arrival, he sighted "a boate with Savages of those partes" rowing toward them. He put out a boat to catch the people, but they proved too swift and got away. Landing, they found a fire, with a half a bear's carcass on a spit; they also discovered at the same place a decorated leather boot and "a great warme mitten." This was clearly Eskimo gear. Eskimo were to be found in the summer in northern Newfoundland and southern Labrador, overlapping in Newfoundland with the Beothuk Indians. There was little vegetation of interest except fir and pine trees. For some unexplained reason, the ship appears to have remained in the one place for a considerable time. Apart from stealing the fish catches of an osprey for her young, they apparently had no means of getting

[5] Biggar, *Cartier*, pp. 4–7, 79, 93, 236–40.

[6] The next part of the narrative follows Hakluyt's texts.

food—their stores appear to have been exhausted. They began to go hungry and went ashore to collect herbs and roots. In the course of this one man killed another on shore and made a meal of him. This onset of cannibalism was followed by the disappearance of a number of men, until eventually someone informed the captain. He thereupon, according to Dawbeny, made a pious speech against these unnatural acts and urged the men to abstain in future, hoping that God would forgive them. "And such was the mercie of God," he went on, that the same night a French fishing vessel put into the bay. The English, by "policie," that is, trickery of some sort, seized the French ship. They exchanged their own *Trinity* for it, seized most if not all of the stores, and set out for England.

All this is unlikely to have taken place on the northeast coast of Newfoundland, from which they had only to sail on down the coast to meet the fishing fleets. If the *Trinity* was damaged and out of commission for some reason the case might be different, though we do not hear that she was. As it is, it would seem that the ship had been taken by Hore into or through the Strait of Belle Isle, following the instructions of Alain Moine, even though he was not aboard her. Their hardships are then likely to have taken place along the desolate southern shore of Labrador, the coast Cartier had described as "the land God gave to Cain." The presence of the French ship is credible: Cartier had found a fishing vessel from La Rochelle on the Labrador coast after he passed through the strait in 1534. The return voyage of the new *Trinity* began in high latitudes, the master probably taking the vessel northeastward from the mouth of the Strait of Belle Isle. Great icebergs were seen, on which hawks and other birds rested. Birds larger than herons, thought to be storks from their red bills and legs (conceivably snow geese), were also sighted. Eventually this French prize reached St. Ives, Cornwall, about the end of October. They had arrived in the vicinity of Cape Breton in mid-June, and their voyage back would have taken them about a month. The exploration in which they were involved, and their ordeal by hunger, would therefore have lasted through the months of July and August.

This tale may have had a good deal of padding and some distortion, but it seems to have a basis in fact. The *William*, under Eliot's command and with Moine on board, parted company with the *Trinity* at some point, probably after the bird-taking expedition at Funk Island. It would seem to have been arranged that all the sight-seers should be accommodated on the *Trinity* while the *William* went fishing, but if so it is strange that Moine, if his function was what I have suggested, did not go on the *Trinity* also. The *William* proceeded down the coast to her fishing station at "the Isle of Spere," one of the three small Spear Islands off Cape Spear and a little to the south of the great harbor of St. John's, which was the center of the shore fishery.

All we know of what took place there arises out of a case of damage to the ship and her condition after she had completed her voyage, and hinges on the behavior of Alain Moine and his status on board, so that it is largely incidental to our main concerns. One point in the case was that Moine was really the ship's carpenter and only incidentally a pilot. He admitted he had done carpenter's work, but only to avoid idleness; pilotage was his main task. The *William*, he said, was "as staunche as any ship myght be comonlye." William Butler, the master's mate, and Christopher Lorde, a seaman, testified against him. Richard Eliot, the master, had asked him to inspect the ship as a carpenter but he refused, saying it was none of his business to do so. He occupied himself by going "on lande emongest the Bryttons his countreymen and made mery with them a day or ii," consorting with them "in bowling and drynkyng vntill he was drounken." He also amused himself by making "a new jerkyn and a payre of sloppes in New Founde lande of new canvas vppon borde the said shyppe."

These sidelights on the social life of the cod fishery are of only minor interest for the story of the voyage. The outcome is a little more relevant. William Butler reported that "in the sayd vyage made unto New fownde lande the sayd shyppe, by reason of laboryng of the see and long lyeing in New founde lande, had thre leaks came upon her after that she came furthe of her haborowe in New Founde lande callyd the Ile of Spere, within a days saylyng." [7] He blamed Moine for his lack of care of the ship, which ship and goods were put in peril. When it came to the point and "he saw the same leaks and [he] dyd helpe to cutte tymber for to stoppe them, and he sayth that the said Alen dyd stoppe the same leaks with byffe [buff leather]." The result was that the *William* duly completed her return voyage to London with her cargo of fish on 29 September 1536.

The survivors of the *Trinity* were emaciated after their ordeal, Sir William Butts and his wife recognizing their son, it was said, only by a secret mark on his body. But they recuperated in Cornwall in a castle of Sir John Luttrel's. According to Hakluyt the French fishermen left on the *Trinity*, or some of them, got home, for they appeared in England some months later. The king is said to have forgiven the Englishmen for their actions, and to have himself given compensation to the French. No

[7] The depositions of Moine, Butler, and Lord are all relevant; the ship's master Richard Eliot in his deposition made no reference to the *William* being in Newfoundland.

confirmation of this part of the story has been found in the English records. Meantime the *William* lay with her cargo of fish in the port of London for some five weeks, while Richard Hore made no attempt to pay off the £160 owing for the charter or to return the ship (said, with her lading, to be worth £500) to William Dolphyn.[8] The probable reason is not any delinquency on his part but simply that he was not there, though he appears to have reached London before the end of October, having possibly got passage from St. Ives. Dolphyn began an action against Hore in the High Court of Admiralty, but it seems likely that it was compromised when Hore returned, and that the charter was extended for a voyage to San Lucár. The *William*, however, put into Falmouth about the beginning of December and stayed there. Her crew refused to sail, saying that the ship was unfit, and proceeded, apparently in lieu of wages, to dispose of gear alleged to be worth £200. Dolphyn, on learning of this, began a further series of actions against Hore and members of the crew, and it was in the course of answering charges of neglect on the *William* during the Newfoundland expedition that the depositions of Moine, Butler, and others were made.

How much of a storm in a teacup Dolphyn's charges against Alain Moine were—at least on a surface reading—may be seen by the schedule which he attached to the Interrogatories in his case against him.

These parcelles following Alane Moine imbesseled and toke away out of Master Dolphyns shipe at the viage to newe found land.

In primis certen remenentes of canvas to the number of xxx elles or ther aboute wherwith the said Alane made hym dyuers ierkns and slopps, and parte of the said Canvas at new found land and at Falmouth for the which he receyved v[s] / All which xxx elles were worth—xxx[s] /

Item certeyn sheffe arrowes to the valewe — xij[d]

These parcelles he toke on the second viage

Item certeyn other sheve arrowes precium xx[d]

Item other thinges to the valew of — xx[s]

Even at sixteenth-century prices, a total embezzlement of goods worth £2 12s. 8d. was scarcely worth the paper and parchment, apart from the legal time, devoted to it, but at least the case brings the words "newe found land," not yet finally fused as Newfoundland, into regular use in the High Court of Admiralty. Though the cases help, they still only tell us a part of the full story of the 1536 voyage.

The composite picture which emerges on our present evidence is that Richard Hore injected into a routine fishing voyage to Newfoundland, the pattern of which was now firmly established, the combination of a sight-seeing and exploration tour. The arrival of the ships in American waters marked the earliest penetration, if our assumptions are correct, of the Strait of Belle Isle by Englishmen and their rediscovery, after Cartier, of the bleak southern shores of Labrador. If we are correct also in attributing this phase of the voyage to information which Alain Moine had brought of Cartier's voyage in 1534, then the objective was to see what the Gulf of St. Lawrence was like, with its great bird and walrus colonies, its whales and fertile-appearing islands, rather than to make an intensive exploration with serious economic or political objectives.

The result, if we can go by the stories of two old gentlemen who remembered imperfectly what had happened, was distinctly unhappy. Both ships lacked leadership, it is clear; the failure to make an effective penetration of the Gulf of St. Lawrence may perhaps be attributed to faults on Hore's side. The abandonment of the *Trinity* suggests that she was not thought sufficiently seaworthy for the return voyage. The seizure by her crew of the French Newfoundlander may be seen as an act of desperation. If the French prize was eventually restored in 1537, then the costs to those concerned and also to Hore may well have been high, and so may offer us some chance of picking up this case, too, in the surviving records. The *William*'s voyage, despite the successful catching and lading of cod, is unlikely to have made up the losses incurred for the *Trinity*. The adventure certainly gave some educated Englishmen a view of the New World, but it was a sufficiently unfavorable one to act as strong negative propaganda for further North American exploring expeditions. There were no more, so far as is at present known, before the end of the reign. If Henry VIII was involved in clearing up the mess created by that of 1536, it may have finally removed any further desire on his part to participate in overseas exploration in this area. Francis I was similarly, though more drastically, disillusioned by the return of Cartier in 1542 and Roberval in 1543 from the attempted exploitation of the St. Lawrence valley for France. North America had still to reveal its attractions, economic, physical, and political, to the western European powers.

Although we lack altogether any record of English plans to explore any part of North America or attempts to do so between 1536 and 1563, it is not at all unlikely that some probing of the coast was being carried on by the more enterprising of the fishermen who went yearly to Newfoundland. It would be strange if a few at least did not join the Breton and Basque frequenters of Cape Breton who came to trade furs as well as to fish and dry their fish—some of whom perhaps ranged the New England shores too. It is not wholly unlikely. They have left no records that can be found, nor under Edward VI or Mary have any moves to penetrate North America come to light. At the same time there was probably more contact than we realize. An illustration of this arises in 1560.[9] An Englishman was found by the Spaniards who had been on the shores of North America between latitudes 33° and 37° in 1546.

John—we do not know his surname—in 1546 at the age of ten left Dartmouth to join a French squadron which went to sea, as so often, in order to seize Spanish merchant or treasure ships coming from the western Indies. But as they got into the Atlantic the weather turned foul. Eventually the ship in which John was cabin boy reached land. It was prepared for trade as well as plunder, and was thus able to take advantage of its changed circumstances. At latitude 37° N or thereabouts—that is, at or near the entrance to Chesapeake Bay—they found a harbor where more than thirty Indian canoes came out, each of which had fifteen to twenty men, every man armed with bows and arrows. The French commander was cautious and would allow no more than two men to come aboard at once. The Indians came prepared to trade, so that visits by French ships at least were no novelty, and they exchanged over a period of two days a thousand marten skins for shirts, fishhooks, and knives. Thus it would seem that the Algonkian Indians of the Virginia tidewater were in contact with white men for at least sixty years before the Jamestown settlement was made. From the vicinity of Cape Henry the French ship moved down the coast to approximately 33°, to Santa Elena, most probably Port Royal Sound. Once more Indians—probably members of the Coosa tribe—came out in their canoes. Some of them wore mantles of highly dressed deerskin, others good skins and leather from different animals. This time the Indians wanted especially fishhooks, the metal hooks being more effective than their bone ones, and they took other trifles too in return for pearls, marten skins, maize, and pumpkins.

This was only the first of several visits made to the coast of southeastern North America by this Englishman, whose French employers alternated plunder with commerce; according to the Spaniards they obtained gold at times from the Indians. In the end John was captured by

[9] *The Luna Papers, 1559–1561*, 2 vols. (DeLand, Fla., 1928), ed. Herbert Ingram Priestley, I, 149, 176–9, 184–5, 192–3.

the Spanish and remained in their service in Mexico, eventually marrying and settling down in Campeche. This is the first English contact we know of with the Indians of the southeast, though Rut is likely to have made calls along this shore in 1527. John is a reminder that exploration did not entirely depend on kings.

Summary

ENGLAND DID NOT follow up the early voyages of discovery in any systematic way. She had learned, perhaps, both too much and too little about North America under Henry VII: namely, that it was vast in extent but barren of any rich trading communities, and that its forests and barbarian peoples were not easy to exploit with profit. Immediately profitable returns were confined to Newfoundland fish. Nor did the new continent appear much more attractive under Henry VIII. Sebastian Cabot's supposed discovery of the opening of a sea passage around the north coast of the forbidding landmass had aroused so little interest in England that he transferred to the Spanish service. He had expressed no great enthusiasm, apparently, for the more temperate shores, which he had coasted down to Chesapeake Bay or farther south. Nor did John Rut, who coasted the same American lands in 1527 and perhaps made a closer investigation of them, excite any enthusiasm for either trade or colonization upon his return. We might conclude that to both Cabot and Rut the shores of the coastal plain showed only endless variety of sameness, none of it interesting to a country still obsessed with the need to export cloth and concerned more with importing tropical exotics than the produce of temperate climes. The intermittent expeditions we know were made were not followed up. No estimates of what North America contained in the way of forests and furs and native societies were made, or were even easily available in other tongues. Apart from what was seen of Newfoundland by fishermen, and of Labrador by the expedition of 1536, there seems to have been little knowledge or enduring curiosity.

English knowledge of North America in 1505 had been greater than that of any other European country; by 1560 England knew little more than she had fifty-five years before. Priority had long been ceded to others, especially the French. Sebastian Cabot alone remained for a long time a living link with the earlier western explorations. His return to England marked the first slight revival of interest in the west, yet it was not followed up, so far as we know, by any western voyages of exploration. By the time Elizabeth I came to the throne on 17 November 1558, he too had become only a memory. English western enterprise had to start anew.

PART III

Sailors and Colonies

Prologue

The Elizabethan period is traditionally dominated by the personalities and exploits of its seamen. We may now see them in somewhat less of a romantic haze than did their Victorian successors, but their deeds make up the foreground at least of maritime and colonial enterprise. This is when the English colonial movement began; more especially it is when North America first emerged in men's minds and experience as a continent open for exploitation and settlement. The men concerned in early English attempts to extract wealth from the New World and settle Englishmen there in order to make the exploitation continuous were not only the prominent promoters like Sir Walter Ralegh, Sir Humphrey Gilbert, and Sir Richard Grenville, but smaller subleaders: men who captained vessels, like Edward Hayes; or piloted them, like Simão Fernandes; and the miscellaneous rank and file of rough seamen and rougher soldiers, farmers, craftsmen, servants to richer men—gentlemen adventurers and adventurers without any qualifications at all. The middle sort in particular are worth more study than we have given them thus far.

The Roanoke voyages—the attempts of the English, under the influence of Sir Walter Ralegh, to occupy Roanoke Island and parts of the shores of Chesapeake Bay between 1584 and 1590—are in the forefront of English colonial experiments in North America. They yielded experience, not all of it happy, some of it tragic. But they produced in the drawings of John White the finest example we have of an artist playing a major colonizing role as settler and governor and also uncovering and preserving for Europeans the main features of human, animal, and plant life before settlement had begun to alter the old ecological pattern. White's detail and sense of color have left us a picture as well as an intellectual understanding of a small segment of wilder America. Thomas Harriot, too, in his *Briefe and true report* pointed the way to the western scientist in digesting the data of the natural world set out before the eyes of the settlers and partially recorded by White.

The Elizabethan attempts at settlement did not succeed, but lessons were learned which helped—not without many ups and downs—to make possible effective occupation in a new century when the Spanish war was out of the way. The Roanoke ventures had brought English activity in North America under the close scrutiny of Spain. In the years before the outbreak of open war, and during the course of the long sea war between England and Spain, the latter had to take account of the presence of an enemy power on the North America mainland. Just as English efforts from 1584 onward were not marked by any very conspicuous success in colonization, so the Spanish attempts to find out exactly where the English were, in what strength, and for how long were not conspicuously successful either, until in fact the exigencies of war led the English to abandon their last group of colonists and virtually to cease voyaging to the parts of North America within reach of the Spaniard. Spanish plans to deny the coast to the English were similarly thwarted by the demands and requirements of the European struggle. The result was, in effect, to leave the shoreline north of the Spanish Florida garrison open to competition in the early years of the seventeenth century.

CHAPTER SEVEN

Sailors and the Sea in Elizabethan England

I

THE SHIP WAS the all-purpose means of transportation to those who lived along the coasts or on the estuaries of Tudor and Stuart England. Movement by water along rivers and by coastal navigation was, at most seasons, easier than by land. The Thames was the main highway of London and its environs, crowded with boats and lined with ships. The Thames fairway led not only to France, Spain, and the Low Countries, to Muscovy and the Indies, but to Harwich and Hull, Newcastle and Leith, to Dover, Portsmouth, Exeter, Plymouth, and Bristol. Ships and sea travel were taken for granted by those who lived on the coast and estuaries. And these people formed the larger part of the population at the time.

Coastal trade was carried on for the most part, in small ships of some 20 to 80 tons. Some were little more than sailing barges or small boats under sail. Others were stouter and more seaworthy. There were a few large coasters, of 100 to something over 200 tons, attached to the larger ports.[1] Some of these were old merchantmen, now too slow or uncertain

[1] A report of 1582 showed that of 1495 merchantmen and coasters only 235 were over eighty tons (Sir William Monson, *The Naval Tracts of William Monson* [Navy Records Society (N.R.S.), 1919], ed. Michael Oppenheim, III, 188–92; see D. W. Waters, *The Art of Navigation in England in Elizabethan and Early Stuart Times* [London, 1958], p. 111). Of the 160 or so vessels mobilized against the Armada, of which the tonnage is known, half were of eighty tons or under and only six were of three hundred tons or more (*State Papers Relating to the Defeat*

for long voyages; others were specialized transports, like the Newcastle coalmen. The common rig of two masts for the smaller and three for the larger gave most of the coastal shipping a stereotyped look, but the knowing eye could spot local variations in build and sail plan which brought variety to the picture.

Most striking about the ports of the sixteenth century is the number of ships in them. Coasters were small, distribution required many individual vessels, and the merchantmen which carried on the overseas trade of England were themselves of no great size. The majority were of 80 tons or less, and it took a great many ships of this size to supply the needs even of England's three or four million people at the time. Mainly three-masters, they too had a characteristic outline, with square stern, a somewhat beaked bow, rather high upper works aft, and similar works—though much lower—forward. The Levant Company employed bigger ships, ranging from 250 to 400 tons in late Elizabethan times up to 500 tons under the first Stuart, as did the East India Company also.

The queen's or king's ships were still somewhere in between a great personal squadron and a permanent institutionalized fleet. A part-time navy of merchantmen, temporarily converted, was still an essential part of the country's maritime defense. Perhaps the professionalism of the Elizabethan navy board can be said to have provided the bureaucratic structure of a navy proper, but the fleet depended very much for its continuation and growth on the whims of the sovereign rather than on the expertise of officials. A rebuilding and refitting program, such as Hawkins carried out in the years before the Armada, was still exceptional, although there had been something like it under Henry VIII. Ships were kept on the strength for decades, even a generation or more, in case they should come in useful—as some old stagers did in the Armada year—but there was also some systematic attention to new design. The employment of expert ship designers, Matthew Baker, Peter Pett, and his son Phineas, brought a measure of continuity and progress. The new galleons of the pre-Armada years, longer, lower, more beaked, more systematically and heavily gunned, were formidable ships of 400 to 800 tons (there were even two ships of 1000 and 1100 tons, respectively, in the Armada campaign). The lesser vessels differed scarcely at all, except in armament, from merchant vessels. The small pinnaces, independent vessels of 25 to 50 tons, showed more variation in design, while the still smaller pinnaces

of the Spanish Armada [N.R.S., 1894], ed. J. K. Laughton, II, 326–31), while two-thirds of the known vessels which went privateering from 1589 to 1591 were of eighty tons or less, and scarcely more than 10 percent of two hundred tons or more (K. R. Andrews, *Elizabethan Privateering* [Cambridge, Eng., 1964], pp. 241–73).

carried or towed by great ships were little more than large boats fitted with one or two masts, with fore-and-aft or square sail rig.[2]

The public image of the royal navy was well conveyed by Sir Jerome Horsey in his dialogue with the Tsar Ivan IV, in 1576.

IVAN. Yt is reported your Quen, my sister, hathe the best navie of shipps in the world.

HORSEY. Yt is true, and please your Majesty. . . . For strength and greatnes to breake and cutt thorow the great occean, turbulent seas.

IVAN. How framed so?

HORSEY. For art, sharpe-kielled, not flat-bottomed; so thicke and strong-sided that a cannon shott can scarse pearse thorow.

IVAN. What ells?

HORSEY. Everie shipe caries cannon and fortie brass peces of great ordinance, bulletts, musketts, powder, cheyne-shott, piekes, and armor of defence, wild fier worckes, stancions for fights, a thowsand marrinors and men at arms, souldiers, captaines, and officers of all sortts to guide and govern; discipline and dailie devine preyers; bear, bread, bieff, fish, bakon, pease, butter, chese, vinegar, oatmeall, aqua-vita, wood, water and all other provicion, plentifull, fitt and necessarie for foode and maintenance of men; ancers, cabells, takells, masts, five or six great salls spread, aunctients, fleggs, costly silke banners displayed with the Quens ensignes and arms, wherat all other kings shipps bend and bowe; dromes, trompetts, taber, pipe, and other instruments of warlicke designes and defiance to the enymie; abell to assault and batter the strongest mariten towns and castells that ar; most tirrable and warrlicke for the aied, conduction and defence, of her Majestys alyance and frends.[3]

Queen Elizabeth's navy-royal was never quite like this, but the spirited propaganda picture, perhaps, most vividly calls it to mind.

[2] For the Queen's ships, see J. S. Corbett, *Drake and the Tudor Navy*, 2 vols. (London, 1898), and *The Successors of Drake* (London, 1900), both invaluable, if in need of correction; Michael Lewis, *The Navy of Britain* (London, 1948), *A History of the British Navy* (London, 1957), and *Armada Guns* (London, 1961); Garrett Mattingly, *The Defeat of the Spanish Armada* (London, 1959); G. J. Marcus, *A Naval History of England*, I (London, 1961). Little of a systematic character has been published on the merchant navy, 1558–1625. Dorothy Burwash, *English Merchant Shipping, 1450–1550* (Toronto, 1947), and G. V. Scammell, "Shipowning in England 1450–1550," *Transactions of the Royal Historical Society*, ser. 12, 105–22, provide the background. For privateering vessels, see K. R. Andrews, whose *Elizabethan Privateering* (Cambridge, Eng., 1964), is invaluable.

[3] From "The Travels of Sir Jerome Horsey," in *Russia at the Close of the Sixteenth Century*, Hakluyt Society (1856), ed. E. A. Bond, pp. 185–6.

Ships' names, too, bring home some of the sea flavor of the time.[4] Many of the queen's ships of the Armada period had names which stuck for centuries in the royal navy—*Dreadnought*, *Rainbow*, *Revenge*, *Tiger* (also a popular merchant ship name), *Triumph*, *Victory*, *Vanguard*, but *Bull* would soon seem undignified for a royal ship and *Ark Royal* would not be revived until the twentieth century. The *Virgin God Save Her* was one of Sir Richard Grenville's prizes, in her name cocking an irreverent snook at the Spaniards. The *Golden Hind*, the *Mayflower*, the *Delight* are good merchant ship names, as are the more intimate family names like *Margaret and John*, *Susan Parnell*, *Pansy*, *Hearty Anne*. Others seem a little odd or frivolous to us—the *Bark Buggins*, the *Makeshift*, the *Black Dog*, the *Rat*, the *Heathen*—while *Three Half Moons* sounds more like an inn than a ship. Some of the privateering vessels had deliberately bizarre names like Sir Robert Dudley's *Earwig* and *Frisking*, and John Chidley's pair, *Wildman* (alias *Susan*) and *Wildman's Club* (alias *Susan's Handmaid*).

Just as the ports—and the roads nearby, and the estuaries—held many ships, so did the coastal towns breed and keep many sailors.[5] The boatmen and lightermen of the Thames were a numerous tribe, and quarrelsome as well. The thickest population of merchant seamen was in the Thames-side parishes east of London Bridge: St. Katherine's, Wapping, Ratcliffe, Limehouse, and Rotherhithe, and besides merchantmen they supplied privateers (largely financed by London merchants) and the royal ships (often by impressment) as well. The quality of the seamen engaged in the coastal trade, and the ships they used, seems to have been lowest of all—apart from a specialized group, those in the coal trade—but it was an hereditary craft and families might remain in one branch of it for generations. For a substantial part of the population the sea, we may remind ourselves, offered the natural way of earning a living. The dull or the conservative stayed where they were born and sailed to no great distance; the more venturesome, ambitious, and unruly moved on to other

[4] Compare Laughton, *Spanish Armada*, II, 324–31, for the names of the Armada ships, and T. D. Manning and C. F. Walker, *British Warship Names* (London, 1959).

[5] For the English seaman see H. H. Sparling, "Mariners of England Before the Armada," *English Illustrated Magazine*, VIII (1891), 647–54; C. S. Goldingham, "The Personnel of the Tudor Navy," *United Services Magazine*, CLXXXVII (1918), 427–51; F. E. Dyer, "The Elizabethan Sailorman," *Mariner's Mirror*, X (1924), 133–46; K. R. Andrews, *English Privateering Voyages, 1588–1595*, Hakluyt Society, 2d ser., CXI (1959), 22–8; Andrews, *Elizabethan Privateering*, chap. 3; Christopher Lloyd, *The British Seaman* (London, 1968); G. V. Scammell, "Manning the English Merchant Service in the Sixteenth Century," *Mariner's Mirror*, LVI (1970), 131–54. The last item is of exceptional value.

branches. On the shorter merchant shipping routes the life was not a bad one. These ships were not overmanned, the pace was slow, the turn-round at foreign ports leisurely (and there were foreign drinks and women and sights to entertain the seamen, even if they were often short of money), while the dangers from weather, though the Channel was always treacherous, were not excessive.

English waters and those of the adjacent shores were mostly charted, if by no means always adequately. The merchants trading to the Low Countries, France, and Ireland, at least in years of peace or comparative peace, do not seem to have had trouble in getting crews. For the longer voyages, to Spain, Portugal, the Atlantic Islands, the Baltic, and Russia by the northern route, the case was rather different. If the ships were somewhat bigger, the danger from weather was greater too. Cooped up in inadequate quarters in bad weather for considerable periods, the seamen cannot have been comfortable. In northern waters especially, they were often unable to keep warm or to get hot food, the seas being too rough to light fires. But conditions were not always so bad; voyages to the Straits—that is, to Morocco, North Africa, the Mediterranean generally—seem to have been popular enough. The merchant seaman's pay was normally rather poor; the somewhat longer voyages, when his pay piled up, were probably the more profitable.

The toughest of the merchant seamen were the fishermen. The North Sea herring fishing vessels might not go far, but the men worked hard, under heavy pressure and in inferior boats (hence the demand at the end of the sixteenth century to copy the Dutch herring buss). The east coast too had a long tradition of deep-sea fishing off Norway and Iceland, while in the southwest Devon and Cornish fishermen gathered in pilchards when they came and then pushed out to fish off the Atlantic coasts of Ireland in competition with French and Spaniards and Portuguese. They went also, increasingly, to Newfoundland, often in ships of no more than eighty tons, sometimes less, but with some larger ships also engaging in the trade in the new century. The Newfoundland run was a risky one: if the weather held westward it could occasionally be easy, but it usually meant adverse winds at some stage, while riding home with the westerlies might also mean having to cope with storm and tempest. At the fishing grounds, the labor of taking cod by hook and line from boats was considerable, as was the shore-drying of the bulk of it on wooden flakes. The ships tended to be overmanned to make the loading as short as possible, which in turn made living conditions worse on board. But if the season was a good one, cod fishing was profitable for all concerned, since the appetite for cod in meat-starved Europe seemed insatiable.

Apart from the Newfoundland fishery, voyages outside European waters were still, in late Elizabethan times, unusual. Russia and the Mediterranean were only just within the normal range of English shipping. The beginning of the privateering war in 1585 saw a change. From 1585 down to 1602 at least, ships—perhaps two hundred each year—went off both singly and in packs to hunt and rob the Spaniards in the West Indies and on the high seas. The sailors saw in the Caribbean new significant parts of the non-European world and learned to adapt themselves in some measure to tropical conditions for the first time. It is true that there had been trade with Guinea since the 1550's, and intermittently with Brazil from earlier still, but the number of ships employed was small and the mortality of the seamen engaged—at least for Guinea—excessive, so that it had not become a "normal" commercial route. Yet Guinea in the southern Atlantic and the West Indies to the west became the foci for expanding exploration. The Roanoke voyages to what is now North Carolina and Virginia between 1584 and 1590 were extensions merely of the West Indies privateering run, just as Gilbert's voyage of 1583, the St. Lawrence voyages of 1593–7, and the later expeditions to New England from 1602 onward were all extensions of the old Newfoundland passage.

The same might be said of Northwest Passage exploration from 1576 on. The Guinea and Brazil routes again acted as leads into the South Atlantic, both east and west, and helped to make possible the final circumnavigation of the earth and the would-be and actual East Indian voyages which, from 1601, made that route one of only comparative novelty. The real breaks with the older shipping routines had come with Drake's passage of the Pacific and Cavendish's successful imitation of his feat. To the seaman, to sail out into the unknown or imperfectly known was an adventure, but it is doubtful if it affected him as anything more than another job, one with more danger than usual perhaps—with, at the same time, a little more reward. The fact that Drake's men came back rich in 1580 had a great influence in making far-ranging voyages of exploration attractive.

The seamen had much to endure on long voyages. Accommodations were limited and poor; on privateering ventures ships were overmanned to provide fighting men and prize crews, while those going to the tropics also took extra personnel on account of the high mortality there. Rough weather meant that fires could not be lit for cooking or warmth, and on northern voyages the men suffered much from cold. In the tropics beer went sour, dried fish rotten, and biscuits moldy. North or south, the men became more lousy as the voyage continued. Luke Fox summed up in

1635 the seaman's lot as "but to endure and suffer; as a hard Cabbin, cold and salt Meate, broken sleepes, mould[y] bread, dead beere, wet Cloathes, want of fire."[6] There were demands for more space and some degree of privacy, but Ralegh did not think it was possible to satisfy them: he said, "Man may not expect the Ease of many Cabbins and Safety at once in Sea-service. . . . And Albeit the Mariners do covet Store of Cabinns, yet indeed they are but sluttish Dens that breed Sickness."[7] The Armada campaign showed how deadly bad food alone could prove. Hundreds died from virulent food-poisoning as the hastily gathered stores interacted on the crowded, press-ganged crews. On board ship hygiene was poor at any time, and especially so in these circumstances. On long runs, shortage of water and the bad quality of what there was were serious matters. The foods carried—salt beef and pork, wet-salted or dried cod, biscuit, beans, peas, with beer, wine, and some oil—were nutritious enough while they were new and if they could be cooked, if supplemented by even a little fresh fruit and vegetables.

On long voyages the diet produced scurvy, which could decimate a crew if it were neglected too long, and as the food deteriorated, wet beriberi and food-poisoning followed.[8] An enlightened commander such as Richard Hawkins tried to curb scurvy with citrus fruits (oranges and lemons), but his example was not widely followed. Physicians advocated various decoctions of scurvy-grass and watercress, which might in sufficient quantity have been effective had not, one suspects, too much of their vitamin C been boiled out of them. Plague might well be picked up in temperate latitudes; typhus was a commonplace of nautical life; in tropical waters malaria more deadly than that endemic in the Thames basin, or even yellow fever, might be had from mosquitoes. Dysentery, often associated with infected food, might in tropical varieties prove mortal, so that the "bloody flux" was especially feared at sea. The men could rarely change their clothes, even if they had a change of clothing. This increased the risks of infection in low latitudes and the impact of chills and pneumonia in high. The run of accidents on a sailing vessel was often great; wounds from shot, sword, or splinters were widespread after an action. Surgeons were carried by many ships on long voyages or on sea campaigns. They were expected to have served their apprenticeship and to have satisfied the Barber-Surgeons' Company of London of their

[6] *North-west Fox* (B. Alsop and T. Fawcet, 1635), sig. A2r; *S.T.C.* 11221.

[7] "Observations on the Navy and the Sea-service," in Ralegh, *Works*, 2 vols. (London, 1751), ed. Thomas Birch, II, 96.

[8] J. J. Keevil, *Medicine and the Navy*, 3 vols. (London, 1957–61), I, 44–148, is the best authority.

qualifications. There were a few outstanding surgeons, like William Clowes, who learned much of their craft at sea, but the quality was often low, and many surgeons at sea had little or no training. Expected to treat only the outer man, they left disease largely to the captain. On important expeditions a physician might be carried; more often there was an apothecary with some knowledge of herbs and nostrums. So captains had to do what they could from the book. George Wateson's *The cures of the diseased in remote regions* (1598) [9] was the first working textbook of tropical diseases and did not help very greatly with its simple program of bleeding, diet, and elementary medication.

Sir Francis Drake was most interested in the problems of keeping food and water at sea. He knew the versatile inventor Sir Hugh Plat,[1] who produced for him "a certain victual in the form of hollow pipes," a form of pasta, which was reckoned to retain its qualities for up to three years at sea. It may have been used as early as the Drake circumnavigation, though this is not certain, and it was undoubtedly employed in the Drake–Hawkins expedition of 1595. Plat maintained that he found also that the mixing of a certain amount of vinegar with the water made it keep better and longer: this notion, too, Drake took up. Whatever the effects of such experiments, it is noteworthy that Drake kept the *Golden Hind* a healthy ship on her three years' voyage, which was unprecedented and ranks as one of his most outstanding achievements.

Danger at sea was not confined to the elements and to poor food and disease. Piracy was endemic along the coasts of Europe at this time and flourished especially in the west—Devon and Cornwall, South Wales, and south and southwest Ireland. Coasters were continually being robbed when they were not taking their turn to rob. In the English Channel there were not only English pirates but French and Flemish as well. Piracy usually involved a certain amount of violence, though sometimes intimidation proved enough; it is possible at times to suspect collusion between seaman and pirate at the expense of the shippers of cargoes. Merchant ships on voyages outside home waters usually carried arms and were able to put up some resistance to attacks, in which seamen

[9] F. Kingston for H. Lownes, 1598; *S.T.C.* 25106.

[1] Hugh Plat, *Sundrie new and artificiall remedies against famine*, P. Short (1596), *S.T.C.* 19996; Plat, *Certaine philosophical preparations of food and beuerage for sea-men in their long voyages*, Wellcome Historical Medical Library (London, 1607); Keevil, *Medicine and the Navy*, I, 108–9; D. W. Waters, "Limes, Lemons and Scurvy in Elizabethan and Early Stuart Times," *Mariner's Mirror*, XLI (1955), 167–9; C. F. Mullett, "Hugh Plat: Elizabethan Virtuoso," in C. T. Prouty, ed., *Studies in Honor of A. H. R. Fairchild* (Columbia, Miss., 1946), pp. 93–118.

were occasionally killed and more often hurt. From 1585 onward the comparatively mild dangers of piracy gave place to a militant free-for-all at sea.[2] Dutch, Flemish, and French (royalist or Catholic League) ships as well as English vessels had license to take enemy ships at sea, which they were apt to interpret as generously as possible. English "ships of reprisal" were first released in quantity in 1585 and were supposed to restrict their attacks to Spanish and Portuguese vessels, but in fact they attacked every vessel going to or coming from Iberian ports, or even thought to be doing so: French, Flemish, Dutch, Hanseatic, Scottish, Danish, all with the utmost impartiality. Moreover, hostility between English ships and those from the Catholic League ports in France provided fresh excuses for mutual violence in European and North American waters, English attacks on foreign shipping in Newfoundland having an almost continuous history in the twenty years from 1582. Which ships belonged to pro-Spanish Flemings and to anti-Spanish Dutch remained obscure, and neither side allowed their final allegiance to stand in the way of a chance of booty. The voyage of the *Brave* and the *Roe,* two small English pinnaces, which were supposed to go to North America but got only to the Azores, is an astonishing record of violence at sea in the Armada year, every ship's weapons being turned against all others—Scots, French, English, Hansards, Flemings, each attacking and being attacked indiscriminately.[3]

It is remarkable that, with so much lawlessness current at sea, so many ships could still carry on with their ordinary tasks. Henry IV and Queen Elizabeth, however, spent the last years of the old century and the first of the new in trying to wipe the slate clean of old injuries between their subjects and to render the Channel safer, if not safe. This process was then taken up between James I and Philip III, when the Treaty of London had brought peace again, in European waters at least, between England, Spain, and Portugal. The Iberian trade soon settled into its peacetime channels. But the privateering tradition died hard. James I was not wholly able to cope with sea robbery, though greater English control in Ireland helped to limit its range, and some sea-rovers were driven to seek bases as far away as Algiers, Morocco, and even Newfoundland. The continued struggle of Dutch and Spaniards until the truce of 1609, however, meant

[2] See Andrews, *English Privateering Voyages, passim.*

[3] Richard Hakluyt, *The principall navigations* (G. Bishop and R. Newberie, Deputies to C. Barker, 1589), 1589, Hakluyt Society, extra ser. 39, 2 vols. (Cambridge, Eng., 1965), ed. D. B. Quinn and R. A. Skelton, I, 771–3; *S.T.C.* 12625. Reprinted in D. B. Quinn, *The Roanoke Voyages, 1584–1590,* Hakluyt Society, 2d ser., no. 5, 104–5, 2 vols. (Cambridge, Eng., 1955), II, 526–9.

that excuses for sea-fighting and robbery, under flags of convenience where necessary, continued in western European waters.[4]

The activities of the East India Company from 1601, the enhanced activity of Guinea merchants after the peace, and the regular Virginia voyages after 1607, together with continued West Indies venturing which came to concentrate rather on illicit trade with the Spanish settlers than on plunder, all turned the exceptional runs of the Elizabethan seaman into more or less routine voyages for his Jacobean successors. But up to 1623, in the Far East at least, there were fresh probings of distant seas still to be made, with the chance of clashes with Portuguese and Dutch which might well be deadly, while the South Pacific was still out of bounds for all. The expanding sailors' world had not yet quite reached its limits.

Joseph Hall was among those who wondered if all this sea enterprise for commercial gain was worth while, writing of "the greedy Merchant that for gaine Sailes to both Poles, & sounds both Indian seas." [5] In the end, it is true, "his long beaten bark from forth the maine Unlades her weary fraight," but only that he "shall as he please, Raise by excessive rate his private store, And to enrich himself make thousands poore." Such doubt about the virtues of capitalistic maritime enterprise seems to have been rare—the prerogative, perhaps, of satirists alone.

The common sailor was bred to the sea, following in his father's wake at a tender age, but if he was tough, intelligent, ambitious, and lucky he could move fast enough up the long ladder of promotion from ship's boy to master. If he was no more than a competent craftsman he might rise no higher than master of a coaster, or master's mate on a merchantman, but if he was capable of picking up some degree of technical skill in navigation as well as of commanding men, he might quite early become master of one of the bigger and farther-ranging merchantmen, mounting, with good fortune, to command her as captain. If he were to go farther he would need to show some capacity for trading or managing his ship's affairs so as to make himself indispensable to a merchant or a mercantile partnership, since many merchants were also shipowners. He could then expect to buy part-ownership of a vessel: he might even be encouraged or helped to do so by the merchants in order to give him a stake in their enterprises. From there he could pick up shares in other

[4] G. D. Ramsay, *English Overseas Trade During the Centuries of Emergence* (London, 1957), p. 45.

[5] *The kings prophecie* (T. Creed for S. Waterson, 1603), *S.T.C.* 12678, reprinted in *The Collected Poems of Joseph Hall* (Liverpool, 1949), ed. Arnold Davenport, p. 117.

ships, until he might perhaps set up as a shipowner, going ashore to run his vessels from Thames-side or Bristol, and even build his own ships, qualify for state subsidies, take on government contracts, and die rich. Such a career seems to have been that of Peter Hill, mariner, of Rotherhithe.[6] Born in 1535, he evidently worked his way up to owning a fleet of merchant ships trading to Hamburg, Spain, and Newfoundland by the time he was in his fifties and became master of Trinity House, and so, in a sense, reached the peak of the seafaring profession in 1589. He could then afford to speculate by sponsoring walrus- and whale-fishing ventures in the St. Lawrence, get bounties for the ships he built at Rotherhithe, and contract to bring soldiers from the Low Countries to Ireland. He died at eighty, in 1615, the eldest brother of Trinity House, in his will founding a school for the children of poor sailors.

Or there was Christopher Newport of Limehouse, another Thames-side sailor.[7] K. R. Andrews has traced him from his first appearance as a common seaman in 1581 to his death in 1617 as a shipowner and probably wealthy, but still at sea, in command of East India Company and Virginia Company squadrons, until the year of his death. Privateering ventures in the West Indies gave him, as it gave others, the chance of advancement. Master of a privateer in 1587, he became captain of the *Little John* in 1590. Though he lost an arm in a fight with the Spaniards, he did well enough to go out in command of a squadron of four privateers on cruise in 1592. This made his fortune, and from then he scarcely looked back, investing in shipping from 1596 onward and taking a rich haul of silver from the town of Tabasco in Mexico in 1599. In 1605 he presented James I with a gift of crocodiles, and in 1607 was chosen to transport the first English colonists to found Jamestown and Virginia. His last ten years at sea saw him win much distinction in western and eastern seas alike; he was not prepared to stay ashore to spend his profits.

William Borough is yet another example.[8] Sailing before the mast on Richard Chancellor's epoch-making voyage to Russia in 1553, he taught himself everything he could about navigation and chartmaking, rising

[6] On Peter Hill, or Hills, see also pp. 330 *n.*, 331–2, 324–6, and 329 below.

[7] D. B. Quinn, "Christopher Newport in 1590," *North Carolina Historical Review*, XXIV (1953), 305–16; K. R. Andrews, "Christopher Newport of Limehouse, Mariner," *William and Mary Quarterly*, 3d ser., XI (1954), 28–41; Andrews, *English Privateering Voyages, passim.*

[8] *D.N.B.;* Waters, *Art of Navigation, passim;* E. G. R. Taylor, *The Haven-Finding Art* (London, 1956), pp. 196, 204–6; Taylor, "Instructions to a Colonial Surveyor in 1582," *Mariner's Mirror*, XXXVII (1951), 48–62; Taylor, with M. W. Richey, *The Geometrical Seaman* (London, 1962); A. H. W. Robinson, *Marine Cartography in Britain* (Leicester, 1962), pp. 29–31.

rapidly to be master, captain, and finally a chief pilot of the Muscovy Company in the 1570's. He had a clear scientific mind, as is shown in his writings, and turned his attention fruitfully to problems of educating pilots, the assessment of compass variation, and the building up of the navy. He transferred to the royal service as Clerk of the Ships in 1582, and in that and other offices had, with Hawkins, much to do with improving naval administration between then and his death in 1599.

A significant problem in Elizabethan England was to adapt the traditional training and lore of the seaman to new responsibilities and techniques. Ocean sailing required quite different handling from coastwise and short-haul navigation. English seamen were slow to adapt themselves to new circumstances. "English masters and pilots," E. G. R. Taylor has written, "remained of the old-fashioned sort. . . . That is not to deny that the Englishman was a good sailor, he was. But his ideal of a good sailor was a good coaster, a man who knew the tides, the landmarks, the shoals, currents and 'dangers,' who could box the compass, tell the time by sun and star, and take his ship into every harbour by soundings of depth and 'ground.' Such a seaman had a deep distrust of instrumental navigation, clinging obstinately to 'the old ancient rules,' which had become quite insufficient once ocean enterprise was seriously engaged on."[9] The story of how techniques of navigation developed, through the reorganization of Trinity House at Deptford (which was responsible for training in pilotage), the education of new-style masters in the navy, the translation of foreign navigation manuals, beginning with that of Martin Cortes in 1561, and the ultimate growth of a native navigation literature, has been told in detail by Lieutenant-Commander D. W. Waters.[1]

Dr. John Dee attempted to put Euclidean geometry at the service of the seamen, yet most navigation techniques remained dependent on Continental teaching until the 1580's. In the last twenty years of the sixteenth century Englishmen began to make valuable independent contributions to both the theory and the practice of navigation. Much attention was given to the problem of the variation of the compass and its dip (the latter being first established by Robert Norman in 1580).[2] The theoretical work of Borough, Norman, and William Bourne was greatly facilitated by the combination of good sea charts and improved tables from Dutch

[9] "Instructions to a Surveyor," p. 49.

[1] *The Rutters of the Sea* (New Haven, 1968) and *Art of Navigation;* see also Taylor, *Haven-Finding Art*.

[2] See his *The new attractive* (J. Kyngston for R. Ballard, 1581), *S.T.C.* 18674; and W. Borough, *A discourse of the variation of the cumpas* (J. Kyngston for R. Ballard, 1587), *S.T.C.* 3389.

sources in *The mariners mirrour* (1588).[3] Thomas Harriot has left us much information on how he taught Sir Walter Ralegh's pilots to work out problems of compass variation and the estimate of latitude by Pole Star and sun, using new, refined methods which reduced errors to a minimum. He did not, unfortunately, publish them.[4] Both he and Edward Wright worked on the problem of the construction of a sea chart which would record direction correctly on a plane surface. Mercator's map in 1569 provided an empirical solution of the problem by showing how the necessary distortions of latitude and longitude could be related to one another. Wright, in his *Certaine errors in navigation* (1599)[5] showed how the practical seaman could, using a chart on the Mercator-Wright projection, construct a nautical triangle which showed latitude and longitude, direction, and course correctly.[6]

The famous map of 1599 ("the new map with the augmentation of the Indies," *Twelfth Night*, III, ii, 85–6), added to the second edition of Richard Hakluyt's *Principal navigations*,[7] was a demonstration of the new seaman's view of the world. Already Wright, with Emery Molyneux, had produced an improved view of the earth in the round in the globe published in 1592, of which the sole surviving specimen is in Lord Egremont's possession at Petworth, while the second edition is represented by the globe in the Middle Temple (1603). Robert Hues, who had sailed the world round with Cavendish, in his *Tractatus de globis* (1594)[8] expounded how the globes were constructed. Globe and book alike were honored by being adopted on the Continent.[9] William Gilbert, also, was stimulated to experiment on magnetism by the issues raised by the practical navigators. His *De magnete* (1600) is mainly a discussion of his thesis that the earth is a magnet and that planetary motions can be explained by magnetism, but it is also concerned with practical navigation problems of

[3] L. J. Wagenaer, *The mariners mirrour*, trans. A. Ashley (J. Charlewood, 1588), *S.T.C.* 24931.

[4] See "The Doctrine of Nautical Triangles Compendious," I, E. G. R. Taylor, "Thomas Hariot's Manuscript," II, D. H. Sadler, "Calculating the Meridional Parts"—all in *Journal of the Institute of Navigation*, VI (1953), 131–47; Taylor, *Haven-Finding Art*, pp. 184, 218–25.

[5] V. Sims; *S.T.C.* 26019–26019*a*.

[6] See also Taylor, *Haven-Finding Art*, pp. 223–7, and Waters, *Art of Navigation*, pp. 219–29.

[7] Vol. II (G. Bishop, R. Newberie, and R. Barker, 1599), *S.T.C.* 12626.

[8] T. Dawson; *S.T.C.* 13906.

[9] See Helen M. Wallis, "The First English Globe," *Geographical Journal*, CXVII (1951), 275–90; Wallis, "Further Light on the Molyneux Globes," *Geographical Journal*, CXXI (1955), 304–11; Wallis, "Globes in England up to 1660," *Geographical Magazine*, XXXV (September 1962), 267–79.

magnetic declination and dip.[1] By 1603 the up-to-date navigator had to know a little trigonometry in order to employ the detailed and reliable tables which were then available. He was still incapable of establishing his longitude at sea by instrumental means, so that the errors of dead reckoning still held him back from knowing his precise position, but with his "true" chart and effective instruments and tables for finding latitude, the Jacobean sailor was well enough equipped for world-wide voyaging.

The captain of a ship of war, whether one of the queen's ships or a privateer, was more often than not a soldier, not a sailor. He was chosen to lead men, not ships, so that in sea campaigns and privateering, seamanship was the business of the master and his mate—fighting that of the captain. But masters, as we have seen, could become captains, and soldiers turned captains could become expert at sea, too, some being willing to learn navigation and chartmaking in order to have more effective direction of their ships, especially on long voyages of exploration. Drake was an expert seaman; Hawkins never lost his skill at sea for all his many years in a government office. Ralegh felt so strongly about the matter that he put himself to school under Thomas Harriot and sent his captains and masters to pick up the new science from him also. Even the wild, unstable Cavendish became a competent cartographer. On the other hand, some sea adventurers appear to have known and cared little about how their ships were sailed. Martin Frobisher was probably, for all his experience, a poor navigator.[2] Even on Drake's West Indian expedition in 1586 it was possible, through errors in navigation and disregard of the cumulative effect of compass variation, for the fleet to set out from Cartagena for Havana and end up at Cartagena again sixteen days later.[3]

At the other end of the scale, impressment brought into the navy many useless landsmen. Ralegh was to complain in James's reign, "For many of these poor Fishermen and Idlers, that are commonly presented to his Majesty's Ships are so ignorant in Sea-service as that they know not the

[1] *G. Gilberti de magnete* (P. Short, 1600), *S.T.C.* 11883; English trans. by P. F. Mottelay (New York, 1893). A useful short account of *De Magnete* is in G. Sarton, *Six Wings* (London, 1957), pp. 94–8.

[2] For Drake see H. R. Wagner, *Drake's Voyage Round the World* (San Francisco, 1926); K. R. Andrews, *Drake's Voyages* (London, 1967); H. P. Kraus, *Sir Francis Drake: A Pictorial Biography* (Amsterdam, 1970). For Hawkins see J. A. Williamson, *Sir John Hawkins* (Oxford, 1927) and *Hawkins of Plymouth* (London, 1949); Michael Lewis, *The Hawkins Dynasty* (London, 1970). For Frobisher see V. Stefansson, ed., *The Three Voyages of Martin Frobisher*, 2 vols. (London, 1938); for Cumberland see G. C. Williamson, *George, Third Earl of Cumberland* (Cambridge, Eng., 1920).

[3] Waters, *Art of Navigation*, p. 162.

Name of a Rope and [are] therefor insufficient for such Labour."[4] Privateering, with its high profits for sailors paid by shares from the richer prizes, attracted landsmen too, some of them men of good education, others of poor character. Some scarcely adapted themselves to a sailor's life. Most privateersmen had a reputation for rough, piratical behavior. Discipline was poor; the men were frequently drunk, especially after taking a prize, and liable to fight each other brutally over the pillage they were allowed to pick up. Masters and captains frequently quarrelled and sometimes fought; K. R. Andrews has given many instances.[5] Thus Captain Barnestrawe, a Dutchman, of the *Tiger* of London "was not regarded by the Englishe men but greatlye reviled and called copernose and . . . he was fitter to drincke ale than to be a Captaine." On one of the queen's ships such conduct would have been punished very severely.

It is possible, just, to get a picture of what the Elizabethan seaman looked like: it is also possible to get an impression of the smell of "a tipe of Thames-street stinking of Pitch and Poor-John."[6] The London Museum has a seaman among its models whose blouse and breeches turned up in an old collection of theatrical costumes, quite probably the original tar-stained garments of a sailor, run up by a sailmaker at sea before 1600.[7] That this was a common way for seamen to get their clothes is shown by the case against Alain Moine (mentioned earlier), who on the 1536 voyage to Newfoundland cut up new sail-canvas to make a jerkin and a pair of slops for a seaman.[8] The model has a knitted coif with hanging ear-flaps, a knitted and felted Tudor bonnet worn above it, and a piece of knitted material worn like a scarf, all Tudor, but not specifically seamanlike, though close to those worn by seamen shown in engravings of the time. Thomas Churchyard, in "A Pirates Tragedie" has left us a verse which fits well enough with this picture:

With horie beard and scorched face,
With poudred hede, and heare unshorne,

[4] *Works* (1751), ed. Birch, II, 104.

[5] Andrews, *English Privateering Voyages*, pp. 22–8.

[6] F. Beaumont and J. Fletcher, *The Scornful Lady*, in *Works* (Cambridge, Eng., 1905), ed. Arnold Glover, I, 255. Compare: Trinculo: ". . . A fish: he smells like a fish; a very ancient and fish-like smell; a kind of not of the newest Poor-John." (*The Tempest*, Act II, Scene 2, ll. 26–8.)

[7] Mr. Martin R. Holmes, formerly of the London Museum, personal communication. See G. E. Manwaring, "The Dress of the British Seamen," *Mariner's Mirror*, VIII (1922), 324–33; IX (1923), 162–73, 322–32.

[8] This occurs in a case relating to the voyage of the *William* to Newfoundland in 1536 (P.R.O., H.C.A. 13/2, fols. 51–153v). See p. 187 above.

With hackes and hewes, in every place,
He seemed like, a man forlorne. . . .

A Sea mans cappe, on hedde he ware,
A slidyng sloppe of Friers graie:
A checker Kaep, both thinne and bare,
To furnish up, his quaint araie.

A cables end, his girdle made,
His shirt besmerde, with Pitch and Tarre:
Close by his side, a rustie blade,
This carle in youth, a man of warre.

A Pilotes compass, he did holde,
To showe what science he profest.
The skill whereof, had made him bolde,
To saile the seas, both East and West.[9]

This casual figure did not differ much in appearance from the men of the queen's ships. Admiralty contractors had concessions to sell clothes to these seamen, and this must have produced some degree of uniformity in dress. But there was no uniform except for those few men whom it pleased the captains to deck out in the queen's liveries, or their own.

At sea the sailors sang and played instruments, listened and danced to them. Sir Richard Grenville could serve a banquet to the Spanish officials in Hispaniola in 1585 "with the sound of trumpets, and consort of musick,"[1] while Luke Warde tells of a similar celebration in Brazil, with Fenton "in his Pinnesse with his musike, and trumpets, and I in my skiffe with trumpets, drum and fife, and tabor, and pipe, accompanied them."[2] Though primarily for the disciplining and encouragement of the men in battle and for entertaining the captain and his associates at meals, the consort of music (or ship's band) brought a taste of relaxation to the men on long voyages which was very valuable for morale.

How far were the seamen literate? It is surprising, perhaps, how many of the thousands of witnesses in sixteenth-century cases in the High Court of Admiralty, the great majority of them common seamen, could and did sign their names rather than make a mark. This does not prove much, but it is probable that among the privateersmen at least, though not necessarily

[9] Thomas Churchyard, *A generall rehearsall of warres, wherein is five hundred severall serrices of land and sea* (E. White, 1579), sig. 2B4^r; *S.T.C.* 5235. "A gables end" has been corrected to "A cables end."

[1] Hakluyt, *Principall navigations* (1589), p. 735; Hakluyt, *Principal Navigations,* 12 vols. (Glasgow, 1903–5), VII, 314.

[2] *Ibid.,* p. 666 (and XI [1904], 191–2).

among those engaged in the coastal trade, the level of literacy and intellectual capacity was moderately high, so affecting the records of sea travel they have left us. The master of a merchantman was expected to keep a log of his position by dead reckoning, checked for latitude and position by celestial observation, with some written indication of weather and a note, very much at his discretion, of "occurrences." The latter might easily expand into some sort of journal of the voyage. The Muscovy Company seems to have insisted on a journal being kept, though this was not usually done by the captain or master, but by someone assigned to the task of recorder, such as the purser, cape merchant, or chaplain if there was one. Using the data in the ship's log as a basis, the official journal might be brief or discursive as the writer thought fit or had time.[3] He might even have so much time on his hands that he kept a private diary as well as his official narrative. And of course, on an exploring voyage a few other unofficial journals were always likely to be kept as well. On a short merchant voyage the log was only a document to record for the owners or charterers the actual performance of the ship. When the expedition's object was exploration or the exploitation of a new and distant branch of commerce, the detailed journals were of great importance as primary records of what occurred and was observed. These journals became in turn the basis of published accounts of completed voyages. But this development of the record and its exploitation in print came late in England.

II

DESCRIPTIVE PROSE NARRATIVE in the vernacular was already a feature of English writing long before the middle of the sixteenth century. Yet objective prose accounts by participants in maritime events are still very rare—or at least have not survived—for the period before 1550. This in spite of the fact that Englishmen had been journeying to the Mediterranean, to Iceland, and to the wilder waters of the western Atlantic long before that date. We have, for example, no single account of a voyage to Iceland in the fifteenth century, though hundreds were made. At least seventeen voyages into or across the North Atlantic were attempted or made between 1480 and 1509, but we have not a single narrative by a man who himself took part in one of them, with the sole exception of some rather imprecise remarks by Sebastian Cabot on his Northwest Passage venture. Our information is all secondhand or thirdhand, and here

[3] For an example printed as it was composed, see John Davis's "Traverse-Booke" for his 1587 voyage, in Hakluyt, *Principal Navigations,* VII (1904), 424–39.

we may compare the case of Columbus, for whose voyages between 1492 and 1504 we have extensive firsthand narratives, most of them by the navigator himself. There is no single reason for this lack. For one thing, no one thought it important to preserve such logs and journals as were compiled on these voyages. For another, they were not then thought worth putting in print. Readers of books in early Tudor England were scholars or persons looking for technical, often legal, information; or they read for edification—not in general for details of recent happenings. The ballad, printed or oral, was a secondhand vehicle for such events, but sea voyages seldom seem to have been featured even in ballads at this period.

A change takes place, somewhat slowly, from about 1550 onward. Perhaps this is mainly because English overseas maritime activities became more spectacular and widespread. They grew worthy of the attention even of the learned world. There is a thin trickle of narrative about overseas voyages of the sixteenth century from the time Richard Eden in 1555 included with his translation of Peter Martyr's *Decades* accounts of the first two Guinea expeditions of the 1550's.[4] Other expeditions now tended to be celebrated in ephemeral ballads, very many of which have been lost. It took some time, certainly, to find an acceptable vehicle for the voyage narrative. When Richard Chancellor wrote an account of his voyage to Russia in 1553, Clement Adams turned it into Latin and published it in 1555.[5] Robert Baker, however, threw his story of the Guinea voyage of 1562–3 directly into English verse, afterward carrying on with this method for his journeys elsewhere.[6] John Hawkins, on the other hand, set down a plain prose narrative in English of what had happened to him on his fateful third voyage to the Caribbean,[7] and this became the more usual pattern for the period.

George Turberville was one of the few Elizabethan poets to spend some time overseas. He was evidently much affected by his experiences, which he retailed in a series of verse epistles and other poems to his friends, many of them about the sea; but they were not published until they ap-

[4] Peter Martyr Anglerius, *The decades of the newe world or West India*, trans. R. Eden, 1555; *S.T.C.* 645–8, various imprints.

[5] No copy of this edition seems to have survived. Hakluyt reprinted it in *Principall navigations* (1589), pp. 270–9.

[6] Hakluyt reprinted the Guinea verses in *Principall navigations* (1589), pp. 130–42. For a collection, probably published though without a copy surviving, see Edward Arber, ed., *Transcript of the Stationers' Register, 1554–1640* (London, 1875), I, 363.

[7] *A true declaration of the troublesome voyage of M. J. Haukins* (T. Purfoote for L. Harrison, 1569), *S.T.C.* 12961.

peared, appended to his *Tragical talks*, in 1587.[8] Already in his *Epitaphes* (1570), probably written before he went to Russia, he has several sea verses.[9] The Frobisher voyages called out a number of published narratives: that of Dionyse Settle was not, he told his readers, that of a seaman;[1] but George Best's was, and it was literate, almost prolix at times.[2] Thomas Ellis, too, wrote a narrative of the third voyage (1578), *A true report of the third and last voyage into Meta Incognita*,[3] and apologized in would-be flowery language for being a mere sailor: "I being a Sailer, more studied and used in my Charde and Compasse, and other thinges belonging to Navigation, than trayned up in *Minervas* Court, or taught by the sage Philosophers the fathers of eloquence, whose sweets and sacred sappe I never sucked. But yet, because I knowe, that the best part of men, will weigh my good will, rather then finde fault with my simple skill." How genuine this ingenuousness was does not appear, but he too tells a plain tale well enough.

Much less plain was that told by David Ingram in the autumn of 1582 to Sir Francis Walsingham and other worthies and then published in 1583.[4] One of Hawkins's men left on shore in 1568, he claimed to have walked with two others (conveniently dead when he gave his story) from the Gulf of Mexico to Cape Breton, from which he was rescued by a French ship in 1569. The elephants and red sheep and other unusual features of North America are, one feels, the end product of a long run of tavern tales where the original story has been eventually overlaid by the "truth" of fiction. There is no doubt that he believed his own story and was prepared to go with Sir Humphrey Gilbert in 1583 almost to Cape Breton to prove it. Thomas Churchyard managed to celebrate in verse and prose in 1578 the expeditions of both Sir Humphrey Gilbert and Sir Martin Frobisher without leaving English shores himself,[5] though

[8] A. Jeffs; *S.T.C.* 24330. [9] Newly corrected. H. Denham; *S.T.C.* 24327.

[1] *A true reporte of the laste voyage by Capteine Frobisher* (H. Middleton, 1577), *S.T.C.* 22265–6.

[2] *A true discourse of the late voyages of discoverie* (H. Bynneman, 1578), S.T.C. 1972.

[3] T. Dawson; *S.T.C.* 7607, Huntington Library only.

[4] Printed by Hakluyt in *Principall navigations* (1589), pp. 557–62, though no copy is known to survive. For evidence of its publication see W. A. Jackson, "Humphrey Dyson's Library," American Bibliographical Society *Papers*, XLIII (1949), 285.

[5] He tried his hand at the description of a storm in the Gilbert tract *A discourse of the Queenes majesties entertainement in Suffolk and Norfolk . . . whereunto is adioyned a commendation of Sir Humfrey Gilberts ventrous journey* (H. Bynneman, 1578), *S.T.C.* 5226. In *A prayse, and reporte of Maister M. Forboishers voyage to Meta Incognita* (J. Kingston for A. Maunsell, 1578), *S.T.C.* 5251, he put

this led it to be rumored facetiously that he was going to sea in the Virginia voyage of 1585.[6] Job Hortop, whose "voyage," with various imprisonments interspersed, lasted from 1568 to 1590,[7] did much better as a seaman author in 1591 than Ingram had done, making a plain tale exciting and conveying his own courage and resourcefulness without boasting. Arthur Barlowe was a soldier before he became a sea captain in 1584, but his narrative of the 1584 reconnaissance voyage up the American coast is a polished one,[8] though perhaps the polish was applied by Ralegh, who seems to have circulated it in manuscript to would-be subscribers to the 1585 Virginia voyage.

Other sailors' narratives that got into print were taken down by non-seamen from the lips of seamen who could tell but not write them. Indeed there is a tendency in later Elizabethan years for the overseas narratives to be written by men who are not primarily sailors. *A summarie and true discourse of Sir Frances Drakes West Indian voyage* (1589),[9] on Drake's 1585–6 expedition, was by at least three hands, none of them seamen's; the account of the last fight of the *Revenge* by Ralegh, no ordinary seaman; the Guiana voyages written up by him or by Lawrence Keymis, sea-captain, but again no common seaman.[1] It was Richard Hakluyt, however, who in the first edition of *The principall navigations, voiages and discoveries of the English nation* in 1589 spread out a feast of sea narration.[2] Every type of sea and land journal, with much of the

in a word for the common mariner, the chief sufferer in difficult voyages, who was liable to be forgotten in tales about his commanders. He attempted a general record of English land and sea exploits in *Generall rehearsall of warres, wherein is five hundred severall services of land and sea* (E. White, 1579), *S.T.C.* 5235.

[6] F. P. Wilson, "An Ironicall Letter," *Modern Language Review*, XV (1920), 79–80. See Jack Roberts to Roger Williams, December 1584, Bodleian Library, TannerMS 169, fols. 69v–70.

[7] *The travailes of an Englishman* (T. Scarlet for W. Wright, 1591), *S.T.C.* 13828.

[8] Printed by Richard Hakluyt in *Principall navigations* (1589); see Quinn, *Roanoke Voyages*, I, 11, 15–17, 91–116.

[9] By Walter Bigges and others; *S.T.C.* 3056–7. For the sequence of the published editions see Quinn, *Roanoke Voyages*, I, 294. N. Breton, *A discourse in commendation of the valiant . . . Maister Frauncis Drake, with a reioysing of his happy adventures* (J. Charlewood, 1581), has little of narrative value on the voyage around the world. See Kraus, *Drake*, pp. 82, 197.

[1] Ralegh, *A report of the truth of the fight about the iles of Acores* (for W. Ponsonbie, 1591), *S.T.C.* 20651; Ralegh, *The discoverie of the large rich, and bewtifull empire of Guiana* (R. Robinson, 1596), *S.T.C.* 20634; Keymis, *A relation of the second voyage to Guiana* (T. Dawson, 1596), *S.T.C.* 14947.

[2] G. Bishop and R. Newberie, deputies to C. Barker; *S.T.C.* 12625. Facsimile, with an introduction by D. B. Quinn and R. A. Skelton, Hakluyt Society, extra ser. 39, 2 vols. (Cambridge, Eng., 1965).

correspondence associated with the voyages, appears for the Muscovy Company expeditions from 1553 to 1588. Drake is there, and Cavendish, Hawkins, Frobisher, Gilbert, and much besides on the Levant and Guinea ventures. The nautical element in the narratives varies greatly, but a great deal was written by the sailors themselves. Some of the finest northern voyage journals—Christopher Hall for the 1576 Frobisher voyage, Hugh Smith and Nicholas Chancellor for the Northeast Passage voyage of 1580—give extended and vivid impressions of the rigors and monotonies of northern sailing, in contrast with Luke Ward's account of the leisurely cruise in tropical waters of Edward Fenton's expedition.

Those mentioned, too, were never to appear again in print unpruned. An encyclopedia of the sea and distant lands, written for the most part by travelers, many of them sailors, was from 1590 onward at the disposal of all those interested in overseas matters or in seafaring. In the decade between the preparation of the first and the appearance of the second edition of *The principal navigations,*[3] which in three smaller volumes more than doubled the material made available, Hakluyt was able to add much that was notable: "The booke of the great and mighty Emperor of Russia" by Richard Chancellor; Andrew Barker's narrative (1576), Pretty's account of Cavendish's circumnavigation, reprints of Best and Bigges, and of course much excellent material for the 1590's, a good deal of it reprinted. Moreover, nearly a fifth of the bulk was made up of "foreign voyages," narratives of non-English explorers included to cover areas hitherto inadequately touched upon by Englishmen.

Hakluyt's "voyages" are often spoken of as if he had written them all himself. This is probably the greatest flattery an editor can receive. But Hakluyt went on no voyages that we know of. Yet he took immense trouble in assembling the narratives in his collections, and gains his outstanding success from the juxtaposition of so many accounts by the same sorts of people on the same sort of field, however various the areas and circumstances they cover. The result is that we hear the seaman, the captain, and the scholarly observer sent on some expeditions report directly on their experiences in strange places. The first, immediate impression had, in his eyes, much more interest—usually more value—than the considered and generalized impression of men who had gone over a particular course many times and had got used to it and absorbed its atmosphere into themselves, taking much indeed for granted. Between the two editions of his great voyage collection we can see him gradually setting standards for his narrators. They should not be allowed to spend

[3] G. Bishop, R. Newberie, and R. Barker, 1598–1600; *S.T.C.* 12626.

too much time on the day-to-day progress of the ship through monotonous seas; nor, when the vessel was in contact with distant shores, should they record only the dull incidents of depths and anchorages, weather and suchlike. They should describe the people of the strange country in as much detail as possible and make comments on the fitness of the place for trade or settlement, the nature of its shoreline and its topography. He did not expect assessments of scenery, though he appreciated some indication of the impressions it made.

In 1589 we find him setting forth almost all that was contained in the narratives. By 1600 he has formed his standards and given himself considerable license to copy-edit his material, cutting the duller passages or those that were repetitive, highlighting those in which he was interested—what he regarded as the essentials and novelties of a situation, not its commonplaces. There is thus some justification for looking upon the narratives as Hakluyt's, since they were what he made them. But he was a very good subeditor; he trimmed to tighten the effect of the narratives, not to emasculate them. He had a great respect for what was actually said by the men who had seen the sights they recorded, and so far as we can make out did not rewrite so much as pare down and select. Thus many of the pieces as we have them are the result of a conscious editorial policy.

There was loss as well as gain in Hakluyt's editorial methods. For the historian the lengthy monotony of ocean sailing and the cumulation of small navigational "occurrences" are important, even essential, parts of the reconstruction of life at sea at this time. The curtailing of such detail as between the two editions of the voyage collection did reduce their value purely as documents on maritime history. On the other hand, to prune and reemphasize was usually to make them more attractive to the nonexpert reader and to make the ensemble more appealing in its revelation of the world to English seamen. There is indeed in the narratives a certain uniformity of style and texture which is not only the result of their being shaped by Hakluyt. They have a basic similarity of aim. Events are recorded with immediacy. The logic of the time framework; the stress on objective reporting which derived from the logging of occurrences; the impact of fresh sights and peoples on men with rather similar backgrounds—these common elements give an impression of uniformity, or at least of congruence. Yet the writers emerge as individuals also; the personality of many of the authors, their likes and dislikes, their special interests, come through with greater or less clarity through the necessary reticence of the medium. The prose is simple and Hakluyt does little to make it more complex; it is relatively unlatinized, even though many of the writers were men of some education; there is little room for courtly or scholarly sophistication. The result is to give us an extensive anthology, well prepared and presented, of a particular category of Elizabethan prose: the narrative of direct observation, which carries its own simple distinction, the educated eye bringing its impressions immediately in words to the reader, stimulating vividly and expressively his own awareness of the world of the Elizabethan seaman and explorer.[4]

By 1600, then, there was an extensive library of the sea. Thereafter the contribution of the seaman himself to English overseas sea-narratives survived in, for example, the first East India Company pamphlets, *A true and large discourse of the voyage . . . set forth the 28 of April 1601* (1603) and *A letter . . . to the . . . East Indian merchants in London* (1603), and in *The last East-Indian voyage.*[5] But James Rosier's account of Waymouth's American voyage in 1605, *A true relation of the most prosperous voyage . . . in the discovery of Virginia* (1605),[6] if close to the log, is not a seaman's narrative, nor are John Smith's *A true relation of such occurrences as hath hapned in Virginia* (1608) and *A map of Virginia* (1612),[7] though both have a soldierly directness. John Nicholl, *An houre glasse of Indian newes* (1607), on a Guiana voyage,[8] and Silvester Jourdan, *A discovery of the Bermudas* (1610),[9] have a nautical touch—and are probable *Tempest* sources.[1] It seems to be generally agreed that Shakespeare had seen, before he wrote *The Tempest,* a manuscript copy of William Strachey's "A true reportory of the wracke, and redemption of Sir Thomas Gates Knight; upon, and from the Ilands of the Bermudas,"

[4] Modern estimates of Hakluyt include those in George B. Parks, *Richard Hakluyt and the English Voyages* (New York, 1928, 1962); E. G. R. Taylor, *Late Tudor and Early Stuart Geography* (London, 1934); Taylor, ed., *The Original Writings and Correspondence of the Two Richard Hakluyts,* Hakluyt Society, 2d ser., nos. 76–7, 2 vols. (1935); Richard Hakluyt, *Principall navigations (1589),* I (1965), ix–lii; Quinn, *Richard Hakluyt Editor,* 2 vols. (Amsterdam, 1967), I.

[5] Imprinted for T. Thorpe, sold by W. Aspley (the first two, *S.T.C.* 7459, 7448); T. P[urfoot] for W. Burre, *S.T.C.* 7456.

[6] Impensis Geo. Bishop; *S.T.C.* 21322.

[7] Imprinted for J. Tappe, sold by W. W[elby], *S.T.C.* 22795. Oxford, J. Barnes; *S.T.C.* 22791.

[8] [E. Allde] for N. Butter; *S.T.C.* 18532.

[9] J. Windet, sold by R. Barnes; *S.T.C.* 14816.

[1] There is a large literature on the sources of *The Tempest.* R. R. Cawley, "Shakspere's Use of the Voyages in *The Tempest,*" *Proceedings of the Modern Language Association* (*P.M.L.A.*), XLI (1926), 688–726, is probably still the best study. See also G. L. Kittredge, ed., *The Tempest* (Boston, 1939); Frank Kermode, ed., *The Tempest* (London, The Arden Shakespeare, 1954); D. G. James, *The Dream of Prospero* (Oxford, 1967).

unprinted until 1625. This was written in the summer of 1610 and brought to England in the autumn.[2] With it Shakespeare may have seen two Virginia Company pamphlets, *A true and sincere declaration of the purpose of the plantation begun in Virginia* (1610) and *A true declaration of the estate of the colonie in Virginia* (1610).[3] Robert Harcourt's *A relation of a voyage to Guiana* (1613) is mainly a record of land travel,[4] as indeed are the major Jacobean travel books by William Lithgow, George Sandys, and Fynes Moryson. And if Samuel Purchas indicated in successive editions of his *Pilgrimage* (1613, 1614, 1617)[5] that he had many sailors' narratives in his hands and may thus have opened them to judicious or persistent inquirers, it was not until 1625 that he released in his *Pilgrimes* a whole new fleet of sea narratives. By then Shakespeare was dead, and the Elizabethan sea tradition was becoming a part of history, not of life.

The sailor's image in the popular mind passed through several stages in the Elizabethan and Jacobean periods. For the most part, he was regarded simply as the conveyor of goods and passengers, little more animate than his ship. As a frequenter of taverns he was known as a man with time on his hands, between voyages, in which to flaunt his trophies (if his voyages were the sort from which parrots or silks derived) and his tales (long-winded and exaggerated no doubt, if also exciting and disturbing). He was also the smelly, independent, drunken, loud-singing, and quarrelsome individual encountered near the quays and in and out of drinking places and brothels. From time to time the ventures he had taken part in would strike the imagination of the individual or the crowd, leading to ballads or poems, or even popular enthusiasm for his kind of exploit, and so by transference for his manner of life. But it is doubtful if this happened at all until Drake's return from his world-circling voyage in 1580. It is likely to have become general in 1585, three years before the Armada. In that year the seafaring man came into his own, or at least into all the headlines. The London ship *Primrose* escaped from the hands of Spanish officials when an embargo was clamped down suddenly in Spain on English shipping, and soon Humphrey Mote had written up and published *The Primrose of London with her valiant adventure on the Spanish coast*[6]—inaugurating, with the government action at the time the pamphlet appeared, nearly twenty years of unremitting sea-warfare against Spain. The letters of reprisal issued by the Privy Council released several

[2] Samuel Purchas, *Hakluytus Posthumus, or Purchas his pilgrimes,* IV, 1735–57 (*S.T.C.* 20509); (Glasgow, 1906), XIX, 5–72.

[3] Imprinted for J. Stepneth; *S.T.C.* 24832. Imprinted for W. Barret; *S.T.C.* 24833.

[4] J. Beale for W. Welby; *S.T.C.* 12754.

[5] *S.T.C.* 20505–7.

[6] Imprinted for T. Nelson; *S.T.C.* 18211.

hundred privateers to recover the value, and more, of ships and goods impounded in Spain.

The rash of privateers which now spread out over western European waters—almost all of them converted merchantmen—gave a new prestige, a national one, to the sailor and a new interest to the sea itself. The privateersman too became a more colorful figure for a material reason: if he now appeared in tavern or brothel it was, likely as not, with some pillage, silver, jewelry, fine clothes, or ornaments to peddle or give away as gifts. The favorable popular image of the sailor was enhanced and magnified as the queen's ships came into action, first against Cadiz in 1587 and later in the Armada campaign. But the privateering seaman found his chronicler in Henry Roberts, the journalist in whom Louis B. Wright says "the spirit of the seagoing commoner, of the Elizabethan citizen adventurer, speaks at first hand."[7] The first prose tract of his to survive is probably the anonymous *The seamans triumph*[8]—though the ascription to him is by no means certain—a gloating tribute to the men who took the great carrack, *Madre de Dios*, in 1592. His hastily written and carelessly printed report of another capture of the same year was the fruit, it appears, of a casual visit to Clovelly. In *Our Ladys retorne to England, accompanied with saint Frances and the good Jesus of Viana*,[9] the religious names of the ships lent a blasphemous jibe to the title. He celebrated the Mediterranean voyages of Edward Glenham in *The honorable actions of Edward Glemham* [*sic*] and *News from the Levane seas*,[1] even if these expeditions involved piracy against Venetian shipping as well as legitimate prize-taking from Spaniards. Next he turned to narrate and extol James Lancaster's experiences in Brazil, in *Lancaster his allarmes*.[2] The series of pamphlets, with their racy titles, helped to build up the privateering sailor and his commanders as popular figures.

[7] Wright, *Middle Class Culture in Elizabethan England* (Chapel Hill, 1935; Ithaca, 1958), pp. 517–18. Roberts's first surviving effort was the verse *A most friendly farewell . . . to . . . Sir Francis Drake* (N. Mantel and T. Lawe, 1585), *S.T.C.* 21084; his verses on Cavendish's return, 1588, are not known to be extant (Wright, p. 517).

[8] R. B[lore] for W. Barley, 1592; *S.T.C.* 22140.

[9] A. J. for W. Barley. Not in *S.T.C.;* in Huntington Library only. Reprinted in Andrews, *Elizabethan Privateering*, pp. 150–5.

[1] A. J[effes] for W. Barley, 1591; *S.T.C.* 11921. Printed for William Wright, 1594 (*S.T.C.* 20572), the latter attempting to justify Glenham's actions. They had already been denounced as piratical by the privy council (*Acts of the Privy Council, 1592* [A.P.C.] [London, 1901], p. 180). See Wright, *Middle Class Culture*, p. 518, *n.* 1.

[2] A. J[effes] for W. Barley, 1595; *S.T.C.* 21083.

Newes out of the coast of Spaine (1587), by Henry Haslop,[3] is the first of the popular news-pamphlets to help establish the image of the queen's ships and their personnel, although armed merchantmen also took part. The Cadiz action it celebrated was a mere curtain-raiser to the Armada campaign. The Armada brought out not only such morale-builders as Anthony Marten's *An exhortation, to stirre up the mindes of all her majesties faithfull subjects to defend their countrey*,[4] but also news reports of the effects of the campaign on the retiring Spanish fleet, like *Certaine advertisements out of Ireland* (1588),[5] and polemical tracts on the respective achievements of the fleets such as *A packe of Spanish lyes* and *The copie of a letter to Don Bernardin Mendoza*.[6] A detailed narrative had to wait until Petruccio Ubaldini's *A discourse concerninge the Spanish fleetes* appeared in 1590,[7] which however paid its due, if tardy, tribute to the seamen. The sailor could scarcely look back after this, and so for the Lisbon expedition of 1589 we have *A true coppie of a discourse written by a gentleman, employed in the late voyage of Spaine and Portingale* (1589).[8] The purely naval events of the 1590's, after the epic story of the *Revenge*, were not all favorable subjects for publicity. Henry Roberts's verse on the "outset" of the Drake expedition in 1595, *The trumpet of fame*,[9] could be followed only by Henry Savile's *A libell of Spanish lies* (1596), a defensive retort to Spanish claims on their great victory over Hawkins and Drake in 1595–6, which had revealed the weaknesses of the Elizabethan war fleet.[1] An official declaration of the

[3] W. How for H. Haslop, sold by E. White; *S.T.C.* 12926.

[4] J. Windet, 1588; *S.T.C.* 17489. He attacked dissension among captains: "For while one saith: I have beene longer in the warres. . . . An other: I have traveled furder upon the Sea, and have doone greater exploits. . . . What is this, but to teare in sunder the Common weale" (sig. D1r.). He exhorted men to care for the navy—"Looke to the amending and new buildinge of ships. Make them strong, light, and nimble for the battaile" (sig. D4r.).

[5] T. Vautrollier for R. Field; *S.T.C.* 14257. Two issues (B.M., G.6512/4 and G. 6512/2) followed closely on one another.

[6] *A packe* . . . (deputies of C. Barker, 1588), *S.T.C.* 23011; Richard Leight, *The copie* . . . (T. Vautrollier for R. Field, 1588), *S.T.C.* 15412–13. Medina Sidonia's instructions too were published as *Orders set down by the Duke of Medina* (T. Orwin for T. Gilbert, 1588), *S.T.C.* 19625.

[7] Trans. [R. Adams] (A. Hatfield, sold by H. Ryther, 1590), *S.T.C.* 24481.

[8] T. Woodcocke, *S.T.C.* 6790, to which can be added T. F., *The copie of a letter sent from sea by a gentleman who was employed in discoverie on the coast of Spaine* (R. Field, 1589), *S.T.C.* 10653, and *Ephemeris expeditionis Norreysii & Draki in Lusitaniam* (T. Woodcocke, 1589), *S.T.C.* 18653. See Kraus, *Drake*, pp. 160–1, 199–200.

[9] T. Creede, sold by W. Barley, 1595; *S.T.C.* 21088.

[1] J. Windet, *S.T.C.* 6551. A broadside, *In memoriam celeberrimi viri Domini Francisci Drake militis,* appeared in 1596 (copy in Library of the Society of

fleet's objectives prefaced the Cadiz action of 1596,[2] but the not unmixed result led to the suppression of all accounts, even the version published by Hakluyt in 1598 and afterward withdrawn.[3] A few small naval-privateering actions were celebrated between 1600 and 1602: *A true credible report of a great fight at sea between certain ships of England and five ships of warre of the king of Spaines* (1600);[4] the sailor Richard Mansell's *A true report of the service done upon certain gallies* (1601);[5] and the recently recovered account of Sir Thomas Shirley's Mediterranean action in 1601, *A true discourse, of the late voyage made by . . . Sir Thomas Sherley . . . on the coast of Spaine* (1602);[6] all of them keeping alive the reputation of the men of the queen's ships.

But the days of the sailor as hero were rapidly passing. Already in 1598, Henry IV of France and Queen Elizabeth tried to cut down the Channel sea war, and a proclamation on 8 February 1599 of peace at sea was the first move to end the chaotic state of affairs which existed in the English Channel.[7] The effect—only partial, it is true—was to turn the tide still further against piracy, as was shown by the proclamation of 20 March 1602 restricting the activities of privateers, especially in the Mediterranean.[8] The privateers, after the pirates proper, became a nuisance rather than a national asset, and a very early result of James I's accession was the annulment of all letters of marque against Spain on 23 June 1603.[9]

Antiquaries, London), as did Charles Fitz-Geffrey's *Sir Francis Drake his honorable lifes commendation* (Oxford, J. Barnes, 1596), *S.T.C.* 10943–4, reprinted in A. B. Grosart, *Poems* (1881).

[2] *A declaration of the causes moving the Queens Majestie to send a navy to the seas* (deputies of C. Barker, 1596), *S.T.C.* 9203; Latin, Dutch, French, Italian, and Spanish versions, *S.T.C.* 9204–8.

[3] Though an official account was prepared—J. S. Corbett, *Successors of Drake* (London, 1900), pp. 129, 439–40—its publication was withheld. Hakluyt's appeared in *Principal navigations*, 3 vols. (1598–1600), I, 607–19, and was announced on the title-page. On its suppression a cancel title-page was printed (C. E. Armstrong, "The 'Voyage to Cadiz' in the second edition of Hakluyt's 'Voyages,'" Bibliographical Society of America *Papers*, XLIX [1955], 254–62). An engraving of Lord Howard of Effingham appeared in 1596 with an inscription beginning *Si domitos Bello Hispanos, Gadiumque; ruinam* (reprinted in A. M. Hind, *Engraving in England*, I [Cambridge, Eng., 1952], pl. 150).

[4] E. A[llde] for W. Burre, 1600; *S.T.C.* 20891.

[5] F. Kyngston, sold by J. Newbery; *S.T.C.* 17259.

[6] Thomas Panyer; not in *S.T.C.* See R. A. Skelton, "An Elizabethan Naval Tract," *British Museum Quarterly*, XXXII (1960), 51–3, which has an account of the unique copy. It is printed in Andrews, *Elizabethan Privateering*, pp. 53–60.

[7] *S.T.C.* 8267; R. R. Steele, ed., *Tudor and Stuart Proclamations, 1485–1714*, 2 vols., I (Oxford, 1910), no. 200.

[8] *S.T.C.* 8290; Steele, *Tudor and Stuart Proclamations*, I, no. 925.

[9] *S.T.C.* 8321; Steele, *Tudor and Stuart Proclamations*, I, no. 956.

This marked the end of the long semiofficial sea war begun in 1585. It meant that all hostile English maritime activity in European waters was henceforth purely piratical, though it did not clarify the situation outside Europe in the same way. The positive side was the restoration of peaceful trade, signalized for example by *A proclamation or edict touching the opening of the trafficque of Spaine with these countries* (1603[–4]),[1] which meant a different, nondramatic role for the privateersman. The sailor was again, with few exceptions, only the common carrier of the sea.

If, in the years after 1604, the sailor did something new in non-European seas, he stood some chance of being celebrated in print, even when the emphasis in travel literature had shifted decisively to land travel. If he engaged in piracy in spite of all the proclamations against it, he might win mention in a newsletter or even a pamphlet, but if he returned openly to England he was quite likely to come to the gallows.

The seamen on royal ships too had a thin, uneasy time. The better and more vigorous of them drifted off into the merchant service. Nathaniel Butler, writing in 1634, is looking back over the past thirty years when he speaks of "that loathness or rather loathing which of late days hath so possessed this kind of people [the common mariner] against all service in his Majesty's ships and fleets."[2] The officers, officials, and naval suppliers all combined in graft, corruption, and neglect to leave the navy successively weaker as James I's reign went on. There was little for it to do; intermittent reports on the bad state of the navy in 1608 and 1618 did bring a little improvement (and the construction of a few fine ships), but this was not persisted in, and the decay continued. In these postwar years the prestige of sea service in the royal ships was at its lowest ebb. The Elizabethan navy-royal was out of date, out of fashion, and almost out of mind. Pride in the past and effective reshaping of the navy as a service had to await a new generation. The merchant fleet was, by contrast, active and growing in numbers and tonnage against stiff Dutch competition, and penetrating in some strength the routes pioneered by the Elizabethan seaman.

[1] W. White for T. Archer, *S.T.C.* 22998. Further proclamations, 1603–5 (*S.T.C.* 8334, 8363, 8369), attempted to deal with piracy and the reversion of mariners to civil employment.

[2] W. G. Perrin, ed., *Boteler's Dialogues*, N.R.S. (1929), p. 35.

CHAPTER EIGHT

Edward Hayes and the Americas

I

THE NAME OF Edward Hayes is frequently met with in the study of Elizabethan overseas enterprise, more especially in connection with attempts to colonize North America, but his life has remained obscure and his career unchronicled. Enough is now known about him so that one may attempt to place him in his setting. His part in the history of Elizabethan colonization was by no means insignificant.

Hayes came from a family which had built up a moderate holding of land in the manors around the borough of Liverpool. His grandfather, Richard Heye, described himself as a yeoman. In 1557 he turned over his lands in West Derby, Kirkdale, and Everton (Yearton) to his eldest surviving son Edward.[1] This Edward was born about 1530, and to him and his wife Alice, in turn, was born a large family, at least five boys and a girl. Richard was the eldest and John the youngest, with Ralph, Lawrence, and Edward somewhere in between. My own opinion is that he was probably the second son. His father is found selling land in the manors of West Derby and Kirkdale—largely to the powerful families of Moly-

[1] Lancashire County Record Office (Lancs.R.O.), Preston, Molyneux Muniments, DDM 52, no. 18 (see *Victoria County History of Lancashire*, III, 16, *n.* 1). Edward had already been admitted to land at Sandeland in the manor of West Derby, held at a yearly rent by his deceased brother Rauff Hay (Liverpool City Record Office (L.R.O.), Moore Deeds, no. 941, 2 November 1557).

neux and Moore—between 1559 and 1580,[2] but he kept a substantial foothold in West Derby and left his interest in it to his children, including our Edward.[3] The elder Edward had moved into Liverpool by 1567 and was apparently trading from there with Ireland and London.[4] In 1570 he became a burgess of Liverpool, and is thereafter usually referred to as Edward Heyes instead of Heye, and calls himself "Edward Heyes, of Liverpool, gentleman," as did his son after him.[5] He lived most of his life in Liverpool, dying only in 1602 and leaving most of what he then owned to another wife, Samewell Heyes.[6]

The younger Edward may well have gone to the grammar school in Liverpool. At that time an eldest son's inheritance was his father's land. A younger son's was largely based on what education his father could give him. Young Edward was clearly destined for the church or for one of the learned professions. In 1565 he was admitted to King's College, Cambridge, as a scholar commoner: [7] he would then have been about fifteen. His presence there does not seem to have been continuous, since he

[2] Twenty-two parcels of land and a messuage in Kirkdale transferred to John Moore of Bank House for £50 (Moore Deeds, nos. 745–7, 8 June 1559); transfer of seven acres, held at customary rent, to Robert Bolton of Thingwall (L.R.O., Hatfield MSS on deposit, Court Roll, West Derby, 5 December 1569; Edward Hay still appeared as a customary tenant of the manor in 1570 (*ibid.*, 10 July 1570); controversy with John Moore in 1570 on whether certain land in West Derby was held as tenant at will or by copy of court roll (Moore Deeds, nos. 943–4); feoffment by Edward Heye of Westdarbie gent., Alice his wife and Richard his son and heir, to John Molyneux of Croxsteth of "The Accres Fieldes" in West Derbie, part of a messuage called "le Town rowe," for £100 (Lancs.R.O., Molyneux Muniments, DDM 52, nos. 25–6, 6 April 1579, 9 July 1580).

[3] Feoffment to uses, Edward Heyes (signed "Edwarde Heyis") of Westdarbye, gent., to Rauf Standishe and Henrye Longworth of Westdarbye, gents., of capital messuage in Westdarbye for Edward Heyes for life, then to John his youngest son and heirs male and successively to his sons Richard, Rauf, Lawrence, Edward, and their heirs male and to Alice his daughter and her heirs male (Lancs.R.O., Molyneux Muniments, DDM 52, no. 22, 14 June 1577).

[4] P.R.O., S.P. 63/213, 2. Richard Peel to William Winter and Edward Baishe, from Liverpool. The passage is "I have wrety[n] a nother lett*er* vnto you by one that dylleth here/hes name es edward heyes w*hi*che letters I trost es Come to yo*ur* hande." The calendar (*Calendar of State Papers, Ireland, 1601–3, and Addenda, 1564–1654* [*Cal.S.P.,Ire.*], p. 586), gives "dealeth" for the "dylleth" of the letter but that appears less likely than "dwelleth."

[5] *Liverpool Town Books, 1550–1603*, 2 vols. (Liverpool, 1918–35), ed. J. A. Twemlow, I, 457, as "Edward Heys," but he is "Edwardus Heye" in the rolls of 1572–7 and 1589 (II, 835,839).

[6] Will 7 November 1598, inventory 21 July 1602 (Lancs.R.O.).

[7] F. L. Clarke, "King's College: Non-members of the Foundation, 1544–1649," MS in King's College.

appears again as a fellow commoner in 1571.[8] It is likely that he stayed some time further at Cambridge, but he is not known to have taken a degree. Ordination or transfer to the Inns of Court would have been the normal next step on the way to a profession. Instead, he attached himself to a rather remarkable household.

Bisham Abbey in Berkshire was the home of the Hoby family.[9] Sir Thomas Hoby had done much to embellish it as a fine Italianate mansion during the nine short years of his marriage, which ended with his death in 1566. His widow, Lady Elizabeth Hoby, was an interesting and formidable woman, born Elizabeth Cooke. Her two sisters had married Sir Nicholas Bacon and Sir William Cecil respectively, those pillars of the Elizabethan establishment, and like her sisters, she had an academic knowledge of the classics unusual in a woman of her generation, and a directness in speech and writing which made her widely respected and feared. Between 1566 and 1574 she devoted herself to bringing up her children: Edward, born in 1560, and Thomas Posthumus, born in 1566 just after his father's death. It would seem almost certain that Edward Hayes was introduced to Bisham as a tutor to one or both of these boys, though before he went to Oxford in 1574 Edward Hoby was for a time at Eton. It seems likely that Edward Hayes was responsible mainly for Thomas. There is certainly a didactic touch about Edward Hayes's writing which suggests the schoolmaster, and there is also more than a touch of ostentatious piety which may mark the former aspirant of holy orders. He may indeed have had something to do with shaping the rigid puritanism of Thomas Hoby's later life, for Thomas grew up much less of a connoisseur and wit than his brother. Slightly deformed physically, he was bad-tempered, suspicious, hard to discipline, and yet able and tenacious in his own curious way.

He cannot have been easy to control or teach, especially after his mother married Lord Russell in 1574. Yet Hayes must have satisfied Lady Russell's high standards, for he looked back with pride to his time in her service, saying, "the remembrance of Bisham shall ever be honoured of

[8] Matriculated May 1571. (J. A. Venn, ed., *Alumni Cantabrigenses*, 4 vols. (Cambridge, Eng., 1922–7), pt. i, II, 339.) Mr. John Saltmarsh informs me that there was no distinction, except in the scale of payments, between scholar commoner and fellow commoner, and that both were normally undergraduates.

[9] For the Hoby family see *D.N.B.;* Historical Manuscripts Commission, London (Hist.MSSComm.), *CecilMSS*, I, 137–9, III, 73, IV, 395; *Calendar of State Papers, Domestic, 1547–80* (*Cal.S.P.,Dom.*) (1856), pp. 301, 407; *Cal.S.P.,Dom.,Addenda,1566–79* (1871), p. 5; A. L. Rowse, "Bisham and the Hobys," in *The English Past* (London, 1951), pp. 15–45.

me where I had my first bread."[1] Moreover, she brought him into the potent circle of the Cecils. Long after, he traced his connections with Lord Burghley back to this period, and Burghley was, we may remember, the greatest dispenser of patronage of the time. But something, somehow, turned Edward Hayes's interests overseas. The most likely thing, though there is no evidence for it, is that he accompanied Edward Hoby to the Continent in 1576 or 1577. There is a suggestion in his references to European countries in his writings that he had been out of England at some time, which lends a touch of substance to the assumption. If so, he had the grand tour without the expense, though Edward Hoby is unlikely to have gone farther afield than France and Italy.

Our next piece of concrete information on Hayes is that as "Master Haies gentleman of Leerpolle," in the spring of 1578, he subscribed to the expedition which Sir Humphrey Gilbert was planning with the object of planting the first English colony in North America.[2] It is highly probable that it was his father's money, gained partly from Liverpool trade, that enabled him to participate in such a forward-looking, though in the short run unsuccessful project.

At this point it may be useful to say what kind of information we have about Edward Hayes's later career, since we cannot deal with it in detail. In the first place, we know that he was tied up closely for five years, 1578 to 1583, with Sir Humphrey Gilbert. At the end of the period he is a poorer man, but he is also Captain Edward Hayes, who thenceforward regards himself as an experienced seaman and a leader of men at sea. Between 1583 and 1599 we do not know precisely how he made his living. He probably enjoyed some minor patronage at Burghley's hands. In 1585 he was living at Charing Cross.[3] He acted as captain and part-owner of a privateer in the English Channel in 1589 and 1590, and in the same years may have had a home in Essex;[4] by 1596 he writes from "my house

[1] CecilMS 291, fol. 94 (Hist.MSSComm., *CecilMSS,* X, 461–2, incomplete). The originals are cited, by permission of the late Marquess of Salisbury, where the calendared version is inadequate for my purpose.

[2] D. B. Quinn, ed., *The Voyages and Colonising Enterprises of Sir Humphrey Gilbert,* Hakluyt Society, 2d ser., nos. 83–4, 2 vols. (London, 1940), II, 333. The fact that Edward Hoby's commonplace book (B.M., AdditionalMS 38823) contains an important document on the preparation of Gilbert's projected voyage of 1582 might suggest that Hayes and Hoby had developed together their interest in overseas enterprises.

[3] Edward Hayes to Burghley, 10 May 1585 (B.M., LansdowneMS 37, fols. 166–7).

[4] Edward Hayes to mayor of Southampton, 18 February 1590 (*Letters of the Fifteenth and Sixteenth Centuries,* ed. R. C. Anderson, Southampton Record Series, XXII (1922), 183; P.R.O., H.C.A. 1/42, depositions of Thomas Canfield,

in Hamsell Park, Sussex."[5] In the same letter he indicates that he and his father have been for some time working closely together. One may therefore suggest that he was helping to look after his father's mercantile interests. His father appears to have accompanied Lord Derby to court when he took up his office as Lord High Steward in 1589,[6] and may well have set up house for a time with his son in Sussex after Lord Derby's death in 1593. But the elder Hayes was back in Liverpool by the time he made his will in 1598. By it he left his son Edward nothing but his gold signet ring.[7] Edward was apparently in and out of Liverpool several times between 1599 and 1601 to see his father. He made a series of journeys to and from Ireland at that time which provided him with opportunities for doing so. On one of these visits the signet ring reached him at his father's hands.[8]

The years 1599 to 1603 were busy ones for the younger Edward. He acted as commissioner for the musters in Leinster, and on one occasion conveyed a large sum of money to Ireland.[9] With his kinsman, Thomas Hayes, he was also deeply involved in coinage business at London and Isleworth. After four years' hectic work he emerged, at James's succession, with a comfortable pension of a hundred pounds a year,[1] and

---

16 June, and Thomas Haryson, 26 June 1590; B.M., LansdowneMS 133, fol. 110v. (as Edward Hayes of Fittington in Essex, gent., 19 July 1589), LansdowneMS 142, fol. 116v. (prize with wine, 1590), 109 (as Edward Hayes of Writtington in Essex, gent., 26 June 1590).

[5] CecilMS 40, fol. 83 (Hist.MSSComm., *CecilMSS,* VI, 183, has "Hamsett"). C. Pullein, *Rotherfield* (Tunbridge Wells, 1928), pp. 399–417, deals with Hamsell, but does not throw any clear light on how and when Hayes came there (indeed he is not mentioned), but he may have leased Hamsell Farm, where there was an iron furnace and hammerpond, on the death of William Maynard in 1593. I am indebted to Mr. F. W. Steer for his help on this point.

[6] In his will of 7 November 1598 (Lancs.R.O.) Edward Heies refers to "my Cheane which my Lorde and Maister did gyue mee when I waited on him at the courte." This was a gold chain of 18 links, weighing 7 ozs. 15 dwt. and worth £20 (Inventory of 12 October 1602, attached to will).

[7] "Also I doo gyve and bequeth to Edward Heyes, my signett ringe." It was valued at 50s.

[8] It had been handed over by the time the inventory was made, and was probably transferred before his father's death.

[9] Hist.MSSComm., *CecilMSS,* X, 441–2 (late 1598 or early 1599), IX, 148; *Cal.S.P.,Ire.,1599–1600* (1900), pp. 205, 240, 458; *Cal.S.P.,Ire.,1600* (1900), p. 261; B.M., CottonMS, Galba D. XII, fol. 42; *Calendar of Carew Manuscripts, 1601–3* (1870) (*Cal.CarewMSS*), p. 84; Hist.MSSComm., *CecilMSS,* XV, 9, 51–2, 54, 85–6.

[1] P.R.O., Privy Seal Index, Ind. 6744, August 1603; *Cal.S.P.,Dom.,1603–10* (1857), p. 619.

settled down in London for the next ten years, having married a sister of Sir Oliver, later Lord, Lambert.[2] Then we lose sight of him. After 1613 he may have come home to Lancashire to spend his declining days.

Edward Hayes was, first and foremost, a "projector." The main, abiding interest of his life was in thinking up speculative schemes of one sort or another and, usually, putting them before government officials. Some of these merely urged the adoption of a new line of government policy. Should one of them be taken up, he might get rewards in the shape of office or even power. More often he put up plans under which he and his associates would get monopoly powers from the government to exploit some new commercial or industrial or administrative device. This, if adopted, might quickly put a great deal of money into his pockets, some of it at least at the expense of the community. Many of his projects concerned coinage: the manufacture of debased silver coins for use in Ireland,[3] improved methods of manufacturing English silver coins,[4] the introduction of a copper coinage in England or Ireland,[5] the revival of

[2] In 1601 (*Cal.S.P.,Ire.,1601–3* [1912], p. 224) and again in 1605 (Hist.MSSComm., *CecilMSS*, XIII, 412) he and Thomas Hayes lodged at "the Lady Scottes house in Clerken-Poules near unto the bishop's house towards Ludgate" (*Cal.CarewMSS, 1603–24* [1873]), pp. 138–40), and he is also mentioned in October 1612 as still living there (Hist.MSSComm., *HastingsMSS*, IV, 7–8).

Refers to "my Brother in lawe, Sir Oliver Lamberte," 7 January 1603, CecilMS 91, fol. 36 (Hist.MSSComm., *CecilMSS*, XII, 590).

[3] For the Irish coinages see Henry Symonds, "The Elizabethan coinages for Ireland," in *Numismatic Chronicle*, 4th ser., XVII (1917), 108–25, where the mistakes on the debasements of 1598 and 1601 in the standard coinage works are corrected. The Hayes partners were probably associated with the debasement of 1598 (see B.M., CottonMS, Titus B.X., fol. 185; P.R.O., State Papers, Ireland, S.P. 63/212, fols. 244–5); and certainly with that of 1601 (*Cal.S.P.,Ire.,1600–1* [1905], p. 238; *Cal.S.P.,Ire.,1601–3* [1912], pp. 84, 224; Hist.MSSComm., *CecilMSS*, XI, 549).

[4] Their inventions comprised a rolling mill for making metal plates for uniform stamping, a screw mill, employing water-power, for stamping coins, and a new alloy. The material on these inventions is somewhat obscure and needs further study. The essentials can be traced from P.R.O., S.P. 12/93, 25; 276, 64; 281, 108; S.P. 63/212, 99; B.M., CottonMS, Otho E.X., fol. 260; P.R.O., Ind. 6744, 7 February 1601; Hist.MSSComm., *CecilMSS*, XII, 590; Sir John Craig, *The Mint* (Cambridge, Eng., 1953), p. 129. The experimental pieces mentioned by Sir Charles Oman (*Coinage of England* [Oxford, 1931], p. 297) were almost certainly struck by Edward and Thomas Hayes. The moneyers strongly resisted their competition in plating and coining one of the Irish issues (Bodleian Library, Oxford, AshmoleMS 1148, p. 460, through the courtesy of the late F. J. Routledge).

[5] In May 1601 copper coins for Ireland were put in hand by the London mint for Ireland (Craig, *Mint*, p. 129; H. A. Grueber, *Handbook of the Coins of Great Britain and Ireland in the British Museum* [1899], p. 232). Edward Hayes later

the Irish mint,[6] schemes for discovering concealed lands rightfully belonging to the crown,[7] plans for an improved water supply for the city of London.[8] These are probably only a few of many which have sunk into oblivion.

The English copper coinage scheme was his favorite. He began petitioning Lord Burghley about it in 1579 and kept on for nearly twenty years; he then turned to Sir Robert Cecil (later Lord Salisbury) and continued with him until 1612. From 1599 to 1608 he was bothering the Earl of Dorset, and in 1613, after Salisbury's death, his successor as Lord Treasurer, Lord Howard de Walden.[9] He was in general unsuccessful. Thirty-four years of fruitless effort in this direction might well suggest that he was the victim of an obsession. The titles he gave to successive editions of the project, too, have a touch of the fantastic about them. At first it was called "The Bee Hive," then "The complaint of the poor," and finally "A suit called the comfort [spelled "comphort"] of the poor, the lamed and the blind."[1]

Yet he did not invariably fail. His proposal that debased silver coinage should be made for Ireland was adopted in 1601, and so was his suggestion that copper coins should be minted for Ireland in the same year. This involved a big change in monetary policy. It is probable that it saved the state a good deal in the short run, and its termination after 1603 limited its long-term inflationary effects.[2] His efforts to obtain contracts for making the new money won the support of Lord Buckhurst, the Lord Treasurer, although they appear to have been frustrated by the opposi-

---

implied he had much to do with the issue but precisely what is not clear. His "motion" regarding it in 1599 is mentioned in Hist.MSSComm., *CecilMSS*, X, 441–2.

[6] *Cal.S.P.,Ire.,1601–3* (1912), pp. 543–50; *Cal.CarewMSS,1601–3* (1870), p. 420; *Cal.CarewMSS,1603–24* (1874), pp. 3–5 (not assigned to Hayes), 138–40; Hist.MSS Comm., *HastingsMSS*, IV, 7–8.

[7] B.M., CottonMS, Titus B.X., fol. 185.

[8] B.M., HarleianMS 4807, fol. 12; *Select Charters of the Trading Companies*, ed. C. T. Carr, Selden Society (1913), p. cxxiv.

[9] An English copper coinage scheme was being discussed with Burghley as early as 1576 (B.M., CottonMS, Otho E.X., fol. 305), while Hayes claimed to have raised it in 1579, thirty years before his project of 1609 (B.M., HarleianMS 4807, fol. 12, also fols. 52–4, 6–11). He brought it up again in 1612–13 (B.M., CottonMS, Otho E.X., fols. 316–19 v.).

[1] See Hist.MSSComm., *CecilMSS*, XVII, 412; B.M., HarleianMS 4807, fol. 12; B.M., CottonMSS, Otho E. VIII, fol. 319v, Otho E.X., fol. 316.

[2] See T. Hayes to Sir R. Cecil (1601) (P.R.O., State Papers, Ireland, S.P. 63/212, fols. 244–5v); Petition of 1606–7 (B.M., CottonMS, Titus B.X., fol. 185), where he claimed to have saved the state £200,000.

tion of the moneyers.[3] The handsome pensions of a hundred pounds a year each which he and his partner, Thomas Hayes,[4] enjoyed after 1603 were rewards for what was regarded as public service.

II

Edward Hayes was, we may put it, a speculator in futures—perhaps in this the precursor of something in the make-up of the modern Liverpool merchant. North America was one of the futures in which he speculated.

Although it was not until 1607 that Englishmen began to settle in North America, there were in Queen Elizabeth's reign more Englishmen interested in that continent and its possibilities as a site for English settlement than is commonly supposed: Burghley and Walsingham at the highest level of government; Hawkins and Drake, Ralegh and Grenville a little further down the scale, to mention only a few of the best-known names. The Reverend Richard Hakluyt was passionately concerned for over thirty years that Englishmen should explore and settle that part of the New World which had first been discovered by an English expedition in 1497. Edward Hayes was another enthusiast. His name is less well known, but he is by no means unimportant in the prehistory of English settlement in America. Before we consider his contributions we must glance at a rough outline of English activity in regard to North America between 1558 and 1607.

What happened, roughly, was that one part of the North American coastline after another provided a temporary focus of interest. Between 1562 and 1572 it was "Florida," that is, southeastern North America up to about modern North Carolina. But this faded out when the Spaniards were seen to have dug themselves firmly in at San Augustín, which they had settled in 1565. Before 1572, older projects for exploring the northeast coast of North America in order to find a passage to Asia were revived by Humphrey Gilbert and others, and the Frobisher voyages of 1576 to 1578 saw unsuccessful attempts to find the Northwest Passage. Sir Humphrey Gilbert next, from 1579 to 1583, aroused great interest in the region between 40° and 50° N, roughly from the southern shores of New Eng-

3 Bodleian Library, Oxford, AshmoleMS 1448, p. 460; Craig, *Mint.*, p. 129.

4 Thomas is always referred to by Edward simply as his kinsman and has not been further identified. It may be worth suggesting that Sir Thomas Hayes, draper, Lord Mayor of London (b. *ca.* 1548, d. 1617), had a second son, Thomas, who could have been he, though Lancashire links for Sir Thomas have not been found (G. E. C[okayne]., "Lord Mayors and Sheriffs, *temp.* James I," in *London and Middlesex Notebook* [1892], pp. 258–62).

land to the Strait of Belle Isle. Though his voyage of 1583 was directed to modern New England, he became vitally interested in Newfoundland and hoped to settle colonies there. On his death at sea his half-brother Walter Ralegh, between 1584 and 1590, switched attention farther south to modern North Carolina and Virginia. But colonies there, which might have been used as bases against Spain, proved unsuccessful. The Davis voyages between 1585 and 1587 in search of a Northwest Passage did make progress, but disillusioned their backers in the end. From 1585 we find Newfoundland again being discussed as a possible site for a colony, then after 1590 the St. Lawrence, and finally New England. Probing voyages between 1597 and 1605 led the Virginia Company of 1606 into an unsuccessful attempt to settle Maine in 1607. Meantime Ralegh, before his fall in 1603, had reopened the possibility of colonies farther south. Thus it was to Jamestown in Virginia that the Virginia Company sent one of its colonies in 1607. And this was the one that survived.

This bare outline is necessary before we can assess the contribution of Edward Hayes to English knowledge of America. As a voyager he played a useful and even important part in Gilbert's last expedition in 1583; that was all, although he may have been on the abortive voyage of 1578 as well. He put some money into both the 1578 and 1583 voyages and lost it, and may not have invested further in American projects. What he did do was to remain in close contact with successive twists and turns of English policy on America for nearly thirty years. He wrote up one sector of North America after another as proper fields for English enterprise, to keep his views before his patrons' eyes and give them some degree of publicity. His account of Gilbert's expedition of 1583 is his one claim to fame, as distinct from notice. His bulky papers on Newfoundland in the mid-1580's and on New England and the St. Lawrence in the early 1590's are almost unknown. His shorter boost for New England in 1602 is less obscure, but is known only to specialists in early American history. And his plans for financing the Virginia Company in 1606 form a mere footnote to the history of that enterprise.

Before looking at his writings in detail there are two general questions to ask. The first is, why did he never associate himself with plans for settling any part of the North American coast south of New England? The second is, who inspired him? The answer to both is basically the same. He was reflecting primarily the attitudes and approach of Lord Burghley, who was his principal patron. Ralegh's ventures, centered round Roanoke Island in modern North Carolina during the years 1584 to 1590, represent primarily the policy of Sir Francis Walsingham, Queen Elizabeth's pugnacious Secretary of State, who was anxious to take the offensive against

Spain and to obtain English bases on the North American coast suitable for attacking ships coming from the Spanish Indies. Lord Burghley, on the other hand, was anxious to keep out of the way of Spain, at least until 1587, and was interested in the English summer fishery in Newfoundland, in ships' stores (tar, hemp, timber), in the fur trade, and in the possibilities of settlement in temperate lands where agricultural production would be on much the same lines as at home.

Hayes was concerned to meet Burghley's views and to provide him with ammunition. He was also, quite sincerely, a protagonist of the "northern" as against the "southern" party on the prospects of American settlement. It was only after Walsingham's death, and when Burghley was very old and feeble, that Hayes made overtures—unsuccessful ones—to follow up Ralegh's Guiana voyage of 1595 to the tropical reaches of the Orinoco.[5] Hakluyt stood away from parties. He encouraged everyone who was interested in any part of North America for whatever reasons. For over twenty years he helped Hayes to keep alive his interest in the New World.[6] It was he who published Hayes's account of Gilbert's voyage of 1583 in his *Principall navigations* in 1589 and republished it in 1600. It may well have been he who saw to the appearance of Hayes's New England treatise in 1602, while in turn, Hayes's plea for public financing of the Virginia Company in 1606 may well reflect Hakluyt's views.

No one reading Hayes's account of Sir Humphrey Gilbert's last voyage can fail to be struck by its sincerity and force, as at once a narrative and an advertisement of America.[7] It starts with a general case for the occupation of North America by the English, and with the missionary objectives which were customary if not wholly formal. Hayes maintained that the natives could be converted only when Englishmen possessed the land, while the failures of the French to establish themselves argued "that the countries lying to the north of Florida, God hath reserved . . . to be reduced to civility by the English nation." Sir Humphrey Gilbert was to

[5] ". . . being now an olde p*ro*fessed Sea man and zealous towards the voyage of Guyana. Whearyn . . . I am veary willyng to follow Sir Walter Raulegh w*i*th the best meanes I can p*ro*cure" (CecilMS 40, fol. 83 [Hist.MSSComm., *CecilMSS*, VI, 183]).

[6] As early as 1582 Hakluyt included Hayes, by anticipation, with Gilbert among "certaine late travaylers" (*Divers voyages touching the discoverie of America* [1582]).

[7] Hakluyt, *Principall navigations* (1589), pp. 679–97; Hakluyt, *Principal navigations*, III (1600), 143–61 (see Quinn, *Gilbert*, II, 385–423). It is probable that he wrote the first version about October 1583 when he, as "a right honest and discrete Gentleman," gave his first oral account to Sir George Peckham (Quinn, *Gilbert*, II, 444–6).

be praised as the first to bring English people across the ocean to settle, and even if he failed much could be learned from what he did and did not do. Norumbega (New England), on which Gilbert had first fixed, was, Hayes thought at this time, too far south; Newfoundland was the place to start.

Generalities out of the way, Hayes got down to narrative. He tells how five ships set out for Newfoundland in June 1583 and how all but one reached the harbor of St. John's at the beginning of August. His story tells of the annexation of the island to the English crown in the presence of a motley crowd of Portuguese, French, and English fishermen. The explorers then went ashore to look at the land and brought back ore samples which were thought to contain silver. Hayes put down all he could learn about the natural history and resources of the island—the knowledge was to be his stock-in-trade for not only one but all his papers on America. When it came to going farther Gilbert had only three vessels, but on they went, making for Sable Island and then the coast southward from Cape Breton, which would lead them down around Cape Cod. Hayes commanded the *Golden Hind,* his own small forty-ton vessel. His

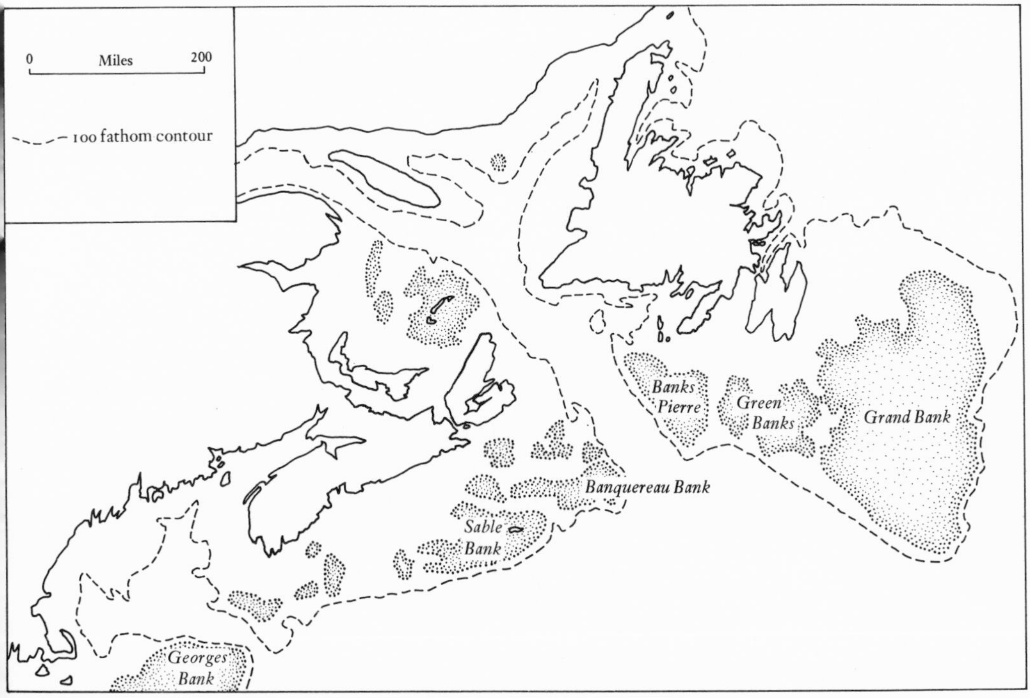

The Newfoundland Banks.

sailing-master was one William Cox of Limehouse, a rough, undisciplined, but daring and able seaman. It is to Hayes's credit that he managed the master and the ship so well. But misfortune lay ahead. On Sable Island, as they thought, the flagship struck and broke up, losing at a blow most of the resources and men of the expedition. Gilbert, luckily, was in the tiny *Squirrel,* a frigate of only eight tons. In spite of the loss, he wanted to go on but was overborne, and the two small vessels turned for home. Gilbert came on board the *Golden Hind* several times to talk with Hayes of how next year's squadrons were to go, one to New England under Hayes, one to Newfoundland under himself, saying "that this voyage had won his heart from the south and he was now become a northern man altogether." Gilbert insisted on returning to his "lucky" frigate. The sea got up, and Gilbert, sitting abaft with a book in his hand, cried out, Hayes said, to those in the *Hind,* "We are as near to heaven by sea as by land." Shortly after, the *Squirrel* disappeared. Professor Sir Walter Ralegh comments, "The last vivid scene has been stamped forever on the memory of his countrymen by the narrative of Edward Hayes."[8] The *Golden Hind* got safely home. The account written by her captain is excellently done—swift, illuminating, and moving.

The Newfoundland papers which Hayes put together in 1585–6 are rather different.[9] They are pure promotion. Addressed to Lord Burghley, they contain Hayes's description of the island and his plan for exploiting it. The former is wholly devoted to economic resources and climate—somewhat affected by his old-fashioned view that the sun went round the earth. (Copernican ideas had been current in England for nearly thirty years.) Fish—herring, bonito, turbot, and lobster as well as cod—could be profitably exploited. The European fishing fleets at Newfoundland had a turnover of some £200,000 a year (an exaggeration) and a tax of 10 percent would produce a useful annual revenue of £20,000. Naval stores such as resin, pitch, tar, deal boards, and masts could be exported; "metals of sorts and happily some rich" might be worked.

To get the scheme going Burghley must find some great man who could inspire the merchants and fishermen to work together in a monopoly company. This would pay if the fish brought home could be distrib-

[8] *The English Voyages of the Sixteenth Century* (London, 1910), p. 58. "The most moving of all narratives printed by Hakluyt," says Samuel Eliot Morison in *The European Discovery of America: The Northern Voyages, A.D. 500–1600* (London, 1971), p. 573.

[9] Hayes to Burghley, 10 May 1585 (B.M., LansdowneMS 37, fols. 166–7, damaged); "Discourse of the Newfounde lande," 10 January 1586 (B.M., LansdowneMS 100, fols. 83–94, damaged).

uted effectively. To secure good distribution he proposed to bring in not only southern ports such as Plymouth, Bristol, and London but also northern ports—Newcastle and Chester (of which Liverpool was still a dependency). Shippers would have to pay the company for the privilege of sending vessels to the fisheries; they would also carry out emigrants free. Investors who could not afford a twenty-five-pound share in the company were invited to club together, their portion falling to their partners, until the survivor took all. This tontine—or survivor-take-all type of investment—is a very early example of its kind. It suggests that perhaps the insurance we know as a "tontine" (after a later Frenchman) should really be known as a "hayes." His own contribution to Newfoundland was to be a collection of two hundred convicts. They would be needed for service in galleys and on public works. The venture was not a humanitarian one.

The whole thing was well worked out, but on much too large a scale. English fishermen were far too individualistic to tolerate an all-embracing monopoly. Moreover, there was little reason why the French, Portuguese, and Spaniards should pay toll to the English in Newfoundland when they had the whole of the rest of North America to provide them with bases. Burghley is likely to have thought well of the scheme in theory but to have seen it was not practical; he did nothing to put it into effect.

The document Hayes wrote in 1592 or early 1593—probably, once more, for Burghley—is something else again.[1] Reports had been reaching him of French and Spanish-Basque voyages to New England, the Maritimes, and the St. Lawrence, and Burghley was becoming interested in the prospects of new English ventures in those regions. By this time Hayes was prepared to admit that Newfoundland was not after all a very good speculation. It *was* cold in winter, and it was not possible to get the fishermen to combine for a big venture such as he had thought of in 1585. He now knew a little more than he had done about the cost of establishing settlements and keeping them supplied during their tender years. The colony left in Ralegh's Virginia in 1587 was found, by 1590, to have faded away for lack of such supplies. What was needed was, first of all, a site for a settlement in a temperate climate. He had all the northern English-

[1] "A discourse conserning a voyage intended for the planting of chrystyan religion and people in the Northwest regions of America: in places most apt for the Constitution of our boddies" (Cambridge University Library, MS Dd. 3. 85, no. 4). A later tract (P.R.O., C.O. 1/1,9) may have been influenced by Hayes. The additional material on French voyages to Canada and the Maritimes was presumably supplied by Richard Hakluyt, and possibly also by Stevan de Bocall (see p. 336 below).

man's contempt for enervating southern heat: 40° N or thereabouts was as far south as it was advisable to go—"seeing," as he said, "that the heat of summer in Italy and in all places else of Europe under forty degrees . . . is unto our bodies offensive, which cannot prosper in dry and scalding heats more natural to the Spaniard than us." He wished to start in a small way, somewhere between 40° and 44° N. A small colony would be enough to begin with, and to supply it he proposed to attract the English Newfoundland fishermen, or some of them, away from the Banks to the fine fishing off the New England coast. There the settlement would provide them with a base. They in turn, at low cost, might bring out settlers and supplies for them each year. He hoped the settlers would soon be able to make a living by agriculture alone. If they did more and exploited, for example, the fur trade, or attracted other fishing vessels to an entrepôt trade there, so much the better. This was much more realistic, in regard to settlement at least, than the earlier Newfoundland plans.

An additional feature of the plan was its stress on the St. Lawrence. This offered a thousand-mile passage into the interior in a southwesterly direction. At the limit of French penetration it was at 45°, which made it suitable for settlement. Why should the French alone have the chance of pushing west by waterways which might lead to a watershed whence the Pacific could be reached? Or might there not be other rivers which would be as good as the St. Lawrence, or better, for this purpose? If so, it would be as well to make plans for trading posts at the portages, so that a short-run trade could be established with the Pacific. This was highly speculative, and suggests that the problem of selling a North American settlement project to an English buyer was still difficult: it clearly had to be wrapped up in some vaguely attractive sales talk.

The next word from Edward Hayes on the Americas came when there was appended to an account of a new voyage to North America in 1602 "A treatise of Master Edward Hayes containing important inducements for the planting in these parts, and finding a passage that way to the South Sea and China."[2] This expedition had been led by Bartholomew Gosnold who is almost certain to have known Hayes and who was the link that tied Richard Hakluyt with the enterprise. Sailing to New England, Gosnold did a valuable piece of exploration, though at the last mo-

[2] John Brereton, *A briefe and true relation of the discouerie of the North part of Virginia . . . Whereunto is annexed a treatise, of M. Edward Hayes, conteining important inducements for the planting in those parts, and finding a passage that way to the South sea, and China* (London, George Bishop, 1602), pp. 15–24. The second edition, in the same year, added a further twenty-four pages of American material from other sources. *S.T.C.* 3610–11.

ment he evacuated the small trading post which had been built on Cuttyhunk Island and so deprived himself of the honor of being the father of New England colonization. The tract which Hayes added to the Reverend John Brereton's published account of the voyage was an abbreviated version of his earlier one, prepared perhaps on his return from Ireland late in 1601 at Hakluyt's request. It was briefer and more workmanlike, but with a few important changes essentially the same. However, the stress on the St. Lawrence has gone—that was left to the French: the stress on the need for the colonists to be self-supporting as soon as possible is greater. It is true that there are still vague speculations about a watershed and an isthmus on the way to the Pacific, but the main emphasis is on settlement in New England. Hayes, in 1602, is in one sense back where Gilbert had been twenty years before, yet in another he is pointing the way to a new line of fruitful and eventually successful experiments.

The last attempt made by Edward Hayes (joined this time by his partner Thomas) to prescribe for North America came just before the grant of the first Virginia Company charter in April 1606. At the end of 1605 and the beginning of 1606 it was at last decided to proceed from experiment to effective settlement in America. Efforts were being made to get old and new American enthusiasts, "northerners" and "southerners," and interests in London, Bristol, and Plymouth to come together to put settlers in both North Virginia (New England) and South Virginia (on Chesapeake Bay). Thomas and Edward Hayes must have been in close touch with Sir Thomas Smith, the leader of the "southerners," at the house of whose sister, Lady Scott, they had been living. They were both known to Sir John Popham, the Lord Chief Justice and head of the "northern" group, while Richard Hakluyt, acting as a link between both sections, had long been Edward Hayes's friend and mentor. In these circumstances it would have been strange had such inveterate projectors remained silent.

As usual, they began their campaign with a letter to Cecil, now Earl of Salisbury,[3] apologizing for mentioning to him a matter "so remote from your great Affayres as America is from England." Yet, remote as it was, America offered a field for missionary activity: "planting of Christianitie amongst heathens" was a great task upon which "som of us have many yeares past ventred both life and substance without Fruite." This was putting an idealistic gloss on Hayes's previous projects, but it

[3] Thomas and Edward Hayes to Salisbury, 1606 (CecilMS 119, fol. 6; Hist.MSS Comm., *CecilMSS*, XVII, 412); printed in Alexander Brown, *The First Republic in America* (Boston, 1898), pp. 3–5.

was perhaps not wholly hypocritical. The point which the partners now wished to make was that "so great a business . . . can never be duly effected by private meanes." "We have," they say, "devised another way without offence to publike or private, wherby the Cause may be compleatly set forward, supported and Seconded, untill it be grown to such perfection as yt may stand of itself and give large Recompense to all Coassistauntes." Their plan required "the Consent of Parliament." They had drawn up a motion, and in addition "a brieff discourse of inducementes allso, for satisfaction of sondry objections which have ben made heretofore," and these they intended "to deliver amongst diverse of our Frendes memberes of the same." [4] First of all, they desired Salisbury's blessing.

It is unlikely that they obtained it, since relations between government and Parliament on financial matters were uneasy and it is most improbable that King James would have wished Parliament to take any hand in the Virginia enterprise. Hakluyt had favored public financing of colonial enterprise ever since 1584, but the Hayes project is the first to bring Parliament into the picture. That the scheme was not pressed or adopted does not detract from its interest. The Virginia Company, when it emerged from the discussions of 1605–6, was a public joint-stock company in which a wide range of individual and corporate interests were represented and which was supervised by a royally appointed council. It was something much nearer a national venture than the small Elizabethan enterprises which depended on the fortunes of a handful of gentlemen.

If we look back over his career it is evident that Edward Hayes occupies a position of some significance in the early colonizing movement. He was actively concerned with North America over the whole first phase of that movement, from the grant of a colonizing patent to Sir Humphrey Gilbert in 1578 down to the issue of the Virginia Company charter in 1606. It was a period of reconnaissance, small-scale experiment, and discussion rather than substantial achievement, but it was an essential prelude to effective English colonization outside Europe. Hayes took a longer continuous part in the debate than anyone else except Richard

[4] Dated 5 January 1607–[8], a document which Brown (who printed it in *The Genesis of the United States*, 2 vols. [Boston, 1890], I, 36–42) called "Reasons for raising a fund" is B.M., LansdowneMS 160, fols. 356–7, and which he thought later (*First Republic* [Boston, 1898], p. 5) must be the Hayes plan. Unfortunately the paper is endorsed and dated by "T. Gerolyn," and is in his hand, while there is internal evidence that it belongs to early in 1608. At the same time it may be based, for the benefit of Sir Julius Caesar to whom it was sent, on the Hayes documents, since its method and arguments are similar to others of theirs, and it has the appeal to Parliament promised in 1606.

Hakluyt, and apart from Sir Walter Ralegh, he was the only one of the participants in Gilbert's first venture in 1578 to remain actively concerned with America down to 1607. The small band of "Americans," as we may label those interested in settlement across the Atlantic, had grown during this period into a considerable movement. Hayes, through his propaganda and his continued belief in colonization, had some influence on that growth. We cannot tell how great this was, but it may not have been small. His American writings combined good sense and farsightedness with much that was repetitive, rhetorical, and impractical. Their importance lies in their emphasis on the suitability for settlement by Englishmen of the more northerly parts of America—Newfoundland, the St. Lawrence, the Maritimes, New England. In a climate not too unlike England's, English agriculture, commerce, and industry could be reestablished without fundamental alteration.

He was thus a pioneer in the advocacy of a new England (though he did not use the term) overseas. This was to be one of the most fruitful ideas behind the English settlement of North America and was to lead to the creation of powerful colonies not many years after Hayes retired from the scene. Even by 1613, he had the satisfaction of seeing a mainland colony in being under the Virginia Company (although it was the southern colony at Jamestown that survived and the northern one at Sagadahoc that died), and an island colony in Newfoundland, his earliest colonial objective. The age of intellectual speculation and experiment had indeed given place to one of achievement, and something in that transition was due to the tirelessly projecting mind of Edward Hayes of Liverpool, gentleman.

III

HAYES HAS LEFT US little information on his personality, but we can learn something from his impact on others. The Cecils, father and son, rarely took up his projects, yet they usually read them and treated them seriously. Other men in high position were ready to give him excellent testimonials. Sir John Popham, the Lord Chief Justice, wrote about an Irish scheme of his in 1600, "if it might be effected it may, in my opinion, fall out to [be] a service of moment."[5] The Irish Solicitor-General, Sir Robert Jacob, as late as 1612 could say that he was "a good understanding gentleman who can invent as many good projects and overtures for his majesty's true profit as any man in England."[6] Yet his techniques were

[5] CecilMS 80, fol. 33 (Hist.MSSComm., *CecilMSS,* X, 185).

[6] Hist.MSSComm., *HastingsMSS,* IV, 7–8.

somewhat crude. We have noticed already his fancy titles: rhetorical overwriting was another fault, though common to his age. To approach Sir Robert Cecil, least emotional of statesmen, with the cry "The scope of our desires is that your honour may be induced to be A FOUNDER and A PATRON, A FOUNDER OF A LOST AND FORLORN KINGDOM [Ireland]" was undoubtedly a mistake.[7] To go on to say in the same document that if Cecil agreed to plant the required number of ex-soldiers in Ireland he would have a good field for preferring his friends, "for the kingdom of Ireland shall there afford places of high preferment to the better sort," was perhaps too direct an invitation to jobbery. The lack of tact is shown again in a further incidental comment in the same document, where he says, "Our state evermore hath occasions ministered to intermeddle with [and] check and curb the mightiest kings of Europe, amongst whom I have heard it said by the greatest statesman of this land that we have no friends." Many a minister in charge of foreign affairs may have felt so, but few would relish hearing it said to them. Still again, Hayes was inclined to parade his patriotism and high sense of purpose in putting forward a project and then let it bump to earth with an appeal to the self-interest of the recipient. Thus, on an Irish coinage scheme, he said to Sir Robert Cecil, "for your honour's private [ear], it shall deserve much grace at her highness's hands and moreover fill your coffers with treasure."[8] Nor could he avoid calling Sir Robert's attention, in another appeal, to his little sweetener (not a bribe): "Vouchsafe the acceptance of my simple present, knowing that a loving cur may sometimes do his master service, if but [by] barking he 'fraye' away the wolf."[9]

Finally, it is as well to admit, too, that he was something of a bore, but one who could not be ignored. One evening in April 1602, the Earl of Nottingham sat working late at Greenwich. As Lord High Admiral he had been sent down by the Lord Treasurer a scheme drawn up by Edward Hayes for an English militia. He was yawning when an urgent messenger arrived. Dutch ships which were cooperating with the English, a note told him, had arrived at Dover, but their instructions had gone astray and must be redone and sent back at once. But Nottingham did not write them. Instead, he scribbled a note to Cecil asking him to have them copied—"the letter," he added, and one can sense the benumbed fatigue with which he wrote, "came to me as I was reading Master Hayes's project and mine eyes so weary as I could not endure to write all with mine own hand." So on the note went to London, marked "Post haste,

[7] CecilMS 91, fol. 36 (Hist.MSSComm., *CecilMSS*, XII, 590).
[8] CecilMS 40, fol. 83 (Hist.MSSComm., *CecilMSS*, VI, 183).
[9] CecilMS 251, fol. 94 (Hist.MSSComm., *CecilMSS*, X, 461–2).

for life, life," while Nottingham nodded in his chair with Hayes's latest project in his hand.[1]

We can leave Hayes here. He had an eye for futures. Most of the schemes he advocated were taken up sooner or later, even if not in the form in which he suggested them. Though a gentleman through his father's efforts, he never passed up an opportunity to trade his wits for money. The "projector," Parliament was to say many times, to Tudor and Stuart sovereigns alike, is a parasite on the healthy state—and this was probably correct. Yet Hayes's approaches to statesman after statesman, his willingness to take risks (though preferably with public money to cushion his losses), his nose for the new, made him of some significance. North America in his day was a risky speculation, yet he saw it as a possible one, and in this he was right. In treating it as a business proposition he did something to make it so.

[1] CecilMS 92, fols. 162–3 (Hist.MSSComm., *CecilMSS*, XII, 125).

CHAPTER NINE

A Portuguese Pilot in the English Service

I

PILOTS WERE A versatile breed. In the discovery and exploration of eastern North America they were in great demand, more particularly if they were prepared to switch their expertise and possibly their allegiance from one power to another—indeed, to be a foreigner was a significant qualification for employment. Portuguese pilots were particularly in demand, especially if they were natives of the Azores. There was not only a venturesome tradition in the islands, but considerable numbers of Azoreans, sometimes from families which had been in the business for generations, went first to Portugal to be trained as pilots and then moved into the service of other nations. An exceptionally large number were employed by Spain, whose imperial need for pilots was very great. Her famous school for pilots in the Casa de Contratación at Seville, several times headed by a Portuguese, does not appear to have attracted sufficient native candidates to supply her demands for pilotage on the high seas.

One Portuguese who served first Spain and then England was the man who appears frequently in English records as "Fernando" or "Simon Ferdinando" or "Simon Fernandez," and in Spain as "Simon Fernández." He was the son of Gaspar Fernandes, "el Rubio" (the Fair), of Alcuña, Terceira. The son, Simão Fernandes, was born about 1538.[1] He appears

[1] Discourse of Gomez de Ávila (1582), A.G.I., Patronato 265, ramo 60 (2.5.1.20); Bernardino de Mendoza to Philip II, 30 April 1582, in Manuel Fernández de Navarrete and others, *Colección de Documentos Inéditos para la Historia de España*, XCII (1888), 347–8.

to have been trained in Portugal before switching his services first to Spain and later to England.

Fernandes came to England sometime after 1570, probably about 1573. He remained there for at least seventeen years, residing first at Plymouth and then in London. He became an English subject, married in London, and sometimes described himself as a merchant of London. He is several times described as a Protestant. He may have come to England because he was a Protestant and wished to escape religious persecution. More likely he drifted into piracy, joined the cosmopolitan company of pirates who based themselves in the English Channel, and reached England by chance rather than by design. He was a trained pilot, and there are many tributes to his knowledge and skill, though also criticisms of his actions in particular circumstances. He had clearly been in the Spanish service in the *carrera de Indias*. He was credited with, and claimed, a substantial knowledge of the western Atlantic; there are indications, too, that he had been in Brazil, and this may well have been when he was a young seaman, before his entry into the service of Spain. Most important, though precise evidence of it is lacking, he appears to have been on one of the Spanish expeditions up the eastern coast of North America, north of Florida proper (there were such expeditions in 1561, 1566, 1570, 1571, 1572, and 1573).

On one of these voyages he claimed to have discovered an inlet into the Carolina Outer Banks, which was known between 1584 and 1587 as Port Ferdinando in his honor, after (so he asserted) he had rediscovered it when in the English service. The only expedition sent by the Spaniards from Florida which is known to have made a landing in the Outer Banks, naming the river and land there "San Bartolome," is that of 1566.[2] The pilot of that expedition was a very expert navigator, Domingo Fernández, of whose origin nothing is known. Also present was "Baltasar Fernández, son of Antonio Hernández and Catalina Dominguez, who reside at Tenerife." This raises the possibility that Simão's information came not from his own efforts but from one of the two Fernández of this expedition. Baltasar, being from the Canaries, was certainly not Simão Fernandes, though he might have been a relative; it is more likely that Domingo Fernández, the pilot, was some connection of Simão. But this must remain only conjecture until further evidence is produced.

Simão Fernandes was not a very estimable character. He had few scruples and greatly enjoyed robbery at sea; he was distrusted by many of those who sailed with him. At the same time, he was a man of con-

[2] See the important paper by Louis André Vigneras, "A Spanish Discovery of North Carolina in 1566," *North Carolina Historical Review*, XLVI (1969), 398–415.

siderable force of personality who appealed to and kept the friendship of powerful men in England. One enduring attitude he retained throughout: a hatred of the Spaniards. What the origin of this was we cannot say, but in a period of growing hostility in England against Spain it was an asset to the pilot. His value to the English was twofold: first, he could provide information on the Spanish fleets in the Indies and on conditions of navigation there; and second, he could, and did, guide expeditions up the North American coast so as to find suitable sites for colonies. In this capacity he is closely associated with both Sir Humphrey Gilbert, 1578–80, and Sir Walter Ralegh, 1584–7, in their first attempts to plant English settlements on North American soil. In the end his instability of character discredited him with the promoters, but significantly enough, on the last occasion he is heard of it is in the English service in the struggles against Spain in the Frobisher-Hawkins expedition of 1590.

Between about 1573 and 1578 Simão Fernandes, or Simon Fernandez as he is almost invariably known in England, was a pirate, in association with English, Dutch, and other freebooters in the English Channel and off the shores of France, Spain, and Portugal.[3] What he was doing before the autumn of 1574 we do not know, but he had already met the notorious pirate John Callice. In October 1574 he took service as pilot on the *Elephant*, partly owned by Henry Knollys, son of the queen's treasurer of the household, Sir Francis Knollys, to go to the Indies to rob the Spanish. With him were Callice as master and Ferdinando Fielding as captain. Off the Azores, on 20 December 1574, they seized a rich Portuguese ship coming from Brazil with sugar and brazilwood. They turned

[3] His career may be traced between 1575 and 1578 from the following documents (numbered for convenience and all in the P.R.O.): (1) *ca.* January 1575—Francisco Giraldi to Sir Francis Walsingham, State Papers, Foreign, Portugal, S.P. 89/1, 265; (2) 6 February 1575—*A.P.C.,1571–1575* (1894), pp. 342–3; (3) 15 October 1576—Castelnau de la Mauvissière to Walsingham, in *Calendar of State Papers, Foreign, 1575–1577 (Cal.S.P.,For.)* (1880), p. 401; (4) 13 December 1576—*A.P.C.,1575–1577* (1894), pp. 248, 267–8; (5) 5 March 1577—Examination of Simon Ferdinando at Cardiff, State Papers, Domestic, S.P. 12/112, 5 and 5(2); (6) [May 1577]—Indictments of John Callice, Simon Fernandez, John Sallmon, and William Peacock, H.C.A., Oyer and Terminer, H.C.A. 1/2, 37, 40; (7) 30 May 1577—Examination of John Challis, H.C.A. 1/40, fols. 22–5; (8) 16 October 1577—Giraldi to Walsingham, *Cal.S.P.,For.,1577–1578* (1901), pp. 262–3; (9) 10 December 1577—Personal answer of John Challis, H.C.A. 13/100, fol. 57; (10) 20 December 1577—*non molestis* for John Challis, H.C.A. 1/2, 66; (11) 2 January 1578, 11 August 1578—reports on pirates in South Wales, S.P. 12/135, pp. 330, 332, 401. On John Callice (or Challis) see C. L'Estrange Ewen, *The Golden Chalice: A Documented Narrative of an Elizabethan Pirate* (Paignton, Devon, 1939), p. 17.

back and brought her to South Wales, where she was sold at Penarth. The Portuguese ambassador alleged that Fernandes had killed seven Portuguese sailors with his own hands, but nothing was done to arrest him. He may or may not have accompanied Callice, now captain of the *Elephant*, on a further cruise to Rochelle, the Azores, and Newfoundland in 1575; direct evidence is lacking.

In this same year he bought a small bark of his own and got some merchants and officials in Cardiff to fit him out. It was probably with her that he took the Dutch flyboat *Fortune*, which was brought into the Irish port of Cork and thence to South Wales. In the spring of 1576, according to his own story, he set out in his bark to make a peaceful voyage to the Canaries, but in reality to join with the *Elephant* and accompany Callice once more to the Azores. There, off Fayal, in waters he must have known well, on 19 April they seized a Portuguese caravel—Manoel Corderoe, master—with a lading of woad, belonging to Francisco Guillett, a native of the Azores. The prize and prize-goods were sold in South Wales, though Fernandes claimed to have returned to Cardiff without profit.

Perhaps this was why his former backers, the local admiralty officials, threw him into jail in May. But instead of being tried, he was first released on bail and then dismissed from appearing before the judges in the summer, after the charges against him had been changed from piracy to "suspicion of piracy" only. It seems likely that he lived for some time quietly in Cardiff after this, though proceedings were begun for the recovery of the Portuguese goods. Finally he was examined by government officials at Cardiff on 17 March 1577 and gave a very garbled account of his activities. He was, however, sent up to London as a prisoner in April, and evidence provided by the Portuguese ambassador ("enough to hang him," he said) was produced. Nevertheless the judges released him, probably on some technical point, whereupon the Portuguese ambassador Francisco Giraldi wrote a furious protest to Sir Francis Walsingham, the Secretary of State, on 16 October 1577. By this time, too, Fernandes's old comrade John Callice had been captured and charged with a long list of robberies, but he also was in touch with Sir Francis Walsingham and was formally pardoned on 14 December 1577. Walsingham had no special hostility to Portugal, but he had to Spain: he was prepared to forgive sea-robbers like Callice and Fernandes their crimes against other nations' shipping if they would turn their undoubted ability toward the robbery and discomfiture of the Spaniards. Not long after this, we do not know precisely when, Simão Fernandes entered the service of the Secretary of State, and is subsequently referred to as "Master Secretary Walsingham's man." It is highly probable that he provided him with detailed information on Spanish America.

II

BETWEEN 1578 AND 1580, Simão was concerned in the first English attempts to explore North America as a preliminary to settling it. Sir Humphrey Gilbert in June 1578 had been given a royal patent to discover and settle unoccupied lands. With Walsingham's help he got together a fleet of ten ships, and was being fed with information on the Spanish empire by Simão Fernandes—"a thorough-paced scoundrel," as the Spanish ambassador, Bernardino de Mendoza, reported. Simão's old friend Henry Knollys was to captain the *Elephant*, with John Callice as pilot. He himself was to be master and pilot of the *Falcon*, belonging to William Hawkins, whose captain was to be Gilbert's young half-brother Walter Ralegh. The plan seems to have been for the squadron to make for the West Indies, seize as much Spanish shipping as possible, and then work up the North American coast looking for sites for a colony.

When the vessels set out in November,[4] most of them, led by the *Elephant*, embarked on their normal trade of piracy in home waters. The rest, Gilbert's *Anne Aucher* among them, were forced to turn back to an Irish port because the *Falcon* was sailing badly and lacked stores. Storms scattered them after they again put to sea. The *Falcon* alone kept on her course. The evidence is obscure, but it seems that Fernandes intended to sail her directly to North America, to a site for settlement which he already knew. Failing to make progress, he turned south, intending to use the trade winds to reach the West Indies and proceed from there.

According to Ralegh, he and Fernandes cooperated effectively on the voyage; he said afterward in the course of a lawsuit "that he and the Master of the said Shipp dyd ther best and diligence both for the good governement of the . . . vyctualles and provisions, and also to Draw the same to convenient length as possibly they could for the furtherance

[4] On 19 November 1578 Sir Humphrey Gilbert left Plymouth with seven ships: the third was the *Falcon*, "which was the Quenes ship of c Tunes havinge in hir of Caste peces -15. fowlers 4. doble bases 12. Capitayne Walter Rawlye brother to sir Humfrye Gilberte a capitayne of An Ancient by Lande. Fardinando the Portugale his master" (the ship was in fact at that time the property of William Hawkins of Plymouth and was chartered by him to Ralegh). See D. B. Quinn, ed., *The Voyages and Colonising Enterprises of Sir Humphrey Gilbert*, Hakluyt Society, 2d ser., nos. 83–4, 2 vols. (London, 1940), I, 211–12; P.R.O., Chancery, Town Bundles, C. 24/150.

of that voyage."[5] Eventually they reached the Canaries, where Ralegh says they "did take in a new supplye of Canary wynes at the Graund Canaries with some relief of swet meates, which wine was about the nomber of xiiii or xv tonnes, and that was not without gret nede, because the drink was all nere spent." What they paid with is not clear, since in a deposition in the same case Fernandes declared they had on board no merchandise except 200 yards of Holland linen, a few unfinished embroidered silk doublets, two pieces of calico, "and certen Manylios of brasse, certen morys belles, which manylios and Belles came into ii° firkins"; while there were also spare hose, shoes, and canvas for shirts for the seamen.

There is later evidence that Fernandes intended to make for Puerto Rico, but instead of sailing westward with the southeast trades, he and Ralegh took the *Falcon* well to the south "as far as the Ilands of Cape de Verde."[6] We then hear of their "manie dangerous adventures, as well by tempests as fights on the sea." Eventually, in the late spring or early summer of 1579, the *Falcon* was back at Plymouth without having made, apparently, a serious attempt to cross the Atlantic.

In 1580 Gilbert was ready to try again, but this time he intended merely to send Fernandes out on a reconnaissance. He put him in command of his own small frigate, the *Squirrel*, of only eight tons, with ten men. He set out sometime in March and was back before the end of June, having explored a suitable site on the North American coast. While he was away Gilbert had to give guarantees that Fernandes, now the servant of one of the queen's ministers, would not engage in ordinary piracy. The voyage was a remarkable one and illustrates Fernandes's skill as a pilot. But evidence of precisely where it was headed for is incomplete. In 1578, if we read the indications correctly, he was making for the Carolina Outer Banks or Chesapeake Bay, where he had been (or said he had been) with the Spaniards; in 1580, the evidence seems to say, he went to New England, possibly to Narragansett Bay—Verrazzano's old "*Refugio*" of 1524—Gilbert having decided on a more northerly objective.[7] Certainly after Fernandes's return Gilbert set all his hopes on the New England area.

[5] Depositions in 1581 in Jilbert *v.* Hawkins in P.R.O., Chancery, C. 24/150 (first noted by Agnes M. C. Latham in "A Birth Date for Sir Walter Ralegh," *Études Anglaises*, IX [1956], 243–5). Fernandes signs his deposition (on the equipment of the *Falcon*) in a bold hand as "Simão Fernandez."

[6] As related by John Hooker (see Quinn, *Gilbert,* I, 237).

[7] The sources for the 1580 voyage are few and quite general in their references. They are printed in Quinn, *Gilbert,* II, 239–40, 282, 309, and discussed in I, 50–1. It is conceivable that Dr. John Dee included an indication of his landfall in the chart he prepared for Sir Humphrey Gilbert in 1582 or 1583, now in possession

On 20 November 1580 Fernandes came to visit Dr. John Dee, one of Gilbert's advisers, bringing with him a Spanish sea-chart of the Atlantic and doubtless telling him where he had been. Dee copied the outlines and details of the North American portion and may have used them in a map he compiled for Gilbert.[8] But Fernandes did not help him further, probably on account of the long delays, and perhaps also because of involvement in the affairs of Portugal (recently invaded by Philip II of Spain) and the various plans to assist Dom António in asserting his claims to the Portuguese throne. With the Spanish conquest, whatever his thieving from Portuguese merchants in the past, Fernandes could now play the loyal supporter of Dom António in future actions against the Spaniards.

III

Fernandes was soon involved in helping Captain Martin Frobisher to get a great ship, the *Galleon Leicester*, ready for a voyage around the Cape of Good Hope to the East Indies and China. Drake had recently returned from his circumnavigation, and the English hoped that the Portuguese in the East would welcome English aid and traders in defiance of

of the Philadelphia Free Library Company, Philadelphia (the best reproduction of which is in W. P. Cumming, *The Southeast in Early Maps* [Princeton, 1958], pl. 8). He includes on what would be the coasts of Maine and New Brunswick four rivers on the largest of which is a place named (apparently) "Stannata," which do not appear on his earlier map of 1580. A certain John Walker was on this coast in 1580 also (see Quinn, *Gilbert*, I, 51–2, II, 309–10), and might have been an alternative source for Dee's material. An early investigation of this problem was made in B. F. DeCosta, "Simon Ferdinando and John Walker in Maine," *New England Historical and Genealogical Register*, XLIV (1890), 149–58.

[8] Dr. John Dee's servant recorded that on 20 November 1580, "Master Fernando Simon" (Simão Fernandes) lent his master a "Sea Carte" of which a copy was made which is now B.M., Cotton Roll XIII, 48, the nomenclature being inserted only for the areas in which Dee was interested. It is a Spanish-type sea-chart extending from 36° south latitude to 69° N through the Atlantic Ocean. This may, on closer study, yield some evidence of Fernandes's own early visits to North America and possibly Brazil. It is reproduced in Armando Cortesão and Avelino Teixeira da Mota, *Portugaliae Monumenta Cartographica* (Lisbon, 1960), II, 129–31, pl. 240. It may have been that Dee had seen the original (or a map of a very similar type) before he completed his larger map, presented to Queen Elizabeth on 3 August 1580 (B.M., CottonMS, Augustus I, i. 1, the relevant part reproduced in Quinn, *Gilbert*, II). The coastline in the vicinity of C. de Arenas (placed by Dee at 38° N) is almost identical with that on Fernandes's map, and might be taken to refer to a voyage made to this region by Fernandes if it were not that it lacks the name Bahia de Santa Maria, the Spanish name for Chesapeake Bay.

the Spanish conquerors. A letter from Fernandes to Frobisher at this time shows him well able to write English.[9] Mendoza reported that he was thought one of the best pilots in England.[1] When the expedition of two ships sailed in May 1582, under the command of Edward Fenton—not Frobisher—Fernandes was copilot of the flagship.

Fenton's orders were to sail to the Moluccas and from there to make trading contacts with China. In fact he did nothing of the sort. By way of the Cape Verde Islands he reached Sierra Leone, Fernandes being later blamed for inciting him to embark on a campaign of robbery.[2] Both chaplains spoke disparagingly of his braggart language and glorification of his piratical exploits.[3] When the vessels crossed westward to Brazil, there were discussions on whether to go for the Cape or for the Strait of Magellan. Fernandes favored the Caribbean as the best place to rob Spaniards. "Whatever comes from the South Sea," he argued, "passeth through the Bay of Mexico, and therefore as good steal it here as there." [4] They reached the Brazilian coast fairly far south (28°), and Fernandes was against going down to the Plate: "Nando [his nickname] hath counselled to go back again and rob São Vicente." The diarist, Richard Madox, declared that Fernandes, "the flatterer," was busy seducing Fenton finally from his original purpose toward open piracy in the Atlantic. "Had he meant honesty at first these doubts now had not needed," but "Ferdinando, a ravenous thief, hath brought the matter to this pass."

[9] His letter to Martin Frobisher about providing yards and stores for the vessel is printed for the first time in E. G. R. Taylor, *The Troublesome Voyage of Edward Fenton, 1582–1583*, Hakluyt Society (Cambridge, Eng., 1959), pp. 22–3. It seems likely that he had earlier been at sea, at his old piratical trade, since among the vessels temporarily confined to harbor but released on 2 September 1581 was "a barke, Capten Ferdinandes" (*A.P.C.,1581–1582*, pp. 195–6).

[1] Bernardino de Mendoza to Philip II, 20 April 1582 (Fernández de Navarrette and others, *Documentos Inéditos,* XCII, 347–8): "y por piloto de la principal nao á un Simon Fernandez, portugués, natural de la Tercera, hereje que há años que está aqui y estiman ser de los majores pilotos del Reino." See Taylor, *Fenton,* p. 38.

[2] Taylor, *Fenton,* pp. 169, 76–82.

[3] The Rev. Richard Madox on the *Galleon Leicester* and the Rev. John Walker on the *Edward Bonaventure* both kept diaries, largely printed for the first time in Taylor, *Fenton.* Walker asked Fenton "to deal with Ferdinando the pilot to deal with more continence in his conversation and with more modesty in his speeches, for that they were (as I affirmed) offensive to God, and nothing Christian-like, for that he rejoiced in things stark naughty, bragging in his sundry piracies." Madox did not even regard him as a competent pilot, writing of the difficulty of finding their position on the way to Brazil, "Fernando sailed a month on dry land." (*Ibid.*, pp. 202, 187.)

[4] *Ibid.*, p. 187.

Challenged about his attitude, Fernandes declared "I am at war with the King of Spain"; he implied that he had become a naturalized Englishman, but even so, boasted "I . . . have a free pardon from five Privy Councillors for carrying on war with Spain" (whatever that might mean).[5] To São Vicente they went, where they met three Spanish warships and one was sunk, but Fernandes acted as the intermediary for peaceful trade with the Portuguese townsmen on shore.[6] Here his aggressive advice was finally discarded and Fenton decided to return home, prizeless and unsuccessful. Fernandes, to some of the Englishmen "the head and origin of all evil" and named "the Swine,"[7] nevertheless retained the friendship and confidence of his commander, Edward Fenton, and his copilot, Thomas Hood. Nor, after his return to England in June 1583, did he forfeit his association with Walsingham and Ralegh.

IV

In the Roanoke voyages between 1584 and 1590 the English for the first time seriously attempted to explore and settle any part of the eastern coast of North America. Sir Walter Ralegh inspired and sponsored these voyages, but Fernandes played a significant part in them. According to a Spanish pilot who knew him in England, he was "the author and promoter of the venture"; this is going too far, but it indicates how important he made out his influence to have been. It would seem, however, that it was he who led the English to the harbors in the Outer Banks of North Carolina and on Chesapeake Bay, where he claimed he had previously been with the Spaniards. He acted as principal pilot of the three main expeditions which sailed from England for exploration and settlement in 1584, 1585, and 1587. And he was, perhaps, partly responsible for the failure and disappearance of the settlers of the third colony, that of 1587.

In 1584 Fernandes piloted two vessels, which were under the command

[5] *Ibid.*, pp. 192–4, 196–7. He claimed that he had a Portuguese permit to trade in Brazil (suggesting that he had been engaged in trade there before he entered the Spanish service), but that now he was, since 1580, as objectionable as any other foreigner. "'How is that' I [Richard Madox] asked. 'Because,' said he, 'I am at war with the King of Spain.' 'What,' said I, 'are you not a subject of our Queen [implying that he had received letters of denization]?' 'That is so,' [he replied,] 'and we are at peace with Spain,' I said. 'But,' he said, 'I have a free pardon from five Privy Councillors for carrying on war with Spain.' 'Which I do not believe,' I said, 'for if it is true it is not possible for anyone to live honestly in this ship which has a permit for illicit war.' 'And I,' said he, 'do not doubt to see you too become a willing thief . . .' 'That is unnecessary,' I said." (*Ibid.*, pp. 196–7.)

[6] *Ibid.*, pp. 137, 252. [7] *Ibid.*, pp. xxxvi, 182, 193, 321.

of Captains Philip Amadas and Arthur Barlowe, across the Atlantic. Leaving England on 27 April they sailed on the trade winds to the Caribbean, evidently calling at Puerto Rico before making their way into the Florida Channel, or modern Straits of Florida. According to Barlowe, land was sighted on 4 July, and after coasting "a hundred and twentie English miles" a landing was made on 13 July, possession taken, and contacts of a friendly nature made with the Indians of the Carolina Outer Banks and Roanoke Island. No precise details are given of how long they remained, but the events described might have been spread over two or three weeks or possibly a little longer before they left, accompanied by two Indians. The narrative says only "we resolved to leave the Countrey, and to apply ourselves to returne for England, which we did accordingly, and arrived safely in the West of England, about the middest of September." [8]

We may compare this account with a deposition made in Spain some years later by Richard Butler, who had been on the 1584 voyage. He says

> . . . he left England with a captain named Amadis who commanded two ships. With instructions from Guater Raule [Walter Ralegh], the owner of the two ships, they went in search of Florida. They coasted along the whole of the Florida coast, and disembarked in the central part of Florida at a place called Ococa [Wococon], so named by the natives of the country. Twenty leagues further on, towards the northern part, they disembarked again in another place, known to the English as Puerto Fernando, and to the savages as Ataurras [Hatarask]. From there they moved twelve leagues to the north and found a port, with a depth of nine feet, which the savages called Cacho Peos [Chesapeake]; and these savages were enemies of those of Puerto Fernando. From there, in accordance with the instructions they were carrying, they set sail for Bermuda, but were unable to reach it because a storm arose when they arrived in the passage in the latitude of the island. From there they set their course for the Azores, where they remained as long as their provisions lasted in the hope of capturing a ship. They were there for six weeks, and then, having failed to take a prize and lacking provisions, they sailed for England. The voyage lasted nine months. In both ships there were about one hundred sailors and soldiers, and the pilot they carried was one Fernando, a Portuguese, whose proper name he does not know. During the voyage the deponent served as a corporal.[9]

This builds up a very different picture. The first landing is said to have been made at Wococon, an island now partly represented by

[8] Barlowe's narrative, in Quinn, *Roanoke Voyages,* I, 91–116.

[9] A.G.S., Estado Inglaterra, E. 839 (unnumbered depositions at the end of the legajo). I am indebted to Dr. Alastair MacFadyen for the translation.

Ocracoke Island, and lying some 70 to 80 miles south of Roanoke Island. We might take it that this represents the land sighted on 4 July, according to Barlowe, and there seems no reason to doubt Butler that a landing was made there, as one was the following year. The traverse of 120 land miles up the coast, making allowance for avoiding the Cape Hatteras Shoals, would fairly represent the distance from Wococon to Hatarask. This was the island in the Carolina Outer Banks extending from modern Cape Hatteras northward to an inlet nearly opposite the southern end of Roanoke Island, which lies in the Sound behind, a little to the north of the modern Oregon Inlet. This inlet was itself known as Hatarask, but it was called by the English from 1584 to 1587 Port Ferdinando. It was thus discovered, or rather rediscovered, by the pilot, we may suspect from knowledge gained on a previous expedition in the Spanish service or from indications derived in some way from the discoveries made by the Spanish expedition of 1566 (though the inlet then discovered was probably not Hatarask).

Butler passes over the contacts made with the Indians which are the main theme of Barlowe's narrative, and moves on. According to him, the ship commanded by Amadas and having Fernandes as pilot went northward some thirty-six miles along the coast and found an entry with a bar of nine feet which the natives, who were enemies of those on Roanoke Island, called Cacho Peos or, we would imagine, Chesapeake. The distance given is insufficient (but so is that from Wococon to Hatarask), and the location of a bar of this nature is difficult to establish, but it appears most probable that Fernandes was able to bring the first English ship into Chesapeake Bay on this occasion, and that this was the origin of later English interest in this area.

There is some additional evidence on this topic. A member of the next voyage to Roanoke Island, in 1585, was cast away on Jamaica. When finally examined by someone who could make linguistic contact with him, he reported that, presumably in 1584, the Portuguese pilot "Hernando" had made the voyage he originally intended (in 1578) and had reached the Florida coast at a headland which on the Spanish chart was at 38°30′ north latitude (though the English chart had it at 36°). He went on to say that "from that point there is a large bay with some islands, and the water is fresh. This bay is four leagues long and opens into the sea, and according to the Indians is the largest along that coast and is a channel to the other sea." [1] It is most difficult to decide whether he is

[1] A.G.I., Patronato 265, ramo 44 (2.5.1.20), for which see Irene A. Wright, *Further English Voyages to Spanish America, 1583–1594* (London, 1951), pp. 175–6, and Quinn, *Roanoke Voyages*, I, 80–1: the depositions have not been published in full.

talking of the entry near Roanoke Island and of Albemarle Sound penetrating into the land north and westward from the island, or whether he is referring to Chesapeake Bay. The latter is at least a possibility. The Englishman then went on to say that, when the Portuguese discovered this port and wished to land on one promontory, "the wild Indians ate thirty-eight Englishmen, and he went on to the other promontory, where there is a good port, and found the savages there gentler."

The two promontories could scarcely have been those at Wococon, where there were no Indians residing, and Hatarask. We might suggest that the witness has them in the wrong order and that the gentle Indians were at the second landing at Port Ferdinando and the savage Indians at the third landing, at—it seems—Chesapeake Bay. That thirty-eight Englishmen were killed also seems very doubtful, or indeed that either the Chesapeake Indians then living near Cape Henry or the more powerful Powhatan group farther into the Bay, made a feast of them. But that there was some hostile contact does not appear unlikely.

The ship on which Amadas and Fernandes were did not sail direct to England, according to Butler, but under Ralegh's orders to Bermuda to try to pick up some straggler from the Spanish homeward bound convoy, but were unable to remain in the vicinity of that island owing to bad weather. Fernandes then brought the ship to the Azores, though we do not know whether or not he landed at his native island of Terceira. Most probably not, since Butler says they stayed looking for a prize for six weeks until their provisions were exhausted, and reached England only in December. This does not fit in with Barlowe's narrative as we have it, though the latter shows signs of having been extensively rewritten, probably by Ralegh. It may be that Barlowe's ship sailed directly for England after leaving Port Ferdinando and did not go to the Chesapeake. Or if it did, it certainly did not linger around Bermuda and the Azores, since its arrival in England in September seems well attested. What is clear is that Fernandes played a major part in the discoveries in 1584 and exploited very usefully for the English reconnaissance expedition the discoveries he had made himself or the information he picked up from others before he left the Spanish service.

How large a part Fernandes played in the discussions leading to the 1585 voyage, which was to establish the first settlement, we cannot say. The settlement was to serve at least three purposes: as a base from which the surrounding country might be explored, as an experimental station where the problems of living on American soil might be studied, and as a port of call for English privateers operating in the Caribbean and along the return route of the Spanish *flota* to Europe by way of Bermuda and the Azores. It is in regard to the latter use that Fernandes is likely to have been most seriously consulted. But for this the new site had a fatal defect: the chosen harbor, Port Ferdinando, was too shallow and too exposed—the pilot's judgment on it was at fault.

In the fleet of seven vessels which left England in April 1585 under the command of Sir Richard Grenville, Simão Fernandes was pilot major and master of the flagship, the *Tiger*, a royal ship.[2] He brought Grenville to the southwestern end of Puerto Rico to refresh his men in May. From there they proceeded to attack Spanish trading vessels; Fernandes took part in these attacks (and may have led some of them); he is found on one occasion interrogating prisoners and reading documents taken from them.[3] He may also have been responsible for introducing Grenville to Spanish officials and merchants on the north coast of Hispaniola, who agreed to trade with him. The English journal of the voyage has several hostile comments on Fernandes's actions after leaving Hispaniola. He misled Grenville about finding salt ponds on the Caicos Islands, "deserving a halter for his hire, if it had so pleased us," says the writer. When the *Tiger* reached Wococon on 14 June there was a disaster which might have proved fatal: weighing anchor to bring her into the harbor, "through the unskilfulness of the Master, whose name was Fernando, the Admiral [the flagship] struck on ground and sank," says the author of the journal. There is no corroboration that Fernandes was responsible, and the ship was in fact got off, though with damage to her lading.

By the time Ralph Lane had landed with the colonists at Port Ferdinando and began to write letters from there to England in August it is clear that Fernandes was on bad terms with Sir Richard Grenville. But so were others; Grenville was said to have acted in an imperious and arbitrary fashion. Ralph Lane was one of those who was hostile to Grenville and friendly toward Fernandes. Writing to Sir Francis Walsingham, an important supporter of the voyage, Lane praised the harbor found by Fernandes as the best on the coast and said "your honour's servant Simon Ferdinando . . . truly has carried himself with great skill, and great government, all this voyage, notwithstanding this great cross

[2] Quinn, *Roanoke Voyages*, I, 158–253, deals with the voyage in detail. Richard Butler (p. 250 above) notes his presence, this time remembering his given name: "The pilot was Fernando, the Portuguese, who, he believes, was called Simon Fernandez."

[3] Don Fernando de Altamirano, a prisoner, reported, "When they took Don Fernando and his companions prisoner they stripped them of all letters and papers in their possession, which a Lutheran Portuguese, whom they had as their pilot, translated" (*ibid.*, II, 742).

[Grenville's alleged conduct] to us all."[4] In spite of these charges it seems that Fernandes was still with Grenville on the return voyage, when a valuable Spanish prize was taken, but he never sailed with Grenville again.

After his return to England in October 1585 until the beginning of 1587 we lose sight of Fernandes once more. It would seem that Walsingham lost interest in the Roanoke ventures and perhaps had other employment for the pilot. In the meantime the colonists at Roanoke Island had done much exploration and had been to Chesapeake Bay without danger from the Indians there. Grenville did not arrive with supplies when they were needed, and so in June 1586 Lane and his men left with Sir Francis Drake, who had called to inspect their harbors on his way back from an attack on the Spanish Indies. Grenville, arriving late, left only a handful of men to maintain continuity of settlement.

John White had been the artist and cartographer of the 1585 colony: he returned to England in July 1586 full of enthusiasm for continuing colonization. With the aid of Sir Walter Ralegh he planned a settlement to be called the City of Ralegh, under himself as governor and with the aid of twelve assistants, drawn mainly from would-be settlers. Among these twelve was Simão Fernandes. His appearance at this stage shows both that he continued to enjoy the confidence of Ralegh and that he genuinely supported a colonizing venture to settle men, women, and children in America. A grant of arms was made to the company for their new city to be founded in America, and arms were also granted to its officers, that to the pilot being to "Simon Ferdinando of London, gentleman."[5] Three ships were equipped and some 117 settlers taken on board before they sailed on 8 May, with White as captain and Fernandes as master of the flagship, the *Lion*.[6]

[4] *Ibid.*, I, 188–9, 201–2.

[5] The company was honored on 7 January 1587 with a corporate grant of arms (*ibid.*, II, 506–12), while its governor and assistants also received grants. Fernandes's was to Symon Ferdinando of London, Gentleman, the blazon being: a field argent two bars wavy, azure, on a canton gules three fusils of the first.

[6] Pedro Diaz, a Spanish pilot captured by Grenville in December 1585, accompanied him on his 1586 expedition to Roanoke Island. According to Diaz they returned to England on 26 December 1586. He says that "the captain [Grenville] went thence to London where he recruited people for the settlement, 210 in number, both men and women. He then despatched three ships in charge of a Portuguese called Simon Fernandez, who had married in England and was a skilful pilot, and, further, was the author and promoter of the venture. This man left London for the settlement in March 1587." Deposition of Pedro Diaz, 21 March 1589 (*ibid.*, p. 793). Grenville is not otherwise known to have played an active part in preparing the 1587 expedition, and it is probably a considerable exaggeration to say that

Friction soon developed between White and the pilot. Fernandes evidently wished throughout to attack every Spanish vessel he could catch; White, on the other hand, disliked privateering, and in any case did not wish to expose the colonists, who included his own daughter, to risks of death or capture. White accused Fernandes of wishing to shake off the flyboat by "deserting" her off Portugal—which does not seem sensible. The ship duly arrived at Port Ferdinando on 25 July and "God disappointed his wicked premisses," in White's words. White was full of complaints about Fernandes's conduct as they worked their way through the West Indies. Some were frivolous—traces of Carib visitors on Santa Cruz when Fernandes had said it was uninhabited, absence of sheep on Vieques Island in spite of his assurance that there were plenty there. But there are indications also of obstruction: preventing White from loading salt on Puerto Rico; from landing in search of plants near San Germán; from trading on the north coast of Hispaniola. These would seem to indicate that White's undoubted hostility to prize-taking and Fernandes's desire to pay for the voyage by robbery were the primary source of friction and that Fernandes, using his power as pilot, was working off his chagrin by inflicting minor discomforts on the colonists.[7]

The plan had been for White to call in at Roanoke Island, collect the small group left by Grenville in 1586 (he did not know they had been driven away by the Indians), and then move on to plant a colony on Chesapeake Bay. At last, on 22 July, they reached Port Ferdinando. When White and a party of his men were ready to set off for Roanoke Island they received an ultimatum from Fernandes. He would take them no farther; they must establish their settlement on Roanoke Island.[8] The ostensible reason, that the season was too late to allow the ships a chance to attack Spanish vessels on the way home, does not seem to be the real one, since the vessels waited for a month, getting shipshape, where they were. White assumed it was mere vindictiveness, and he may have been right; perhaps Fernandes's actions were not wholly rational. It may be, however, that White misjudged him. If he had been in Chesapeake Bay with the Spaniards long before, he must have known of the Indian destruction of the Jesuit mission there in 1570 and the subsequent Spanish reprisals. Moreover, he had had some evidence of Indian hostility to the English in this region in 1584. His action may, in part, have been intended to limit the risks for the little party of settlers. But on Roanoke Island, though they settled there, they were not happy. They insisted that John

---

Fernandes was the primary promoter of the venture. Moreover, the expedition finally sailed from England only on 7 May though its ships may have left London as early as March.

[7] *Ibid.*, pp. 517–18, 520–2. [8] *Ibid.*, pp. 523, 525.

White should return to fetch them supplies. And White insisted on sailing in the flyboat, leaving command of the *Lion* to Fernandes. The latter made for Terceira, perhaps out of sentiment, in hope of taking prizes off the Azores. Instead, sickness descended on the vessel and no prizes were taken. The *Lion* limped into Portsmouth in October.[9]

This brings to an end Fernandes's connection with Ralegh and with North American voyaging. It is highly probable that Ralegh repudiated him for his part in deflecting the colony from its objective. White remained vindictive, and since the colonists perished this is understandable. But Fernandes did not lose all his friends in England. When the English fleet was being assembled to meet the threat from the Spanish Armada, his services were again required. He joined his old acquaintance Martin Frobisher, now captain of the *Triumph*, the queen's largest galleon, as boatswain. He saw plenty of fighting, being almost continuously in action from 21 to 29 July—off Plymouth, off Portland, off the Isle of Wight, and at the last battle of Gravelines engaging the Spanish flagship, the *San Martin*, herself.[1] He had at last full opportunity to work off his hatred of Spain.

He survived to serve at least once more against Spain. In 1590 Sir John Hawkins and Sir Martin Frobisher took out a fleet of thirteen ships. Frobisher led the bulk of them to the Azores; Hawkins remained with the others off the coast of Spain. Fernandes served this time as master under Captain William Winter on the *Foresight* (300 tons).[2] We may take it that he accompanied Frobisher rather than Hawkins. His vessels were reported between July and the beginning of September off São Miguel; Terceira (so Fernandes saw his birthplace again); Fayal (where the shore commander had Frobisher's messenger executed); and Corvo—taking prizes finally off the last island. If Fernandes survived this expedition, he has not yet been identified on a later one.

There is a reference much later, in 1611 or 1612, to "an old plott" shown to William Strachey by Lord De La Warr, "wherein by a Portugall our seat is layd out, and in the same 2. silver mynes pricked downe."[3]

[9] *Ibid.*, pp. 536, 538.

[1] *State Papers Relating to the Defeat of the Spanish Armada*, N.R.S. (1894), ed. J. K. Laughton, II, 325. For the *Triumph*'s part in the campaign see Garrett Mattingly, *The Defeat of the Spanish Armada* (London, 1959), pp. 189, 239–40, 256–8, 264–5, 282.

[2] Michael Oppenheim, ed., *The Naval Tracts of William Monson*, N.R.S. (1902), III, 242–8. I am indebted to Pierre Lefranc for bringing this to my attention.

[3] William Strachey, *The Historie of Travell into Virginia Britania (1612)*, ed. Louis B. Wright and Virginia Freund (London, 1953), p. 131 (written between 1610 and 1612). See Quinn, *Roanoke Voyages*, II, 854; Cortesão and Teixeira da Mota, *Portugaliae Monumenta Cartographia*, II, 129.

This could conceivably represent a map of the southern part of Chesapeake Bay, showing the north bank of the James River between Old Point Comfort and Jamestown as suitable for English settlement. We know of no other Portuguese besides Simão Fernandes who was involved in the English Virginia enterprises, so this may have been a sketch based on his experiences in the Spanish service or gained during the 1584 voyage and compiled for the information of Ralegh at any time between 1584 and the departure of the third group of colonists in 1587. The evidence is suggestive rather than conclusive, but it remains just possible that Fernandes's influence on English ventures in these parts of North America lasted long after his disappearance or death.

Simão Fernandes—a violent, quarrelsome, and unattractive though able man—is one of a series of Portuguese pilots from João Fernandes onward who helped English explorers to penetrate unfamiliar waters outside Europe. He was the most prominent of those who helped Queen Elizabeth I in her struggle with Philip II, though like others of his kind he had been trained in the Spanish service. His importance in English history arises from the part he played in voyages to examine and attempt to settle eastern North America, and he was important in no less than five of the eight principal English voyages for this purpose between 1578 and 1587. The English were concerned with two distinct parts of eastern North America, the southeast (Florida to Virginia) and the northeast (New England to Cape Breton and Newfoundland). Simão Fernandes was able, from his earlier experience, to pilot them by way of the trade winds, the Caribbean, and the Florida Channel up the southeast coast. Moreover, he appears to have claimed, and to have had, detailed knowledge of the shore of what is now North Carolina, which enabled him to discover or rediscover in 1584 the inlet which the English named after him, Port Ferdinando, near Roanoke Island. This was to be the site of three colonizing attempts, all ultimately unsuccessful, between 1584 and 1587.

Further, it seems that he had some comparable knowledge, perhaps not gained at first hand, of what is now the tidewater area of Virginia, and that he was the first to teach the English something about Chesapeake Bay, where they planned to settle in 1587, but did not finally succeed until Jamestown was established in 1607. Though his conduct on the expeditions of 1584–7 may have contributed to the failure of the colonies, he had a significant role in the sequence of attempts which led eventually to effective English settlement in southeastern North America. Besides approaching North America by way of the West Indies, the English were interested in a direct route to the northeast coast between Cape Cod and

Cape Breton. It is conceivable, though this is pure speculation, that Fernandes had been on a Portuguese fishing voyage which gave him some knowledge of these coasts also. For Sir Humphrey Gilbert, in 1580, he certainly proved able to make a remarkably swift and daring voyage, apparently to the southern shore of New England. This gave the English valuable information, even though Gilbert's attempt to follow up the reconnaissance without his assistance as pilot ended in failure in 1583. Fernandes thus substantially extended the geographical knowledge of the English in the west and acted as a bridge by which some of the Spanish and Portuguese experience in North American navigation, topography, and cartography was communicated to them. As such, he deserves some little prominence in the history of the discoveries.

CHAPTER TEN

Some Spanish Reactions to Elizabethan Colonial Ventures

I

SPAIN'S CONCERN WITH the eastern shores of North America during the early part of the sixteenth century had been peripheral. Exploration under official and private auspices, both along the coasts and into the interior, had yielded a rich harvest of information, but down to 1561 projected and attempted settlements and missionary enterprises alike had failed to establish any permanent foothold in Florida or on the coast farther north. Spain was nevertheless determined, then and later, to deny the North American lands to any foreign power. But if the desire to preserve her monopoly rights underlay the resistance of Spain to foreign intervention, her occupation of Florida from 1565 onward and her continued concern to eliminate attempted foreign settlements there and farther north in the later sixteenth century were governed by more specific and practical considerations. The stabilizing of the Spanish fleet system in the 1560's brought its own problems. The *galeones*, with treasure from Nombre de Dios, and the *flota*, with Mexican produce from Vera Cruz, met at Havana early in the year and were supposed to sail jointly to Spain between March and June. Their route took them northeastward with the Gulf Stream along the North American coast, sometimes as far north as 36° N, though they usually swung eastward toward Bermuda at about 34° N.[1] Frequently late in

[1] C. H. Haring, *Trade and Navigation Between Spain and the Indies in the Time of the Hapsburgs* (Cambridge, Mass., 1918), pp. 201–30. There is much new information in the massive work by H. Chaunu and P. Chaunu, *Séville et l'Atlantique*, 12 vols. (Paris, 1955–9).

leaving Havana, the fleets tended to pass along the American coast during the hurricane season in late July and August, littering the coasts with wrecks and treasure and shipwrecked men often as far north as Cape Hatteras.[2] The creation of a series of posts which could salvage the ships and protect the crews thus left to the mercy of the Indians seemed a desirable insurance, and this provided one significant reason for maintaining the Florida garrisons after 1565.

The other danger was that of pirates and privateers, first mainly French but later English as well, who could wait to catch the fleet emerging from the Florida Channel and pick off stragglers as it sailed northeastward. A coastal squadron based on a Florida settlement offered some hope of limiting losses by these means, though the choice of San Agustín as the *Presidio* of the Florida colony was unfortunate from this point of view. Its advantage was its comparative ease of access to Havana, the nerve-center of Spanish activities in the Caribbean. Its disadvantage was that its harbors were inadequate for any substantial war vessels, though it could and did act as a useful base for light coastal craft. To build and maintain a base at a good harbor farther to the north was a frequent motif in Spanish plans and explains the continued Spanish preoccupation with Chesapeake Bay from about 1560 onward. But it was too expensive an undertaking to be attempted lightly.

Finally, if foreign raiders, not content to cut out an occasional straggler from the treasure fleets, were to establish naval bases of their own on the mainland coast, the fleets might be at their mercy. And not only that. The Spanish Indies might be systematically rather than just spasmodically ravaged from such bases. As the English attack on the Indies mounted in the 1580's, the fear of such a development became a Spanish obsession. The possibility of strong foreign bases, too, opened up the prospect of extensive civilian settlement by French or English nationals. This in turn would make a continually widening breach in the Spanish monopoly, which would be progressively harder to maintain even in the Indies—as indeed the following century was to show.

While Spain was inclined to exaggerate the immediate threat to her empire of foreign intervention in North America, there is no doubt that French and English alike aspired to do just what the Spaniards most feared. It is possible to dwell too much on long-term economic and social motives inspiring the rather tardy English colonizing movement of which the two Hakluyts, Sir Humphrey Gilbert, and Sir Walter Ralegh were the moving spirits, and to push into the background their short-term

[2] Haring, *Trade and Navigation*, p. 228; Hakluyt, *Principal Navigations*, 12 vols. (Glasgow, 1903–5), VIII, 303, 307, X, 58.

objective: the overriding consideration of robbing the Spanish empire. While detailed evidence from both English and Spanish sides has not all been uncovered, this chapter is an attempt to indicate some Spanish reactions to Elizabethan colonial ventures in North America.

II

The establishment in 1562 of the French post of Charlesfort on Port Royal Sound, in modern South Carolina, was followed by the abortive English enterprise under Thomas Stukeley in 1563 and by a second French settlement, at Fort Caroline on the St. John's River in modern Florida, in 1564. All this stung the Spaniards into action. Pedro Menéndez de Avilés was given the forces both to wipe out the French settlers, which he did, and to establish a permanent garrison in Florida in 1565. Surviving a damaging blow delivered by the French Dominique de Gourges in 1568, his colony was built up by a chain of coastal posts from Santa Elena on Port Royal Sound southward to his capital of San Agustín. He also embarked on exploration of the coast farther north, flinging out an advance screen of missionaries to calm and control the Indians. Farthest north was the Jesuit post on Chesapeake Bay—the Bahia de Santa Maria (or Bahia de Madre de Dios) of the Spaniards—established in 1570. After it was wiped out by Indians, Menéndez himself went north in 1572 to take revenge, and this venture provided a body of information about the coastline which was to be of service later.[3] His attempts to extend the settlement failed, however, and when he left Florida in 1572 the Spanish colony remained a weak outpost, tardily supplied with men and stores from Spain. For the next five years it fell into neglect, until his nephew, Pedro Menéndez Marqués, returned with reinforcements in 1577.[4]

From 1562 on, the Spanish ambassadors in London had kept a sharp lookout for any sign of English interest in eastern North America, to the whole coastline of which they gave the name Florida. Álvaro de la Quadra in 1563 maintained a steady fire of protests to Queen Elizabeth against Thomas Stukeley's proposed expedition, maintaining that Spain's title to North America was fully established, while at the same time he sent home reports on the preparations.[5] Similarly, when Guzman de Silva

[3] Ruidiaz y Caravia, *Florida; su Conquista y Colonización;* Woodbury Lowery, *Spanish Settlements in the United States, 1562–1574* (Washington, D.C., 1905); C. M. Lewis and A. J. Loomie, *The Spanish Jesuit Mission in Virginia, 1570–1572* (Chapel Hill, 1953).

[4] Mary Ross, "French Intrusions and Indian Uprisings in Georgia and South Carolina, 1577–1580," *Georgia Historical Quarterly,* VII (1923), 236.

reported that Hawkins had visited the French colony in 1565, Philip II required him again to make inquiries about English intentions regarding Florida and the adjoining coasts.[6] These preliminaries, however, were not soon followed by further alarms, and successive ambassadors confined themselves to reporting fact and rumor about English raids on the Indies and on Spanish shipping.

Although in 1578 Bernardino de Mendoza kept a close watch on Sir Humphrey Gilbert's preparations for an expedition, it is not clear from his surviving dispatches that he knew the objective to be a reconnaissance of the North American coast with a view to establishing a colonial base such as the Spaniards feared.[7] But when, in 1582, Gilbert's plans were revived in a more elaborate form he was soon aware of their nature and implications. He wrote on 26 April 1582 to say that Gilbert's objective was Florida, where the French had been, and that the queen would give him a substantial army once he had established a foothold. Times had changed, and when Mendoza went to court to protest, he was refused a hearing.[8] This did not prevent him from doing his utmost to sabotage Gilbert's preparations. When a group of English Catholic gentry, headed by Sir George Peckham and Sir Thomas Gerard, proposed to go with Gilbert, he not only threatened that they would get their throats cut by Spanish soldiers but accused them of being traitors to their faith. Moreover, he wrote personally to Dr. William Allen, as adviser to the Pope on English Catholic affairs, and to the Spanish representative at the Vatican to bring the strongest ecclesiastical pressure to bear against their participation. These measures were, he claimed, effective in frightening off all but a handful of Catholics from any further connection with the project.

Mendoza could not prevent Gilbert from sailing on his last unsuccessful voyage, nor could he stop Sir George Peckham from trying, also unsuccessfully, to follow up Gilbert's plans early in 1584, but his use of ecclesiastical sanctions to further the imperial interests of Spain is not without interest.[9] No reactions by Philip II or his ministers to the news from London have so far been traced, but it is not too much to assume that from 1582 onward they were once more sharply aware of the impli-

[5] *Cal.S.P.,Span.,1558–1567* (1892), pp. 323, 333–6, 442, 447, 448; A. Rumeu de Armas, *Viajes de Hawkins a América* (Seville, 1947), pp. 134–7; Jean Ribaut, *The Whole and True Discouerye of Terra Florida* (DeLand, 1927), ed. J. T. Connor.

[6] *Cal.S.P.,Span.,1558–1567*, pp. 470, 486, 493, 495–6, 503.

[7] D. B. Quinn, ed., *The Voyages and Colonising Enterprises of Sir Humphrey Gilbert,* Hakluyt Society, 2d ser., nos. 83–4, 2 vols. (London, 1940), I, 186–8, 194.

[8] *Ibid.*, II, 244–5. [9] *Ibid.*, pp. 58–9, 62, 71–6; cf. p. 377 below.

cations of an English settlement in North America—even if it should be, as Gilbert had planned, in "Norumbega" (New England) rather than on the doorstep of the Florida garrison.

When, in March 1584, Walter Ralegh fell heir to Gilbert's patent, the Spaniards were presented for the first time with a sequence of persistent though small-scale English attempts to establish a permanent foothold on the American coast north of their Florida outposts. These continued as the scale of English raids on the West Indies appeared to be mounting toward the climax of an all-out assault, for which the Armada of 1588 finally seemed the only remedy. In spite of its failure to conquer England, this had the desired result of diverting the main English attack from the Indies. The Spanish government, therefore, took most seriously any news of English settlements in North America, and indeed it was only by a series of mischances that they did not wipe out the Roanoke colony and themselves establish a strong, continuing fortress on Chesapeake Bay.

Spain was handicapped in discovering and thwarting English plans for American settlements by the very complexity of her own political and administrative system. In January 1584, Bernardino de Mendoza, her ambassador, was turned out of England. Though he had left agents behind, his reports on English activities from Paris, where he was soon installed as ambassador, were intermittent, incomplete, and often tardy. Álvaro de Bazán, Marquis of Santa Cruz and head of the Spanish forces, had his own spies in England, but in general the paucity of information gathered by the Spaniards constitutes a high tribute to the quality of English counterespionage. For the most part they had to depend on reports picked up from the Atlantic islands and the West Indies, where outward-bound English expeditions called for food and water or to trade and plunder. Across the Atlantic such reports trickled through local officials to Havana, and thence with majestic slowness, by way of the annual fleets, to Spain, where they got enmeshed in the network of councils and committees and the painstaking paper work of King Philip, until the news was stale when decisions came to be made.

Nor was it then simple to get action taken. Much of the delay was due, not to inefficiency but rather to the technical problems of governing from such vast distances. Great efforts were made to speed things up during the years from 1585 onward. Swift packet boats were increasingly used for inward and outward correspondence. The Junta de Puerto Rico of the Council of the Indies was built up as both a deliberative and an executive board, through which decisions on such matters as threats from English colonies could be translated into protective action. But the process did not, and could not, make for speed in a rapidly changing situation.

From 1568 to 1577 the Florida colony had substantial freedom from foreign intervention.[1] Hawkins, it is true, was suspected in 1570 of a plan to attack and settle Florida in association with the French, without implicating the queen in his preparations, while at the end of 1571 or early in 1572 three English ships, possibly belonging to Sir William Winter, attacked San Agustín and were driven off by Pedro Menéndez de Avilés only with difficulty. But when in 1577 Pedro Menéndez Marqués went north to stamp out an Indian rising in the vicinity of Santa Elena, he found that the French had established a fort on the coast north of the Spanish outpost.[2] A band of French privateers under Nicolas Estrozi (Strozzi), who had been fitted out by his brother at Bordeaux,[3] had moved from the West Indies to establish a base on the mainland. Attacked and taken prisoner by the Indians, Strozzi and his men made friends with their captors and were endeavoring to incite them against the Spaniards. After destroying the empty fort and inflicting some losses on the Indians, Menéndez Marqués induced them to make peace in 1579 and to hand over their French allies, all but five of whom he executed, refusing a large ransom from Strozzi. In 1580 other French vessels tried to find Strozzi's base, and the Spaniards were kept in a continuous state of alarm. Finally Gilberto Gil, a Catalan, coming out with supplies for Strozzi, ran his vessel aground at San Mateo and in July 1580 was defeated, captured, and with all but four of his men, executed.[4]

These events were not without relevance to the Spanish reaction to later English enterprises, since they revived the concern of the Spanish government with foreign threats to the colony. In 1577 Rodrigo de Junco was sent from Florida to Spain to report the arrival of the French,[5] and urged the sending of additional galleys to the Cuba station which could be used for a regular six-monthly or annual patrol of the Florida coast.[6] In 1581 Menéndez Marqués had asked in vain for permission to come home to report information he had obtained from the French,

[1] *Cal.S.P.,Span.,1568–1579* (1894), p. 277; Irene A. Wright, ed., *Documents Concerning English Voyages to the Spanish Main, 1569–1580* (London, 1932), pp. xxxvi–xxxvii, 37–9.

[2] Ross, "French Intrusions," pp. 256–69; J. T. Connor, ed., *Colonial Records of Spanish Florida, 1577–1580,* 2 vols. (DeLand, 1925–30), II, 78–9.

[3] He appears to have been the brother of the famous Philippe Strozzi, cousin of Catherine de' Medici, who died only three years later attempting to drive the Spaniards out of the Azores.

[4] Ross, "French Intrusions," pp. 270–5; Connor, *Colonial Records of Spanish Florida,* II, 318–23.

[5] Ross, "French Intrusions," p. 258.

[6] *Colección de Documentos Inéditos de Indias,* 42 vols. (Madrid, 1864–84), 1st ser., XI, 229–32.

which he said "he did not dare to trust to paper." [7] We know, too, that he had been alarmed afresh in 1584, and again sent Rodrigo de Junco—accompanied or followed by his brother-in-law Juan de Posada—to Spain to request reinforcements and shipping to deal with a renewed threat of foreign intervention.[8]

Reports to Madrid from Paris in the spring of 1584 had been quick to associate Ralegh with new English preparations for expeditions to the Indies,[9] but there is no evidence in the surviving dispatches that they conveyed anything about the voyage made by Amadas and Barlowe to the Carolina Banks between April and September 1584. Menéndez Marqués's action may have proceeded from some fresh French ventures, but it is more likely to reflect some news or rumor of the Amadas-Barlowe expedition. In either event, both the governor of Florida and the Council of the Indies were on their guard before the first English colonizing expedition left Plymouth in April 1585.

English plans for a North American colony were finally decided early in 1585, but the surviving documentation is incomplete. It is clear, however, that—among other things—they involved the creation of a fortified settlement in newly named Virginia.[1] It is also probable that Sir Richard Grenville intended to leave there the greater part of the force with which he set sail from England, together with some shipping, so that a permanent base for raids on the treasure fleets and on the Indies could be maintained.

While there was much improvisation in the intensified sea war mounted against Spain in 1585, and it is doubtful if there was any close coordination between the separate strokes delivered, it seems not unlikely that the Virginia colony was intended to serve as one element in a broadly-conceived plan—a plan developed after news came of the Spanish seizure of the English merchant fleet in Spanish ports in May 1585. Such a plan would have included Bernard Drake's attack on the Spanish fishery at Newfoundland as well as Sir Francis Drake's attempt to find the treasure fleet, to demolish the main centers of Spanish power in the West Indies, and possibly to establish permanent English footholds there. Drake's avoidance in 1586, on his way out of the Caribbean, of an attack on Havana in favor of an attempt to render the Florida colony untenable by the Spaniards, suggests that his visit to the English colony on the Carolina Banks in June 1586 was made in expectation of finding a good port of call in English hands. That he was to be disappointed by both the absence of

[7] Ross, "French Intrusions," p. 281. [8] Quinn, *Roanoke Voyages*, II, 726–7, 746–8.
[9] *Ibid.*, pp. 725–6. [1] See *ibid.*, I, 130–9.

an adequate harbor and the weakness of the colony was not to be foreseen. These conjectures cannot be proved, but they certainly represent, if not the precise character of the English plans, the course which the Spaniards came to anticipate and appeared to see unfolding during the years 1585–6.

Mendoza had been able to report to Madrid quickly and with some approach to accuracy on Ralegh's preparations between February and April 1585, though he believed his ships were destined for "Noranberga" —the New England objective of Gilbert's projects.[2] But efforts by his agents to glean more precise information from the English ambassador in Paris met with no success.[3] He was able to report the departure of Grenville's squadron only a fortnight after it had gone, and added mistakenly in June that his ships had put back to port, this information being accepted gratefully by Philip II in July.[4] From this time onward his English correspondents began to fail him, and he was able to contribute little further to Spanish knowledge of English North American plans and voyages.

Certain precautions were being taken, however, before news from the West Indies proved that Grenville had not returned. In January the Junta de Puerto Rico had obtained the king's approval for the dispatch, with the outgoing fleet, of a frigate which would carry reinforcements and supplies to Florida, make a reconnaissance along the coast, and return to Spain in the autumn. Then, too, the Casa de Contratación sent out warnings, which reached Havana by the end of May, that English raiders were on their way to the Indies.[5] Pedro Menéndez Marqués, at last granted leave of absence from Florida, arrived at Havana to sail home with the fleet just in time to hear that Grenville had reached Puerto Rico and might well be going on to North America.

Reports of the fortified camp which Grenville had built in May at Guayanilla in Puerto Rico suggested that the English intended to establish themselves there, but after building a pinnace they abandoned the camp and moved on to trade along the coasts of Puerto Rico and Hispaniola. There they made no secret of their intention to establish a colony, and bought livestock and collected plants to take with them. Later a report from a Spaniard taken by Grenville and released on Puerto Rico indicated that his men refused to say precisely where they were going, suggesting Trinidad, Dominica, or some other unoccupied part of the

[2] *Ibid.*, II, 728–31.

[3] E. G. R. Taylor, ed., *The Original Writings and Correspondence of the Two Richard Hakluyts*, Hakluyt Society, 2d ser., 76–7, 2 vols. (London, 1935), II, 345.

[4] Quinn, *Roanoke Voyages*, II, 731–2.

[5] *Ibid.*, pp. 733–8.

Spanish empire. The fact that they had two North American Indians with them led Menéndez Marqués to suspect that they might be going to settle on the mainland north of Florida, so, after adding his reports to those of the Havana authorities, he again deferred his leave and returned to San Agustín to take precautionary measures.[6] He settled down to construct a new wooden fort there[7] and in December sent a vessel northward to see whether an English post had been established. Among the forty men on board was a Frenchman, Nicholas Bourgoignon, afterward taken by Drake, whose presence suggests that the search was made first in those harbors north of Santa Elena frequented by the French. The vessel apparently worked up the coast only as far as the vicinity of Winyah Bay and then turned back,[8] leaving the colony on Roanoke Island, some three hundred miles farther north, still undiscovered.

The advent of Drake with a formidable fleet on the north coast of Spain in September 1585 and his subsequent departure for an unknown destination forced the Spaniards to revise the scale of their preparations to meet the English threat to their empire. A month after Drake had gone, the Marquis of Santa Cruz was already sketching out the far-reaching plans which led toward the Armada of 1588 and was urging the speedy dispatch of a seagoing fleet which would search for and strike the English fleet in the West Indies.[9] This followed shortly on the news of Grenville's activities in the Indies and of his colonizing plans. It was thus easy to associate Drake's probable objectives with those of Ralegh and Grenville, and to conceive of the colony which Grenville was believed to have planted in North America as a link in a chain of English plans for intensifying the attacks on the Spanish Indies. Toward the end of November the possibility of dealing with Drake by means of a fleet which should leave Spain not later than 1 March 1586 was already being discussed at a high level,[1] while at the same time the sending of further aid to Menéndez Marqués in Florida was being considered. A decision on the latter was taken by the Junta de Puerto Rico on 24 December.[2] Two ships—one a strongly armed frigate—were to carry arms, supplies, money,

[6] *Ibid.*, pp. 738–43.

[7] Verne E. Chatelaine, *The Defenses of Spanish Florida, 1565–1763* (Washington, D.C., 1941), pp. 50–1.

[8] Quinn, *Roanoke Voyages*, II, 765–6.

[9] Hakluyt, *Principal Navigations*, X (1904), 88–97; Joan de Castellanos, *Discurso de el Capitán Francisco Draque*, ed. Ángel González Palencia (Madrid, 1921), pp. lxxxi–lxxxiii.

[1] *Ibid.*, pp. lxxvii–xc, 360–1.

[2] Quinn, *Roanoke Voyages*, II, 744–8, 750–2; Irene A. Wright, *Further English Voyages to Spanish America, 1583–1594* (London, 1951), pp. 12–15.

and men to Florida in order to render the colony alike defensible and capable of taking the offensive against the English settlement.

Though the reinforcements had not reached Florida by May 1586, packet boats went out to the Indies to inform officials in the islands, on the main, and in Florida that the English had settled on the North American coast and that a formidable fleet was coming from Spain to destroy the archpirate Drake.[3] But it was not until April 1586 that Philip II finally decided that Santa Cruz in person should command this expedition, which was not to interfere with the decision already taken to launch the great Armada against England itself. By this time, according to the Venetian representative in Madrid, Spanish opinion was even more apprehensive of rumored English conquests in North America than of Drake's victories in the Indies,[4] while Santa Cruz believed that Grenville had left not only five hundred men but five ships in Virginia, and was aware that he was preparing a further expedition to reinforce the colony.[5] He concluded that the English intended to set up strong permanent bases in both the West Indies and Virginia which could play a vital part in the mounting campaign against the Indies.

Although part of the fleet Santa Cruz was to command had been assembled at Cadiz by the end of April, its preparation was never completed and it was finally cancelled. Substantial precautions had been taken. Álvaro Flores de Quinones took out a specially reinforced squadron to escort the mainland fleet in April, while six galleys were posted to the most seriously threatened ports in the Indies. Of the abandonment of Santa Cruz's expedition the king said later, "if this was given up it was because it was understood that he, Drake, would retreat before he could be seized." [6]

Drake's actions after passing out of the Caribbean through the Florida Channel in May appeared to bear out Santa Cruz's worst expectations. Warned that Drake might descend on him, Menéndez Marqués wisely withdrew from San Agustín and its protecting fort, after a token resistance, when the English fleet appeared on 28 May 1586. Drake could not chase him and his Indian allies into the wilderness, and so contented himself with destroying fort and town before deciding to go on to

[3] See Césareo Fernández Duro, *La Armada Española*, 9 vols. (Madrid, 1895–1930), II, 482. On the warnings reaching the West Indies, see Quinn, *Roanoke Voyages,* II, 748–9.

[4] *Calendar of State Papers, Venetian, 1581–1591* (*Cal.S.P.,Ven.*) (1895), p. 140.

[5] C. Fernández Duro, *La Armada Invencible*, 2 vols. (Madrid, 1884–5), I, 330–3.

[6] *Ibid.*, II, 482. The king's statement was made in a letter transcribed in B.M., AdditionalMS 36315, fols. 76–88.

Santa Elena and the Roanoke colony. For lack of a pilot he left Santa Elena alone, but soon made contact with Ralph Lane's lookout parties on the Carolina Banks. There any hopes he had of finding a strong base on a good harbor were disappointed. As we have seen, failure of the promised supplies to arrive had disheartened the colonists, though Drake offered them a ship in which they might search for a better site on Chesapeake Bay. But a storm drove the ship to sea, and Drake took off the remaining colonists and brought them home. The supply ship, followed by Grenville's squadron, arrived too late, and Grenville left only a small party of men to maintain the empty fort on Roanoke Island.[7]

Had the Spaniards known of these developments they might have ceased to concern themselves with the Virginia settlement as a serious threat to their own predominance. Instead, the reconstruction of the Florida colony and the planning of a descent on the English post became a close preoccupation during the following years. They received exaggerated reports in 1586 that Grenville was in command of no less than twenty-eight ships,[8] while at Havana at the opening of 1587 officials were convinced that Drake would return that year, using as his main base the English North American settlement. The Venetian representative in Madrid said a little later it was believed in Spain that the English held the approaches to the Florida Channel itself, and from this they could do immense damage.[9] Philip's mind was certainly running along such channels and on 16/26 May 1587 he urged the Junta de Puerto Rico to "consider the importance of the rumor—if it is true—about the English viscount," apparently Grenville. "It is to be feared," he wrote, "that, if he has established a settlement on the coast, the fact that he has changed its site is no indication of a decision to abandon it, but rather of his intention to improve his position." The Junta was to report on countermeasures to be taken.[1]

Pedro Menéndez Marqués was meantime carrying out his own precautionary measures. Encouraged by the inflow of supplies and men after Drake's raid, he had begun the construction of a stronger fort at San Agustín,[2] but was clearly much concerned about what the English might be doing further north. He set out early in the summer of 1587 on a reconnaissance in a single frigate, and reached the latitude where he expected to find the English colony, in the vicinity of Chesapeake Bay, about the time when John White's expedition, with the third ("lost") colony on board, was making its quarrel-ridden way through the West

[7] Quinn, *Roanoke Voyages*, I, 294–312, 477–80. [8] *Ibid.*, II, 757–60, 766–7.
[9] *Cal.S.P.,Ven.,1581–1591*, p. 250. [1] Quinn, *Roanoke Voyages*, II, 768–9.
[2] Chatelaine, *Defenses of Spanish Florida*, pp. 50–1.

Indies. Menéndez Marqués was, however, driven out to sea by a storm, and being unable to recover his position, ran for Havana and thence back to San Agustín.[3] It was then that he decided to abandon his northern outpost at Santa Elena as untenable, and was able to report in February 1588 that the evacuation had been completed.

In Spain, in spite of preoccupation with the Armada, close attention was being given to the task of destroying the English settlement and replacing it by a Spanish one. A Venetian report in December 1587 stated that "the king is thinking of building three or four forts in Florida, and he has the plans in his room."[4] It is probable that these were not merely new forts for the San Agustín zone but fortifications for the area to be conquered from the English. The Duke of Medina Sidonia, who took over in March 1588 the command of the great Armada, sent orders to Menéndez Marqués that he must be ready by 5/15 May 1588 to leave San Agustín in person on an expedition against the English colony. After a presumably successful attack he was to sail home to Spain. But the Spanish government was by now so deeply involved in the Armada campaign that neither reinforcements nor instructions arrived in Florida. Menéndez Marqués, after waiting until 28 May, decided to send a packet boat which had come from Spain on a reconnaissance of the English position, under the command of Vicente González, a pilot who was familiar with the coast.[5]

The ship was a small one, a *barca luengo,* which could be sailed or rowed and was admirably suited for coastal exploration. With González went Juan Menéndez Marqués, *sergente mayor* of the fortress, the governor's nephew; Gines Pinzón, a pilot; and twenty-eight men. Their instructions were to run along the coast past the mouth of the Chesapeake as far as 39° N and to pick up any information they could about the English. They called at a number of points between Santa Elena and a place somewhat north of Cape Romain—probably Winyah Bay—but learned nothing of any English activities. Farther north they sailed quickly along the Carolina Banks, making no attempt at a search and passing the inlets which led through to Roanoke Island, thus indicating that the Florida authorities had no precise knowledge of the location of the English settlement. González, who had been there in 1573, took the

[3] Quinn, *Roanoke Voyages,* II, 804–13.

[4] The reference is to Battista Antonelli, being the Italian named as the engineer (*Cal.S.P.,Ven.,1581–1591,* p. 329). With Juan de Texeda, he (in his Spanish guise of Bautista Antoneli) planned the rebuilding of Cartagena after Drake's raid (Castellanos, *Discurso,* pp. cii–ciii).

[5] Quinn, *Roanoke Voyages,* II, 778–81.

vessel into Chesapeake Bay. The exploration of this great inlet was a remarkably swift and effective operation, extending up the western shore, past the Susquehanna River to the end of the Bay, and then, less systematically, down the island-strewn eastern shore and again back to the western shore, without finding any trace of the English.

Running out into open sea, González made no attempt to turn north, but coasting southward was caught with a freshening wind and so forced to furl his sails, dismast, and row for shelter. It was this accident which led to the discovery of some traces of the English settlers, since by chance he found shelter at Port Ferdinando (or Hatarask), the more southerly and more important of the two inlets that led through the Carolina Banks to Roanoke Island. This had been the harbor used by successive groups of colonists from 1585 to 1587. Since White had sailed back from there for reinforcements in August 1587, no help had come for the colonists, White's two pinnaces in May 1588 having got only to the vicinity of the Azores before turning back. González's discovery was of a slipway, made for small vessels (*varadero señalado de chalupas*), which had probably been used since 1585 for transporting men and goods to the fort, which was about ten miles away at the northern end of Roanoke Island. In the sand round about were sunk a number of casks, evidently used for catching water. This discovery does not certainly indicate that the "lost colonists" were still at Roanoke, but it gave the Spaniards the evidence they needed to locate a settlement which they presumed must still exist. This was all González required. Taking his latitude—as 35°30′ N (for 35°50′), he set off down the coast and reached San Agustín again before the end of July, after a very swift and effective, though somewhat lucky, reconnaissance.[6]

Pedro Menéndez Marqués had meantime gone to Havana and from there he wrote to the king on 7/17 July to report that the final instructions for his voyage against the English settlement had not arrived and that he had sent González on his mission. He stated too that five English vessels were plying off Cuba attempting to cut off ships arriving at Havana to join the Spain-bound fleet. His comment on this news was interesting, since he concluded that these ships must be based on the English Virginia settlement. Otherwise he could not understand how they

[6] The main authority is Luis Gerónimo de Oré, *Relación Histórica de la Florida*, 2 vols. (Madrid, 1931), I, 78–82 (trans. Maynard Geiger, *The Martyrs of Florida, 1513–1616* [New York, 1936], pp. 44–9; trans. Quinn, *Roanoke Voyages*, II, 804–13), supplemented by the relations of Vicente González (*ca.* 1600) (*ibid.*, pp. 822–5) and of Juan Menéndez Marqués, 28 May–7 June 1606 (*ibid.*, pp. 816–21; E. Ruidías, *Florida: Su Conquista y Colonización*, 2 vols. [Madrid, 1893], II, 495–500).

had been allowed to leave England in the Armada year.[7] He indicated that he would have to defer his own voyage against the English settlement until 1589 as the season for northward voyages was passing.

He returned to San Agustín, where he received the reports of González, Juan Menéndez Marqués—*tan puntual y prolija*—and Pinzón, which he appears to have dispatched to Spain, where they have not yet been found. His long-expected orders, when they came, merely told him to return as soon as possible to Spain, so he left San Agustín on 18 October, taking his nephew with him and leaving Juan de Posada in charge of Florida. Once again he was unfortunate. He was driven by a storm back to the West Indies and had to put in at Havana, where he was detained for some months.[8] His time was not wasted, however, since valuable information was now becoming available at Havana on English activities on the mainland coast.

In the first place, Alonzo Ruiz reported in July 1588 that he had been taken in June 1587 by William Irish, commanding three ships belonging to Sir George Carey in the West Indies.[9] They had passed through the Florida Channel on the way home, and being short of water had put in at the place where the English colony was thought to be settled. This was, he said, at 37° in the Bay of Santa Maria, i.e., Chesapeake Bay. Though no English settlers were found, the discovery of some "traces of cattle and a stray dark-brown mule" convinced him they were not far away. His story indicated two things to the Spaniards: first, that the site of the English settlement was on Chesapeake Bay; and second, that English raiders of the Indies expected to use the English colony, as the Spaniards had feared, as a base for revictualling and refitting, which would help to prolong their raids on the Indies.

A more systematic statement was made by the pilot, Pedro Diaz, in March 1589.[1] Taken in the *Santa Maria* by Grenville on his return voyage in 1585, he knew the whole story of the English colonizing effort so far. He had been brought by Grenville to the Carolina Banks on his second voyage in 1586, and could explain why the González expedition had been unable to find the English settlement on the Banks, since it was on Roanoke Island inside the Sound. He was aware not only that Drake had

[7] See p. 298 below.

[8] Oré, *Relación*, I, 82–3 (Geiger, *The Martyrs of Florida*, pp. 49–50; Quinn, *Roanoke Voyages*, II, 813–14). But royal letters of 19–20 October 1588, recalling him, which possibly reached Havana before the end of the year, reiterated the instruction to make a personal reconnaissance of the coast before coming home. Gutierre de Miranda was named governor to succeed him (A.G.I., Santo Domingo 2528).

[9] Quinn, *Roanoke Voyages*, II, 781–4. [1] *Ibid.*, pp. 786–95.

removed the first colony in 1586, but also that Grenville had left only eighteen men to form the second. He could tell of the departure of White's expedition from England with the third colony in 1587 and of the failure to supply or reinforce it in 1588. He himself had piloted one of White's small supply ships, the *Brave*, in 1588, until it was stripped by a French privateer off the Azores. There he made his escape and eventually got to Havana. His opinion was that the English colony in Virginia had come to an end, or was at least in great straits.

This information put the authorities in Havana in possession of nearly as much knowledge as the English had themselves, so it is not surprising that arrangements were made to ship Diaz home to Spain as soon as possible. The whole perspective of the scale of the English enterprises, with all its limitations, was now clear to the Spaniards. Pedro Menéndez Marqués, however, considered himself justified in returning to San Agustín, possibly to reassure his deputy that the English offered no present threat to the Florida colony. From there he set out at last for Spain on 8 May, arriving at San Lucar on 25 June and going on with his nephew to Madrid. Juan Menéndez Marqués gave a verbal account of the 1588 voyage to two of the king's ministers, Juan de Idiaquez and Juan de Ibarra, while Pedro Menéndez Marqués appeared before the Council of the Indies.

The council clearly believed that action was urgent, apparently rather to forestall further English settlements than to come to grips with a puny and perhaps nonexistent colony. Pedro Menéndez Marqués was given instructions to prepare an expedition in Spain, with four supply ships, soldiers, and stores. With these he was to sail to Havana and there pick up such galleys and merchant ships as he would require. He was then to go to San Agustín, taking only the galleys over the difficult bar and allowing the other vessels to proceed along the coast. At San Agustín he was to land a number of the new troops and take on an equivalent number of seasoned men from the garrison. The expedition was to proceed to Roanoke Island and wipe out such English as were found there, after which it was to go on to Chesapeake Bay, and when a suitable site had been found, establish a strong fort with a garrison of three hundred men. The governor of the fort was to be required also to make an extensive search for precious metals, the hope of finding which had been aroused by reports of the 1588 expedition.[2]

Had these instructions been carried out, the fate of the "Lost Colony" might be known, and the Spaniards would have been established in force

[2] *Ibid.*, pp. 184–5.

in the area to which the Virginia Colony of 1607 came. That they were not was due to the exigencies of the maritime war with England.

The intensified English blockade had now forced the Spanish government to devise some quicker and surer means of getting the New World treasure to Spain. So Pedro Menéndez Marqués was taken from his North American enterprise and put in command of two fast *galizabras,* and between May and September sailed triumphantly to the Indies and back with the silver.[3] The expedition to the Chesapeake Bay, first postponed, was then abandoned. Pedro Menéndez Marqués was retained for more important service on the Atlantic treasure route.

The Spaniards, it is true, learned that the privateering vessels belonging to John Watts and William Sanderson, which undertook in 1590 to go on to Roanoke Island to search for the Lost Colony after seeking prizes in the West Indies, carried a "governor," John White, and (they believed) artillery for the settlement.[4] The governor of Puerto Rico, writing on 22 August/1 September 1590,[5] expressed all the old Spanish fears that the English were using the colony as a fortified base at which to take on fresh water and refresh their men to prolong their privateering raids. Once more he urged the king to take action against the settlement, but without result. Spain was too deeply involved in Europe.

It is an interesting and ironical result that the sea war between England and Spain, which obstructed and finally ended the first series of English attempts to settle colonists on the North American mainland, also in the end prevented the establishment of Spanish forts and settlements there, which in their turn might have made the English Virginia settlement of 1607 impossible.

III

THERE IS STILL a postscript to write on the continuing concern of Spain with real or presumptive English settlements in North America. In Florida, Indian risings and lack of supplies and reinforcements hampered Menéndez Marqués's successors, so that no attempt was made to resume a forward policy until Gonzalo Méndez de Canzo took over the government.[6] Starved of resources as usual, he decided that the only way to arouse Spanish interest in the colony was to urge the material advantages

[3] *Ibid.,* p. 815. [4] *Ibid.,* pp. 580–2, 704–12. [5] *Ibid.,* pp. 797–801.

[6] For Méndez de Canzo see J. T. Lanning, *Spanish Missions of Georgia* (Chapel Hill, 1937), pp. 111–35; Maynard Geiger, *Franciscan Conquest of Florida* (Washington, D.C., 1937), pp. 71–116; C. W. Arnade, *Florida on Trial* (Coral Gables, 1959), *passim.*

of expansion. In 1598 he sent home glowing reports of the riches to be gained from exploring and developing the interior of what is now Georgia and opened up the prospect of an easy land route to New Mexico. The government of the new king, Philip III, on 30 October 1598, was sufficiently interested to instruct him to collect further information and to make concrete proposals.

In the course of his search Méndez de Canzo discovered in his garrison an Irishman, Darby Glavin. He had been a member of Lane's colony on Roanoke Island in 1585–6 and in July 1587, on the way back to Virginia with White's colony, had deserted with another Irishman, Dennis Carroll, in Puerto Rico. There he had been sent to the galleys before being enrolled as a soldier and eventually sent to Florida. He now told the governor of his experiences at Roanoke and expressed his belief that the colonists of 1587 were still there. Moreover, he had since heard from some survivors of Richard Hawkins's Pacific expedition of 1593–4 that in June 1593 two ships had left England "with supplies of people, ammunition, clothes, implements, axes and spades for the settlers of Jacan" (i.e., Virginia). This indicated to Méndez de Canzo that the English colony, which it was assumed must still survive near the 36th parallel, was worth seeking, especially as Glavin was confident that gold and pearls were to be found nearby.

It is surprising that the governor did not check this story with Juan Menéndez Marqués, now serving as treasurer of Florida, who knew a great deal more than Glavin about the history of the English colony and had been near Roanoke Island in 1588. But Glavin's story provided Méndez de Canzo with bait which might be sufficient to tempt the Spanish government into a new North American venture. Accordingly, while enclosing Glavin's deposition, he completed his dispatch of 18/28 February 1600 with a detailed scheme for an expedition of one thousand men, with ships and equipment listed down to the last *escupile* or padded jacket. This force would go north and wipe out the English and then establish a great fort on Chesapeake Bay, from which expeditions would soon open the way to the treasures of the interior and establish an easy land route to New Mexico.[7]

Méndez de Canzo's ignorance of North American geography was as great as his optimism. He tried hard during the next year or so to collect further information on the English settlement, but failed to find any. It seems probable that he led the authorities in Spain to interrogate Vicente González, who had headed the 1588 expedition. The latter's rambling

[7] Quinn, *Roanoke Voyages*, II, 833–8.

and inaccurate account of that voyage did not add much that was of value, though he gave it as his opinion that the English settlers were probably located on a river north of the 38th parallel in Chesapeake Bay.[8]

But no expedition was authorized. Instead, a commission was sent from Cuba to consider whether it might not be well to wind up the Florida colony altogether. In the course of the investigation the commissioners took some evidence from Juan Menéndez Marqués, which included reminiscences of the 1588 voyage and inspired him on 10/20 September 1602 to make a report on Florida and the ports and coastline to the north.[9] Two days later Méndez de Canzo completed a long dispatch to the king in which he surveyed the whole situation of Florida.[1] He recommended its continuance as a base for rescuing Spanish ships and sailors, as a mission center, and as a starting point for future exploitation of the interior, but he had convinced himself, or had been convinced, that the English were no longer established on the coast to the north. Further, he expressed some doubts as to whether, if the Florida garrison were withdrawn, the English would step in to replace it. He gave as his reasons: first, that there were no harbors suitable for large vessels; second, that the country round about was incapable of producing food supplies sufficient to maintain any large body of inhabitants; and third, that San Agustín itself was an impossible site, most unsuitably placed for mounting any attacks on the treasure fleets or on the Indies.

By 1602 the wheel had again come full circle. The Spaniards had been prepared in 1589 to destroy the English settlement, after it had in all probability been deserted. Now, at the very time that Ralegh and others were reviving their voyages to the Virginia and New England shores preparatory to a new settlement, there was a strong possibility that Spain would abandon altogether her footholds on the Atlantic coast. Florida was not in fact abandoned, but the new Virginia settlement from 1607 on had little to fear from the isolated and neglected garrison which was maintained there.

[8] *Ibid.*, pp. 826–33. [9] *Ibid.*, pp. 822–5. [1] A.G.I., 54.5.9 (Santo Domingo 224).

CHAPTER ELEVEN

The Failure of Ralegh's American Colonies

I

WE HAVE SEEN that the beginnings of English colonization in North America, from which such great results eventually grew, were tardy and tentative in their early expression. The Portuguese were the pioneers in building an administrative system around widely scattered European posts far from the homeland. The Spanish were the first to transplant large bodies of people outside Europe to the newly found American continent, and to build their new cities and dependent colonial societies. England, unless her government could oust Spain from her American lands, had, perforce, to concentrate on colonizing, if she was to colonize at all, the temperate latitudes of North America, and to do so not on the basis of great discoveries of wealth, but on the founding of agricultural societies. The only successful colonies (and this only partly) made by Englishmen in the sixteenth century were inside Europe, in Ireland. American efforts failed. Yet they were made, and this chapter attempts to illustrate some of the factors that stirred and impeded the first impulses of the English colonizing movement.

The planning of English colonies in North America, as we have noted, really begins with Sir Humphrey Gilbert. In his abortive schemes of the years 1578 to 1583 we get the first body of significant information on the difficulties of equipping and financing an overseas venture with a colonizing objective under the limiting conditions which Tudor England afforded. Gilbert was also the first Englishman seriously to dispose—if only on paper and on the basis of inadequate information—of American land to English settlers. It was an accident that he himself was drowned on his return voyage from American waters, but it was scarcely accidental that he did not succeed in establishing a colony. His resources were altogether too meager and his projects at once too grandiose and too inadequate to provide any real chance of success.

Gilbert's half-brother Sir Walter Ralegh had the advantage of learning a good deal from these deficiencies, and the colonizing expeditions he sponsored between 1584 and 1590 were the first serious English attempts to grapple with the realities of settlement on American shores. That these, too, failed was not perhaps inevitable, though they probably would have done so even if the violence of the Anglo-Spanish war between 1588 and 1602 had not checked and diverted the impulse that sent them forth.

The story of Ralegh's colonies, in bare outline, is well known. A reconnaissance expedition of two ships under Amadas and Barlowe arrived off the long sand-reef which shelters the greater part of the North Carolina coast in July 1584. The islands north and south of Cape Hatteras were explored and friendly contact made with the local Indians before the expedition returned to England.[1] Queen Elizabeth accepted Ralegh's suggestion that the new land be known as Virginia. In 1585 Sir Richard Grenville brought out a fleet of seven vessels, and between June and August explored the coastal islands and the adjoining mainland. He left behind on the island of Roanoke 108 men (the first colony) with Ralph Lane as their commander. This settlement attempted to establish itself by the construction of a fort and village, by attempts at cultivation, and by trade with the Indians, but failed to remain on friendly terms with the local inhabitants. Exploring parties examined, to the south, the coastal fringes of Pamlico Sound and River; to the west, Albemarle Sound, penetrating some distance into the interior up the Chowan and Roanoke rivers; and, to the north, up Currituck Sound, from which they rounded Cape Henry to the southern shores of Chesapeake Bay. Food shortages and the nonarrival of supplies expected in April led to their deserting the colony and returning to England with Drake's West Indian fleet in June 1586. They thus missed a relief ship sent by Ralegh, which turned back when Roanoke was found deserted. A larger "supply" under Grenville, consisting of three ships, arrived in July and deposited a group of fifteen men (the second colony) to act as a holding party until it should be found what had happened to the first settlers.

Finally, a new expedition of three ships arrived off Cape Hatteras in July 1587, carrying a third colony of 117 men, women, and children, with John White as governor. They found no survivors from those left in 1586. Intending to move from Roanoke to a better site, they sent their

[1] See pp. 254–7 above.

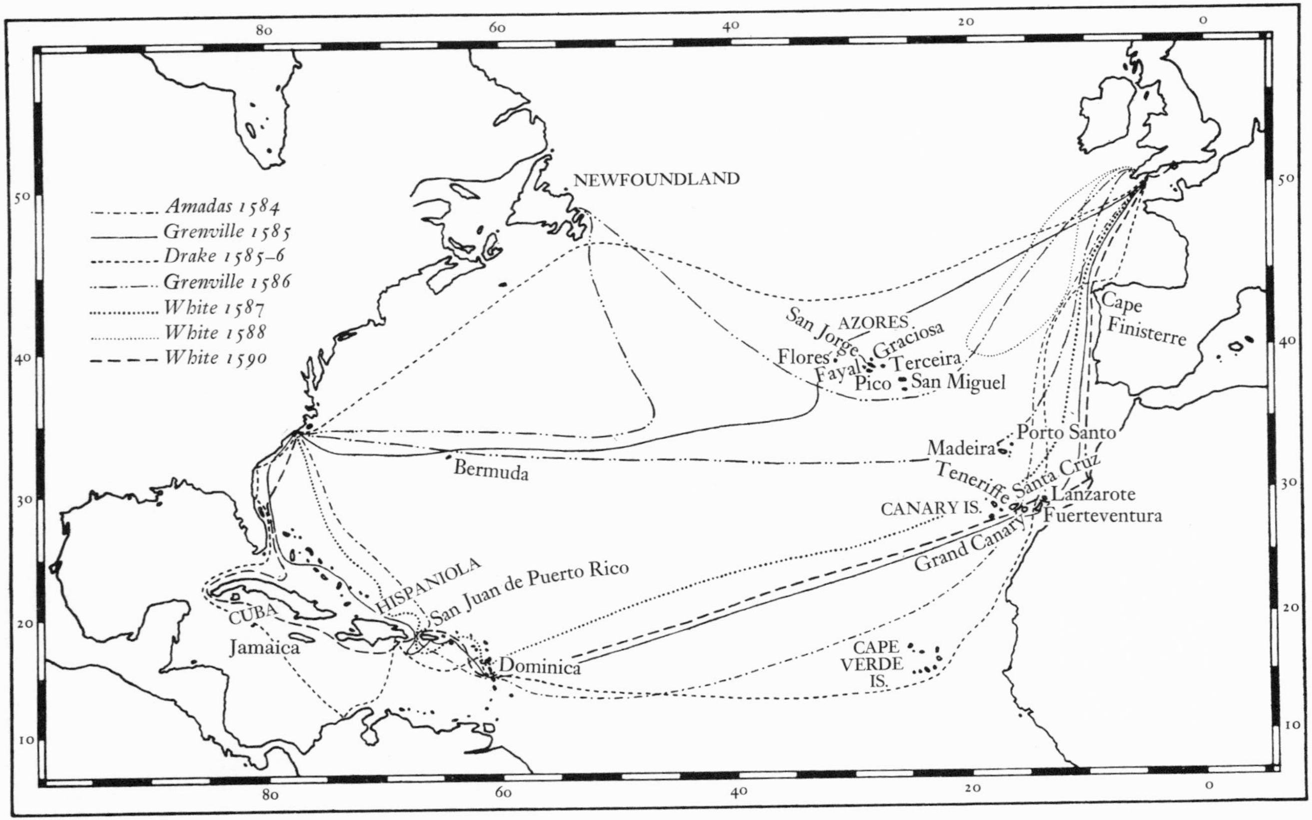

The Roanoke Voyages, 1584–1590. From D. B. Quinn, ed., The Roanoke Voyages, 1584–1590 *(1955).*

governor home to hasten supplies from England at the end of August.[2] This was the last that was seen of the colony. White was unable to get relief sent out at once, and the supply vessels prepared by Ralegh and Grenville in the spring of 1588 were detained in England by the government to help to meet the peril from the Armada. White contrived to ship some stores in two small vessels in April, but their crews went privateering and returned to England without having crossed the Atlantic. Not until 1590 did he get away from England, and then only as a passenger on a privateer. He landed on Roanoke in August and found that the colony had disappeared. He was hustled away by the seamen before making any extended search for the settlers, and in effect the settlement was abandoned.

What stands out immediately, even from this bald outline, is the small scale on which the colonizing attempts were made. Less than 250 persons were concerned in three successive attempts to establish a settlement. This is an indication at once of the relative poverty of English resources even at the end of the sixteenth century, and of the small fraction of those resources which could be mobilized for building an American colony. Accident played an appreciable part in the failure of the colonists to establish themselves, but this was largely because of the weakness of the enterprises and the consequently narrow margin of safety provided, even with the best intentions and with many precautions.

Faulty choice of a site had much to do with the early lack of success. In order to estimate this at all accurately, we must examine the geographical knowledge available at the start of the experiments and also the economic and strategic objectives it was hoped to attain by the successful planting of colonies in the area chosen.

How much did Ralegh and his associates know about North America at the time the colonizing expeditions were sent out? The answer is largely to be found in the writings and collections of the two Richard Hakluyts and in a few of the maps we know to have been available to the planners. Richard Hakluyt, the elder, advised and wrote on overseas matters between about 1570 and 1591; his younger cousin of the same name was active between 1580 and 1614, working mainly on publishing travel narratives, notably *The principal navigations* (1598–1600).

John Dee's maps of 1580 and 1583, the latter of which he compiled for Gilbert, and Lok's map published by Hakluyt in 1582[3] are a mass of

[2] See pp. 259–61 above.

[3] The maps of 1582 and 1583, with part of the 1580 map, are reproduced in D. B. Quinn, ed., *The Voyages and Colonising Enterprises of Sir Humphrey Gilbert*, Hakluyt Society, 2d ser., nos. 83–4, 2 vols. (London, 1940).

unproved assumptions, the coastlines only very broadly correct and revealing all kinds of theories about water passages around and through the landmass of North America. They were quite inadequate as charts for sailors or maps for settlers. Detailed cartographical knowledge available in England about the North American coast was largely confined to the southern and eastern shores of Newfoundland, and shaded off from certainty into conjecture at the northern shore at the St. Lawrence and the southern fringe of New England. From the tip of the Florida peninsula to South Carolina, again, the available knowledge was fairly well grounded. Jacques le Moyne de Morgues, a survivor of French attempts to settle Florida in the 1560's, was in England and had made workable maps of the coastline south of Cape Fear.[4] But for the area roughly between Cape Fear and Cape Cod, Ralegh's cartographical information appears to have been inadequate, a good deal of it going back to primitive maps of the discoveries and conjectures of Giovanni da Verrazzano some sixty years before. The Spanish had, it is true, explored the coast and entered Chesapeake Bay,[5] and Lane had seen, or possibly had with him, some Spanish chart.[6] Deficiencies were made good by the cartographical work of John White on the coastline between Cape Fear and Cape Henry, but his maps were only available after one colony had proved abortive and the penalties of a faulty choice of site had begun to be paid.

Literary material on America as a whole, much of it at second or third hand, was more plentifully at Ralegh's disposal. Over thirty years of work by Richard Eden, Richard Willes, and the two Hakluyts had accumulated a considerable store of information.[7] The plundering expeditions of several thousand Englishmen among the Caribbean Islands and on the Spanish Main had built up a sizable body of firsthand knowledge of conditions there. North America, however, was much less well known than the Spanish-occupied coastlines farther south. The French attempts

[4] Map engraved in Theodor de Bry, *America*, pt. 2 (Frankfurt am Main, 1591).

[5] See C. M. Lewis and A. J. Loomie, *Spanish Jesuit Missions in Virginia* (Chapel Hill, 1953), *passim.*

[6] A crossed-out note in one of Lane's letters to Walsingham (Quinn, *Roanoke Voyages*, I, 201, *n.* 10) states that "Thys Porte [Ococon] in ye Carte ys by ye Spanyardes called St. Marryes baye."

[7] This has been explored in George B. Parks, *Richard Hakluyt and the English Voyages* (New York, 1928, 1962); in E. G. R. Taylor, ed., *The Original Writings and Correspondence of the Two Richard Hakluyts*, Hakluyt Society, 2d ser., 76–7, 2 vols. (London, 1935); and in Richard Hakluyt, *Principall Navigations, 1589*, Hakluyt Society, extra ser. 39, 2 vols. (Cambridge, Eng., 1965), ed. D. B. Quinn and R. A. Skelton, Introduction.

to establish a colony in Florida in 1562 attracted attention in England and led, in 1563, to the first English project for an American colony. Hakluyt did much between 1584 and 1587 to add to the sources available on these experiments for Ralegh's information, while Jacques le Moyne de Morgues had in London not only maps but drawings of the Florida Indians, descriptive notes, and a narrative, all of which eventually became available to Ralegh.[8]

From the sources on Florida a good deal was to be gathered about the products, people, perils, and problems of North America as a whole. The vegetable riches of the country were attractive, the possession of some gold by the Indians alluring. Problems of supplying, organizing, and disciplining a military colony several thousand miles from its homeland were well illustrated. The outlines of Indian society—primitive, warlike, and mobile, storing little agricultural surplus for its winter needs, and at once friendly, suspicious, and treacherous—were there to be studied. The younger Hakluyt did learn much from the Florida record, but neither he nor any other English colonial planner knew, without experience of conditions on the spot, the right questions to ask; they were naturally inclined to take from these materials the more rather than less favorable and hopeful information.

For the region immediately north of Florida there were few recent details of any value. Hakluyt set himself to bridge the gap by assembling materials on the more northerly coasts of North America. For the St. Lawrence he learned something from the records of the Cartier–Roberval expeditions of 1534–43. For Newfoundland he could draw on the narrow, practical experience of hundreds of English fishermen, mainly concerned with fishing problems, as well as the more informative accounts of Anthony Parkhurst (1577–8) and Edward Hayes, who had recorded Gilbert's discoveries in 1583. But for New England he had little good information beyond the report of the reconnaissance voyage made by Simão Fernandes in 1580 for Gilbert. The material that could be collected on the Cape Breton–New England zone for Gilbert's information in 1582 was not at all impressive, and Hakluyt could do little to add to it in the following years. In 1586 he published in Paris an account of the travels of Antonio de Espejo in the interior of North America during 1582–3. For the rest he depended on old, often garbled scraps of information or on analogies, frequently misleading, from Spanish America.

Ralegh's colonists, therefore, went to North America very imperfectly briefed. The results of the reconnaissance voyage of 1584, described by

[8] Acquired after his death by De Bry and engraved for *America,* pt. 2 (1591).

Barlowe, were the only really apposite knowledge on which Lane had to rely in 1585. The work of the first colony in 1585–6 did provide a comprehensive account, with maps and drawings, narratives, and specimens of the coastal region of North Carolina;[9] while the third colony, which went out in 1587, was forearmed with much invaluable knowledge and experience. But mistakes, accidents, and the lack of drive behind the colonizing movement in England led to much of it being wasted.

Whatever lack of information there may have been in 1584–5 about conditions in America, there was little hesitation about the broad economic and strategic objectives of Hakluyt and Ralegh. The "Particuler Discourse" called the *Discourse of western planting*, which Hakluyt wrote in the early autumn of 1584, stated them clearly for the queen.[1]

We have seen that a primary consideration in the establishment of a North American colony was the creation of a bulwark against the further extension of Spanish colonial power along the Atlantic coast and the building of a base which could be used for attacks on existing Spanish colonies and the valuable plate-fleets that sailed from them. I have already noted that this was an important, possibly decisive factor in determining the approximate site of the first colony.

French experiments in Florida in the early 1560's had alarmed the Spanish authorities, and from 1565 a determined effort had been made to establish a strong Spanish administration in that area. Attempts to settle a substantial civilian population there had failed by 1585, but a small town had been created at San Agustín, which had a trading and administrative community as well as a garrison, and a smaller, mainly military outpost at Santa Elena guarding Port Royal and St. Helena sounds in the Carolina low country. The overriding purpose of this rather expensive military establishment was to deny the ports to France or England,[2] and thus protect the plate-fleets which, sailing through the Florida Channel,

[9] A sketch-map, a small engraved map showing detail, a map of the wider surroundings of the colony, engraved versions of this, and a general map of eastern North America—all derive from the White-Harriot activities. With the drawings of Indians (and engravings after them), many drawings of birds, fish, and other natural history specimens, and Harriot's *Briefe and true report of the new found land of Virginia* (London, 1588), an impressive body of material was assembled. It is all collected in Quinn, *Roanoke Voyages*, I, and Paul H. Hulton and D. B. Quinn, *The American Drawings of John White*, 2 vols., (London and Chapel Hill, 1964).

[1] Taylor, *Hakluyts*, II, 211–26.

[2] A narrative of Drake's voyage speaks of Florida as "serving there for no other purpose, then to keepe all other nations from inhabiting any part of all that Coast" (Quinn, *Roanoke Voyages*, I, 299).

were often swung by currents and winds as far north as Cape Hatteras.

The choice of a site for an English colony was therefore limited to being sufficiently far north of the Spanish zone to free it from the menace of constant attack, yet far enough south to make it a convenient base for attacks on the plate-fleet. In cold fact, the site chosen was useless as a base for lack of a suitable harbor, but this had to be learned by hard experience.

Hakluyt set out a very wide range of economic objectives to justify colonization. His third chapter, indeed, is headed: "That this westerne voyadge will yelde unto us all the commodities of Europe, Affrica, and Asia as farr as we were wonte to travell." [3] But among all the many products which he believed America could be made to yield, one group was specially emphasized: namely, those coming from areas of Mediterranean climate. Continental wars and the growing hostility with Spain were unfavorably affecting English commerce with southern Europe, while the balance of trade was in any event unfavorable. Hakluyt wanted to recreate in North America sources of wine, olive oil, sugar, lemons, oranges, figs, salt, iron, woad and other dye-stuffs, and possibly even silk and rice. The value was stressed of developing trade in cloth and other English produce with the Indians, more especially as they became civilized, since this, it was hoped, would cure unemployment at home, while the export of colonists would both relieve the supposed pressure of overpopulation and rid the country of various undesirable elements—convicts, beggars, and Puritan clergy among them.

However, the objective of building up across the Atlantic a new Mediterranean type of agriculture was a primary factor, on the economic side, in the choice of a site in the region of 36° north latitude. This involved the development of a highly specialized and carefully organized type of farming with which few Englishmen were thoroughly familiar. However sound in theory, it was not easily practicable. There was no conception in Hakluyt's mind of the long struggle for a bare subsistence, under primitive conditions, which marked all the later and ultimately successful English colonies in America, and which made the rapid construction of such a settlement as he envisaged quite unrealistic. The possibilities of ultimate agricultural development along these lines undoubtedly did exist in parts of modern North Carolina,[4] but they were not to be achieved with the means to hand between 1584 and 1591.

[3] Taylor, *Hakluyts,* II, 222–33.

[4] Cultivation limits, e.g., for citrus fruits, were not the same in America as in Europe. The differing climatic zones in North America were only slowly understood.

The theoretical planning which lay behind the choice of a site was, therefore, doubly at fault. The absence of any adequate harbor between Cape Fear and Cape Henry ruined the value of the colony as a strategic base for attacks on the plate-fleets. The lack of agricultural techniques and the inappropriateness of intensive garden and plantation cultivation for a small, weak, and struggling community made the economic plan equally misguided. These miscalculations undoubtedly played an appreciable part in the failure of attempts to establish a colony on the North Carolina coast.

The safety of Ralph Lane's colony—the first settlement—was jeopardized from the beginning by the absence of a suitable harbor. At the first bay in the reef at Wococon Island, where Grenville's fleet attempted to anchor, the largest vessel, the *Tiger* of 160 tons, went aground and was nearly wrecked, being saved only with the loss of the greater part of the provisions designed to tide the colonists over the first winter. This might have proved fatal to their survival, if it had not been possible to get considerable quantities of food from the Indians.

The two openings in the reef which offered some shelter and were least unsuitable were those they named Trinity Harbor, with an eight-foot bar at high water, and Port Ferdinando (later known as Hatarask), with a twelve-foot bar. The latter was sufficient to shelter vessels of about 70 tons, and also to let a pinnace of some 20 tons pass through to Pamlico Sound beyond.[5] Otherwise, ships had to anchor several miles out on windswept roads. When Drake arrived in June 1586 he offered Lane a ship small enough to enter Port Ferdinando, but after a storm had broken his cables and this vessel had seized the opportunity to put to sea for England, Drake could only replace her by a much larger vessel, the *Bark Bonner* of 170 tons, quite unsuitable for their purposes, which finally decided the colonists to sail back to England with his fleet.[6]

Lane was astute enough to see that the colony's chances of survival and development depended to a considerable degree on having adequate harbor facilities, whether for the supply of the settlers, the development of commerce, or as a base against Spain. He therefore carefully collected information on other sites and eventually decided that the desired harbor was to be found on Chesapeake Bay. His plan was to wait until shipping arrived from England, then send round a bark and two pinnaces by sea to find a harbor and make soundings, while he himself would lead an expedition up the Chowan River and thence overland to the Bay, where he would build a fort and then remove the rest of the colonists to the

[5] Quinn, *Roanoke Voyages,* I, 201–2. [6] *Ibid.,* pp. 290–2, 301.

new base.[7] When the relief ships did not come, and when Drake, in June 1586, offered a small ship and pinnaces for the use of his party, he proposed to carry this plan into effect, establish his base, and then send the ship back to England to ensure that further supplies would arrive at the new settlement. The storm and the desertion of the *Francis* made it impossible to proceed with this plan, so Lane decided to come home.

His report to Ralegh stressed the need to shift the site of the next settlement to Chesapeake Bay. Ralegh consulted Hakluyt, who advised that Lane's plan be followed.[8] John White left Plymouth on 8 May 1587 at the head of the third colony. He had specific instructions from Ralegh to pick up the second colony of fifteen men left on Roanoke by Grenville the previous summer and then proceed direct to Chesapeake Bay.[9] But the sailors insisted they should disembark at Roanoke and begin to rebuild a settlement there. When White left them on 28 August they were planning a move to a mainland site some fifty miles away.

II

THE FINANCING OF such a series of expeditions was not one which could easily be undertaken by a group of private gentlemen. We know that Ralegh was in receipt of lucrative perquisites from the crown during these years, which enabled him to make large investments. It is clear that important figures in the administration like Sir Francis Walsingham (in 1585 at least) and Lord Howard of Effingham, the Lord High Admiral, were among the contributors. Grenville is likely to have put up a good deal of his own money, and other adventurers, like Thomas Cavendish in 1585, contributed a ship or a share in a ship. A substantial amount was recouped on each voyage by privateering, but we cannot claim that any particular voyage made a profit, though that of 1585 may possibly have done so. The search for investors widened after 1586 and focused largely on London City merchants, men like William Sanderson and the young Thomas Smith. How far the colonists of 1585 and 1586 were investors or how far paid servants of Ralegh and his associates is not certainly known. Those of 1587 were clearly men and families who had invested their own possessions in the venture, as did the handful of recruits to the settlement who attempted to join them in 1588. In the end the voyages to Virginia became mere appendages to privateering adventures in the Caribbean and entirely subsidiary to them.

Through the researches of K. R. Andrews, we have a good means of

[7] *Ibid.*, pp. 261–3. [8] *Ibid.*, II, 493–4. [9] *Ibid.*, pp. 502–3, 522–4.

estimating the cost of equipping privateers for six-month cruises.[1] These figures can be applied (with some margin of error, since all the details of them are not known) to the seven separate voyages made to Virginia by twenty-four vessels, ranging from substantial ships of 200–300 tons' burden down to small pinnaces of 30 tons or less. About 1750 tons of shipping were employed, and some 1050 seamen and soldiers, convoying between 240 and 250 colonists (108 in 1585, 15 in 1586, and 117 in 1587 reached Virginia), which cost in the neighborhood of £16,000 gross and something over £8000 net, provided all the heavy equipment like guns were brought home and the vessels reasonably sound after their voyage.[2] Later, under the Virginia Company, £20 was reckoned sufficient to maintain an able-bodied man for a year, as £12 10s. had been earlier, in 1583. This would add about £5200 to the costs. Supplies, most of which never reached Virginia and a large part of which were probably lost or damaged in some degree, might be reckoned as enough (about £4200) to bring the colonizing costs up to perhaps £10,000.

The ventures, then, represented an investment of some £26,000, from which a substantial amount was recouped by privateering (though there are not enough data to provide anything like an adequate estimate, this figure might be in the region of £6000 to £8000). Ships and stores returned safely to England, and so to be set off against costs, might represent, we could guess (again an estimate would not be easy), between £5000 and £7000. It would thus appear that the net costs were in the region of £12,000 to £15,000.[3] This was a great sum for one person to provide, and a substantial amount for a small syndicate, but it was all on a very small scale for a major company. The Virginia Colonies of the years 1584–7 were planned and executed on a shoestring, and this may be seen as a major factor in their failure to endure. The settlement of 1607 survived only because there was a continuous priming of the colony with fresh supplies irrespective of returns.

The 1584–7 expeditions were, however, pioneer ventures for Englishmen. They were the first attempts made to maintain men across the ocean. The experiments threw up the information that there were special difficulties in the way of financing colonies. To establish a party of settlers

[1] K. R. Andrews, *Elizabethan Privateering* (Cambridge, Eng., 1964), pp. 46–50.

[2] The data are extracted from Quinn, *Roanoke Voyages*.

[3] It cannot be claimed that this estimate is more than a very rough one. If wages were paid to crews on the seven voyages and to the men who remained on Roanoke Island in 1585–6, for example, these figures would be substantially increased. Even so, it would not seem likely that the total net cost exceeded £20,000.

on land meant a substantial capital outlay, and each mischance which involved renewing the colony from its foundations meant a repetition of that expenditure. To keep a colony alive required the dispatch of annual supplies, and its reinforcement involved a continuous drain. Expenditure might continue along these lines for an indefinite number of years, while returns were problematical. Short-term returns in the shape of American products brought to England by vessels returning from the colony were unlikely to do more than offset the losses through accidents and mischances incidental to its original establishment. Unless some rich mineral resources were found and exploited or some easily grown and highly profitable staple crop developed, the maintenance of even a single small, localized colony was likely to cost from five thousand pounds upward a year, over and above any returns. Given an income of this size it should have been possible to nurse such a colony to pay some little dividend, after perhaps a decade, but this was not a commercial proposition. It was a venture which investors, however farsighted, could and would sustain for only a limited period.

In such circumstances, and assuming the absence of important mineral discoveries, there were three ways only by which money might be found to get a colony on its feet. There was the possibility of direct financing or subsidy by the state. There was the possibility of running a nonprofit colonial experiment out of the surplus profits of some larger money-making enterprise. Finally, there was some prospect of inducing families to go to America with means sufficient to pay for their supplies over a number of years until they were well established.

Sir Humphrey Gilbert's search for subscribers for his 1583 venture had been a wide one. Merchants of Southampton, Exeter, Bristol, and London were approached, as were the privateering gentry of the south-west, courtiers, and Catholic landowners who had some idea of moving to America to escape crippling penal taxation. Yet Gilbert found money very hard to come by. His contacts and his reputation were not sufficient to bring him in an adequate working capital, while his personal resources were relatively small. Walter Ralegh was from the beginning in a much stronger position. His place at court as a member of the queen's immediate circle meant that he could command an influence which Gilbert never enjoyed, and a range of contacts wide enough to give him a reasonable chance of raising at least adequate initial subscriptions for his colony. But it is clear that, from the beginning, he appreciated in some degree the precarious prospects of an American settlement dependent entirely on the resources of himself and his friends. He therefore hoped for state assistance for the venture. It was to secure this that Hakluyt wrote for him the *Discourse of western planting*, presented to the queen in October 1584.

This stressed throughout the national motives for colonization; the extension of the crown's dominions into an area to which historical claims, in virtue of the Cabot discoveries, might be made; the spread of protestantism into new lands as a counterpoise to the spread of Catholic influence, as well as the economic and strategic objectives already described. "If her Majestie take these westerne discoveries in hand. . . . Yf wee plante, and people ryally. . . . If her Majestie woulde put in a foote in that enterprise"—these were his presuppositions for success.[4]

While there is every reason to believe that Elizabeth favored the project, it is not surprising that she did not sponsor it as a state venture. Her revenue available for administrative and military expenses was small, and the wide range of expensive contingencies which had to be provided for —Ireland, the Netherlands, Scotland, the navy, and the approaching all-out struggle with Spain, made her reluctance to take on the primary burden of developing an American colony a natural and even inevitable one. But this did not mean that she could not and did not help. Each year from 1583 to 1587 saw her add to the offices and perquisites from which Ralegh could draw further financial resources.[5] Much of this advancement was due to his rising position and influence at court, and much of the money was required to keep up this position, but it is a legitimate assumption that some at least of his sources of income were put at his disposal to enable him to continue his American ventures.

It is clear, however, that the main source of revenue on which a colony could be built was intended to be derived from the plunder of the Spanish merchant fleet and colonies. Up to 1584 piracy and privateering by English seamen against Spain had been only covertly and intermittently connived at by Elizabeth and her chief officials. The expulsion of the Spanish ambassador from England early in 1584 was one of a chain of events which led to a radical change of attitude toward the plundering of Spanish and Portuguese resources. After 1584 the crown and most courtiers invested lavishly in joint-stock, ostensibly private, ventures of an aggressive nature, and so did many merchants, sailors, gentlemen, and noblemen all over the country.

Ralegh's position as chief representative of the crown in the southwestern counties gave him peculiar opportunities for taking advantage of this new situation. In 1585, therefore, he can have had little difficulty in

[4] Taylor, *Hakluyts*, II, 237, 248, 258, 289, 313–19.

[5] See D. B. Quinn, *Raleigh and the British Empire* (New York, 1962), pp. 37–8.

As in fraunce Irlonde and in spayne
Portyngale seuyll also in almayne
Freslonde flaunders and in burgoyne
Calabre poyle and erragoyne
Brytayne byske and also in gascoyne
Naples grece and in myddes of scotlonde
At cape saynt vyncent ⁊ in the newe foūde Ilonde
I haue ben in gene and in cowe
Also in the londe of rumbelowe
Thre myle out of hell
At rodes constantyne and in babylonde
In cornewale and in no northumberlonde
Where men sethe russhes in gruell
Ye syr in caldey tartare and Inde
And in ẏ londe of women ẏ fewe men dothe fynde
In all these countres haue I be
¶ Syr what tydynges here ye now on the see — Frewyll.
¶ We mette of shyppes a grete naue — Hyckscor.
Full of people that wolde in to Irlonde
And they came out of this countre
They wyll neuer more come to englonde
¶ Whens were ẏ shyppes of them knowest ẏ none — Imagy.
¶ Herke ⁊ I wyll shewe you theyr names eche one — Hyckscor.
Fyrst was the regent with the myghell of brykylse
The george with the gabryell and the anne of foye
The starre of salte asshe with the Jhesus of plūoth
Also the hermytage with the barbara of darmouth
The nycolas and the mary bellouse of brystowe
With the elyn of london and James also
Grete was the people that was in them
All true relygyous and holy women

ABOVE: The first illustration [INSET] of an Englishman who claimed to have been to America, with the first mention of "the newe founde llande" (North America) in a book printed in England. From the unique copy of *Hyckescorner*, *ca.* 1510–1515, in the British Museum.

OVERLEAF: Letter from John Day to the Grand Admiral (Christopher Columbus), December 1497 or January 1498. Archivo General de Simancas.

Magnifico Señor

Su criado de vra. Sa. [illegible] y visto lo q por ella me manda quisiera q
fuera siendo seruiçio de my dicho y de my dicha letra el libro de Ynbinçion Fortunata
no le hallo y creo q le traxe con mys cosas y desplazeme mucho no le
hallar por q le quisiera mucho seruir. el otro de Marco Paulo y la copia
de la tierra q es fallada le enbio y plazeme no le enbio por q con mys o-
cupaçiones no tuve lugar de bolver a buscarlo como queria por q la hize de priesa al par-
tir pero por la dicha copia comprendera vra. Sa. lo q quiere saber
q en la misma copia estan nonbrados los cabos de la tierra firme y las yslas
y por alli asy mysmo vera donde fue la primera vista por q a la buelta
se fallo la mayor parte de la tierra q se descubrio y asy sabra vra. Sa. q el
cabo mas cercano a Yrlanda esta 1800 millas al hueste de cabo
Dursel q es en Yrlanda y la parte mas baxa de la ysla de las Siete Cibdades
esta al hueste del rio de Burdeos y sabra vra. Sa. q no decendio en ella
syno en solo un logar de la tierra firme q es cerca donde se fizo la
primera vista en el qual logar decendieron con un crucifixo y alçaron
banderas con armas del Padre Santo y con las armas del rey de Ynglaterra my señor y fallaron arboles grandes de q fazen los mastiles de las
naos y otros arboles de [illegible] y la tierra muy buena de yerbas en el qual logar
segund q escrive a vra. Sa. hallaron un camino cerrado q entraba en
la tierra y vieron un logar donde se avia fecho fuego y fallaron estier-
col de alimañas q juzgaban ser campesinas y fallaron un palo
de longor de un codo foradado en anbos cabos y labrado y el qual palo
hera tinto con brasil y por estas señales se juzga ser la tierra po-
blada y como se fallaba con poca gente no oso entrar dentro en la
tierra saluo de un tiro de ballesta y tomo agua dulce y boluiose a su
nao y de luengo de la costa fallaban muchos pescados tales q en Ysla-
nda se acostumbra secar al ayre y se venden en Ynglaterra y en otros
ptos y estos pescados se dize en ynglés stocfisshe y asy mismo a la
tornada vieron en tierra dos bultos uno en pos de otro q no supie-
ron si eran honbres o alimañas y paresçia q avia labranças donde
pensaba q avia poblaçiones y vieron una floresta q las fojas de ella
les paresçian buenas. y al tiempo q partio de Ynglaterra era en
fin de mayo y estovo en el camino 35 dias antes q fallase tierra
y el viento hera est y nordest y las mares hera bonança asy a
la yda como a la venida salvo un dia q hizo tormenta y esto fue
dos o tres dias antes de fallar la tierra y yendo tan adelante le faltaba
en el aguja de marear el punto de norte q se le declinaba dos puntos
por baxo y andaria en descubrir la costa un mes poco mas o me-
nos y del sobredicho cabo de la tierra firme q es mas cercano a Yrlanda estando con la venida y llego fasta la costa de Europa 15 dias
q traya el viento a popa y alli goberno en Bretaña por q los marineros
le fizieron desconçertar deziendo q venia mucho de norte

y de alli se vino a Bristol e se fue al Rey a le dezir todo lo sobre
dicho y el Rey le hizo merced de xx libras esterlinas cada año
para se reparar fasta el tiempo quando de esto se sepa mas de negocio porque se
espera poner con diligencia con diez o doze navios para descubrir la dicha
tierra mas largamente el año venidero Dios queriendo porque en este
dicho viaje no llevo sino un solo navio de cinquenta toneles e
veynte personas e vituallas para siete o ocho meses y por grande
diligencia se quiere poner en obra de presente creese aver seydo fa
llado e descubierto en otros tiempos el cabo de la dicha tierra por los
de Bristol que fallaron el Brasil como dello tiene noticia Vra. Sa.
la qual se dezia la ysla de Brasil e presumese e creese ser tierra fir
me la que fallaron los de Bristol

E porque quiere saber Vra. Sa. del viaje primero de que Vra. Sa. quiere saber es que fue con
un navio y la gente que llevaba le desbarato e yba mal
vituallado y fallo los tiempos contrarios y ovo por el de
se bolver. Magnifico Señor cerca de otras
cosas para cumplir al caso quisiera servir a Vra. Sa. si no lo impi
diera la ocupacion de los negocios y fechos de mucha impor
tancia que agora de cargazones y escrituras que para Inglaterra tengo
de hazer con mucha prisa los quales me impiden mucho el servir de Vra. Sa.
pero tenga de mi Vra. Sa. como magnifico Señor el deseo de mi natural
yntencion que es de servir y en hallandome en otra disposicion y mas des
ocupado de negocios yo me pondre a todo trabajo que aber por ser
vir por servicio y quando tenga noticia de las cosas de Inglaterra Vra.
to a las sobredichas yo soy cierto ha de venir todo a mi noticia yo lo
haré saber a Vra. Sa. lo que non fuere en perjuicio del Rey mi señor
suplico a Vra. Sa. que en remuneracion de algunos servicios [illegible]
hazer le plega escrivirme algunas cartas [illegible] con otros [illegible]
[illegible] que [illegible] mucho la [illegible]
de [illegible] de que tenga noticia [illegible] el [illegible]
de Vra. Sa. [illegible] quando Vra. Sa. [illegible]
[illegible] el libro [illegible]

besa las manos de
Vra. Señoria

Johan Day

E 2

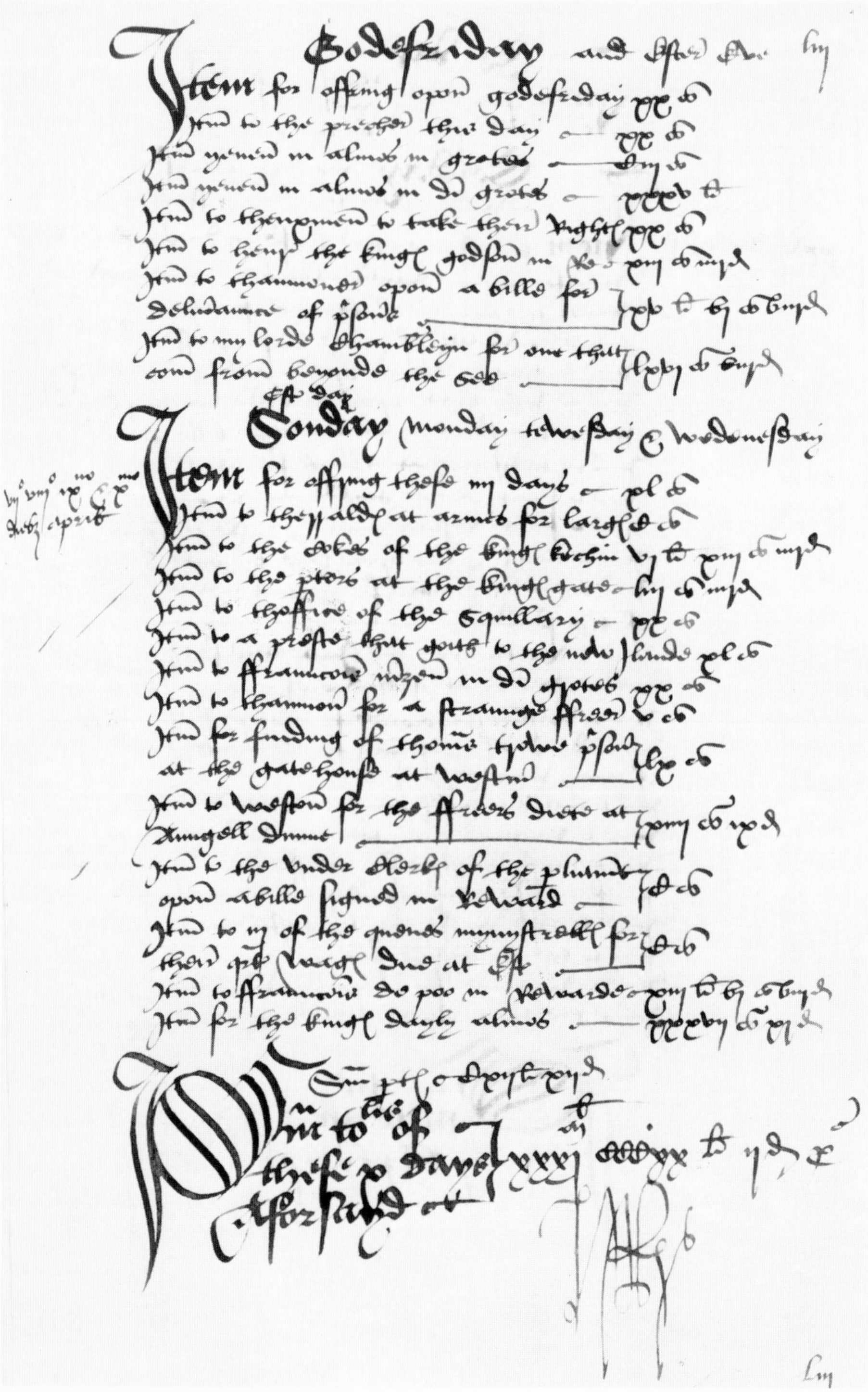

Godesfriday and Ester Eve [illegible]

Item for offring upon godesfriday xx s
Item to the precher that day — xx s
Item yeven in almes in grotes — [illegible]
Item yeven in almes in d grotes — [illegible]
Item to the yomen to take their right xx s
Item to hange the kinges godsond in [illegible]
Item to Thamoner upon a bille for deliverance of prisoners — [illegible]
Item to my lordes Chamberlain for one that come from beyonde the see — [illegible]

Ester day
Sonday Monday Tewesday & Wednesday

Item for offring these iiij days — xl s
Item to the haraldes at armes for largesse [illegible]
Item to the cokes of the kinges kechin [illegible]
Item to the porters at the kinges gate [illegible]
Item to thofficers of the Squillary — xx s
Item to a preste that goth to the new ylande xl s
Item to ffraunceys [illegible] in d grotes [illegible]
Item to Thamoner for a strange frere [illegible]
Item for fynding of thomas thre prisoners at the gatehouse at Westm[illegible]
Item to Weston for the freres diete at Aungell Inne [illegible]
Item to the under clerk of the [illegible] upon a bille signed in rewarde — [illegible]
Item to iij of the quenes mynstrelles for their [illegible] at Ester [illegible]
Item to ffraunceys [illegible] in rewarde [illegible]
Item for the kinges dayly almes — [illegible]

Summa [illegible]

Summa totalis of these dayes aforsaid [illegible]

Phillipps Manuscript 4104, folio 32v., 15–20 September 1503:
to "Sir Walter Herbert's servant for bringing of a brasil bow and two red arrows."
Courtesy of Mr. Philip Robinson and the Robinson Trust.

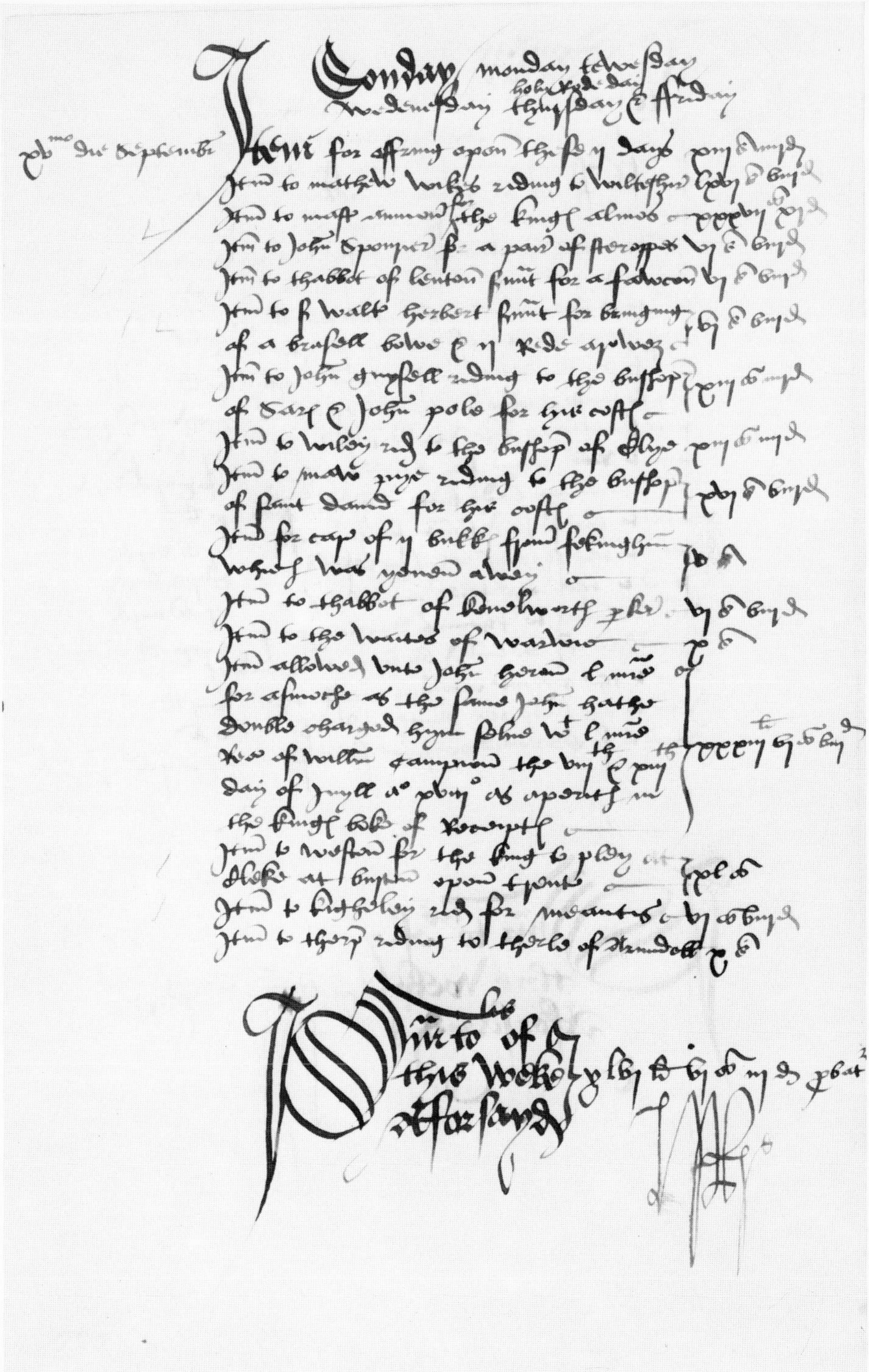

Phillipps Manuscript 4104, folio 53v., 7–10 April 1504:
to a "priest that goeth to the new Island."
Courtesy of Mr. Philip Robinson and the Robinson Trust.

Phillipps Manuscript 4104, folio 96v., 15–20 August 1505:
to "Clays going to Richmond with wild cats and popinjays of the new found Island."
Courtesy of Mr. Philip Robinson and the Robinson Trust.

ABOVE LEFT: Sebastian Cabot in old age. From Samuel Seyer, *Memorials Historical and Topographical* (Bristol, 1821–1823).

ABOVE RIGHT: English ship, *ca.* 1530. King's College Chapel, Cambridge.

BELOW: The *Tiger*, 1580. From Public Record Office Maps, M.P.F. 75.

ABOVE LEFT: Sir Humphrey Gilbert. From Henry Holland, *Herωologia* (London, 1620).

ABOVE RIGHT: Sir Walter Ralegh, *ca.* 1598; anonymous painting. National Gallery of Ireland.

BELOW: English galleon, *ca.* 1588, possibly the *Ark Royal*. British Museum.

finding subscribers for Grenville's expedition to plant the first colony, which, if successful, might itself become a base for further predatory activities against the Spanish empire. But the expedition had also to pay dividends, and this explains much of Grenville's program on his way to North America and also his prize-seeking on his way home. A Spanish report in February 1585, indeed, asserted that Elizabeth had promised Ralegh that if he was not allowed to lead the expedition in person she would pay all its expenses,[6] but there is no other indication of this. The queen, however, was an investor in the expedition, the *Tiger,* Grenville's flagship, being a royal vessel and representing part or the whole of her adventure.[7] Grenville, when he got to West Indian waters, was concerned not only with meeting the need of his company for fresh water and that of the colonists for certain West Indian products, but was bound to try to accumulate plunder as well. The two Spanish frigates which he took yielded cargoes of cloth and some passengers, who were later ransomed at San Germán, Puerto Rico.[8] In Hispaniola he found Spanish merchants willing to trade, and besides purchasing stores for the colonists he took on board hides, sugar, ginger, pearls, and tobacco for sale in England. Arriving at Virginia, Grenville evidently did a brisk trade with the Indians, for such things as deer skins in exchange for "puppetts and babes," cloth, and above all copper and metal goods of every description, while his men collected specimens of the vegetable and animal products of the region. He returned, in Lane's words, with "a grete amasse of good thynges y^{t} hee bryngethe hys shippe presently frayegheted *with* all; to avoyde all suspycyone of fraude."[9] This cargo from Virginia clearly had some monetary value even if most of its components were for show.

On his way back to England Grenville, by chance or design, was fortunate enough to pick off a straggler from the Santo Domingo vessels on their way to join the *flota* at Havana, the *Santa Maria de San Vicente,* a vessel of three to four hundred tons, near Bermuda. She was boarded and a prize crew, led by Grenville himself, installed. After being blown off his course to the Azores, he got her safely to England on 18 September 1586.[1]

[6] *Cal.S.P.,Span.,1580–1586* (1896), p. 532; Quinn, *Roanoke Voyages,* II, 738.

[7] See Tom Glasgow, Jr., "H.M.S. 'Tiger,'" *North Carolina Historical Review,* LIII (1966), 115–21.

[8] Quinn, *Roanoke Voyages,* I, 184, 740–3.

[9] *Ibid.,* pp. 200, 735–6, 747; Irene A. Wright, *Further English Voyages to Spanish America, 1583–1594* (London, 1951), pp. 9–11, 16.

[1] See Quinn, *Roanoke Voyages,* I, 199–200, 207, 216–17, 219, 233, 273, 325–35, 418.

The prize was an important one containing a valuable cargo of sugar, hides, and ginger, cochineal, and some pearls, gold, and ivory. As soon as Ralegh heard of her arrival he went down to Plymouth, and the usual tussle took place between the crews, endeavoring to embezzle as much as possible of the proceeds of the voyage, and representatives of the adventurers, including the queen, anxious to get their hands on the lot. We do not know any details of what happened, but the share-out between the crews, who normally got a third; the Lord Admiral, who got a tenth; the crown, which got customs; and the adventurers, who divided what was left, was usually a long-drawn-out process. Grenville evidently grew alarmed at the reports that were going to court about the bullion and jewels supposed to have been taken, and wrote to Walsingham that there was no gold or jewels beyond what the passengers had had on their persons, of which the crew had relieved them. He put the value of her sugar and ginger at 40,000 to 50,000 ducats (£12,000–£15,000), and was able to inform the Secretary of State that his adventure would be repaid "with some gain." A circumstantial Spanish account declared that there were gold, silver, and pearls aboard worth 40,000 ducats and that the total value of the cargo was 120,000 ducats.[2]

Thus four profitable components were brought home: the goods acquired by trade in the West Indies, the profits of prizes taken in the Caribbean, the prize taken in the Atlantic, and the products and specimens from the American colony. If we take the total value as £40,000 and deduct the payments usual before the adventurers were reimbursed, we would get a figure of approximately £20,000. This would not only repay all investments but leave a handsome profit. At the very least the combination of privateering and colonization had paid well, but probably the least favorable item in the account was the relatively small value of produce from Virginia, since this would indicate to those concerned that colonization was scarcely worth while, even as a sideline, when so much more was to be gained from the direct plunder of Spanish resources.

Expeditions to supply and reinforce the colony were probably intended to be prepared, financed along the same lines, for 1586. But sooner or later English mercantile interests had to be seriously interested in the North American colony if it was to develop any substantial trade with England. Armed with the knowledge that a colony had been established on the other side of the Atlantic, Ralegh could invite merchants to con-

[2] *Ibid.*, pp. 169–71, 177–8, 192–3, 218–22, 229, 231, 743, 744, 757. The value of the silver ducat was then about 6s. 5s.; 10d. and 6s. 2d. are cited as its value at Cadiz in 1583–4 (P.R.O., H.C.A. 13/25, 19 October 1585, S. Lucke, 21 January 1586, A. Bowen).

tribute money and assistance to building up its trade. We know that his brother, Carew Ralegh, approached the merchant adventurers of Exeter on his behalf. "Certaine articles" were brought before the guild court on 16 January 1586, "touchinge a pretended voyage to Wyngandacoia [the presumed Indian name for Virginia] and a noate of the marchantable and other comodities there founde." But the merchants refused to contribute, since they had already put money into John Davis's expedition in search of a Northwest Passage to China.[3] Doubtless a similar approach was made to merchants in other towns, with what success has not been ascertained.

Ralegh had, however, one important link with London merchant capital. William Sanderson, a prominent merchant adventurer, married Ralegh's niece and acted as his man of business. He is said at times to have stood security for him for as much as a hundred thousand pounds, and to have lent him large sums. Deeply interested in overseas expansion, he was the main backer of Davis's expeditions, but nonetheless made considerable ventures in the American enterprise, to the extent of approximately a thousand pounds.[4] It was probably he who gradually interested a number of other London merchants in the colonial project.

From the point of view of the colony, 1586 was a disappointing year. Lane's settlers returned with Drake in July. The supply ship Ralegh had sent them came back with its stores intact after missing them. Grenville's three vessels, bringing further supplies, did likewise, and after leaving the small holding party on Roanoke, turned to the task of making their expedition pay. The sack of Azores towns and the prize laden with sugar, ginger, and hides which Grenville brought into Bideford in December may well have covered the greater part of the year's expenses.[5]

Drake's outstanding success in despoiling the Spanish empire in his expedition of 1585–6 is likely to have diverted many of Ralegh's fellow adventurers from any further concern with the colonizing aspect of American expeditions. As John Hooker put it, Drake's exploits so "inflamed the whole countrie with a desyre to adventure unto the seas, yn hope of the lyke good successe, that a greate nomber prepared shipps marynors and soylders and travelled every place at the seas where any proffite might be had." He does not fail to add cynically that by these means "many were undonne and theym selffes yn the ende never the better." [6] There was, in fact, an outbreak of overspeculation, mainly in privateering, which rendered it more difficult to get support at court and from the gentlemen of the southwest for an unprofitable colony.

[3] Quinn, *Roanoke Voyages,* II, 471.

[4] A. H. Markham, *The Voyages and Works of John Davis* (1880), pp. xiii–xiv.

[5] Quinn, *Roanoke Voyages,* II, 480–4, 494.

[6] *Ibid.,* pp. 312–13.

For the third colony, that of 1587, Ralegh planned differently. He wanted to experiment with settlers who would themselves make a sufficient investment in the enterprise to impel them to build up a self-perpetuating and commercially stable settlement. It is reasonable to assume that Ralegh's motive was at least partly financial, and to connect it with the boom in privateering and his own inability to carry the whole weight of financing the colony. It may also be associated with his commitments in 1586 to take part in the plantation of Munster. A corporation, "the Governor and Assistants of the Citie of Ralegh in Virginia," was established on 7 January 1587, and to it was delegated the task of bringing the settlers to America and taking responsibility for their maintenance.[7] The governor, John White, and most of the assistants were themselves to lead the settlement, but they left representatives in London, and possibly arranged with London merchants to use part of their personal capital to send them further supplies as they were needed. If this was so it does not mean that Ralegh and his circle had ceased to be major investors in the enterprise, but only that some part of their administrative and financial responsibility had been delegated.

From what we know of the voyage to Virginia, by way of the West Indies, in the summer of 1587, it appears that White insisted on avoiding privateering and intended to concentrate on supplying the needs of the colonists. Yet on the way home Fernandes took the *Lion* "to linger about the Island of Tercera for purchase," though he was unlucky and arrived in Portsmouth empty-handed, with only the timber shipped from Virginia as a return for the voyage.[8]

Governor White had sailed from Virginia in the other vessel so as to bring back supplies at the earliest opportunity. Ralegh offered to send a pinnace with some stores as soon as possible and to follow it up with a larger supply under Grenville. But the vessels were prevented from sailing by the Privy Council on 31 March 1588, in view of the danger to England from the Armada.[9] The two small pinnaces which White eventually got permission to take out with supplies in April went privateering, and the "theeuerie of our euil disposed mariners" ruined, as White said, the carrying through of the plan.[1] The episode, so tragic in its implications for the colonists, who were never seen again, indicates clearly Ralegh's continuing desire to assist the venture.

[7] Letters of reprisal had already been issued to at least 82 ships between July 1585 and February 1586 (P.R.O., H.C.A. 14/23, 43); see K. R. Andrews, *Elizabethan Privateering*, pp. 3–5 and *passim*.

[8] Quinn, *Roanoke Voyages*, II, 536–8.

[9] *Ibid.*, pp. 559–64.

[1] *Ibid.*, pp. 564–9.

Shortly afterward he took another step to divest himself of direct responsibility for the colony. White agreed to a scheme, which may have been suggested by Sanderson, that twelve new associates be joined to the original assistants for guidance of the colony's affairs. They included Sanderson, Thomas Smith, soon to be one of the foremost overseas speculators, nine other merchants, and Richard Hakluyt. The agreement, made on 7 March 1589, transferred full authority over the colony to the new corporation and thus relieved Ralegh of further obligations to finance it, apart from the sum of £100 which he contributed as a gift.[2] As the colony's overlord and sponsor he retained a general responsibility. To transfer the financing of it to a group of wealthy London merchants was a sensible and realistic proceeding. Unfortunately, they seem to have taken their duties rather lightly, and apparently made no immediate attempt to send out supplies or reinforcements. There is not enough evidence to assign the blame definitely either to them or to Ralegh.

At length, in 1590, John White found the means to reach first the West Indies and then Virginia.[3] He sailed in John Watts's *Hopewell*, the flagship of a small privateering squadron, and we find that when they were in contact with the Spaniards the English did not guard their tongues in referring to the "governor" who was to take up office in the colony in Virginia and whose heavy artillery was said to be in ballast below decks. Some of this was bluff, but exactly how much is not at all clear. William Sanderson's *Moonlight* was sent out specifically to make the Virginia voyage, and there are indications that she carried supplies for the settlement. But she, too, had to await the raids and battles of the privateers in the Caribbean. Only in August was the *Hopewell* free to cruise, along with the *Moonlight*, up the Florida coast in search of the lost colonists. For indeed they were lost. When White went ashore on Roanoke Island they were not to be found. Their heavy palisaded enclosure was impressive but empty. Some heavy cannon and bars of metal were found, and eventually White's heavy baggage, armor, maps, and pictures, excavated by Indians from pits where it had been laid by the colonists. They had gone, so a notice carved on a tree said, to Croatoan near Cape Hatteras, where Manteo's people lived—the Indian chief whom White had installed in 1587 as ruler, under Ralegh, of Roanoke Island and its adjacent territories.

This was a great disappointment but not a tragic one. Any sign that would have indicated departure in distress was lacking. But to sail, or

[2] *Ibid.*, pp. 570–6.

[3] There is a full account of the 1590 voyage, with documents, *ibid.*, pp. 579–716.

row, down Pamlico Sound did not prove easy. A boat's crew had already been largely lost when overset in treacherous water. A northeasterly had set in, anchor chains were parting, men's tempers were frayed after a season's campaigning against the Spaniards. White did his best to hold the *Hopewell* in western waters over the winter, so that the search could be renewed in the spring, but this did not prove acceptable; in the end he had to return, leaving the colonists still missing.[4]

The failure to find them thereafter may have been due partly at least to Ralegh's desire to assume they were alive, for if so, his patent would remain in force—one of its stipulations being that of continuous settlement. If the colonists were proved to have died or been killed, this would lead to cancellation of the patent. Thus the colony perished in the midst of a profitable privateering war in the west, when colonies were scarcely worth considering.

A voyage set out by Ralegh in cooperation with Watts's syndicate in 1591 throws some light on the relative incentives of privateering and colonization, with its lack of profit and loss of settlers. The West Indian squadron, again led by the *Hopewell,* took goods valued on their return at £31,150. Of this, £16,198 went in shares to the crew and the Lord Admiral, customs, and the cost of transport, leaving £14,952 for the adventurers. They were twelve in number. The queen had insisted that a careful reckoning be kept, possibly because she reserved the right to take a proportion of the profits. Ralegh wrote to Lord Burghley[5] about the returns on 16 October, declaring that he and the other adventurers had spent nearly £8000 in fitting out, and that the profit "amounteth not to the increas of one for one, which is a small returne. Wee might have gotten more to have sent them a fishing." In fact the profit amounted to some 85 percent on the outlay. This gives a very clear illustration of why he and other adventurers were, for a time at least, unwilling to go on pouring out money into colonization without some immediate return. Between 1584 and 1587 it seemed worth while to invest a few thousands which could be covered by incidental privateering profits from prizes taken on the way out and back. But when there was really big money to be made—when privateering was a booming, large-scale business—the drain of colonizing experiments became unattractive. After John White's return it appears to have been nearly a decade before Ralegh was again ready to spend money on Virginia.

[4] See pp. 439–40 below.

[5] Edward Edwards, *The Life of Sir Walter Ralegh . . . with His Letters,* 2 vols. (London, 1868), II, 43–5; see Andrews, *Elizabethan Privateering,* chaps. 7–8.

The link with privateering affected colonization in another way. The crews of the vessels which brought the colonists and their stores to America were entirely uninterested in this phase of their voyage. Their willingness to take the risks of an Atlantic crossing was due almost entirely to the expectation of plunder, and they were reluctant to serve for long on other tasks except under the tight rein of an exceptional commander. Ralegh put this eloquently many years later when he said:

> We finde it in daily experience that all discourse of magnanimitie, of Nationall Vertue, of Religion, of Libertie, and whatsoeuer else hath beene wont to moue and incourage vertuous men, hath no force at all with the common-Souldier [and he might have added "sailor"], in comparison of spoile and riches. The rich ships are boorded vpon all disaduantages, the rich Townes are furiously assaulted, and the plentifull Countries willingly inuaded. Our English Nations haue attempted many places in the Indies, and runne vpon the Spaniards head-long, in hope of their Royalls of plate, and Pistolets, which had they beene put to it vpon the like disaduantages in Ireland, or in any poore Countrie, they would haue turned their Peeces and Pikes against their Commanders contesting that they had been brought without reason to the Butcherie and slaughter.[6]

It was only the firm discipline imposed by Grenville and Lane and the capacity for leadership which the former showed, together with his skill and luck in taking prizes, that kept the expedition of 1585 reasonably attentive to its task, and even then there were quarrels. Lane, the second in command, headed a party which accused Grenville of "intollerable pryede and unsaciable ambycione" and of endangering the safe arrival of the fleet near Roanoke.[7]

The intractability of privateering crews is illustrated in the incident we have already seen, when Drake visited the colony in June 1586. The crew of the *Francis*, which was to be left with Lane, seized the chance offered by a storm which broke their cables to make for home and avoid being impressed for probably unprofitable service. And when it was decided to take off the colonists, the sailors, impatient at even ten days' delay, tipped most of the settlers' belongings into the sea.[8]

How disastrous indiscipline of this sort could be was shown very clearly in the later attempts to reestablish and supply the colony. The story of White's expedition in 1587 is, if we can believe his account, one of continuous sabotage. He accused Simão Fernandes, master of the lead-

[6] *Historie of the world* (1614), pt. 1, bk. 4, chap. 2, sec. 4 second pagination, p. 178.

[7] Quinn, *Roanoke Voyages*, I, 212.

[8] Compare *ibid.*, pp. 291–2, 302.

ing vessel (and called by the English Simon Fernandez or other Anglicized variations of the name), of leading the expedition to Santa Cruz, Vieques Island, Puerto Rico, Hispaniola, and the Caicos Islands; and yet making it impossible for White to get any of the things for which they had gone to the West Indies, namely plants, livestock, and salt.[9] At least some of the incidents mentioned by White appear to have been malicious. They would be senseless if they did not imply the existence of a conflict between White, who wanted supplies, and the sailors, who desired plunder. Then at Roanoke, Fernandes and the sailors insisted on leaving White's colonists, instead of carrying them on to Chesapeake Bay.[1] This action may well have been the cause of the loss of the whole colony. The attitude of the crews of the vessels in which White tried to get relief brought out in 1588 and 1590 has already been sufficiently noted. So long as the sailors employed on American voyages refused to accept their task as sufficient in itself and persisted in combining privateering with it, whatever the cost to intended colonists, there could be little chance of building up an English community so far from the British Isles.

If investors were greedy and sailors unruly, the colonists and their leaders were not without weaknesses. Ralph Lane was a soldier who organized the first colony on a military basis. He maintained a harsh discipline, enforced through provost marshals, on the men whom he commanded on American soil in 1585–6. This enabled him to organize a series of exploring expeditions up the Pamlico, Chowan, and Roanoke rivers, and to the mouth of the Chesapeake. Considering their limited equipment, this achieved a good deal, and clarified the topography of a considerable area, while his mapmaker and painter, John White, and his naturalist and scientific observer, Thomas Harriot, collected much accurate information on Indian society and on the fauna, flora, and minerals of the region. In less than a year they had gained an accurate knowledge of American conditions within a limited area.

But if they did their work of exploration well, they made little attempt to establish a firm social or economic basis for the colony. There were evidently few men with skilled agricultural knowledge among the settlers. The plants and cuttings they had gone to such trouble to obtain in the West Indies and to keep alive on shipboard, died or wilted. The sugar canes did not take root. Their wheat had become musty when the *Tiger* struck and sprang a leak, and they had little else to spare for seed, while they were clearly too late to plant maize in the Indian manner. In the spring of 1586, it is true, they did get seed from the Indians to plant maize

[9] See p. 260 above. [1] Quinn, *Roanoke Voyages*, II, 515–38; see p. 261 above.

enough to see them through, as they estimated, another winter, but their competence as farmers does not impress anyone who studies their record.[2] Their whole method of organization was against success, for, as J. A. Williamson has well said, "a military force could not grow crops." [3]

They did not make any attempt to appropriate land and allocate it among individuals. Their fort was built near the Indian village of Roanoke, and their houses were possibly scattered among the Indian dwellings. The land they sowed in the spring was cleared and allocated for their use by the natives.

It is not surprising, therefore, that they became largely parasitic on Indian society. Among the Indians of this area there was greater dependence on agriculture than in many parts of North America. Their plots of maize, beans, squashes, sunflowers, and tobacco around their villages played an important part in their community life. Where the soil was very fertile, cropping could go on for some years, but not indefinitely on the same soils without manuring. There was little pressure of population, however, and new land could be cleared and villages easily moved if need arose. Hunting, fishing, and collecting also played a large part in their economy.

Although in the autumn of 1585 they made no difficulty about supplying the colonists with considerable amounts of corn, vegetables, roots, fish, and deer-flesh in return for trinkets and prized metal objects, the pressure of the demands made on them became serious over the winter. The Indians did store some corn for the winter, and of course for seed, but not in such quantities as to provide an appreciable surplus for trade. In the spring and early summer, before new crops were ready, they went short and had to concentrate on hunting and collecting. It was at this season that they began seriously to resent English demands for food, accompanied as they probably were with threats and offers of higher prices in copper, which were sufficient to arouse savage cupidity. The result was an attempt to starve out the Roanoke settlement by the concerted effort of several tribes during Lane's expedition up the Roanoke River in March.

The survival of the expedition, despite the absence of supplies from the Indians on the way, led to a temporary entente and to the sowing of corn by the Indians for the use of the colony. But a renewed economic blockade began in May, and the colonists were forced to disperse in order to search for food for themselves. When this happened, Pemisapan, chief

[2] *Ibid.*, I, 187, 336, 407, 408, 742; Hulton and Quinn, *American Drawings of John White*, I, *passim.*

[3] J. A. Williamson, *The Age of Drake* (London, 1938), p. 246.

of the Roanoke Indians, conspired to attack and overwhelm the English, but Lane's intelligence was good and he sprang the plot at the beginning of June by bearding the chief in his village and putting him and the elders of the tribe to death. This cowed the Indians and saved the colony, but it did not establish any *modus vivendi* between the two societies.[4]

The failure of Lane's colony to support itself turned the Indians into the unwilling hosts of the settlers, but their land was not yet in jeopardy. With the arrival of White's' colonists in 1587, determined to appropriate substantial farms to each family, a more serious prospect developed, although we do not know what part this played in the disappearance of the colony. In any event, it was clear from the events of 1585–6 that the Indians would neither submit to economic enslavement nor to being ejected from their lands without a serious struggle. The small scale of the colonies of 1585, 1586, and 1587 showed that this was not at all clearly foreseen in England. For a colony to succeed economically, it must be large enough to provide adequate defenses and competent enough to organize its social resources and activities so as to be self-sufficient. None of the three colonies in any degree fulfilled these requirements.

Lane's letters in August and the early part of September 1585 were most enthusiastic about the wealth of timber and the variety of commercially usable plants to be found in North Carolina.[5] He told Walsingham on 8 September that God "dothe dayely blesse here w*ith* a dayely dyscov*er*ye of sumwhat rare growy*n*ge [here] y[t] Chrystendom wantethe." A good quantity of specimens and trade goods was collected or obtained from the Indians, as we saw, for Grenville to take back at the end of August. But once the party was left to itself there is little evidence of attempts to cut and season timber for export, to store skins and furs acquired by trade, or to prepare the plants which had, or were believed to have, medicinal properties. In fact the only articles we hear of as having been collected between September and June are two strings of pearls.[6] As the settlers were not adequately prepared for agricultural tasks, so they were not equipped for other activities which might help to pay their way.

Lane ultimately became pessimistic about the colony ever becoming an economic success on the basis of the export of local products. His final conclusion was "that the discovery of a good mine, by the goodnesse of God, or a passage to the Southsea, or someway to it, and nothing els can

[4] Quinn, *Roanoke Voyages*, I, 265–7, 275–88.

[5] The letters and sketch-map of August–September 1585 may be found, *ibid.*, pp. 197–217.

[6] *Ibid.*, pp. 260, 331–2.

bring this country in request to be inhabited by our nation. And with the discovery of any of the two above shewed, it willbe the most sweete, and healthfullest climate, and therewithall the most fertile soyle, being manured, in the world: and then will Sassafras, and many other rootes & gummes there found make good Marchandise and lading for shipping, which otherwise of themselves will not bee worth the fetching."[7]

The record of the exploring expeditions shows that this view was shared by his men. The Roanoke River expedition was made by Lane because he had heard from the Indians that the river rose from a great rock near the seaside. He also heard that up-country from its basin there was rich alluvial metal, which sounded as if it might be gold. The lure of a route to the Pacific and of finding gold was such that his men, boycotted by the Indians and almost starving for lack of food, insisted on going as far as they possibly could before turning back. Harriot tells us that for many these were the only aims that seemed worth while, and that "after gold and silver was not so soone found, as it was by them looked for, [they] had little or no care of any other thing but to pamper their bellies."[8] In such circumstances the hard task of raising a subsistence and creating a profit from agriculture, trade, and exploitation of natural resources could not be undertaken.

Harriot and John White were more optimistic. They believed that a serious group of colonists, working their own land in family groups, could feed themselves, grow crops for export (mainly of specialized Mediterranean produce), trade and exploit timber and native plants, and so survive and make a good living. Harriot, with his book, *A briefe and true report of the new found land*, which he finished in February 1588 and which was critical as well as eulogistic, became the propagandist for this view in England. White was not content to talk or write but was willing to stake his whole resources, his family, and his life on trying to bring such a colony to fruition. The third colony of 1587 had some prospect of doing better than the first, but we cannot tell how far it was equipped to survive, since it was never seen after August 1587. It was in any case so small as to be in a precarious position from the beginning.

The experiments made in these years produced no direct successors in America. The Jamestown colony in 1607 started with many advantages, such as much better knowledge of the topography and natural resources of the area chosen for settlement, but the colonists there had to learn much from the beginning by bitter trial and error. Had they read the lessons of the failures of 1584 to 1590 better, they might have saved them-

[7] *Ibid.*, p. 273. [8] *Ibid.*, p. 323.

selves much hardship. Ralegh's colonizing enterprises failed, partly because of insufficient appreciation of the complex problems that had to be surmounted in recreating a new society far from the homeland, and partly because the whole scale was too small and the financing so precarious as to leave the colonies only a slim chance of survival.

Summary

IN THE LATER sixteenth century, ignorance was only slowly giving place to knowledge so far as North America was concerned. But experiment and inquiry brought knowledge, even if they brought it hardly. Richard Hakluyt, who had done so much to inform Englishmen about America—to induce them to go there to trade, explore, and settle, and to tell of their exploits when they had been there—was able to include a fine world map in his *Principal navigations*, Volume II, when it appeared in London in 1599. This showed, amongst much else, an intelligible North America crowded with names and features. Most of the names were given by explorers from Portugal, France, and Spain, yet many had been placed on it by English enterprise and by Englishmen. But effective spheres of influence—genuine colonies (except for Spanish Florida)—were still to seek. After the sea war was over, the real struggle, the struggle for space, could begin in earnest.

PART IV

Economic and Religious Discontents

Prologue

TRADE AND RELIGION—religion and trade—these two motifs jostle each other in the prolonged sequence of experiments that led up to the permanent settlement of North America by northern Europeans. For a long time it was thought that settlement was not possible without trade. But religious enthusiasts, hampered at home by rigid church establishments or under more positive pressure from Inquisition or High Commission Court, were sometimes willing to trust themselves "to the wild," and without being assured that trade would be adequate to secure them supplies from Europe, attempt to survive in conditions of mere subsistence.

Englishmen working their way into the Gulf of St. Lawrence for walrus, cod, and whale, opened a possible door for Protestant Separatists, but they could not make use of it at the time, nor did they succeed in doing so until the Pilgrim settlement of 1620 at Plymouth in lower, slightly more kindly latitudes. Catholics, who were also preparing themselves for exile, alike in 1582 and in 1605, thought longingly of the prospect of great estates in the woods and along the rivers of the American North, but they did not attain them, perhaps because their sights were then set too high. They tried, at about the time the Pilgrims were edging painfully into New England, to put down some roots in Newfoundland, but found the fishing economy, the land, and the climate all too arduous to bear, and eventually turned toward the safer shores of Chesapeake Bay, where already Virginia, thanks to tobacco, was turning from a starving settlement into a rich plantation. There, alongside it, Catholic Maryland was to flourish also.

The urge to convert the Indians, too, was embedded in this outward movement, but it was a weak motive with limited drive and ultimate effect. The settlers, both Separatist and Catholic, were self-centered, filled with their spiritual, organizational, and personal problems. What they wanted, what they sought and eventually found, though not necessarily in the forms aspired to, was a place of their own, a self-centered community where labor could bind society together, trade feed it—make it rich in the end, perhaps—and where experiment or toleration of one sort or another was open to religious radicals or religious conservatives, as the case might be, whose roots at home were weakening or had been pulled up, or whose desires were incapable of fulfillment in the increasingly monolithic states of Europe.

CHAPTER TWELVE

England and the St. Lawrence, 1577–1602

I

ENGLAND'S IRRUPTION into a region which had been a reserve of French and Spanish Basque enterprise for perhaps half a century is a fact which requires some explanation, although it is perhaps not possible to trace all the circumstances surrounding it, even with the new material which has gradually accumulated in recent years. In so far as there is a pattern in England's concern with North America in the sixteenth century, it is that of scrutiny of one section of coastline after another to see whether certain limited objectives could be attained by more concentrated exploitation on land or offshore. The objectives varied from the circumnavigation of the Americas to the all-embracing settlement of the eastern seaboard of North America, and from the finding of sites where Mediterranean olive trees, vines, and citrus fruits could be profitably introduced to the establishment of a walrus fishery.

The only large and lasting achievement of the English in American waters in the sixteenth century was the development of a substantial hold on the cod fishery in one sector, southeast Newfoundland. The walrus fishery for which English expeditions were sent into the St. Lawrence in the 1590's is best seen as an extension of the cod fishery, but it also became involved in the problem of settling Englishmen—nonconformists who could not easily be fitted into English society—outside their own country. The story of experimental voyages to the St. Lawrence is in the end that of an unsuccessful attempt to have walrus caught by a band of

Congregationalist Pilgrim Fathers. It is a curious story, and the failure of the attempt may have been the principal reason why it has not hitherto been expounded at length.

The question of whether or not the English had a sufficiently acute interest in Jacques Cartier's discoveries to try to follow where he led into the St. Lawrence valley cannot usefully be discussed here. But it must be realized that the English fishermen who congregated at and off the Avalon Peninsula every summer were in intermittent touch with Breton, Norman, and French Basque seamen whose shore bases were on the south of the island, while the cod fishery shaded off into the area of mixed whale and cod fishing based on western Newfoundland under the domination of Spanish and French Basques. The latter in turn had a sphere of influence extending throughout the Gulf of St. Lawrence, covering the fur trade and white-whale (*beluga*), whalebone-whale, walrus, and cod fishing. The Breton ship which Cartier found fishing beyond the Strait of Belle Isle in 1534 and the courses plowed through the gulf by the Cartier-Roberval expeditions between 1534 and 1543 were the first-known examples of a long run of European interventions in this region. The Basques, whose claims to priority are probably good, appear to have left few records of their Canadian sphere of influence, but most likely a good deal of information and speculation as to the products of the gulf which they exploited reached English seamen in Newfoundland, though the majority of Englishmen seemed quite content to return each year to the same fishing stages.

Anthony Parkhurst must take pride of place among the English who had a lively interest in northeastern North America. He looked at Newfoundland in the 1570's with a seeing eye, commending its potentialities for commerce and settlement, and also saw beyond it. From 1574 on he collected information about the gulf and river of St. Lawrence, until in 1578 he declared himself willing to lead an English expedition to the river, having already advocated the seizure of Belle Isle, the occupation of Anticosti, and the implied declaration (for this is what it amounted to) of commercial war against the Basques.[1] Just at this time Sir Humphrey Gilbert obtained a patent giving him the right to colonize or control the colonization of America by Englishmen. The two Richard Hakluyts, lawyer and clergyman, were busy collecting materials to help point the way for him and his associates and clients. The elder Hakluyt was probably responsible for Gilbert's selling of licenses "to sundry persons of

[1] E. G. R. Taylor, ed., *The Original Writings and Correspondence of the Two Richard Hakluyts*, Hakluyt Society, 2d ser., nos. 76–7 (London, 1935), I, 123–34 (esp. pp. 133–4).

mean ability . . . to plant and fortifie . . . about the river of Canada." [2]

One of these was Edward Cotton, a Southampton merchant much engaged in overseas venturing, but we know little of his companions. Their plan was to enter the gulf and imitate the Basques (and compete with them by force too, perhaps) in trading with the Indians, whaling, and making train oil as it was known (whale or other fish oil). An expedition was, indeed, sent out. Richard Whitbourne, who sailed on Cotton's ship, tells us only that it failed "by the indiscretion of our Captain, and faint-heartedness of some gentlemen of our Company." [3] One might suggest that the vigorous reaction of the Basques to English competition may have been the decisive factor. We cannot, on present information, tell whether this venture took place in 1579 or 1580. In the latter year, however, the younger Richard Hakluyt, taking his first independent initiative in the field of geographical publicity, arranged for John Florio to publish the Jacques Cartier material already available in print in Italian, so as to let Englishmen know clearly what the French had found in the St. Lawrence basin over forty years before. The Cartier narrative was prefaced by an appeal for English settlement there [4] and was probably closely linked with the anti-Basque expedition already described. Nevertheless, though Christopher Carleill paid much attention to the St. Lawrence in the colonizing tract he published in 1583,[5] and though the younger Hakluyt carried on a vigorous campaign of economic espionage on French voyages to North America while attached to the English embassy in Paris (1583–8), no evidence of English voyages to the St. Lawrence is known during these years. Gilbert had turned his attention to Newfoundland itself; after his death interest had shifted south to what is now North Carolina and Virginia, and that "Mediterranean" zone occupied the attention of colonialists until the Spanish war blanketed off the English settlement on Roanoke Island and forced abandonment of the southern colonial experiment.

[2] Richard Hakluyt, *The Principal Navigations*, 12 vols. (Glasgow, 1903–5), VIII, 40. See D. B. Quinn, ed., *The Voyages and Colonising Enterprises of Sir Humphrey Gilbert*, Hakluyt Society, 2d ser., nos. 83–4, 2 vols. (London, 1940), I, 49–50.

[3] *Discourse and discovery of New-found-land* (London, F. Kyngston for W. Barret, 1620), *S.T.C.* 25372, sig. C5r. (See Quinn, *Gilbert*, II, 426–7; Quinn, *Richard Hakluyt, Editor*, 2 vols. [Amsterdam, 1967], I, 3–5).

[4] *A shorte and briefe narration of the two navigations to New France* (London, H. Bynneman, 1580); *S.T.C.* 4699, entered 7 June 1580; reprinted in Quinn, *Richard Hakluyt, Editor*, II.

[5] *A discourse vpon the entended voyage to the hethermoste partes of America* (London, 1583). Not in *S.T.C.* For the passages in question see Quinn, *Gilbert*, II, 362–4.

II

News about the Gulf of St. Lawrence which reached England in 1591 through the coincidences of privateering restarted the long-suspended project of competing with the Basques. Sir Francis Walsingham, who as Secretary of State had sponsored first Gilbert's and then Ralegh's colonizing projects and had come to concentrate on the southern ventures, died in 1590. Official initiative for the more northerly ones came from Lord Burghley, the Lord Treasurer. He had for long been interested in the western fishery, and as far back as 1563 had pushed through Parliament an act for having two "fish days" a week, in order to build up the English fishery against the competition of the five hundred ships and fifteen thousand seamen the French were thought to employ at Newfoundland. He was concerned with fish, train oil, and the naval stores obtained in northern waters and is found subscribing both to the Frobisher voyages in search of a route around North America and to the Gilbert ventures.[6]

An example of Burghley's continued interest in this field is given by John Davis. In the course of his second voyage in search of a Northwest Passage in 1586, the latter discovered a great cod bank in the strait which now bears his name. He salted down a sample of the "great cod" he had taken, so that he could exhibit them to possibly interested parties when he returned to England. Telling Sir Francis Walsingham of his find (as he relates in *The worlds hydrographical description*, published in 1595):[7] "master Secretary . . . commanded me to present unto the most honourable lord high treasurer [Lord Burghley] some part of that fish, which when his Lordship saw and heard at large the relation of this second attempt, I received favourable countenance from his honour, advising me to prosecute the action, of which his Lordship conceived a very good opinion." One of Parkhurst's papers on Newfoundland in the 1570's is among the Burghley manuscripts, and it was to Lord Burghley that Edward Hayes addressed lengthy pleas to sponsor intensive settlement of Newfoundland so as to keep control of the fishery in English hands.[8]

In the autumn of 1591 two separate pieces of information drew Burghley's attention to the Gulf of St. Lawrence. The English, since the sea war against Spain had become general in 1585, had been seizing every

[6] See Conyers Read, *Mr. Secretary Cecil and Queen Elizabeth* (London, 1955), pp. 271–4; Taylor, *Hakluyts,* I, 123–7; Quinn, *Gilbert,* I, 329.

[7] Not in *S.T.C.* Copies in B.M. and Folger Shakespeare Library, Washington, only.

[8] See Quinn, *Gilbert,* II, 329; B.M., LansdowneMS 100; and pp. 238–9 above.

ship they could in any way associate with Spanish ownership or with commerce to Spanish ports. Basque vessels coming from the western fisheries were especially good targets for English privateers. Although many of the ships were in French ownership, French and Spanish Basques were so intermingled that there were usually a few Spanish and a few French aboard each vessel, while fish brought by French and Spanish vessels alike was mainly destined for Spanish consumption. The blitz against the Basques from 1585 to 1603 has still to find its historian, but one of its fruits was the French-Basque ship the *Catherine de St Vincent* (or *Catalina de San Viçente* in its Spanish guise). She was taken on her return from America in the autumn of 1591 by the privateer *Golden Hind*, Edward Lewes, captain, and brought into Weymouth. From there it seems likely that Michel de la Ralde, captain and part-owner, made his way to London and, through his own efforts or those of the French ambassador, induced the Privy Council on 22 October to order the release of the ship and cargo intact. It also seems likely that this was done promptly, since there is no record of the sale of the ship or her cargo as prize goods, though it is not unlikely that she had suffered to some extent from pillage.

Scarcely had this been achieved than a stream of correspondence reached Lord Burghley from St. Jean de Luz and Bayonne urging him to intervene to rescue the ship. Catherine, Princess of Bourbon, Henry IV's sister, who administered the southern provinces for him, wrote that the ship was under her protection (its name may even have been bestowed by her) and was carrying merchandise for her service. M. de Chasteaumartin, who represented English interests in Bayonne, told Burghley that if the *Catherine* was not released there would be reprisals against English vessels trading to French Biscayan ports.[9] The reason for all this activity emerges only in a letter from the capable English intelligence agent at St. Jean de Luz, Edmund Palmer. Writing to Burghley on 9 October he said that the ship had been built only recently at St. Jean de Luz, and was bringing back from American waters, (evidently by report of some of her consorts who returned safely) train oil, salmon, and Newfoundland fish, and in addition "a great stores of rich furs, as beaver, marternes, otters and many other sorts."[1] This explains why the French were so anxious to recover the ship and her cargo, and emphasizes in a dramatic way how profitable the commerce of the St. Lawrence region had become. Palmer deliberately incited Burghley to interest himself in the

[9] *A.P.C.,1591–1592* (1901), p. 35; Madame to Burghley, n.d., P.R.O., State Papers, Foreign, France, S.P. 78/26, fol. 95; Chasteaumartin to Burghley, *ibid.*, fols. 62–3.

[1] P.R.O., State Papers Foreign, Spain, S.P. 94/4, fols. 64–6.

Catherine's cargo of furs by saying that "sometimes they do bring black fox skins—no such things to ease a man of the pain of the gout as these black fox skins." This must have had some appeal to an aging and gouty man.

Before these letters arrived, Burghley's attention had already been forcibly drawn to the Gulf of St. Lawrence by another capture, and he had been urged to encourage English enterprise there. The initiative in this case came from a prominent Bristol merchant, Thomas James, who informed him on 14 September that a ship of his had taken a Breton prize coming from the Gulf of St. Lawrence and so had revealed a profitable branch of commerce—a walrus fishery—on the Magdalen Islands, which he implied would be advantageous for the English to exploit.[2] James later obtained a description of the Magdalen Islands and of the Breton voyage,[3] which he no doubt forwarded to Burghley on receiving a favorable reply to his first letter. He was also probably responsible for bringing the younger Richard Hakluyt into the affair. Then a prebendary of Bristol Cathedral, Hakluyt was frequently in that city. He is likely to have taken an active part in publishing the Magdalen Islands material, preserving for us most of the documents we have and contributing himself, perhaps as part of the advertising material for English ventures, his little essay on the walrus: "A briefe note of the Morsse and the use thereof."[4] On the basis of the information obtained about the French venture of 1591, English expeditions to the St. Lawrence were initiated two years later.

From the documents we can construct a good deal of what happened in 1591. In that year a Breton syndicate headed by M. de la Court, Sieur de Pré-Ravillon et Grand Pré, who has not yet been identified in the French records,[5] sent two small vessels for a season of walrus fishing to the Magdalen Islands in the St. Lawrence. It seems clear that their knowledge of the fishery had been culled from the Basques, and it is likely that they had Basque charts of the islands and possibly a Basque pilot. The two vessels left St. Malo with "the fleet that went for Canada," the Bretons having resumed their fur-trading in the St. Lawrence River from 1581 on. One of the two ships, the *Bonaventure*, passed Cape Ray on 6 May and soon sighted Bird Rocks, but was held back by a storm, and it

[2] For James, see Hakluyt, *Principal Navigations*, 12 vols. (Glasgow, 1903–5), VIII, 155; K. R. Andrews, *English Privateering Voyages, 1588–1595*, Hakluyt Society, 2d ser., no. 111 (Cambridge, Eng., 1959), p. 185.

[3] Hakluyt, *Principal Navigations*, VIII, 150–4. [4] *Ibid.*, pp. 166–7.

[5] I am indebted to M. Robert Le Blant for this valuable negative information. He has searched the St. Malo records for La Court in vain. It is possible that the narrator gave a false name for him. See *D.C.B.* (Toronto, 1965), I, s.n.

was not until the end of the month that she was able to sail down the western shores of the Magdalens, rounding Amherst Island into Pleasant Bay, and enter the inner Basque Harbor. There she evidently found her consort, in which perhaps La Court had sailed,[6] which had coasted the eastern shores of the group and arrived some weeks before. The Bretons called the group, and also it seems Amherst Island in particular, Ramea (Spanish *rama, ramo,* French *rame, rameau,* branch), perhaps suggesting Spanish Basque influence. What are now Grindstone and Wolf islands were known collectively as Île Hupp (Spanish *rupe,* touchwood? French *huppe,* crest?). The long beaches, with good shingle banks behind, were excellent for drying cod, and on several of them herds of walrus were thick on the ground. The Bretons set hard to work killing, flensing, and boiling.

They must have had a good number of boats with them, for they took cod in some quantity as well as walrus, drying it on flakes on the beaches. Most of the walrus, it would seem, were hit on the head on land, though some may have had to be chased and harpooned at sea. The tusks were hammered out of their massive heads, the skin separated from the blubber and roughly salted, the blubber boiled down to oil and casked, and some of the meat from the pups used for food and barreled for provisions. By the end of the walrus season, which began in April and lasted for two months, they had taken fifteen hundred walrus, a great catch. Before all was prepared for lading, and their cod dried, it was probably mid-August. It does not appear that they had, this season, any competition from Basques or from the local Indians; at least we are told of none. Ignorance of the fact that both Spanish and French Basques normally came there in some strength was to bedevil the English enterprises.

On 6 September, off the Scilly Islands, the *Bonaventure* was chased by an English privateer and taken;[7] her consort escaped and apparently got safely home to St. Malo. The *Pleasure,* which took the *Bonaventure,* was owned and victualed by Thomas James and Thomas Jennings of Bristol, and her captain was William Trench. The prize was brought to Bristol with her cargo of "trayne oyell, feshydes and teethe," to cite the document precisely,[8] and appraised there as worth £793. The cargo was both

[6] The author refers to "my Masters" as being on board the other ship, of whom La Court (or a person of some other name in his place) could well have been one (Hakluyt, *Principal Navigations,* VIII, 152).

[7] *Ibid.*, p. 155.

[8] *Sic* in B.M., HarleianMS 598, fol. 15v (prize brought in October 1); note by Burghley on list of prizes that Thomas James's prize belonged to Frenchmen of St. Malo, B.M., LansdowneMS 67, fols. 146–7; the prize noted on another list, *ibid.*, fol. 109r.

valuable and unusual, and it is not surprising that James brought it to Burghley's attention or took the trouble to get one of her complement—probably the master, though we do not know this for certain—to write "A relation of the first voyage and discovery of the Isle Ramea," giving the account of the Magdalens voyage referred to above which was afterward printed by Hakluyt.

The fifteen hundred walrus produced a good quantity of oil, two barrels for five carcasses, some eighty tuns in all, judging from the more than forty tuns in the *Bonaventure*. Train oil from cod, seal, and whale sold in England for from £9 to £14 a tun, though the customs valuation was only £5.[9] If we reckon the selling price of forty tuns at £12 a tun we should get £480. The walrus ivory might weigh an average of five pounds a pair for the tusks of the adults among the fifteen hundred killed—perhaps seven hundred pairs in the *Bonaventure*, about thirty-five hundred pounds, conservatively reckoned. Elephant ivory had a customs value of 5s. a pound, but apparently was worth retail no more than 1s. 6d. in 1591, while a prize valuation in 1590 put it at only 9d.[1] Nonetheless the retail price for walrus ivory was, we are told, 2s. 9d. to 3s. in London.[2] If we take 2s. a pound as the selling price we get about £350 for what the *Bonaventure* carried. As for walrus hides, oxhides were rated for custom at 20s. each, and prize valuations gave from 5s. to 8s. a hide according to quality.[3] If we reckon another seven hundred hides at 10s., giving £350, we should be safe enough. The walrus meat is not likely to have been very bulky or valuable. Allowing £250 for her cod, we get a total sale value for the cargo of some £1,430, which probably errs on the side of caution, since the prize valuation of under £800 includes the ship and was usually about half the sale value or less.[4] It is likely that the vessel that got home to St. Malo paid the way of both ships. Nor is it surprising that Thomas James, Lord Burghley, and Richard Hakluyt became excited about the *Bonaventure*'s rich and unusual cargo.

The main value of the walrus, at first sight, was the oil. "Train oil" was used for lighting and lubrication, but the greatest need for oil was probably for soap, relatively large quantities of which were required for the cloth industry. Oil from cod and seal was too fishy to be freely used in

[9] T. S. Willan, *A Tudor Book of Rates* (Manchester, 1962), pp. xxxi, xli, 43, 79.

[1] *Ibid.*, p. 36; Hakluyt, *Principal Navigations,* VIII, 156; Quinn, *Roanoke Voyages,* II, 692–4.

[2] Hakluyt, *Principal Navigations,* VIII, 156–7.

[3] Willan, *Tudor Book of Rates,* p. 11; Andrews, *English Privateering Voyages,* pp. 118–19; Quinn, *Roanoke Voyages,* III, 692–4.

[4] For official appraisements see Andrews, *English Privatering Voyages,* pp. 20, 56–8.

this way, though whale was better; walrus oil was, miraculously, sweet—that is, it did not stink of fish. The Company of Soapmakers of Bristol, a center for soap manufacture, had set itself against the use of any except olive oil,[5] but from 1585 this was shut off by the Spanish embargo except for what came round from the Mediterranean or was reexported from France, mainly from the Biscayan ports. It was thus both scarce and dear,[6] and this explains Thomas James's jubilation at the quality of the walrus oil: "if it will make soap, the king of Spain may burn some of his Olive trees." [7] Soapmaking was thus the major incentive for English penetration of the Gulf of St. Lawrence, which the capture of the *Bonaventure* provided. Minor ones were stressed by Richard Hakluyt—the comb-and-knife makers would buy the ivory at high prices; moreover, the walrus tusks were proved to his satisfaction by Dr. Alexander Woodson of Bristol to have valuable medical qualities, being "as sovereign against poison as any Unicorn's horn"—a reminder that pharmacy was still prescientific.[8] Finally the hides, later much valued for their toughness in preventing rigging from chafing, were in demand. "The Leather-dressers take them to be excellent good to make light targets," said Hakluyt, noting that he had seen a piece thicker than two ox hides.

With these incentives on top of the discovery of the valuable cargo of furs on the *Catherine*, also from the St. Lawrence region, an English venture to catch walrus on the Magdalen Islands was planned. What is strange is that we have no evidence that anything was done in 1592. It may be, indeed, that there was some attempt to make a reconnaissance of the islands and that this did not succeed for lack of charts or a pilot or for other reasons. But it may also have been necessary to spend some time in convincing the businessmen of London and Bristol that this activity might bring profits as high as those of privateering. When the project for a voyage finally emerges in 1593, it has taken shape as a fairly professional venture. It has a backer from the London area: "Master Hill of Redrife," as Hakluyt calls him—Peter Hill (or Hills) of Rotherhithe, Surrey, as we now know him.[9] He was born in 1535 and pulled himself up the

[5] *The Company of Soapmakers, 1563–1642*, B.R.S., X (Bristol, 1940), ed. H. E. Mathews, pp. 4, 5, 26. A fine was levied in 1572 for using fish oil in soapmaking. The editor doubts, however, whether the prohibition was rigidly maintained.

[6] Rated at £8 to £12 a ton, its sale value was rather more like £20 (Willan, *Tudor Book of Rates*, pp. iii, 42).

[7] Hakluyt, *Principal Navigations*, VIII, 155.

[8] *Ibid.*, pp. 156–7.

[9] Brass in St. Mary's, Rotherhithe, *Surrey Archaeological Collections* (London 1924), XXXII, 80–1; he was engaged in privateering between 1585 and 1589 (B.M., LansdowneMS 73, fols. 196–8; his and his partners' trading activities can be followed in P.R.O., H.C.A. 3/19, 14 and 20 January 1586; H.C.A. 13/25, 19 October 1585,

ladder from seaman to shipowner. Active in the Thames pilotage organization, in 1589 he became Master of the Trinity House at Deptford. Before that his ships ranged to Hamburg and Spain, and in 1584 his *White Hind* had been to Newfoundland to fish and had taken its cargo to sell in Spain, thus being an early starter in the triangular trade from the Banks which was later to flourish. Cut off from Spain in 1585, he may have been only too willing to employ his ship *Marigold* in the St. Lawrence in 1593.[1]

Setting out from the Thames in the spring, she had on her a couple of butchers for flensing walrus and three coopers to knock up barrels in which to put their oil. Peter Hill's representative on board was Richard Fisher, who wrote a narrative of the voyage. Hill seems to have had close connections with Topsham in Devon, since Richard Strong, master of the *Marigold*, and Peter Langworth his mate both came from there. This makes it the more likely that Hill was responsible for bringing George Drake of Topsham into the venture as commander of the second ship to be employed on the voyage.[2] He was probably a relative of Sir Bernard Drake, who had seized Portuguese vessels at Newfoundland in 1585. Behind him we can see Bristol capital put up by Thomas James, by another prominent merchant, Rice Jones, and perhaps by Richard Hakluyt, but in modest quantities. Burghley may well have brought Hill into the game, but we do not know whether he ventured his own money in it.

Unfortunately we do not have Lord Burghley's letters to Edmund Palmer during the period from October 1591 on. It is likely, however, that he told Palmer about the *Bonaventure*'s capture when reassuring him as to the *Catherine*'s release, and may have suggested then (or raised the matter later) that Palmer should find him a Basque pilot to bring walrus-fishing vessels from England to the St. Lawrence. Certainly by the

15, 17, and 21 January, 1586, 18 February 1586; H.C.A. 13/28, fols. 39v., 75r.; Hakluyt, *Principal Navigations*, VIII, 157, 161 (and see p. 208 above and p. 346 below). He received a bounty for building large ships, 6 April 1594 (P.R.O., S.P. 38/4); he was contracting to carry soldiers from France to Ireland for the Queen in 1598 (Hist.MSSComm., *CecilMSS*, VIII, 28). One of his ships carried planters to Ireland on 22 April 1607 (H.C.A. 1/46, fols. 330v–331r). He sold his share in the *Mayflower* (the Pilgrims' ship?) and other ships to Robert Bell on 8 December 1610 (Bibliotheca Phillippica, new ser., pt. v (Americana), no. 1056, sold at Parke-Bernet Galleries, New York, 28 October 1969).

[1] Hakluyt, *Principal Navigations*, VIII, 157–61.

[2] Hakluyt wrote a brief note on this voyage (*ibid.*, pp. 161–2) after George Drake had failed to supply a promised narrative; Fisher (*ibid.*, pp. 157–8) tells us most of what we know.

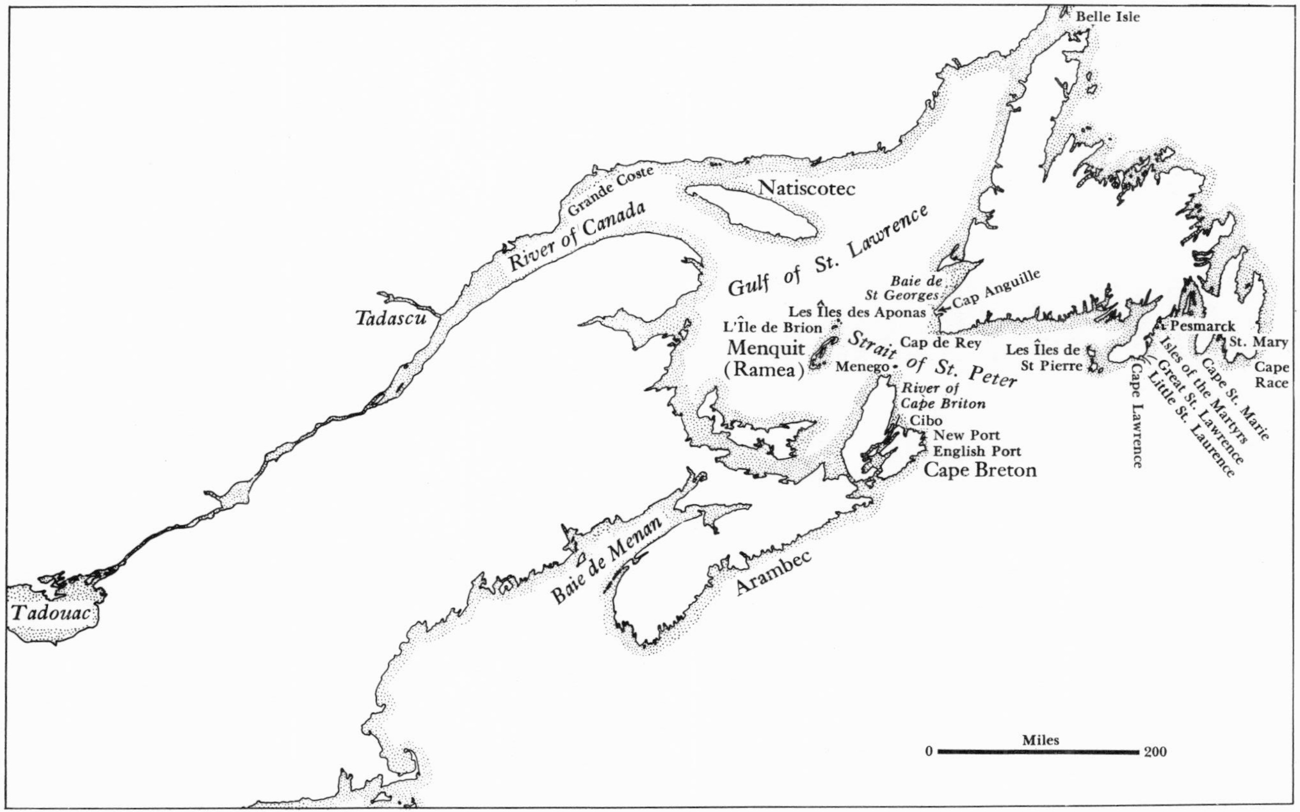
Belle Isle
Natiscotec
Grande Coste
River of Canada
Gulf of St. Lawrence
Tadascu
Baie de St Georges
Cap Anguille
Les Îles des Aponas
L'Île de Brion
Menquit (Ramea)
Strait of St. Peter
Menego
Cap de Rey
Les Îles de St Pierre
Pesmarck
St. Mary
Cape Race
Cape St. Marie
Isles of the Martyrs
Great St. Lawrence
Little St. Laurence
Cape Lawrence
River of Cape Briton
Cibo
New Port
English Port
Cape Breton
Baie de Menan
Arambec
Tadouac
Miles
0
200

The English in the Gulf of St. Lawrence, 1581–1597.

spring of 1593 a Basque pilot well known to Palmer, Stevan Bocall, was at Bristol, and we now know that he sailed with George Drake as pilot to the Magdalens.[3] Drake was tardy in preparing his ship and thus held back the *Marigold* so that it was almost too late for walrus-hunting when they left Falmouth on 1 June. Drake sailed ahead and, with his pilot to show him the way, rapidly reached the Magdalens. Strong was delayed: the *Marigold* reached St. Francis Bay, Newfoundland, only on 11 July, worked her way around and through Cabot Strait ("the Straits of St Peter"), but could not light on the islands and so turned back to Cape Breton and thence down the Nova Scotia coast, doing a little desultory cod-fishing and finally making an unsuccessful attempt to take prizes off the Azores. Peter Hill got his ship back without a cargo (except perhaps for a few cod) at the end of the year.

George Drake did better. There was a single Breton ship in the harbor at Ramea (very likely in Basque Harbor). Like the *Bonaventure* in 1591, she came from a Catholic League port—probably from La Court's St. Malo syndicate. Her lading of walrus was three quarters complete: at the rate of the *Bonaventure*'s lading she had on board the proceeds of between five hundred and fifty and six hundred carcasses, worth £800 to £900. On sight of Drake's ship she raised anchor and took flight, getting away without difficulty. But three of her boats, with twenty-three men, were out on a walrus hunt. These, with the carcasses they had, Drake and Bocall seized on their return, and then proceeded to do some hunting for themselves, taking "certain sea-oxen but nothing such numbers as they might have done, if they had come in due season." Once again we hear of no Basque or Indian competition. However, Drake had at least begun a trade: Englishmen had got, by fair means and foul, a cargo of walrus. How much there was, and how ready a sale in Bristol for the oil, skins, and ivory we cannot say. It seems likely, though, that we can trace the disposal of tusks of perhaps 250 walrus from this cargo in Russia in 1594. In May and June of that year, 1311 pounds of "morsse teeth" were shipped there by Thomas Pitt and Richard Merick, to be sold for £159 4s. (about 2s.5d. a pound) to an English agent.[4] It may have been that London did not absorb as much walrus ivory as expected, and it seemed best to sell it where there was already an established market. The price realized was a good one. We do not hear of any further effort to fish walrus in 1594.

Instead, another St. Lawrence venture was planned. Bocall had evi-

[3] Palmer to Burghley, 6 March 1595, P.R.O., S.P. 94/5, fols. 9–10v.

[4] T. S. Willan, *The Early History of the Russia Company, 1553–1603* (Manchester, 1956), pp. 363–4.

dently returned to Bristol and put in hand an expedition to reconnoiter the Basque whale fisheries in the Gulf of St. Lawrence. Probably he wanted to get a large vessel under his control and to teach the English whaling, but he did not succeed. Though it is likely that Peter Hill and Thomas James again invested in the venture, along with Rice Jones, Bocall was able to get to sea only Jones's small ship of thirty-five tons, the *Grace*, with Sylvester Wyet as master. Wyet informs us that she left Bristol on 4 April and sighted Newfoundland on 19 May, working southward and westward round the island to the Bay of Placentia, a Basque fishing center.[5] The two ships there were French Basques from Ciboure. Sailing on round Cape Ray to the west coast, the *Grace* was in waters not known to have been fished hitherto by English ships. Bocall piloted her to the southern end of St. George's Bay, where two Basque whalers had been wrecked in 1593, as he had apparently learned from news carried by survivors to his home port, St. Jean de Luz. The wrecks were badly damaged by rockfalls as well as by the sea (though there were some iron bolts considered worth salvaging), and the train oil had leaked from the barrels. Yet there remained intact "seven or eight hundred whale fins," that is, pieces of whalebone, which were all recovered and provided them with a valuable cargo that "made" their voyage.

Bocall then took the ship across the Gulf to the southern shore of Anticosti, telling Wyet that whales wounded by the Basques were often cast up on the beaches. Nothing was found, and after a little exploration round the north side of the island, where again the English were in new territory, the ship returned toward Cape Ray, having sighted Bird Rocks on the way. Back in Placentia Bay they found many Basque ships, both French and Spanish—more than sixty vessels in all. They were able, no doubt with Bocall's assistance, to borrow two pinnaces from which they fished for cod, but left the bay after some thieving by the Beothuk Indians. They completed their lading at Farillon, where there were twenty-two English ships, and made an easy run home with a valuable cargo to Bristol by 24 September.

From the letter of Edmund Palmer which tells us all we know of Bocall's participation in the voyages of 1593–4—since Hakluyt suppressed all mention of him in the published narratives—it is clear that the pilot was dissatisfied with his experiences in the English service.[6] We are told that "these two years he hath sailed from Bristow [Bristol], but he could not have that as he would have for the victualling, and when he came

[5] Hakluyt, *Principal Navigations*, VIII, 162–5. See *D.C.B.*, I, s.n.

[6] 6 March 1595; P.R.O., S.P. 94/5, fols. 9–10v.

thither [to the Gulf of St. Lawrence] his men would do nothing, and in a bark of 35 tons." These remarks remain somewhat cryptic. He despised the *Grace* because she was too small, most probably for whaling. The men would not do something or other—perhaps they would not attempt to capture whale for themselves. It is just possible that Bocall, who as we shall see was very anti-Spanish, wanted his English associates to cut out one of the Spanish Basque whalers or fishing vessels as a prize, but they would not take the risk of doing so. What he means about the victualing we cannot tell precisely. It may be, however, that he had plans to winter in Canada, and that the English backers would not provide the necessary stores to enable him to do so. If this is the explanation, he may have planned to take one of the two expeditions up the St. Lawrence River, so as to bring this too within the range of English contacts. None of these possibilities is out of the question, but none is supported by evidence. There is no doubt, though, that he considered the scale of English activity in the Gulf so far as altogether too small.

In 1595 Burghley is again our link with what was planned. In the letter from Palmer already cited, of 24 February 1595, a new project is broached. Bocall (Palmer said) had returned for the winter to St. Jean de Luz and was now going to England with a new proposition which he could commend to Burghley. He told him that "there is wintered in Newfoundland in the Grand Baye [probably in western Newfoundland, though the name could apply to land anywhere round the gulf] a new ship of St Sebastyans [San Sebastian, on the Spanish side of the frontier], one of 400 tons, who went thither to kill the whale, and the ship cannot but be rich with train oil. Another small ship is preparing to get to her with victuals, and other two bound to the killing of the sea cows [the walrus on the Magdalens], out of whom they do get great store of 'Balyne' [baleen, here walrus ivory] which is a rich commodity."

Bocall had discussed with Palmer a scheme for taking a ship out from England to seize the Basque whaler and "bring home these Spanishes." He had promised to "repair first to your Honour" when he reached England, and he "hath such a mind to these 'Spanyses' that he cannot be in quiet till he hath the new ship with her lading." The pilot could have reached England by the middle of March, and it would have been possible for Burghley to obtain letters of marque for an English privateer in time to make the proposed expedition, provided a ship could be found already equipped to make such a voyage. Peter Hill had suffered losses from the Spaniards and might have been willing to take part. We shall see that William Craston, a privateer officer of considerable experience, was engaged for a St. Lawrence expedition in 1597 and showed on it substantial knowledge of the Gulf, which might suggest he had been there before with Bocall in 1595. However, there is no evidence as yet which points directly to a voyage of the kind Bocall contemplated being undertaken in 1595. All we can say is that it might have taken place, though if it was successful it is surprising that something should not have been heard of it.

Bocall was clearly an exceptional man who had a wide range of experience in North America, to which Palmer paid generous tribute in the letter already quoted. He was "called here at St Jean de Luz the Prince of Conde," we are told, which implies he was a Huguenot. This would explain his hatred of the Spaniards and his difficulties in working in the mixed French-Spanish Basque fishing trade manned by Roman Catholics, while it might also point to arrogance on his part and a capacity for giving himself airs. Yet he was, too, says Palmer, "the oneliest pilot in this land," the best they had—"he knows where the copper mines be in the Newfoundland, whereof I have show, but I never saw better in my life." These mines, again, could have been on the island of Newfoundland, but might also have been anywhere else in the Maritimes or in the St. Lawrence basin. There is, indeed, a possibility that they were on the Bay of Fundy, since Bocall may well be the source of the evidence for such mines which Edward Hayes, who like Palmer had seen specimens of ore, cited in several of his writings.

Bocall had also had much contact with Indians—"this man hath had great traffic with the savages and will warrant any man to pass that way over a point of land to the South Sea." We can only guess where he thought the portage to the Pacific was—perhaps over the *saults* to Lake Ontario. But Palmer thought he knew his way: "for that country and these passages I think he has not his fellow in the world." Finally, he was an expert trader. "I have known him," said Palmer, "bring out of the Canada [thus giving proof of Basque fur-trading well up the St. Lawrence] in a paltry barque three thousand pound worth in furs besides other things of rich value." This reconstruction of an otherwise unknown personality is of considerable interest for this early period of European contact with Canada.

The tantalizing gap in our sources for events of Atlantic voyaging in 1595 is repeated in 1596. There is one further reference to Bocall. Palmer had said in the letter already quoted that "all the best men of this country as pilots are against him and have 'wrotte' [wrought] all the means they can to keep him at home." Doubtless they did not wish to see their hard-won knowledge of the west transmitted to the English. Bocall had nonetheless gone to England in March 1595, but was back in St. Jean de

Luz in the spring of 1596. This time he was subject to pressures from Spanish agents. They had been maneuvering since 1594 to get him to enter their naval service because of his knowledge of the coasts of England and Ireland, and had renewed their offers in 1596, asking especially for detailed information, and no doubt charts as well, on the approaches to the Bristol Channel, Barnstaple, Dublin, and Limerick. Palmer, by this time on leave in England, wrote on 1 May 1596, apparently to Sir Robert Cecil, about this latest development, adding: "Which Stephen Bocall serveth here in England for merchants voyages and, being of late on a voyage there [to St. Jean de Luz], they procured all that ever might be, by money and other promotion, to have him to serve their said purpose, but he would not consent to serve them in any manner of means." [7] It would seem from this that Bocall had returned to England, perhaps accompanying Palmer, but it is not certain. And we cannot presume that he or his English associates made a voyage to the St. Lawrence in this year. At the same time, the walrus-fishery project clearly had not been abandoned. It was revived in a new guise and with new personnel in 1597.

III

The novelty of the 1597 venture to the Magdalen Islands lay in two things. First, the project was planned as a colonizing rather than solely a commercial venture. Since the Bretons and the Basques were known to frequent the islands and to dominate the walrus fishery, if the English were to gain at least a major share in the fishery it seemed desirable that they should attempt to overreach their competitors. The walrus season was short and English ships not accustomed to attempt the Atlantic crossing so early in the year as their rivals. If, therefore, an English settlement could be left on the islands, the colonists would be able to kill a large number of walrus as soon as they appeared, and also build flakes for drying their cod and so start the fishery in good time. The islands were known to contain land that was promising for agriculture, and there was also some timber. It is unlikely that at this time there was any serious idea of holding off other fishermen and walrus-hunters by force. It seems to have been thought that the mere presence of an English settlement, and the priority its members would gain in harvesting the sea, would ensure the forbearance of the Basques and Bretons, making it possible to reinforce the settlement annually by vessels from England for which it would provide a base.

[7] Palmer to Cecil, 1 May 1596, P.R.O., State Papers, Domestic, Elizabeth, S.P. 12/257, 64.

The second new feature was the proposal to take from England a group of settlers who were willing and eager to leave the country and could be counted on as likely to apply themselves conscientiously to the hard pioneering life demanded of them on the islands. The plan was to send out two vessels in good time in 1597:[8] the *Hopewell*,[9] with Captain Charles Leigh, and the *Chancewell* with Captain Stephen van Harwick, which would attempt to carry through a season's walrus- and cod-fishing, while at the same time a small party of four settlers would be carried in order to examine the islands, choose a site for a settlement, and assess the supplies necessary to bring out for the larger party which was to come in 1598. The four planters were expected to stay over the winter along with one of the ships—apparently the *Chancewell*—and her company. The spring might then be spent in fishing and hunting walrus. This would provide, it was thought, all the necessary experience required for establishing a secure colony and steady trade, the prosperity of the settlers being assured by the sale of their products each year in England.

The project shows signs of Bocall's influence; the plan for the ship to winter in the Gulf might have been borrowed from his experience of Basque whaling practice, and his hostility to the Spanish Basques would have led him to advocate an English settlement in order to deny them access to the islands. It may be that he had already advocated some such measure in 1593 or 1594, the failure of the English to attempt anything on an adequate scale being a main cause of his earlier discouragement. But whatever his influence, Bocall was not intended to accompany the expedition. Indeed, since he is not heard of after May 1596, we cannot usefully speculate on the reasons for his failure to appear on the scene in the following year.

A number of men appear in the picture in 1597 who are somewhat difficult to identify and associate. We cannot say definitely that Peter Hill was concerned in the venture, but as other persons linked to it in some way had associations with Rotherhithe, and as Peter Hill had been in the walrus project as early as 1593, there is good reason to suppose that he may again have been one of the promoters, and that Ralph Hill, who took part in the voyage, was his representative. Abraham van Harwick certainly was a sponsor. He was a Dutch merchant, not

8 Charles Leigh's narrative (Hakluyt, *Principal Navigations*, VIII, 166–80) is the main authority, except for George Johnson, *A discourse of some troubles and excommunications in the banished English church at Amsterdam* (Amsterdam, 1603), *S.T.C.* 14664.

9 For the *Hopewell* see Quinn, *Roanoke Voyages*, II, 589–98, 662–3 (armament); Andrews, *English Privateering Voyages*, pp. 95–104.

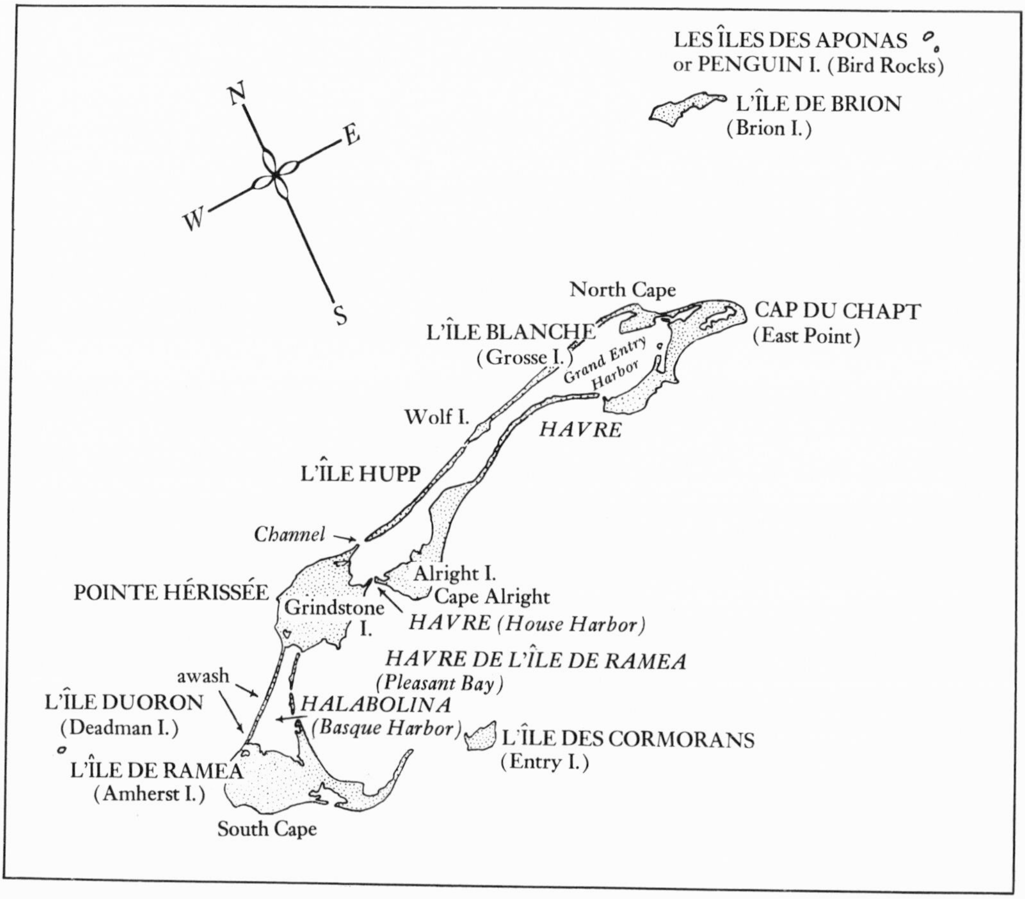

The Magdalen Islands, Gulf of St. Lawrence, in 1597 and today.

naturalized, who had been settled in London for some years and was active at various times in importing wine, purchasing prize goods, and establishing "mineral battery works" (stamp-mills) powered by water for working copper or brass at Rotherhithe.[1] Stephen van Harwick, also a

[1] Hist.MSSComm., *CecilMSS,* XIV, 318; *A.P.C.,1596–1597* (1902), p. 141; B.M., AdditionalMS 12505, fol. 450; *A.P.C.,1597–1598* (1904), pp. 491–2; M. B. Donald, *Elizabethan Monopolies* (London, 1961), p. 191 (who says Van Harwick had a license from the Mineral and Battery Company). On 7 February 1601, Edward and Thomas Hayes were authorized to erect "an Engine at Redreth [Rotherhithe]," which was either a rolling or stamping mill for preparing metal for coinage or for coining money (P.R.O., Privy Seal Indexes, Ind. 6744). The topographical association of Edward Hayes, Van Harwick (and a similarity between his business and that of Hayes), Peter Hill, and William Craston with Rotherhithe suggests that they were all acquainted. Cf. pp. 209 above and 331 below.

merchant, is likely to have been his brother, but has not otherwise been met with than as a sponsor and captain of the *Chancewell.* Ralph Hill we can trace as the second son of Edmond Hill, originally of Shere, Surrey. Born about 1573, he was apprenticed to a London goldsmith in 1585 and became free of the Goldsmiths' Company in 1594. He raised some money in February 1597, probably to invest in the voyage, and was later accused by his elder brother Richard of leaving him in financial difficulties in 1597, when he "departed England upon strange and desperate adventures."[2] If he was a relative of Peter Hill, which is not yet established, he might have been a nephew.

The fact that William Craston was only master of Captain Leigh's ship, the *Hopewell,* should not lead to his significance being minimized.[3] He had himself been captain of the *Hopewell,* a vessel of a hundred and twenty tons, as far back as 1590, when she made a privateering voyage to the West Indies and called at Roanoke Island in search of the lost colonists. He, too, was a Rotherhithe man, born in 1561, who undoubtedly knew Peter Hill but is not known to have sailed on his ships. Craston had sailed for John Watts in 1590 and had undertaken other privateering voyages for him, gaining a reputation for sharp practice on the way. If John Watts, an important London merchant of his time and an especially large investor in privateering ventures, still owned the *Hopewell,* as is likely, he may have invested her in the Magdalens venture or else hired her to the other promoters. It has already been suggested that Craston was just the sort of man Bocall needed for his cutting out project in 1595. His presence on the 1597 expedition indicates that resistance was expected, since the *Hopewell* carried twenty to twenty-four guns, and that it was hoped to take some Spanish Basque prizes to pay part of the expenses of the voyage.

Captain Charles Leigh was the leading personality in the expedition, yet very little is known of his early life.[4] Born in 1572 at Addington, Surrey, the third son of John Leigh and Joan Oliph, he is described in

[2] P.R.O., Chancery Proceedings, Bill and Answer, C.2 Elizabeth/Hh. 24/31.

[3] For Craston see Andrews, *English Privateering Voyages,* pp. 157–8, 172.

[4] In 1602 he described himself as aged thirty years or thereabouts (P.R.O., H.C.A. 14/35, 127–8): the date is confirmed by the best genealogical study of his family, G. Leveson-Gower, "Notices of the Family of Leigh of Addington," Surrey Archaeological *Collections,* VII (1880), 77–123. The owners of the *Marigold,* which he commanded in his 1601 Mediterranean voyage (Hist.MSSComm., *CecilMSS,* XI, 408), probably included Peter Hill, as she is likely to be the same ship that Strong commanded in 1593. If this is so, the continuity of association with Hill would suggest that Leigh had been employed by him before as well as after 1597. See *D.C.B.,* I, s.n.

1597 as a merchant, and it is probable that besides serving an apprenticeship in London he had already had some experience at sea (or conceivably as a soldier). It is at least possible that he had sailed for Peter Hill. By 1597 he was sufficiently well known as a responsible man to be entrusted by the Privy Council, along with the Van Harwicks, with the execution of the Magdalens venture. Leigh is the only link between the two sides of the project. He was known to and sympathized with the Puritans who were designated to found the colony, while his commercial and maritime interests may have joined him with Peter Hill and John Watts—if indeed they were concerned—as well as with the Van Harwicks, in the business enterprise.

The voyage of 1597, after so much preparation had been put into it, was an almost complete failure. The *Chancewell* was wrecked on Cape Breton, though her men were recovered later. The *Hopewell* alone penetrated the inner harbor in the Magdalens and was in the end driven out by the French and their allies. She did not acquire a single walrus, whale, or cod. Her men refused to take the expedition farther up the Gulf to a possible whaling ground there; in the end Leigh seized a French Newfoundlander as a prize to make up for the loss of the *Chancewell.* The strategy of the expedition was at fault. It arrived too late and with too little force, neither forestalling the Bretons and Basques nor able to master them. The proposed colony was probably a potential liability rather than an asset. The economics of maintaining a colony in such a rigorous winter were not understood, and a colony on the Magdalens, if it was not to be starved and robbed, would probably have cost more than it produced. The main interest of the voyage lies in the personalities of the Separatist Protestants who went with Leigh and in the precedents set by their venture for the Pilgrims of 1620. This is recounted elsewhere.[5]

Leigh had brought home no walrus and founded no settlement, although the prize he had taken, with her lading of cod and no doubt train oil probably paid most of the costs of the voyage (no appraisement has been found). He had been emotionally involved with the Separatists and may well have been deeply disappointed when the settlement was frustrated, yet he did not despair of returning to the St. Lawrence. On 4 October, indeed, he submitted a further plan for settlement on the Magdalens.[6] Found among the papers of Dr. Julius Caesar, it may indicate that that astute lawyer and judge was a friend and possible sup-

[5] See pp. 345–57 below.

[6] B.M., AdditionalMS 12505, fols. 77–77v. See John D. Rogers, *The Historical Geography of Newfoundland* (Oxford, 1911), pp. 249–50.

porter; it was intended in the end to reach the queen. Leigh stated he had received promises of support from friends (the Van Harwicks presumably, and possibly Peter Hill and John Watts) who were willing to put three ships under his charge in 1598. His plan was influenced by what he had seen: the French must be expelled from the islands by force. A small garrison strongly installed on Entry Island would hold the southern harbors and another manned post those farther north. The English must be there thirty days before the French and must have authority to seize French Basque as well as Spanish ships. The island was fertile enough for agricultural settlement, which could be built up by some of the settlers while the rest concentrated on fishing. The emphasis now is wholly on cod-fishing (walrus are not mentioned), the cod coming there first and allowing the ships early on the scene to complete their lading at the end of the season off Newfoundland. The colony should, in time, take the trade of "all the inland countries"—the fur trade of the St. Lawrence River, we may assume, being chiefly in his mind. In November, Leigh and Stephen van Harwick got a Spanish Basque hostage they had brought from Newfoundland to register a statement on their behalf in the High Court of Admiralty about the taking and loss of the *Catalina* in case they should be accused of assaulting a French Basque vessel.[7]

No record has yet been found of how Leigh fared with his latest scheme. Sir Robert Cecil, now in control of external affairs, would not have favored an assault on Henry IV's Basque subjects, but the notion of transporting the crown's incompatible subjects overseas was still current. The Hakluyts, years before, had advocated compulsory colonization by criminals and vagrants. Now in Parliament, in November and December, a drastic bill for dealing with the unemployed, the "sturdy beggars," was on the stocks. One of its provisions (at what stage it was inserted is not clear from the surviving proceedings on the bill) was for the banishment of rogues, vagabonds, and sturdy beggars at the cost of the counties afflicted with them. The act, as it finally received the queen's approval on 9 February 1598, stated that they were to be conveyed into such parts beyond the seas as should be at any time thereafter assigned for the purpose by the Privy Council.[8] If the Magdalens could be so designated,

[7] Deposition of Francisco de Cazanova, 7 November 1597, P.R.O., H.C.A. 13/32.

[8] 39 and 40 Elizabeth I, c.4 (see G. W. Prothero, *Select Statutes and Other Constitutional Documents Illustrative of the Reign of Elizabeth and James I*, 3d ed. (Cambridge, Eng., 1906), pp. 100–2. For the course of the bill through Parliament, see John E. Neale, *Elizabeth I and Her Parliaments, 1584–1601* (London, 1957), pp. 347–9; E. P. Cheyney, *History of England from the Defeat of the Armada to the Death of Elizabeth* (New York, 1926), II, 69.

the act would provide a more dependable source of settlers, with the costs of their transport already provided for.

But the act came into force too late to help a 1598 expedition, whether or not the proposers of the transportation clause had Leigh in mind when they put it forward. He had argued that an expedition to forestall Basques and Bretons must leave in January to reach the islands early in March. There is no evidence that he got away on a venture of his own that year, and this was final. Certainly the idea of shipping the poor across the ocean was in the air. Joseph Hall, the satirist, attacked the landlord who was clearing his land of unwanted poor tenants "and ships them to the new nam'd Virgin-land." [9] A proclamation for the enforcement of the act was published on 9 November, but it did not specify locations to which deportees should be sent,[1] though a subsequent proclamation of 1603 did include "Newfoundland" (which could have covered the Magdalens) among the places to which "rogues . . . shall be banished and conveyed." [2] The English were to do without their walrus and cod fishery, whether manned by pilgrims or paupers, in the Gulf of St. Lawrence.

There was still some residue of interest in the affair. Edward Hayes, who had served with Sir Humphrey Gilbert and was an old advocate of settling Newfoundland with the aid of convicts, wrote a long treatise on American colonization, probably in association with Christopher Carleill, in 1592 or 1593.[3] It urged the settlement of what are now the Maritimes as containing good land for agriculture and as bases for fisheries, and it also emphasized the advantages of the St. Lawrence basin as providing access to the interior (and to the Pacific). The general tone of the references to the St. Lawrence suggests the influence of Stevan de Bocall, while mention of mines discovered by the French on the Bay of Menan (Bay of Fundy) and of Lake Tadoac (Lake Ontario) far in the interior suggests more specifically the knowledge Bocall brought to England be-

[9] *Virgidemiarum*, V, I, 113, in *The Collected Poems of Joseph Hall* (Liverpool, 1949), ed. Arnold Davenport, p. 78. The satires were entered on 30 March 1598 and published soon after (*ibid.*, p. lxv).

[1] *Tudor and Stuart Proclamations*, 2 vols. (Oxford, 1910), ed. R. R. Steele, I, no. 899; B.M., G. 6413 (356).

[2] Proclamation of 17 September 1603, with Order attached, the latter specifying "The New-found Land, the East and West Indies, France, Germanie, Spaine and the Lowe countries or any of them" as possible destinations for the deported poor. Reprinted in C. S. Brigham, ed. *British Royal Proclamations Relating to America, 1603–1783* (Worcester, Mass., 1911), pp. 1–3. There is a copy of the Order in the collection of Mr. Paul Mellon.

[3] Cambridge University Library, MS Dd. 3.85.

tween 1593 and 1595. Hakluyt also passed material to Hayes, and in 1596 Thomas Harriot put down a note "M*aster* Hackluit / of Canada some mappes of it,"[4] which sounds like a Hakluyt treatise which has been lost and suggests a collection of maps known to him, most likely connected at least in part with the Magdalen Island voyages.

Hakluyt clearly remained longer than Leigh an active supporter of the project. He gathered all the material he could get about the experiences of the years 1591–7, omitting for reasons we do not know any mention of Bocall's part, and Charles Leigh contributed not only the narrative of the 1597 voyage which is our main authority (though it, in turn, suppresses the role played by the Separatists), but also a short account of the natural resources of the Magdalen Islands,[5] which helps to make them one of the better-documented parts of Canada in the sixteenth century. Hakluyt inserted in this collection, which may originally have been put together for propaganda purposes at the end of 1597 or in 1598, an appeal for the continuation of English enterprise, complaining that England had allowed the French and Spaniards to take advantage of the resources of the islands "while we this long time have stood still and have been idle lookers on, making courtesy who should give the first adventure, or once being given, who should continue or prosecute the same."[6] This appeared in print in 1600 in the third volume of *The principal navigations*, but did not arouse any particular response. An obscurely worded document, which can be dated within the years 1598–1600,[7] it provides a commentary on the scheme Hayes had advocated and which Leigh had attempted, in his own way, to put into effect. Since the French are said to carry on a secret trade to the place thought of as the location for an English settlement, the Magdalen Islands may well be intended. That Puritans of some sort were meant to take part is indicated by a reference to "the precise," but they were not to be the only colonists. The author emphasized the special problems of getting enough capital together to enable settlers to accommodate themselves to novel conditions. He reached the conclusion that royal aid was necessary to bring such a colony to fruition, and urged that a commission be given to "a worthy general" to bring out settlers.

The atmosphere of the tract is not optimistic, and there was little chance that Queen Elizabeth, as her life drew toward its end, would subscribe to a state colonizing enterprise. Edward Hayes and Hakluyt, as we have

4 B.M., SloaneMS 2292, fol. 41.

5 Hakluyt, *Principal Navigations,* VIII (1904), 166–80.

6 *Ibid.*, p. 162.

7 P.R.O., State Papers, Colonial, C.O. 1/1, 9, endorsed "Plantacion in America," without date or indication of authority.

seen (pp. 240–1), had something to do with an English venture in 1602 which explored New England and proposed a trading post on Elizabeth's Isle, off the southern shore of Massachusetts. Hayes refurbished his old treatise for the pamphlet published on the return of the voyagers; he added a few details about the mines in the Maritimes, culled, I have suggested, from Bocall, but he trimmed out of his analysis all reference to the availability of the St. Lawrence to English enterprise.[8] The English concern with the gulf and river, which dated at least from 1578 and had brought about some limited penetration and an abortive colonial enterprise in the 'nineties, had at length fizzled out. Or perhaps it is best to say that English attention had been rediverted to the New England shores on which Gilbert had counted so much twenty years before and which, after still further failures, were to provide a major site for English Separatists and nonseparating Puritans alike a generation later.

There is a curious parallelism between the decline of English enterprise in Canada and the revival of French activity.[9] Even before peace came to France in 1598, La Roche had re-emerged as the titular governor of New France, and in the very year the vagrants act came into force in England he set French criminals seal-hunting on Sable Island. If this project had a limited success, it ended in tragedy and horror a few years later. Tadoussac, the first fur-trading post since Cartier, had a grim winter in 1600–1 and was wiped out except as a summer trading mart. But in 1602 new blood was coming into French enterprise. Champlain and De Monts were about to demonstrate that the future of Canada for a long time lay in French hands.

[8] John Brereton, *A briefe and true relacion of the discoverie of the north part of Virginia . . .*, 2 issues (London, G. Bishop, 1602), S.T.C. 3610–11.

[9] Marcel Trudel, *The Beginnings of New France, 1524–1663* (Toronto, 1972), pp. 54–70; G. Lanctot, "L'Établissement du marquis de la Roche à l'île de Sable," *Annual Report of the Canadian Historical Association for 1933* (Ottawa, 1933), pp. 33–43; Lanctot, *Realisations françaises de Cartier à Montcalm* (Montreal, 1951), pp. 29–50.

CHAPTER THIRTEEN

The First Pilgrims

Let Amsterdam send forth her brats,
Her fugitives and runagates;
Let Bedlam, Newgate and the Clink
Discharge themselves into the sink;
Let Bridewell and the stews be swept
And sent all thither to be kept.
So shall our church be cleansed and made pure
And keep both itself and state secure.[1]

I

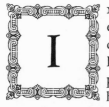

IN THE SIXTEENTH CENTURY each of the "national" Protestant churches, after it had established itself, settled down to persecute other kinds of Protestants or Catholics. Few Catholic powers, meanwhile, ever ceased persecution. Always there were dissident groups in hiding or running to find refuge. The French Huguenots, then one of the most powerful dissident groups in western Europe, were on the offensive in the decade from 1555 to 1565, trying to establish colonies in Brazil, in South Carolina, and in Florida, both as forward bases against the religious and national enemy, Spain, and also as places of refuge should things in the end go badly for them in France. They were the first to see America in this light. In 1572, before they had had any lasting success overseas, the massacre of St. Bartholomew took place. If it cut off their leaders, yet it established in the remainder the determination to survive and succeed. They won through in the end to the Edict of Nantes because they were determined to remain both Frenchmen and Protestants: they demonstrated that religious dissent was not incompatible with national loyalty. In doing so they turned decisively away from the Americas. In England, as Queen Elizabeth's church broke with Catholics on the right, with Presbyterians in the center, and with

[1] Samuel Eliot Morison, *Builders of the Bay Colony* (Boston, 1930), p. 386; and a further version in P. A. Kennedy, "Verses on the Puritan Settlement of America, 1631," Thoroton Society, Record Series, no. 21 (Nottingham, 1962), 39. Professor Leland H. Carlson gave valuable advice at the time this chapter was being prepared.

Separatists to the left, so too we find the issue of political loyalty complicating the religious picture. Because they remained loyal to the queen, many of the Catholic gentry refused to fly the country even though they were fined for not attending church and were forbidden to hear Mass; we find radical Protestants worshiping in secret in their own way and attacking the bishops, yet firmly asserting their allegiance to the state.[2]

To reconcile the claims of conscience in questions of religion and the demands of the state in matters both civil and religious was, we all know, a long and painful process, with many partial advances and almost as many retreats. It was in Elizabethan England that serious consideration was first given to the export of religious dissidents, not to foreign states, but to outlying areas within the jurisdiction of the crown, places of refuge that would not be entirely cut off from the homeland.

As early as 1569 Sir Thomas Gerard offered to bring Catholics from Lancashire to settle in Ireland,[3] there to do the queen service against the Irish and receive toleration in return—though his project fell through in 1570. In 1572 George Carleton, a Puritan-minded member of Parliament, considered in an appeal to Lord Burghley whether toleration for Presbyterian dissidents might not be possible: he decided that in the interests of good order toleration inside England was not possible (the Tudor "Order" theme was "Obedience joins: disorder separates"), while exile to foreign lands would lose the queen loyal bodies she could not spare.[4] He, too, saw Ireland as a possible place of refuge where 3,000 Puritans might engage to "live under the Queen's subjection . . . and laws of the Realm, the Church's constitution only excepted." This, too, bore no immediate fruit, but both suggestions were seminal ones.

[2] For an example, see Henry Barrow, *A petition directed to her most excellent Majestie* . . . [1590?], sigs. C2v.–C3r.: "When the Spaniards intended an invasion, the establishment of a foreign potentate in the Seat Royal, and the conversion of this land into Aceldama, a field of blood, the ministers that seek reformation gave great assurance of their affection and loyalty to the Queen's Majesty and the State. They were importunate with the Lord by private and public prayer and fasting for the safety of her royal person before the Bishops or their followers were seen to go about any such matter. . . . Also when the expedition was made into Portugal, they renewed these exercises a fortnight or three weeks before the Bishops sent to their favourers any precepts or instructions to do the like. Is it likely that these men do malice her Majesty?"

[3] See pp. 368–70 below.

[4] P.R.O., State Papers, Domestic, Additional, S.P. 15/21, 131. See W. K. Jordan, *The Development of Religious Toleration in England from the Beginning of the English Reformation to the Death of Queen Elizabeth* (Cambridge, Mass., 1932), pp. 132–5, 155.

Ireland was in a real sense the moving frontier of Tudor England. In the Munster Plantation from 1585 onward there were chances for Presbyterians, Separatists, or English Catholics to settle in the Irish west (though not in peace or in autonomous colonies). Indeed, a hostile critic in 1598 accused the bishops there of allowing "papists, puritans, Brownists, atheists . . . to preach, to reason, to prate, to gather conventicles." [5] How far this is accurate we cannot say. A few Separatists at least found refuge in the older towns in the eastern part of the island.

The Catholic gentry in England after 1572 sometimes had to pay as much as £240 a year for each member of their families for the privilege of not going to church. Though these fines were only intermittently enforced, the incentive they offered to treason or exile was considerable. In 1582 Sir George Peckham and Sir Thomas Gerard (of the 1569–70 Irish plan) prepared a scheme to set up a Catholic colony of refuge in association with Sir Humphrey Gilbert on the shores of Narragansett Bay.[6] But this fell through when Sir Humphrey was lost at sea in September 1583.

Separatism had clearly emerged in England by 1580. Presbyterians, driven out of the church, might hold services in secret, but they regarded themselves as still part of the national church. Congregations such as that headed by Robert Browne at Norwich considered themselves as almost wholly separated—a church community of believers drawn together into a religious and social unit, sufficient to itself. Prepared to bow to the "magistrate" (the state) in civil matters, they felt bound to resist state intervention in spiritual affairs. There was some dissension in Browne's congregation in 1580 on whether the church should go into exile in Middelburg in the Netherlands, the members reconciling themselves to leaving England only when they were convinced that it was God's purpose for them to do so—namely, when a sufficient number had been imprisoned.[7] Though they trickled back—and Browne returned in the end to the Church of England—Separatism and its doctrine of the "gathered church," hostile to and severed from the undiscriminating "national" church, had arrived in England.

In 1583 John Whitgift became Archbishop of Canterbury and began

[5] *Cal.S.P.,Ire.,1598–1599* (1895), pp. 428–31. [6] See pp. 371–81 below.

[7] Robert Browne, *A treatise of reformation without tarrying for any* (Middelburg, 1582), and *A true and short declaration both of the gathering and joyning together of certain persons: and also of the lamentable breach and division which fell amongst them* (Middelburg, 1584). See Albert Peel and Leland H. Carlson, eds., *The Writings of Robert Harrison and Robert Browne* (London, 1953), esp. pp. 155, 164, 167.

a long and arduous attempt to isolate and expel the Presbyterians and their supporters inside the Church of England, and also to repress all organized bodies of Protestants outside the Church. The Reverend Richard Hakluyt, who had not approved of sending potentially disloyal Catholic gentlemen to North America (which he regarded very much as a potential Protestant preserve), told Queen Elizabeth in 1584 that some Protestant dissidents could usefully be removed to North America (he did not regard their loyalty as in doubt).[8] The Puritan clergy, "always coining of new opinions," as they were at home, ought to be sent to America, where "they will become less contentious" and where they can engage in "reducing the savages to the chief principles of our faith." Presbyterian or Separatist Indians were clearly not thought of as too great a potential danger. The proposed colonies in "Virginia" (North Carolina), too, might become a refuge for foreign Protestants who were "forced to flee for the truth of God's word." Yet no English Puritans and few foreign Protestants have so far been traced among the Roanoke colonists of 1585–87.[9] Christopher Carleill, when promoting in 1583 a colony in Nova Scotia or Maine parallel to Gilbert's Catholic one, had already offered inducements to Puritans to come with him, promising that "the godly minded . . . shall be at their free liberty of conscience,"[1] but we do not know if he had any such persons with him when his expedition broke up no farther westward than Cork Harbour in the summer of 1584.

The Spanish wars created such a strong feeling of solidarity among southern English adherents of the established church that it became possible to identify more completely loyalty to the Church of England with loyalty to the state, while the Marprelate tracts, with their savage and witty satire on the episcopate, strengthened the desire of churchmen to isolate and punish Puritan, and especially sectarian, nonconformists as sources of disunity and weakness.[2] The sectaries were regarded as social radicals, either subversive of the established system of property

[8] "A particuler discourse," known as "Discourse of Western Planting," in E. G. R. Taylor, ed., *The Original Writings and Correspondence of the Two Richard Hakluyts,* Hakluyt Society, 2d ser., 2 vols., nos. 76–7 (London, 1935), II, 217–18, 239, 326.

[9] Compare Quinn, *Roanoke Voyages,* I, 194–7, II, 539–43; William S. Powell, "Roanoke Colonists and Explorers: An Attempt at Identification," *North Carolina Historical Review,* XXXIV (1957), 202–26, esp. 213.

[1] *A discourse upon the entended voyage to the hethermoste partes of America* (London, 1583), sig. A3; Quinn, *Gilbert,* II, 355.

[2] See William Pierce, *An Historical Introduction to the Marprelate Tracts . . .* (London, 1908).

relations or else deluded by concepts of a Utopian society which was a mere fantasy.[3]

The Welsh writer of a long tract about 1590 against Spain, one Richard Griff or Griffith, may be taken as typical of a not unduly extreme aspect of this approach. He urged the queen to isolate and if necessary punish those who might aid the enemy:

Namely, our covert Catholics, counterfeit Protestants and English "Mauranes" [Moreans?], whereof we have many in England, are diligently to be searched and suppressed as a sort of people most dangerous, for they that can play with their conscience and mask their religion will soon be brought, upon occasion offered, to scorn and oppugn the State. . . . And as for our disciplinaries, being the best name I can give them, they have at their first flight found fault with our silent and unlearned ministers (and overmuch living, many of them and of some that were more worthy of Bridewell than of a benefice, and of prison than of a parsonage), which hath emboldened them to make a further progress and, as though they lived in Plato's Commonwealth or Sir Thomas More's Utopia, to desire and imagine a fantastical perfection, sometimes found in [a] few assisted with God's abundant grace, living under the Cross when the Church was persecuted, and can never be found in the multitude when the Church is warranted with public authority. And also to recontinue outworn and ancient orders, without consideration there of the difference of some few good and godly and the multitude that challenge the name of Christians, or of the diversity happened in the time and state of the Church, or of the authority, as well of the Church in changing rites and orders according to behoof and decency as also of Kings and Princes, in all those matters that be indifferent.[4]

The detachment of the "gathered church" from the society in which it existed made it easy to characterize its members as Utopians. The sectaries themselves wished to live in a setting where their oneness could be more and more emphasized. Nonsectarians, on the other hand, could logically proceed on the assumption that expulsion to the wilder-

[3] This can be illustrated from a dedication to Sir Edmund Anderson, Chief Justice of Common Pleas and a strongly antisectarian member of the judiciary, by William Clever of his *Foure profitable bookes* (London, Thomas Creed, 1597[–8], unique copy in Folger Library, Washington, D.C.): "This is a manifest experience, that when Sectarists furiously do rage in God's Church, they not only do ransack public authority, holy assemblies, and loving associations, but also, through rapine, violence, and extortion, level both Church and Commonwealth equal with the ground."

[4] The tract took the form of a long letter, written about 1590, by a man signing himself "Rich: Griff: a poore gentleman." Huntington Library, EllesmereMS 1598, fols. 27–8.

ness was one way of ridding society of its sectaries and at the same time satisfying the latter's desire for exclusiveness without further danger to either church or state. To label sectaries as Utopians, as Griffith did, was one step toward proposing to export them—whether they wished it or not—to a Utopia, if they could make it so, in Ireland, America, or elsewhere.

The paper war waged by Presbyterian Puritans against the bishops in the Marprelate tracts of the late eighties brought out the basic loyalties of many Englishmen to the Elizabethan church, so that Protestant opponents of the church could now be and were regarded as potential allies of Spain. Richard Harvey, attacking the Protestant left in *A theological discourse of the Lamb of God and his enemies* in 1590, wondered if those opponents of nonconformity were not right "who would banish it into the Novus Orbis,[5] where the ten tribes of Israel," as he said in an aside, "had gone before the Portugals." The notion of getting rid of nonconformists to America was thus still abroad. But Archbishop Whitgift could think of nothing but prison and the gallows for the Separatists, at least to begin with. They were rounded up into jail, among them a little congregation of some fifty-six persons taken with their pastor Francis Johnson early in 1592.[6] Henry Barrow, John Greenwood, and John Penry were executed for their seditious writings in April 1593, while an act of Parliament was forced through which for the first time penalized Protestants as such. Between imprisonment and death there was added the intermediate penalty of banishment, if the person would not conform after a first offense. The bill was not passed easily (as Sir John Neale has shown), and even when it was on the statute book no decision had yet been taken on the countries to which nonconformists should be sent or allowed to go.[7]

Sir Walter Ralegh had asked that question while the House of Commons debated the bill.[8] "If two thousand or three thousand Brownists

[5] Richard Harvey, brother of Gabriel Harvey, the writer and critic, owned a copy of Peter Martyr, *De orbe novo . . . decades* (Paris, 1587), now in the B.M.

[6] *Mr Henry Barrowes platform* . . . (1611), sig. D, 3v. See John Waddington, *Congregational Church History from the Reformation to 1662* (London, 1862), pp. 28–34; Henry M. Dexter and Morton Dexter, *The England and Holland of the Pilgrims* (Boston, 1905), pp. 422–9; Henry C. Burrage, *The Early English Dissenters* . . . (Cambridge, Eng., 1912), I, 136–54.

[7] John E. Neale, *Elizabeth I and Her Parliaments, 1584–1601* (London, 1957), pp. 280–97; Geoffrey R. Elton, *The Tudor Constitution: Documents and Commentary* (Cambridge, Eng., 1960), pp. 447–50.

[8] Simonds D'Ewes, *The Journals of all the Parliaments during the Reign of Queen Elizabeth* . . . (London, 1682), p. 517.

meet at the Sea, . . . at whose charge shall they be transported, or whither will you send them? I am sorry for it. I am afraid there be ten thousand or twelve thousand of them in England. When they be gone, who shall maintain their wives and children?" Was he, perhaps, angling for state support to enable him to begin large-scale colonization with their aid, now that his small-scale colony in Virginia had been lost? The figure of ten thousand plus dependents, making at least twenty-five thousand and perhaps even fifty thousand, may very well be questioned. There is not likely to have been anything like that number of Brownist sectaries in England, but if to the sectaries were added the Presbyterians who had already been driven out or were ready to leave the church, the figure is not wholly unrealistic. If Ralegh had thought for a moment of acting as the sponsor of a vast North American Puritan colony, he soon shifted his attention decisively to the tropical forests of Guiana, where there was no place for Puritans.

The problem of going or not going out of England was also worrying Francis Johnson as he lay in prison. He wrote to Lord Burghley (whose instinct was strongly against persecuting Protestants) on 7 December 1593, asking him to pass on a petition to the queen pleading that he and his congregation should not be forced to leave England, but should be tolerated at home, or at least within reach of it.[9] He urged that "this heavy chain laid upon our loins may be removed, that we be not still forced to go into fire and water as hitherto we have been—and that only for our obedience to the commandments of Christ." He asked, instead, that "we may be suffered together in peace . . . to live under her Majesty's government in any place of her dominions." He was making the old case for toleration, if not in England then in some place where he and his people could still remain loyal subjects—perhaps meaning Ireland, possibly already casting his thoughts to America. Only if this were impossible would they go under alien rule to foreign parts, or as he put it eloquently enough, "to whithersoever it shall please God to bring us and to give us a resting place for the service of his name and in peace and tranquility."

About the same time, John Johnson petitioned Sir Robert Cecil on behalf of his two sons, "scholars and Masters of Arts in the university of Cambridge and there brought up in learning at the great charges of your said Orator their Father."[1] George had evidently proved particularly recalcitrant in jail and had been dealt with harshly, being "kept sometimes

[9] B.M., HarleianMS 1849, fol. 143, printed in Waddington, *Congregational Church History* . . . , pp. 32–3.

[1] CecilMSS, Hatfield House, Petitions, no. 1055 (Hist.MSSComm., *CecilMSS,* XIV, 281).

twenty nights together without any bedding and as long without any change of linen and all this sixteen months in the most dankish and unwholesome rooms of the Prison they could put him into not suffering any of his friends to come unto him, and now of late not permitting your Orator his Father so much as to see him." He urged that since their only offense, in his eyes at least, was "that upon Conscience they refuse to have spiritual communion with the present Ministry of the Land," they should be either released, Francis from the Clink and George from the Fleet, or else "suffered to be at some honest men's houses in the City upon sufficient assurance there to be forthcoming upon warning duly given." John Johnson was put off by Cecil and told to bring the matter to the Privy Council as a body.[2] But though they had to wait some three years for their realization, the suggestions put forward by both Francis and John Johnson were eventually acted on.

A few Separatists did get away to Ireland, but by strict interpretation of the act residence there was equally illegal, since they were required to abjure "this realm of England and all other the Queen's Majesty's Dominions for ever." [3]

II

GRADUALLY THOSE WHO remained in prison in London declined in number. As individuals accepted banishment abroad, so they were released and made their way to Holland. Francis Johnson remained behind to lead in the Clink Prison a small band of those who would not voluntarily leave England.[4] He managed to marry, while he was there, the well-to-do widow of a London merchant, a member of the congregation who had died in prison, and to smuggle out sheet by sheet his contributions to sectarian controversy.[5] Meantime the exiled group consolidated un-

[2] Endorsed thus on back of petition.

[3] While they were in prison the Brownists "Delivered to Mr Wood a Scottish preacher in Ireland, *anno* 1594," a copy of the complaint they had sent to Parliament early in 1593, giving an account of the seizure of Francis Johnson's congregation on 3 April 1592, and of their sufferings in prison. In it they asked: "Are we malefactors? Are we in any wise undutiful unto our prince? Maintain we any errors? Let us then be judicially convicted thereof and delivered to the civil authority?" *Mr Henry Barrowes platform, which may serve, as a preparative to purge away prelatisme* . . . ([London?] 1611), sigs. D3–D4.

[4] His career can be followed in Rev. Alexander Gordon, *D.N.B.*, s.n.; and see *D.C.B.*, I (1965), "George Johnson."

[5] A. H[ildersam] and F[rancis] J[ohnson], *A treatise of the ministery of the Church of England* . . . (Middelburg, 1595), contains matter written by "one Mr. F. Jo[hnson] prisoner for the same cause," which had clearly been smuggled out of

der the teaching of Henry Ainsworth, who came from Ireland to lead them in Amsterdam. Ainsworth in 1596 assembled and published the forty-five articles of religion on which the members of the congregation in England and in exile were agreed (thus giving a popular and enduring model for a Calvinist church in a congregationalist setting), *A true confession of the faith, and humble acknowledgement of the alegiance, which wee hir majesties subjects, falsely called Brownists, do hold towards God, and yield to hir Majestie and all that are ouer us in the Lord. . . .*[6] The preface called attention to the determination of the Separatists to acknowledge the intervention of the crown only in civil and not in spiritual matters. The preface is notable also in that it provided an epigraph for the whole Separatist dispersion when it stated, poignantly and prophetically: "We are but strangers and pilgrims warring against many and mighty adversaries"—the self-given name of "Pilgrims" which was later to attach to those of 1620. At last, in prison in England, the remaining members of the church came to think of themselves too as Pilgrims. Their attitude of stubborn resistance to exile softened. A destination was at length suggested to them where they might settle within the queen's allegiance. At the beginning of 1597 they were proposing to accept exile in the Gulf of St. Lawrence on the Magdalen Islands. There, on that unlikely soil, Francis Johnson saw at last the opportunity for establishing (and the words are his own) "a company of faithful people, by the word of God called out and separated from the world and the false ways of the Gospel by a voluntary profession of the faith and obedience of Christ." [7]

Even the elect must eat. How could such a church transferred overseas find sustenance for its members, who would include men weak-

---

prison. In it Johnson showed his continued defiance of the 1593 Act: "Yet do we not deny neither, but it is to be accounted an happy benefit and greatly to be desired, that the Church and people of God may have rest and be suffered to lead a godly life in peace and quietness, keeping the faith, order, commandments and statutes which our Lord Jesus Christ hath given and appointed to his Church. But if this cannot be had in peace without persecution, yet must we not therefore refuse or turn from the way and commandment of Christ, but set our feet therein notwithstanding, and always be ready to walk through the midst of afflictions with joy in the Holy Ghost, by the grace and assistance of Christ our Lord; knowing that if we suffer with him, we shall also reign with him." (Sig. S1r.)

[6] Published in Amsterdam in 1596, it was issued in a second edition there in 1598. See Marshall M. Knappen, *Tudor Puritanism: A Chapter in the History of Idealism* (Chicago, 1939), p. 314.

[7] *An answer to Maister H. Jacob his defence of the churches and ministery of England,* "By Francis Johnson, an exile of Jesus Christ" ([Middleburg], 1600), p. 196.

ened by prison and also women and children? The Separatists were mostly craftsmen, with a sprinkling of educated members of the merchant class and gentry among them. If they went to Holland, each had a chance of working at his trade, or perhaps of receiving rents from English lands or houses, if he had them. But if they went farther afield, what then? There must be a fairly specific economic objective, together with some kind of partnership with English promoters and shippers, which would not only bring them out of Europe but also sustain them, or enable them to sustain themselves, in some profitable occupation overseas. If they were to live wholly on their own in the wilderness it could be only after some years. Later, William Brewster, John Carver, and William Bradford knew that their bond to Thomas Weston's syndicate, however burdensome, was essential if they were to have a chance of life. A similar tie and a similar opportunity existed in 1597 for Francis Johnson and his would-be Pilgrims.

It occurred to someone that the obstinate Brownists of Francis Johnson's congregation, who resisted exile to a foreign land and wished to remain under the Queen's obedience, might make suitable colonists. Consequently a plan was worked out, by businessmen and friends of the prisoners, to move their church from the Clink Prison to Halabolina in the Island of Ramea—that is, to Amherst Island in the Magdalen group in the Gulf of St. Lawrence.

The walrus- and whale-fishing ventures initiated in the Gulf of St. Lawrence in 1591 [8] formed the bridge which was to take the Separatists out of prison to an independent community of their own, where their "gathered church" could function as both a religious and a social unit, still within the wider society under the English crown which a transatlantic colony might offer. Lord Burghley was almost certainly the key that opened the prison door for them. Which of those involved in the walrus project was the prime mover in linking the Separatists with the entrepreneurs is not known. It could have been the shipowner Peter Hill, the goldsmith Ralph Hill, or the Dutch merchant Abraham van Harwick, who had settled in London and of whom there is a faint suggestion that he was a sympathizer. The commander of the 1597 expedition, Charles Leigh, was certainly on their side. If he had been in the service of Peter Hill for some time before 1597, this could have been the tie that drew him and eventually the Separatists into the venture. Leigh is described by Francis Johnson's brother George as "a brother in the faith with us," [9]

[8] See p. 317 above.

[9] *A discourse of some troubles and excommunications in the banished English church at Amsterdam* (Amsterdam, 1603), p. 106; *S.T.C.* 14664.

namely, as a Separatist, but this may have been going rather too far. He was certainly a sympathizer, a fellow traveler, but in all probability not a member of a Separatist congregation.

So far as we know no formal corporation was established to run the colonizing venture, but the promoters seem to have formed a voluntary company not unlike the syndicate which backed the Pilgrims in the 1620's. This was described by John Smith as "some gentlemen, some merchants, some handicraftsmen . . . knit together by a voluntary combination in a society without constraint or penalty, aiming to doe good and to plant Religion" [1]—and (though he does not add this) to make a profit from the labors of the colonists at the same time. In 1597 the economic objective came first, the Separatists as colonists being only a possible instrument for its attainment.

In detail, as we have seen (p. 329), the plan had been to bring out a small advance party of Separatists so that they could plan the settlement and assess the problems the islands presented. The smaller of the two ships was to be left behind over the winter, and her crew would start the fishery in the spring while the four Separatists made what preparations they could for the arrival of the remaining members of the little church early the following summer. They, in turn, would build themselves homes and prepare to stay over the first long winter away from England.

The earliest document we have, though it comes from a time when the project was already fully planned (perhaps February or early March 1597), is a petition to the Privy Council, probably composed by Francis Johnson, asking permission to go "to a foreign and far country which lieth to the west from hence in the Province of Canada." [2] The Separatists desired there "to worship God as we are in conscience persuaded by his Word." They offered to do their country what service they could and "in time also greatly annoy that bloody and persecuting Spaniard about the Bay of Mexico." What this latter belligerent statement means precisely is not clear. To deny the Gulf of St. Lawrence to the Spanish Basques might indeed inflict some small peripheral damage on Spain, but only that; it may be that the Magdalen Islands were thought by John Watts and Craston as a possible refitting base for English privateers operating in the West Indies.

[1] John Smith, *The generall historie of Virginia, New England, and the Summer Isles* . . . (London, 1624), p. 943; Edward Arber, ed., *Captain John Smith . . . Works* (Birmingham, 1884), p. 783.

[2] P.R.O., State Papers, Domestic, Elizabeth, S.P. 12/246, 46; Burrage, *Early English Dissenters,* II, 125–6.

In March the Privy Council gave its assent to the voyage and so authorized a flexible interpretation of the act of 1593. The London customs officials were told on 25 March by the council that the queen had licensed a number of "artificers and other persons that are noted to be sectaries" to go on the voyage "to plant themselves in an island called Ramea or thereabouts" (thus not limiting them solely to the Magdalens), where they were "to establish a trade of fishing."[3] Four of them were to make the voyage now; others were to follow next year. All were to undertake to stay away from England unless they were prepared to conform in religion; none was to serve the queen's enemies. They were to take an oath that they would continue to be Queen Elizabeth's loyal subjects, while the merchants under whose charge they went were to put in bonds to see that these conditions were observed. The settlers were to be allowed to take with them, duty free, "such household stuff and other implements as may serve for their necessary use."

Those members of Francis Johnson's old congregation who had remained in prison appear at last to have been allowed out on parole after their five-year ordeal. Though most of them were not to sail for America until the following year, there was evidently enough sympathy now felt for their plight for the authorities to leave them in peace for the time being, probably after exacting undertakings that they would not spread their views by propaganda in the interval. Even if they had friends who had looked after their possessions since 1592, readjustment to their old crafts and occupations must have been difficult and the temporary character of their release unsettling. For their leaders, however, release offered an opportunity to continue the debate on Separatism and other issues which had arisen between them and which had been restricted by their confinement. Another Separatist leader, Henry Jacob, who had been like Francis Johnson an Anglican clergyman before he became a Brownist, joined Johnson and his associates. Jacob, who had left England when the 1593 act came into force and had since been living at Middelburg, now slipped back illegally from the Netherlands early in 1597, possibly because he had heard of the American plan and wished to take part in it, but also no doubt because he wished to continue his debate with Francis Johnson on the limits of separation, which prison had hampered but not prevented.

Jacob's break from the historic church was not complete: he regarded its claims as having some validity; the "gathered church" was not for him wholly set apart from the "national church." Francis Johnson re-

[3] P.R.O., Privy Council Register, P.C. 2/22, p. 167; *A.P.C.,1597* (1903), pp. 5–6.

garded Jacob with suspicion verging on hostility. On 3 April, when the ships were about to leave London for America with the four pioneering Separatists on board, Johnson and Jacob met in controversy on the great theme of separation, apparently before an audience of Separatists, possibly including more than Johnson's own congregation. The debate was inconclusive: each felt he had done enough to convince the other, yet neither was convinced. Jacob felt there was no place for him in the American scheme and returned to the Netherlands. After a long exile, he was to see America at last when he arrived in Virginia in 1622 to found, as a particular plantation, the settlement of Jacobopolis.[4] This episode, indicating very clearly that their views on church organization and government took priority over the need for unity in adversity, indicated that the would-be Pilgrims would find cooperation far from easy.

The four men who were setting sail for the Magdalen Islands comprised two artificers and two others. The pastor, Francis Johnson, had bravely offered to head his congregation in America and to be one of its pioneers. He and his brother George, who was also to go, were men of middle-class origins, their father, John Johnson, being a Yorkshire merchant and former mayor of Richmond. Both were Cambridge men: Francis had been a Fellow of Christ's College. He was intelligent and tenacious, with a genuine if somewhat limited capacity for leadership. George was a schoolmaster in London when he was arrested—a neurotic personality, unstable, with touches of attractive idealism in his writings, but almost certainly a paranoiac. The other two men had come into the church from the class of intelligent but lowly townsmen who were often attracted to the sects. Daniel Studley, a girdler by trade, was literate and had been a schoolmaster, a fighter who hit back when he was repeatedly interrogated during a long imprisonment, and was sentenced to death in 1593 but afterward reprieved. He appears as a man somewhat obsessed, crude, vindictive—but then we see him mainly from the pen of George Johnson after he had become his enemy. John Clerke was a husbandman, a farmer of Walsoken (Walsham?), Norfolk, in jail since 1590 and subjected to hard labor on the treadmill at Bridewell prison—chosen no doubt for his knowledge of the land. We know nothing else about him except that on the outward voyage he followed the lead of George Johnson. Francis Johnson and Studley were to sail on the *Hopewell* with Leigh; George Johnson and Clerke on the *Chancewell* with Stephen

[4] See Henry Jacob, *A defence of the churches and ministerye of Englande . . .* (Middelburg, 1599), p. 3; Francis Johnson, *Answer to Maister H. Jacob,* pp. 172, 216–17. See Gordon Goodwin, *D.N.B.,* s.n.

van Harwick.[5] Craston, master of the *Hopewell*, was well-equipped as a pilot but Stephen Bennet, on the *Chancewell*, was new to American waters and quite possibly a bad navigator.

The ships sailed from Falmouth about 28 April and kept company in a rapid voyage which brought them to the Grand Bank on 18 May, but they wasted much time in Newfoundland trying to buy boats for fishing at the Magdalens. They acquired only a single large shallop which needed repair. The ships finally lost each other in a fog off Placentia Bay on 5 June.

It will probably be best if we follow first the fortunes of the *Chancewell*.[6] She was not a happy ship. At Falmouth, George Johnson had attempted to circulate Ainsworth's *A true confession*, with its seditious preface, amongst the sailors. Only the pastor's intervention saved him from rough treatment at the hands of Captain van Harwick. There was more trouble in Newfoundland. Francis had to intervene again when George attempted to convert the crew and there were renewed threats of punitive action. The *Chancewell*, on parting from Leigh, sailed southwestward and passed Cape Breton, but failed to find the Magdalens and returned to Cape Breton Island. She was reconnoitering (apparently) St. Anne's Bay when, as George Johnson tells us, the ship, "through the headiness of the Master, in a fair summer day, run upon the rocks." The master, Stephen Bennet, made some amends by helping to get her off on the next tide, and she was safely beached. But no preparations were made to put her in a state of defense before she was overrun by boatloads of French Basques who had been fishing in the Bay. They virtually stripped the ship, leaving the crew their boats—a shallop and a ship's boat—with the clothes they wore and little else. George Johnson and Clerke lost all their settlers' gear. Captain van Harwick was now in a desperate position, but he was evidently a responsible-minded man, conscious of his obligations to his prickly and ungracious passengers. His solution was to try to turn the tables on the Basques and capture one of their ships when she was sufficiently weakened by her boats' crews going off to fish. At the same time he realized that he should, if possible, gain the cooperation of his passengers.

To his disgust, George Johnson took up a pacifist attitude and would not countenance an attack on the Basques. Finally, the captain gave the

[5] The *Chancewell* was a Yarmouth vessel of about fifty tons burden, which had, in 1593 or 1594, made a Mediterranean voyage to Civita Vecchia for alum, when Abraham van Harwick had sailed in her. P.R.O., H.C.A., Examinations, Oyer and Terminer, H.C.A. 1/46, fols. 174–5, 204–6.

[6] In George Johnson, *A Discourse of some troubles*, p. 109. A notice of Johnson will be found in *D.C.B.*, I, s.n.

Separatists three choices: to be put on shore "so that," as Johnson says, "they should be subject to be devoured by the wild" (though it is not clear whether he means the wilderness, wild beasts, or Indians). Or they would be handed over to the French to be brought to Europe, in which case "by them on seaboard they should be urged to hear Mass," says George Johnson, evidently regarding it as a worse fate than abandonment in wild America. Or, lastly, they must "adventure" with the crew and try to take a prize, indeed give their active assistance in doing so. Both George Johnson and Clerke refused to make a decision; like Oliver Cromwell in a later age they would wait upon events. They said that "they could not have their own hands in choosing but which he [Van Harwick] would put upon them, that by God's help they would undergo (hoping he would work all for good)." Van Harwick was uneasy still, "being unwilling to bring any one upon us," as George puts it. He respected their stoic obstinacy and put off a final decision while the boats were being rigged out as well as possible in the circumstances; they evidently dismantled the wreck to make them seaworthy—conceivably even built another.

Three or four days later, when the men and boats were almost ready, an extraordinary thing happened (or as George Johnson put it "God's Providence showed itself"). Van Harwick and he were walking on the cliffs, "talking of these things" since a decision had now to be taken. The captain, who was "quick sighted . . . saw a ship far off in the sea." He told Johnson what he had seen, to which George replied, "It may be the Lord will send us help thereby." He urged the captain to man the shallop and send her out forthwith. This was done, while the captain, George, and other sailors watched from the heights. One of the sailors "discerned it to be an English ship and put us in hope that it was our fellow." The ship was, indeed, found to be the *Hopewell* returning from the Magdalens. "What tears there were," said George, "not for the loss but for joy that we so met, specially between the brothers, I cannot express." Even six years later he said, "I cannot now write without tears remembering such a wondrous providence of God then in a strange land." In this little incident we have a clear picture of the Separatist as he later showed himself in New England, obstinate, tenacious, with his individual reliance on God and his sense of being personally advised, watched over, and regarded by Him.

The *Hopewell*, on losing the *Chancewell* on 5 June, had sailed directly for the Magdalen Islands so confidently that it is clear she had an experienced pilot on board.[7] He must almost certainly have been William

[7] Richard Hakluyt, *Principal navigations*, III, 195–6, VIII, 166–72.

Craston, trained as has been suggested by Bocall. Passing Bird Island, they saw not only birds in quantities but walrus, though the fact that the herd put off and pursued the ship cannot have been altogether reassuring to the two exiles on board. On 18 June they rounded the southwestern end of the Magdalen group and put into the inner harbor —now Basque Harbour (then known to the Basques as Halabolina). Inside the harbor Captain Leigh, who perhaps was unwise to have entered it, found two Breton ships from friendly (pro-Bourbon) ports and two Basque vessels, one from Ciboure on the French side and the other possibly French, possibly Spanish, Basque. There were a number of other Breton and Basque ships in the northern harbors; drying flakes for cod had been erected at various points, and there were probably also fires for the oil-rendering necessary for exploiting the cod and walrus kill. Moreover, there were anything from three to five hundred Micmac Indians come over from the mainland for the summer fishing.

We have, most unfortunately, no record of the reactions of either Francis Johnson or Daniel Studley to the revelation that the wilderness to which they had come to escape from the crowded tyranny of Europe was teeming with human as well as animal life, all of it engaged in purposeful economic activity. (Francis Johnson is not known to have written anything about the voyage; Studley did, but nothing of his is known to have survived. All we have, therefore, is a plain narrative of Leigh's actions only.) The circumstances were clearly unexpected, and while his ship was heavily gunned, without his consort he was unable to maneuver effectively. His four potential antagonists in the harbor, the two Basques and probably the Bretons as well, were at least as well prepared for a clash as he.

Leigh was highly suspicious of his neighbors but also, to begin with, cautious. The Breton skippers came aboard for refreshments, assured him of their good will, and told him that the other two vessels were French (not Spanish) Basques. The Basques first ignored his overtures, but one ship later sent some men across to the *Hopewell* and convinced Leigh that their ship was from nominally friendly Ciboure. Of the fourth ship he could get no assurance and so sent her an ultimatum. Unless she could satisfy him of her friendly intentions she must surrender her arms and munitions into his charge while they remained in the harbor. But this was too much to ask; they refused, whereupon Leigh sent in a boarding party under Craston who, with his experience and ruthlessness, soon prevailed. Leigh learned that his men were taking more than arms—were in fact looting the ship—and so intervened, established his ascendancy over his men (a remarkable achievement) and took the arms alone back to the *Hopewell*. But there he had a mutiny brewing, since Craston joined the majority of the crew in demanding that the Basque be taken as a prize. He persuaded them to sleep on it, and by morning (20 June) the decision was taken out of his hands.

He found that Basques and Bretons had joined forces and had called in reinforcements from ships in other harbors, together with some three hundred Micmac Indian auxiliaries. They had mounted three guns on shore and soon opened fire on the *Hopewell*, which responded with her own armament, though there do not appear to have been any serious casualties on either side. Leigh was then invited to send delegates ashore to parley, and rather trustingly let Ralph Hill (evidently acting as his cape merchant) and a seaman go ashore, while a Breton sea captain (one Captain Charles) came on board to dictate terms. Leigh must give up the arms and also surrender his shallop before leaving Ramea. While this was taking place, a Breton ship had worked her way alongside and was ready to board when she was spotted and obliged to sheer off by the threat to fire her sails—Captain Charles slipping away in the confusion. Leigh had to cut his cable (attached on shore) and, under threats to the hostages, work out of the harbor, when at last Hill and the other man were allowed to return on board. Trouble had not yet ended, however, for the *Hopewell* ran aground on the bar at the entry to the outer harbor (Pleasant Bay), but fortunately the victorious Frenchmen did not take advantage of Leigh's plight and the ship was floated off on the tide. As the *Hopewell* sailed up the eastern shores of the island group Leigh found further guns mounted to protect the northern harbors.

The "battle of Ramea," small as it was, was a rout for the English. A Separatist colony in the Magdalens was no longer easy to envisage: no English colony, indeed, was going to be easy to set up without a good deal of bloodshed. There was still another chance—the exiles were not tied to the Magdalens alone. Another walrus fishery was known to exist at Grande Coste: this was apparently the island of Anticosti or, more specifically, its northwest shoulder—a still less promising site we might think. Captain Leigh, most probably with the consent of Francis Johnson and Studley, ordered course to be set northwestward across the Gulf. Here William Craston came decisively into the picture. He argued against going to Grande Coste as he said fresh supplies were needed; instead they should go back to Cape Breton and get some more. (Fish at least could be obtained there, also prizes.) Yet Leigh insisted and the *Hopewell* set out, but now the crew (probably incited by Craston) took a hand: they would seize the ship unless the captain changed her course back to Cape Breton. He gave way, saving his face by declaring he intended to return later on, though he was in fact finally defeated, and his Separatist charges also. On the twenty-seventh as they were nearing Cape Breton the accidental encounter with the *Chancewell*'s men took place. In St. Anne's Bay (if this indeed is where it was) Leigh formally released the reunited exiles from their undertakings to remain in America and himself undertook (in spite of his own obligations to the contrary) to bring them back to England.

The voyage now turned into a search for justice and revenge. A few articles from the looted *Chancewell* were recovered, under the *Hopewell*'s guns, from French Basque ships at Cape Breton, Leigh holding off his men by force of his personality from further plunder. Finally he promised that when they reached southern Newfoundland they could seize a Spanish Basque or hostile Breton ship. They did indeed take a Spanish Basque ship at St. Lawrence Harbour, but she was freed by a combination of French Basques and Bretons. Finally they took and held a Breton ship from a Catholic League port (or so we are told). Leigh surrendered the *Hopewell* to Craston (to take privateering) and brought the exiles on board the prize, probably with the *Chancewell*'s crew. He made a good voyage eastward across the Atlantic and entered the English Channel, though by this time the exiles were at each other's throats and his own.

George Johnson says nothing at all about his transshipment to the prize or the circumstances of the voyage except in so far as they concern the disputes on board.[8] The exiles were preoccupied with their own affairs. Daniel Studley, Johnson says, stood aloof from the reunited brothers and incited George (so he alleged) to "exhort and admonish Captain Leigh about certain of his shortcomings." Whether these concerned his spiritual welfare or the circumstances under which he had become involved in prize-taking we do not know. We do know that the captain resented his passengers' interference with his authority, whatever his sympathies with their views. The result was that he quarreled with George Johnson, "who before," as George said, "had long been dear friends."

It was Studley (once again he may be George's scapegoat) who re-

[8] *A discourse of some troubles* is largely a series of bitter complaints by George Johnson against his associates. In the course of it, he said that Daniel Studley "also spied and kept things in writing against me which fell out in our banishment, when we were at sea and in Newfoundland." This notetaking (or diary-keeping) George resented bitterly: "Prison, banishment and shipwreck are (I confess and have felt them) heavy, yet thus to be spied into by a false brother as this Master Studley did is rather heavier" (p. 185).

vived a futile controversy which had already emerged in the congregation in the Clink Prison on the propriety or otherwise of the pastor's wife's style of dress. Clearly, from George Johnson's account, he wrangled with Studley as well as with his brother. Clerke alone seems not to have been involved. George conveys a vivid picture of the three of them lying in their cabins and putting out their heads to hurl scriptural arguments at one another, George and Studley at first combining against Francis. By the time they were nearing the English coast George had become hysterical in his accusations.[9] He was ostracized by the others, and Francis Johnson even consulted Captain Leigh about the desirability of keeping him under restraint on board ship when they reached England so that he should not break up the congregation. Leigh had plenty of other worries on his shoulders, being under bond to keep the Pilgrims in America and liable, if they returned, to lose money if not his liberty as well.

It was finally decided that they should be put ashore on the Isle of Wight to make their way to London by road, George having been somehow quieted and induced to accompany the others, while Leigh took the prize round to the Thames. This prize, laden with cod and possibly also oil, is likely to have been somewhat more valuable than the *Chancewell*, with her fishing and settlers' supplies, so that the voyage was not, from the point of view of the syndicate, wholly lost. The *Hopewell* may even have brought in another prize to improve the take. But it was the end of the American road for these Pilgrims. The four exiles made their way to London, where the other members of the church were on parole. They quickly decided to join Ainsworth and the rest in Amsterdam before the authorities could rearrest them. This they did rapidly and efficiently, Francis Johnson taking charge of the reunited congregation and Henry Ainsworth remaining with him as teacher. The "Ancient Church," as it soon came to be called, had taken on a new lease of life, but not in an American context.

Would the Magdalens scheme have worked had the Pilgrims been installed there? It is extremely doubtful whether an isolated community

[9] While the main story is on pp. 111–13, a few further side lights on the voyage appear elsewhere: "At sea Master Studley having stirred up the matter [of Mrs. Johnson's clothes] was angry that George Johnson spoke of it, seeming unwilling to have speech thereof, but rather to let it be buried" (p. 117). At one point, Francis Johnson, exasperated no doubt beyond endurance, threatened George, "at the sea in the presence of Master Charles Leigh and Master Studley," that "either I should be excommunicate or he would be no Pastor" (p. 180). Such, at any rate is George Johnson's account.

of men and women could have maintained itself on the basis the promoters envisaged. Tough Basque whalers might be able to winter successfully on board ship in the frozen Gulf, but the church members, weakened by prison and not selected for physical hardiness, would most probably have died off. Moreover, the Pilgrims were most unlikely to develop the sheer physical strength to cope with the Basques, Bretons, and Indians who would compete with them for walrus and cod. (The Pilgrims of 1620, even with Indian help, barely survived.) Moreover, they could not rely on aid and supplies coming soon from England. Between 1593 and 1597 all English ships bound for the Gulf arrived in June or July or missed the way altogether, while the Basques seem to have slipped in before the end of May. Even if the London syndicate did its best—and there was no guarantee that it would go on doing so unless the settlement paid its way quickly—the chance of mishap to ships bound for the Magdalens was too high to risk.

Then, too, the congregation did not have the cohesion of the Leiden church which launched the 1620 Pilgrims. Francis Johnson had to put up with disorder and disunity in Amsterdam, and later in life was to divide the church himself. Judging by what we know from George Johnson's *A discourse of some troubles and excommunications in the English church at Amsterdam* (1603), wordy battles interested him and some other members of the group more than the struggle for physical survival. The Leiden leaders, John Robinson, William Brewster, and William Bradford, were statesmen compared to the first Pilgrims with their limited political capacity. Francis Johnson, it is true, had organizing ability and tenacity. He had also a strong authoritarian tendency (which split the Amsterdam church between 1610 and 1612). It is just possible that he could have held an American community together. Henry Ainsworth, too, showed signs of the liberal statesmanship which built the Plymouth Colony.

George Johnson was at least a little mad, suffering from a strong sense of persecution and never recovering from it.[1] Studley was also somewhat unbalanced, and one cannot be sure of his capacities. These two alone could have split any community in any setting into fragments. Had they gone to the Magdalens, there is little doubt that the colony would have been at least partly immobilized by disorder. And there was no virgin land, at least semihospitable, on their borders to which dissidents could wander as they could later in New England. The strongest asset which

[1] Francis evidently realized his brother's mental instability, and it was one of George's many complaints that Francis and Daniel Studley told the Amsterdam congregation "that I had a crakt brain." (*A discourse of some troubles*, p. 184.)

a separated church had as an instrument for colonization, its internal cohesion as a community, could scarcely have been maintained. The economic backing which the 1597 venture had in both London and Bristol was appreciable, but not at all firm or consolidated, and the failure to follow it up on a purely secular basis illustrates the weakness of the movement to exploit the St. Lawrence basin. Captain Leigh, though he emerges in his own account of it as a resourceful commander in the 1597 voyage, was clearly disillusioned by the dissensions among the Separatists and is not found to have maintained any further ties with them.[2] He was no John Smith or Christopher Newport, though he did, we may remember, establish a small colony in Guiana which was still in existence when he died there in 1605.

III

Leigh did not, after the departure of Francis Johnson's church, give up at once. By 4 October 1597 he had put in a new scheme for the control of the Magdalen Islands which he hoped would win approval at court.[3] This time an armed and non-Separatist garrison was to be installed on Entry Island to hold the southern harbors in the Magdalens against all comers. The ships bearing the men for this purpose must leave in January 1598—though how they were to get out of the English Channel then he does not say (for contrary winds often made egress difficult in winter). They would be able, he was confident, to secure a monopoly of the early cod-fishing for the English—walrus are not now mentioned. The colonists would be able to spare enough attention for agriculture to plant crops which would help them to survive the following winter. His friends—most prominent among them probably Peter Hill and company—would get three ships to sea in 1598. The main thing he needed was authority to treat French Basque interlopers as enemies and therefore lawful prize.

This alone was sufficient to damn the project in the eyes of Sir Robert Cecil and other members of the Privy Council, since England's ally Henry IV would resist vigorously any such interference with his subjects.

[2] If the "Master Leigh" who was for a time a member of the Amsterdam congregation (*A discourse of some troubles*, p. 185) is Charles Leigh, this statement would not be correct, but it is probable that he is another person. Even while the London Brownists were adjusting themselves to exile, John Payne (*Royall exchange* [Harlem, 1597], p. 48) accused them of "an untempered zeal . . . with overweening and wrangling . . . want of love, peace, concord and humility."

[3] B.M., AdditionalMS 12505, fol. 77. See John D. Rogers, *The Historical Geography of Newfoundland* (Oxford, 1911), pp. 249–50.

He was treating with Spain, their common enemy, for peace. Nothing more is known of any further voyages being made to the St. Lawrence by Leigh or others in pursuit of either the religious or economic objectives already considered.[4]

Richard Hakluyt continued to believe in the economic value of the Magdalens project and commended it in 1600 in the third volume of his *Principal navigations*, where he printed a number of narratives—suppressing all mention of the Brownists and of the pilot Stevan de Bocall—along with a somewhat glowing account of the agricultural possibilities of the islands by Charles Leigh.[5] There were other protagonists of a St. Lawrence project too. A somber and critical discussion of the chances of settlement in parts of America with a temperate climate belongs to 1600 or thereabouts.[6] It mentions "the precise"—that is, Puritans though not necessarily Separatists—as possible contributors to a state-assisted settlement on the St. Lawrence, but no practical scheme for their participation emerged. A little later George Johnson's *A discourse of some troubles* set out his narrative of the events of 1597 and may have helped to keep the memory of the Pilgrims alive, though not in a favorable light.[7]

Francis Johnson was upheld in his beliefs partly by the thought that in England there were "many thousands" who supported the Separatist cause, but he was realistic enough to know that only a tiny minority could stand out and suffer persecution for their views. In 1600 he said "many will not endure imprisonment, banishment, loss of goods, or the like for that truth which themselves have heretofore professed, preached,

[4] There is a slight suggestion that the bringing out of a further group of Brownists was being contemplated in November, since Thomas Nelmes, a Brownist, described as "a principal of that sect" was in Newgate Prison under sentence of death "for publishing seditious books," and it was proposed he be released "to depart the Realme and not return again." He had been one of those intended to join Leigh on a second voyage. He did not go and indeed he may well have refused to go into exile on any account since his sentence was still hanging over him in January 1598 when he obtained a further reprieve. *A.P.C.,1597–1598* (1904), pp. 153, 256. He has not been identified under the name of Thomas Nelmes.

[5] Richard Hakluyt, *Principal navigations*, III, 189–201, VIII, 150–82, esp. 156–7, 161–2, 180–2.

[6] P.R.O., State Papers, Colonial, C.O. 1/1.9.

[7] The two copies surviving in England are in Trinity College, Cambridge (whose librarian kindly made it available for extended use by me), and Sion College, London. Neither copy is complete, though each ends at the same page, and the assumption has been that George Johnson ran out of money before he could bring the discourse to an end. Professor Carlson has now located further copies in the United States and Canada and has opened the way for an effective collation of the texts.

sued for to the Parliament."[8] This may have been the reason why, after James I's accession, when the chances of some relaxation of episcopal intolerance seemed brighter, "Master Francis Johnson, one of the pastors of that people . . . came with his other assistants to make their humble suit to the King, and were ready to entertain conference with the prelates that his Majesty might the more perfectly have understood the innocency of their cause and the evilness of their adversaries."[9] Though the Hampton Court Conference in January 1604 brought no relief, the death of Archbishop Whitgift on 29 February seemed to Johnson and others a judgment of God on the bishops, but it was not followed by any concessions and so Francis Johnson returned to Amsterdam to resume his exile. We cannot say whether, in London, Johnson renewed his contacts with the "American" groups, now slowly swelling as a result of the voyages of Bartholomew Gosnold and Martin Pring and their exploration of New England shores, but he was not tempted to revive his old plans of exchanging Amsterdam for an American exile.

The enemies of the Brownists had not, however, forgotten the proposed permanent solution for their turbulent transportation to the American wilds. Joseph Hall, both when he was sketching out his famous satirical Utopia, *Mundus alter et idem* in the latter years of Queen Elizabeth's reign and again in 1605 when he put the finishing touches to his map of the "Other World," had them very much in mind.[1] His "Other World" —a grandiose "Terra Australis" or Antarctica—has identifiable sections of North America on its coastline. Along one great river estuary appears the site of "Doxia," land of the opinionated sectaries, which is translated by John Healey in 1609 as "Sectarioua."[2] This Hall describes as "a country of much variety, but little delight. Every valley, every house, has his peculiar fashion, quite different from the rest." He proceeds to particularize the peculiarities of various sects and says of the exiles of 1597, "here also have certain Virginian exiles laid a plot for to erect themselves a body politic."[3] The side note has "Certain English Brownists exiled to

[8] Francis Johnson, *An answer to Maister H. Jacob,* p. 77.

[9] *Mr. Henry Barrowes platform* (1611), sig. I4v.

[1] Mercurius Britannicus [Joseph Hall], *Mundus alter et idem* (Francofurti, apud haeredes Ascanii de Rinialme [but believed to have been brought out in London by H. Lownes, 1605]).

[2] [Joseph Hall], *The discovery of a new world* (*Mundus alter et idem*) (London [1609?], Cambridge, Mass., 1937), trans. J[ohn] H[ealey], ed. Huntingdon Brown.

[3] *Mundus,* pp. 185–9; *Discovery of a new world,* pp. 120, 122, 228–9. Joseph Hall was already aware of Virginia by the time the first Pilgrims sailed and in his satire, the second part of *Virgidemiarum* (London, 1598), sig. E6v., attacks the enclosing landlord who: ". . . *might dislodge whole Colonies of poor/And lay their roofs*

America," so there is no ambiguity about the reference. Hall, for all the levity of his satire, is very much the orthodox Anglican and was later to be a bishop. He goes on to say seriously that the best thing to do with sectaries is to get rid of them to America. "O all you earthly potentates, that know the contagious nature of heresy, and love to have your states secured from so dangerous an infection, punish those damnable perturbers of holy peace unto this Country and let them take up their stations there where they can do no mischief." If his advice was not followed, at least he did not let the matter die.

Hall, too, was the first to tie together the old woes of the Johnson congregation with the new difficulties of John Robinson's Scrooby church as it transferred itself to Leiden. His *A common apologie of the Church of England: against the unjust challenges of the . . . Brownists* (London, 1610) is mainly an attack on Robinson's views on separation,[4] but he criticizes Francis Johnson as well and uses his brother's *Discourse* (cited eight times) against him, showing that George Johnson's account of the 1597 voyage was well known to him. Moreover, he met Robinson's plea for a humble corner in England in which to worship with the challenge that Separatists (Johnsonians and Robinsonians alike) could live at peace nowhere. "Our land you could like well," he said, "if you might be Lords alone. Thanks be to God it likes you not, and justly thinks the meanest corner too good for so mutinous a generation. When it is weary of peace it will recall you. You that neither in prison, nor in the Seas, nor in the Coasts of Virginia, nor in your way [both references to the 1597 voyage], nor in [the] Netherlands could live in peace. What shall we hope of your ease at home?" He challenges Robinson to defend "the hellish impieties" of the Separatists, which he might try to explain away as merely incidental inflictions "not prejudicing your Goshen." But this Hall denies: "I fear they would soon make the Ocean your Red Sea and Virginia your Wilderness." Hall indeed is speaking in 1610 as if the Amsterdam congregation were again thinking of America as potentially their promised land. It is even possible that he had the Scrooby congregation at Leiden also in mind. His reference may be rhetorical only, but it is significant that it was in print ten years before the Plymouth Colony came into existence.

The feeling that the sectaries did not "belong," that they could be at

---

quite level with their floor,/While yet he gives, as to a yielding fence,/Their bag and baggage to his Citizens/And ships them to the new-nam'd Virgin-land." The Collected Poems of Joseph Hall (Liverpool, 1949), ed. Arnold Davenport, p. 78.

[4] Sig. R3r., s.v. reprinted in Joseph Hall, *The Works of Joseph Hall . . .* (London, 1625), pp. 549–612, esp. pp. 558, 565.

home nowhere, that they were fit only for an unworldly setting to which they could never attain, was cultivated by their antagonists. Thomas Scot, whose *Philomythie* went into two editions in its year of publication (1616), put these sentiments forward in terms of mild satire: "The Chameleon is in England a Familist, at Amsterdam a Brownist, at [ ] [5] an Anabaptist. He lives by the air, and there builds Castles and Churches. None on the earth will please him. He would be of the triumphant and glorious Church but not of the terrene militant Church . . . he must find out Sir Thomas More's Utopia, or rather Plato's Community, and be an Elder there." From such a point of view—and the satire is less severe than Joseph Hall's—the removal of the Amsterdam congregation to wild America was the most rather than the least likely thing to happen. It is interesting too that the same terms as those used by Richard Griffith a quarter of a century before for the ideological affiliations of the Separatists, namely Plato's *Republic* and More's *Utopia*, should still be used to mark their separation from the established order in politics no less than in religion.

There was a sense in which the Anglican clergy who trumpeted the advantages, both civil and religious, of taking part in the colonization of Virginia from 1607 onward were ambiguous in their attitudes. The Reverend William Crashaw, in *A sermon preached at the Crosse, Feb. xiiij. 1607* (London, 1608), denounced sectaries "such as be now termed of the separation, formerly called Brownists, who forsake our Church and cut themselves from our congregation, or as they call it, into a covenant and communion of their own devising." To form a "gathered church," to detach men and women in either ecclesiastical or civil matters from English society, no matter where they lived, was clearly regarded as disloyal. Nonetheless, when the same William Crashaw preached on Virginia's prospects in *A sermon preached in London before the right honorable the Lord La Warre, Lord governor . . . of Virginea . . . Febr. 21, 1609* (London, 1610), the running head to whose printed pages was "A New-Yeeres Gift to Virginia," he stressed the opportunity offered to planters in Virginia to become "Fathers and Founders of a new Church and Commonwealth." Neither a "new church" nor a "new commonwealth" in Virginia was really desired by the Anglicans, and Crashaw had no desire to encourage separation in church or state, but it may be that in 1610 he was influenced unconsciously by Separatist terminology. But if, by moving from London to Jamestown, settlers really acquired

[5] Blank in text, presumably for the reader to fill in himself. The 1622 edition has "further on an anabaptist." (Sig. E5v.)

the right to add something "new" to the church, then by flying from London to Amsterdam or Leiden a "gathered church" might claim the right to inject something "new" into its polity either in the Netherlands or in America if it should move there. Indeed, the thought of Virginia being a place of refuge for moderate, conforming, nonseparating Puritans inside the Church of England may well have been in the minds of some of its mercantile subscribers from the beginning, though their idea of "a new church" might be something much more conservative than that of the Separatists.

From William Bradford's "Dialogue," there seems little doubt that the "Ancient Church" at Amsterdam, which Francis Johnson continued to lead until 1612 or 1613, was one of the major influences that led the Scrooby congregation in 1608 first to Amsterdam and then to Leiden. Bradford, with John Robinson, William Brewster, and others heard from Francis Johnson in 1608 an account of his experiences and difficulties, and pays tribute to the tenacity of the "Ancient Church" in surmounting its many difficulties. "The truth is their condition, for the most part, was for some time very low and hard. It was with them as, if it should be related, would hardly be believed. And no marvel. For many of them had lain long in irons, and then were banished into Newfoundland, where they were abused [a concise comment on the Ramea venture], and at last came into the Low Countries, and wanting money, trades, friends or acquaintances, and languages to help themselves, how could it be otherwise."[6] For Francis Johnson, Bradford retained a strong admiration—"a brave man he was," he said of him, "and an able teacher." Robinson and Brewster knew Johnson even better, for they were called in to mediate between him and his congregation. (A split took Johnson with part of the church to Emden at some time between about 1613 and 1617.)

The notion that the Leiden church might imitate the 1597 Pilgrims may have been, as we saw, in the air in 1610, but the situation in Virginia was not then favorable to the creation of a Separatist colony. From 1607 to 1616 the colonists at Jamestown remained individually servants of the Virginia Company and were ministered to by Anglican clergy. Robert Cushman hinted in 1621 that some Separatists who went to Virginia soon lapsed "into worldliness" there.[7] Such examples would not have

[6] Alexander Young, *Chronicles of the Pilgrim Fathers of the Colony of Plymouth from 1602 to 1625* (Boston, 1841), pp. 425–45. The manuscript is in the collections of the Massachusetts Historical Society, but there has not been a modern critical edition.

[7] Robert Cushman, *A sermon preached at Plimmoth in New England. December 9, 1621* (London, 1622).

encouraged larger bodies to follow them. Only after the Company divided out its lands among its subscribers from 1616 onward and then launched its scheme for "particular plantations" was there hope of a religious refuge for Separatists in Virginia.

It is possible, though not certain, that the old experiences of Francis Johnson played a part in leading Robinson, Brewster, and Carver to approach the Virginia Company in 1617 so as to obtain a grant of a "particular plantation" to which they could remove a part or the whole of the Leiden church.

There may have been an even closer connection. Francis Blackwell, a member of Johnson's church at Emden, seems to have approached the Virginia Company before the Leiden men. Though accused of handing over at least one exiled Separatist to the Anglicans, Blackwell took an overloaded ship to Virginia in the winter of 1618–19, and died with many of the company at sea. It seems likely that he carried among them some of the Emden congregation, and he may have intended to bring Francis Johnson also to a new American exile—twenty-one years after the first effort—if he had not died at Amsterdam in January 1618. Blackwell may, indeed, have been planning a joint effort between Johnson's men and the Leiden church. If so, the latter edged out of it just in time.[8]

The element of continuity is clearly there, though in the absence of more specific evidence there remains an element of conjecture in estimating precisely how it operated. Yet it was clear to Bradford that the "Ancient Church" was one of the principal progenitors of the Plymouth venture, and that the pioneering if abortive voyage of Francis Johnson in 1597 was one of the pointers for the Second Pilgrims.

[8] All that is known of the mysterious Blackwell episode is given in William Bradford, *History of Plymouth Plantation* (Boston, 1912), ed. Worthington Chauncey Ford, I, 83–93, and Bradford, *Of Plymouth Plantation, 1620–1647* (New York, 1952), ed. Samuel Eliot Morison, pp. 37, 356–9.

CHAPTER FOURTEEN

The English Catholics and America, 1581–1633

I

IN PIECING TOGETHER the activities of individuals and groups concerned in any way with early English plans to explore and settle North America, it is necessary at times to sort them out into economic or religious groupings. Some of these—as we have already seen—were Puritan and some were Roman Catholic. They were attracted in one way or another by the idea of going to settle in the New World. With some the impetus was mainly that of adventure; with others it was the desire to get rich, to get great estates, to elevate their social position. For still others the American field offered an opportunity to live a life unhampered by the restrictions of European government, particularly in the matter of religion. This operated for both Catholic and Puritan groups concerned in plans for early settlement in America.

This is a field in which there are many loose ends and a great shortage of adequate material. It is chastening, perhaps, to find that in many areas we know very little about the past, and in some fields, such as this first English Catholic involvement with the New World, what can be assembled so far is a collection of bits and pieces of information rather than a coherent story or an entirely intelligible pattern of knowledge.

A brief reference to the position of English Catholics in the period from 1558 to 1640 is essential here.[1] The first phase after Queen Eliza-

[1] For the problems of recusancy in this period, see especially Patrick McGrath, *Papists and Puritans Under Elizabeth I* (London, 1967); William R. Trimble, *The Catholic Laity in Elizabethan England* (Cambridge, Mass., 1964); John Bossy,

beth's accession was one of gradual and increasing alienation. The state veered its course in a Protestant direction, creating out of largely traditional material an Anglican establishment, which it then proceeded to favor in such ways that those who became recusants and declined to participate in it were isolated in their religious observances and excluded from service to the state. During this period, occasional conformity combined with private adherence to the older religious practices was tolerated —even, one might say, almost encouraged by the state as a second-best to complete conformity or as a preliminary to it.

The second period, from 1570 to 1585, sees the Elizabethan state embattled. Threatened by the papal bull of 1570, which declared Elizabeth excommunicated and incapable of retaining the allegiance of her Catholic subjects, the state steadily increased its pressure on recusants, at the same time trying to prevent their going into exile on the Continent, as many had done since 1559. The idea was to force them to conform, fully if at all possible, or at least occasionally and nominally. Token conformity tended to become more and more a test of loyalty to the state, and those who did not comply to this extent were liable to find themselves spending longer and longer terms in prison. Moreover, any proof of the use of old forms of service—the hearing of Mass in particular—was more consistently and steadily penalized. At the same time, the missionary priests were regarded by the state as enemies and also as obstructors of the complete anglicization process, which before the northern rising of 1569 seemed to be slowly, inevitably engulfing the greater part of the population.

But just as the priests provided a new reason for state pressure, so also they worked against the practice of occasional conformity. It was a test of the loyalty of adherents to the Catholic faith that they should not appear in a state church even in the most nominal way. The state, of course, gradually stepped up the penalties on the priesthood and the parallel penalties on those who protected it, so that a sentence of death hung over every priest and that of imprisonment or more over almost every layman who had effective contact with a priest. In these circumstances the degree of pressure inflicted on men who wished to remain loyal both to the state and to their religious beliefs was appalling. They

---

"The Character of Elizabethan Catholicism," *Past and Present,* no. 21 (1962), pp. 39–59; Philip Hughes, *The Reformation in England,* III (London, 1954); M. J. Havran, *The Catholics in Caroline England* (Stanford, 1962).

I am indebted to Dr. E. W. Ives and Mr. Patrick McGrath for commenting on a draft of this chapter and for a number of valuable suggestions, though they cannot be held responsible for the opinions expressed in it.

were faced with a dilemma which seemed inescapable. Moreover, the missionaries were persuading additional men and women to apostasize from Protestantism, and these conversions offered a positive threat to the Church of England.

The third phase, 1585 to 1603, was one of open war with Spain and with the Papacy as Spain's political ally. Up to the coming of the Armada in 1588, pressures on the Catholics as a whole increased; after that date they tended slightly to diminish. Enough Catholics came forward with money, offers of personal service, and other assistance to make it possible for the state to discriminate slightly in favor of loyal as against disloyal Catholics, though the pressure against those regarded as disloyal was, if anything, accelerated. The executions of priests declined as more of those caught were kept alive in prison. On the other side, some Catholics who had exhibited their loyalty in material or physical ways, paid their toll also by occasional conformity in the established church.

What the queen and her advisers found was that they could not eliminate Roman Catholicism. They had to govern the country on the assumption that a Catholic minority was an established part of its structure. This recognition was part of the reason why the period from 1603 to 1640, under both James I and Charles I, saw a good deal of *de facto* recognition of the right of Catholics to retain their distinct religious observances so long as they did so in private. This semitoleration led some Catholics to positions of influence at court. It could also lead to circumstances in which priests were exiled or penalized and fines for recusancy enforced. It was a period of uneasiness, of relative prosperity for some while others still paid heavily in fines and local discrimination. The unease was due to the fact that in the country as a whole there was much basic deep-seated hostility to Catholics and Catholicism among the many branches of the growing Puritan movement.

In this shifting pattern of policies and attitudes, the part played by America as a Utopia—a new land where Catholics might obtain freedom—was a changing one, generally very marginal to the main events of the time, though sometimes illuminating them from unusual angles. Exile to Catholic Europe was the choice of many Englishmen and more than a few Englishwomen, even though it meant loss of property and proscription. Movement to America or even to nearby Ireland, where repression was less likely to take such an extreme form as in England and ties of allegiance would be retained, seemed at various times a possible solution for certain groups of Catholics. And it was listened to with some favor by members of the government under both Elizabeth and the early Stuarts. Those involved in these moves on the Catholic side were mainly members of the country gentry and nobility. They had one very special characteristic. Many, possibly most of them were social conservatives who believed strongly in maintaining old hierarchical values: the entire dependence of the tenant on his lord, the complete loyalty and devotion of the lord to his sovereign. One reason why they remained so resolutely Catholic during the period of alienation after 1558 was precisely their conservatism.

So far as their social outlook was concerned, in many areas they were not isolated. Other nobles and gentlemen who conformed to the Established Church had not dissimilar views about social problems—they too regretted the loosening of social bonds and of tenant and gentry loyalties, the rise of "upstarts" to wealth and power. This was one reason why the Catholic upper classes were able to maintain their identity. They had friends who agreed with them on everything except religion, and in their moves to get away from England they found some sympathy and support from conforming Protestants of this sort. At the same time the Catholic gentry, in certain regions at least, did their best to wall round their estates and their social and religious concepts from a world which in their eyes was becoming increasingly revolutionary, no less in its social than in its religious aspects. It was these attitudes, held in extreme form or in areas where moves toward conformity were slow and tardy, that led them in many cases to remain Catholics rather than become Anglicans. But with the new Counter-Reformation spirit, they too in many cases went through some degree of spiritual revolution of their own: the missionary priests instilled into them a new militant attitude toward their faith. If they did not respond in this way, they tended to drift away from their Catholic allegiances.

In general one may say that the missionary movement helped to weld English Catholics into a coherent and only slightly fluctuating group after the 1570's, until they emerged on the side of conservative monarchy in 1642 and gave their king a chance to win a war against parliamentary Protestantism. Their problem, their agony at times, was to remain both Royalist and Catholic. They also retained a strong sense of feudal obligation to their tenantry and other dependents. In the south of England, on some estates tenants conformed while the lord remained Catholic, and the link between social and religious obligation was thus weakened. In the north, however, especially in Lancashire, where the lord remained Catholic the tenants did also. We might indeed say that in many cases, *because* the lord remained Catholic the tenantry did so too. The gentry and the nobles had resources in land and money and connections which enabled them to resist many of the pressures of the state. Yet when these were stepped up beyond a certain level against their tenants in the way of fines, imprisonment, and the threat of death, it became impossible for their lords to protect them. The obligations of loyalty to the crown and of loyalty to their dependents were put to such a test that emigration *en masse* of lords and tenants to another environment held great attraction, especially if the traditional society could be reconstituted there. To some extent, especially in the early years, when removal to America was discussed this was Utopian, scarcely capable of being successfully realized. Yet it did not remain so. Gradually North America became a practicable colonial location for some Catholics, and in the end a substantial number of English Catholics took advantage of the opportunities across the Atlantic.

II

Sir Thomas Gerard of The Bryn was one of the most prominent of the Lancashire Catholic gentry.[2] He was also most anxious to break out of the restrictions imposed by the Elizabethan settlement on persistent Roman Catholics. Several times in his long career he was accused of being involved in plots against Queen Elizabeth, but he was never convicted of anything more serious than harboring priests or hearing Mass in his own houses, though he spent a good deal of time in prison. No close investigation has yet been made of his career, so that it is hard to judge the tenor of his association with opponents of the queen. What is clear is that he developed—and perhaps was a pioneer in this—the idea of moving himself and his tenants and friends out of Lancashire to a new settlement while still retaining allegiance to the crown.

His first objective was Ireland. After Shane O'Neill was killed in 1567, Sir Henry Sidney as Lord Deputy there was much occupied in meeting two problems. The first was the intrusion of the Scottish islanders into Antrim, the northeast corner of Ireland, and the second was the replacement of the power of O'Neill by an English presence. His recipe for both was massive English colonization. The queen was not wholly con-

[2] Usually spelled at this time "Gerrard," though with many variations. The family name in Lancashire and Derbyshire is "Gerard" and has been used here. Sir Thomas needs, but has not found, a biographer. Much information on him will be found scattered through *The Victoria County History of Lancashire*, 8 vols. (London, 1906–14), ed. William Page, III, IV, VI, and VII, with important references in IV, 122, 144–5. Also J. S. Leatherbarrow, *The Lancashire Elizabethan Recusants* (Manchester, 1947), pp. 42, 86, 103, 115, 150; Catholic Record Society, *Miscellany* (London, 1905), II, 257, 259, 264, 281, 284; J. Brownbill, ed., *The Moore Manuscripts* (Liverpool, 1913), p. 166; Trimble, *Catholic Laity*, pp. 65, 75, 163, 192, 210.

vinced of the practicality of this idea. She did not want to subsidize an experiment on these lines. So Sidney looked around for private speculators. Among those who came forward in 1568 was Sir Thomas Gerard, who with other gentlemen of Lancashire whose names we do not know offered to settle in Antrim and to defend it on the east against the intruding MacDonalds of the Isles, and on the west against the Irish O'Neills. It was suggested that he go to Ireland to discuss the position and then return to London to try to work out terms with the government. But his first plan was rejected in the spring of 1569, apparently because it would be too costly for the crown.

He renewed his offers early in 1570, for Sidney had thus far found no takers. This time we have some details of what he wanted. He asked for concessions to export goods to the new settlement free of duty, which was not unreasonable; but he also desired a commission to levy soldiers, laborers, and craftsmen in the counties of Yorkshire, Lancashire, and Cheshire, which was surely overambitious. He requested one hundred horse soldiers, four hundred footmen, and certain ships and artillery with which to fortify the coastline, the soldiers to be paid for by the crown for three years. Inside his settlement he asked for a fair measure of autonomy. He and his company would choose their own officers annually and make their own laws, so long as they did not conflict with the laws of the realm of Ireland, and could impose martial law without any right of appeal against their decisions. This asked the queen to pay too much, and also perhaps to give away too much autonomy for a settlement so near her government in Dublin. Gerard's second plan was rejected.[3] It is,

[3] The first offer of Sir Thomas Gerard and other gentlemen of Lancashire reached Sir Henry Sidney, Lord Deputy of Ireland, about the end of 1568. He forwarded it to Queen Elizabeth in March 1569, asking her for a speedy decision so that Gerard and his friends might make a start in May (thus expressing his personal approval). The Queen's reply on 6 June was that Gerard and his friends had better visit Sidney in Ireland for detailed discussions before any decision could be reached. The result, following such a visit, of further correspondence with Sidney was Sir Thomas's second book of demands, received by Sir William Cecil as Secretary of State on 15 March 1570. This asked that Gerard and his associates should be incorporated as a company with the right to elect officers annually, to make ordinances not conflicting with the laws of the realm of Ireland, and to use martial law without the risk of reprisals being directed against them. These proposals anticipate in many respects those afterward envisaged for American seignorial settlements. His additional requests for royal authority to levy soldiers, horses, and arms in northwest England, the supply of two ships to transport his company, wages for his men as soldiers for three years, with arms and munitions supplied by the crown for his castles, were also included. On 2 June, the Queen sent Sidney a virtual rejection of the plan saying "We cannot be . . . at the charges of fortifying

however, significant as the first attempt we know of to move a large number of English Catholics out of England to an area where they would be still under the queen's control but might enjoy some real degree of religious and indeed secular autonomy. There is no indication in the surviving documents that formal toleration was asked for, but it is clearly implicit in the demand that the settlers should have powers of self-regulation. Nominally, Ireland had its own legal compulsions to establish Anglicanism and eliminate Catholics from office; but in practice all areas, native Irish and Anglo-Irish alike, which retained any local autonomy (as did most of the island) were free to worship as they chose.

These plans are mirrored in later plans for settlement by Sir Thomas Gerard and other Catholics in North America. Gerard next emerges into view as a leading member of the syndicate which more than a decade later proposed to set up in North America a settlement very similar to what he had envisaged in Ireland. In this case, there was no question of the queen being asked to contribute funds. Rather, she was expected to forgo, or merely defer, fines that she would otherwise have levied on the Catholics.

III

THE 1581 ACT which raised the penalty for not attending church from one shilling a time to twenty pounds a month and imposed a fine and imprisonment for hearing Mass was ostensibly aimed at those who disloyally seduced subjects of the queen into allegiance to the Papacy. It was directed primarily against the missionary priests and those who sheltered them. There was a possible loophole for Catholics if they gave nominal tokens of their acceptance of the Church establishment by appearing publicly at Anglican service four times a year.[4] The imposition of these

[Gerard's castles] and of the North." See P.R.O., State Papers, Ireland, Elizabeth, S.P. 63/27, 64; S.P. 63/30, 32; T. Ó Laidhin, ed., *Sidney Papers 1565–1570* (Dublin, 1962), pp. 109–10.

[4] Clause IX reads: "Provided also that every person which usually on the Sunday shall have in his or their home the divine service which is established by the law in this realm, and be thereat himself or herself usually or mostly commonly present, and shall not obstinately refuse to come to church and there do as is aforesaid, and shall also four times in the year at the least be present at the divine service in the church of the parish where he or she shall be resident, or in some other open common church or such chapel of ease, shall not incur any pain or penalty limited by this act for not coming to church." On four Sundays a year all Catholics, under penalty, were to appear in a parish church: on forty-eight Sundays they were supposed to have Anglican services held in their own houses and were forbidden to

penalties could be crippling to most Catholic landowners, and impossible to enforce on most of their tenantry. Sir John Neale has called the fine "a ruinous penalty when enforced."[5] The dilemma of the Catholic gentry was now extremely painful. Nor were they given time to consider their position. The recusancy fines were rapidly enforced after the bill became law on 18 March 1581.

The initiative in trying to extricate the Catholic gentry from this predicament by means of an American venture came from Sir George Peckham, a Buckinghamshire squire, and Sir Thomas Gerard. Sir Humphrey Gilbert was preparing an expedition to discover a site for a settlement on the east coast of North America. His first venture in 1578 had been forced to return without result. Sir George Peckham had already shown his interest in overseas voyages by subscribing to that expedition,[6] though there is as yet no evidence that he intended at the time to become a colonist or that a refuge for English Catholics in the New World was then considered. It was evidently through this connection that the possibility arose of exploiting the new expedition just being planned in 1581, to ease the burden of the Catholic gentry.[7]

Peckham had conformed nominally at various times, but in 1580 had been imprisoned for harboring priests and was on parole, under promise of conformity, after March 1581. How he knew Sir Thomas Gerard is not clear, but Gerard had already expressed his interest in bringing Catholics to Ireland—and also in overseas voyaging, by subscribing to

---

have Mass said there. Technically, as Mr. Patrick McGrath has pointed out to me, the act offered no concessions even to Catholics who conformed on the four occasions annually, though there was no requirement to take Communion according to the Anglican rite until 1606. He suggests that the privilege to hold services at home was primarily intended to allow some concessions to Puritan-minded Protestants who did not wish to follow precisely the Book of Common Prayer, and was not meant for Catholics. At the same time, it will be obvious that, except in time of crisis, it was possible for well-disposed local authorities to overlook what kind of services were held in the home, even though there were frequent raids to see whether Mass-saying priests were present in the houses. The "church Papists" who appeared in church on the set occasions were in many cases under less severe pressure—again except in critical times—than those who did not, though conditions varied from place to place. Church appearance was, however, one important indication of potential loyalty to the crown.

5 J. E. Neale, *Elizabeth I and Her Parliaments, 1559–1581* (London, 1953), p. 389.

6 D. B. Quinn, ed., *The Voyages and Colonising Enterprises of Sir Humphrey Gilbert*, Hakluyt Society, 2d ser., nos. 83–4, 2 vols. (London, 1940), II, 332.

7 For this episode see R. B. Merriman, "Some Notes on the Treatment of English Catholics in the Reign of Elizabeth," *American Historical Review*, XIII (1907–8), 480–500; Quinn, *Gilbert*, I, 71–6, II, 243–80, 313, 341–7, 364–5, 369–75, 375–8, 435–82.

Martin Frobisher's second expedition, in 1577, to find gold or a passage to China in the vicinity of Baffin Island.[8] The first contacts between Peckham and Gerard and Gilbert in 1582 were private ones and were reported by an intelligence agent on 19 April to a member of the government.[9] "There is a muttering amongst the Papists that Sir Humphrey Gilbert goeth to seek a newfound land. Sir George Peckham and Sir Thomas Gerard goeth with him. I have heard it said amongst the Papists that they hope it will prove the best journey for England that was made these forty years."

Thus within a little more than a year after the new act came into force, a project for Catholic emigration to America had emerged and was receiving some appreciable degree of support. The next stage was to get some measure of official approval for the venture, and this was done by the end of May 1582, so that by June specific contracts could be entered into by Catholics with Gilbert and the details of their relations with the state worked out. These were arranged by Peckham and Gerard with Sir Francis Walsingham, the queen's strongly anti-Catholic but realistic Secretary of State.[1] They had asked that an official register of emigrants be kept, and that those entered on it should be free to leave England and return freely from their new home across the Atlantic. Existing laws required a passport to leave the country, and this would not normally be granted to Catholics, while Catholic exiles who got away without a passport would not usually be allowed to return. A system of licensed freedom to come and go was vital for the future of the Catholic colonizing project.

All gentlemen of substance ("recusants of ability") would pay out-

[8] Quinn, *Gilbert*, I, 72. Sir George Peckham's career, like Gerard's, has remained largely untraced. He both enjoyed an annual pension from the Crown and was obligated to pay an enormous debt, which he had inherited, to the Queen. At various times he appears in possession of estates in Buckinghamshire and elsewhere; at many other times he appears to have had no money and to have been living in the direst poverty. He may have been unfortunate in his commitments. He was certainly afflicted by the recusancy fines. But he was probably somewhat shiftless also. At the same time, he kept open his lines of communication to members of the government (e.g., his petition to Sir Robert Cecil, 16 January 1597, CecilMS 37, 76 [Hist.MSSComm., *CecilMSS*, VII, 23]; also, see Trimble, *Catholic Laity*, pp. 106, 171), and the City of London (e.g., his petition to the Fishmongers' Company, of which he was a member, 8 August 1604, Records of the Company of Fishmongers of London, Ledger I, 1592–1610, Guildhall Library, London, MS 5570/1, fol. 396).

[9] Quinn, *Gilbert*, II, 241.

[1] Compare the first agreement between Gilbert, Peckham, and Gerard, 6 June (*ibid.*, pp. 245–54), with their petition to Walsingham, which followed immediately on it (*ibid.*, pp. 255–6).

standing fines before they left. Other recusants who had not the money to pay their fines would enter into an obligation to pay them from America when it was possible for them to do so—a somewhat naïve though face-saving suggestion for both parties. They undertook that they would not use their license to take French leave to the Continent, and all of them would undertake to avoid any act prejudicial to Queen Elizabeth and her allies. They undertook, finally, to help to relieve the problems of unemployment and poverty at home by including in every ten persons one who had "not any certainty whereupon to live" or maintain himself in England. These requests were evidently accepted in some such form, since a number of them are mentioned in the draft agreement drawn up between Peckham and Gerard on one hand and a further group of gentlemen with whom they were subcontracting part of the rights acquired from Gilbert.

This group was headed by Sir Edmund Brudenell, a prominent Northamptonshire gentleman. He was not a Catholic, though he had Catholic relatives, but he was willing to associate himself with gentlemen who were. One of these was a representative of an important Northamptonshire family, Sir William Catesby of Ashby St. Ledgers, with whom Brudenell had frequent dealings, sometimes friendly, sometimes not. Catesby, like Peckham, was on parole from prison in expectation of his conformity. Another party to the contract was William Shelley—apparently William Shelley of Michelgrove, Sussex, who had been sent to prison in August 1580. The third party was Philip Basset, who appears to have been a Devonshire man, released from the Fleet Prison under bond on 15 July 1581.[2]

Gilbert's timetable for his American voyage provided that very shortly after the completion of the contract in June he would make his way to Newfoundland and work down the mainland coast of North America to pick out sites for a settlement, returning to England late in 1582. The Catholic group associated with him was to follow early in 1583, setting out from England not later than 31 March. They were to assemble a fleet of ships to occupy a suitable headquarters in America and leave a group to winter there, so that a permanent colony could be built up.

A well-known commander was to be found to make the Catholic expedition effective. Three men were to be taken into the syndicate who

[2] Two important documents on this matter from the BrudenellMSS, Deane, Northamptonshire, were calendared in Quinn, *Gilbert,* II, 256–60 (and see I, 73). With two others (which are represented by official versions elsewhere) they were sold separately at Sotheby's in London on 2 November 1964 and have been scattered. See also Joan Wake, *The Brudenells of Deene* (London, 1953), pp. 51–84, esp. p. 66.

had qualifications for this task. One, Martin Frobisher, was highly experienced in American waters, but the degeneration of his Northwest Passage ventures of 1576 to 1578 into an abortive hunt for gold had somewhat discredited him; in any case, he did not get on well with the experienced sailors on his voyages. The second to be named, Richard Bingham, had wide experience as a mercenary soldier in fighting both for and against Spain, but was not employed at this time. (He was in fact to conclude his career by taking a prominent part in Irish affairs, where he distinguished himself as a tough, even brutal administrator of an Irish-Catholic population.) The third man was another northern Catholic, Sir William Stanley of Hooton, Cheshire. He too had been in Spanish service, but had been employed more recently in the Irish service of the English crown, helping to stamp out the last embers of the Desmond Rebellion in Munster. He had come to England to enlist reinforcements for the army. Stanley was to go over spectacularly to Spain in 1587, with the Deventer garrison, and to remain at the head of a regiment in the Spanish service for a generation.

An obscure secondary project under Anthony Brigham was also linked with this venture, some minor reconnaissance which may have been dispatched by June 1582;[3] we hear of two ships which had not returned by March 1583, and these may well have been his if he had indeed set out. This may not have been part of the main colonizing project, but a subsidiary commercial scheme to set up a whaling base on the west coast of Newfoundland. Certainly Brigham was back in England in 1584, when he planned to go whale-fishing off the Newfoundland coast, though perhaps not with Catholic support.

Among the interesting detail that survives of these plans is an elaborate set of instructions for a surveyor called Thomas Bavin.[4] It is just possible that he provides a further link with south Lancashire, whence part of the Catholic initiative derived, or with nearby Cheshire. His name may be one which is found in both Elizabethan Liverpool, where a Thomas Bavande, merchant (flourished 1563–86), was mayor at various times from 1571 to 1586, and Elizabethan Chester, where Richard Bavande, who also spelled his name "Bavin" and "Bavan," was mayor several times

[3] On Brigham see Quinn, *Gilbert,* I, 61–3, 73, 90, 99, II, 258, 339, 349, 375, 486.

[4] Commonplace Book of Edward Hoby, B.M., AdditionalMS 38823, fols. 1–8 (incomplete); Quinn, *Roanoke Voyages,* I, 51–4; E. G. R. Taylor, "Instructions to a Colonial Surveyor in 1582," *Mariner's Mirror,* XXXVII (1951), 48–62; Taylor, *Mathematical Practitioners of Tudor and Stuart England* (Cambridge, Eng., 1954), p. 184; D. W. Waters, *The Art of Navigation in England in Elizabethan and Early Stuart Times* (London, 1958), pp. 164, 534–40.

from 1581 to 1601 and once M.P.[5] Was this young man, possibly a Catholic also, a son of Liverpool's Thomas or Chester's Richard? Further research may conceivably tell us. But the fact that Gerard's base was in south Lancashire and that Gilbert's chief lieutenant, Edward Hayes, came from Liverpool may well point to an association with this area.

Bavin and another man were to conduct a complete geographical survey of the parts of the American coast touched at by the first Catholic expedition. We have instructions such as this: "Let Bavin carry with him good store of parchments, paper royal, quills, and ink, black powder to make ink, and of all sorts of colours to draw all things to life, gum, pencil, a stone to grind colours, mouth glue, black lead, two pairs of brazen compasses, and other instruments to draw cards [charts], and plots [maps]." Another item reads: "Also let Bavin draw to life one of each kind of thing that is strange to us in England, by the which he may always garnish his plot, as he shall so cause upon his return. . . . And also draw to life all birds, beasts, fishes, plants, herbs, trees and fruits . . . Also . . . the figures and shapes of men and women in their apparel . . . in every place." The fate of this versatile artist-surveyor is unknown; prolonged search by the late Eva Taylor failed to uncover a single map or chart drawn by him.[6]

The lands contracted for by Gerard and Peckham in June 1582 amounted to no less than two million acres each, and the documents we have enable us to see something of the kind of settlement they envisaged. Each of them, under Sir Humphrey Gilbert as Lord Proprietor and Governor of the whole colony, was to be lord paramount of a great seignory; each would have under him a hierarchy of adventurers and subadventurers who would be assigned land under them (paying one shilling per hundred acres to them every year); each would be a member of the supreme council and court of the colony, and each would hold courts for their own tenants.[7] This notional hierarchy well illustrates the conservatism of the adventurers—shared with Gilbert and his Protestant supporters also—as well as their grandiose conceptions.

As insurance in case anything happened to Gilbert, Peckham was named as one of three trustees to hold the rights on Gilbert's grant from the crown, if he died on his first voyage. Later, when Gilbert's departure had been delayed, on 28 February 1583 Sir George Peckham and his son

[5] *Liverpool Town Books, 1550–1603*, 2 vols. (Liverpool, 1918–35), ed. J. A. Twemlow; R. H. Morris, *Chester in the Plantagenet and Tudor Reigns* (Chester, 1893), *passim; Chester Customs Accounts, 1301–1566* (Liverpool, 1969), ed. Kevin P. Wilson, pp. 59–60 (an earlier Thomas, of Chester), 88, 92, 99 (Thomas, of Liverpool).
[6] See p. 374, *n.* 4, above. [7] Quinn, *Gilbert*, II, 266–73.

George contracted for a further million and a half acres and defined more closely the rights due them and their duties owed to Gilbert in the new colony.[8] Gerard had already placed his family land in the hands of trustees in 1582.[9]

The two leaders were not without their anxieties. Rumors had begun to circulate in Catholic quarters that Spain owned the land it was proposed to settle. On 16 July 1582 Peckham, on his own behalf and Gerard's, visited Dr. John Dee, the eminent astrologer and geographer, at his home in Mortlake.[1] They wanted assurances that Spain had no title to the land Gilbert proposed they should occupy in America. Eventually, Dee assured Peckham that Spain had no rights in the area; on the maps it was New France, having been claimed for Francis I by Verrazzano in 1524 but not occupied. Moreover, Dee was able to point out to them on the large map of North America he had drawn in 1580 the precise place he thought their settlement should lie. Verrazzano had stayed for some time on Narragansett Bay in modern Rhode Island, which he called his "*Refugio*," and there it was decided that Peckham should lay out his seignory. Thus in the agreement of 28 February 1583 it was solemnly set out that the Peckhams were to have one and a half million acres around the Dee River and the Bay of the Five Islands, renamed, presumably by Gilbert, after Verrazzano's discoveries. This seemed to give him some reasonable assurance that his title would stand up to Spanish claims.

As early as July 1582 the would-be emigrants were encountering a campaign against their project. This was mounted by Bernardino de Mendoza, the Spanish ambassador, who was keeping a close watch on all English overseas plans. He wrote to Philip II on 11 July 1582 that the Catholic gentry had been drawn into Gilbert's venture by Sir Francis Walsingham and confirmed in it by the queen herself.[2] Mendoza described the participants as men who "were anxious to live as Catholics without risking their lives" and who were being promised that they could live in America "with freedom of conscience, enjoying the use of their English properties. . . . The Queen restores them to her favour and accepts them as loyal subjects and vassals." The project was deeply distasteful to Mendoza. In the first place, it would interfere with Spain's so far unsubstantiated claim to the whole of North America. Second, it would weaken the Catholics in England whom he hoped to use in the interest of

[8] *Ibid.*, pp. 341–6.

[9] In favor of Elizabeth his wife and Thomas his son. *Victoria County History of Lancashire*, 8 vols. (London, 1906–14), ed. William Page, IV, 144, citing P.R.O., County Palatine of Lancashire, Feet of Fines, P. L. 17/44, m. 266.

[1] Quinn, *Gilbert*, II, 280. [2] *Ibid.*, pp. 278–9.

Spain to overthrow Elizabeth. He considered that the plan was invented only because, in spite of persecution, Catholicism was increasing in England. If it succeeded, the departure of the Catholic gentry would destroy the effectiveness of the seminaries on the Continent and remove all shelter and encouragement for the missionary priests. And Spain would lose the Catholic instrument Mendoza hoped to use against the queen. He thought it his duty to stop the venture if he could.

His tactics were to spread word through the priests with whom he was in contact that the lands to which they were bound belonged to Spain, and that the Spaniards would come and cut the colonists' throats if they settled there (as they had done, he said, with the French in Florida in 1565). Further, "they were imperilling their consciences by engaging in an enterprise prejudicial to His Holiness." He claimed to have scared some off by these threats, but was writing to Dr. William Allen at Douay to exercise his great influence among English Catholics against the project, and was also writing to the Abbot Briceño in Rome to use his influence there. It has not so far been possible to trace any of these contacts in published papers. But there is an echo of the official Catholic attitude of the time in a paper of Father Parsons written in 1605, to which we shall come later. In 1582 he had recently been to Spain to discuss the invasion of England. The proposed "evacuation of Papists," as Parsons called the colonization scheme, had made them a laughingstock to the heretics (or perhaps it was urged that this would happen if they submitted to the indignity of being exported to America), so it was a matter of dignity for them to stay; and in any case the "attempt became . . . most odious to the Catholic Party." How far Parsons played a part in this campaign is not known.

The vicissitudes of Sir Humphrey Gilbert's fortunes complicated and in the end helped to destroy the Catholic plan. Failing, through defects in organization, to get to sea during the months between May and August, when access to Newfoundland and thence to New England by a direct voyage was possible, he made a desperate attempt to set out between September and December, though this meant approaching North America by the long voyage through the West Indies, the only practicable winter route. But even then contrary winds bottled him up in Southampton and blocked all exit from the English Channel. He gave up, finally, at the end of 1582. Before doing so he had received a reassuring message from Peckham that he and his friends would not back down from the expedition. Maurice Browne wrote on 19 December to John Thynne, his friend and fellow investor in the enterprise: "This last night [18 December] Sir H[umphrey Gilbert] had A messenger from Sir George Peckham and others of his good friends that there is divers good ships preparing to follow Sir H. and a new supply to assist him in this Action."[3] This is a valuable glimpse of what was happening, as it indicates that Mendoza had been less successful than he claimed in driving away Peckham's associates, though it is possible that he was now coming to depend less on Catholic than on Protestant gentry support.

Sir William Stanley, mentioned as possible leader of the Brudenell syndicate, had gone with fresh troops to Ireland in November 1582.[4] It is not unlikely that Sir Thomas Gerard had also been discouraged by the delays, and possibly the threats, and had returned to his Lancashire estates. We hear no more of Catesby, Shelley, and Basset in connection with the project, or of non-Catholic members like Sir Edmund Brudenell. On the other hand Peckham, as we saw, made another agreement with Gilbert on 28 February 1583 regarding the location of his American grant,[5] which seems to have paved the way for the revival of Gilbert's project in March. Peckham was still active in May, when Gilbert was almost ready to sail at last, and brought into the venture William Rosewell of Forde, an important Devonshire landowner who was apparently not a Catholic.[6] In the same month Mendoza, admitting that his earlier hopes of killing the project had been optimistic, reported that the Privy Council had suggested a lump-sum contribution by the Catholics to Gilbert's enterprise as the price of some temporary concessions to them individually or as a group.[7] Few, he said, were coming forward in response. Whether there is anything in this or not we do not know. Mendoza admitted that "some spendthrift and ruined Catholics have gone with Jorge [= Humphrey] Gilbert, selling for this purpose what remained to them."

It seems not improbable, therefore, that when Gilbert finally sailed on 11 June he had at least a few Catholic associates with him, but who they were we do not know. His plan was to go first to Newfoundland and then coast southward to inspect the lands which he himself proposed to occupy and also those assigned to the various syndicates, several of them composed at least mainly of Catholics. It is unlikely that more than a reconnaissance was planned at this time, in spite of all the delays that had taken place.

Gilbert asserted his authority over St. John's Harbour and over the Newfoundland fishery in August and then set out on his long coasting

[3] MSS of the Marquess of Bath, Longleat House, Wiltshire, Thynne Papers, V, fol. 233r. See D. B. Quinn and Neil M. Cheshire, *The New Found Land of Stephen Parmenius* (Toronto, 1972), p. 202.

[4] *Cal.S.P.,Ire.,1574–1585*, pp. 411, 424.

[5] Quinn, *Gilbert*, II, 341–6.

[6] *Ibid.*, pp. 369–73.

[7] *Ibid.*, pp. 364–5.

voyage. Before reaching the mainland the loss of the *Delight* forced him to turn back across the Atlantic. The *Squirrel*, with Gilbert on board, parted company from the *Golden Hind*, which Edward Hayes alone brought home at the end of September with news that no reconnaissance of the New England shore had been achieved and that the commander of the venture and the linchpin of its hopes was missing at sea and believed dead.

Before this news came, Peckham had been slowly making progress. In July, Sir Philip Sidney made him a gift of the title to the very large grant of land which represented his own investment in the Gilbert enterprise [8] —it is not likely that this brought Peckham any benefit, though his possession of the title might have attracted a few supporters to him. Before the return of the *Golden Hind*, too, he had bought at least one ship, the *Emanuel* of Yarmouth,[9] which, however, became involved in legal proceedings, and he appears never to have had the use of it. He—and his son George—were already preparing fresh publicity for their venture in order to exploit the news they expected Gilbert to bring home from his reconnaissance. Edward Hayes in the *Golden Hind* reached England on 22 September, and when he arrived in London early in October with the ship's master, William Cox of Limehouse, both were interrogated by Peckham. The presumed loss of Gilbert and the failure of the expedition to reach the mainland and report on the prospects in the territories laid out for settlement—if only on paper—were bitter blows. But the Peckhams were confident they could surmount them.

With Walsingham's assistance they threw themselves into a final attempt to succeed where Gilbert had failed, opening their venture more widely to non-Catholics. They obtained verbal support at least from Drake and Hawkins, Bingham and Frobisher, and a number of London merchants. Before the end of the year they publicized the project in print. The small book, or large pamphlet, which appeared late in November or in December 1583 was the fullest statement so far to get into print making out a case for English settlement in America.[1] The title was *A*

[8] *Ibid.*, pp. 376–8. [9] *Ibid.*, I, 92.

[1] Reprinted, *ibid.*, II, 434–82. The dedication to Walsingham was signed at Oxford on 12 November by "G. P.," who appears almost certainly to have been Sir George's son, George Peckham, whose Catholic associations would not appear quite so obvious as his father's. Professor George B. Parks considered that "G. P." could have been George Peele and believed Peele and his friends might have completed the text and written the preliminary poems. Whatever may be said of the poems, the dedication makes sense only if it is by one of the Peckhams. See George B. Parks, "George Peele and His Friends as 'ghost'-poets," *Journal of English and Germanic Philology*, XLI (1942), 527–36.

true reporte of the late discoveries . . . of the Newfound Landes.[2] This told something of Gilbert's experiences in Newfoundland and went on to give a summary of early English, French, and Spanish experiences in the New World. The Peckhams said that these evidences convinced them that the continuance of this project to settle between 30° and 60° north latitude in America was "honest and profitable" and worth the cooperation of "all good minds" who are willing "to be assistants to this so commendable an enterprise."

A great deal is said about the desirability of converting the American Indians to Christianity, but nothing at all about the vital question of toleration as between Catholic and Protestant settlers. This was left to be worked out privately and in practice. The Peckhams had evidently read a good deal on the theory and practice of empire by Spain and considered that, while the Indians should be well treated, European Christians had a right to force their trade and their religion on them and to take over such parts of their land as were needed to set up a colony (scriptural proofs being adduced for these conclusions). The crown of England was said, through the mythical voyage of Madoc in the twelfth century and the real voyages of John Cabot at the end of the fifteenth, to have good prior title to North America. The potential trade and natural resources of North America were sufficient to make the settlers rapidly prosperous, and the advantages of possessing great landed estates there were constantly stressed. Finally, the colonization of North America was a patriotic, even a religious duty for all Englishmen who could do so. The pamphlet concluded, prosaically, with a list of the terms on which subscribers and adventurers would be accepted.

At its best this was vigorous propaganda, though it had its dull patches. With Walsingham's help, Peckham in January 1584 approached the Corporation of Exeter for support, but received very limited promises from the merchants. We know little more of the details of the venture, except that he got into some trouble over his title to the ship *Emanuel.*

The climate of opinion was now turning sharply against the Catholics.[3] In November 1583, Francis Throckmorton had been arrested, and under torture gradually gave away the details of an elaborate plot to oust Queen Elizabeth in which the Guises, Mary Queen of Scots, and the Spanish ambassador were all implicated. Mendoza was expelled from England in

[2] John C[harlewood] for J. Hinde, 1583; *S.T.C.* 19523. There were at least three different issues, which might reflect a greater and more prolonged interest in the tract than has hitherto been acknowledged. Quinn, *Roanoke Voyages,* I, 3–44; information from Miss K. F. Pantzer, Houghton Library, Harvard University.

[3] Quinn, *Gilbert,* I, 92–3, II, 480–2.

January 1584. Moreover, Throckmorton's revelations compromising two of the greatest Catholic lords, the earls of Northumberland and Arundell, tended to raise a new wave of suspicion of the loyalty of the remaining Catholic aristocracy and gentry. This made it less likely that Peckham would receive adequate support for his colonial plans, since his Catholic associations were so widely known. Finally, a little later in 1584, on the accusation of a certain John Nichols, Sir George Peckham was denounced for pro-Catholic activities and arrested. This effectively put an end to plans for an English Catholic colony for some twenty years. Peckham was in and out of prison for some years, appearing, together with his son and Sir Thomas Gerard, on a list of prisoners in 1586. Gerard nominally conformed late in life and was rewarded with the office of Captain of the Isle of Man. He died in 1601.

When the Spanish Armada arrived in 1588, the majority of the English Catholics of the upper classes gave assistance to the crown, and this meant that proceedings against the aristocrats and gentry (though not against the Catholic clergy) became less frequent while the war went on, though a number of Catholic gentlemen thought it wise to appear occasionally in their parish churches so that their loyalty might be publicly demonstrated. But very few changed their basic beliefs or their essentially conservative outlook on social questions. A minority of courtiers developed Catholic sympathies or became Catholics in the 1590's, though they were driven out of the court in the last years of the reign on account of their associations with the Earl of Essex. But American colonization could not be revived for any Englishmen until the war was over.

To some extent, the elaborate schemes of 1582 to 1584 were daydreams. Much more needed to be known of North America before anyone could launch out into empire-building there. The notion of great estates in a new land appealed to feudally minded gentlemen. But only with much more capital than most of them had, and the chance of a return on it from a staple crop, was large-scale aristocratic settlement possible. And it needed a somewhat greater degree of good will and tolerance on the part of the state than could be attained in Elizabethan England before Catholics would feel really free to go pioneering in a strange region while still nominally under the English crown. The period from 1585 to the end of the war with Spain was not suited to colonial adventures, at least by English Catholics. To remove them or encourage them to go in time of war, when their loyalty was to some degree in doubt, would have been quixotic and unrealistic. Moreover, during the early 1580's when the Peckham-Gerard plans were envisaged, colonization on an aristocratic basis was in fact Utopian and very difficult to achieve. In the next century, not only would more have been found out about North America, but better techniques for its exploitation were being developed and capital was accumulated in amounts which made effective colonization feasible, to some extent at least.

IV

WITH THE DEATH of Queen Elizabeth in March 1603, the situation of the English Catholic aristocracy and gentry appeared to change for the better. The pressures of war and the constant threat of being charged with treasonable activity were replaced by a more permissive atmosphere. James I's uncompromising view of monarchical power the most conservative aristocrat might respect. From the time of his arrival in England, he encouraged some members of the Catholic upper class to come to court and singled them out for notice and honors (among them Sir Thomas Arundell, who had been created a count of the Holy Roman Empire for his services against the Turks, and who in 1605 was made Lord Arundell of Wardour).

What the Catholics did not at first realize was that, while James could bring himself to tolerate their religious practices, he also retained many serious reservations about their church. The revelation that obscure intrigues (the Main Plot and the Bye Plot) were being mounted against him under Spanish auspices, in which Catholics as well as Sir Walter Ralegh and Lord Cobham were apparently involved, led to the revival of fears of a Catholic *coup d'état*. James's deep-seated resentment of the temporal claims of the Papacy and his fierce polemic with the Jesuits (whom he accused of sponsoring the doctrine of tyrannicide) made him especially suspicious of the Catholic priesthood. He was at any moment liable to put heavy penal legislation into effect against the priests. Consequently, though Catholics by and large benefited from his accession, his policy, or perhaps lack of a consistent policy, left some of them without any real sense of security. It is not surprising that they again began to think of a place of refuge overseas. With the Spanish war moving toward its end in 1604, American colonization once more became a legitimate sphere of speculation.

Henry Wriothesley, Earl of Southampton—"Shakespeare's Southampton" as A. L. Rowse has labeled him[4]—may have been the catalyst who brought the American idea to life again for the English Catholics. A prisoner in the Tower after the rebellion of the Earl of Essex, Southamp-

[4] A. L. Rowse, *Shakespeare and Southampton* (London, 1965), pp. 234–6.

ton appears to have invested in a small expedition to America under Captain Bartholomew Gosnold in 1602. This was a reconnaissance to the area which had already in 1582 been thought of as the site for a settlement. It was proposed to try out its resources by setting up a small trading post on its shores. Gosnold returned to England leaving no settlers behind, but bringing a description of an attractive, sunny, and accessible land across the ocean in what is now Massachusetts. His discoveries were rapidly given publicity in a little book by John Brereton which went into two editions,[5] while Sir Walter Ralegh, Edward Hayes (Gilbert's old companion), and the Reverend Richard Hakluyt, whose second edition of *The principal navigations* had been completed in 1600, all involved themselves in the scheme.

But in spite of the publicity, little or nothing was done by any of these people in 1603. In July, Ralegh toppled off his pinnacle and disappeared as a prisoner to the Tower. Edward Hayes is not known to have taken any further action after contributing some notes to Brereton's booklet. Richard Hakluyt did have something to do with a small ship which was taken out by Martin Pring from Bristol in 1603 and which traded happily for furs at Cape Cod during the summer,[6] but it was not concerned apparently with pioneering a colony. However, during the winter of 1604–5, Southampton seems to have made his brother-in-law, Sir Thomas Arundell, keenly interested in the idea of a Catholic expedition to America, and the latter began during the winter to collect Catholic support in England for such a venture.[7]

Arundell's activity remains obscure, but it is probable that rumors of his projects, probably vague at first, circulated not only in England but on the Continent, and indeed our first knowledge of the Catholic projects comes from the Continent and not England. In August 1604, agreement on a treaty of peace was reached between England and Spain. Although

[5] John Brereton, *A briefe and true relation of the discoverie of the north part of Virginia . . .*, 2 issues (London, G. Bishop, 1602); *S.T.C.* 3610–11.

[6] See Samuel Purchas, *Hakluytus Posthumus, or Purchas his Pilgrimes*, 4 vols. (1625), IV, 1659–67 (*S.T.C.* 20509); 20 vols. (Glasgow, 1906), XVIII. See p. 425 below.

[7] Rowse, *Shakespeare and Southampton*, pp. 236–7; also see Henry C. Burrage, *The Beginning of Colonial Maine* (Portland, 1914), pp. 37–9. In 1602, Arundell had been sheltering Lady Peckham during one of Sir George's spells in prison. When Peckham was released, Arundell refused to have him at his house on the grounds that he was too notorious a Catholic and would compromise him. Peckham appealed to Sir Robert Cecil to intercede for him with Arundell (Trimble, *Catholic Laity*, p. 171). An earlier association with Peckham may initially have aroused Arundell's interest in American prospects for Catholics.

ratifications were not exchanged until June 1605, it was clear that many men in the Spanish service would be disbanded, and there might be an opportunity for some of these ex-soldiers who were English Catholics to return to England. It would take some time to know how many, if any, would be allowed to return and how many wished to do so. The notion that some at least should join with Catholics from England to leave the Continent, not for their homeland but for America, seems to have arisen through the efforts of a Cornishman, Tristram Winslade.

He was a veteran Catholic soldier who had served for some thirty years in Continental armies and was a pensioner of the Spanish crown.[8] How he got wind of Arundell's ideas for a settlement we do not know. But he aimed to mobilize from among Catholic Englishmen on the Continent a thousand "husbandmen, laborers and craftesmen" who would be put under "the better and richer sort" of Catholics who intended to go to America. He thought the money for this venture could be found on the Continent. He proposed a wide appeal to Catholic Europe—to the Emperor Rudolf II and to the Archdukes who now ruled the Spanish Netherlands for Philip III, and some Italian princes. He even hoped to have an appeal launched from the pulpit for the aid of the colonists and for the expenses of a mission to convert the North American Indians to Christianity. In the form we know of, this was an interesting though scarcely a realistic project. It made no provision for acquainting the king of Spain with the plan or getting him to permit or tolerate it, and in the circumstances this was a very considerable handicap. But Winslade did take the plan to the most famous English Jesuit, the rector of the English College at Rome, Father Robert Parsons, who had for a generation been strongly pro-Spanish in his views. He knew of the older project of 1582 and still remembered it with hostility.

The document by Father Parsons entitled "My Judgment about Transferring English Catholiques to the Northern Partes of America for inhabitinge those partes and convertinge those barbarous people to Christianitie" is our authority both for Winslade's plans and for Parsons's

[8] Tristram Winslade was an activist among the exiles, concerned to overthrow the Protestant settlement and assist Spain to conquer the country. He wrote a treatise, "De praesenti statu Cornubiae et Devoniae," which commends the large number of nobles, gentlemen, and yeomen in Cornwall and Devon who are, he says, ready to assist the Spaniards during and after an invasion. The treatise, undated but assigned to *ca.* 1595, though it is likely to be prior to 1588, is in the Hans P. Kraus Collection of Drake Manuscripts (H. P. Kraus, *Sir Francis Drake: A Pictorial Biography* [Amsterdam, 1970], pp. 152–4, 193–4). See also A. J. Loomie, *The Spanish Elizabethans* (New York, 1963), pp. 248, 263.

hostile and almost conclusive reply.[9] Father Parsons was not too closely in touch with England at the moment. He did not believe that James would allow ex-soldiers to emigrate, nor did he think that James would let the Catholic gentry go to America after realizing their property in England. He was certainly wrong about the second point, though James's view was not tested so far as we know on the first. Father Parsons doubted, too, if "the better and richer sorts" of Catholics at home would really be willing to take the risk of going into the American wilderness; though again he was not wholly in touch with events there. Winslade needed the full cooperation of Catholics in England if he was to make any progress, and we do not know how far he had made soundings there, or indeed whether he was yet in touch with Sir Thomas Arundell.

Father Parsons was on firmer ground when he spoke of Spain. He was correct when he said that Winslade would not find it possible for discharged soldiers from the Spanish forces to leave Spain for America without the specific consent of the Spanish king. Nor was he likely to get much help from King Philip, who took the view (as Parsons said) that "no strange nation [shall] take footing in any part of the Indies." It was not sufficient for Winslade, or the English, to say that "those parts are not presently occupied by the Spaniards." In fact, "the care of the Spaniards is that no other European nation have footing in that continent beside themselves where a fleet may rest and refresh or fortify herself against the rest of the Indies possessed by them." On this account they had massacred the French in Florida in 1565, and, repeating the old threat Mendoza had made, which he may have recalled, Parsons said, "The like no doubt would they do to the English if they should go thither without their leave." He was probably right in thinking Spanish permission would not be forthcoming—though he did not expect Winslade to take him at his word and even thought he might well go to Spain to see for himself how the land lay.

One thing only, Parsons said, attracted him to the project. This was the possibility of bringing the Christian religion to the Indians: "the intention of converting these people liketh me so well, and in so high a degree as for that only I would desire myself to go in the journey, shutting my eyes to all other difficulties if it were possible to obtain it." In the end he offered Winslade one slight loophole. He could not bring him-

[9] This document was known to and used by J. G. Shea but without a reference to location (*The Church in the Colonies, 1531–1763* [New York, 1886], pp. 24–8). It was printed from Stonyhurst College, MS Anglia III, no. 53, in Thomas Hughes, *History of the Society of Jesus in North America, Documents,* I (New York, 1908), 3–5, and see also *Text,* I (New York, 1907), 153–5.

self to raise the matter either in Spain or in England, but if Winslade did so and received any encouragement in either place, he would bring up the matter in Rome and do what he could. The memories of a long career as an exile at the side of Spain and against the Tudor state made the new situation, with Stuart and Hapsburg trying to reestablish peace and friendship, unpalatable, and one can see that even to consider these propositions coolly was bitter to him.

The comfort he could offer Winslade was indeed slight, and we do not know that Winslade made any further moves in the matter. The reply by Father Parsons on 18 March 1605 virtually brought to an end this attempt to mobilize for an American enterprise Catholic ex-soldiers who, with the peace of 1598 followed by that of 1604, were now surplus to the Spanish forces. It is not wholly unlikely that further documents in Spain or in the Vatican archives may be found to throw some additional light on this.

V

WE MAY HERE turn aside for a moment to take notice of the situation in Ireland. The Nine Years' War which began there in 1594 had brought Queen Elizabeth and her government to appreciate that some *modus vivendi* should be made with those of her subjects in Ireland who were prepared to remain loyal even when tempted into rebellion by the formidable rebel forces in the field. At the same time, it was difficult to formulate terms of toleration while fighting was still in progress. Lord Mountjoy, Lord Deputy in Ireland 1600–6, was very conscious of this problem. On the one hand, he wanted to get rid of as many of the hostile Irish soldiery as possible and was prepared to consider shipping some of them to America. On the other, he wanted to strengthen the loyal Catholic element, especially in the port towns. Besides English Protestant colonies to prevent future risings, he contemplated the construction of protected Catholic cities and zones. There could be limited toleration in Ireland, he told Sir Robert Cecil, "in some principal towns and precincts after the manner of some French edicts" (especially the Edict of Nantes which made such arrangements for Protestants), but he thought these might be the better for an English Catholic infusion, saying, "Neither if any English papist or recusant shall for liberty of his conscience transfer his family and fortunes thither, do I hold it a matter of danger, but rather an expedient to draw on undertaking [i.e., colonization by the English] and to further population." [1] Even though no formal arrangement of this

[1] Hatfield House, CecilMS 139, fol. 136 (Hist.MSSComm., *CecilMSS*, XIV [London, 1940], 240).

type was reached, it is probable that a number of English Catholics were among those English who reinstated the Munster Plantation in the years after 1603, though this still requires investigation.

When Sir Robert Cecil was defending his government's record in dealing with the Irish war during discussions in the Star Chamber in November 1599, he took up this position: "But some will say that the Queen mighte have rooted out the whole Nation by this time. So hath the Spaniard done in the Indies, but her Majesty is more merciful for they must have some place to live in." [2] Mountjoy in the following years was also concerned that too many militant Roman Catholics should not continue to live in Ireland, and indeed many Irish soldiers took refuge on the Continent, followed by many noncombatants who fled for their lives from the devastated lands of Munster. Some "swordsmen" he thought might be lured away to the Low Countries or even to the Indies.[3] Spain in 1604 seems to have contemplated offering them some place in which to settle,[4] though it is not clear where this was to be.

Nor did other Continental powers know how to deal with them. Portugal enrolled many to go to Brazil. An English agent, Maillard Rickward, wrote from Lisbon on 10 October 1604: "Here are certain galleons now setting forth, together with 10 Dutch ships which carry 17 or 1800 soldiers toward Rio di Plata of Jenere [Rio de Janeiro]: because it is advertised that the Indians are risen against the Christians and defeated many: among these 1700 men, there are about 300 Irish, very naked, which may well be spared from hence." [5] We do not know the outcome in this case.

Similarly, the Irish were causing great problems in France, especially in Paris. In November 1605 it was reported that there were twelve hundred to two thousand Irish on the streets of Paris; attempts were to be made to get King James to take them home.[6] "Some," we are told, "have talked of bringing them to Canada." Unfortunately, "Monsieur du Mont [Pierre du Gua, Sieur de Monts] who has come back from there says that they will be useless and on no account will they receive men so useless that they do not know how or wish to work." After his experience of an unusually severe winter at Ste. Croix in 1604–5, De Monts was disinclined to recruit for his new settlement at Port Royal men who were unlikely to stand up to much hardship—refugees, apart from their personal

2 *The Dr. Farmer Chetham MS.*, 2 vols. (Manchester, 1873), ed. A. B. Grosart, p. 37.

3 See D. B. Quinn, *The Elizabethans and the Irish* (Ithaca, 1966), pp. 119–20, 183.

4 P.R.O., State Papers, Foreign, France, S.P. 78/51, fol. 226v.

5 P.R.O., State Papers, Foreign, Newsletters, S.P. 101/90, fol. 231.

6 David Buisseret, "The Irish at Paris, 1605," *Irish Historical Studies*, XIV (1964), 58–60, citing B.N., Fonds Français, MS 15578, fol. 246.

qualities, frequently needing rehabilitation before being fit to be pioneers.

The problems of getting rid of Irish military men to the Spanish Indies, to Brazil, to Canada were partly associated with their religion. By 2 June 1606 Villeroy could report to Boderie that a multitude of Irish beggars were being shipped from Rouen, but the ships were bound for Ireland and not for distant parts.[7] Though James I eventually accepted the return of many Irish from France, a chief reason for keeping them away was that Catholics who could possibly revive the Irish resistance to England were unwelcome, but it might just be possible to accommodate them in American lands, even if this was done by European powers which themselves were Catholic. It is clear that during these early years of the seventeenth century the Americas were being uniquely regarded as a dumping ground for European surpluses, but perhaps especially for Irish and English Catholics.

We should return now to Sir Thomas Arundell, whose plans for a Catholic settlement in America led to the setting out on 5 March 1605 of the ship *Archangell*.[8] She was equipped largely by Arundell in Southampton, though some Plymouth merchants were also involved in the venture. The captain, George Waymouth, was certainly not a Catholic. He came from a Protestant Devonshire shipowning and shipbuilding family.[9] His father had subscribed to Gilbert's venture in 1582, and George himself had gained experience on an unsuccessful voyage in 1602 in search of a Northwest Passage. He was a good practical sailor and had no navigational difficulties on the voyage except that, so far as we can see, he was expected to concentrate on finding the elusive "*Refugio*" which Gilbert and Gosnold had looked for earlier in vain. Instead, Waymouth concentrated on the coast of Maine, to the north. His main job was to find a

[7] B.N., Fonds Français, MS 7108, fols. 21–5; N. E. McClure, *The Letters of John Chamberlain*, 2 vols. (Philadelphia, 1939), I, 231.

[8] James Rosier, *A true relation* (1605) (see p. 389, *n.* 1, below); Purchas, *Pilgrimes*, IV, 1659–67, and XVIII, 335–59.

[9] A seagoing family in Cockington, Devon, which had raised itself from coastal fishing to shipbuilding and shipowning in two generations. Waymouth's initial experience at sea may have been gained in the Newfoundland trade, though this has not yet been established. In 1602 he led a small expedition to seek a Northwest Passage to China for the East India Company, which failed but was not discreditable to him (Purchas, *Pilgrimes* [1625], III, 809–14; [1906], XVIII, 306–18). The credentials he carried with him for the Emperor of China were brought back and are now in the Lancashire County Record Office, Preston. He presented a treatise on navigation, "The Jewell of Artes," to King James in 1604 (B.M., AdditionalMS 18859); another copy from the collection of Mr. Henry C. Taylor is now in the Beinecke Library, Yale University.

place where land was available for Catholic settlers, but he was also to find, if he could, fishing grounds for his merchant backers. This is probably what brought him farther north than Arundell had expected him to go, for something was already known of the good fishing of the Gulf of Maine.

The most interesting individual amongst the personnel of the *Archangell* was James Rosier, whose task it was to write a journal of the voyage and to find out what he could of the natural resources of the area and the people who lived there. His identity is a matter of difficulty, so we cannot tell whether he was a Catholic, though it is not impossible that he was and had been in Arundell's service.[1] Two of Arundell's own men, a Welsh boy called Owen Griffen and a man by the name of Booles, almost certainly Catholics, were with them.

In many ways the voyage of the *Archangell* was idyllic. Leaving Dartmouth on 31 March, they reached Cape Cod on 14 May and worked across the Gulf of Maine to Monhegan Island, where they put ashore on 18 May. As soon as they were on land Rosier went round examining the trees, which would make fine masts and provide planking, resin, and tar to support a shipbuilding industry. The spring vegetation gave promise of summer fruit. The water was plentifully supplied with oversize cod and other fish. After the explorers had oriented themselves, they could see land, high mountains they thought, on the mainland to the north, with a number of smaller islands between them and the mainland. They eventually set out northward and found a low attractive island (now Allen Island) alongside which was an excellent anchorage, which they named St. George's Harbor, as it is still called today. Waymouth went ahead in the shallop, a large boat, to reconnoiter the mainland and came back with news that there was a large inlet into the land to the north. They had by this time made contact with the Penobscot Indians, who had come out to gather shellfish on the islands and were doing some

[1] This was apparently the James Rosier who took his M.A. at Cambridge in 1596. (J. and J. A. Venn, *Alumni Cantabrigienses,* III [1924], 488). He was formerly identified with a James Rosier who became a Catholic in 1602 and, as James Ross, was ordained a priest at Rome in 1609 (*D.N.B.*). Correspondence with Miss P. Renold, Honorary Secretary of the Catholic Record Society, and inquiries kindly made by her on my behalf, indicate that the identities of James Ross and of our James Rosier are now believed to be separate. There are some indications in the version of the Rosier narrative preserved by Purchas (*Pilgrimes* [1625], IV, 1662–6; [1906], XVIII, esp. 344, 355) that Rosier understood he was preparing the way for a Catholic colony, was sympathetic to that objective, and may have been himself a Catholic. It is unfortunate that more specific information about him is not so far available.

trade with them, and found out something about the area by means of signs and sketch maps. Eventually they set off to explore the opening into the mainland. They entered a wide river, with attractive woods but also with parklike flat plains on its banks, and numerous coves.

Rosier was enchanted with this, and some of the men thought it a fairer river than the Severn or the Thames. He says they worked up the river twenty-six miles, though actually it was not more than about ten miles in all from the river-mouth to the wide bay where they eventually anchored. Rosier neglected to note in his narrative that they here came to a natural limit, the Fall Line, and that beyond the bay, the wide river turned rapidly into a modest stream. They went ashore to try to reach the Camden Hills, the "mountains" they had seen from Monhegan, but their armor proved too hot for them and after a three-mile walk they returned to their boat, though bringing with them a very good impression of the fertility of the land. The St. George River, as it is still called from Waymouth's naming, is a very pleasant estuary and was once important for its shipbuilding, but never became a center of population and is not so today. Waymouth made charts of the coast while Rosier made notes of the natural resources, picking up all he could from such Indians as they met and from the five whom, rather callously, they seized as guides for later expeditions. They sailed for home on 16 June, arriving back at Dartmouth on 18 July. America, they had shown, with good fortune was within easy reach.

When Waymouth got home, he found that Lord Arundell of Wardour was no longer in England and had given up the project altogether. He and Rosier had to look for other means of support. They had some backing for another fishing voyage on behalf of the Plymouth merchants, and while Waymouth turned to raise support at court, Rosier made contact with Sir John Zouche of Codnor in Derbyshire, who came in as chief promoter in Lord Arundell's place.[2] Waymouth claims to have found the king sympathetic and a number of the members of his Privy Council and other courtiers willing to give some help. It is likely that some at least were Catholics, though Zouche was not, but the Gunpowder Plot in November 1605 brought almost all Catholic courtiers under some degree of suspicion, and it would certainly have been unwise for any Catholic

[2] Agreement between George Waymouth and Sir John Zouche signed, *inter alia,* by James Rosier, 30 October 1605. Formerly in P.R.O., Manchester Papers, P.R.O. 30/15, 2, no. 203. The collection was dispersed in 1970 (Parke-Bernet Galleries) as *The American Papers of Sir Nathaniel Rich,* and this item (no. 60) was sold on 5 May 1970 for $6000 to Mr. John Fleming, bookseller, New York. It is now in the University of Virginia Library, Charlottesville.

lord or prominent gentleman to take part in publicity for an American venture for the time being. Rosier and Waymouth, instead, published an attractive pamphlet about the end of 1605, *A true relation of the most prosperous voyage made this present yeare 1605, by Captain George Waymouth in the discovery of the land of Virginia.*[3] Written, it was said, "by James Rosier, a gentleman employed in this voyage," it was intended to appeal to gentlemen and merchants in general who were prepared to invest in an American gamble, and (as we have seen in describing the voyage) it was an attractive prospectus. But behind the scenes another move was under way. Lord Salisbury and Chief Justice Popham were bringing together various merchant interests, mainly in London and Plymouth, into a new, large-scale Virginia Company. This was well on the way by March 1606, and a charter was granted to it on 10 April.

Sir John Zouche's promise to get two ships to sea by the end of April was not performed, but in June plans were in hand to petition the king to allow three hundred Catholic households to go to Virginia.[4] Though we do not know whether James saw or commented on the petition, and though evidence is not conclusive, we may assume that the continued pressure brought by Zouche on the Lord High Admiral, the Earl of Nottingham, to obtain a passport was linked to this Catholic plan. When finally, on 14 August, he got his passport and license under bond not to misbehave at sea, he seems to have had two ships and a pinnace almost ready to leave.[5] But we do not hear of them sailing; the 1605–6 Catholic plans were as stillborn as those before them.

The Irish project with which Sir Ralph Bingley was associated involved sending many ships from Ireland to Virginia in 1606,[6] and it seems likely that this was linked both to a London Fishmongers' plan and to Sir John Zouche's venture in a combined scheme to get Irish Catholics to settle in Maine or some other part of New England; but all was dissipated in inefficiency, piracy, and the gradual and inevitable loss of confidence by the parties concerned.

We may note that, though Winslade failed to get an American opening for English ex-soldiers, his activities may have helped to detach Lord Arundell from his American plans. For it was decided that instead of

[3] Imp. G. Bishop, 1605; *S.T.C.* 21322. Purchas, *Pilgrimes* (1625), IV, 1459–67; (1906), XVIII, 335–59.

[4] Hist.MSSComm., *CecilMSS*, XVIII (London, 1940), 173, 181–2.

[5] See James Franklin Jameson, in *Virginia Magazine of History*, XIX (1911), 195–6.

[6] See D. B. Quinn, "The Voyage of *Triall* 1606–1607, an Abortive Virginia Venture," *American Neptune*, XXXI (1971), 85–103.

sending ex-soldiers to America, some of them should be reenlisted as an English regiment under the Archdukes in the Spanish Low Countries. Some of these men were to come from England and would probably be Catholics; others would be reenlisted from Continental armies; all would be under Lord Arundell's command, and he would be the guarantee that their ultimate allegiance was to King James. This provided for Catholic soldiers a genuine alternative to the chance to win American lands for themselves. By autumn of 1605, Lord Arundell was installed in his new command at the head of fifteen hundred men, though his command did not sit too easily upon him and he did not hold it for very long.

Meantime, Virginia had at last been settled. In May 1607, Jamestown had been founded by the London branch of the Virginia Company, while a fort was also built on the Kennebec River in Maine by the Plymouth branch. Jamestown was kept alive by strenuous efforts as a permanent English settlement in America, but Fort St. George in Maine was soon abandoned. It was probably the failure of the Plymouth group to establish itself in Maine, together with regrets at the opportunities he thought he had missed by going to Brussels rather than America in 1605, that briefly roused once more in Lord Arundell the idea of going to America. His plan, as reported by the Spanish Ambassador, Zúñiga, on 7 January and 5/15 March 1609,[7] was to take out five hundred men from England—mainly Catholics we may assume—and to add to them the same number of Irishmen (reviving earlier plans), and with this joint force to fortify America. The Spanish thought this was to be fortification against the Spaniards, and in southern Virginia—that is, the modern state—not, as was more likely, in Maine where the French were now considered by the English a threat to their interests. However, there were two great difficulties. Lord Arundell wanted a patent separate from that of the Virginia Company, and this was not easy to arrange. Further, he wanted money from King James to start a colony, which the king would never spare, and an overt promise of freedom of conscience in America, which he might think it impolitic to give. In the end this scheme, like all the others, lapsed. Arundell settled back in Wardour Castle to live the quiet life of a Catholic nobleman for a further thirty years.

[7] Letter of 7/17 January, in Alexander Brown, *The Genesis of the United States,* 2 vols. (Boston, 1890), I, 198; Philip L. Barbour, ed., *The Jamestown Voyages Under the First Charter, 1606–1609,* 2 vols. (Cambridge, Eng., 1969), II, 254–5, 269. Mr. Barbour was unable to locate the earlier letter translated in Brown.

VI

No excessive pressures on Catholics to emigrate for religion's sake existed after perhaps 1609, but there remained strong incentives to invest in business enterprise. Many of the estates of the landed gentry among them had run down during the time of fines and intermittent imprisonment; there was considerable temptation to rebuild their fortunes by speculation. The landed class as a whole was inclined at this time to risk money in overseas ventures, along with many merchants,[8] and it may well be that Catholics were rather more likely to make such investments than non-Catholic landowners. Nor were the Catholics entirely free of pressure: not all possible fines were exacted at all times, but some well might be, either through informers who shared part of the penalties imposed or by the action of hostile local authorities. As the difficulties of the Stuarts increased, they were inclined to use the recusancy fines as a reserve form of revenue to be imposed for financial rather than strictly ecclesiastical reasons. This was especially the case after 1629. Thomas Wentworth as president of the Council of the North was particularly active in doing so, making Lord Baltimore, an old friend and associate, protest and call for "true justice," not severity, in his dealings with the Catholic magnates.[9] Intermittent denunciations of priests and occasional orders for their expulsion kept aristocratic Catholics continually aware of the risks of their situation. The result was that some members of the Catholic upper class continued to bear in mind the possibility of a foothold outside England to which they might retire in case of necessity.

George Calvert is the outstanding example. He served King James in a number of offices and from 1619 to 1625 held the important post of Secretary of State.[1] His Catholic sympathies went back well into this period, but he would not openly declare his allegiance to the Catholic

[8] Theodore K. Rabb, *Enterprise and Empire* (Princeton, 1967), an analysis of eight thousand investors, 1575–1630, which was not able, however, to segregate Catholic investors from others.

[9] Cited in Havran, *Catholics in Caroline England,* p. 95, from W. Knowler, ed., *The Earle of Strafforde's Letters and Despatches* (1739), pp. 52–3. How early the climate changed, however, in the seventeenth century is illustrated in Edmund Gardiner, *The triall of tobacco* (H. L[ownes] for M. Lownes, 1609), *S.T.C.* 11564. A Catholic physician, already in 1609 he could get a license for a book in which he wrote "I speak as a Romist," and recalled his "long endurance in prison of the king's Bench" (sigs. L1v., Q1v.). Though interested in Virginia, he did not apparently attempt to go there.

[1] See *D.N.B.*, s.n. There is no satisfactory modern biography.

Church while he held office under the crown. Only in 1625 did he give up his office, avow himself a Roman Catholic, and—though he received the title of Lord Baltimore—leave the royal service. He seems to have had close connections with Lord Arundell, and Arundell's influence may have led him into overseas investment and finally to colonization.

It is not surprising that Calvert should have begun his overseas enterprises in Ireland. Many landowners, English and Scottish, and mainly Protestants at first, were involved during James I's reign in colonizing parts of that country which were confiscated by the crown. Calvert had served as an official in Ireland and put himself forward as an undertaker, a potential colonizer, when the king confiscated part of County Longford (O'Ferrall's country of Annaly) in 1619. He was given an extensive grant of lands there, though he was not in a great hurry to take them up. In 1622 it was found that he held 2304 acres but that he had not yet begun to reside on his land or indeed to build anything there.[2] He did later get some tenants and set up a household, while in 1625 he took his title as Baron Baltimore in the Kingdom of Ireland from an obscure holding on his estate.[3]

But by this time he had already gone farther afield to look for a site for a plantation. This he found in Newfoundland. English settlement there had begun in 1611, but the Newfoundland Company had not gone ahead very fast and had sold off part of its rights to aristocratic speculators. Sir George Calvert purchased a substantial part of the Avalon Peninsula in the southeast part of the island, next to the holding of Lord Falkland, who had also served in Ireland and was in 1623 to attempt to bring out Irish settlers. Calvert got a royal grant of his land in the same year. He acted at first through agents. In 1621 Captain Edward Wynne had installed a dozen men for him at Ferryland, and Captain David Powell brought fifty more in 1622. Their main task was to lay out village settlements, to begin cod-fishing on a commercial scale, and to build a manor house for Sir George. The location of this house has recently been discovered, or rediscovered,[4] and it is clear that it occupied a site with a very fine view northward. It was protected to some extent from the prevailing westerly winds, but exposed to those from the north and east.

2 "Longford. Sir George Calvert 2304 [acres.] The Patent is lately passed, no Residence nor Building." Survey of Plantations in Ireland, 1622, B.M., SloaneMS 4756, fol. 126v.

3 Hamill Kenny, "New Light on an Old Name," *Maryland Historical Magazine*, XLIX (1954), 116–21.

4 J. R. Harper, "In Quest of Lord Baltimore's House at Ferryland," *Canadian Geographical Journal*, LXI (1960), 106–13.

When Lord Baltimore felt free to leave England in 1625, he intended to go himself to Newfoundland, but for various reasons found it difficult to get away at once. He sent Sir Arthur Aston to speed up the construction of his house and paid it a first short visit in 1627. He was impressed with what he saw; the situation in summer was attractive, and he decided to make the great move to America. Thus in 1628 he set out to found a Catholic colony in Newfoundland with his family: his wife, his sons, his daughters, sons-in-law, two priests, and servants and associates to the number of forty. There was a protest from an Anglican clergyman already there, the Reverend Erasmus Stourton, at the appearance of priests and the open saying of Mass, but Baltimore was strong enough to expel him from the island.

He in turn, however, was beaten by the weather. A long period of snow and ice lasting, he said in 1629, from October to May was too much for him. He sent the women home as soon as he could in the spring, and he himself set sail in August for Virginia. He had lost ten persons during the winter, and at one time had fifty sick on his hands. But he left behind him small Catholic settlements at Ferryland and Petty Harbour which had some continuous existence.[5] The Calvert title to Avalon survived after the Restoration but was eventually set aside.

Lord Baltimore turned to Virginia as a more clement place to settle. The crown had taken over its administration from the Company in 1625, and it was now a flourishing colony—or, as some said, a rich tobacco plantation. Baltimore thought there would be room for him somewhere along its borders. He wrote, therefore, to Charles I before leaving Ferryland that he considered himself cut out to be a colonist, "my inclination . . . carrying me naturally to these kind of works." He was bringing forty persons with him to Virginia, "where I hope to lay my bones I know not how soon, and in the meantime may yet do the King and my Country more service there by planting of Tobacco." He had made the economic choice between cod and tobacco.[6]

Yet he did not find acceptance there. The colonists were stoutly Anglican and would admit him only if he took the oaths of allegiance and supremacy which, in the form then current, he had renounced when he gave up his secretaryship of state. So he had unwillingly to turn his ship back to England, and it was two more years before he got a grant of his own for a colony to be established to the north of the colony of Virginia,

[5] Gillian T. Cell, *English Enterprise in Newfoundland, 1577–1660* (Toronto, 1969), pp. 92–5.

[6] Lawrence C. Wroth, *Tobacco or Codfish: Lord Baltimore Makes His Choice* (New York, 1954).

beyond the River Potomac. Charles I gave it the name Maryland in honor of his queen, Henrietta Maria, but it can scarcely have escaped his notice that this name explicitly associated it in the minds of Catholics and Protestants alike with the Marian cult, and this made it an avowedly Catholic colony.

There was to be no ambiguity about the name of its first settlement: St. Mary's.[7] But George Calvert was not himself to plant it. He died on 15 April 1632, and the Maryland patent was passed shortly afterward to his son Cecilius, second Lord Baltimore, who went ahead with his father's plans. Continuity is evident here too, since he had married Ann Arundell, second daughter of Lord Arundell of Wardour.

By 1632 it might be thought that the Catholics were secure enough in England, with a Catholic queen installed at court and with Parliament indefinitely suspended. But upper-class Catholics knew that they were feared and hated by the majority in the country and that the observance of their religious practices was on sufferance only. Moreover, the idea of a patriarchal, feudal principality where a conservative social order could be enshrined in permanent institutions had its special attraction for them. The main thing, however, was that their religion would be free from interference. And America might provide a place of refuge for others, too, if the laws were again enforced in England. In Maryland they could remain as attached to their customs and religion as they wished, and would at the same time maintain their traditional allegiance to the crown. Now at last they could be colonists with a reasonable hope of subsistence, or even wealth; for tobacco was, and would be for some time, a gold mine.

Though Maryland was to be a Roman Catholic colony, with a Catholic Lord Proprietor and a Catholic governor under him, and with Catholic gentlemen bringing their tenants to settle, it was not to be exclusively Catholic. It was a business proposition. Money invested in it could, even must, come to some extent from Protestants. Protestant settlers and servants would be needed as much as Catholics to get the colony under way. Any undue exclusiveness in selecting settlers could rebound in a

[7] The name St. George's River (now St. Mary's River) was given to the inlet from the Potomac on which St. Mary's has stood since 1634. (The name had first been applied to the river in Maine—still the St. George River—found by the Waymouth expedition sent out by Lord Arundell in 1605; cf. pp. 388–91 above.) Among the prominent early settlers was a Dr. Thomas Gerrard, and it would be interesting to know whether he had any family connections with Sir Thomas Gerard. These and other indications of possible continuity between the earlier and the later Catholic ventures may be traced in Henry Chandler Forman, *Jamestown and St. Mary's: Buried Cities of Romance* (Baltimore, 1938).

wave of opposition at home. Discretion must be the watchword; full toleration for Anglicans was essential, since any attempt to prosecute or even curb upholders of the established church might produce an invasion from Virginia, if nothing else. Anglican churches would appear as a token of conformity. Few Protestants and fewer Catholics at this period believed in religious toleration in principle; for most people on both sides it meant tolerating the intolerable. But the Catholics who were emigrating to Maryland had more recently lived under some degree of toleration in England and realized they must experiment with it in Maryland. Any serious discrimination against Protestants could bring with it the threat of active reprisals.

Discretion was the first requisite in the instructions given by Lord Baltimore to his brother Leonard on 13 November 1633 for the plantation of Maryland.[8] In dealings with the Virginia Colony, only practicing Anglican Marylanders were to be used (even this did not prevent fierce quarrels, but they were not primarily religious). The priests who joined the colonists, Fathers White and Altham, were to be brought on board quietly at the Isle of Wight, not to take ship openly at London. It was laid down that "all Acts of Romane Catholique Religion to be done as privately as may be, and that they instruct all Roman Catholiques to be silent on all occasions of discourse concerning matters of Religion." Strict instructions were given "that they should suffer no Scandall, nor offence to be given to any of the Protestants, whereby any complaint may hereafter be made by them in Virginia or in England." And also that "the said Governor and Commissioners treate Protestants with as much mildness and favour as Justice will permitt. And this to be observed at Land as well as at Sea." These were the provisions of a tolerance of caution rather than of conviction; but they worked. When Maryland had an assembly of its own, in 1649, toleration was written into the Statute Book of Maryland.

With the creation of a Catholic colony, English Catholics at last established a degree of freedom for the exercise of their religion that they did not enjoy in the British Isles until 1829. Accident, the vicissitudes of war and policy, and the slow approach to a practical, businesslike attitude toward the exploration and exploitation of America had delayed Catholic settlement there from 1581, when the first rumors of it emerged in England, until the *Ark* and the *Dove* reached Maryland in 1634, fifty-three years later.

[8] First printed in *The Calvert Papers,* I, Maryland Historical Society (Baltimore, 1889), 131–40; most readily available in C. C. Hall, ed., *Narratives of Early Maryland, 1633–1684* (New York, 1906), pp. 16–17.

Summary

THE LOVE of the strange, desire to escape from the old, the lure of gold, and the reward of honest toil for fish or furs—these were among the incentives that drew men westward. The cramped economic life of old Europe and the new thrusts of greedy and forceful merchants and speculators, the ease with which the sailing ship could now move through the oceans, the desire for a Utopia—whether as a place to live well, to prepare for Heaven, or merely to escape enemies—these impelled men less immediately. The threats of wild nature checked their enthusiasms, made them turn back: disease, plants that might prove poisonous, beasts that might attack—above all, the unknown quantity which the native inhabitants were. So the movement toward and away from America was a kind of seesaw of incentives and repulsions which eventually led to a plunge forward, a decision to take risks. Was this chance, or the working out of expansionist trends in the European economy, or the competing rivalry of jealous states? The answer is not clear; it must be looked for in a total context of social life, techniques, and economic prodding. But in the late sixteenth and early seventeenth centuries religion, too, could prick men on to western wanderings.

PART V

Preludes to Permanent Settlement

Prologue

THE TURN of the century—the year 1600—was a genuine turning point. Thereafter, French and English were to compete continuously with each other and with Spain for settlement rights and territory. In the beginning they had almost too much choice. It took the English some years, from 1602 to 1608, to establish where and how they would attempt to settle, and the French took as long. On the English side we have a series of reconnaissances—Mace and Gosnold in 1602, Gilbert and Pring in 1603, Waymouth in 1605, Challons and Hanham in 1606—before a band of permanent settlers put ashore in either Virginia or New England. We know little about certain aspects of these preliminary voyages, though it is slowly becoming possible to add some slight documentation on a few of them.

Samuel Mace's expedition is one of these. Some rough notes among Thomas Harriot's papers help us to make a better estimate of its objectives in trading with the Indians south of Roanoke Island: to gain certain economic advantages and also to make contact (if they had survived) with the lost colonists of 1590. For the following year, 1603, we now have the surprising information that some Indians were brought to London, and this may possibly be a clue to another ship, part of Gilbert's venture of 1603, which might have made a reconnaissance of Chesapeake Bay. That such a probe had at some time been made always seemed likely, in view of the confidence with which Newport entered it in 1607. Exactly where some of the early New England reconnaissance voyagers went remains in many instances far from clear. The expedition of Martin Pring, it seems, may have made its summer camp on Provincetown Bay—not Plymouth Harbor—and if so, the Pilgrims of 1620 were greater pioneers than they have appeared in their final choice of site.

We know also that expeditions were planned and even sailed from England after the Virginia Company was chartered in April 1606. And we can follow the shadowy, haunting memory of the Lost Colony, as it has come to be called, from the experiments of 1584–90 into the new period that began in 1607. These ghostly inhabitants of Virginia or North Carolina or wherever continue to appear vaguely out of the mists to the new settlers at Jamestown. They never materialize in the shape of living men. They begin to fade out of consciousness in America and in England only when the Virginia Company is itself in decline, and then have to await resuscitation at the hands of romantics of the nineteenth and twentieth centuries.

CHAPTER FIFTEEN

Thomas Harriot and the Virginia Voyages of 1602

THE VOYAGE of Samuel Mace in 1602 in search of the lost colonists has remained very poorly documented, being attested only by a note printed in John Brereton, *A briefe and true relation of the discoverie of the north part of Virginia* . . . (London, G. Bishop 1602),[1] a few months after Mace's return, and by a brief indirect mention in a letter by Sir Walter Ralegh in August 1602.[2] We do not know the name of the ship: Brereton describes it as "a small bark" and Ralegh as a "pinnace." We might therefore think of it as being a vessel of some thirty to fifty tons burden. Brereton tells us that it was under the command of Samuel Mace (who elsewhere appears as Mayce) of Weymouth, "who had been at Virginia twice before, and was employed by Sir Walter Ralegh to find those people which were left there in the yeere 1587." Mace left Weymouth, Dorset, in March 1602 and made an American landfall "fortie leagues to the Southwestward of Hatarask, in thirty foure degrees or thereabout." [3] Hatarask is not Cape Hatteras but the inlet named Port Ferdinando or Hatarask in John White's maps of the 1585–6 Roanoke Island settlement: it corresponded very roughly with

[1] This is a composite work, and it is not clear whether John Brereton, who contributed the first item and is named on the title page, was also the compiler. For convenience, Brereton is credited with having placed the item (which appears on p. 14) in the volume.

[2] Edward Edwards, *The Life of Sir Walter Ralegh . . . with his Letters*, 2 vols. (London, 1868), II, 251–3.

[3] "Myne [pinnes] fell 40 leaugs to the west of it," Ralegh said. *Ibid.*, p. 251.

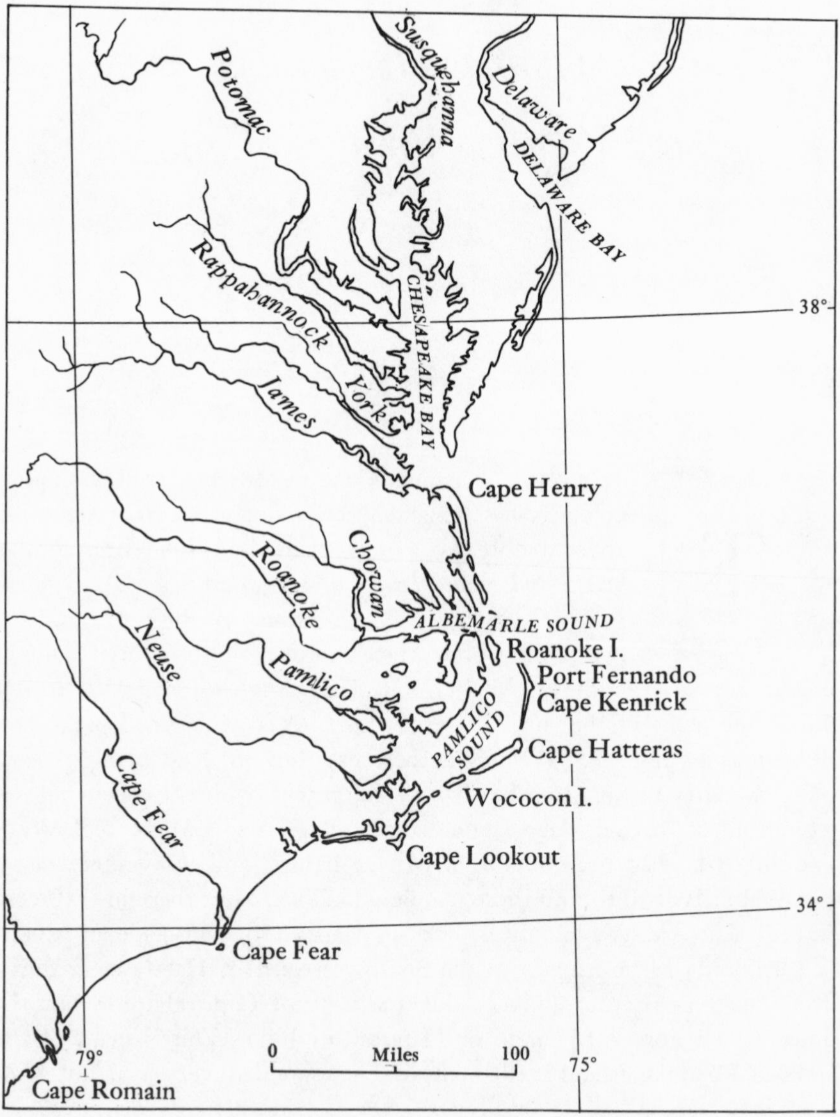

The Virginia shore, 1584–1625.

the modern Oregon Inlet in the Carolina Outer Banks, though it was a little farther north, almost opposite the south end of Roanoke Island. The actual location of the landfall must remain in some considerable doubt. Forty leagues (120 miles) south of Hatarask would place it at or near the modern Cape Lookout. Modern Cape Fear is at 34° north latitude but is approximately one hundred miles coastwise to the southwest of Cape Lookout. A latitude error of that magnitude was possible at this time, but is sufficiently large to be improbable. All we can say is that the landfall is unlikely to have been farther north than Cape Lookout and could well have been somewhere appreciably farther south, though not so far as Cape Fear. It took place, therefore, on the southern section of the Carolina Outer Banks.

Very little is known of the Indians who at this time inhabited the area between Cape Fear and Cape Lookout and the sounds behind the lower section of the Carolina Outer Banks. The Cape Fear Indians (linked with the Waccamaw of South Carolina) were of Siouan stock and were unlikely to have been familiar with Carolina Algonquian. The Coree (Coranine) and the Neuse (Neusiok) Indians of the sounds behind the Outer Banks are believed to have been in close contact with the Algonkian tribes farther north and so, probably, familiar with their speech.[4] If any contacts were made by Mace's men with the Indians it is likely to have been with the latter tribes. The shoreline vegetation would not vary greatly over the possible range of territory: thick forests would be found on the inner, sound side of the Carolina Outer Banks.

We are told that the members of the expedition stayed on land for a month, and that "from that place where they abode" they collected a considerable cargo of the vegetable products of the area. These indications would seem to point to their having built a summer camp on shore, no doubt reasonably well-defended in case of Indian attack. A similar program was followed by Martin Pring in the Cape Cod area in the summer of 1603. The Englishmen were briefed with at least a few words of the Carolina Algonquian language and perhaps with a systematic vocabulary and phrasebook.[5] We have no indication that they made contact with the Indians: had they met with possibly Algonquian-speaking Indians of the Cape Lookout area they might have used these aids to ask questions, including inquiries as to the whereabouts of the lost colonists of 1587. But we have no indication whether or not they learned anything.

[4] Quinn, *Roanoke Voyages*, II, 872; John R. Swanton, *The Indian Tribes of North America*, Smithsonian Institution, Bureau of American Ethnology, Bull. 145 (Washington, 1952), pp. 75, 78, 82, 89, 100–1.

[5] See p. 411 below.

The main practical purpose of the expedition was to bring back roots, bark, and leaves of vegetable products of the area which had some value for medicine or for their odor. Thomas Harriot's *A briefe and true report of the new found land of Virginia* (London, 1588) had provided a guide to the "merchantable commodities" to be found in the Roanoke Island area.[6] They included sassafras, commended for its sweet-smelling timber and for the medicinal value believed to lie in its wood, bark, leaves, and roots, its special quality being antisyphilitic. Amongst the roots known to the Indians, Harriot drew attention to the woody smilaxes which he identified with the China root, brought from the Far East and extensively used in medicine in Europe. He also referred rather cautiously to "Sweet Gummes of diuers kinds, and many other Apothecary drugges," without giving further details,[7] though it is likely that he knew more than he cared at this time to put down. The only other available guide in print was Nicholas Monardes's *Joyfull newes out of the newe found worlde*—the third English edition was published in 1596—giving data on a few Florida plants of medicinal value.

The expedition evidently settled down on shore to cut down trees and excavate their roots. It is probable that they had someone on board who had some medicinal knowledge of plants, perhaps trained by experience with Harriot in the Roanoke Island colony of 1585–6. We are told very little of the kinds and quantities brought to England. They included sassafras, probably in some appreciable quantity, since it was in demand and commanded a good price in the English market. "Radix Chinae or the China Root," which had similar attractions, was also obtained. We learn further of three spicelike products. One was "Benzoin"—this being a gum with medicinal qualities brought from Sumatra. The American plant was probably the wild spicebush (*Lincera benzoin*), the obvious botanical analogue to its Oriental counterpart; another was "Cassia lignia." The cassias of North America are small plants only; the trees with cinnamonlike bark are natives of the West Indies and Central America. This might possibly be the sweet gum (*Liquidambar styraciflua*) or perhaps a dogwood (*Cornus*). The final product specified is described simply as "a rinde of a tree more strong than any spice yet known," which strongly suggests a magnolia, probably the sweet bay (*Magnolia virginiana*), whose bark is noticeably aromatic and bitter.[8]

[6] Quinn, *Roanoke Voyages*, I, 314–87. [7] *Ibid.*, pp. 329, 334, 348–9.

[8] Merritt L. Fernald, ed., *Gray's Manual of Botany*, 8th ed. (New York, 1950), pp. 678–9, includes with the main species of spicebush another, Jove's Fruit *(Lincera melissafolium)*, as local to North Carolina, while Francis P. Porcher, *Resources of the Southern Fields and Forests . . .* (Richmond, 1863), pp. 354–5, indicates older

Besides these we are told they brought "diuers other commodities which hereafter in a larger discourse may come to light"—which is not very informative. The extended account of the voyage has never been found; that it was announced suggests that it was to be composed by a member of the expedition who had some knowledge of the natural history and medicinal flora of the area. The products named are more likely to have been found in the sheltered woods of the interior of the broader stretches of the Carolina Outer Banks and on the inner (sound) side than very near the ocean, so that some exploration was necessary before a suitable site for the camp could be located.

The second phase of the voyage involved an attempt to sail farther north along the coast to the Hatarask entry into the Outer Banks, to search for the lost colonists. "When they came along the coast," Brereton tells us, "to seeke the people, they did it not, pretending that the extremitie of weather and losse of some principall ground-tackle, forced and feared them from searching the port of Hatarask, to which they were sent." The writer in using the word "pretending" is not, in contemporary usage, saying more than that they stated that weather and the breaking of anchor cables was the cause of their failure, but he implies a certain criticism all the same. Sir Francis Drake had found in June 1586 that a storm sweeping along the Outer Banks could inflict very severe casualties on his fleet,[9] and it is not unlikely that, faced with comparable conditions about the same time of year, Mace had no alternative but to put out to sea. His failure to persist when the weather had improved may be a more genuine fault. Instead he returned with such cargo as he had, reaching Weymouth sometime in August after a voyage of perhaps rather more than five months.

Samuel Mace is first heard of as master of the *Brave* of the Isle of Wight in 1590;[1] so by 1602 he was something of a veteran seaman. He was later concerned with Ralegh's Guiana enterprises, and may have taken part in the reconnaissance of 1594 as well as in Ralegh's own voyage of 1595; while he was apparently master of the ship *Darling* of London which Lawrence Keymis took for a third voyage to Guiana in 1596.

---

uses of the spicebush in medicine. Fernald stresses the aromatic character of the magnolias (pp. 675–80), and Porcher the medicinal uses (pp. 36–41). Porcher attributes quinine-like qualities to dogwood-bark (p. 9), but there are no indications of early medicinal uses; he shows that the sweet gum was extensively employed (pp. 9, 344–5). Fernald, pointing out that the ligneous forms of *Cassia* do not occur in the United States, simply says that cassia "was an ancient name for some aromatic plant," leaving its precise identification open (p. 885).

[9] Quinn, *Roanoke Voyages*, I, 291–3, 302, 307–8. [1] *Ibid.*, II, 564.

In July of that year Harriot, who was looking after Ralegh's Guiana interests while he was engaged in the Cadiz expedition, reported to Sir Robert Cecil that the master of Keymis's ship was disseminating information about the voyage to Ralegh's prejudice. Cecil sent orders that the narratives and maps in the hands of Mace and William Downs should be seized. The two men were found in the same house at Weymouth and claimed a certain property in the materials that were impounded. The maps and narratives were posted off to London early in August with one of the two mariners—it is not known whether it was Mace or his partner—following them in an attempt to assert ownership.[2]

When Mace could have been on two voyages to Virginia before 1602, as Brereton states, is not clear. He has not been identified on any Virginia voyage between 1584 and 1590: it may be, however, that Ralegh was sending out annual expeditions before 1602, and that we can place Mace's earlier expeditions in 1600 and 1601. It may be worth notice that in September 1601 Ralegh went down from Sherborne to Weymouth, whence he wrote to Cecil on 26 September.[3] It may well be that he expected to find Mace there, returned from an American voyage, though proof is so far lacking that the latter was at sea in this year. In any event, there is no doubt that Mace was an experienced seaman and had been for a long time associated with Ralegh's overseas enterprises.

Harriot certainly knew of Mace in 1596 and may have met him then and subsequently. From 1598, Harriot had been officially in the service of Henry Percy, ninth Earl of Northumberland, but he continued to perform various services for his former master, Ralegh. Northumberland and Ralegh were in close contact and shared a common interest in Harriot's scientific work. Harriot was an inveterate and often careful notetaker. Besides making full records of his scientific experiments and mathematical calculations, he had the habit of jotting down notes as reminders of his miscellaneous activities on the back of his mathematical worksheets, a large number of which have survived. One of these is apparently (though nowhere explicitly) a set of memoranda on the preparations for Mace's voyage of 1602 and adds something to our exiguous information on that enterprise. It is headed by a two-by-three-inch sign in the form of a crude trefoil, and reads: [4]

[2] Harriot to Cecil, 11 July 1596, in Edwards, *Ralegh*, II, 420–2; Hist.MSSComm., *CecilMSS*, VI (1895), 256–7; Sir George Trenchard and Sir Ralph Horsey to Cecil, 31 July and 10 August 1596, *ibid.*, pp. 300, 321; Edwards, *Ralegh*, II, 423. For Keymis's voyage see Richard Hakluyt, *The Principal Navigations*, 12 vols. (Glasgow, 1903–5) [orig. publ., London 1598–1600], X, 452, 495.

[3] Edwards, *Ralegh*, II, 240–1.

[4] B.M., AdditionalMS 6788, fol. 417.

Whe*th*er compasses or diales.[5]

Copper not brasse 20 or 30 pound in plates.
some as thin as paper & small & great.

Hatchet*es*. 5. doz.	Mattockes. 20
Kniues. 50. doz.	Iron shouelles 20.
lead and powder.	Sheres.
powder and shot.	Sawes.
clothes for me*n*.	
Booke of voyages.	

What is this Kecow hit tamen. Wh*at* is your name.[6]

Ianuary .29 ♀.[7] $\frac{1601}{1602}$.

Copper in plates. 32li.

del*y*f*er* they*m*
at 16d the pound.
276 pieces. } + 42s + 8d

a payne of glass [8]
and p*un*ches--- } + 3s + 4d

46s + od

[5] The suggestion is that Harriot was considering whether he needed to schedule or order any more compass cards and/or needles or else running glasses. As a scholar he would know the Latin term "dial" better than the seaman's term "running glass." Lists of sea stores commonly united requirements of compasses and running glasses. (Data from George P. B. Naish and David W. Waters, National Maritime Museum, Greenwich.)

[6] Barbour writes that *kecow*, "what," corresponds with Powhatan *kaquere* (for *kaquew*?) or *caquaih* in the Smith and Strachey vocabularies, and is a dialectal variant of Natick (Massachusetts Alkonquian) *cháwas* or *teagwe*. *Hit tamen* should be one word, and is remarkably close to Natick *hettamun*, "it is called." See Philip L. Barbour, ed., *The Jamestown Voyages Under the First Charter, 1606–1609*, 2 vols. (Cambridge, Eng., 1969), II, 333; William Strachey, *The Historie of Travell into Virginia Britania (1612)* (London, 1953), ed. Louis B. Wright and Virginia Freund, p. 206; James Hammond Trumbull, *Natick Dictionary*, Smithsonian Institution, Bureau of American Ethnology, Bull. 25 (Washington, D.C., 1903), pp. 21, 27. The end result would make it "It is called what?"

[7] The sign for Venus, probably Friday.

[8] "Payne" is a probable but not a certain reading. If it is correct the piece of glass, if it measured 14″ by 20″, could have provided a template for 3″ to 7″ sizes of copper plates, the precise outlines of which could be inscribed on it with a diamond.

videlicet.		
of 7 inches, square.		10.
round.		05.
6 inches. square.		20.
round.		10.
4 inches. square		40.
round.		20.
3 inches. square		100.
of a smaller. size and iblonge and different beg*n*esses.	}	71.
		276.

The first group of notes on the upper part of the page concerns the materials needed to set out an expedition. "Whether compasses or dials," asks a question about the instrumentation of the voyage, though its precise implications are not clear. The next raises the question whether brass or copper should be brought with them and is answered by the statement that it should be copper in plates, some thin, some large, some small. Hatchets and knives are clearly, like the copper plates, for trade. Mattocks, iron shovels, shears and saws are probably, in view of what we know of Mace's activities, intended largely for the cutting and digging of trees, shrubs, and roots, perhaps also to assist in building a camp. Lead, powder, shot, and clothes for the men are all items of ship's equipment. We then have a "Booke of voyages." As the third volume of Richard Hakluyt's *Principal navigations*, published in 1600, contained full accounts of the Roanoke voyages between 1584 and 1590, with what was known of the Lost Colony, there is no doubt that this is what was intended. Under it is the apparently mysterious sequence: "What is this. Kecow hit tamen. What is your name." Philip L. Barbour maintains that the middle phrase is Algonquian and means something approximating the first of the English phrases. This gives a clue to its purpose. Harriot is trying to recollect phrases of the Carolina Algonquian language, which he studied from 1584 to 1586 and for which he had developed a special orthography.[9] He may have gone on to compile a short wordbook which would help the expedition's leaders to trade with the Indians and make inquiries about the lost colonists.

On the lower part of the page, and under a line, is a dated note regarding the plates of copper mentioned above. The date, 29 January 1602, fits well with the preparations which would be under way to get Mace to sea by March. Thirty-two pounds of copper were obtained for

[9] See Quinn, *Roanoke Voyages,* I, 389.

£2 2s. 8d., and some additional materials, a pane of glass and a punch, for 3s. 4d., making £2 6s. in all. From this there were to be made 276 individual plates, round, square, and oblong. Details of the numbers of those measuring seven inches, six inches, four inches, and three inches across are given. The remainder, "of a smaller size and iblonge [*sic*] and different begnesses," were probably made from the fragments left after cutting the larger plates.

It is not clear whether Harriot took on the task of making the plates himself or simply laid down specifications for their manufacture. He had himself experienced in 1585–6 the demand of the Indians of the Roanoke Island area for copper in the form of plates for head and chest ornaments,[1] while John White had drawn an Indian elder or chief wearing a copper gorget, about six inches square, suspended from two holes by a string round the neck.[2] It seems clear that he was here providing for Mace a supply of gorgets of the sort and shapes he had seen in America, which were clearly suitable and profitable articles of trade. In 1586, in company with Hakluyt, Harriot had also heard a Frenchman who had been for many years in the Spanish service in Florida describe how the Indians there particularly wished to trade in red woolen and cotton cloth, copper, and hatchets.[3] With the last two of these he was seeing Mace well provided. Whether, in fact, any of these articles were traded with the Indians we have not enough material to say.

It is therefore clear that Harriot was using, for Sir Walter Ralegh's benefit, knowledge of Indian language and trading preferences which he had obtained at an earlier period in his life when he had been a member of the Roanoke Island colony. He was a remarkably assiduous and talented scientific scholar, but also a practical man, ready to put his experience at the service of planners and leaders of expeditions. He was interested, we have seen, in listing instruments, books, linguistic aids (did he also supply some natural history data?), clothes, and tools, as well as trade goods to be taken. The linking of the list with Mace's voyage is wholly circumstantial, but it is nonetheless convincing.

Ralegh himself supplies us with our final piece of information on Mace's voyage: namely, that he returned to Weymouth in August and that Ralegh visited the town "to speake with a pinnes of myne arived from Virginia,"[4] but he gives us no further information on what Mace brought home. Instead, he found that a similar cargo had come from an unauthorized voyage. Made by Bartholomew Gosnold and Bartholomew

[1] *Ibid.*, pp. 102–3, 209, 260, 266, 268–70, 281, 284, 332, 367.

[2] *Ibid.*, pp. 438–9; Paul H. Hulton and D. B. Quinn, *The American Drawings of John White* (London and Chapel Hill, 1964), I, 107–8, II, pl. 50.

[3] Quinn, *Roanoke Voyages*, II, 765.

[4] Edwards, *Ralegh*, II, 51–3.

Gilbert in the *Concord*,[5] its objective had been to find the *Refugio* of Verrazzano on the coast of Norumbega, establish a trading post there, and bring back whatever goods could be traded from the Indians. Gosnold had explored the coast of New England from southern Maine round to Buzzards Bay, but failed to get his men to remain in the fort he had built on Cuttyhunk in the Elizabeth Islands. The *Concord* had brought back among other things twenty-two hundredweight of sassafras and twenty-six cedar trunks. Some of the sassafras had been divided with the adventurers at Southampton. Ralegh met Gilbert, still in possession of part of the cargo, at Weymouth and heard about the voyage. He declared Gilbert's portion confiscated and sent in haste to Sir Robert Cecil and Lord Howard of Effingham to hold the rest, when it should reach London, for his use. At the same time he must have written to Harriot to act for him in having the sassafras impounded. Once more in one of Harriot's memoranda there appears a record of his task. The notes read:

> S*ir* Walter Ralegh.
> Sassafras come to London in carte.
> re*mem*brances to arest.
> Tobacco.
> pipes.[6]

The first three items give the information that Ralegh had written to him that sassafras had come to London in a cart which he, Harriot, was to have arrested. "Tobacco" and "pipes" are likely to be separate reminders of his own requirements which often appear in the memoranda. Ralegh's right to a monopoly of trade depended on his interpretation of his Virginia patent of 1584, whose validity in turn depended on the presumption of the continued existence of the Lost Colony as proof that he had achieved an unbroken settlement. Whether Harriot succeeded in impounding the sassafras (the unloading of which on the London market would drastically reduce the price and deplete especially the value of that brought by Mace), or Ralegh established his right to it, we cannot say for certain, but it seems probable that he did. In his letter of 21 August to Cecil, Ralegh admitted that he was prepared to return his share of the cargo to Captain Gilbert. But this was in consideration of Gilbert's willingness to enter his service and command the *Concord*, along with the pinnace or bark in which Mace had sailed ("I do sende both the barks away agayne"), on a further attempt to continue trade with North America and perhaps find the Lost Colony in the process.

An attempt was made by Ralegh to deal with the problem of a glut

[5] For the Gosnold voyage see Warner F. Gookin and Philip L. Barbour, *Bartholomew Gosnold* (Hamden, Conn., 1963).

[6] B.M., AdditionalMS 6789, fol. 514.

of sassafras on the English market, consequent on the arrival of both Mace's cargo and also presumably that confiscated from the Gosnold expedition, by disposing of the surplus on the Continent. It is not clear how far, if at all, Harriot was involved in this transaction, but it is possible that he may have had some hand in it. Sometime toward the end of 1602 or the beginning of 1603 Ralegh arranged to dispose of a considerable quantity of sassafras to a German merchant, J. B. Zechelius, to be delivered to his Hamburg agent, a man named Lul, for forwarding to Leipzig. Correspondence on this transaction was carried on by one of Ralegh's servants named Spilman. The sassafras was to have arrived in February, but Ralegh added a postscript to a letter of Spilman's dated 30 March 1603, saying delays had occurred and that it would be sent very shortly. Zechelius (who had arranged for the diversion of the cargo to Nürnberg) heard nothing further for over three months. He then wrote to Ralegh on 10 July. He stressed the delay and the failure of communication and suggested that the sassafras be sent as soon as possible. He recommended that it be packed in a dry vat instead of in four or five sugar chests, as this would cut down weight and lower transport charges by some four or five pounds sterling. While it is not easy to get any precise indication of quantities, it would appear that several hundredweight of sassafras at least, and possibly more, were involved. By the time the letter arrived in London, Ralegh had gone to prison and the letter did not reach him. It was recovered from one of his agents, James Sutton, by Sir William Waad, who forwarded it to Lord Cecil (as Sir Robert had become) on 10 September,[7] possibly because it might be a

[7] P.R.O., State Papers, Domestic, James I, S.P. 14/3, 63, 63(1). Sir William Waad to Cecil, 10 September 1603: "It may pleas y*ou*r good L*ordship* this l*ett*re to s*i*r Walter Rawley came to the handes of Jaymes Sutton from beyond the seas, w*hi*ch I thought good to send y*ou*r L*ordship*." Enclosed, J. B. Zechelius to Sir Walter Ralegh, 10 July 1603:

Right Honorable Lord, as your fauour heretofore hath beene most greatlie extended towardes me, so I humblie desire a continuance thereof; and there be no means in me to deserue the same, yet the Vttermost of my seruices shal not be wanting, where and whensoeuer it shall please your Lordship to dispose thereof: For as much, as in m*aster* Spilmans last letter, the date whereof was the 30 of March, yowr Lo*rdship* did in a postscript aduertise me that the Sassafras, wich (according to yowr Lo*rdshi*ps former letters.) I haue expected anie time this 5 moneths, should with the Verie first winde be send awaie, I am humblie to aduertise yowr L*ordsh*ip that hetherto I haue receaued nothing, no, not so much as a letter of aduice, what I should doe (. wich doth greefe me to the hart.) Indeed I doe gesse, that this delaie is partley cawsed, trough other manifold and waightie affaires where with your Lo*rdsh*ip is (. and especially at this troublesome time.) dailie incombred withal, yet neuerthelesse, seeing that it is a great hinderance, to the setting forth of this owr new begun trade, I would wisch, that yet it might be

cover for some of the alleged Continental intrigues in which Ralegh was said to have been engaged. But there is no reason to believe it is not precisely what it says it is—what Zechelius refers to as "owr new begun trade," an early exercise in the reexport of North American produce from England. Harriot's known part in the disposal of American cargoes is small but of some marginal interest: it may, in practice, have been somewhat larger than appears.

There is a possibility that Harriot had a further slight connection with the aftermath of the Gosnold voyage. Ralegh, once he had asserted his monopoly claims, was only too willing to take the participants under his wing, since their reports could be used as a basis for the promotion of further expeditions. Brereton, indeed, dedicated to Ralegh his *Briefe and true relation of the discoverie of the north part of Virginia.* His own short narrative was followed by the note on Mace's voyage already referred to and by several promotion documents. These were compiled either by Brereton himself or more probably by Edward Hayes, a veteran of Sir Humphrey Gilbert's Newfoundland voyage of 1583. The pamphlet evidently aroused some public interest, for a second enlarged edition was soon issued which contained further promotion material, including notes on commodities mentioned in Harriot's earlier tract, *A briefe and true report of the new found land of Virginia.* It is clear that the compiler or compilers had the support of and access to the library of Hakluyt, whether or not he played a direct part in preparation of the book. The last section of all (pp. 46–8) was entitled "Certaine briefe testimonies touching sunndry rich mines . . . ," said to exist in North America. Reference was made to an account of the expedition of Hernando de Soto

---

send awaie with speede, Likewise if it be not alreadie gone from London, I would if it were possible, that it were packt in a driefatt, of wich there is enough to be had, euerie where abowt London, and maie be had for 4 or 5 shillings a peece, that will hold as much as 4 or 5 Sugarchests; it will saue charges, at least 4 or 5 pound, for these Sugarchests, I know are verie heauie, to be carried so farre ouer Land.

Thus humbly desiring pardon of my tediousnesse, I leaue yowr Lordship to the tuition of the Almightie, Datum Norenberg this 10 of July A*nn*o d*omini* j603.

Yowr Lordships euer to be Commaundet in all humblenes.

J. B. Zechelius

PS: To Master Arnold Luls brother which dwellet at Hamborough I haue giuen order long agoe to send such thinges as he shal receaue from your Lo*rdsh*ip hether to Noremberg (and not to Leipzig). therefore I beseeche yowr Lo*rdsh*ip that it maie be directed by his brother onlie to him and to none els.

The letter "y" is written "ij" linked, otherwise the hand of the letter is a clear italic. I am indebted to Professor Pierre Lefranc for drawing this letter to my attention.

(Fidalgo de Elvas, *Relaçam* [Evora, 1557]), which it is said "can be seen in print in the hands of Master Richard Hackluyt." There was also a reference to the narrative of the Espejo expedition, printed in Hakluyt's *Principal navigations*, III (1600), 304 ff., and adding (p. 47): "The large descriptive chart of which voyage containing great numbers of towns and diuers great riuers discouered in that action made in Mexico by Francisco Xamuscado [Chamuscado] 1585 being intercepted afterward by the English at sea, we haue in London to be shewed to such as shall haue occasion to make vse of the same."

This map provides a link with Harriot. In 1599 in his dedicatory epistle to Sir Robert Cecil, Hakluyt himself drew attention to his earlier reprinting of the Espejo narrative in 1586,[8] and spoke also of the information to be found "in a secret mappe of those partes made in Mexico the yeare before [1585] for the king of Spaine, which originall with many others is in the custodie of the excellent Mathematician M. Thomas Hariot." It will be noticed that in 1602 the map was said to be accessible in London, but it is not said that it was in Hakluyt's possession. It would be a natural inference that it was still in Harriot's hands and was made available by him for consultation, quite probably at Durham House, Ralegh's city residence, which Harriot was still using. There is a speculative element in all this, of course, but it appears probable that Harriot, after being engaged by Ralegh to arrest part of the cargo brought by Gosnold from New England in the summer, was making amends, a little later on in 1602, by assisting in a propaganda drive by the same group to get further voyages under way. The Chamuscado map has, regrettably, disappeared.

Harriot was to lose much of his involvement in overseas voyaging with the fall and imprisonment of Ralegh in 1603, but he did not give up all interest in the New World. The Virginia Company charter was at length granted in April 1606, and in December Christopher Newport took out the first expedition under it to what was now known as South Virginia. Among his principal associates was Captain Gosnold. It seems probable that Harriot had got to know him through the 1602 affair. At some time before Newport sailed, Harriot made a further set of notes which read:

m*aste*r Pool.

Cap*tai*n Bartholomew Gosnold.
M*aste*r Roger Stranson. } for Virginia

[8] Richard Hakluyt, *Principal navigations,* II (1599), dedicatory epistle; Hakluyt, *Principal Navigations,* I (1903), lxvi.

Pool could be Jonas Poole (or Powell) who went to the falls of the James River in May 1607,[9] but may not be linked at all with the other two persons. Roger Stranson (whose name Harriot first wrote as "Robert") has not been identified as having gone to Virginia in 1607 or later. But Gosnold was a prominent member of the group which founded Jamestown and took a significant part in its affairs until his death on 22 August 1607.[1]

These are Harriot's latest notes so far identified as having reference to North American affairs, but in February 1609 at a meeting in the house of Thomas Cecil, Earl of Exeter, he reported what he had heard of American Indian methods of placer mining, as he recollected them from his experience some twenty-three years earlier in the Roanoke Island settlement.[2] The stress on copper and on the need to find mines in the instructions given to Sir Thomas Gates in May 1609[3] may reflect this discussion.

Harriot in his little book, *A briefe and true report of the new found land of Virginia*, in 1588 did much to describe and explain the natural resources and inhabitants of a part of eastern North America to English readers. His work was translated into Latin, French, and German and, with his notes on the engravings from the drawings of White, reached a wide European audience and built up a substantial segment of western knowledge of the Americas. Theodor de Bry's *America* (Frankfurt am Main, 1590), part i, was well launched with the work of the Harriot-White partnership in the Roanoke settlement. Harriot helped Ralegh between 1594 and 1596 to gain background on his Guiana enterprise and drew maps from the information and sketches brought back. The notes published above trace a continued concern with America over the years from 1602 onward, ending only in 1609 with his last appearance as an adviser on Virginia. Unfortunately, all the detailed descriptions and sketches he brought back from Roanoke Island in 1586 and his chronicle of the Roanoke voyages, 1584–7,[4] have disappeared, while his materials on the Indian language, which were extant in the later seventeenth century, have not been found. On this account his full contribution to the knowledge of America may not be possible to assess.

[9] Alexander Brown, *The Genesis of the United States*, 2 vols. (Boston, 1890), II, 968. For Harriot's notes see B.M., AdditionalMS 6789, fol. 390.

[1] Gookin and Barbour, *Gosnold*, pp. 191–218.

[2] Quinn, *Roanoke Voyages*, I, 388.

[3] Susan M. Kingsbury, ed., *The Records of the Virginia Company of London,* III (Washington, D.C., 1933), 17, 19–20, 22.

[4] Quinn, *Roanoke Voyages*, I, 387.

CHAPTER SIXTEEN

"Virginians" on the Thames in 1603

THE INFORMATION THAT there were American Indians in England in September 1603 and that they gave a demonstration of their skill in handling a canoe on the river Thames adds an entirely new item to our knowledge of English contacts with North America at the opening of the seventeenth century. The document which provides this information was identified by Miss Clare Talbot, former librarian and archivist at Hatfield House, home of the late Marquess of Salisbury, with whose permission given in his lifetime it is published.

Among the Cecil Family and Estate Papers at Hatfield House (Accounts 6/31) is a document (see pp. 430–1) headed "A note of all the rewardes geuen the last progresse from the 20th of July to the sixt of September 1603" (the endorsement helps a little further by describing it as "A note of rewardes geuen the last progress, and one weecke after," indicating that the "progresse" came to an end on 30 August). The third leaf contains three items dated 1 September, and then has the date 2 September with sixteen items, followed by two more, completing the account on the reverse of the leaf. From the heading, we are probably entitled to assume that the eighteen items following the 2 September date in fact covered the five days from 2 to 6 September, the last marking the conclusion of the account. The items referring to the "Virginians" are the fourth, fifth, thirteenth, and eighteenth of those belonging, we believe, to these five days, nos. 4 and 5 being probably 2 September, but possibly 3 September, and no. 18 being apparently 6 September, with no. 13 lying somewhere between, probably nearer 6 September than 2 September.

The first (no. 4) records that "Miles" gave two watermen (professional boatmen who conveyed passengers across and along the river Thames) a reward of five shillings for bringing a canoe to "my Lord's house," and then (no. 5) includes a payment of four shillings by "my Lord" to "the Virginians." My Lord is Lord Cecil, formerly Sir Robert Cecil and best known by his later title of Earl of Salisbury. My Lord's house would in this case mean Cecil House in the Strand, a very short walking distance from the Thames, but easily accessible to it. The next entry to refer to the Indians (no. 13) is the note of a further reward of five shillings to them, without the circumstances being specified, while the final entry (no. 18) records a payment of twelve pence to "a payre of ores," two oarsmen, perhaps professional boatmen also. They had "waited on the Virginians when they rowed with their Cannow."

What we can reconstruct of the story, therefore, would seem to be that on 2 or 3 September a Thames boat, probably a wherry normally used for passengers, came upstream from some distance down the river, having in tow or on board an American Indian canoe—a dugout canoe would need to be towed, a birchbark canoe could possibly be carried—and also two or more Amerindians, whose description as "Virginians" could mean at this time that they came from anywhere between Cape Fear and Maine. The wherry put to land on the north bank of the river, below the houses that lay along the bank and behind which were the gardens and grounds of the houses fronting on the Strand. They conveyed their Indian charges and the canoe into the hands of Miles, one of Lord Cecil's servants, who gave them the generous reward of five shillings, and the Indians were then handed a gift of four shillings on behalf of Lord Cecil, or possibly goods to the value of this sum. A few days later they were given five shillings or further presents in kind to this value. Finally, they gave a demonstration on the river of their handling of their canoe. Two oarsmen were employed in another boat either to keep them company or to pace them. This was not a long-drawn-out or arduous task, since they were given the modest reward of sixpence each only.

The arrival of the Indians we can place on 2 or 3 September, and the payment of the oarsmen at the time of the demonstration of their canoe was apparently made on 6 September, so that the canoe's paces were probably tested on the same day or conceivably on 5 September.

We might naturally assume that Lord Cecil was at home to greet the Indians on their arrival and to give them their first gift personally; and we might also conclude that he was present to watch them show what they could do with their canoe on the Thames. But this does not seem to have been so. On 1 September Lord Cecil was at Basing House, the seat of William, fourth Marquess of Winchester, some forty-five miles from London. This was perhaps two days' riding from London or three days' by coach, and we have no evidence so far that Cecil returned to his London home before 6 September.

Throughout the summer of 1603 the plague had raged through the city and the area around it. The city fathers and the principal magistrates of Middlesex had moved from London and its environs to escape infection. Many Londoners who fled spread the plague outward around the city, much to the dismay of the villagers on whom they quartered themselves.[1] King James I, not long established on the English throne, had ventured down the Thames to be crowned at Westminster on 25 July before returning to Hampton Court. But soon, on 10 August, he set out with his court on a short progress through the southern counties so as to keep a distance between him and the infected capital. During the remainder of August and most of September the court moved slowly through Hampshire and Wiltshire and back again, the king staying for a few nights at each of a number of great country houses—and incidentally carrying infection with him—until on 22 September he came to rest for a considerable time at Basing House.[2] Lord Cecil, as Principal Secretary of State, accompanied the king on some of the earlier stages of this progress, but at the end of August he left him to stay at Basing House, from which a certain amount of government business was being carried on. He wrote from Basing on Thursday, 1 September, to Sir Thomas Parry, the English ambassador at Paris, giving him some court and diplomatic news and indicating that it would now be possible to proceed with certain state trials: "they shall [be] proceeded withall in Justice, which hetherto hath ben portrac[ted] by reason of the great infection of the Plague in these pa[rts] being very dangerous at such tymes, to draw any multitu[de] of people together." [3] It does not appear that on this date Cecil had any intention of returning to London, and no evidence has been found that

[1] F. P. Wilson, *The Plague in Shakespeare's London* (London, 1927), pp. 84–113, especially Sir William Waad, clerk of the Privy Council, to Lord Cecil, from Hamstead, 31 August 1607, cited on pp. 94–5.

[2] John Nichols, *The Progresses, Processions, and Magnificent Festivities, of King James the First, his Royal Consort, Family, and Court: Collected from Original Manuscripts, Scarce Pamphlets, Corporation Records, Parochial Registers &c . . . ,* 4 vols. (London, 1828), I, 250.

[3] B.M., CottonMS, Caligula X, fol. 200.

he had done so by 6 September when the account containing the references to the "Virginians" ends. His draft letter of 2 September to Sir James Elphinstone does not give the place from which he is writing, but it appears still to be Basing. He makes similar reference to the plague and to the deferment of trials and states that the judges are to meet on Tuesday, 6 September, at Maidenhead (about half-way between Basing and London) to decide on them, thus showing that much of the business of government was still being undertaken outside London.[4]

It would appear therefore that, although the Indians were sent to Cecil House, Lord Cecil could not have been there in person to greet or reward them. And it follows that he also missed the demonstration in their canoe. If Cecil was not at his house, we may ask why the Indians were kept there for several days at least, and induced to exhibit their canoe's paces. The reason is apparently that there were other persons residing in or visiting the house who were interested in such curiosities. One such man was Sir Walter Cope. He appears twice in the account between two entries relating to the Indians, on 2 September (items 11 and 12), being recompensed for several payments which he made on Cecil's behalf. One, of ten shillings, was made to the Cecil House housekeeper, possibly to enable him to pay out rewards to the Indians.

Cope was an inveterate collector who had a private museum. Already in 1599 he had at his London house, among other ethnographical items, "A long narrow Indian canoe, with the oars and sliding planks, hung from the ceiling."[5] He would surely have greeted the Indians and made them perform, and perhaps in the end have added their canoe and other gear to his collection. Moreover, Cope had an enduring interest in Virginia. He played an active part in the preparations for launching the Company in 1606 and was a member of the Council of Virginia in that year.[6] Whether ultimately Cecil encountered the Indians we cannot say, nor have we any further information about them. Normally, the arrival of "Virginians" in London might have attracted sufficient notice for their presence to be remarked by writers of gossip or news, or even referred to in a ballad or play.[7] A probable reason for the absence of all references to them is that during a plague epidemic there were much more

[4] Hist.MSSComm., *CecilMSS*, XV (London, 1930), 243–4.

[5] Clare Williams, ed., *Thomas Platter's Travels in England, 1599* (London, 1937), p. 173.

[6] Hist.MSSComm., *CecilMSS*, XVIII (London, 1940), 84. See Alexander Brown, *The Genesis of the United States*, 2 vols. (Boston, 1890), II, 862–3.

[7] *Westward Hoe*, a play by Thomas Dekker and John Webster with topical references, could well have had some mention of the Indians, but it is thought to have been completed too early in the year.

serious things to write about, while in any case writers of newsletters were themselves unlikely to have remained in the capital.

If the presence of American Indians in London could be easily explained by reference to known voyages, it would scarcely be necessary to go into so much detail in trying to put down as precisely as possible the circumstances under which they were received in London. But it has not been possible to find direct evidence which associates them with any known expedition of the year 1603.

We know that Samuel Mace had gone on a voyage for Sir Walter Ralegh to Virginia in 1602, to the coast between Cape Fear and Oregon Inlet, and had returned with sassafras and other goods in August, though without having made contact with the lost colonists. Bartholomew Gosnold, Bartholomew Gilbert, and Gabriel Archer had explored the coasts of Maine and Massachusetts in the same year, bringing back sassafras and other American commodities, and had been charged by Ralegh with infringing his monopoly, though he pardoned them and took Bartholomew Gilbert into partnership. On 21 August, Ralegh, in a letter to Sir Robert Cecil as he then was, said that he had arranged for both ships, the *Concord* on which Gilbert had sailed and the bark in which Mace had returned, to go again to Virginia in his service ("Butt I do sende both the barks away agayne"). Later in the year John Brereton, who had been with Gosnold and Gilbert, as we have seen (pp. 405–7) published narratives of the Gosnold voyage,[8] a brief note on Mace's voyage, and a substantial amount of propaganda material on the economic advantages and products of North America. This was *A briefe and true relation of the north parte of Virginia,* which with the same date of 1602 rapidly went into two editions.[9]

It is probable that this little book was one inspiration for the expedition led by Martin Pring from Bristol to Cape Cod Bay between March and June 1603,[1] just as it is certain that the Reverend Richard Hakluyt

[8] Edward Edwards, *The Life of Sir Walter Ralegh . . . with his Letters,* 2 vols. (London, 1868), II, 251–3; Warner F. Gookin and Philip L. Barbour, *Bartholomew Gosnold* (Hamden, Conn., 1963). Gilbert sailed in the *Elizabeth,* not the *Concord,* in 1603.

[9] John Brereton, *A briefe and true relation of the discoverie of the north parte of Virginia . . . ,* 2 issues (London, G. Bishop, 1602), p. 14; *S.T.C.* 3610–11.

[1] Samuel Purchas, *Hakluytus Posthumus, or Purchas his Pilgrimes,* 4 vols. (1625), IV, 1654–6 (*S.T.C.* 20509); 20 vols. (Glasgow, 1906), XVIII, 329–35. Pring appears with a John White (who could conceivably have been the artist on his way to still another search for the lost colonists) in the Caribbean in 1601. They did not, however, attempt a reconnaissance of Virginia, but helped to take a prize back to England. See Paul H. Hulton and D. B. Quinn, *The American Drawings of John White* (London and Chapel Hill, 1964), I, 22–3.

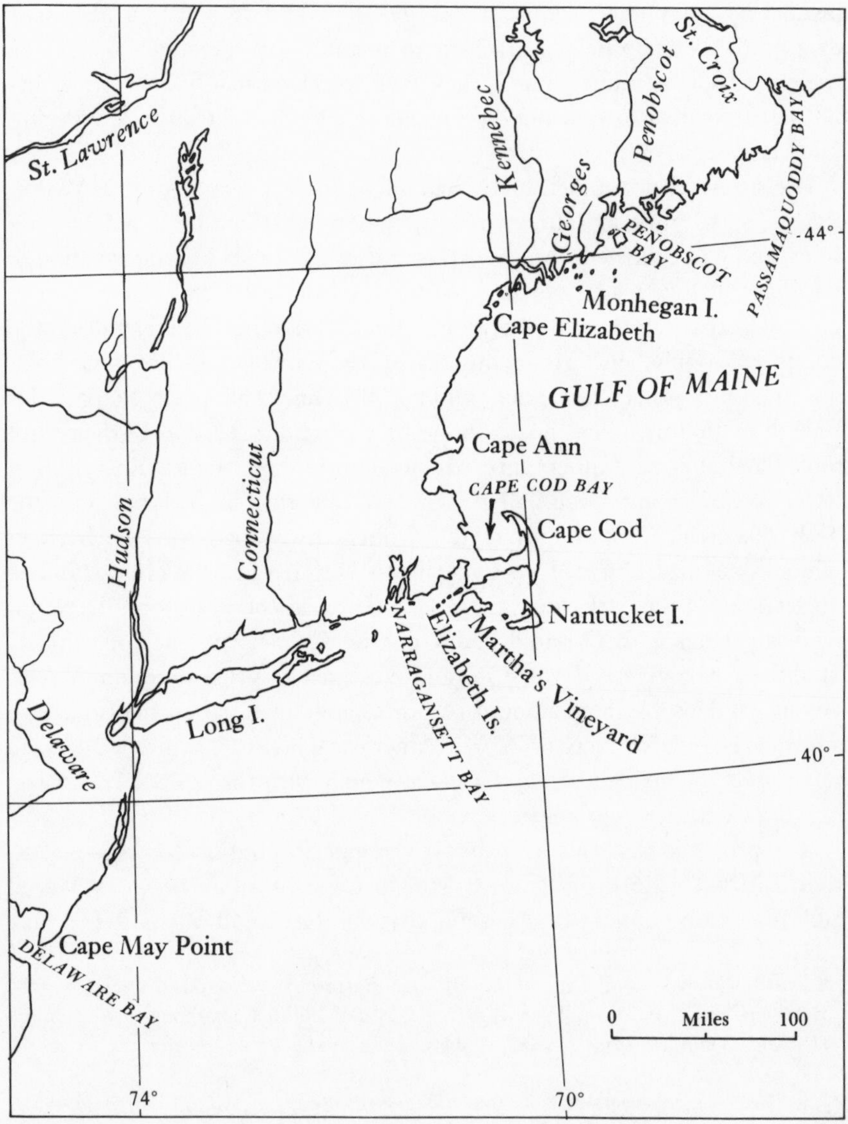

The New England shore, 1600–1630.

was another; permission having been duly obtained from Sir Walter Ralegh. His objective was trade rather than exploration. It has been accepted that he made his summer trading camp at the site of the Plymouth colony of 1620, but it may now appear that it was at Provincetown bay that the *Speedwell* and *Discoverer* cast anchor. About the end of June the two ships were sailing down from a point on the Maine coast they knew as Savage Rock, which is either Cape Elizabeth or Cape Neddick. They soon passed Cape Ann and entered a "greate Gulfe." This was Massachusetts Bay and Cape Cod Bay combined. Captain Bartholomew Gosnold was said to have "overshot" it in 1602 when he discovered Cape Cod. Certainly he sailed directly from Savage Rock to the vicinity of Barnstable without making any detailed exploration of the coast, and then turned and came out round the Cape to explore the islands to the south which he had seen from a hasty reconnaissance of the Barnstable hills.

Pring was determined to probe more closely. As he examined the coasts from Cape Ann southward he was on the lookout for Cape Cod. When he picked up the Cape he decided that his reconnaissance of the mainland could be left for the time being. The narrator says that he was "coasting on the North side," but being "not yet satisfied in our expectations we left them [some Indians he met] and came to an Anchor on the South side." [2] The south side seems undoubtedly to have been Cape Cod, with Race Point and the higher ground behind it showing up to the southeast as Pring coasted southward from Cedar Point on the mainland toward Brant Rock and the Gurnet (which would lie west-south-west of Race Point). This relative rather than precise use of "north" and "south" seems to make more sense than any other explanation. In due course the ships reached land on the "south" at a bay they called Whitson Bay. This we can identify as Provincetown harbor. It is described as an "excellent Haven at the entrance whereof we found twentie fathomes water and rode at our ease in seven fathomes being Landlocked, the Haven winding in compasse like the shell of a snaile." In one place this is described as being "in the latitude of 41. degrees and odde minutes," at another "in latitude of one and forty degrees and five and twentie minutes." [3] The twenty-fathom depth fits present-day soundings at the mouth of Provincetown harbor: the seven fathoms inside the harbor suit a long stretch of water close inshore eastward to the mouth of the Pamet River. However, Sandy Point has changed, as sand from Race Point has drifted south; the curving character of the outer shore of the harbor is evident in almost all

[2] Purchas, *Pilgrimes* (1625), IV, 1656; (1906), XVIII, 324.

[3] *Ibid.* (1625), IV, 1655–6; (1906), XVIII, 324, 329.

seventeenth-century and subsequent maps. A hill seen on the land was named Mount Aldworth. If the ships were lying close inshore to Provincetown, hills of eighty feet or more would be seen (the present Monument Hill would be possible). If the ships anchored some miles to the south, there are hills of over a hundred feet both north and south of the Pamet River.

Pring was acting under instructions to find a fertile place, well inhabited by Indians, where he could settle down to investigate the resources of the area and trade with them. To do this, if he was to keep his men ashore, he must set up a camp. And unless he could trust the Indians completely, he must give his camp some protection. Many Indians were encountered at some place not too far from the original anchorage and on or accessible to the seashore. There, we are told, "wee thought it convenient to make a small baricado to keepe diligent watch and ward in, for the advertizement and succour of our men, while they shoulde worke in the Woods." This is later described as "Our House or Barricado, wherein were foure of our men alone with their Muskets to keep Centinell." [4] Clearly there was a palisade enclosing some sort of building, which was apparently strong enough to be defensible.

Is it possible to pin down the location of this site from which the English operated for about five weeks in July and August 1603? No certain identification can be made, but it is well within the bounds of possibility that this "small baricado" is the same as that which the Pilgrims found seventeen years later and described as an "old Fort or Palizide," [5] near the mouth of the Pamet River, probably on Corn Hill, an elevation of over one hundred feet.[6] The location would be a very likely one, some four to five miles across from Sandy Point (depending on its precise location in 1603), in the center of a well-occupied Indian area and with sandy soil suitable for obtaining sassafras roots—a major objective of the voyage, and found we are told only where it was sandy. The planks discovered in 1620 some distance away could have been brought by the Indians from the site. It does not seem useful to say anything about the kettle, which might have been traded in at any time over the previous eighteen years. The survival of remnants of the palisade and house for this length of time is quite possible; intended for defense, they were probably stoutly constructed.

[4] *Ibid* (1625), IV, 1655–6; (1906), XVIII, 324, 328.

[5] *Mourt's Relation or Journal of the plantation at Plymouth* (Boston, 1860), ed. H. M. Dexter, pp. 3, 23.

[6] Geological Survey, North Truro Triangle.

Though this robs Edgartown (favorite from 1798 [7] to 1878 [8]) and Plymouth (favorite from 1878 to the present day) of the honor of providing Pring with a site for his trading camp, Provincetown bay seems a much better choice, and the entry to the Pamet River is a site with some circumstantial evidence that it was used in Pring's time for a palisaded camp.

The first vessel home to Bristol, about the middle of September, was the *Discoverer*, so that the Indians who appeared in London could not have been aboard her. Bartholomew Gilbert had duly gone out in Ralegh's service with the *Elizabeth* in 1603. She ranged along the coast from Cape Fear northward, maybe as far as the shores of New Jersey, failing to find the entrance to Chesapeake Bay. Gilbert went ashore, perhaps on Delaware Bay, possibly on the Virginia Eastern Shore, and was killed by Indians. Henry Suite brought his ship home, but she did not reach the Thames "until about the end of September 1603." [9] Once again, she could not have brought the Indians with her.

One other possibility remains. We hear nothing of Samuel Mace in 1603. Ralegh had said in August 1602, as we have seen, that he too was being sent back to Virginia with his bark, as was Bartholomew Gilbert in the *Elizabeth*. It may be that Mace set out with Gilbert, or independently retraced his route in 1602, and at some place on the North American coast where he was not in contact with the *Elizabeth* picked up two or more Indians with their canoe and brought them to London about the end of August 1603. This is supposition, but it remains the only obvious possibility in the present state of our knowledge. If Mace reached London in August 1603, however, he would not have been able to make any personal contact with Ralegh. On 15 July Ralegh had been arrested on charges of plotting against King James, and by August was undergoing interrogation in the Tower of London.

That the Indians, in this case, should have been brought to Cecil was natural enough. He had been closely associated with Ralegh's Guiana ventures some years before. In 1599–1600 Richard Hakluyt had dedicated Volumes II and III of *The principal navigations* to him, in both dedications appealing to him to support the colonization of North America by Englishmen. In August 1602, Ralegh had written to Cecil about the Mace and Gilbert ventures of that year in terms which showed that Cecil was well aware of Ralegh's reviving interest in North American

[7] Jeremy Belknap, *American Biography* (1798), II, 128–9.

[8] B. F. DeCosta, "Gosnold and Pring, 1602–1603," *New England Historical and Genealogical Register*, XXXII (1878), 79–80.

[9] Purchas, *Pilgrimes* (1625), IV, 1656–8; (1906), XVIII, 329–35.

trade and exploration. Cecil was afterward to play a vitally important part in the creation of the Virginia Company. If Ralegh was in prison, then Cecil's house was an obvious destination for Mace's (if they were Mace's) Indian guests or captives. Indeed, only a few days after we find the Indians at Cecil House on 10 September we find Sir William Waad, Clerk of the Privy Council, writing to Cecil and, knowing his interest in North America, enclosing the letter which had been intercepted on its way to Ralegh with the information that some of his American sassafras, consigned to Nürnberg for sale, had failed to arrive at its destination.[1] The link therefore has some plausibility, and may—if confirmation can later be found for it—fill in another small gap in the still incomplete story of the voyages that preceded the Jamestown settlement.

It remains to be seen whether the episode can be fitted into our general picture of events in the years 1602–6. If Bartholomew Gilbert was particularly briefed to penetrate the Chesapeake in 1603, Mace (if he was in fact at sea in 1603) might be presumed to have similar orders. So far as we know no earlier English ship had reached there to trade or to look for the lost colonists since 1590. There is one striking piece of evidence that a European ship did reconnoiter the Chesapeake before 1606 and remove some Indians. In December 1607 Captain John Smith was taken prisoner by the Pamunkey Indians and was exhibited to the neighboring Indians to see whether anyone could identify him as a member of the ship which had been there previously. Edward Maria Wingfield reported that the Pamunkey chief, "hauing him prisoner caryed him to his Neybors Wyroances to see if any of them knew him for one of those which had bene some twoe or three yeeres before us in a rivere amongst them Northward, and taken awaie some Indians from them by force."[2] Two or three years "before us" would be the period before 1607, i.e., 1604 or 1605, but it would not be stretching the evidence too greatly to suggest 1603 as a possible date and the predicated Mace voyage a possible origin of the episode.

There is nothing exclusive in this suggestion, since there may well be other indications of what this voyage was. But it provides an answer, though not the only one, to a question which scholars have often legitimately raised: "Why was Jamestown founded without previous reconnaissance?" Namely, that there was a reconnaissance and that it took place in 1603. This visit to Chesapeake Bay would most probably have been made by a ship under the command of Samuel Mace, which sailed

[1] See pp. 414–16 above.

[2] Philip L. Barbour, *The Jamestown Voyages Under the First Charter, 1606–1609*, 2 vols. (Cambridge, Eng., 1969), I, 227.

in consort with Bartholomew Gilbert's *Elizabeth* but became detached from it and pursued the latter part of its voyage independently, so that no mention of it appears in the narrative of the *Elizabeth*'s voyage. This remains a hypothesis until confirmed by further evidence.

If we can see the bringing of the Indians to the Thames in 1603 as the fruit of a further voyage under Ralegh's auspices, then we gain a possible indication of the build-up of his North American activities. It might well have been that in 1600, after a long interval, he first sent Mace out to look for the lost colonists; that this and a subsequent expedition in 1601 were unsuccessful; and that the expedition of 1602, on which some additional evidence has emerged, brought some hints of the survival of Englishmen in the Chesapeake Bay area. From this would follow the instructions given to Bartholomew Gilbert to concentrate on exploring that area; if similar orders were given to Mace in 1603 and carried out, then the taking of the Indians and bringing them to England was part of an intentional policy. What we would have here is the gradual building up of a body of information and of trading contacts with the Indians along the Carolina and Virginia shores which would prepare the way for a fresh colonizing venture.

If all this is so, Ralegh's imprisonment brought an abrupt end to the planning. The men who had gained fresh experience (if we are right) of the Chesapeake Bay in 1603, and who had brought Indians back with them who could have helped to open up knowledge of the region, were left without leadership and their knowledge dissipated. Consequently the renewal of attempts to settle the Chesapeake area was deferred for a further four years. It is possible that some information was brought back on the survival of some of the lost colonists of 1587. It is possible also that from contact with the Indians and the men who found them in 1603 Sir Walter Cope (and through him Cecil) received part of the impetus which in the end made them so influential in the establishment of the Virginia Company.

A single item such as that on which this discussion is based must inevitably rest its tentative conclusions largely on conjecture, which new evidence in the future may confirm or dispose of in other ways. But the Indians on the Thames in 1603 were a reality. The Indians seized by George Waymouth on the Maine coast in 1605 played an important part in opening northern New England to detailed exploration and attempted settlement in 1606–8. Can we trace any comparable influence of the 1603 Indians on the Jamestown settlement?

This is not precisely possible. No Indian is known to have accompanied Newport in 1606. If the 1603 Indians were from the Chesapeake Bay area, it would seem that they had died before Newport set out in December 1606, since none returned with him. At the same time it is surprising that the Jamestown settlers made themselves so easily understood, at an elementary level at least, to the Powhatan Indians they encountered in 1607. If the narratives of the earliest months of the colonists' activity in Virginia are scrutinized closely it might appear that some vocabulary of Algonquian words was at the disposal of the settlers.[3] Thomas Harriot undoubtedly had a repertoire of Carolina Algonquian words and phrases at his command, dating back to the Roanoake Island colony of 1585–6. We saw that he jotted down one Indian phrase, apparently for the use of the 1602 Mace expedition, and he may well have provided this particular expedition with a vocabulary. A Carolina Algonquian word list would be of some use in 1607 in Powhatan territory, but a more up-to-date and precise vocabulary could have derived from the Indians brought back in 1603 (if they were Powhatan Indians), elicited from them by either Harriot or some other person with linguistic skill. Such a vocabulary would then have been included in the equipment with which Newport left England in 1606.

These implications of the hitherto unrecorded appearance of "Virginians" in London in 1603 may require on further scrutiny to be modified, but they emphasize some respects in which our knowledge still remains incomplete for the background of the Virginia Company of 1606 and the first settlers of 1607.

The document from Hatfield House follows:

[folio 1, recto]

A note of all the rewardes geuen the last progresse from the 20th of Iuly to the sixt of Septembre 1603 . . . .

[folio 3, recto]

	1 Sept*embre*		
[1]	geue*n* to S*ir* Will*iam* Fleetwoode*s* men that waited all the progresse on the wagon	xl	s
[2]	geue*n* to *Mas*ter Iaques his man that brought grapes	ij	s
		vj	d

[3] When toward the end of May 1607 George Percy notes in his journal the following—"But yet the Savages murmured at our planting in the Countrie, whereupon this Weroance made answer againe very wisely of a Savage, Why should you bee offended with them as long as they hurt you not, nor take any thing away by force, they take but a little waste ground, which doth you nor any of us any good"—it is difficult to accept the view that no verbal intercourse between Englishmen and Indians was possible. See Purchas, *Pilgrimes* (1625), IV, 1689; (1906), XVIII, 415.

[3]	geue*n* to S*i*r Robart Knowles his man that brought a muske melon	v	s
	2 Sept*embre*		
[1]	dely*er*ed to Tegg for my Lo*r*d to geue the poore	iij	s
[2]	geue*n* to the post boye	xij	d
[3]	geue*n* to on that caryed a lette*r* to S*i*r Michel Hick*e*s	xij	d
[4]	geue*n* by Myles to ij watermen that brought the cannowe to my Lo*rds* howse	v	s
[5]	geue*n* by my Lor*d* to the virginians	iiij	s
[6]	geue*n* to M*aster* Ockyes man that brought grapes	ij	s
		vj	d
[7]	geue*n* to S*i*r Nowell Carons man that brought fructe	v	s
[8]	geue*n* to S*i*r Richard Ieffor*d*es man that showed my Lor*d* his hawcke flye	xx	s
[9]	geue*n* to my Lo*rd* of Northumberland*e*s man that brought grapes	v	s
[10]	geue*n* to M*aster* Ockyes man that brought grapes	ijs	vjd
[11]	geue*n* by S*ir* Walter Cope to the keeper of the House.	x	s
[12]	geue*n* by him to S*i*r Babtist Hick*e*s his servant*e*s for my Lor*d*	v	s
[13]	geue*n* to the virginians	v	s
[14]	geue*n* to M*ast*er Harris his man that brought grapes	ijs	vjd
[15]	geue*n* for a hud for the tassell	xij	d
[16]	geue*n* for a brace of partridges to entice the same hawcke	iij	s
[folio 3, verso]			
[17]	geue*n* for a basket and the caredge of the partridg to Winsor	xiij	d
[18]	geue*n* to a payre of ores that waited on the Virginians when they rowed with ther Cannow	xij	d
	Sum*m*a iij^xx^xiiij^li^iiij^d^	[£74.0s.	4d.]

[Endorsed:] A note of rewardes geuen the last progress, and on weecke aftere.

CHAPTER SEVENTEEN

The Lost Colony in Myth and Reality, 1586–1625

I

WHAT HAPPENED TO the lost colonists? This is one of the queries of early American history which has called forth many solutions, has produced fiction and drama, and has led also to more than a little faked evidence of one sort or another. It is not a problem to which answers can be given simply and decisively, yet they can be indicated with some degree of probability, even with some authority.[1]

The "lost colonists" in most reckonings were the eighty-five men, seventeen women, and eleven children last seen alive by the governor of the Roanoke colony, John White, on 27 August 1587 when he went on board ship on his way to England to fetch supplies for them which he was never able to deliver.[2]

[1] This attempt to set out what is and what is not known of the lost colonists stems from a discussion held on the stage of the Fort Raleigh Theatre on 17 July 1959 in which the late Christopher Crittenden, William S. Powell, and David Stick also took part. In 1962 a section on "Sir Walter Raleigh and the Lost Colony" was added to the paperback edition of D. B. Quinn, *Raleigh and the British Empire* (New York, Collier Books, 1962), while not long after, the author was privileged to see unpublished material by Dr. Bernard G. Hoffman on early tribes in eastern North America which indicated that his views had been proceeding along parallel lines. Some further comments on the subject were added to Paul H. Hulton and D. B. Quinn, *The American Drawings of John White*, 2 vols. (London and Chapel Hill, 1964), I, 60–1. Philip L. Barbour's *The Jamestown Voyages Under the First Charter, 1607–1609*, 2 vols. (Cambridge, Eng., 1969), with reliable texts of many scattered documents, provides an opportunity for a further review of the subject.

[2] Material on the Roanoke Island settlements will be taken without further reference

This group was not, however, the only one abandoned by the English during the course of their colonizing attempts at Roanoke Island between 1585 and 1587. At least three others can be segregated as probable or certain "lost colonists" at stages earlier than 1587. If they, or any one of them, were still alive in August 1587 they may or may not have coalesced, in whole or in part, with the lost colonists of 1587, or may have gone their own ways separately.

It is desirable to consider what potential Sir Francis Drake had for reinforcing the colony when he arrived at the Carolina Outer Banks in June 1586. In his series of attacks on Spanish fortresses he had begun by freeing and taking with him Negro slaves from the Cape Verde Islands.[3] He launched out in a grand program of equipping himself with additional men at Santo Domingo. There he freed some 200 Moors and Negroes from among the galley slaves (offering to bring the Moors back to their own country). "Many negroes belonging to private persons" we are told "went with them of their own free will," and though their owners offered to buy them back, "the English would not give them up except when the slaves themselves desired to go." [4] With the Negroes taken at the Cape Verde Islands, some 150 persons, they amounted to 350 in all, to whom he added at Cartagena "300 Indians . . . mostly women" and some Negroes as well [5]—so that the total could have been as high as 650 to 700 human beings. Though there may have been some deaths among the people he collected, he can scarcely have had less than 300 to 400 persons, allowing for Spanish exaggerations in the earlier figures, when he reached San Agustín in May 1586. His actions there convinced the Spaniards that he was equipping a colony as he went. We hear:

> Because the corsair carried off so many small things of all sorts, leaving nothing, nor any craft, large or small, that he could take along, we certainly believe it to be his intention to make a settlement. . . . He has taken with him everything required, by land or sea, to establish a settlement including even negroes which he seized at Santo Domingo and Cartagena.
>
> If there is not [a settlement], and Francis Drake did not intend to proceed thither . . . there would be no sense in his taking the pains he took to carry off launches and frigates, implements, locks and all sorts of hardware and negro labourers who in his country are free.[6]

---

from Quinn, *Roanoke Voyages,* except where a specific reference to the fate of the lost colonists is involved.

[3] Irene A. Wright, *Further English Voyages to Spanish America, 1583–1584* (London, 1951), p. 212.

[4] *Ibid.,* pp. 35, 54, 212.

[5] *Ibid.,* p. 173. The Indians were intended for an abortive attack across the Isthmus of Panama.

[6] *Ibid.,* pp. 181–2, 185, 187, 189.

Although Drake scarcely had time to disembark many or possibly any of his reinforcements in the shape of South American Indians and blacks on the Carolina Outer Banks between the arrival of Ralph Lane to meet him on 11 June and the beginning of the four-day storm on 13 June, it seems unlikely that all were lost during its course. We learn, indeed, that four ships put out to sea, having broken or cut their cables, and that "Manie also of our small Pinnaces and boates were lost."[7] Between 16 and 18 June, Drake pulled his forces together and arranged to take Lane and his settlers back to England. What did he do with his South American Indians and his freed Negroes? We hear of something like a hundred Moorish galley slaves who were, indeed, shipped back to the Mediterranean.[8] A few Negroes may easily have been assimilated into the seagoing population of Devonshire or the Thames. But a large number of Indians and blacks would certainly have caused comment in England, which is entirely lacking. The only reasonable explanation is that a considerable number of Indians and Negroes were put ashore on the Carolina Outer Banks and equipped with the pots and pans, locks and bolts, boats and launches of San Agustín. There is no direct evidence at all that this was done, but it is difficult to imagine what else happened to all those on board Drake's fleet. It is unlikely that very many were lost in the storm, certainly not all. So we have the possibility that, unknown in later times, a settlement strangely compounded of aborigines from South America and predial and household slaves from Spanish Caribbean cities and estates was left to form an isolated colony in what is now North Carolina, since there is no indication that contact was ever made with other groups. Though it was never located as such, the many legends of lost colonists in the area behind the Sounds may conceivably, though perhaps not probably, go back to a colony resulting from these events of June 1586.

Not all even of Ralph Lane's men were taken off by Drake on 18 June 1586.[9] An anonymous journal of a member of Drake's fleet records that the colonists were all taken off "except iij [who had gone furt]her into the countrie and the winde gre[we so that] wee coulde not staie for them." We have no precise indication of who these men were or where they had gone. We can speculate with some probability. Lane had had the son of Menatonon, the chief of the Chowan Indian tribe, as a hostage. This young man, Skiko, had given him valuable information that the Roanoke Indians were planning an attack on him, and Lane countered this by taking the initiative, attacking and killing Pemisapan at Dase-

[7] Quinn, *Roanoke Voyages*, I, 291–2, 307–8. [8] *Ibid.*, pp. 251–5.

[9] *Ibid.*, p. 307.

monquepeuc on 1 June. It is highly probable that immediately afterward he released Skiko and sent him back with the three Englishmen, who may well have been charged with some messages to Menatonon. Lane makes no mention of Skiko after 1 June or of the men sent off and eventually deserted. At the same time it must not be forgotten that the reports, very much later (as we shall see on pp. 473–4 below), of Englishmen located at the headquarters of this tribe and retained apparently as metalworkers might well have concerned those involved in this episode.

In 1586 Sir Richard Grenville, arriving too late with supplies for Lane's men, left only a small holding party on Roanoke Island, "15. men . . . furnished plentifully with all maner of prouision for two yeres"[1] (though Pedro Diaz, a Spaniard who was on board Grenville's ship, says it was "eighteen men . . . [with] four pieces of artillery of cast-iron and supplies for the eighteen men for a year. In charge of them he left Master Cofar, an Englishman, and another called Chapeman"). John White picked up information on this group from the Croatoan Indians when he returned in 1587 with those who later became known as the "lost colonists." Of the fifteen he believed had been left, two had been killed in an Indian attack. Their "house" was set on fire by the Indians, and the remainder were able to reach their boat, probably a smallish pinnace, and make their way to a little island in the Outer Banks opposite Roanoke Island. There they "remained a while, but afterward departed whither, as yet we knowe not."[2] They may have attempted to make an Atlantic crossing or to work their way to the Caribbean in the hope of meeting with English privateers; but they are just as likely to have gone north or south along the coast and to have made some sort of life for themselves, either on their own account or in association with a friendly Indian tribe. Again, nothing is known of what happened to them, but it is not impossible that some survived for some time on the North American mainland.

The circumstances under which the "lost colonists" proper were left on Roanoke Island in August 1587, and the evidence of their possible destination after they left the island, discovered in 1590, are very well known and have been referred to elsewhere, but must be included in any discussion of their subsequent fate. It is necessary, first of all, to consider where the English envisaged possible locations for a colony after Lane's men reached England with Drake in July 1586. Clearly the Moratuc (Roanoke) River was thought of as a possible route to the supposed copper mines of the interior, but Lane apparently thought its basin had not been

[1] *Ibid.*, I, 480, II, 791. [2] *Ibid.*, II, 528–9, 793.

well enough explored to be possible as the first location for a new colony. The Chowan River was more hopeful. Menatonon, chief of the Chowanoac tribe, had been helpful about the lands and waters that lay beyond his own villages and especially toward the north. So much so, indeed, that Lane thought of going overland by way of the Chowan to a bay to the northeast which sounded very suitable for settlement,[3] while sending some vessels round to it by sea from Roanoke Island. The distances in Lane's narrative are not entirely clear, but somewhere on Chesapeake Bay is obviously meant. If we lack precise indications of where it was, the "Iland" on the bay may possibly have been Old Point Comfort, then detached from the mainland and probably shown in the John White map made at this time.

The party Lane sent to explore the Chesapeake Bay area appears to have spent part of the winter of 1585–6 on its southern shore. They found the passage up Currituck Sound dangerous, and worked their way around Cape Henry to a total distance of 130 miles (Lane said) from Roanoke Island. They were under the command of a colonel (whose name we do not know), and we have indirect evidence that Thomas Harriot and John White were among them, since their general map gives a valuable picture of the southern part of the bay area. An Indian village, Chesepiuc, presumably the tribal village of the Chesapeake tribe, is marked in the vicinity of Lynnhaven Bay. An important Indian village, Skicóak, is marked to the south of a well-defined Elizabeth River, which would place it some miles south of modern Norfolk. Unnamed villages are placed on each side of the Nansemond River. Hampton Roads are shown, and the island that lies offshore between the Nansemond and Elizabeth rivers is presumably an exaggerated Old Point Comfort. The peninsula is clearly indicated, with an opening in the east end which is possibly Back River (with an unnamed village marked). The York River is shown also, but here information gives out, as this entry is conflated with the northern continuation of Chesapeake Bay, just as the north bank of the York is assimilated to the southern part of the Eastern Shore, making a continuous land barrier across the bay. The map provides evidence of a thorough exploration by boat of the southern shore of the bay and a brief reconnaissance of Hampton Roads and the Peninsula. The waterways lying to the south of the bay were particularly well prospected.

The result of this reconnaissance was that Lane commended the area highly in his report, "for pleasantnes of seate . . . not to be excelled by any whatever."[4] When Drake appeared in June 1586, Lane begged him

[3] *Ibid.*, I, 259–63. [4] *Ibid.*, p. 257.

for ships and boats to make a further reconnaissance. This would undoubtedly have been to Chesapeake Bay. He proposed to stay there for two months and then return to England. The next stage, presumably, would be to bring out a strong colony to settle on the bay if a suitable site had been found.

After Lane's return, as we saw, Richard Hakluyt strongly urged Sir Walter Ralegh to proceed with the colonization of the bay area, saying "your best planting wilbe about the bay of the Chesepians."[5] Consequently, when in 1587 John White took out the first real colony—that is, one containing women and children as well as men—the intention was to go to Chesapeake Bay to establish the City of Ralegh there. Sir Walter Ralegh had given instructions that they were "to make our seate and forte" at "the Bay of Chesepiock," as White said.[6] They first called in at Roanoke Island to see what had become of the fifteen (or eighteen) men left by Grenville in 1586, intending then to work up the coast and into the bay. But Simão Fernandes (Simon Ferdinando), the dominant figure in the expedition, forced White to disembark his colony on the Carolina Outer Banks and convey them to Roanoke Island. As the reader will recall, the reason White gave for this change of plan was that Fernandes considered the season rather late for catching Spanish ships crossing the Atlantic to Europe (it was now 22 July) and wanted to waste no more time transporting colonists, so that he could go privateering.

This we have already considered; there was also possibly a less callous reason. Fernandes, having apparently been in the Spanish service under Pedro Menéndez de Avilés at some point between 1565 and 1572, and having ostensibly gone with him on one of the voyages to the Chesapeake Bay region, or had detailed information about it,[7] would know that in 1570 the Indians there—presumably from the Powhatan group of tribes—had killed off a party of Jesuits, and had in turn been subjected to severe reprisals by the Spaniards. Moreover an attack was made in this area on the English expedition of 1584. He may well have considered that, however well Lane's party of 1585–6 got on with the Chesapeake Indians (and this must have been very well in view of the reports brought back), there were also potentially hostile tribes on the bay which might well attack and destroy White's weak colony. Whatever the case, as we have seen, the colonists established themselves once more on Roanoke Island and insisted that White should leave for England to report their altered plans and bring out early reinforcements and supplies, and he accordingly did so on 27 August 1587.

[5] *Ibid.*, p. 494.

[6] *Ibid.*, II, 523; see p. 247 above.

[7] *Ibid.*, I, 80–1. See pp. 260–1 above.

We have two indications of how he expected to be able to find them when he returned, which he mentioned three years later when he was finally able to set foot again on Roanoke Island.[8] The first was that they should carve on trees or doors the name of the place to which they were going to move. The second was that, already before White left, they had decided not to stay on Roanoke Island, but "were prepared to remove from Roanoak 50 miles into the maine." This is difficult to interpret precisely. By water, up the inside of the Outer Banks to the northernmost outlet and then up the coast to Chesapeake Bay was a longer journey than that, and so was the voyage up Albemarle Sound and the Chowan River to Menatonon's village and thence to the bay. The phrase "into the maine" seems to mean into the interior, and taken literally might suggest the Chowan, but if so it might well be as a halfway house to Chesapeake Bay by such an overland route as Lane had already sketched out with Menatonan. It seems less difficult to take White as meaning that the colony was going to settle on Chesapeake Bay, as originally intended, but was moving by stages, the first estimated to be some fifty miles in length. Thus their first stage could have been either up Albemarle Sound on the way to Chowanoac or to the head of Currituck Sound, on the way to Cape Henry, and a second to their final destination on the bay.

At least one English ship may have put in at Chesapeake Bay later in 1587 and found traces of the colonists already there, though it did not succeed in making contact with them. This was the expedition of Captain William Irish, who took the *Commander* and two other ships on a privateering voyage in the West Indies in 1587.[9] The sponsor of the voyage, Sir George Carey, was linked with the White venture, and it appears that Irish was carrying some stores for the colony. On the way back to England, with some Spanish prisoners on board, Irish and his ships sailed along the Florida coast, "making their way . . . until they came to the Bay of Santa Maria in latitude 37°. There they stayed to take in water and found traces of cattle and a stray dark-brown mule." This statement was made by Alonso Ruiz, one of Irish's prisoners, in July 1588 after he got back to the Spanish West Indies.[1]

Now Irish would expect White's men to have gone to Chesapeake Bay as they originally intended, and it would be natural for him to put in there to look for them. The Bahia de Santa Maria was the Spanish name for Chesapeake Bay. The discovery of traces of cattle and a stray mule is very puzzling. For the colonists to have got such animals so far north of Roanoke Island as, say, Lynnhaven Bay by the time Irish arrived (we do

[8] *Ibid.*, II, 613. [9] *Ibid.*, p. 498–9. [1] *Ibid.*, p. 782.

not have the exact time but it would probably be not later than October and could have been earlier) suggests that they left Roanoke Island very soon after White sailed in late August. The only other explanation would be that the animals were left over from the 1585–6 exploring party, but this seems to have gone by boat and was very unlikely to have taken animals so far. It is possible, therefore, that Ruiz was mistaken in the latitude where Irish landed, and that he put in instead at the Outer Banks near Roanoke Island, where stray animals were more likely to be found. But if so, it is very hard to understand why he should not have gone across the Sound to Roanoke Island to make contact with the settled colonists. The evidence points, though not without some ambiguity, to the lost colonists being already established, or at least some of them, at some place near the Cape Henry entrance to Chesapeake Bay within a month or two of White's departure. The obvious site would be in the vicinity of the village of Chesepiuc, near the shore of Lynnhaven Bay, though the inference is based on too many uncertainties to be conclusive.

White was unable to reach Roanoke Island in his relief attempt in 1588, being forced to retire, plundered and injured by sea-robbers, when his vessels had got almost to the Azores. Mysteriously and somewhat tragically, he could get no help at all to go out in 1589. Finally in 1590 he got passage on the *Hopewell*, which with William Sanderson's *Moonlight* reached the Outer Banks on 15 August, and Roanoke Island on the evening of the seventeenth.[2] The search made on the morning of the eighteenth brought him first to a tree on the highest point overlooking the north point of the island on which was "curiously carved these faire Romane letters CRO." This White interpreted as indicating the place where the settlers were now located, as "a secret token agreed upon betweene them & me at my last departure from them," provided that "in any wayes they should not faile to write or carve on the trees or posts of the dores the name of the place where they should be seated." White then located what had been the residence of the settlers, a palisaded enclosure, "and one of the chiefe trees or postes at the right side of the entrance had the barke taken off, and 5. foote from the ground in fayre Capotall letters was graven CROATOAN without any crosse or signe of distress."

White could scarcely be more specific; moreover he had indicated that the arrangement was that not only should the location of their destination be stated, but that "if they should happen to be distressed in any of those places, that then they should carve over the letters or name, a Crosse ✠ in this forme." He was emphatic that "we found no such signe of dis-

[2] For a summary account of the circumstances of the voyage, see *ibid.*, pp. 579–97.

tresse." He decided that "I had found a certaine token of their safe being at Croatoan, which is the place where Manteo was borne, and the Savages of the Iland our friends." White made great efforts to get down the coast to the vicinity of modern Cape Hatteras, where the Indian center on the then Croatoan Island was, but lack of boats, very rough weather, loss of cables and anchors, earlier losses of men, and the reluctance of the seamen, all forced him to agree to give over the search. They planned to winter in the West Indies but were not able to make their way against contrary winds; eventually they sailed out to the Azores and thence to England, and the search was virtually over.

This poignant episode is so well known that further gloss on it is scarcely necessary, but two points may be made. The first is that White did not expect that whatever signs would be left would indicate that they had gone southward across Pamlico Sound to Croatoan. He is quite clear that their intended destination in 1587 was elsewhere: he says that "at my comming away they were prepared to remove from Roanoak 50 miles into the maine." Whether this meant that they intended to move either to Chesapeake Bay, their original destination, or to the Chowan River, the other area which had attractions for settlers, it certainly did not cover the islands in the Carolina Outer Banks to the south.

It is easy to see objections to the whole colony moving south to Croatoan. They are most unlikely to have done so before making a reconnaissance to see whether suitable land was available there for them to settle, even if they believed they could rely on Manteo's good will in accepting them. The island, now the southern part of Hatteras Island, was undoubtedly more extensively wooded and had therefore much more soil cover than today (though in the Buxton area it is still wooded). It may also have been appreciably wider, since it has been steadily cutting back westward since the sixteenth century. At the same time, it is doubtful whether it would seem likely to provide adequate agricultural land for a settlement of some hundred English colonists in addition to maintaining its Indian occupants. The main colony is much more likely to have followed its original plan and to have gone either north or west, being at least fifty if not more miles away in one of these directions by the time White returned after three years' absence in August 1590. The departure of the whole colony to the south and their subsequent removal to the mainland in the vicinity of the Pamlico and Neuse Rivers cannot be wholly excluded as a possibility, but the existing evidence makes it appear slight and, even in an area of insubstantialities, improbable.

There is a possible solution which might follow logically from such evidence as we have, and would seem preferable to the view that the whole colony migrated southward to Croatoan. This is slightly more complex. If we assume that the colony moved shortly after August 1587, as White expected, either to the Chowan or the Chesapeake, this does not mean that all the colonists removed at the same time or that they left Roanoke Island entirely deserted. They could very well have left a small party behind. White found in 1590 that a strong defensive enclosure had been erected which could have been regarded as adequate to protect a holding party against a fate such as had overtaken Grenville's comparable party in 1586. The purpose of leaving such a party would be partly to safeguard the heavy equipment, bars of iron and cannon which could not be taken with the main party, which presumably had only the pinnace and one or two boats at their disposal. They would also be expected to look after the chests containing John White's personal possessions. Their other function would be to await his return with supplies and reinforcements in 1588, both so that they could direct him to the settlement which the main body had created and also to keep the fort site on Roanoke Island available as a base he might wish to use for part of the new body of settlers expected to come with him.

For some reason, it is suggested, this party decided to abandon its post, most probably because White did not appear in the summer of 1588. They may have been harassed by Indian enemies, or had insufficient food, but they may also have had other reasons for going south rather than trying to rejoin the main party. White had been on very friendly terms with Manteo in August 1587 and had recognized him as the Indian ruler of both Roanoke Island and the mainland village which had been the headquarters of the Roanoke tribe whose chief Lane killed in 1586, in addition to his own tribal holdings on the Carolina Outer Banks. The holding party could assume that, whatever else he did, when White did come, he would make contact with Manteo, as indeed he tried to do in 1590. They could therefore move to Croatoan and settle down temporarily alongside the Indians there without abandoning their primary function of making contact with White when he came. They would not (if the foregoing argument is correct) have had more than a boat or two with them, since the pinnace would have gone with the main party; and so could not move guns, iron bars, or White's chests, even if they wanted to. They could leave signs—those found by White in 1590 would be appropriate—no Maltese cross, since they were not in distress, and the name of CROATOAN as their destination. The assumption would be that White, seeing the signs on Roanoke Island, would make contact with Manteo as soon as possible and thus obtain the full story, so far as the holding party could tell it, of what had happened to the colony since

August 1587. If this was the case, the party could still have been at post on Croatoan Island when White returned in August 1590, and the whole mystery, or the greater part of it, would have been solved when he found Manteo there.

This reconstruction is largely fictional, but it rests on a reasonable body of inference from the extremely few facts at our disposal; the addition of a very few more could easily destroy or confirm it. It is desirable to make the reconstruction as specific as can be made to seem reasonable in view of one element that should be made plain. Whatever happened to the "lost" groups already considered in addition to the 1587 colony, we may plan to look for the surviving lost colonists of the early seventeenth century in *two* groups rather than one: the main body, which most probably went north or west, for which the basic evidence is reasonably good; and a smaller group—on which the evidence is considerably more indirect, though not negligible—which went south.

II

THE LOST COLONISTS lived on in various ways after 1590. They provided by their presumed continuing existence a legal title from the English crown to Sir Walter Ralegh over the greater part of the east coast of North America until its resumption by James I late in 1603. Had their continued existence not been assumed, Ralegh's patent would have expired in March 1591, since its continuing in force depended on his having established an English colony in North America within seven years. By assuming that the 1587 colonists were still in being as a corporate unit, and that the City of Ralegh had substantial existence, Ralegh was able to maintain his claim to control all English expeditions to eastern North America (except Newfoundland). We have seen that he wrote indignantly to the Lord High Admiral in 1602 to complain that Bartholomew Gosnold had gone on a voyage to what was later New England without his permission. It can be argued that the lost colonists should really be thought of as the "deserted" colonists, because Ralegh neglected to make any serious attempts to rescue them after 1590, in the belief that sometime or other he might find it profitable to take up again the probing of North America for trade and colonization.

It is true that, in his *The discoverie of Guiana* (1596), Ralegh claimed that he intended in 1595 to call in at Virginia on his way from South America to see if he could find any trace of the colony,[3] but there is no

[3] Sir Walter Ralegh, *The discoverie of Guiana* (1595), p. 5.

indication that on his voyage homeward from the Caribbean between July and September 1595 he made any approach to the North American coast. It was claimed long afterward, in 1602, that five attempts in all were made under his auspices to find the colonists. We know of those in 1588 and 1590, and in 1602. The others, as we have seen, are more likely to have taken place as late as 1600 and 1601 rather than earlier. Ralegh's responsibility for leaving the colonists in danger was considerable, though of course there is no way of estimating what the chances were of locating them or determining their fate, had other expeditions been sent out in 1589, 1591, and subsequent years. By 1593, when he had retired to Ireland, John White had given up all hope of getting adequate help from Ralegh or anyone else and had been forced, fatalistically or realistically—or both—to write off the whole episode, which had engulfed his own daughter, son-in-law, and granddaughter with the rest.

The colonists survived in the minds of both Englishmen and Spaniards. To Englishmen who remained interested in North America throughout the long war between England and Spain, the belief that the lost colonists might be still active in North America kept alive the desire to renew speculative voyages of exploration along the American coast. The continued belief of some Spaniards that the English had never finally left the Outer Banks area operated in the contrary sense. It suggested to them that English occupation of part of the North American coastline would continue to infringe their monopoly of the western continents and that a colony in being could pose a threat to their Florida garrison and to their trading fleets returning from the Spanish Indies on the Gulf Stream. Suppression of the supposed colony appeared desirable. As we shall see, too, the chances are high that the lost colonists did in fact live on for some time in North America—certain groups of them at any rate—and that they even survived the reversion of Ralegh's exclusive patent to the crown in 1603.

John White concluded his narrative of his unsuccessful voyage in 1588—or perhaps it was Richard Hakluyt, when he included the narrative in his *Principall navigations* (1589) [4]—by saying that his expedition for the relief of the planters had to be given over, "which thereby were not a little distressed," thus providing a keynote for subsequent assumptions that they must still be in existence. Of his second unsuccessful expedition, which had brought him to Roanoke Island, John White wrote on 4 February 1593 that his failure had been "noysome to the planters" and "discomfortable to them," [5] again keeping alive the impression of their con-

[4] Quinn, *Roanoke Voyages*, II, 613. [5] *Ibid.*, p. 715.

tinuance as a colony. In a somewhat tragic conclusion to his letter to Richard Hakluyt he commends "the reliefe of my discomfortable company the planters in Virginia, to the merciful help of the Almighty," having evidently given up hope that human agency would aid the members of his family and the rest of the little group he last saw in 1587. This letter was published by Richard Hakluyt in the third volume of the second edition of *The principal navigations* in 1600.[6]

The crew of the *Dainty*, when she was setting off on her ill-fated Pacific voyage under Richard Hawkins in 1593, had two ships in company with them for some little way, which, they said some years later, they believed were carrying "supplies of people, ammunition, clothes, implements, axes and spades for the settlers in Jacan [the Spanish name for the Chesapeake Bay area]." This they passed on to Darby Glavin, a former member of the 1585–6 Roanoke colony who had entered the Spanish service, and who expressed the opinion that it justified him in thinking (in 1600) that the Roanoke colony still survived. It has not been established if such ships did in fact accompany Hawkins. The *Dainty* left Plymouth on 12 June 1593, and it is possible that the two ships were those of George Drake and Richard Strong, which left Falmouth on 1 June on a walrus-hunting expedition in the St. Lawrence, had been delayed in their progress westwards, and were picked up by the *Dainty* later in the month.[7]

John Gerard, barber-surgeon and herbalist, who was a member of the syndicate which had undertaken to assist in the maintenance of American settlement in 1589 but had done very little about it except to help White to go out in 1590, took the line in 1597 that the lost colonists might be still alive. In his *Herball* he wrote of "Virginia . . . where are dwelling at this present Englishmen, if neither untimely death by murdering, or pestilence, corrupt aire, bloodie flixes, or some other mortall sicknes hath not destroied them."[8] Gerard can scarcely be described as overoptimistic about their chances of survival, but he did not wholly write them off. George Abbot, future Archbishop of Canterbury, offered no such hope. While the English had "sent thither at two severall times, two severall companies as Colonies" and named the land Virginia after the queen, "this voyage being interprised in the charge of private men, and not

[6] Richard Hakluyt, *The principal navigations*, 3 vols. (1598–1600), III, 287–8.

[7] Cf. Quinn, *Roanoke Voyages*, II, 836–7; and Richard Hawkins, *Observations* (London, 1933), ed. J. A. Williamson, p. liii. See pp. 323–4 above.

[8] John Gerard, *Herball* (1597), p. 752; Quinn, *Roanoke Voyages*, I, 446, and for a further association of Gerard and White, E. G. Morgan, "John White and the Sarsaparilla," *William and Mary Quarterly*, 3d ser., XIV (1957), 414–17.

thoroughly being followed by the State; the possession of this Virginia is now discontinued, and the country at the present left to the olde inhabitants."[9]

The law took the same view as Abbot in the case of one of the lost colonists, Ananias Dare. In April 1594, his nearest relative, Robert Satchfield, was given letters of administration of the estate of Ananias Dare, late of the parish of St. Bride, Fleet Street, London, who had died beyond the seas (or was presumed by law after the lapse of seven years to have so died). This assignment was varied on 27 June 1597 when the administration was removed from the hands of Satchfield and put in those of John Noke, another kinsman, during the minority of John Dare, son of Ananias.[1] Formally, then, in the eyes of the law the Lost Colony was held, well before the end of the century, to have died out.

By the time Richard Hakluyt came to publish the third volume of *The principal navigations* in 1600 his thoughts had already turned toward further colonizing attempts in America, possibly based on the rediscovery of the Lost Colony if it was there to be discovered. In reprinting Thomas Harriot's account of the resources of Virginia, first published in 1588, he put in the margin beside Harriot's remark that the settlers of 1585–6 had lacked proper means for hunting and fishing: "This want is hereafter to be supplied."[2] I would suggest, without being able to prove it, that Sir Walter Ralegh began his attempts to rediscover the Lost Colony in the same year, 1600, and that Hakluyt's comment may have been made in the light of new preparations.

It is possible that Mace went out in that year and in 1601 to search for traces of the lost colonists, for with the sea war running down Ralegh once again thought of reviving the colonizing process and so exploiting his dormant rights to control trade and settlement on the North American shore. So far we know only that Ralegh was in Weymouth, from which Mace operated, in September 1601 at a time when a reconnaissance expedition would return from Virginia. In 1602 Mace, "who had beene twice before at Virginia,"[3] sailed to somewhere in the vicinity of Cape

[9] Abbot, *A briefe description of the whole worlde* (1600), sig. H2v.

[1] P.R.O., Prob. 6/5, fols. 95, 213; *Index to Administrations in the Prerogative Court of Canterbury, 1581–1595*, ed. C. H. Ridge (London, 1954), p. 45; *Index to Administrations in the Prerogative Court of Canterbury, 1596–1608* (London, 1964), ed. Marc Fitch, p. 37; William S. Powell, "Roanoke Colonists and Explorers: An Attempt at Identification," *The North Carolina Historical Review*, XXXIV (1957), 225–6.

[2] Hakluyt, *Principal navigations*, III (1600), 280; Quinn, *Roanoke Voyages*, I, 384.

[3] John Brereton, *A briefe and true relation of the discoverie of the north parte of Virginia . . .*, 2 issues (London, G. Bishop, 1602), p. 14; *S.T.C.* 3610–11.

Lookout equipped with trade goods and probably a vocabulary of Indian words supplied by Harriot, and sought for and conceivably found some hints on the possible location of the colonists;[4] in particular he heard that there may have been white men living in the Chesapeake Bay area.

There is a further curious episode in 1602 which could conceivably have been another attempt by John White to make contact with the colonists.[5] Martin Pring, who made a trading voyage to Cape Cod in 1603, was associated in 1602 with a John White who could have been the artist, in a venture which might have begun as one more attempt to search for the colonists. In that year Martin Pring, John White, and Nicholas Narborne were on board the privateer *Susan Parnell* in the West Indies. Off Cuba they transferred to the ship *Archangell*, captained by Michael Geere, who put them in charge of a prize crew to take a Spanish prize home to England. The vessel had little in the way of supplies on board, so they went with her to Campeche Bay to get what they could, and were successful in acquiring a quantity of logwood (Campeche wood) but very little in the way of food. They set out to cross the Atlantic in her, had an extremely bad time through lack of food, and eventually disposed of ship and logwood in Morocco, they said, in order to get food and a passage home, since the ship was sinking beneath them.

This enterprise may have been a simple privateering episode having nothing whatever to do with the lost colonists. It may, however, have a somewhat different implication, though it is quite impossible on present knowledge to prove it. If White was the artist and governor and took passage on the *Susan Parnell* in hope of getting her to call in at Roanoke Island on the way home, so that he could see whether the colonists were there or with Manteo, then the transfer to the *Archangell* would make sense. The *Susan Parnell*'s activities might well have made the return call difficult. But the captain of the *Archangell*, Michael Geere, had been master of the *Little John* in the small squadron that had promised to bring White to Roanoke Island in 1590 (though in the end only the *Hopewell* and *Moonlight* made that brief, inconclusive visit). Geere worked for John Watts and Company and would be well aware of the problems of reaching the colonists. One can see the handing over of the Spanish prize to White and his associates as providing a means by which they might make their way to Roanoke Island on their way home. The visit to Campeche Bay in search of logwood and food would fit with such an intention.

[4] See pp. 406–14 above.

[5] Dr. K. R. Andrews discovered the relevant documents in P.R.O., H.C.A. They are discussed in Hulton and Quinn, *The American Drawings of John White*, I, 22–3.

Why, then, did the vessel not follow a homeward route through the Florida Channel and call at Roanoke Island? In the first place we do not know that she did not try. The documents in the case have nothing to do with the Lost Colony but are concerned with what happened to the prize and her lading in Morocco. If she made the attempt, or indeed even succeeded in making the call, we can be reasonably sure that she found no clear evidence that the colonists had survived, since this would almost certainly have been publicized after White got back to England; yet she, too, might have picked up some scraps of information and rumor.

But it would seem more probable, even if this reconstruction of the purpose and nature of the voyage were correct, that the ship took the shortest and most rapid route available at the time and did not make a North American call, since failure to obtain adequate supplies of food would make any diversion to the Carolina Outer Banks risky, putting the lives of the prize crew in greater danger. White may even have been overcome by the pressure of his companions and prevented from reaching North America, as he had been once before. Whatever the pattern of this voyage—and it must be stressed again that the association of it with the search for the Lost Colony is only conjectural, based on the association in it of men previously involved in the attempts to explore and settle North America—there is an outside chance that the North American coast was reached and some rumors added to the stock already current, even if firm information was not obtained.

Thus, late in 1602 Ralegh may have been in possession of some slight indications that the lost colonists lived on somewhere within reach of Chesapeake Bay. He had proposed in this year to send out both Samuel Mace and Bartholomew Gilbert to search for them on Chesapeake Bay, or to prospect this area in order to revive his old colonizing plans, or both. We know the sequel, so far as it now appears. Gilbert never entered the bay in spite of several attempts, and was killed by Indians somewhere on the Atlantic shore well to the north of Cape Charles. We have no direct evidence on Mace's voyage, but the bringing of "Virginia" Indians to the Thames at London with their canoe in September 1603 [6] raises the question of whether they may not have been brought by Mace from Chesapeake Bay. If so—and the inference is still highly conjectural—then it would have been possible for one such as Thomas Harriot, who knew some Algonquian, to question them to some purpose, so that if the lost colonists were living on or near Chesapeake Bay a clear channel of contact could at last have been envisaged.

[6] See pp. 419–23 above.

But if there were any indications of this sort it was a very unpropitious time to pursue them. By September 1603 Ralegh was a prisoner in the Tower of London charged with treason and was on the point of losing all his Virginia rights to the crown. He was in no position to encourage further Virginia voyages. At the same time, it is not impossible that some knowledge of the survival of the lost colonists was available in England before the end of 1603 and was used by Lord Salisbury, as will be indicated, in the peace negotiations with Spain in 1604.

III

THE SPANIARDS HAD their own channels of information about English colonizing activities far to the north of the Spanish posts at San Agustín and Santa Elena. They were constantly on the lookout for French pirates or colonizers and kept a record of all non-Spanish ships seen working their way northward along the Florida coast. Moreover, Indians with whom they were in contact reported activities by foreign ships along the shores well to the north of the Spanish settlements, and occasionally brought news of the presence of white men—usually described as Frenchmen—among the more northerly tribes. Clearly, information could have filtered down from the Roanoke Island and Chesapeake Bay areas of continuing English occupation, though it would be rather vague and of little exact value by the time it reached San Agustín.

The Spanish expedition under Vicente González which explored Chesapeake Bay in 1588 returned with the rather imprecise belief that Englishmen were located in a settlement somewhere on or near the bay, and this belief persisted in the minds of participants in the expedition for many years. Moreover, they had found more concrete traces of an English presence, in the shape of a boatslip, farther south on the Carolina Outer Banks on their way home. The captivity of the Spanish pilot Pedro Diaz, taken by the English in 1585 and brought on several expeditions to Roanoke Island, on his escape enabled the Spaniards to get a picture of English activities in the Roanoke area from 1584 to 1588, revealing that the colony site on Roanoke Island had been screened from observers on the Outer Banks.[7] Diaz made his way to freedom when the small ship in which he was sailing as part of John White's abortive rescue expedition was overrun by French pirates, from whom he eventually escaped at the Cape Verde Islands. He realized that White had not been able to complete his voyage in 1588 and gave his opinion on 21 March 1589 that

[7] Quinn, *Roanoke Voyages*, II, 816–18.

"the people who remained in the settlement should have, by this time, died of hunger, or been exposed to great need and danger."

This view was not shared by Spanish officials in the Caribbean. In 1590 news of John White's presence on the *Hopewell* on his way to Virginia filtered through from Spaniards in contact with ships of the privateering squadron with which he sailed,[8] and this was taken to mean that the settlement was still in being and in process of being reinforced. In a letter written in September 1590 by Diego Menéndez de Valdes, governor of Puerto Rico, which was intercepted and translated by the English, he wrote that the English were established in "Floryda" and that they "doe fortyfie there apace, and y[t] the same place dothe serve us [the English] notable to take in fresh water and to refreshe our men. And yf anie our shippes do happen to come late, they do wynter there." Virginia, indeed, was thought to be continuing to serve the English in her privateering campaign against Spain, as Ralegh and Grenville had hoped it would do in 1585–6 when the Roanoke Island colonizing experiment was first begun.

Menéndez de Valdes was wrong about the continued use of the settlement for the purpose of refreshing the privateers, although probably individual English ships did put in along the coast north of Santa Elena and as far north at least as Chesapeake Bay in the years after 1590.[9] But there is no evidence—or at least none has yet been found—that they made contact with any of the lost colonists, or especially that they brought any of them home. In 1589 indeed, the governor of Florida, Pedro Menéndez Marqués, had reported on the need to wipe out the supposed English settlement which he believed was located on Chesapeake Bay, and was authorized to take out a strong expedition in 1590 to eliminate it and put up a stout fort, with a garrison of 300, to secure the bay for Spain.[1] But war necessities diverted the general to the more urgent task of running the Indies treasure through the English semiblockade in fast-sailing, specially constructed vessels. The project for taking over the area where the English had been, and were still thought to be active, was abandoned. It was not forgotten.

From time to time scraps of information reached the Spaniards that supplies were being sent to a settlement. We have seen above that members of Richard Hawkins's expedition of 1593 believed that two ships

[8] *Ibid.*, p. 799.

[9] K. R. Andrews, "Christopher Newport of Limehouse, Mariner," *William and Mary Quarterly*, 3d ser., XI (1954), 3–27; Andrews, *English Privateering Voyages, 1588–1595*, Hakluyt Society, 2d ser., no. 111 (1959), p. 195.

[1] Quinn, *Roanoke Voyages*, II, 816–18; see pp. 278–9 above.

which had sailed in their company had brought "people, ammunition, clothes, implements, axes and spades for the settlers," and that the informant to whom they told the story believed in 1600 that the settlers "were still there." [2] But if ships did go out in 1593 we know nothing of what they found, and it is unlikely, in view of White's painfully resigned letter of the same year, that any were sent.

From time to time the Florida authorities reverted to the possible survival of English settlements to the north. At some time after 1593 Vicente González gave a rather meandering account of the expedition he had had led in 1588 to Chesapeake Bay, expressing the opinion that "The English colony . . . is established from this village [near the southern entrance to Chesapeake Bay] northwards on a river from which . . . there is a passage to the South Sea . . . and so he holds it as certain that the Englishmen are there." [3] This is based on what Indians told him in 1588, and possibly later, since two captives were taken from the bay area to Florida. This is probably the vaguest and least substantial of rumors, but Gonzalo Méndez de Canzo, collecting materials on the prospects for further Spanish exploration into the interior and up the coast, was able to get a statement from the Irishman, Darby Glavin, whom I have quoted for the tale about ships leaving for Virginia in 1593.

The governor, in a letter of February 1600, reported that Glavin had made it clear that the English had first entered the country at 35°30′ N, namely at Roanoke Island, but had later moved to 37° N, which would be on Chesapeake Bay—"where," the governor said, "he believes they are at present." Glavin himself, in the deposition he made a little earlier, said "the English are in Jacan [i.e., around the bay]. It does not seem likely that they would abandon so fertile a land where there was so much gold and so many pearls." [4] Glavin, who had deserted White on the way to Virginia in 1587, could not know from his own knowledge that the lost colonists had been deposited at Roanoke Island rather than Chesapeake Bay, whatever he might have picked up from other sources in the meantime. It is also clear that in 1600 Méndez de Canzo did not have any new information on the English settlements. At the same time, the fact that reports were still reaching Spain in 1600 that the English probably maintained contact with a settlement in Virginia were not without relevance to events in Europe.

The significance of the possible survival of the colony emerged in 1604. In that year a peace treaty was at last concluded between England and Spain. The leading Spanish delegate, who came to England only for

[2] *Ibid.*, pp. 836–7. [3] *Ibid.*, p. 825. [4] *Ibid.*, p. 838.

the concluding sessions, was the Constable of Castile, Juan Fernández de Velasco. Like the rest of the delegates, he was entirely opposed to the English case that Spain should recognize their right to trade with and occupy untenanted parts of the Indies, and wished the treaty to prohibit all English intercourse with the Americas—South, Central, or North. At the same time he believed that the English had indeed been in possession of Virginia for some thirty years and that it would be difficult to get them to relinquish their subjects there or their rights to continue their occupation. We can see that, if he had been well informed of the interest which his government had taken over so many years, since 1585 indeed, in the movements of the English expeditions up the coast, the rumors of settlements and of reinforcements sent to them in 1590, and the continuing belief of the Florida authorities as late as 1600 that the English were still located to the north of the Spanish colony, he could have formed this opinion from Spanish sources alone. At the same time we cannot exclude the likelihood that this information was reinforced by some new English evidence, produced in private since it did not appear in the formal discussions, that the Lost Colony still existed. We have seen that some such indications might have reached King James in 1603. It would be natural that, if this were so, his representatives in the negotiations should have brought them forward and, in turn, they could have reinforced Spanish beliefs and information. We have not, however, found anything on paper to this effect.

The Constable, however, when consulted about the new Virginia colony in 1607, recalled these problems, noting "that when he discussed peace in England he considered that if he specifically tried to exclude the English from the Indies, and specifically from Virginia, he foresaw the difficulty that they are in peaceful possession of the latter for more than thirty years." [5] At the same time he indicated "if it was declared that it [Virginia] was not part of the Indies, a gate would be opened leading to ruin." In the end no provision was made about the Indies in the treaty, leaving it to the Spaniards to maintain that the English, as always in their view, were still excluded. The Lost Colony, whether in existence or not, thus played an appreciable part in the diplomatic contest over the Treaty of London, and the circumstances suggest that some new information was in the possession of the English negotiators, though no trace of it has so far come to light.

[5] Barbour, *Jamestown Voyages,* I, 121–2. This throws an important light on the negotiations in England in 1604. The discovery of a dossier used to convince the Spaniards would be a most significant one.

It seems probable that the matter was talked about in London in 1604 and reviewed again in 1605, and that the story of the Lost Colony became somewhat tedious by repetition to Londoners, at least, for in 1605 it was guyed on the stage in the play *Eastward Hoe* by George Chapman, Ben Jonson, and John Marston. It will suffice to cite one speech of Seagull's on the English occupation of Virginia. "A whole Country of English is there man, bred of those that were left there in 79 [*sic* for 1587]; They have married with the Indians, and make 'hem bring forth as beautifull faces as any we have in England: and therefore the Indians are so in love with 'hem, that all the treasure they have they lay at their feete."[6] It might appear that in the current propaganda for the revival of the Virginia enterprise, which bore fruit in the charter of April 1606, the story of the allegedly surviving colony had been somewhat oversold. By what precise means—manuscript tracts, ballads which have not survived, or simply gossip (in view of the fact that the question came up during negotiations for the Treaty of London)—cannot be more than guessed at.

IV

THERE IS NO CLEAR evidence of any further English reconnaissance of Chesapeake Bay before Newport reached Cape Henry with the first settlement of Virginia on 29 April 1607. But there could well have been earlier contacts. We have seen that the European vessel which came into the bay two or three years before 1607 and seized several Indians at a river north of the York, which E. M. Wingfield reported in 1607,[7] might have been Samuel Mace's ship in Ralegh's service. It might also have been a vessel belonging to France or Spain. There is no indication in the surviving documents that it was a Spanish ship.

Christopher Newport led the first settlers impeccably into the Chesapeake in 1607. Had he been there before? His intention to go with John White in 1590 had been frustrated, but Dr. K. R. Andrews has shown that he had many later opportunities to call at the North American coast on the way home from West Indian voyages.[8] He may even have done so on his last venture before the Jamestown settlement. In 1605 he returned from the West Indies to have an interview with King James (to

[6] Act III, Scene 3, ll. 17–22. The play was entered in the Stationers' Register on 4 September 1605. Ben Jonson, *Works,* ed. C. H. Herford, I (1925), 190–200, and IV (1932), 498–9, 569; Edward Arber, ed., *A Transcript of the Stationers' Register, 1554–1640,* 5 vols. (London, 1879–94), III, 300.

[7] Barbour, *Jamestown Voyages,* I, 227. See p. 428 above.

[8] See p. 209 above.

whom he presented a crocodile). It is possible that he also reported on a visit to the Chesapeake of which we have no direct evidence; such a report would have provided a specific reason for his selection to command the first fleet in 1607. These are somewhat empty speculations, except that it is difficult to envisage the Jamestown settlement taking place without some reconnaissance more recent than twenty years earlier. The Spanish ambassador, Pedro de Zúñiga, it is true, reporting Newport's first return in a letter of 22 August 1607, stated "they have not been able to find the 20 men they left there three years ago now." [9] But we know nothing of any men sent out in 1604 to settle in the area. He must have picked up a garbled tale about the inability of the Jamestown settlers to find the lost colonists left behind in 1587—twenty, not three years before—and perhaps confused it with something he had heard of a 1603 voyage.

Yet between 1607 and 1610 there were persistent attempts to locate survivors from the various lost groups of the years 1585–7, and also to assemble information from Indians with whom the settlers were in contact. From these efforts a reasonably coherent outline of what occurred to certain groups of persons who survived for some considerable time can be seen to emerge.

The first and perhaps crucial question is what happened to the Chesapeake Indians? Already by about 1580 a great chief had grouped under him a substantial number of tribes on the region of the lower Chesapeake Bay. Whether he was Powhatan (as is most probable) or his predecessor is not certain. But his authority did not extend over the Chesapeake tribe. According to Strachey, writing in 1610–11, all members of the Chesapeake tribe had recently been wiped out by Powhatan. He says: "Not long synce yt was that his priests told him, how that from the Chesapeack Bay a Nation should arise, which woould dissolve and give end to his Empier, for which not many years synce (perplex't with this divelish Oracle, and divers understanding thereof) according to the auncyent and gentile Custome, he destroyed and put to sword, all such who might lye under any doubtfull construccion of the said prophesies, as all the Inhabitants, the weroance and his Subjects of that province and so remayne all the Chessiopeians at this daie, and for this cause extinct." [1]

[9] Barbour, *Jamestown Voyages,* I, 77. Barbour (I, 212) cites a Venetian report of 17–27 February 1609 which says, "A few years ago in the reign of the present King another ship with a like number of people [eight hundred] and cattle was sent out." This sounds like a garbled reference to the 1606 expedition, but may refer to something different.

[1] William Strachey, *Historie of travell into Virginia Britania* (1612) (London, 1953), ed. L. B. Wright and Virginia Freund, pp. 104–5, 108.

There is no reason to disbelieve Strachey on the wiping out of the Chesapeake tribe shortly before Newport's arrival in 1607, which means that the Indians who attacked the settlers at the first landing were Powhatan's own men, recently—possibly very recently—placed there.

Strachey had what he regarded as authoritative information on the fate of the lost colonists; they were, he maintained, killed by Powhatan. Near the opening of the "Historie of travell in Virginia Britania" he bewails "the poor planters . . . [who] as we shall find in this following Discourse came . . . to a miserable, and untimely desteny." [2] He blamed John White for "neglecting these unfortunate and betrayed people, of whose end yet you shall hereafter read in due place." [3] But the book was never finished, the narrative sections on the Virginia Colony and its immediate prelude not being included in any of the three copies of the draft that survive; this was presumably never written, so he did not keep his promise to provide a full narrative of the lost colonists' fate. He does, however, refer to a report sent to King James which set out what had been found, he believed authoritatively, on the fate of the colonists and also the king's reaction to the report and what he advocated should be done in Virginia as a result of it.

There is good evidence that some such information was in the possession of the Council of Virginia by May 1609. Besides, Strachey, as secretary of the colony in 1610–11, had access to files and registers which have not survived, and it is probable that if he had completed his "Historie" he could have cited in detail the document he claimed was sent. He showed the "Historie" to important men connected with policy-making in Virginia in the years 1608–10, and is most unlikely to have put in it statements of this sort which he did not know for certain to be true. In regard to events of which he had direct knowledge, Strachey can be shown to have been an accurate and conscientious writer, though he was liable to take over other men's opinions and even words in situations where he had not himself been involved.

He tells us that "his Majestie hath bene acquainted, that the men, women, and Children of the first plantation at Roanoak were by practize and Commaundement of Powhatan (he himself perswaded thereunto by his Priests) miserably slaughtered without any offence given him . . . by the first planted (who 20. and od yeeres had peacably lyved and intermixed with thos Savadges, and were out of his Territory)." [4] As to when this took place, he says "at what tyme our Colony (under the conduct of Captain Newport) landed within the Chesapeak Bay." He believed, therefore, that it took place as late as the spring of 1607, possibly even as the

[2] *Ibid.*, p. 15. [3] *Ibid.*, p. 150. [4] *Ibid.*, p. 44.

first report of Newport's ships reached Powhatan, which would fit in with the simultaneous attack on the Chesapeake tribe and its elimination in the few relevant days in late April of that year. This might oblige us to assume that the band of Indians who crept up on the evening of 27 April, wounding Gabriel Archer and a sailor with their arrows, were an advance party of Powhatan's men; and that the Indians who were so busy keeping out of the way of the Englishmen along the south shore of the bay on the twenty-seventh and twenty-eighth were Powhatan's forces going about their task of killing off the Chesapeake Indians—and possibly lost colonists as well—and burning their villages (the reconnaissance party "saw great smoakes of fire"),[5] so that all effective contact between Newport and the surviving English colonists and friendly Chesapeake Indians was cut off for ever.

The deduction of such a story—which would add a dramatic gloss to the circumstances of the first landings in 1607—from what Strachey says in the passages cited would not be an illegitimate use of evidence. On the other hand, it is clearly not the whole story, and it may not be correct.

We cannot be certain that Strachey was speaking precisely when he implied that the attack on the lost colonists took place in those days between 26 and 29 April while Newport's first reconnaissance was being made. He may have meant that the attack took place some little time before the arrival of the colonists. Indeed, whatever detailed evidence had been accumulated for the report sent to the king, it is unlikely that exact dates could be established unless one of the Indians concerned in it specifically linked the time of the massacre with the time of the first landing. We can probably take it that Strachey believed the massacre to have taken place on these dates in April when the Englishmen first came ashore.

We lack an exact statement from Strachey that the killing off of Chesapeake Indians by Powhatan was directly linked with their association with the lost colonists and took place at exactly the same time. This makes it impossible to be certain that all our evidence—and too much of it is Strachey's own—points in the same direction. There is no reason to doubt that Strachey believed Powhatan had overthrown and cleared out the Chesapeake Indians and installed his own men in their villages, and this is very probably true. What we cannot be certain of is whether he was correctly informed about the time when this took place. It could very well have occurred at the same time and under the same circumstances as the killing of the lost colonists, being directly bound up with

[5] Barbour, *Jamestown Voyages*, I, 133–5.

it, but this association remains circumstantial only and is not directly authorized by what Strachey says.

There is also the fact that Strachey does not state that the massacre of the lost colonists took place on or near the south shore of Chesapeake Bay. We may infer this from anterior evidence, and we can produce reasonable indications that the lost colonists are more likely to have been able to live there for a long period undisturbed than in any other area one can name. But we cannot make the association precise for lack of direct evidence—which is why we so badly need to have before us the documentation, particularly the report to the king, which Strachey was using. Nor, finally, is Strachey consistent throughout his unfinished book in defining the place where the lost colonists were killed. In the passages quoted so far—which appear to be decisive about the fact of the massacre—he does not name a place. Elsewhere he indicates that the place was Roanoke Island and not the vicinity of Chesapeake at all, though this problem will require investigation in more detail before it can be fully covered.

The result is that, although Strachey can be used as basis for the report that Powhatan killed or caused to be killed the lost colonists in or shortly before 1607 (and other evidence will be reviewed which on the whole confirms this report), yet the circumstantial deductions which would place that massacre near the southern shore of Chesapeake Bay in the last week of April 1607 and associate it with the killing off of the Chesapeake tribe may or may not be justified. They can be used as one possible or even probable hypothesis, but cannot be taken to exclude other possible interpretations.

Strachey records what he says was the official reaction of the king to news that the lost colonists had come to a tragic end at the hands of Powhatan—to whom, it must be remembered, James himself had sent a crown and various other regal trimmings in 1608, and had him formally established by Newport as a subking under his own ultimate authority. In these circumstances, to deal with Powhatan as a traitor and murderer might appear too sharp a change of front. Nonetheless, Strachey says that the king "hath given order that Powhatan himself with his Weroances, and all his people shalbe spared, and revenge only taken upon his quiyoughquisocks [or priests] by whose advise and perswasions was exercised that bloudy Cruelty, and only how that Powhatan himself and the Weroances must depend on his Majestie both acknowledging him for their superiour Lord." [6]

[6] Strachey, *Historie,* p. 91.

This may appear rather drastic, since the elimination of the priests from the tribes of the Powhatan confederacy involved a fundamental intrusion into the operation of the whole of Indian society—irrespective of the colonists' power to attempt it—while on the other hand the subordination of Powhatan and his subchieftains and elders to the crown appears rather mild, and indeed involved little more than carrying further the process of "subinfeudation," if that is not too grand a term, which the crowning of Powhatan had initiated. There is the difficulty, too, that the documents containing the king's reactions to the report of the killings have not survived, though some sharp response by the king surely lies behind Dale's instructions in May 1609, which indicate a drastic change in policy toward the Indians closely following the sequence outlined in Strachey.

The draft instructions prepared by the royal Council of Virginia for Sir Thomas Gates in May 1609 are a basic document in this inquiry. They approach quite nearly to Strachey's picture of the story which had emerged about Powhatan's culpability for the fairly recent elimination of the majority of the surviving lost colonists. If we lack the report sent from Virginia and the king's response to it, it would appear that the instructions represent the proposed implementation of the king's order as indicated by Strachey. The relevant passages are:

> [1] . . . we think it reasonable you first remove from them their Iniocasockes or Priestes by a surprise of them all and detayninge them prisoners. . . . And in case of necessity, or conveniency, we pronounce it not crueltie nor breache of Charity to deale more sharply with them and proceede even to dache [death] with these murtherers of Soules and sacrificers of gods images to the Divill.
>
> [2] For Powhatan and his Weroances it is Clere even to reason beside our experience that he loved not our neighbourhood and therefore you may in no way trust him, but if you finde it not best to make him your prisoner yet you must make him your tributary, and all other his Weroances about him first to acknowledge no other Lord but Kinge James, and so we shall free them all from the Tirany of Powhatan.[7]

In these passages it is not specifically stated that Powhatan, his Weroances, or his priests killed the lost colonists (though this is indicated later in the document) but the intention to destroy the priests and to limit the power

[7] Barbour, *Jamestown Voyages*, II, 264–5; Susan M. Kingsbury, ed., *The Records of the Virginia Company of London*, III (Washington, D.C., 1933), 14, 18.

of both Powhatan and his chief men fits in precisely with the king's reaction to the news of the killings as set out by Strachey.

That the Council of Virginia knew of the massacre of the lost colonists by Powhatan in terms very similar to, if not identical with those mentioned by Strachey, is evident however from the latter part of the instructions (which will be dealt with in their context), which referred to "the englishe . . . left by Sir Walter Rawely" and to "the slaughter of Powhatan of Roanocke, uppon the first arrivall of our Colonie." Though Strachey's rather oblique references to the contents of the report to the king and his response to it seem to admit of some ambiguity, the draft instructions for Dale in May 1609 support it in essentials and so make it possible for us to adopt it as, in outline, the correct story of events so far as they were known to the English at Jamestown at some time before the instructions were drawn up.

Attention has been drawn to certain ambiguities which remain in Strachey's major statements even after his main points are accepted. These and other difficulties can only be discussed against a background of the statements made about the lost colonists in the successive narratives of George Percy, John Smith, Strachey, and others as a result of the searches made for them, and of the scraps of gossip or information picked up about them during the years 1607–9. The cumulative picture they present is very imperfect and hard to integrate with Strachey's basic statements and the 1609 instructions, though some reasonably coherent picture can probably be put together.

From the time of their first landing the Jamestown settlers were on the lookout for any trace of European contacts, and particularly for any signs of the lost colonists. George Percy notes as early as 8 May 1607, among the Appomattocs "pieces of yron able to cleave a man in sunder." [8] which were clearly signs of contact with Europeans, though perhaps gained by trading down from the St. Lawrence basin. At Poor Cottage, later in the same month, he noted "a Savage Boy about the age of ten yeares, which had a year of hair of a perfect yellow and a reasonable white skinne, which is a Miracle amongst all Savages." [9] Though the generalization is perhaps rash, Percy took this fair child to be the result of intermixture of Indians and Europeans, and he may have been right. Francis Magnel affected to believe that the Indians considered the knives and other iron objects they had been able to acquire as having come across the mountains to the west from the Pacific coast, and so reflecting white contacts—again perhaps through Iroquois traveling from the St. Lawrence basin.[1]

[8] Barbour, *Jamestown Voyages,* I, 138. [9] *Ibid.,* p. 140. [1] *Ibid.,* p. 156.

Initial leads to the presence of Europeans well to the south of the James, who might prove to be survivors of the Lost Colony, came when Captain John Smith fell into the hands first of Opechancanough and later of his brother Powhatan toward the end of 1607. The authority is Smith's *True relation*, published less than a year after the events. He is not as specific as we could wish. Opechancanough described his dominions to Smith, and told him "of certaine men cloathed at a place called Ocanahonon, clothed like me,"[2] but no direction is specified. Later he had similar conversations with Powhatan. Once again Smith was told "of certaine men clothed at a place called Ocamahowan," which is clearly that named by Opechancanough. This occurs in the text at a point where Powhatan is describing the Susquehanna Indians at the head of Chesapeake Bay, beyond whom are men clothed like the English and with similar ships, who are clearly the French on the St. Lawrence. It might seem that Powhatan had switched from north to south in his topographical descriptions without Smith noticing it, as his own knowledge of Algonquian must at this time have been limited.

This imperfect linguistic knowledge is perhaps reflected also when he reports that Powhatan said "the south part of the backe sea" (did Smith think him to mean the Pacific?) was "within a day & a halfe of Mangoage, two days from Chawwonock 6. from Roonock." Smith, with his knowledge of the White–De Bry map of 1590, could easily place Roanoke Island, the Chowan River, and the supposed location of the Mangoak tribe as described by Ralph Lane, so that the presence of a "backe sea," however unlikely, was a pleasant mirage.[3] Lewis A. Binford has examined these references in detail. He thinks that the Mangoaks of 1586 were people who moved from the Roanoke River to the Nottoway-Meherrin basin, their place taken by the Tuscarora, whose chief village was Ocanahowan; or else the Mangoaks of 1586 were Tuscarora and the "Mangoage" of 1607 represented the Nottoway. The Moratuc Indians of the Roanoke River, also referred to by Lane, Bernard Hoffman thought might be Tuscarora (and equate with the Mangoaks?) if they lived on the south side of the river and an Algonkian tribe if they lived

[2] *Ibid.*, p. 182.

[3] *Ibid.*, p. 186. See Lewis A. Binford, "An Ethnohistory of the Nottoway, Meherrin and Weanok Indians of Southeast Virginia," *Ethnohistory*, XIV (1967), 103–218, esp. 121–4; B. G. Hoffman, "Ancient Tribes Revisited," *Ethnohistory*, XIV (1967), 1–46, esp. 35, 37. On Powhatan's northern contacts (including Anona), see Hoffman, *Observations on Certain Ancient Tribes of the Northern Appalachian Province*, Smithsonian Institution, Bureau of American Ethnology, Bull. 191 (Washington, D.C., 1964), pp. 196–8.

to the north. Clearly the problem of whether or not tribes changed their location between 1586 and 1607 has a bearing on the Lost Colony question, but it is especially difficult to find clear answers for it. Powhatan's further reference to another country, direction unspecified, called Anone, "where they have abundance of Brasse, and houses walled as ours," is probably irrelevant. Powhatan did not reveal that he personally had had any contact with the lost colonists.

When Captain Christopher Newport came out with the first supply in January 1608, it seems not unlikely that he was instructed to have a specific search for the lost colonists made as soon as possible. Smith tells us that in the same month a search was put in hand, saying, "we had agreed with ye king of Paspahegh to conduct two of our men to a place called Panawicke beyond Roonok, where he reported many men to be apparelled. Wee landed him at Warraskoyack, where playing the villaine, and deluding us for rewards, returned within three or foure dayes after without going further." [4] We have no further information directly from Smith on the progress of the search, but the two men went ahead on their own, and it is almost certain that a full report of their experience reached the Virginia Company in London.

Mr. Philip Barbour has argued cogently, too, that the Zúñiga map is a version of the map which Smith compiled between June and September 1608 and sent to England. The depiction of the country south of the James and the inscriptions on the rivers there make up the most valuable evidence we have of the activities of this first reconnaissance in search of the lost colonists early in 1608. One legend marks the point at which the expedition set off, which Mr. Barbour identifies as probably the Pagan River, a south-bank tributary of the James, and reads: "Here paspahegh and 2 of our men landed to go to panawiock." To the south are four rivers entering the sea west or south of Roanoke Island, which might appear to be, in that order: Albemarle Sound with its various divisions and tributaries, Wyesocking Bay, the Pamlico River, and the Neuse River.

The second inscription, set down near or on Wyesocking Bay, has: "Pananiock. and went to se." This is a little confusing. It suggests that the men sent to look where the Paspahegh chieftain indicated actually went to inspect the locale, though this is not the only possible interpretation. The third inscription appears on what we take to be the south bank of the Pamlico River: "pakerakanick. Here remay[n]e the 4 men clothed that came from roonock to okonohowan." [5] An early annotator

[4] Barbour, *Jamestown Voyages*, I, 190. [5] *Ibid.*, pp. 238–40.

of Smith's *True relation,* whose notes have been transcribed by Philip Barbour, probably after hearing some reports of the expedition of January 1608 put a gloss on Opechancanough's "Ocanahonon": "as of certaine men at a place 6 dayes jorney beyond Ocanahonon," suggesting that he had seen the map and was glossing the third inscription on it also.[6]

Clearly the Zúñiga map is of the greatest importance in showing us what was known and surmised in 1608 as to the area south of the James. The Virginia map offered for sale by Mr. H. P. Kraus of New York in 1969 has perhaps some relationship to the Zúñiga map.[7] If so it is more likely to belong to late 1608 or early 1609 than the 1610 date tentatively assigned to it. This has four rivers entering the sea from the west to the south of the James, but they are not sharply differentiated and contain no named locations, though a total of fifteen half circles, apparently indicating Indian village sites on them, are shown. It might be suggested that this part of the map does reflect, though very faintly, the first 1608 expedition to the south, but there is nothing of evidential value in it for that area.

We are left then with a very imperfect body of evidence on this first 1608 expedition. We do not know the names of the two men who carried it out. The Paspahegh chief, Wowinchopunk, set out with them before the end of January, apparently from the Pagan River.[8] He then took them, presumably from the point where his canoe could travel no farther, some way overland before leaving them. If we assume he spent two full days in their company, he may have put them in touch with Indians of the Weapemeoc group of tribes who lived on the inlets on the north shore of Albemarle Sound and arranged for them to bring the Englishmen farther south in their canoes. Judging by the Zúñiga map, Panawiock was located on Wyesocking Bay and can be equated with the village of Pomeioc, which appears prominently on the White map and in the narrative of the Roanoke voyages. There was some confusion with another name, Panauuaioc, which appeared on the De Bry version of White's map as lying on the south bank of the Pamlico River.[9] As indicated above, the inscription at this point on the map is somewhat ambiguous, but it seems to mean that the two Englishmen went to see whether in fact there were any Lost Colony survivors at that point, and were disappointed.

[6] *Ibid.*, p. 182.

[7] H. P. Kraus, *Monumenta Cartographica,* cat. 124, no. 28 (1969), pp. 43–6.

[8] See Philip L. Barbour, *Pocahontas and Her World* (Boston, 1970), pp. 10–17, 87, 89, 99.

[9] Quinn, *Roanoke Voyages,* II, 870 (Pomeioc), 872 (Pannauuioc); Barbour, *Jamestown Voyages,* I, 190, 240.

Granting them some limited knowledge of Algonquian, we may suggest that they learned something of the layout of the rivers from their hosts, and that they heard in particular that four men had come to Oconohowan, which is located on the map well up the Roanoke River, and that they had gone from there overland, the gloss to *The true relation* indicating that it was a six-day journey, to Pakerakanick, possibly on the Pamlico or else on the Neuse River. Clearly the information was received in a somewhat vague form, and referred to areas which they had not seen, so that it lacks precision. We must assume they returned from Panawiock-Pomeioc to Jamestown without further inquiry to the south, though judging by the map they may first have made some cursory inspection of Albemarle Sound and learned something of the rivers running into it. We do not know precisely how or when they returned, or indeed how extensive a report they made on the area to the south when they did so. This was an important reconnaissance, but an indecisive one.

Whatever report reached England in 1608 as a result of this mission, it stimulated the royal Council of Virginia and the Virginia Company to instruct Newport to make a fresh effort. When he arrived in October 1608 he was equipped to crown Powhatan as a royal vassal of King James and was also determined "not to return without a lumpe of gold, a certainty of the south-sea or one of the lost company of Sir Walter Rawley."[1] Smith affected to be displeased with the instructions Newport carried: he did not approve of the coronation, and also indicated to Newport, he says, that his other objectives were useless. The letter Newport claimed to have sent to the Company, first printed in *The generall historie* in 1624,[2] has long been thought to have been invented or at least doctored by Smith. Yet it seems to represent his views.[3] "Expressly to follow your directions by Captaine Newport, though they be performed I was directly against it; but according to our Commission, I was content to be overruled by the major part of the Councell. . . . I . . . have . . . Crowned Powhatan according to your instructions." Newport had failed to portage his boat over the falls of the James, "And for him at that time to find in the South Sea, a Mine of gold; or any of them sent by Sir Walter Raleigh: at our Consultation I told them was as likely as the rest." Smith affects to be as skeptical of the chances of finding any of the lost colonists as he was of discovering the Pacific Ocean.

Once Newport had gone, however, Smith planned to send out not one

[1] Barbour, *Jamestown Voyages*, II, 410.
[2] *Ibid.*, I, 241–5; P. L. Barbour, *Three Lives of John Smith* (Boston, 1964), pp. 233–4.
[3] Barbour, *Jamestown Voyages*, I, 242.

but two expeditions to the south. In December 1608 he met the chief of Weraskoyack, whose village also lay on the south bank of the James. He too proved rather antagonistic to Powhatan, and Smith thanked him for his advice not to trust the latter, "yet the better to try his love, desired guides to Chowanoke, for he would send a present to that king to bind him his friends. To performe this journey, was sent Michael Sicklemore, a very honest, valiant, and painefull souldier, with two guides, and directions how to search for the lost company of Sir Walter Rawley, and silke grass." [4] By this time, apparently, Smith had some information about the Chowan Indians and some knowledge that there was silkgrass (milkweed, its down suitable for a kind of rough silk) in the area; there was also a possibility that members of the Lost Colony might be on the Chowan River or with the chieftain. In his *Map of Virginia* (1612) Smith is most laconic about the result: "Master Sicklemore well returned from chawonock, but found little hope and lesse certainetie of them were left by Sir Walter Rawley." [5] This indicates that he probably made contact with the chief of the Chawanoac tribe, that he found very little evidence that white men had ever been there, though he may have gathered a few hazy rumors, and that he made no fruitful contacts of any sort.

In *The generall historie* Smith is a little more forthcoming about Sicklemore's mission, saying that the river he saw "was not great, the people few, the country most over growne with pynes, where did grow here & there straglingly Pemminaw, we call silke grasse. But by the river the ground was good, and exceeding furtill." [6] This is a fair enough summary of what may have been a quite detailed report. It suggests that Sicklemore may not have reached the wider part of the Chowan River, near its entry into Albemarle Sound, and may also imply that most of the Chowanoac Indians were keeping out of his way, for in Lane's time the river valley was well peopled. If they were not, it is possible there had been some movement northward and the tribe was now centered some way north of the Chowan River.

The second group was not sent out until later, after Sicklemore's return, and so after Smith's own visit to Powhatan. He stated that "Nathaniell Powell & Anas Todkill, were also, by the Quiyoughquohanocks, conducted to the Mangoages to search them there. But nothing could we learn but they were all dead." [7] The Quiyoughcohannock were another of the small tribes on the south bank of the James, the third to be enlisted

[4] *Ibid.*, II, 423. [5] *Ibid.*, p. 449.

[6] John Smith, *The generall historie of Virginia, New England, and the Summer Isles . . .* (London, 1624), p. 87.

[7] Barbour, *Jamestown Voyages*, II, 449.

for providing guides to the south, but we do not know where the expedition went. Lane's impression was that the Mangoaks lived well inland from the Chowan Indians, and that their territory reached the Roanoke River well up its course. We might therefore suspect that they went somewhat to the west of the route followed by Sicklemore, possibly into the area between the Meherrin and Roanoke rivers, the former not standing out in their memory because it runs through a swampy zone, and clearly they did not reach the latter. How accurate *The generall historie* is we cannot be certain, but in it Smith says of the Indian guides, "Three dayes jorney they conducted them through the woods, into a high country towards the Southwest: where they saw here and there a little corne field, by some little spring or small brooke, but no river they could see: the people in all respects like the rest, except there language: they live most upon rootes, fruites and wilde beasts; and trade with them toward the sea for dryed fish and corne, for skins." [8]

This sounds correct and may well represent contact with an inland Iroquoian tribe, but here was none of the superfluity of copper which Lane, from tales told him on the Chowan, associated with that area. Strachey confirms that Powell and Todkill penetrated into the country of the Mangoaks, that is, into the area westward and northward from the Chowan and extending into the piedmont. He says that "in their discoveryes to the Mangoagues they did light once upon two skynns, which by all the Judgements in the Fort were supposed to be Lyons skyns," and would indeed have been skins of the mountain lion, *Felis concolor couguar*.[9]

V

It would appear that the Powell-Todkill mission was intended not merely to look for the lost colonists but to explore more effectively the small sections of the piedmont reached in the earlier expedition, which appeared of some promise as an alternative base well to the south of the Jamestown settlement.

The interest of the royal Council of Virginia, the Virginia Company, and the Jamestown settlers in the Lost Colony was to some extent represented in the printed literature of these years. Smith's *True relation* of 1608, already cited, came first. Robert Johnson maintained in general terms the proposition that the lost colonists still survived: after referring to the earlier settlements, he says that "the same footing and possession

[8] Smith, *Generall historie*, pp. 87–8. [9] Strachey, *Historie*, p. 125.

is there kept and possessed by the same English, or by their seede and offspring, without any interruption or invasion, either of the Savages (the natives of the countrie) or of any other Prince or people (for ought we heare or know) to this day." [1] It can scarcely be maintained however that Johnson, in spite of his close involvement in the Virginia Company, revealed any knowledge of the whereabouts or fate of the Lost Colony.

George Abbot, too, in the third edition of *A briefe description of the whole worlde*, thought it desirable, in view of the Virginia Company's recent settlement, to make some reference to the Roanoke colonies.[2] This pale and muddled mention would be of little interest in itself if it had not been so often repeated: it reappeared in editions of 1617, 1620, and 1624 and so was one source for popular impressions of the fate of the lost colonists until 1625 and after. He confused his material very thoroughly—having failed to read Hakluyt's *Principal navigations* intelligently—and thought the second colony, not the first, had been established by Lane and brought home by Drake; he also believed there were women and children in it. Drake took off the colonists, he says. "Yet some of these English which being left behind, ranged up & down the Country (and hoovering about the Sea coast) made meanes at least (after enduring of much miseries) by some Christian ships to be brought backe againe into England."

If he had not shown himself so muddled, it might be thought he thus provided evidence that some lost colonists had been repatriated, but he was probably referring to Grenville's men in 1586, last seen by the Indians when they took off from an island in the Carolina Outer Banks in their small vessel, as described earlier. If there is anything in what he says, which appears most unlikely, it does not seem possible to track it down to its source. He then goes on to refer to the colonists (presumably those of Lane's colony, though confused with White's): "while they were there inhabiting, there were some children borne, and baptized in those partes: and they mighte well have endured the Countrey, if they might have had such strength as to keep off the inhabitants from troubling them in tillinge the ground, and reaping of such Corne as they would have sowed." It is impossible to say whether he was referring to colonists who had stayed for some months or years and then returned, or who had remained.

It is clear from the foregoing that John Smith's published references to the Lost Colony and to his relations with Powhatan have little connec-

[1] Johnson, *Nova Britannia* (for Samuel Macham, 1609); *S.T.C.* 14699.

[2] George Abbot, *A briefe description of the whole worlde*, 3d ed. (for John Brown, 1608); *S.T.C.* 27, sig. S.1v.

tion with the story of Powhatan's responsibility, told circumstantially if obliquely by Strachey and confirmed in its basic features by the instructions of 1609. The circumstances in which Smith became aware of the fate of the lost colonists at Powhatan's hands, and his subsequent actions—and concealments—must remain a matter for conjecture. It was probably not during Smith's imprisonment in the hands of the Powhatan Indians, and his stay as a prisoner at Powhatan's village, that he learned of the lost colonists' fate. If he had, the friendly and cooperative visit he made with Newport to Weromacomoco in March 1608 would be difficult to accept,[3] though we must admit that he spent the last day of this visit alone with Powhatan and might just possibly have received his confidences. If he did, clearly he did not communicate them to Newport. Further, he concealed them wholly in those of his writings which appear in the 1608 tract.

Friction with Powhatan of a somewhat serious nature developed after Newport's departure in April 1608.[4] He came out, on the second supply, with authority and equipment to crown Powhatan as a vassal under King James I, and did so before any information on Powhatan's responsibility for the deaths of the lost colonists had reached the king. The second visit of Smith and Newport to Powhatan took place late in 1608, and the ceremony passed off without signs of real friction,[5] so that we can probably take it that neither Smith nor Newport had serious charges to bring against Powhatan at that time. It is only after Newport's departure, in spite of the recent ceremonies, that Smith attempts to humiliate Powhatan and bring him to heel, though he does not refer in his narrative writings to any atrocities committed by him. Powhatan was evidently uneasy: after a rather time-serving truce or peace was made, he deserted his usual seat of Weromacomoco on the York River and put himself out of Smith's reach.[6]

It might seem then that very soon after the crowning ceremony, and before the beginning of December, Smith became aware of Powhatan's part in the Lost Colony affair, and this altered his view of the Indian ruler. A possible explanation is that about the time Smith and Newport returned to Jamestown after the crowning ceremony, William White, who had lived with the Indians for some time and had learned enough of their language to understand them, returned to the fort. He brought detailed accounts of Indian ceremonies, customs, and policies. Unfortunately, only brief extracts from his reports survive.[7] They include the

[3] Barbour, *Jamestown Voyages*, I, 190–9, 228, II, 390–2.

[4] *Ibid.*, I, 206, II, 395–6. [5] *Ibid.*, I, 242–3, 410–14.

[6] *Ibid.*, II, 416–18, 421, 424–8, 435, 437, 441–4. [7] *Ibid.*, I, 145–50.

description of the ceremonial torture and sacrifice by the Indians of one of the colonists, George Cassen, to which Smith subsequently referred,[8] saying that Powhatan had also turned his men on the Piankatank Indians, massacring most of them and taking the remnant prisoners—in much the same way that Strachey reported his dealing with the Chesapeakes. Smith spoke of Powhatan reciting this as a great and terrifying achievement for the edification of some members of the colony who had deserted the fort and gone over to him. White also reported that "many other our men were cruelly and treacherously executed by them, though perhaps not sacrificed" [9]—showing that he understood the difference between the killing of persons in war or a raid and after capture, to play a part in a sacrificial ceremony. It seems not at all improbable that White was the channel for the information that Powhatan had in fact taken part in the killing of certain of the surviving lost colonists, though if so, it is also probable that he was told to keep quiet about it, and complied.

If this supposition (that White—or possibly another Englishman at about this time—was the informant) is viable, it can be seen that both Smith and Newport were placed in a very difficult and awkward position. Powhatan had just been crowned and had thus been placed into an honorable position under the king; to repudiate him publicly, on the basis of private reports, for actions which had taken place more than a year earlier, would have been to risk being accused of acting in a derogatory manner toward King James. They would feel bound to act only after the king had been consulted, and in the meantime to keep the matter as confidential as possible. Besides, a public denunciation of Powhatan could easily bring about an all-out attack by the Indian tribes on the still weak colony. A full report to the king by Smith, the remaining councillors, and Newport, with strict injunctions to secrecy on those who knew about the matter, would be the obvious policy to pursue. This would accord with what is told by Strachey of a report made to the king on Powhatan's killing of the lost colonists.

As I have said, this also appears to represent something of what lay behind the 1609 instructions. But it may very well not be the whole story. Smith might also have heard of the episode from Powhatan's own lips in December 1608. In his *Map of Virginia* (1612) Smith gives us the formal exchange of speeches that passed, he says, between him and Powhatan on the occasion of their meeting during that month, when Smith's pressure on the Indians had been stepped up and Powhatan had been got to talk.[1] It is highly probable that the speeches exchanged between

[8] *Ibid.*, p. 372. [9] *Ibid.*, p. 150. [1] *Ibid.*, II, 424–8.

them were much harsher and more realistic than Smith reported, and that Smith accused Powhatan of attacking and killing the lost colonists, Powhatan replying by admitting it—perhaps boasting of it, possibly excusing it in some way. It was possible for him to say that he did not know the lost colonists to be English—that he had a traditional policy among his people, going back to the killing of the Jesuits in 1577, of eliminating foreign intruders—that he had no treaty with the English at the time, or something of the sort. The reason for thinking that he may have made some explanation of his actions as well as admitting them is that this would enable Smith to go on with the establishment of a *modus vivendi* with the Indians, whereas a boastful attitude might have forced him to take a more rigid line. This view, of course, is based on the assumption that he would not know precisely what to do until he heard what the king's reaction to the earlier report had been.

Smith, alike in his *Map of Virginia* (1612) and his *Generall historie*, maintained a complete silence on Powhatan's part in the killing. If he undertook, at the time the 1608 report was sent in, to keep silence, he made good his undertaking so far as his published works are concerned. But he does not appear to have been so reticent in conversation with his friends. He had known and cooperated with the Reverend Samuel Purchas from at least 1613, and at some point told him of what Powhatan had admitted, though perhaps not when the admission was made. In 1623 Purchas was writing his tract "Virginias verger" (the manuscript of which is in the Duke of Devonshire's collections at Chatsworth [2]), and put into it a direct quotation, derived he says from Captain John Smith, stating that "Powhatan confessed to Cap[tain] Smith that hee had beene at their [the lost colonists'] slaughter, and had divers utensils of theirs to shew." This was published by Purchas in 1625 at the end of his *Purchas his pilgrimes*, and so Smith's admission that he had direct evidence from Powhatan on the killing of the lost colonists eventually, and in his own lifetime, came to light.[3] There is no reason to disbelieve Purchas's statement that the information came directly from John Smith, who himself had it from Powhatan.

Thus, while there is not enough evidence to be positive about the circumstances of how and when news of the killings reached Jamestown, it is possible to construct a plausible sequence of events. This cannot be taken as more than a provisional reconstruction; it is presented as making intelligible a sequence of events which has hitherto seemed to have little

[2] Hist.MSSComm., *3d Report* (London, 1872), app., pp. 41, 44.

[3] Samuel Purchas, *Hakluytus Posthumus, or Purchas his Pilgrimes*, 4 vols. (1625), IV, 1813 (*S.T.C.* 20509); 20 vols. (Glasgow, 1906), XIX, 227–8.

shape or pattern. It could very well be disturbed by the discovery of additional evidence, but the main lines of the argument, at least, fit what evidence we have.

Some additional information was sent to England with Newport about the beginning of December 1608 reaching England before the end of January, and more information and tales of the lost colonists came into the hands of Smith, and later of Strachey, subsequent to this. It is difficult to sort out precisely which was which. However, the information lying behind a certain further section of the draft instructions of May 1609 was clearly sent with Newport. The Virginia Company was concerned at this time to exploit the discoveries made to the south by the exploring party early in 1608, so as to establish a secondary base there and build up a trade in commodities which would supplement those obtainable in the vicinity of Jamestown itself. A possible instrument for doing this would be any surviving member of the Lost Colony, whose guidance on opportunities for settlement and trade in the area would prove invaluable. Not having the full reports, or indeed maps other than the Zúñiga map on which the draft instructions were evidently based, we are at a loss to follow every detail, though Philip Barbour has attempted helpfully to disentangle the topographical problems.[4]

There is one passage in Strachey which can be used to parallel a good deal of the information lying behind the instructions, so that the two can be analyzed to some extent together. In the instructions the first southern objective was a place called Ohanahorn or Chinahorn,[5] which cannot be equated with any location on the Zúñiga map, but could possibly have been the Ohanoak of Ralph Lane, situated on the west bank of the Chowan River some distance above its entry into Albemarle Sound. Yet it may have been a different place altogether. The instructions say, "Foure dayes Journey from your forte Southwards is a towne called Ohonahorn seated where the River of Choanocki devideth itself into three braunches and falleth into the sea of Rawmocke in thirty five degrees." The topography of this seems fairly clear: for the compiler, the town of Ohanahorn lay where the Chowan and Roanoke rivers join, the third channel being the bay at the head of which Edenton now stands. The conjoint channel is then Albemarle Sound and the entry into the sea at Trinity Harbor, the cut through the Carolina Outer Banks just north of Roanoke Island, lying however above the thirty-sixth, not the thirty-fifth parallel. If this was Lane's site of Ohanoak, there is some confusion about

4 Kingsbury, *Records,* III, 17; Barbour, *Jamestown Voyages,* II, 264–5.

5 Strachey, *Historie,* p. 34. Some discussion of the locations mentioned, by Binford ("Ethnohistory," pp. 121–4), may be found useful.

its exact location. The Jamestown authorities are told how to proceed: "this place you seeke by Indian guides from James forte to Winocke by water."

Winocke is unidentifiable as it stands. Philip Barbour sees it as a probable mistake for Warraskoyack, and the water the Pagan River, though there would be a good deal of land travel from there to the Chowan River. They are to go "from thence to Manqueocke, some twenty miles from thence to Cathega [or Cathuga] as much and thence to Oconahoen." This would seem to indicate that it was possible to go through the country of the Mangoak tribe (if that is what Manqueocke is), which would be up the Roanoke River according to Lane's earlier information, then to a place not otherwise heard of, Cathega, and finally to what we have already heard of as Oconahoen or Ocanahonon. This we have seen is located on the Zúñiga map on the south bank of the Roanoke River well along its course.

These topographical mysteries were possibly simplified and explained in the final version of the instructions which we do not have, or in an accompanying map. At this place the base was to be established, where "you shall finde a brave and fruitefull seate every way unaccessible by a straunger enemy, much more abundant in Pochon and in the grass silke called Cour del Cherva and in vines, then any parte of this lande knowne unto us. Here we suppose, if you make your principall and chefe seate, you shall doe most safely and Richely because you are in the part of the land inclined to the southe, and two of the best rivers will supply you." Behind this direction is clearly a fuller report of the early 1608 exploratory mission than we have, and some indication that, after visiting Pomeioc, its members went up to the head of Albemarle Sound and even possibly some way up the Roanoke River before returning to Jamestown.

After dealing with Oconahonon, the instructions say that the explorers will then be "neere to Riche Copper mines of Ritanoc [or Ritanoe] and may passe them by one braunche of this River." At the time of these instructions, Richard Hakluyt was in possession of similar information. Dating his dedicatory epistle to *Virginia richly valued* 13 April 1609, he stated in it that "our owne Indians have lately revealed either this [Lane's and Harriot's copper on the Roanoke River, in Mangoak possession] or another rich mine of copper or gold in a towne called Ritanoe."[6] This would seem to be based not on the reconnaissance so much as on Indian tales picked up in the Jamestown region. As we shall see, Strachey appears to have thought this place and its mine were on the Chowan River.

[6] F. Kyngston for H. Lownes, 1609, sig. A3r.; *S.T.C.* 22939.

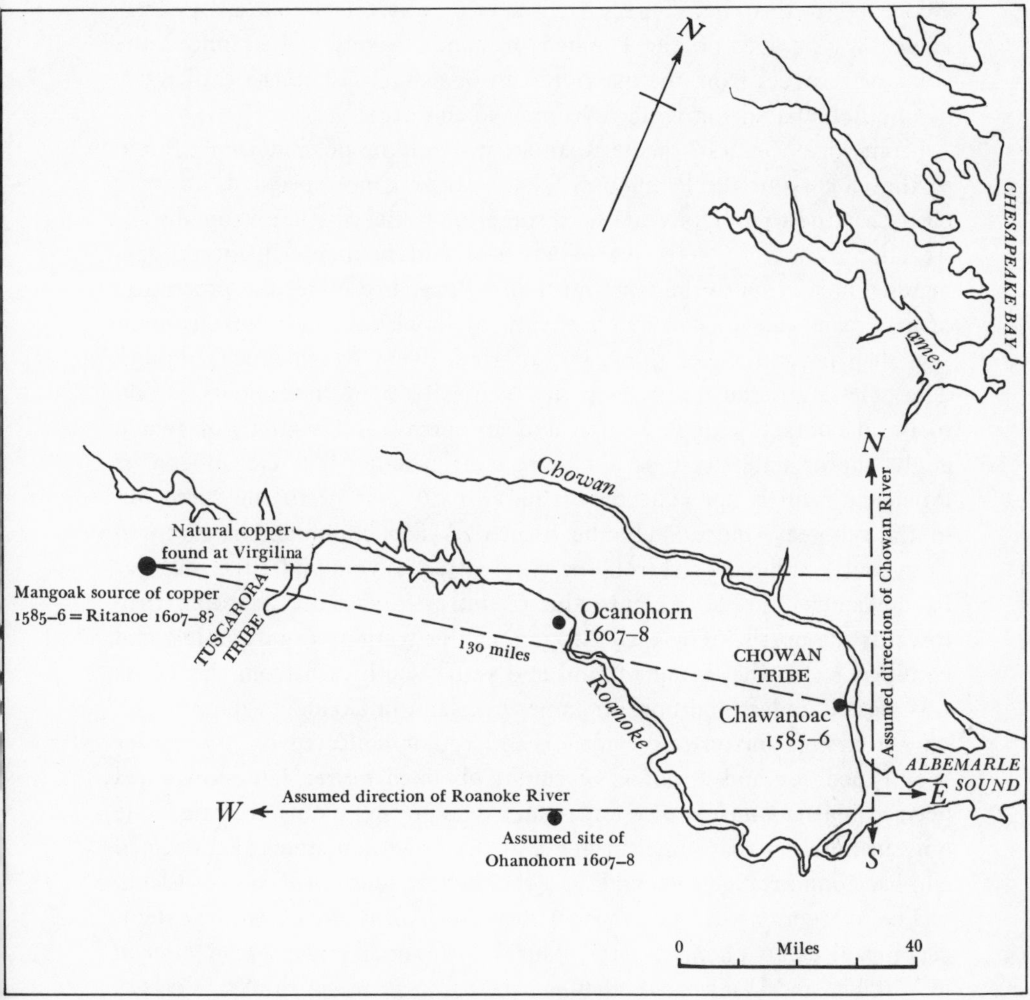

Location of sites associated with the Lost Colony.

The explorers, according to the instructions, were then within reach of Pakerakanick and could come to it by another branch of the river. There the "4 men clothed" of the Zúñiga map have been transformed into lost colonists escaped from Powhatan. The explorers are told that there "you shall finde foure of the englishe alive, left by Sir Walter Raweley which escaped from the slaughter of Powhatan of Roanocke, uppon the first arivall of our Colonie." The earlier indications were that these were simply lost colonists who had at some time drifted away to Pakerakanick, or at least white men. The later report on them or others of similar number had become part of the story of Powhatan's attack.

According to this, the refugees had got well away to the south, if Pakerakanick was in fact on the Pamlico or Neuse River, and if indeed the story of refugees from the massacre can be assimilated to the earlier tale of undifferentiated survivors remaining in this area.

From what "branch" of the Roanoke it would be possible to get down to the vicinity of the Pamlico or Neuse River is not specified, but it is clear that the topography at the disposal of those who drew up the instructions was very defective. There is a still further element of new material in relation to the same survivors: "they live under the protection of a wiroans called Gepanocon enemy to Powhatan, by whose consent you shall never recover them, one of these were worth much labour." The chieftain is thus located on the Neuse River or thereabouts, is said to be in contact with Powhatan and an enemy of his—both of which might appear unlikely. It is not quite clear whether it is Gepanocon or Powhatan who is not expected voluntarily to consent to the surrender of the refugees—more likely the former. A final injunction is given to carry out a still wider search for survivors: "if you find them not [at Pakerakanick], yet search into this Countrey it is more probable than towards the north." There is, throughout this section, a quite unjustified confidence that the layout of land and water southward from the James was clearly understood both in Jamestown and in London, while in fact only a strange mixture of evidence and rumor collected by the earlier 1608 expedition and a morass of rumor obtained nearer Jamestown had been assimilated into a program which was by no means realistic. The only firm item is that some survivors of the Powhatan attack had escaped and had found refuge somewhere to the west or south of Roanoke Island.

The instructions of May 1609 in their final form, which is not extant, accompanied Sir Thomas Gates, who was to act as governor *ad interim* in Virginia, and William Strachey, secretary designate, in the *Sea Venture* when she left Plymouth on 2 June. They did not reach Jamestown, owing to the *Sea Venture* being cast away at Bermuda, until 23 May 1610. In the meantime Strachey had had time to become acquainted with the instructions and to hear from Sir Thomas the story of the report which had reached London some months before their departure of the killing of the lost colonists, and the king's response to this news. Strachey did not himself have a chance to pick up anything about the lost colonists until the summer of 1610, nor did Gates do anything so far as we know to implement the 1609 instructions concerning them.

In the meantime we are somewhat at a loss to know precisely what if anything was done about the lost colonists. The expeditions late in 1608 had brought no very positive evidence on whether or not any survived, though they had shown something of the character and potentialities of the territory to the south. What one may suggest is that in the interim between the beginning of 1609 and the summer of 1610 a good deal of rumor had continued to circulate in Jamestown about them. This seems to have centered around the person of the Indian, Kemps or Machumps, who had been brought into the colony as a prisoner in the winter of 1608–9 and had become a useful bridge between English and Indian, as he had learned English and adapted himself to life in the colony. It is hard to disentangle his stories from other bits and pieces of information which were available when Strachey at length reached the settlement. In the relevant passage, Strachey is talking of the prospects of the lands to the south of the colony and says, "This high-land is, in all likelyhoodes a pleasant Tract, and the Mould fruictfull, especially what may lye to the southward, where at Peccarecanick and Ocanahoen, by the Relation of Machumps, the People have houses built with stone walls, and one story above another, so taught them by those English who escaped the slaughter at Roanoak, at what time our Colony, (under the Conduct of Captain Newport) landed within the Chesapeack Bay, and where the people breed up tame Turkeis about their howses, and take Apes in the Mountayns." [7]

This sounds very much like a contaminated story passed on by the Indian on the basis of what he had heard from his own people and the settlers about the lost colonists. The framework is the basis already established by earlier searches and information; the trimmings are details probably developed by invention among the Indians of the smaller tribal units of the James River, especially those reasonably near Jamestown such as Machumps himself, who was a Paspahegh. Once the initial inquiries by Smith and his agents were over, further "information" supplied by the tribes who had been questioned earlier becomes immediately suspect as being thought up after these inquiries. The stone walls, the two-story houses, the apes, and possibly the turkeys are all elements in this sort of story. A side note has "Peccarecanick betweene 35. & 36. degrees of the Line: and in her warm Vallyes may be planted Sugar-Canes, Oranges, Lemons, & all sortes of Southern fruites." This is Strachey's gloss, essentially, on the passage in the instructions which ordered the Jamestown colonists to establish a further base to the south.

The other element in Strachey's summary is more specific and possibly different in character: he says, "at Ritanoe, the Weroance Eyanoco preserved 7. of the English alive, fower men, twoo Boyes, and one young

[7] Barbour, *Jamestown Voyages*, II, 325, 442–3, 446, 448; Strachey, *Historie*, p. 34.

Maid, who escaped and fled up the River of Choanoke, to beat his Copper, of which he hath certayn mines at the said Ritanoe, as also at Pannawaiack are said to be store of salt stones." Leaving out the last clause, which belongs to a different context, we appear to have more specific information than was sent to London in 1608 and used in the instructions of May 1609. Strachey implies that the chieftain Eyanoco, who is possibly though by no means certainly the Gepanocon of the 1609 instructions, was established on the Chowan River—though we must realize that Albemarle Sound and any of its diverging rivers might be spoken of as such—and that there he had given shelter to seven survivors. The number of men is the same as in the instructions, but to them are added two boys and a girl. This looks like additional information.

The employment of the men sounds credible. Englishmen could know enough about metals to carry out the process of annealing, making the copper soft enough for it to be shaped into better tools or weapons and thereafter hardened by systematic hammering, or even possibly smelting. Ritanoe is said to have mines, but it is not unlikely that Strachey is speaking about the Chawanoac Indians and their chief village of Chawanoac on the Chowan River. Lane had gathered from Menatonon, the chief of this tribe, in 1585–6 that he was in contact with sources of copper through the Mangoak Indians, though he did not control them himself.

In the nineteenth century native copper was in fact found near the Roanoke River within 30 miles of the approximate site of Chawanoac, or perhaps within 150 miles by water: [8] though this is far cry from mineral sources under the control of the Chawanoac chieftain. If this reading of Strachey is correct, then the location of the village where the survivors of the 1607 killings were had been pinned down to within

[8] Native copper and silver were found in the nineteenth century in Granville County in the Virgilina district, but whether they would have been accessible to the Indians is not clear (F. B. Lane, *The Geology and Ore Deposits of the Virgilina District of Virginia and North Carolina*, North Carolina Geological and Economic Survey, Bull. 26 [Raleigh, 1917]). Nodules of copper in smaller quantities were also found occasionally in other areas at no very great distance (see Quinn, *Roanoke Voyages*, I, 332–3). A source of confusion was that the Roanoke River was thought of as flowing from west to east, whereas it flows northwest to southeast for most of its course. The Chowan was thought of as flowing from north to south, whereas it, too, mostly flows northwest to southeast and for a considerable distance parallels the Roanoke within twenty miles' distance. A natural copper source some way up the Roanoke River would be almost as easy of access by way of the Chowan.

easy reach of Jamestown on the Chowan River. It is not certain, however, that this is the right interpretation: he might still mean that they had gone much further inland and that the alleged mines were on the Roanoke River rather than the Chowan, but a reasonable assumption would be to favor the simpler rather than the more complex solution.

There is the possibility that this more realistic location for the place where survivors were thought to have gone in 1607 was the result of further searches made in 1609. If the *Sea Venture* went astray in that year, the other six ships did not and came into Jamestown in August, returning to England before the end of the year. One of them appears to have brought news of a further search. On 14 December 1609 an official Virginia Company pamphlet was entered in the Stationers' Register;[9] it was published early in 1610 as *A true and sincere declaration . . . of the plantation begun in Virginia.*[1] This contained, presumably on the basis of information brought back by those who had reached England in the previous few months—including Captain John Smith—some alleged information on the lost colonists. It said that "intelligence of some of our Nation planted by Sir Walter Raleigh (yet alive) within fifty miles of our fort, who can open the wombe and bowells of this country: as is testified by two of our colony sent out to seeke them, who, (though denied by the Savages speech with them) found Crosses, & Leters, the Characters & assured testimonies of Christians newly cut in the barkes of trees."

This was picked up by Emmanuel van Meteren in the 1610 edition of his *Commentarien,* where he wrote, in Philip Barbour's translation, "They hold it for certain that some English are still alive there, the ones taken there some years ago over fifty miles from their colony (for) they have had word and have found crosses carved on trees."[2] This strongly suggests that the contact was made on the Chowan River, parts of which are within fifty miles of Jamestown, while the site of Chawanoac is some seventy miles by direct line. Who the investigators were is not known. Under what circumstances they found signs like those arranged by White with the original colonists in 1587 and later found on Roanoke Island can scarcely be imagined. Why, after such a discovery, no expedition was sent to surround the village, coerce the Indians into releasing their prisoners, and so obtain at last a live lost colonist is very difficult to understand, even though in 1609 the Jamestown settlers had many problems and crises confronting them. Unless the whole thing was a fiction,

[9] Arber, *Stationers' Register,* III, 425.
[1] For J. Stepney, 1610, p. 18; *S.T.C.* 24832.
[2] Barbour, *Jamestown Voyages,* II, 279.

which seems unlikely in the case of an official pamphlet of such a sort, where fictions were usually couched in less specific terms, the last mystery of the lost colonists was as great as the first.

For no further concrete trace was ever found of them. If this is the true story, then the last survivors—if they were such—lived twenty-two years out of contact with other Englishmen and were again abandoned in Indian hands by their countrymen after they had established themselves only some fifty miles or so from the Jamestown settlement.

VI

We know little thereafter of what was or was not done to continue the search for the lost colonists. The most probable conclusion is that the pessimism engendered by John Smith's *Map of Virginia* in 1612 led to the abandonment of further searches. There were still rumors of white men living to the south of the Jamestown colony, but they had by 1614 changed their character; by that time they were thought to be Spaniards. Ralph Hamor, in *A true discourse of the present state of Virginia . . . till the 18 of June, 1614,* published in 1615, reported that two deserters from the colony were making their way south to a rumored Spanish plantation beyond Ocanahoen when they were intercepted by Indians despatched by the English to catch up with them and head them back. The passage reads: "even this summer Cole and Kitchins Plot, with three more, bending their course towards the Southward to a Spanish Plantation, reported to be there, who had travelled (it being now a time of peace) some five days jorney to Ocanahoen, there cut off by certaine Indians, hired by us to hunt them home to receive their deserts." [3] But no details are given of whether there were indeed Spaniards, or survivors from one or another of the groups of lost colonists, in this territory south of the middle course of the Roanoke River from which rumor had so often come before.

A final visit to the south which had in it some element of search for the lost colonists was made by John Pory in 1622. Pory was deeply interested in the earlier English voyages and seems at times to have thought of himself as possible successor to Hakluyt, though unlike Hakluyt he aspired also to take an active part in colonization. It was appropriate that he should wish to round off his services in Virginia, before returning home after meritorious service as secretary to the colony, by making an expedition into the lands described in outline by Lane and Harriot so many years before and still just possibly containing

[3] John Beale for William Welby, 1615, p. 27; *S.T.C.* 12736.

some trace of the lost colonists of 1587. Smith reports his journey, saying: "In February also he travelled to the South River Chawanock, some sixty miles over land; which he found to be a very fruitfull and pleasant Country, yeelding two harvests in a yeare, and found much of the Silke grass formerly spoken of, and was kindly used by the people and so returned."[4] It must have pleased him, as a traditionalist, to trace in reverse the route which Ralph Lane had planned to follow from the Chowan to Chesapeake Bay in 1586.

We have other details of his discoveries, including part of a letter sent by George Sandys from Jamestown on 3 March 1622, in which he said: "Maister Pory deserves good incouragement for his paineful Discoveries to the South-ward, as far as the Choanoack, who although he hath trod on a litle good ground, hath past through great forests of Pynes 15. or 16. myle broad and above 60. mile long, which will serve well for Masts for Shipping, and for pitch and tarre, when we shall come to extend our plantations to those borders. On the other side of the River there is a fruitfull Countrie blessed with aboundance of Corne, reaped twise a yeere: above which is the Copper Mines, by all of all places generally affirmed. Hee hath also met with a great deal of silke grasse which growes there monethly."[5] Unfortunately his own report is lost, but it is clear that he came on no trace whatever of the Lost Colony. "And thus," runs Smith's epilogue, "we left seeking our Colony, that was never any of them found, nor seene to this day 1622."

The view that the main body of lost colonists met their end on Roanoke Island has usually been accepted by historians who have not examined the evidence in detail. There are three mentions of Roanoke in this connection, one in the draft instructions of 1609 and two in Strachey. The first is the most authoritative, where it speaks of "the slaughter of Powhatan of Roanocke."[6] This is by no means unambiguous and can bear at least three separate interpretations. The first is that "of Roanocke" means "of (the former) Roanoke (colonists)." This seems not at all improbable, such portmanteau constructions being not unusual at the

[4] Smith, *Generall historie*, p. 331.

[5] His mission can be followed in Patrick Copland, *Virginia's God be thanked* (J. D[awson] for W. Shefferd and J. Bellamie, 1622), where Sandys's letter is quoted on pp. 13–14 (*S.T.C.* 5717); Edward Waterhouse, *A declaration of the state of the colony* (G. Eld for R. Mylbourne, 1622), *S.T.C.* 25104; Kingsbury, *Records*, III, 549, 587, 641–2. The full narrative in William S. Powell, "John Pory, His Life, Letters and Works" (dissertation, University of North Carolina Library, Chapel Hill, 1947), has no further references to his search for the Lost Colony, and it would appear that his personal report is irrecoverable.

[6] See Kingsbury, *Records*, III, 17; see p. 458 above.

time. The second is that "Powhatan of Roanocke" applies to a person who is a Powhatan or high chief of Roanoke and is distinct from the Powhatan of the Virginia confederacy. This can be ruled out; there was no such person. Strachey, it is true, says "no part of this South country is supposed to be under Powhatan, but under an absolute Weroance, as powerfull and great as Powhatan."[7] He thus gave his opinion that the tribes in at least part of the area formerly explored during the Roanoke voyages were consolidated under a single chieftainly rule. This may or may not have been so, but there is no evidence at all that there was an official or rank called "a Powhatan"; while the tribal chieftain at Roanoke is named by Strachey himself as quite different from Powhatan: "the Kings name of Roanoac—Nanamachauwh."[8]

The third conceivable meaning is that "of Roanocke" means "at Roanoke," and though this is possible it is probably less firm than the first suggestion offered—at least by no means conclusive. Strachey has four references, two of which are ambiguous: he refers to "the men women and Children of the first plantation at Roanoke [who] were by practize and Commandement of Powhatan miserably slaughtered,"[9] but "the first plantation at Roanoke" most obviously means "the first plantation [established] at Roanoke" in 1587, though it can also be interpreted as meaning "at Roanoke [Island]" in 1607. Only two references are unambiguous, where he speaks of "the slaughter at Roanoak."[1] Here he is explicitly associating himself with the view that the killings took place on Roanoke Island. Even so, the evidence that he really understood them to have been killed on Roanoke Island is not conclusive, since he may have based his view on the evidence of the instructions, which as we have seen are certainly ambiguous.

If the killings took place on Roanoke Island, we are left with a number of difficult historical problems. In the first place, why should the settlers of 1587, having first left the island and being clearly far away from it in 1590, return? It is difficult to find any particular reasons. The Roanoke Island Indians had not been friendly, and yet Strachey speaks confidently of the settlers living peacefully with the Indians for a long time. More cogently, an occupation extending from some time fairly soon after 1590 to about 1607 would have left substantial archaeological traces. The extensive excavations on Roanoke Island under the auspices of the National Park Service have not only revealed no such traces, but have conclusively demonstrated that the site of the fort erected in 1585 was

[7] See Strachey, *Historie*, p. 36.
[8] See *ibid.*, p. 190.
[9] See *ibid.*, p. 91 (with a similar reference on p. 26).
[1] See *ibid.*, pp. 34, 58.

filled in within a very short time of its completion, almost certainly by Grenville's men in 1586, and that there has never been any extensive occupation on the site. Outside the immediate fort area no remains at all have been found. It is just barely conceivable that an intensive occupation site may appear, but this seems highly unlikely. The probabilities are that the colony did not end here in 1607.

For the Chesapeake Bay location there is the fact that the colonists almost certainly went to this area—most of them at least—shortly after White left them in 1587. Their peaceful continuation there on friendly terms such as were anticipated in 1587 with the local Indians of the Chesapeake tribe would be a logical outcome. In what is said above, the argument that the lost colonists were living with the Chesapeake Indians and that the killing of the Chesapeake Indians and of the lost colonists at, apparently, the same time—if it is acceptable—would make a simultaneous or near-simultaneous attack on lost colonists who were at Roanoke Island unlikely. One can of course imagine circumstances in which survivors from the Chesapeake area took refuge at Roanoke Island and were pursued and killed there in their turn, but this seems unnecessarily complex. Only intensive search and a great deal of good fortune can reveal, if it is ever to be known, the village in which they lived.

It will be seen that conclusive argument for either location is impossible. It can be discussed only on the basis of greater or lesser probability. In the view of this writer the more probable location, all known factors being taken into account, is not far from the southern shore of Chesapeake Bay.

This does not quite finish the story. It is conceivable that the persistent suggestions that white men survived on the Chowan, possibly as metal workers, represent the continued presence of one or more of the three men left behind in 1586. We also have the story of the clothes-wearing men who are said to have made their way, first up the Roanoke River and then to some place which sounds as if it might be on the Pamlico or the Neuse. They emerge in 1607 before there is any talk of a massacre. They next appear on the Zúñiga map as the four clothed men who came from Roanoke to Ocanahonan and finally to Pakerakanick—again at a time when the news of the massacre had not come out. In the 1609 instructions they have been transformed into refugees from the Powhatan massacre. To Machumps they are men who build houses with more than one story. In 1614 they are heard of as Spaniards. This is the most persistent separable story: [2] it could very well mean that in the Pamlico-

[2] See pp. 459 and 471–3 above.

Neuse area there was a small group of non-Indian survivors, whether from the lost colonists of 1587 or from one of the other lost groups, not excluding Drake's Negro and Central American Indian group.

Finally, there are the alleged survivors of the massacre. They are first of all four men, but these are perhaps taken over from the earlier story involving four different men. When to the four men are added two boys and a girl, second-generation members of the original group of 1587, the evidence becomes more plausible. We have seen that these people are said to have fled up the Chowan and to have been integrated into the Indian village ruled by a chief called Gepaconon or Eyanoc; that the men were involved in working metal, and that this place was most probably on the Chowan, its site the old village of Chowanoac—though an alternative location, farther from Jamestown and well up either the Chowan or the Roanoke River, cannot be excluded.[3] If this group did reach a safe refuge they are likely to have been the most enduring of all the remnants. But at that point they disappear finally and completely from history.

In the nineteenth century the story of the Lost Colony became a legend. Out of it emerged a number of folk tales which placed the origins of various rural groups back in the sixteenth century with the "lost colonists." The number of counties in modern North Carolina which at some time or other have made claims of this sort is surprisingly large.

VIII

THE FATE of the Lost Colony at the hands of Powhatan may have had some not insignificant effects on the subsequent relations of English and Indians between its discovery in 1608 and the death of Powhatan in 1618. Strachey, writing in 1611 or 1612, thought that because of it, or the precedent it could mark for future action of this sort by the Indians, the fate of the Jamestown settlement might still hang by a slender cord. He says of Powhatan "he doth often send unto us to temporize with us, awayting perhaps but a fitt opportunity (inflamed by his bloudy and furious priests) to offer us a tast of the same Cuppe which he made our poore Countrymen drink off at Roanoak."[4] Friction under Smith's government in the last month of 1608 and the early months of 1609 seemed likely to bring all-out war. But Powhatan was too uncertain of his strength to commit himself to a final challenge.

Indeed, through the good offices of his daughter Pocahontas, a few

[3] See p. 471 above. [4] Strachey, *Historie*, p. 59.

years of tolerably good relations intervened before his death in 1618.[5] From that time onward the English pressure on the Indians developed so rapidly and so intolerably that the rising of 1622, the massacre organized by Opechancanough, was almost inevitable. But though it had some success, it could not achieve total victory and was followed by revenge and the expulsion of Indians from more of their lands, the start of a longer policy of pressure and extermination. Purchas, writing his "Virginias verger" in 1623 just after the massacre, and recalling as we saw Powhatan's part in the earlier killings of the lost colonists, links the two happenings together. His peroration asserts that "their carkasses, the dispersed bones of their and their Countrey mens since murthered carkasses, have taken a mortall, immortal possession, and being dead, speake, proclaime and cry, This our earth is truly English, and therefore this Land is justly yours O English."[6] The lost colonists and their fate become in the end the talking point for aggressive expansionist propaganda.

[5] Effectively examined in Barbour, *Pocahontas.*

[6] Purchas, *Pilgrimes* (1625), IV, 1813; (1906), XIX, 227–8.

CHAPTER EIGHTEEN

The Road to Jamestown

SHAKESPEARE'S LIFE almost exactly spanned the period when the settlement of North America was transformed from an idea into reality. On 23 April 1564, when Shakespeare is believed to have been born, there was not a single European settlement north of Mexico. In 1616, when he died, there were no less than six centers of European settlement, all small but some with a great potential: St. Augustine, Jamestown, Bermuda, Port Royal, Quebec, and the Avalon Peninsula in Newfoundland. One was Spanish, two French, three English.

Bermuda was pretty well isolated. Repeated efforts did not make Newfoundland more than a potential colony. Jamestown alone of English settlements at that time seemed to have a great future. It was the first enduring English colony in the New World. How it came to be so is partly the result of the effort poured into it from 1606 onward; but it is partly also the result of the trial-and-error approach to American colonization described in this book.

I have ranged hitherto over the background of settlement; it is time now to look at the foundation of Jamestown itself. A great transformation occurred in the scale of English colonial activity with the issue of the Virginia Company charter on 10 April 1606. The ventures of Gosnold and Pring in 1602–3 had been small-scale affairs for trading and exploration, with little or no coordination between them. Though they revealed enough to point the way to settlement, and though Waymouth could be sent in 1605 to prepare the way for a new Catholic colony, yet there was no big money or large numbers of settlers involved. Bartholomew Gilbert's attempt in 1603 to discover the mouth of Chesapeake Bay was a failure, and if Newport looked in there on his way back from the West Indies in 1605 we do not know how much new information he could have picked up.

Yet while Waymouth in the autumn of 1605 had been scraping around for a small investment to start a settlement, some six months later there arose, full-blown, a dual Virginia Company (a northern one to exploit the Gosnold-Waymouth discoveries, a southern one for the Old Virginia of the Roanoke colonies, with a supervisory royal council to coordinate their activities and act as a watchdog for the state). We are still at a loss to know precisely how this came about. Recent work has done a good deal to elucidate the involvement in the venture of some of the 1607 settlers, such as Bartholomew Gosnold and John Smith, but who were the architects of the great measure?

Sir Thomas Smith, the great London entrepreneur, certainly supplied the business confidence which led City merchants to invest. Lord Chief Justice Popham and Lord Salisbury, the king's chief minister, between them were vitally important, and without them little would have been done. But we are not quite sure how it was tied together. Captain Waymouth himself may have been the one to get the king interested, and without his interest nothing could have happened. Sir Walter Cope, another official, may well have been the man who ran from sea captain to soldier, from expert to expert (Edward Hayes to Richard Hakluyt), from merchant to statesmen (Smith to Popham and Salisbury). But so much was done by word of mouth that we cannot tell exactly who was responsible for what. Certainly both Salisbury—as nominal High Steward of Plymouth and with his fiery friend Sir Ferdinando Gorges as commander of the Plymouth garrison—and Popham, with his grandson Thomas Hanham entrenched in the Plymouth plutocracy (such as it was) and his links with Bristol through having been Recorder—tied in the independent-minded interests of western England firmly with the Londoners.

There had to be several revisions of the Company charter before it worked at all efficiently; it never was a first-rate instrument for colonization. What it was excellent for was committing the English, at last, to a sustained program of settlement.

While the royal council did not operate very effectively in the day-to-day affairs of the Company, it was, I think, the one thing in the charter which gave reasonable assurance that state support for colonization would be maintained, even without direct assistance from taxation. The element of national prestige which the maintenance of a colony backed by such a body conferred made it almost certain that the crown would not abandon the Company in the face of Spanish threats. The very fact that the Spaniards managed to seize the *Richard*—the first ship sent out by the merchants of Plymouth and Bristol in 1606—and played a cat-and-mouse game with her men for several years, made Lord Salisbury and other members of the government determined not to give up the colonies. The long series of threats by Spain was set aside with smooth talk rather than defiance, and the Spanish government proved unwilling to take the risk of war which the attempted destruction of the colony in 1607 or 1608 would probably have provoked.

By 1606 the various social and regional groupings interested in American colonization had been to some extent sorted out. The London merchants had become converted finally to speculative investment, when it was seen that the new East India Company could make a profit; the western merchants were attracted into speculation by the sudden postwar boom in the Newfoundland fisheries. Dr. Theodore Rabb has drawn our attention to the scale of the landowners' investment in new speculative companies in the years after James's accession. No less than a third of the landowning members of the Parliament of 1604–11 were willing to invest in this open-ended mercantile venture which allowed money to work without requiring direct participation as a merchant.

Besides, the landowners and some merchants too were interested in land speculation as such: certainly many were becoming interested in Irish land, and American land might also prove worthy of investment, with a possibility of resettlement there at a higher social and economic level than in England. We may therefore be justified in probing a little closer into economic and social motives, to bring out at least the major incentives as they presented themselves to the two chief regional groupings represented in the Company.

What was the reason for the emphasis of Londoners on a southern colony—why the stress by the western merchants on a northern? We have seen that there was an aristocratic desire for landed estates in North America, and that demand was not linked very closely to one latitude rather than another, though perhaps directed a little more to areas where there were fewer rather than more Indian occupants who might interfere with the creation of new rural lordships. But the merchants' view of North America was decisive. Without merchant capital, without the sustaining power of a strong economic program, a colony backed by gentry only might be very long in coming into existence. This Gilbert's experiments had shown.

The reason for the bias of the western merchants toward the American shore from Cape Cod northward was that their basic concern was with fish and oil and furs, and their colonizing interest was the expression of a need to find an area which could be exploited for these products all the year round, not merely in the short summer season. The objectives of the Londoners were different. In 1604 great hopes were pinned on the Levant and Spanish trades. The former would be free from Spanish interference in the Straits of Gibraltar; the latter would be open freely to English merchants for the first time since 1585. But these hopes were soon to some extent qualified. North African pirates continued to take a fairly heavy toll from the Levant trade. In Spain and Portugal a maze of duties and lawsuits and the hostility of officials somewhat dimmed the hopes of high profits to be gained at San Lucár, Seville, and Lisbon, while the outlook for Spanish commerce in the years immediately following the peace remained poor and uncertain.

The English aim in Iberian lands and the Mediterranean was to revive the trade in southern European products. The desire for a colony was therefore largely one for a base with an economy complementary to that of England, so as to produce the sugar, wines, raisins, citrus fruit, rice, dyes (woad especially), and possibly leather and iron which came mainly from the Iberian countries and their Atlantic island dependencies. Then, too, the peace excluded the English from the Spanish Indies. Perhaps a colony just outside the Spanish zone in North America would produce some of the minor riches of the Indies, such as tobacco, dyes, and cotton; possibly even its silver and gold, though opinion about potential mineral assets was inclined to be cautious. The foundation of the East India Company in 1600 and the return of its first fleet in 1603 had shown that London capital could produce all the spices, silks, and Oriental dyes that England needed. A Caribbean base was ruled out for the time being by the treaty and by Spanish hostility and ruthlessness in dealing with intruders. A Virginia colony, in latitudes similar to that of the lapsed Roanoke settlement, was the best that could be hoped for.

Both westerners and Londoners expected certain advantages from the timber resources of America. Westerners looked for pitch, tar, turpentine, masts, and the chances of shipbuilding on the spot once a colony was established (the very first product of the Maine colony of 1607–8 was a ship); the Londoners were concerned with clapboard for wainscot, staves for barrels (wine trade), cedar for fine cabinetmaking, use of the forests for smelting iron (either local iron or ore brought from England as ballast), and making glass and potash for soap—all activities which were becoming increasingly expensive at home as English timber was used up in increasing quantities. Sassafras was a medical panacea, for both groups, but its significance was soon seen to be small.

Both westerners and Londoners had national aims too. The Spaniards were established in Florida; they might at any time move up the coast and occupy the sites that could serve English mercantile purposes. In the north the English had abandoned by 1602 any attempts to penetrate the St. Lawrence, since French activity there had increased at such a rate that it was clearly only a matter of time before permanent settlements were created. News that in 1604 the French had begun working down the Atlantic seaboard was clearly an incentive to get in first and preserve it from them.

These national aims also governed to some extent the character of the earliest settlements. With Spanish and French threats to be met, however shadowy, it did not seem possible to send out purely civilian settlements as the first stage of colonization. The nucleus of any settlement must be a body of trained men under a degree of military discipline. Had the Indians been the sole reason for taking precautions, a modest program of arming and training civilians and providing them with some military backbone might have sufficed, as it did with the Pilgrims in 1620. But with the possibility of professional European soldiers to be met with, men with real training in the Low Countries or the Irish wars were essential. They were available in considerable numbers now that peace had come.

The problem which was not faced or solved in practice by the Virginia companies, and which brought them nearest to disaster, was how to exploit these military men productively. Beyond looking after a fort, once built, and making forays with exploring parties, it was hard to expect them (though it *was* expected of them) to become laborers, craftsmen, merchants, and administrators. Some few did prove adaptable; the majority were too professionalized to remain anything but soldiers. Their uselessness (the word may be too emphatic, for they had some uses) was the main reason for the failure of the northern colony, and along with disease it brought the southern colony several times to the verge of collapse.

There was this difference, too, between the westerners' and the Londoners' approach. The westerners hoped to develop colonies as a convenience. They did not greatly care about settlements as such and were quite willing to allow enterprising gentlemen or freedom-seeking Catholics, Separatists, or Puritans to do the pioneering for them, so long as merchant activities were left in their hands. When the Sagadahoc colony went to pieces in 1608, they went on with their fishing and intermittent fur trading. With John Smith's help this New England commerce became quite profitable, though they still felt the need for shore bases to extend the season. The French did not, in fact, move down the coast (Argall scotching in 1613 the attempt to start missions in Maine), so they were not seriously impeded in their profitable activities in American waters by the lack of colonies, though this limited the scale on which they could operate.

The position of the Londoners was quite different. They could not achieve any of their aims without a colony. The whole basis of their economic program rested on agriculture, industry, and possibly mining, even though there was subsidiary Indian trade to be obtained. If Jamestown was to be given up, London merchant activities in America could pack up too. There was only one slight alternative open to them. They might give up settlement, though perhaps trying to keep a small port of call going, if they could revive full-scale trade under arms in the West Indies. Privateering had become just this by 1604: it had not ceased with the treaty, but had to be a clandestine activity in view of the desire of the crown for peace and alliance with Spain. It was not capable of rapid expansion. Some London Company merchants would have been delighted to renew the open privateering war, but the device of the royal Council of Virginia effectively prevented any such move. Unless and until royal policy cooled decisively against Spain, which it did not do until 1624, the Virginia Company of London was stuck with Jamestown (though they were able to launch out on a promising sideline in Bermuda in 1612) and had to make the best of it. These various distinctions were not unimportant in the survival of one Virginia settlement from 1607 on. And they combined closely with the factor of prestige.

When Christopher Newport reached England in July 1607, after quickly and safely establishing the first settlers in Jamestown, he reported not only that the country was extremely fertile but that it was apparently full of gold. This report caused tremendous excitement among the investors at first, and an almost equally great outburst of disappointment when it was shown that analysis of the supposed ore had once again been faulty. Sir Thomas Roe, nonetheless, spoke for the more cautious merchants and aristocratic investors when he said there was sufficient justification for "the honor and profit to our nation to make provincial to us a land ready to supply us with all necessary commodities naturally wanting to us, in which alone we suffer the Spanish reputation and power to swell over us." In other words, the economy of the new Virginia colony would complement that of Great Britain, and in helping it to do so King James might consider his new empire well won. Newport went back to Jamestown; the hundred or so additional colonists he brought infused new life into its dying frame. The crucial turning point had come and been passed. The road to Jamestown was not to be a mere track into a wilderness but a main road into colonial empire.

Summary

The brief treatment of the voyages of 1602 and 1603 underlined both how little we know and also how slowly some light is emerging on the preliminaries to the settlement at Jamestown. The more extended discussion of the lost colonists which follows showed us how the sixteenth-century ventures overlap those of the seventeenth, though the precise nature of that overlap is seen through a dark glass only. The lost colonists, whatever their fate, stand as at least a symbol of continuity. We do not yet know their story fully and may never know it, but at least some outlines have now emerged: they are something more than a myth, if not wholly realizable. And so in the end we are able to use our perspective glass, that magnifying instrument first produced in America by Thomas Harriot in 1585, to take once more a bird's-eye view of the long process of partial discovery, involvement, and planning, illustrated perforce by samples rather than by long continuous narratives, from the first thoughts of Englishmen about America down to the first attempted settlements. We can end with the emergence at last of a solidly backed colonization program, and with the launching of what was to be the first permanent English social unit on North American soil. But in these early years of Jamestown we can see only the enunciation of the determination to settle—achievement still lay, with many hazards, ahead. The morality of colonization, the capitalist techniques for its achievement, the human and societal problems it would create, were still wholly unformulated in detail. Success was a question mark suspended for almost a generation.

Epilogue

THE BEGINNINGS OF English enterprise in the North Atlantic are misty and uncertain. We can pierce them only inadequately by more or less well-justified speculation and guesses. Slowly—but very slowly—a few new facts are beginning to emerge and theories becoming somewhat more substantial, perhaps even taking some positive shape, before we enter the era of the Columbian discoveries.

We have then a long period of trial and error, over the whole of the period covered in this volume. It is a time of many-sided experiment, of strange failures to follow up apparently promising initiatives, of firm achievement in limited areas of exploration: in the building up of a great international fishery, in the gradual definition of diplomatic issues as between England, Spain, and France in North America. It is an era when rash or heroic experiments in colonization fail; when careful surveys of land and resources and people seen in the new continent slowly build up a coherent picture of American realities. The Indians are always present, but only seldom in the forefront of the picture as painted by the European visitors; the Spaniards are in the wings, ready to move ahead but doubtful of the value to themselves of doing so. Individuals stand out—men like Gilbert and Ralegh and Grenville who have, partly through a long glorification of the Elizabethans, an apparent heroic quality. Others emerge, rough but not uneducated sea captains like Frobisher or Edward Hayes, who achieve the ends at which they aim but working under the orders of others. Men like John White, Thomas

Harriot, and James Rosier use their fine intelligence or finer brush to give us some imperishable reflections of the sight and feeling of an unspoiled land.

Men plot in London and Bristol how to make money out of settlements. Men study in Lancashire or Leiden how to get away from a society which hems in their religious life unduly, perhaps unmercifully. Gradually—far more gradually than is often realized—the strands cohere: money is found to keep new settlements alive; men and women are found, willing for a variety of motives to cross the ocean. Tiny new forts and villages emerge; eventually they will grow into a new nation.

From the first known Brasil voyage to the landing of the Pilgrims was a span of 140 years; from 1620 to the Revolution was 156 years. Yet in American history (and British too, perhaps) the second period seems so much longer and fuller than the first. The comparison helps to underline why we need so much guessing, so much speculation, so much research, and so much concern with what in other circumstances would be trivial bits of information. We must clutch at straws when we have no other. Yet we are not only gradually acquiring more information; we are beginning to acquire a little more understanding—some appreciation perhaps of the variety and vitality of the motives and men which eventually established Europeans in North America, in spite of climate and rugged nature and the natural claims of the old inhabitants of the land. The New American World was far to seek.

A BIBLIOGRAPHY OF

Books and Articles on American Exploration and Colonization by David Beers Quinn

I. GENERAL

Covering a Wider Period and Area Than North America, and Prior to 1625:

1. "Die Anfange des britischen Weltreiches bis zum Ende der Napoleonischen Kriege." *Historia Mundi,* VIII (Munich and Berne, 1959), 455–95.
2. "Exploration and the Expansion of Europe." Comité International des Sciences Historiques, XIIe Congrès International des Sciences Historiques, Vienne, 29 Août–5 September 1965, *Rapports,* I (Vienna, 1965), 45–60.
3. (editor) *The Hakluyt Handbook.* 2 vols. Hakluyt Society, 2d ser., nos. 144 and 145. Cambridge, Eng., 1974 (forthcoming).

Partly Concerned with North America, Before 1625:

4. *Raleigh and the British Empire.* London, 1947, 1962, 1973; New York, 1949, 1962.
5. "Sailors and the Sea." In *Shakespeare Survey 17* ("Shakespeare in His Own Age"), ed. Allardyce Nicoll. Cambridge, Eng., 1964. Pp. 21–36, 242–5.
   (See pp. 199–326 above.)
6. *The Elizabethans and the Irish.* Folger Monographs on Tudor and Stuart Civilization. Ithaca, 1966.
7. (with R. A. Skelton) Richard Hakluyt, *The Principall Navigations,*

Voiages and Discoveries of the English Nation: A Facsimile of the Edition of 1589, with an Introduction by D. B. Quinn and R. A. Skelton and with a New Index by Alison Quinn. 2 vols. Hakluyt Society, extra ser. 39. Cambridge, Eng., 1965.

8. (with John W. Shirley) "A Contemporary List of Hariot References." *Renaissance Quarterly*, XXII (New York, 1969), 9–26.
9. (with A. C. Crombie, J. V. Pepper, J. W. Shirley, and R. C. H. Tanner) "Thomas Harriot (1560–1621): An Original Practitioner in the Scientific Art." *The Times Literary Supplement*, 23 October 1969, pp. 1237–8.

II. NORTH AMERICA IN GENERAL

10. *The New Found Land: The English Contribution to the Discovery and Settlement of North America.* John Carter Brown Library. Providence, 1965.
11. "La Contribution des Anglais à la découverte de l'Amérique du Nord au XVIe Siècle." In *La Découverte de l'Amérique: Esquisse d'une Synthèse. Conditions Historiques et Conséquences Culturelles,* by Manuel Ballesteros-Gaibrois and others. Paris, 1968. Pp. 61–76.
12. "The Road to Jamestown." In *Shakespeare Celebrated*, ed. Louis B. Wright. Folger Library Publications. Ithaca, 1966.
    (See pp. 482–8 above.)
13. *North American Discovery, Circa 1000–1612.* New York and Columbia, S.C., 1971.
14. (with W. P. Cumming and R. A. Skelton) *The Discovery of North America.* London and New York, 1971.
15. (with Alison M. Quinn) *Virginia Voyages from Hakluyt.* London, 1973.

III. NORTH AMERICA TO 1550

16. "Madoc," "John Jay," "Thomas Croft," "Lancelot Thirkell," "Hugh Eliot," "RobertThorne," "John Rastell," "John Rut," "Richard Hore." In *Dictionary of Canadian Biography (Dictionnaire Biographique du Canada)*, ed. G. W. Brown, Marcel Trudel, and André Vachon. Vol. I. Toronto and Quebec, 1965.
17. (with P. G. Foote) "The Vinland Map." Viking Society for Northern Research. *Saga Book*, XVII (London, 1966), 63–89.
    (See pp. 28–40 above.)
18. "Edward IV and Exploration." *The Mariner's Mirror*, XXI (Cambridge, Eng., 1935), 275–84.

19. "The Argument for the English Discovery of America Between 1480 and 1494." *Geographical Journal*, CXXVII (London, 1961), 277–85.
(See pp. 5–17 above.)
20. "The English Discovery of America." In *The Expansion of Europe*, ed. De Lamar Jensen. Boston, 1967. Pp. 47–51.
21. "John Cabot's *Matthew*." *The Times Literary Supplement*, 8 June 1967, p. 517.
22. "John Day and Columbus." *Geographical Journal*, CXXXIII (London, 1967), 205–9.
(See pp. 103–11 above.)
23. "État présent des études sur la découverte de l'Amérique au XVe siècle." *Journal de la Société des Américanistes*, LV (Paris, 1966), 343–82.
24. *Sebastian Cabot and Bristol Exploration.* Bristol Branch of the Historical Association, Local History Pamphlets, no. 21. Bristol, 1968.
(See pp. 131–59 above.)

IV. NORTH AMERICA BETWEEN 1550 AND 1600

25. *The Voyages and Colonising Enterprises of Sir Humphrey Gilbert.* 2 vols. Hakluyt Society, 2d ser., nos. 83–4. London, 1940. Photolithographic reprint in one volume, Nendeln, Liechtenstein, 1967.
26. "Preparations for the 1585 Virginia Voyage." *William and Mary Quarterly*, 3d ser., VI (Williamsburg, 1949), 208–36.
27. "The Failure of Raleigh's American Colonies." In *Essays in British and Irish History in Honour of J. E. Todd*, ed. H. A. Cronne, T. W. Moody, and D. B. Quinn. London, 1949. Pp. 61–85.
(See pp. 282–306 above.)
28. "Some Spanish Reactions to Elizabethan Colonial Enterprises." *Transactions of the Royal Historical Society*, 5th ser., I (London, 1951), 1–23.
(See pp. 264–81 above.)
29. "Christopher Newport in 1590." *North Carolina Historical Review*, XXIX (Raleigh, 1952), 305–16.
30. *The Roanoke Voyages, 1584–1590: Documents to Illustrate the English Voyages to North America Under the Patent Granted to Walter Raleigh in 1584.* 2 vols. Hakluyt Society, 2d ser., nos. 104–5. Cambridge, Eng., 1955. Photolithographic reprint in one volume, Nendeln, Liechtenstein, 1967.
31. "Edward Hayes, Liverpool Colonial Pioneer." *Transactions of the*

Historic Society of Lancashire and Cheshire, CXI (Liverpool, 1960), 25–45.
(See pp. 227–45 above.)

32. (with Jacques Rousseau) "Hakluyt et le mot 'Esquimau.'" *Revue de l'Histoire de l'Amérique Française*, XII (Montreal, 1959), 597–601.
33. "Simão Fernandes, a Portuguese Pilot in the English Service, *Circa* 1573–1588." Congresso Internacional de História dos Descobrimentos, *Actas*, III (Lisbon, 1961), 449–65.
(See pp. 246–63 above.)
34. (with Paul H. Hulton) "John White and the English Naturalists." *History Today*, XIII (London, 1963), 310–20.
35. (with Paul H. Hulton) *The American Drawings of John White*. 2 vols. London and Chapel Hill, 1964.
36. "Elizabethan Birdman." *The Times Literary Supplement*, 1 April 1965, p. 250.
37. "David Ingram," "Anthony Parkhurst," "Sir Humphrey Gilbert," "Stephanus Parmenius," "Edward Hayes," "La Court de Pré-Ravillon et de Grandpré," "Sylvester Wyet," "Charles Leigh," "George Johnson." In *Dictionary of Canadian Biography (Dictionnaire Biographique du Canada)*, ed. G. W. Brown, Marcel Trudel, and André Vachon. Vol. I. Toronto and Quebec, 1965.
38. "The Voyage of Étienne Bellenger to the Maritimes in 1584; a New Document." *Canadian Historical Review*, XLIII (Toronto, 1962), 328–43.
39. "England and the St. Lawrence, 1577 to 1602." In *Merchants and Scholars*, ed. John Parker. Minneapolis, 1965. Pp. 117–44.
(See pp. 313–36 above.)
40. "The First Pilgrims." *William and Mary Quarterly*, 3d ser., XXIII (Williamsburg, 1966), 359–90.
(See pp. 337–63 above.)
41. (with Jacques Rousseau) "Les Toponymes Amérindiens du Canada chez les Anciens Voyageurs Anglais, 1591–1602." *Cahiers de Géographie de Québec*, X (1966), 263–78.
42. *Richard Hakluyt, Editor*. With facsimiles of Richard Hakluyt, *Divers Voyages Touching the Discoverie of America* (1582), and *A Journal of Several Voyages into New France* (1580). 2 vols. Amsterdam, 1967.
43. (with Neil M. Cheshire) *The New Found Land of Stephen Parmenius*. Toronto, 1972.
44. "Thomas Harriot and America." In *Thomas Harriot, Renaissance Scientist*, ed. John W. Shirley. Oxford (forthcoming).

V. NORTH AMERICA BETWEEN 1600 AND 1625

45. "Notes by a Pious Colonial Investor, 1608–1610." *William and Mary Quarterly*, 3d ser., XVI (Williamsburg, 1959), 551–5.

46. "Advice for Investors in Virginia, Bermuda, and Newfoundland, 1611." *William and Mary Quarterly*, 3d ser., XXIII (Williamsburg, 1966), 136–45.

47. (with Warner F. Gookin) "Martin Pring at Provincetown, 1603." *The New England Quarterly*, XL, (1967), 79–91.
(See pp. 423–7 above.)

48. (editor) George Percy, *Observations Gathered out of "A Discourse on the Plantation of the Southern Colony in Virginia by the English, 1606, Written by that Honorable Gentleman, Master George Percy."* Charlottesville, 1967.

49. "A List of Books Purchased for the Virginia Company." *Virginia Magazine of History and Biography*, LXXVII (1969), 347–60.

50. "Thomas Hariot and the Virginia Voyages of 1602." *William and Mary Quarterly*, 3d ser., XXVII (1970), 268–81.
(See pp. 405–18 above.)

51. *Jamestown Day Address, 11 May 1969.* Association for the Preservation of Virginia Antiquities. Richmond, 1969.

52. " 'Virginians' on the Thames in 1603." *Terrae Incognitae*, II (Amsterdam, 1970), 7–14.
(See pp. 419–23 and 427–31 above.)

53. "The Voyage of *Triall*, 1606–1607: An Abortive Virginia Venture." *American Neptune*, XXXI (Salem, Mass., 1971), 85–103.

54. "The Value of Some Early Relations for the Study of the New England Indians." *Actas y Memorias* (XXXIX Congreso Internacional de Americanistas), XIV (Historia y ethnohistoria americana). Lima (forthcoming).

Index

[H]

[I]

[T]

[U]

[V]

[W]

[Y]

[Z]

A NOTE ABOUT THE AUTHOR

DAVID BEERS QUINN was born in Dublin in 1909. He took his B.A. at Queens University, Belfast, in 1931 and his Ph.D. at the University of London in 1934. From 1934 to 1939 he was lecturer in history at University College, Southampton; from 1939 to 1944 Senior Lecturer in history at Queen's University, Belfast; and from 1944 to 1957 Professor of History at University College, Swansea, University of Wales. Since 1957 he has been Andrew Geddes and John Rankin Professor of Modern History at the University of Liverpool. He has held research fellowships at The Folger Shakespeare Library, Washington, D.C.; The John Carter Brown Library, Providence, R.I.; and The Henry E. Huntington Library, San Marino, Cal.; and was James Pinckney Harrison Professor of History at The College of William and Mary, 1969–70. He is the author of *The Voyages and Colonising Enterprises of Sir Humphrey Gilbert* (1940), *Raleigh and the British Empire* (1947), *The Roanoke Voyages, 1584–90* (1955), *The Elizabethans and the Irish* (1965), *Richard Hakluyt, Editor* (1967), *North American Discovery, c. 1000–1612* (1971), and, with Paul Hulton, of *The American Drawings of John White* (1964).

A NOTE ON THE TYPE

THIS BOOK was set on the Linotype in Janson, a recutting made direct from type cast from matrices long thought to have been made by the Dutchman Anton Janson, who was a practicing type founder in Leipzig during the years 1668–87. However, it has been conclusively demonstrated that these types are actually the work of Nicholas Kis (1650–1702), a Hungarian, who most probably learned his trade from the master Dutch type founder Dirk Voskens. The type is an excellent example of the influential and sturdy Dutch types that prevailed in England up to the time William Caslon developed his own incomparable designs from them.

Composed, printed, and bound by Kingsport Press, Incorporated, Kingsport, Tennessee.

Typography and binding design by Clint Anglin.